CASS LIBRARY OF AFRICAN STUDIES

MISSIONARY RESEARCHES AND TRAVELS

No. 2

General Editor: ROBERT I. ROTBERG

TRAVELS,

RESEARCHES, AND MISSIONARY LABOURS

DURING AN EIGHTEEN YEARS' RESIDENCE
IN EASTERN AFRICA

TOGETHER WITH
JOURNEYS TO JAGGA, USAMBARA,
UKAMBANI, SHOA, ABESSINIA, AND KHARTUM

AND A COASTING VOYAGE
FROM MOMBAZ TO CAPE DELGADO

BY

J. LEWIS KRAPF

WITH AN APPENDIX
BY E. G. RAVENSTEIN

SECOND EDITION

WITH A NEW INTRODUCTION BY
R. C. BRIDGES

FRANK CASS & CO. LTD.
1968

Published by
FRANK CASS AND COMPANY LIMITED
67 Great Russell Street, London WC1

First edition   1860
Second edition   1968

Printed in Great Britain by
Thomas Nelson (Printers) Ltd., London and Edinburgh

GENERAL EDITOR'S PREFACE

THIS is one of the three or four most significant missionary accounts of nineteenth century Africa. Historians and ethnologists have for long valued Krapf's observations on precolonial East Africa. He and his colleague Johann Rebmann were the earliest European explorers of the Kilimanjaro and Kamba regions; the present text, here reprinted in English for the first time in more than a century, contains a full report of their journeys and geographical researches. There is also information of importance about Ethiopia—where Krapf served before he founded a mission near Mombasa—and which he revisited in the time of the Emperor Theodore.

A modern, properly introduced edition of Krapf's *Travels, Researches and Missionary Labours* has long been needed. It is fitting, therefore, that the present volume should inaugurate a series of republished Missionary Researches and Travels. Within the framework of the series it is intended to provide new, authoritative editions of the historically most valuable nineteenth and early twentieth century narratives written about Africa by missionaries and other church-connected figures. The text of each, as in the present instance, will be a facsimile of the standard version of the original without abridgement or other alteration. Each will be introduced by persons possessing a particular knowledge of the authors and areas involved.

Dr. Roy C. Bridges, a Lecturer in History in the University of Aberdeen, has made the history of the exploration of East Africa his speciality. For the present volume he has placed the labours and travels of Krapf and Rebmann in their historical context, provided the fullest and most informative biographical sketch of Krapf in English, and discussed the contents of the following text in the light of modern scholarship. The present edition is further enhanced by a new map drawn from a sketch by Dr. Bridges.

15 November 1966 R. I. R.

INTRODUCTION
TO THE SECOND EDITION
BY
R. C. BRIDGES

UNTIL the middle years of the nineteenth century, Eastern Africa was little known by Europeans. Yet within the space of three or four decades it was to be explored, evangelised and finally conquered by Britain and Germany. In the story of the growth of European contacts with the region, the name of Johann Ludwig Krapf occupies an important place—indeed, really serious concern with East Africa may be said to begin with his work.

Krapf is a familiar figure to most scholars concerned with the history of Africa or missionary expansion. Yet his place in the record of missionary work and African geographical exploration is often undervalued in general accounts which quickly, and sometimes patronisingly, dismiss him to make way for apparently greater missionaries and explorers like Livingstone, Burton, and Stanley. The current interest in African studies has resulted in a change of emphasis in the approach to the history of Africa with less weight being given to European expansion and more to indigenous developments. This has the paradoxical result of increasing the importance of Krapf's work; the earliness of his acquaintance with the region means that he is the only source of written evidence for the history of certain parts of East Africa in the 1840's and 1850's. Nor is his material on Ethiopia, although less unique, to be disregarded.

Given the period during which he worked, Krapf was an acute observer of the African scene and his work easily bears comparison with later travellers. This book therefore constitutes a valuable mine of information on African peoples as well as the record of the activities of a notable missionary-explorer and his companions. Moreover, many of the adventures Krapf had to recount are well worth reading in their own right. For all these reasons, Krapf's English publication of 1860 deserves to be revived and made available to a wider audience in Europe, Africa, and America.*

I BASLE AND THE CHURCH MISSIONARY SOCIETY

Krapf was born in 1810 and the main details of his early life are set out in the first chapter of the main text. The spiritual progress he describes produced a man whose strong faith was to bear him through some twenty years of missionary endeavour and a further twenty-five of quieter work for Africa and the Gospel. Yet like his great contemporary, David Livingstone, Krapf nearly did not go to Africa. Peter Fjellstädt, having renewed the younger man's missionary ambitions, wanted him to work in Asia Minor. Fjellstädt was a Swede who had worked in South India before attempting, in the face of Orthodox Christian and Muslim opposition, to plant Protestantism in Greece and Ottoman Turkey.† This effort was one of the projects of the Church Missionary Society, founded in 1799 as a product of the evangelical revival in England. This society was to employ Krapf himself in 1837.

It was not unusual for a Swede or a German to work for the C.M.S. during this period. The Society had difficulty for the first fifty years of its existence in obtaining recruits from England, partly, at least, because its aims and methods were suspect to a large proportion of Anglicans including, initially, all of the bishops. Lay control became characteristic and men like Dandeson Coates, Lay Secretary from 1824 to 1846, and his committee had no qualms about accepting non-Anglican ordinands as missionaries. Most of these foreign recruits were from Germany; the earliest contacts were with Berlin where J. Jänicke's Missionary Seminary trained men from 1802

---

* The German version, Johann Ludwig Krapf, *Reisen in Ost-Afrika*, (Stuttgart, 1858), 2 vols., has also recently been republished in one volume with an introduction by Hanno Beck (Stuttgart, 1964).

† Eugene Stock, *History of the Church Missionary Society* (London, 1899), I, 350. Fjellstädt was recalled in 1840.

onwards.* The system was mutually advantageous for English enthusiasm stimulated German missionary interest and English finance allowed this interest to find a practical outlet. In 1825, the C.M.S. opened its own seminary at Islington; it became common for foreign recruits to spend some time there before going into the field and, eventually, for most of them to receive Anglican orders. Krapf was an exception; he did not formally meet his English employers until 1851. The fact that he was a product of the Basle Seminary was taken as sufficient guarantee, for by the 1830's it was a principal source of recruits for the C.M.S.

Basle Seminary was essentially a product of German protestant zeal. Lutherans and Calvinists in the "united relation" characteristic of Württemberg were associated with the seminary, which had been founded in 1815. It was built as a thank-offering by the citizens following deliverance from a threatened bombardment in the war.

Württemberg, two-thirds Protestant and hemmed in by Catholic Baden and Bavaria, tended to provide state and church support as well as popular enthusiasm for pietism. Krapf's millenarian leanings are one indication of the influence of pietism. The emphasis on personal sanctification in pietism meant that the philosophical threat to religion implicit in rationalism and the growth of secular knowledge could more easily be resisted—or rather side-stepped (for, in fact, secular knowledge was used to practical effect in educational institutions). This system tended to make for religious conservatism, but the alliance with the more outward-looking Swiss protestants of Basle no doubt helped to generate enthusiasm for missionary work. The foundation in 1780 of a "German Society for the promotion of pure doctrine and true Godliness" marked an important stage in the development of a concern for spreading the Gospel and uniting Christians. English evangelical influences affected the German Society, which had contacts, for example, with the London Missionary Society. There were also long standing contacts between Württemberg and the missionaries from Halle in Denmark. A number of other regional

* Charles Pelham Groves, *The Planting of Christianity in Africa* (London, 1948), I, 214. Stock, *History*, I, 82–83.

societies, like those at Barmen and Dresden, were later to support and reinforce the Württemberg-Basle missionary initiatives.*

In 1816, only a year after the foundation of the seminary, the C.M.S. made its first contacts with Basle. A donation of £100 was made towards its work and the reward came two years later when the first recruits from the seminary arrived to serve the English society. But the real flow began after the visit to London in 1822 of Basle's director, Theophilus Blumhardt. He promised that any of his trainees sent to the C.M.S. would accept Anglican ordinances and the Book of Common Prayer. At the same time, the scope of the work at Basle was widened; as a missionary institute it began to offer more comprehensive training, including instruction in geography and various crafts. Basle also soon began to send out its own missions as well as men for the C.M.S.†

II FROM ETHIOPIA TO EAST AFRICA, 1837–1844

Among the first of the men from Basle to study at Islington was Samuel Gobat, later Bishop of Jerusalem, who, with four compatriots, was sent to Egypt in 1825 to try to re-vitalise the Coptic Church. Early in 1830, Gobat managed to extend this work to Ethopia. It was continued after his departure because of ill-health in 1835, by other Basle men, particularly Carl Wilhelm Isenberg, who arrived in Ethiopia in 1835, and Krapf who followed in 1837. Broadly speaking, the aim of the C.M.S. work in Ethiopia seems to have been to bring about a "reformation" equivalent to Europe's. It entailed, for example, the use of the gospel in the Amharic vernacular rather than corrupt material in "Aethiopic" (i.e. Ge'ez) understood only by the priesthood. But religious and political conditions in Ethiopia were unfavourable at this time. Islam was attracting more converts and there was the threat of an Egyptian invasion. The established church, though disorganised—there was no head or "Abuna" from 1830 to 1841—was nevertheless generally

---

* Gustav Warneck, *Outline of a History of Protestant Missions* (Edinburgh and London, 1901), 117–122.

† Beck, in Krapf, *Reisen* (1964), VII. Stock, *History*, I, 120,124, 245, 263.

hostile to Protestantism. The emperor was now only a puppet; real power lay with the contending regional rulers, notably those of Tigré, Semien, Begemder, Gojjam, and Shoa. Each ruler was interested in the growing number of rival European visitors only in so far as these were prepared to promote his own particular interests. Thus Krapf was unable to remain in Tigré in 1838 because its ruler, Ubié, allowed priestly hostility and French influence, manifested in the work of the indefatigable Arnaud d'Abbadie and a Franciscan mission, to discredit the protestants. Isenberg, in any case, badly mishandled the situation.*

Further south was Shoa, destined to be the "Piedmont" of the renewed Ethiopian Empire. Shoa was now expanding and better disposed towards British inspired contacts. Its rise was the work of Sahla Selassie, who reigned from 1813 to 1847. Under his patronage, Krapf and Isenberg began work in June 1839, but many obstacles were placed in their way and French rivalry again appeared in the person of Louis Philippe's emissary, Charles E. Xavier Rochet d'Héricourt.† The position was retrieved somewhat by the arrival of a British mission led by William Cornwallis Harris.

British interest in Ethiopia had manifested itself in the activities of the British East India Company from the time thirty years before when Lord Valentia, Henry Salt, and some of their followers had made contacts with Ethiopian rulers. There was also, of course, the stimulus of Bruce's travels of 1769–1772. Now, following the take-over of Aden and, apparently, the advocacy of the missionaries, the Company decided to respond to Sahla Selassie's overtures. In July 1841, Harris' mission arrived. Not until November of that year did he succeed in securing a treaty of amity and commerce with the King on behalf of the British, who also hoped to end the slave trade. It appears that Krapf, now without Isenberg, helped Harris by acting as an interpreter and intermediary with the King. Krapf also provided much material for Harris' sub-

* Donald E. Crummey, "Foreign Missions in Ethiopia, 1829–1868", *Bulletin of the Society for African Church History*, II (1965), 19–20.

† Stock, *History*, I, 351–353, II, 71. Groves, *Planting*, I, 309. *Journals of the Rev. Messrs. Isenberg and Krapf* (London, 1843), 165–167.

sequent book, although Harris denied the assertion that his volumes were all effectively the work of Krapf. The missionary certainly seems to have been much respected by Harris and the other members of his party, particularly Graham.* This favourable impression was to be remembered and to affect Krapf's life in 1867, but, at the time, the treaty and his association with Harris conveyed little advantage to him. Sahla Selassie was disinclined to stamp out slave-trading, and "legitimate trade" interested him little, unless the guns and cannons which Harris brought are included within that category.†

Early in 1842, Krapf left Shoa to meet two new missionaries, J. Mühleisen-Arnold and Johann Christian Müller, who were being sent to help him. His march to the coast near Massawa was the first really long and arduous journey he accomplished. The fascination of travelling over new ground which marks his life was at least one of the reasons which prompted him to take this route rather than the shorter and easier one to Tajurra. On the way, as he describes, Krapf was captured by Adara Bille.‡ This was probably an incidental result of the rivalry between Sahla Selassie and Ras Ali of Begemder over the control of the Muslim Wallo Galla tribes which separated Shoa from the rest of the Christian regions. Krapf was the first European to visit the Wallo.

Neither Krapf nor the two new missionaries were subsequently able to continue their work in Ethiopia. Their exclusion from Shoa in December 1842 seems rather surprising, particularly as Krapf had enjoyed good relations with the King and as Harris was still in the country, but the reasons given by Krapf in the text may well be the correct ones.§ In addition, the King wanted to establish unhampered control over the Galla south of Shoa and knew that Harris and Krapf both believed that these territories might prove profitable fields of European enterprise. Harris' long reports and recommendations advocating this view had little immediate effect as far as the British and

---

* William Cornwallis Harris, *The Highlands of Aethiopia* (London, 1844), 1st ed., xi; 2nd ed., xxx–xxxi.

† *Isenberg and Krapf*, 344.

·‡ *Ibid.*, 367–395. See below, 91–101.

§ Below, 108.

Indian authorities were concerned, but in Krapf's case, the idea was to be the means of carrying him to East Africa. Meanwhile, the C.M.S. had decided to give up the Ethiopian mission altogether because of the hostility it had encountered. There was little tangible result beyond the fact that many bibles had been distributed. Yet the mission is historically important; it had played a part in the process of opening up Ethiopia to the Western world. Krapf's own role in this process had been a major one. The relatively brief space that he gives to it in the following text may be explained by the fact that in 1843 many of the journals that he and Isenberg sent to the C.M.S. were published in English.*

Krapf's interest in the countries to the south of Shoa arose partly because it was agreed that Isenberg should concentrate on the preparation of literature in Amharic (the language used in Shoa) while Krapf would work on the Galla tongue since the Galla tribes occupied large areas of Ethiopia and had been only partly absorbed into Ethiopian society. The Galla had penetrated Ethiopia from the south-east from the sixteenth century onwards. The King of Shoa himself had Galla wives and had attempted to secure the vassalage of certain Galla and Sidama tribes as a source of military strength. Krapf had been able to make his way south in 1840 with one of Sahla Selassie's expeditions. For Krapf the attraction of the Galla living south of Ethiopia was that they appeared to be a numerous, virile people, capable of resisting Muslim onslaughts. They were, he thought, relatively unaffected by any false religious principles. Convert them to Christianity—an urgent task if the world were near its end—and they would, Krapf reasoned, be the means of lighting the lamp of the Gospel and civilisation over a large part of Africa. In a word, the Galla could become the "Germans" of Africa. Krapf's enthusiasm for these pastoralists, whom he never really got to know, was probably misplaced, but there were also other reasons for his interest in the countries to the south of Shoa. The Galla tide had swept through the outlying parts of the old Ethiopian Empire leaving, it was thought, some islands of Christianity. It might be profitable for mission-

---

* *Isenberg and Krapf* in fact fully covers only April 1839 to August 1840, and March 1842 to May 1842.

aries to establish contact with these "Christian remnants" among the Sidama tribes. Travel to these unknown regions was also in itself attractive to Krapf who, like Livingstone at the equivalent point in his career, had begun to speak of the scientific importance of new geographical discoveries.*

In 1843, Krapf and Isenberg made a final attempt to work in Ethiopia, returning once more to Tigré. Hostility from local as well as Roman Catholic clergy led to their expulsion and Krapf decided to follow up his ideas among the Galla instead. While, therefore, his companions, Mühleisen-Arnold, Müller, and Isenberg, went off to work in other fields, Krapf sailed south late in 1843 in order to try to find a way into Galla territory which would enable him to avoid Shoa. Krapf's new wife accompanied him.

The courtship between Krapf and Rosine Dietrich seems to have had little romance about it. Presumably, the number of women prepared to marry missionaries was limited and Krapf, having, to judge from his own account,† cold-bloodedly decided that he needed a wife to help him in his work, must have been prepared to seize the first opportunity of marriage. Letters from Basle told him of the availability of Miss Dietrich. She travelled to Cairo, met Krapf there, and married him in mid-1842. By June 1843, Mrs. Krapf had lost her first child during the period of Krapf's fruitless final attempt to work in Tigré.

When Krapf and his wife reached East African waters by means of a perilous voyage in a dhow from Aden, the missionary had no very clear plans for his subsequent operations although, at the end of his life, he claimed that if it had not been necessary to pay his respects to the Sultan of Zanzibar, he would have immediately set out from the Kismayu area towards the Galla country. The vagaries of the voyage enabled Krapf to visit Brava, Takaungu, Mombasa, Tanga, and Pangani before finally reaching Zanzibar. During these visits he began to learn something of East Africa; in one of these ports he first heard talk of a large lake (Lake Tanganyika) in the country of the Nyamwezi. Most important was the stay at Takaungu, a small

* *Isenberg and Krapf*, 97–98, 112, 160, 470. Krapf, *Imperfect Outline of the Elements of the Galla Language* (London, 1840), iii–xiv.

† Below, 86; *Isenberg and Krapf*, x, 264.

settlement north of Mombasa founded by Mazrui refugees from
the latter town.* Here Krapf first heard of the Nyika people
among whom he was destined to work. Living near the coast,
they were accessible and were also said to be relatively peaceful.
Krapf also learned, by contrast, of the "murderous" propensities of the southern Galla. While it is true that these visits
altered his outlook by widening his interest beyond the Galla
to the whole of East Africa, it is difficult to accept Krapf's
assertion that by going direct to Zanzibar he would have lost
the opportunity of learning something of the "geography and
ethnography" of East Africa.† Indeed, had East Africa been
his real objective in 1844, Zanzibar would have been the
obvious place in which to start learning about it.

When he left Zanzibar in March 1844 Krapf's general aim
was still to penetrate into Galla country. Yet the ease with
which he was dissuaded from sailing to his projected starting
point at Lamu‡ perhaps illustrates the uncertainty he felt at
this time, as does his vague idea for a mission to Usambara in
January 1844. Then came the sudden impulse to make
Mombasa his base and to work among the surrounding Nyika
tribesmen before going on to the "murderous" Galla. Krapf's
wife, again expecting a child, could remain with him if he based
himself in a centre like Mombasa; no doubt this was a factor in
his decision. Yet if this indicates a weakness or a lack of
necessary ruthlessness, it is fair to note that there were other
compelling reasons for the change of plan.

Not until Krapf reached East Africa did he realise that here,
as he wrote at the time to the C.M.S., there was an "immense
field" for missionary labour among the heathen of the interior.
Previously he had assumed that all East Africa was dominated
by Islam. Even so, as late as February 1846, Krapf was
obviously still in doubt about whether he should stay in the
Mombasa area.§ Although later that year the arrival of a

---

* Krapf, *Dictionary of Suahili* (London, 1882), vii; G. S. P. Freeman-
Grenville, *The East African Coast* (Oxford, 1962), 286.

† Below, 111, 116–117.

‡ Below, 127.

§ C(hurch) M(issionary) S(ociety) A(rchives). Salisbury Square,
London: Krapf to Coates, 22 January 1844, 26 August 1845, 25 February
1846.

companion was to be followed by the establishment of a
permanent base, Krapf was never content that his work should
be narrowly confined to one area. The interior of East Africa
held out the attraction of the Galla, numerous other pagans and,
as he came to realise, important unmapped lakes and mountains.

Initially, Krapf settled down at the house in Mombasa which
had housed the British governors of the town in 1824–1826 and
was later to accommodate Burton, Speke, and other British
explorers and consuls.* The early and tragic death of his wife
and new-born child in July 1844 left him the sole agent for "the
promotion of Christianity and Science" on the East African
mainland.†

III   EAST AFRICA IN THE 1840s

East Africa in 1844 certainly offered attractions for the
explorer from Europe. So little was known of this region that it
was possible as late as 1812 for a leading geographical text to
assume that the main coastal towns were still under Portuguese
control.‡ In fact, any effective Portuguese domination had
come to an end when Fort Jesus fell to the Omani Arabs in
1699. In the course of the eighteenth century and the early
decades of the nineteenth, the coastal towns and Zanzibar,
having much less importance than in their mediæval heyday,
passed through a series of vicissitudes involving wars, alliances
and even occasional Portuguese reappearances. The most
notable development, however, was the growing influence of
the Omani Sultans of Muscat who began to base their East
African activities on Zanzibar. The Busaidi dynasty, who had
come to power in 1741, found their greatest check in the refusal
of another Omani clan to recognise their authority in East
Africa. It was not until 1837 that the Mazrui of Mombasa were
finally overcome by the greatest of the Omani Sultans, Seyyid
Said bin Sultan, who reigned from 1806 to 1856.

Seyyid Said is a most important figure in East African history.
In the course of his reign, he converted the maritime Omani

---

* Joseph Thomson, *Through Masai Land* (London, 1885), 41–42.
† CMSA: Krapf to Coates, 10 January 1844.
‡ Robert Kerr, *A General History and Collection of Voyages and
Travels* (Edinburgh, 1811–1824), II, 319.

hegemony over East Africa into something like a separate sultanate—which indeed it became after his death. It was he who, particularly after 1828, speeded up the economic development of Zanzibar and thus encouraged the concomitant Arab penetration of the mainland interior. Seyyid Said became the ruler of an East African empire much wider than the coastal towns; it was an empire, however, of trade and influence rather than political control.

One aspect of Seyyid Said's attempt to develop East Africa economically was the encouragement that he gave to European and American traders, although the diplomatic and strategic implications of their presence were ever clear in his mind.* French interest was of relatively long-standing. The series of wars between Britain and France in the period from 1740 to 1815 established British superiority in the Indian Ocean, but they by no means eliminated the power of France. She retained control of Bourbon (Réunion) and some enclaves on Madagascar. Needing markets for sugar produced on Bourbon and labour for its plantations, France had developed a triangular system of trade which took in her islands, the Persian Gulf and the East African coast. In the 1840's French activity and interference in East African affairs was still much in evidence and was to remain so until the Anglo-French Declaration of Neutrality in 1862. Traders now came direct from France itself as well as Bourbon. Even more notable, the French navy, busy trying to re-establish the country's prestige and position as a world power, was to be seen in East African waters. New establishments at Nossi Bé and Mayotta were acquired and there began the notorious "free labour emigration" scheme—the slave trade in disguise. Krapf himself feared that the French were aiming to occupy the coast and then drive their way across the continent to Senegal. Already, he reported in 1848, African women had to flee from the "voluptuous desires" of Frenchmen.‡

The French made a definitive commercial treaty with Seyyid Said in 1844, and appointed a consul at Zanzibar. Thereafter

* Reginald Coupland, *East Africa and Its Invaders* (Oxford, 1938), 361.

† Zanzibar Archives, ARC. 2: Krapf to Hamerton, 7 June 1848.

they traded throughout Said's dominions except in ivory and gum on the "Mrima"—i.e. the coast from Kilwa to Tanga—where Said wished to preserve the Arab monopoly and prevent Europeans going directly to the sources of supply. This prohibition applied to all the white traders now coming to Zanzibar, although it was not expressly stated in the first of the major treaties that Said signed—that with the United States of America in 1833.

The American trade was the preserve of a handful of merchants, nearly all of whom came from Salem in Massachusetts and who had seriously begun to operate in East African waters in the late 1820's. It was they who first benefited from Said's policy of imposing only a 5 per cent tax on goods brought into Zanzibar. At the end of his reign they were still supreme, handling about 55 per cent of the exports and 37 per cent of the imports in the "western trade" of Zanzibar. Krapf became friendly with the first American consul, R. P. Waters, who took up his duties in 1837. Waters' evangelistic fervour was to Krapf's taste but Krapf wisely rejected the American's suggestion that he should try to convert the Muslims in Zanzibar.*

German trade also developed in the 1840's with the activities of Wilhelm O'Swald and Jacob Hertz (who pioneered the profitable business of carrying cowrie shells from East to West Africa). A treaty between the Hanseatic Republics and Zanzibar was concluded in 1859, but, like the Americans, the Germans as yet had only a trading interest in Said's "empire".

Direct British trade with Zanzibar in this period was almost non-existent, the few attempts made to institute it all ending in failure. Krapf himself had to refuse to be drawn into one misconceived scheme which involved looking for antimony mines in East Africa.† Despite this situation, British influence was supreme at Zanzibar in the 1840's. This was partly because many of the Asian traders or "Banyans" who, like the European traders, had been encouraged by Said to operate in Zanzibar, were British subjects. Banyans dominated retailing, financed Arab ventures into the interior, farmed the customs and

---

* Mrs. Charles E. B. Russell, *General Rigby, Zanzibar, and the Slave Trade* (London, 1935), 344.

† CMSA: Krapf to Coates, 3 June 1846.

generally provided the economic energy which accounted for
the steady expansion of East African trade. The British were
represented in Zanzibar by an official holding the dual post of
East India Company agent and Foreign Office consul. This
appointment was, however, the result of much wider considerations than the activities of Banyans. Strategy required good
relations with Seyyid Said. The Cape route to India could be
menaced by too strong a French position in East Africa but
from the end of the eighteenth century, the Suez overland route
was of at least equal concern. This was one of the reasons for
safeguarding the north-western approaches to India, and Said's
position at Muscat consequently became involved. A treaty had
been signed with his father in 1798. Even when the French
danger seemed remote, the British still found it politic to
co-operate with Muscat in opposing common enemies like the
Jawasmi pirates. Naturally, for his part, Seyyid Said found it
profitable to have such a powerful ally. Thus the British
interest in Said was perhaps rather less because he was an East
African than because he was a Persian Gulf potentate.*

Other considerations which did point more directly to East
Africa itself were beginning to come into play by the 1840's. In
the first place there was the desire for scientific information—
particularly accurate geographical data. This was desired for its
own sake by bodies like the African Association (founded 1788)
which had merged into the Royal Geographical Society in 1831,
and the Bombay Geographical Society. Geographical studies
might, of course, provide a useful guide to future commercial
openings.† Secondly, there was the growing British concern
with the slave trade. In the long run, the price Seyyid Said and
his successors had to pay for the protection afforded by
Zanzibar's membership of the British "informal Empire" was
to lose one of their most profitable sources of revenue. A treaty
limiting the scope of the slave trade was negotiated in 1822 and
more rigorous clauses added in 1839. A new treaty operative
from 1847 was designed to prevent all export of slaves from

---

* Coupland, *Invaders*, 95ff.

† The investigations of Smee and Hardy (1811), and Christopher
(1843), of the Indian Navy may come into the category of commercial
investigations.

East Africa. Between roughly Lamu and Kilwa however, the carriage of slaves in East African waters remained legal, and beyond these limits it proved to be not difficult for slave dhows to avoid capture.

The two British interests of exploration and humanitarianism had earlier combined to produce the curious episode of the Mombasa Protectorate in the 1820's. Captain William Fitzwilliam Owen, leading an Admiralty Hydrographic Survey of the coasts of Africa, was also a keen advocate of abolition. The Mazrui clan in Mombasa sought British protection in 1822 when they were faced with the prospect of Seyyid Said's forces taking control of the city. Owen agreed to give that protection in return for an undertaking that the slave trade at Mombasa would be discontinued. Naturally, a new alliance which cut across the traditional alliance with Seyyid Said was unwelcome to the authorities at Bombay, and British concern and know-ledge of the Asiatic end of the slave trade was not yet enough to overbear this consideration. Nor did the government in London desire any more imperial territory if it could avoid it. Nevertheless, delays and muddles meant that Mombasa remained a British protectorate for the two years 1824–1826.* In 1837 Said finally ousted the Mazrui. Krapf had already met Mazrui refugees in Takaungu and was to find that memory of the protectorate had remained strong in Mombasa itself. It was unfortunate from his point of view that the most lasting relic of the British stay was the love of card playing since displayed by the local Arabs; the British, in his eyes, had done moral harm.†

Krapf was inclined to think that the British representative in Zanzibar twenty years later might also be doing moral harm. The British had signed their commercial treaty with Seyyid Said in 1839, and in 1841 Captain Atkins Hamerton had arrived as consul. Krapf could not but admire his skill in manipulating affairs in the British interest and was grateful for the various kinds of help that Hamerton gave to him and the mission. Cordial messages passed between the Foreign Office and the C.M.S. in 1850 as a result of this help. But the mission-

* Sir John Milner Gray, *The British in Mombasa* (London, 1957), 143–156.

† CMSA: Krapf to Coates, 9 April 1846.

ary was upset by the consul's "strong tendency to drunkenness", his "desecration of the Lord's day" and his use of "military expressions of the old and rough school".* For his part, Hamerton seems to have liked Krapf and even consulted him about the best way to deal with a drunken and dissolute nephew. In the last analysis, the success of Krapf's mission would depend on maintaining Hamerton's confidence since only through his influence could Arab toleration be obtained. Krapf realized this much, but he did not appreciate the British agent's policy well enough to see that his own developing desires to penetrate the interior might involve actions which did not suit Hamerton. The consul preferred not to stir up Arab jealousy and hostility by allowing any moves which could be construed as poaching on their preserves on the mainland.

In any case, all attempts by Europeans to penetrate the interior had so far failed; Lieutenant John Reitz, an officer of the Mombasa protectorate, for example, died after trying to go up the Pangani river. Soon after Krapf's arrival in East Africa, Lieutenant Maizan of the French Navy set out on an attempt to cross the continent. When only a short way inland, in 1845, he was murdered, possibly at the instigation of those in Zanzibar who feared European designs on East Africa.* While knowledge of the coast increased, the interior remained a mystery in the first five decades of the nineteenth century. Arab and Swahili travellers provided information, but it was difficult to translate their data into reliable maps and guides. Indeed, it seemed to many geographical scholars that Ptolemy was still as good an authority as any for East African topography.

One might ask why it was that Europeans had as yet failed to penetrate the interior to any significant extent. The usual answer given to this question is in terms of the physical difficulties of terrain, unnavigable rivers, disease, fierce tribes, etc. These factors have their importance and explain the failures of Reitz and Maizan, but they do not provide a complete answer since these same conditions still operated when the first major journeys by Krapf, Rebmann, Burton, and Speke were

* CMSA: Krapf to Coates, 25 February 1846.
‡ Richard Francis Burton, *The Lake Regions of Central Africa* (London, 1860), I, 73–76.

made in the 1840's and 1850's. The crucial difference seems to be that, in the later period, effort, time, and capital were devoted to overcoming the difficulties. In other words, European concern had become great enough for something like a sustained effort to be made. This had happened a generation before in West Africa. The process now began in East Africa with Krapf and for this reason, if no other, he is an important figure, though it should be noted that for the Arabs, penetration of the interior was common from about 1825. It could be argued, in fact, that European exploration was possible only when Arab traders had blazed the trail. What is less often realised is that Europeans and Arabs alike were themselves following African trade routes.

During the period of the changes on the coast that have been outlined, equally significant developments were occuring in African societies of the interior. These developments were for the first time firmly to link the destiny of the peoples of the interior with events on the coast. The position can best be summarized by saying that until the end of the eighteenth century, migrations had taken mainly a north-south direction. In the eighteenth century however, one begins to discern west-east movement, for example, in the apparent spread of certain forms of political organisation eastwards from Unyamwezi—a spread which may possibly be associated with the development of long distance trade.† At any rate, connections between peoples were certainly ceasing to be only on interior lines, and the growing habit of taking ivory down to the coast from Unyamwezi is one important manifestation of a change which had consequences far and wide. By the end of the eighteenth century, for example, it is clear that goods from the coast were for the first time reaching Buganda, almost certainly *via* Unyamwezi. Probably the majority of East African peoples came to be affected by the outside world to some degree well before any alien traders from the coast actually reached them. Existing inter-tribal trading and raiding contacts now began

---

† Roland Oliver, "Discernible Developments in the Interior, 1500–1840" in Roland Oliver and Gervase Mathew (eds.), *History of East Africa* (Oxford, 1963), I, 205.

to be given added point by the arrival of coastal goods like
cloth and beads.

In the region with which Krapf was to be particularly
concerned, as further south, a coastwards movement seems to
have been apparent. Here a contributory factor may have been
the disquiet caused by the arrival of the Masai. It was the
Kamba people living to the east of the Masai who opened up
regular contacts with the coast at Mombasa. Krapf himself
notes the importance of the famine of 1836 in bringing Kamba
people to the coast,* but it seems clear that the contact was
already well established when British officers reported that
Kamba tribesmen were trading at a place called Kwa Jomvu,
near Mombasa, more than ten years before.† Kivoi, who was to
prove so important in Krapf's adventures, seems to have been
a "chief" who emerged as important among the Kamba as a
result of the organisation of trade caravans to the coast. His
tribe was one not normally characterized by chiefly institutions.

Instances of such changes could be multiplied. Their pace
was increased, of course, by the advent of Arab and Swahili
traders in the interior. Their arrival was also disruptive not only
because it involved a greater demand for slaves and ivory than
could easily be satisfied without upsetting existing social and
economic arrangements, but also because it was a reversal of
the movement by Africans from the interior to the coast. In
other words, there was a substitution of Arab or Swahili middlemen for Africans like the Kamba. This process was only just
beginning in the Mombasa region when Krapf arrived, perhaps
because the rivalry between Mombasa and Zanzibar had until
recently been an all-engrossing concern for the Arabs and
Swahili of Mombasa. Further south, of course, Arab and
Swahili traders had been travelling the routes inland from
Bagamoyo for about twenty years. They had travelled even
earlier from the Kilwa coast.

It was, then, a complex and changing East Africa in which
Krapf began to work in 1844. The Nyika people, with whom
he was at first most intimately concerned, occupied an inter-

---

* D. Anthony Low, "The Northern Interior, 1840–1884", *ibid.*, 314.
† Thomas Boteler, *Narrative of a Voyage of Discovery to Africa and
Arabia* (London, 1835), 205, 211–212.

mediate position. Whilst they received Kamba traders and feared the occasional foray into their territory by interior tribes, they were, on the other hand, subject to a fair amount of control by coastal Arabs. These people were actually nine tribes, collectively called the "WaNyika"—a word denoting people of the wilderness—only by outsiders. They probably settled in what is now the southern half of the Kenya coast after about 1300 A.D. This followed the dispersion of Bantu peoples caused by the arrival of the Galla from the north, some of whose customs, notably the idea of age sets, the Nyika adopted.* The Nyika were an agricultural people living in rather widely scattered settlements with no immediately obvious centres of political authority. Important decisions were normally the responsibility of councils of elders at various levels.†

Krapf's first encounter with the Nyika was determined by his friendship with a trader called Abdulla Ben Pisila who had links with the Kamba traders as well as considerable influence among the peoples of the Rabai tribe who were one of the principal of the nine divisions of the Nyika. The fortuitous onset of a rainstorm together with the Arab's influence made Krapf particularly welcome in Rabai Mpia, a small village on an elevated site about twelve miles north-west of Mombasa, which he eventually selected as the best place for a mission house. Until the arrival of Rebmann in mid-1846, however, Krapf remained in Mombasa, making various excursions to spy out the land and sow the first seeds of Christianity by preaching to the pagans that he encountered. Already he had available his own translations of parts of the Gospels into the Swahili and Nyika tongues.

IV   RABAI AND A STRATEGY FOR THE MISSION 1846–1851

With the coming of Rebmann, the serious work of the mission could begin. House building operations, linguistic work, preaching at Rabai and neighbouring hamlets, attempts

* George Wynn Brereton Huntingford, "The Peopling of East Africa", in Oliver and Mathew, *East Africa*, 89–91.
† Adriaan Hendrik Johan Prins, *The Coastal Tribes of the North Eastern Bantu* (London, 1952), 35, 59, 74–78.

to institute the observance of the Sabbath and to instruct children all became part of the two men's daily life. But Rabai's site had been selected by Krapf partly also with a view to its giving access to the far interior (it was already a resort of Kamba traders), and Rebmann, initially at least, was to show himself no less willing than his colleague to take advantage of this fact.

Johann Rebmann, born in 1820, was also from Württemberg, although Krapf had not met him before. The senior missionary was relieved, he said, to find Rebmann single-minded like himself;* indeed Rebmann was to prove single-minded enough about his work in East Africa to stay on until 1875. This tenacity must have been Rebmann's principal gift; one does not receive the impression that he had many of the other talents required of a pioneer missionary.

Rebmann had trained at Basle Seminary and then moved on to Islington for further study and Anglican ordination before arriving in East Africa. The same was true of the third recruit, Jacob Erhardt (c. 1823–1901) who was sent to reinforce the mission in June 1849 together with Johann Wagner. The latter died of fever less than two months after his arrival, but Erhardt survived to play an important part in the mission during the next few years. He had some medical knowledge and thus added a new aspect to the work of the mission.† More important, he seems to have been a man with much more determined views than Rebmann—views which were to prove incompatible with those of Krapf. Following the first major journeys inland that he and Rebmann had made in 1847–1849, Krapf was now thinking very seriously of the missionary possibilities in the interior which could be opened up from the base at Rabai.

In London, the Church Missionary Society's interest in Krapf's proceedings is evident from its willingness to send him colleagues. Although it is probably true to say that India provided the burning issue for the Society in these years, the supporters of missionary endeavour certainly did not lack knowledge of Krapf's exploits. Very full extracts from his journals were regularly published in the *Church Missionary*

---

* CMSA: Krapf to Coates, 13 June 1846.
† CMSA: Erhardt to Venn, 24 September 1850.

Record, a periodical issued from 1830 onwards. East African activities may almost be said to dominate the early issues of the *Church Missionary Intelligencer*. This was a monthly journal, published from 1849 onwards under the editorship of Joseph Ridgway, which aimed to attract a reading public from among those interested in geography and travel as well as the supporters of missionary activities. Thus the East African mission's geographical exploits and their implications received considerable attention in the new magazine. The discovery of the snow-capped mountains Kilimanjaro and Kenya, by Rebmann and Krapf in 1848–1849 was of particular importance from this point of view.

Sales of the *Intelligencer* presumably helped to augment the financial resources of the C,M.S. The total annual income for the society had been about £75,000 in the 1840's, the major part of which was used in India and Ceylon. Krapf complained in 1849 that shortage of funds was hindering his work and offered to go into the ivory trade on behalf of the Society.* To a certain extent, he personally depended financially upon a certain Rev. John Olive whose living does not appear to have been a rich one. But suggestions for expedients like ivory trading could be ignored by the C.M.S. after 1849. That year marked the beginning of a decade of financial advance for the Society when its annual income often exceeded £100,000. Thus when Krapf visited London for the first time in June 1850, he arrived during a period when the financial situation was much more encouraging than it had been. By 1856, according to one account, the Society would have spent £12,000 on the East African mission.†

Krapf's return to Europe in June 1850 was occasioned not only by his desire to recruit his health after thirteen years in Africa but also by his wish to obtain the support of the C.M.S. for the ambitious plans that he had begun to develop for his mission. Krapf's wanderlust could never for long be stilled and the acquaintance he had made with the Kamba traders,

---

* CMSA: Krapf to Venn, 28 February 1849. Many of Krapf's letters were published in the *Church Missionary Intelligencer*, but complaints of lack of support or offers to trade in ivory were naturally omitted.

† Stock, *History*, I, 477, 480–481. Burton, *Lake Regions*, I, 6–7.

his selection of the site at Rabai, and the six major journeys he
and Rebmann had already made into the interior all point to
his unwillingness to remain cut off from the pagans of the
hinterland. What he proposed to do was to open up a suitable
route from Rabai, initially to Unyamwezi but eventually to
the west coast of Africa. Krapf envisaged exploratory journeys
during which he or his helpers would be preaching and preparing
the way for the later establishment of permanent missionary
stations along the route. Eventually, a chain of Christian
centres across the continent would be formed.

The C.M.S. committee accepted Krapf's ideas. This
acceptance is indicative of the good impression he must have
made and of the interest which he had aroused in East Africa,
for it involved a considerable departure from normal missionary
precedents. The principle adopted was that, rather than settle
down in one spot, Krapf and his companions should try to
reach Unyamwezi, covering as much ground as they could, and
preaching to as many people as possible on the way. To justify
this departure from precedent, the C.M.S. argued that the
snow-capped mountains that Krapf and Rebmann had
discovered showed the interior to be healthier than the coast
(and most of West Africa) because it was higher, that the fierce
Masai were less of a threat than they had been, that there were
indications of strong non-Islamic chiefs who would protect the
missionaries in the interior, that, in any case, the Sultan of
Zanzibar wielded influence inland over a wide area and was
well-disposed towards Krapf, and finally, that the close
relationship of all the Bantu languages spoken in East Africa
which Krapf had noted would make a policy of moving about
among large numbers of people a practicable one. It is also
possible that East African expansion seemed to fit in with the
society's currently successful expansion in West Africa, where
the Yoruba mission was opening new stations in these years.

Krapf left England to return to Mombasa in January 1851.
Ridgway of the *Church Missionary Intelligencer* hailed the new
scheme as "England's answer to the Papal Agression", and
with Prince Albert communicating his interest, no doubt an air
of great importance was given to the whole project. But was
this a geographical investigation rather than missionary work?

At the valedictory meeting, Henry Venn, the Society's honorary secretary and its dominating figure in the mid-nineteenth century, specifically denied that the new mission was concerned with the "adventitious attractions of geographical and linguistic discoveries." To reassure the doubtful, he went on to say that the "sober calculations of wise men" had demonstrated that the extensive aims of the new venture would not constitute a squandering of "sacred funds". (Confronted with the somewhat similar situation of a missionary wanting to blaze a trail rather than to work in a conventional manner, the London Missionary Society was, a few years later, to end its formal connection with David Livingstone.)

In detail, the 1850 plan envisaged that Krapf and a new recruit would prospect for a mission station site to the northwest of Mombasa. They would follow the Kamba trade route which Krapf had already travelled. Erhardt and a second newcomer were to move southwestwards towards Usambara—which Krapf had also visited with promising results in 1848. Rebmann's investigations towards Kilimanjaro must have been assumed to be conclusive enough because Mt. Kadiaro was designated as the site of a future station among the Teita people. Accordingly, Rebmann was to remain at Rabai for the time being, while the other investigations went on.*

V   BREAKDOWN OF THE MISSION, AND A RETURN TO ETHIOPIA, 1851–1855

From the outset of his new scheme great difficulties presented themselves to Krapf. None of the new recruits who was to help implement the plan became an effective member of the mission. Six men had originally been engaged to accompany Krapf back to Africa in 1851. All were from Basle. Of the three missionaries among them, one was adjudged in London to be unsuitable, the second, Conrad Diehlmann, smelt popery in the Anglican Church and therefore left Krapf at Aden while the third, Christian Pfefferle, died soon after reaching Rabai in May 1851. Reflecting the Basle emphasis on practical accompaniments to missionary labour, three "lay mechanics",

* (*Church Missionary*) *Intelligencer*, II (1851), 39–42; 3rd Series, VII (1882), 133.

Hagemann, a carpenter, Kaiser, an agriculturist, and Metzler, a smith, had also been engaged to help the mission. They joined Krapf at Trieste but were not destined to remain with the mission.*

Seriously crippled from the start, the new scheme was nevertheless put in hand by Krapf himself with the planned journey northwest to Ukambani in July–September 1851. This trip wås disastrous and Krapf narrowly escaped with his life. Undeterred even then, he made a visit to Usambara early in the following year with encouraging enough results for him to wish to persevere with the idea of a mission station there as a link in the proposed chain. Yet Rabai was not the best base from which to reach Usambara. In 1848, it is true, Krapf had travelled there overland, but the easiest way of reaching the kingdom was *via* the coastal towns of Pangani or Tanga. Moreover, the Kamba route although accessible from Rabai, certainly did not lead to Unyamwezi. This Krapf now realised, although he pointed out that it did provide a route to other important tribes like the Kikuyu. All routes inland from the Mombasa area were subject to attacks by the Masai (a generic term for the Kwavi and the pastoral Masai). The most convenient way of reaching Unyamwezi was to take a caravan route from one of the towns on the mainland opposite Zanzibar. With Rabai remaining the base this meant an initial and inconvenient sea journey.

It may be that Krapf considered the "Mrima" coast to be so closely controlled by the Zanzibari Arabs that a Christian base there was impracticable. Whether this was so or not, Krapf's own handling of the situation on the "Mrima" coast was so clumsy as to add yet another obstacle to the implementation of his strategy of 1850 and, in particular, to spoil the chance of founding a mission station in Usambara.

Kimweri, King of Usambara, had actually offered Krapf a site for a mission station when the two men first met in 1848. The Muslim advisers at the pagan Kimweri's court were natur-

* Stock, *History*, II, 130–132; *Intelligencer*, II (1851), 44. It is not clear exactly when Hagemann withdrew, but the other two mechanics, wishing to avoid Pfefferle's fate, left sometime soon after September, 1851.

ally displeased by this action for religious reasons. Political considerations were also involved; Seyyid Said's relations with Kimweri were already somewhat delicate; the ruler of Usambara was powerful enough to share with Said a "condominium" over the Tanga-Pangani section of the coast. In practice, this meant that the two authorities bargained over the appointment of governors for the area and Kimweri occasionally exacted tribute.* As long as the dominant outside influence in Usambara remained Arab, Kimweri's actual power and this recognition of it posed no major problem for Zanzibar. But the offer of a site for a mission station might be taken as indicating that Europeans were about to usurp the Omani influence in the kingdom.

Early in 1852, when Krapf, in pursuance of his strategy, made his second visit to Usambara, the offer of a site was renewed. This was enough to arouse Arab suspicions, but Krapf seemed to confirm the worst of these fears by sponsoring the activities of one of Kimweri's officials—the *Mbereko*—who accompanied the missionary back to Zanzibar from Usambara. The *Mbereko* attempted to sell ivory to a French merchant and, claiming to be acting in accordance with Kimweri's wishes, Krapf put him in touch with other European and American traders. Thus the middleman's function of the Arabs and coastal people seemed to be threatened by the development of direct economic relations between Europeans and peoples of the interior.

It happened that Consul Hamerton was away from Zanzibar at this time; had he been present, he would almost certainly have prevented Krapf from upsetting the Arabs in this way. As it was, Hamerton's absence had a further unfortunate effect. With no other companion,† Krapf seems to have spent much time, both before he set off for Usambara in February 1852 and on his return in April, with the French Consul, S. de Belligny. The French were particularly active in East Africa at this time. Anxious to promote their trade, they were not unwilling to consider schemes that would by-pass the hold of

* Coupland, *Invaders*, 351–352.
† Erhardt was not in Zanzibar at this time, as Coupland assumes, *ibid*., 414.

the Arab middlemen by setting up stations on the mainland. Krapf was widely believed to have told Belligny that Seyyid Said did not control the section of the coast where the "condominium" arrangements operated and this was interpreted as being an attack on the Zanzibar Arabs and a recommendation to the French to open up direct trade with Kimweri—with whom Krapf had made the necessary arrangements. All that really happened was that Krapf simply related the true state of affairs regarding Usambara and the section of the coast in question. It would appear that he unwisely repeated his observations in writing after his return to Rabai, although Rebmann and Erhardt warned him not to do so. Ironically enough, Krapf's view (derived from his experiences of 1848) that the Sultan had "not one inch of ground" on the coastal area in question, had already been published in the *Church Missionary Intelligencer* in Britain in 1849.

In the rumpus caused by the Arab wrath with Krapf in 1852–1853, the missionary was not entirely an innocent victim. He obviously thought that it would be desirable if the Muslim stranglehold on the trade of the coast could be loosened. But equally obviously, as he frequently made plain, he would not wish to replace Arab by French Roman Catholic control. Moreover, Krapf had imagined that Belligny's inquiries on such matters were occasioned simply by the consul's desire to collect geographical and ethnographical information for the Paris Geographical Society. This may indeed have been part of Belligny's purpose, for the Society was showing interest in Krapf and East Africa at this period. But the more immediate purposes to which Belligny put the information frightened the Arabs considerably. Consequently, when Hamerton and the Sultan returned to Zanzibar in 1853 and heard the story, Krapf became a victim of their extreme displeasure. Although remaining personally friendly and delivering only a mild rebuke to him, Hamerton was irritated by Krapf's "meddling" because it upset his policy of conciliating the Arabs. His strictures were passed on to the C.M.S. by the Foreign Office.* In fact, little harm was done to the position of either Said or Britain. But Krapf had done himself and his new strategy considerable harm;

* *Ibid.*, 414–417; *Intelligencer*, I (1850), 203.

he remained discredited for some years—as Burton was pointedly to emphasize—and could hardly rely on Hamerton's help for any further ventures into the interior. More particularly, Tongwe in Usambara, which had been offered as the site for the future missionary station, was soon occupied instead by a detachment of Said's Baluchi soldiers.* The Sultan had reacted to the scare by securing the acknowledgement of his over-lordship not only by Kimweri but also by all the authorities along the coast.† The whole episode had shown that Krapf could be naive in political matters if not, indeed, unwise and obtuse.

With Hamerton and the Foreign Office alienated, the only other powerful body in Britain which might conceivably have helped the C.M.S. and its East African mission in some way was the Royal Geographical Society. It was at this time beginning to show an interest in East Africa. But considerable doubts had been thrown on the validity of the discovery of the snowy mountains by Krapf and Rebmann. Moreover, there must have been more general doubts about the missionaries' proficiency as explorers which, after all, is what the new strategy required that they should be.

It is true that when Krapf reached the Tana river, east of Mt. Kenya during his visit to Ukambani in 1851, he had marched some 300 miles from Mombasa. This constituted his longest East African expedition and, given the circumstances in which he travelled, it was an impressive performance. But it may be legitimate to ask whether he, and earlier Rebmann, could not have achieved more than they did once they had actually set out on expeditions; were the obstacles to their reaching Unyamwezi or one of the lakes insuperable?

Lack of money was a great impediment. The missionaries were unable to provide themselves either with sufficient goods to pay their way through the territories of the various tribes or with a big enough force of men to make them at least semi-independent of local chiefs. Neither Krapf nor Rebmann wished to use force in any case; indeed Krapf would not fire his gun when under attack in 1851 and proudly claimed that he

* Coupland, *Invaders*, 352 n.
† CMSA: Krapf to Venn, 14 March 1853.

normally marched along, "carrying nothing about me but my umbrella".* Even with the limited resources at his command and even given his determination not to use force, Krapf might have managed longer journeys had his organisation been rather more sophisticated. The impression is that his expeditions were made with little real preparation, for there were rarely more than half a dozen porters with him, and he had few presents ready to offer. It is true that this was in part a policy; Krapf had believed that the solution to the problem of present giving was to have few things to give.†

That even with lax organisation of caravans the missionaries achieved as much as they did may be attributed in large part to the help of experienced travellers. Krapf and Rebmann both relied before 1849 on the services of an Arab they call "Bana Kheri" (more correctly Bwana Heri), while Krapf later depended on "Chief" Kivoi, a leading Kamba trader whose death was to leave the European bereft and in danger of losing his own life on the 1851 trip.

Krapf first met Kheri in 1847 and he proved to be a willing guide as well as one of the few Arabs in Mombasa who either knew or was prepared to tell much of what he knew of the interior. His death at the hands of the Masai in 1849 was another blow to Krapf's 1851 strategy. Exactly on what basis he was paid for his service before 1849 and precisely how much, it is difficult to determine, although on the first Usambara trip, when he accompanied Krapf, he was paid fifteen dollars while the seven porters received five dollars each.‡ Such a small party of men seems to preclude trade, but possibly Kheri found the trips useful for the purpose of arranging future commercial transactions; Mrs. Stahl has recently pointed out that he always guided Rebmann to the parts of Kilimanjaro where the Chagga groups with whom he had close trading arrangements were situated.§

* *Intelligencer*, I (1850), 401.
† *Ibid.*, 379.
‡ *I.e.* Maria Theresa dollars. Below 267, 277; *Intelligencer*, I (1850), 41, 254. CMSA: Krapf, Journal, 28 September 1847.
§ Kathleen M. Stahl, *The Chagga People of Kilimanjaro* (The Hague, 1964), 159.

On his last trip, because of some disagreement, Rebmann was unaccompanied by Kheri, and was unable to achieve his object of going beyond Kilimanjaro towards Unyamwezi. Whether even Kheri could have helped Rebmann at this point may be doubted since Mamkinga, chief of Machame, was obviously unwilling to let the missionary proceed. The fact that the missionaries were, to a greater extent than they realised, at the mercy of African chiefs or men like Kheri, limited their achievements when they travelled.

In the last resort, however, Krapf's strategy did not fail simply because he and Rebmann were inefficient explorers or because of the political complications arising from encounters with African chiefs, Arabs, or Frenchmen. Krapf's greatest obstacle was the attitude of his own companions. Returning to Rabai in 1851 determined to open a new age for East Africa by bearing the Cross into the interior, Krapf was dismayed to find that his fellow missionaries were far from sharing his enthusiasm. Rebmann explained his doubts to the C.M.S. It was vital, he said, not to weaken the first link in the continental mission chain; Rabai must be consolidated before new ventures were attempted. There was not yet enough "iron" to fashion a chain of a strength sufficient to bear the "immense weight" of East African heathendom. Rebmann concluded on an extremely defeatist note, minimising the importance of East Africa and advising the C.M.S. not to send out any more helpers for the time being.*

Though he was formerly in tune with Krapf's ideas, the difficulties Rebmann had encountered on his last major journey into the interior (April–June 1849) seem to have disillusioned him about the prospects of reaching Unyamwezi. He made no more excursions during the rest of his long career. Yet it was Erhardt whose opposition was the more important. Krapf believed that he had adversely influenced Rebmann regarding the new strategy. Erhardt point-blank refused to undertake his part of the scheme, which was to have been opening up the Usambara link in the mission chain. Pressure from the home committee led to his making an attempt in 1853, but, by this time, Krapf's own journey of the year before and its unfortun-

* CMSA: Rebmann to Venn, 22 March 1851, 13 April 1854.

ate aftermath of Arab hostility had made the task much more difficult. Erhardt was thus able to make the point that Krapf's own political indiscretions had seriously prejudiced implementation of the new strategy. During the period when he was still refusing to move and whilst Krapf was away on his two journeys of 1851–1852, Erhardt demonstrated his view of priorities by building a new mission house at Kisuludini near Rabai. Rebmann meanwhile went to Cairo in October 1851 to marry a Mrs. Tyler who had been helping in the work of the C.M.S. there. The couple then returned to Rabai to assist Erhardt in his construction work. When Krapf re-appeared in April 1852, the other two missionaries began to live in the new house leaving him alone in the old one. Though the three men joined for prayers, Krapf felt that this was an empty formality. The estrangement seems to have been deep and lasting.*

Several possible reasons for the breakdown in friendship may be immediately suggested. There was, first of all, a genuine conflict of principle over the correct policy for a pioneer mission. Perhaps, too, Rebmann and Erhardt felt they had not been sufficiently consulted when Krapf went to London to secure the Society's endorsement of his ideas. Had there been an officially designated leader of the mission, if not necessarily yet a bishop, some of the difficulties might have been avoided. The obvious hostility of the Arabs and Hamerton's now critical attitude did much to confirm Rebmann and Erhardt in their opposition. But behind this there were probably more specifically personal antagonisms. Very little by way of contemporary estimates of the characters of the men involved is available except in the most general terms, but one may guess that Krapf must often have seemed to his companions pedantic and intolerant while visionary and unpractical in his aims. Rebmann appeared to Krapf, on the other hand, to be obstinate and increasingly unadventurous while Erhardt must have demonstrated enough of the brashness of youth to irritate the more experienced missionary. Even worse, he had a dispiriting awareness of the political realities in East Africa. No doubt the normal heightening of tensions and irritations caused by

* CMSA: Erhardt to Venn, 11 April 1851, 9 April 1853; Krapf to Venn 10 April 1851, 10 April, 11 November 1852.

malarial fevers exacerbated the situation between the three men.

All this would hardly be guessed from Krapf's text or from contemporary C.M.S. publications. Yet by those who knew the situation, the pages below (506–514), where Krapf gives advice to future missionaries, were to be read as an indictment of his "dear friends Rebmann and Erhardt". The first of the five major points in his homily warns the aspirant evangelist in East Africa not to become faint-hearted about the magnitude of his task and, in the light of what we know, this can be seen as a clear attack on Rebmann's shortcomings. The second recommendation—with its references to settling down "behind bolt and bar"—is obviously aimed at Erhardt and the new house. In letters to the C.M.S.,* Krapf complained that creature comforts—the new house, Rebmann's wife, and Erhardt's tobacco pipe—inhibited missionary fervour. The third point deals with the problem of present giving and may refer, in part, to Erhardt's view that exploratory journeys ought to be well financed and properly organised, not undertaken by small, ill-provided caravans of the type that Krapf had hitherto led. "Respect an old and experienced missionary" is Krapf's lament at the opposition he had experienced. The threat that God might strike down critical young men like Erhardt, if it reflects Krapf's normal attitude, can hardly have endeared him to his fellows. A final point concerns the possibility of political changes and the problem of whether a missionary needed the backing of European civil power to carry out his work effectively. Erhardt and Rebmann seem to have come to the conclusion that extension of their work must wait upon the arrival of European government; Krapf regarded such an attitude as unrealistic and defeatist.†

By referring to them in this allusive manner, Krapf concealed the disputes from the general reader. He was thus surely charitable to his companions despite the fact that their lack of support must have been deeply wounding. His decision to leave Rabai in September 1853 was ostensibly because a bowel complaint had become much worse. In fact, although relations

* CMSA: Krapf to C.M.S. 22 April 1852, 4 April 1854.
† CMSA: Erhardt to C.M.S. 27 October 1854.

had been patched up a little in March, Krapf's departure was probably as much because the estrangement from his companions made life so unpleasant.* Krapf's subsequent proceedings show that, as yet, he had no desire to end his active missionary career. Moreover, the home committee had not lost confidence in him and his plans; they refused to recall him at the height of the disputes, remonstrated with Rebmann and Erhardt, and proposed in 1854 to send out another recruit to accompany Krapf back to East Africa to carry on with the work.

Heartened by this friendly reception in London, Krapf set out again late in 1854 accompanied by the new recruit, J. G. Deimler, a Bavarian who had been through the seminary at Basle. Deimler left Krapf at Suez to go on to Bombay to learn Arabic, and ultimately did not work in East Africa at all, though he seems to have visited Rebmann in 1857. Krapf had complicated his plans by agreeing to help Gobat, now Bishop in Jerusalem, who wanted to revive the protestant cause in Ethiopia by sending missionaries there again, Gobat had some trainees under his care, most of whom were from Württemberg, ready to fulfil this project. Krapf's experience of Ethiopia would have made it possible for him to act as a guide to Gobat's trainees. In the event, Krapf was accompanied by one of them, Martin Flad, who was to have some importance in subsequent Ethiopian history, and who also seems to have become a lifelong friend. Krapf actually planned to return to East Africa *via* Ethiopia. Thus, besides acting for Gobat, he would have the chance of fulfilling his long cherished desire to visit the Galla and the Christian remnants south of Shoa. It seems that Krapf aimed, once this ambitious journey was accomplished, not to stay at Rabai with his former companions but to found a station further inland about half way to Kilimanjaro on the isolated upland of Mount Kadiaro among the Teita people. This was the point Rebmann had reached on his first venture to the interior in 1847 and recommended as a potential missionary site.

By 1854–55, developments in a Masai (probably Kwavi) civil war had made Kadiaro a dangerous spot,† but in any case,

* CMSA: Krapf to Venn, 14 March, 4 November 1853.
† Zanzibar Archives, Arc. 15: Erhardt to Hamerton, 10 January 1855.

Krapf was not destined to reach there. Conditions in Ethiopia thwarted his plans for what would have been, even in the most favourable circumstances, a very long and risky journey through Galla territory. As it was, he now made one of his longest and most difficult forays in Africa. Landing at Massawa, he traversed northern Ethiopia in the months February to June 1855. He passed through Adowa, Gondar, and Sennar to arrive in the Nile valley at Khartoum. This was an extremely interesting period in Ethiopian history when pressure from Europeans and a new Muslim threat had created conditions in which the redoubtable Kassa could raise an army to defeat the major provincial rulers and have himself crowned Emperor. The coronation came after his victory over Ubié of Tigré and just before Krapf met him in April 1855. The fact that Theodore, as he now styled himself, was turning his attention to Shoa and the Galla in the southern part of Abyssinia explains why Krapf was unable to make his way south overland. But the favourable atmosphere for Protestant Christianity following the expulsion of the Catholics by Theodore must have been an additional reason for returning quickly in order to report to Gobat. In the event, missionary prospects were to prove illusory since Theodore wanted only the technical expertise that Gobat's men could offer, and the attempts to follow them up became part of the story of the tragedy of the fall of Theodore—an event with which Krapf was to be somewhat concerned ten years later. Krapf's account of his journey furnishes some interesting material on Abyssinia during this period.*

The rigours of the trek down the Nile valley in mid 1855, especially the crossing of the Nubian desert, convinced Krapf that the state of his health now positively demanded that he forsake active work in Africa for a time, although until a late stage he was still contemplating sailing to Mombasa from Egypt. It may be, too, that he thought that he could immediately do more for the projected chain of mission stations in Africa by promoting the idea in Europe than by returning to his reluctant companions. Thus in September 1855 he settled in Württemberg, and refused a C.M.S. invitation to take on the

* Below, 432–484.

unadventurous job of teaching freed slaves on the island of Mauritius.*

VI ERHARDT AND REBMANN

In East Africa after 1853, the active life of the mission drew to a close, not to be revived for another twenty years. Whilst Erhardt remained, however, there were some interesting developments. After his initial hesitations of 1851–1852, he went to Pangani in March 1853 but decided that the whole area was too disturbed for him to be able to get inland to Usambara. Yet he was now thoroughly interested in East Africa and prompted, perhaps, by the unwelcome decision of the C.M.S. to transfer him to Bombay, he tried a second time and reached Usambara during a journey which lasted from August to December. Kimweri's renewed offer of Tongwe as a mission station was now useless as Said's troops occupied the place and the Arabs naturally objected to an alternative site. The Sultan later told Erhardt that he could not allow a mission inland anyway or, so he claimed, the French and Americans would demand the same privileges. Despite this, Erhardt, in his somewhat belated enthusiasm for emulating Krapf's example, hoped to obtain permission to go inland again. Meanwhile he went to Tanga to begin learning the language of the people of Usambara. He was there between March and October 1854 but again found the hostility of the Arabs such as to discourage further work in the interior.†

The result of Erhardt's sojourn in Tanga was to have some importance in the exploration of East Africa. The missionary gathered the information which formed the basis of the so-called "slug-map" which will be referred to later. With his health failing, Erhardt finally obeyed a C.M.S. injunction and left East Africa early in 1855. While in Europe he arranged at Ludwigsburg for the publication of a Masai vocabulary for which Krapf wrote a patronising preface. He also communicated his geographical ideas to the Royal Geographical Society together with some bad advice on the methods, and optimistic

---

* *Intelligencer*, 3rd Series VII (1882), 141.

† CMSA: Erhardt to C.M.S., 9 April, 27 December 1853, 24 March, 27 October 1854; Erhardt's Journals, August–December 1853, March–October 1854.

forecasts of the costs, of exploring East Africa.* After 1856, Erhardt fades from the scene; he was sent to India where he worked for thirty-five years before retiring to Stuttgart. He died there in August 1901 "at an advanced age".†

Rebmann remained at Rabai although he often wrote of the hopeless nature of the task in East Africa. He continued to be bitter in his comments on Krapf and it was not until 1864 that the latter was able to report the restoration of "peace and love" with his old companion. In 1855, Rebmann had started for home on the grounds that the C.M.S. was neglecting him, but the Society persuaded him to return.‡ It seems that the committee hoped that Rebmann would at least maintain a footing in East Africa and make studies of languages for the benefit of future missionaries. It was often easy to forget Rebmann; "an honest and conscientious man he had yet all the qualities which secure unsuccess" wrote Burton, who also alleged that Rebmann's one convert was prepared by a long course of idiocy.§ This was Abbé Gunja. Yet by 1864 there were six converts and six under tuition.‖ Abbé Gunja and his son, who was baptised in 1861, ultimately established a nucleus of Christianity among the Giryama. They were aided by two freed slaves, educated in Bombay, who came to Rabai together with two girls designated as wives for new converts.¶

The result of Rebmann's linguistic work was the reduction of two languages to writing. Curiously, although this is again according to Burton, the missionary did not begin seriously to study the language of the Nyika people until 1857. In time, however, he produced a dictionary much used by his successors at Mombasa. The fair copy was lost and the book was not

* Jacob Erhardt, *Vocabulary of the Engutuk Iloigob* (Ludwigsburg, 1857). R.G.S. Archives: Erhardt to Shaw, 10 November 1855, 17 March, 2 April 1856. *Proceedings of The Royal Geographical Society*, I (1855–1856), 8–12.

† Stock, *History*, II, 135; *The Geographical Journal*, XVIII (1901), 543.

‡ CMSA: Rebmann to Venn, 2 January 1854, 18 November 1855, 7 July 1857; Krapf to Venn, 6 December 1864.

§ Richard Francis Burton, *Zanzibar; City, Island and Coast* (London, 1872), II, 56–58.

‖ Roland Oliver, *The Missionary Factor in East Africa* (London, 1952), 6.

¶ *Intelligencer*, 3rd series, I (1876), 697. Stock, *History*, II, 430–433.

published until long after his death, having been edited from a rough version by Krapf and Thomas Sparshott, a subsequent missionary in East Africa. Krapf also brought out Rebmann's *Kiniassa Dictionary* in 1877. Rebmann's informants had been slaves from the Lake Nyasa region. Though it seems odd that he should have begun this work in 1853, before he tackled the local Nyika language, it was undoubtedly useful since so many of the freed slaves later sent to Rabai were from the great slave sources around Lake Nyasa. Krapf's derogatory remarks in the preface on the little that Rebmann had produced show that the old wounds had not altogether healed, although he later relented a little when he learnt of the existence of the KiNyika dictionary. Rebmann's other product was a translation of St. Luke's Gospel into Swahili.*

There were no further exploratory ventures in this later period of Rebmann's life. In 1856, when Burton and Speke set off for Lake Tanganyika, it was suggested that the missionary might accompany them. The C.M.S. gave its permission, but Rebmann objected to being associated with explorers who carried weapons. Burton says that the Arabs and Hamerton would not, in any case, have allowed a member of the mission to go inland after the upset caused by Krapf's indiscretions. However, Burton found all of the information that Rebmann gave him most useful in compiling his various accounts of East Africa, and was accordingly unwontedly restrained in his comments about the missionary.

At the time of Burton's visit to Rabai, there was a threat from Masai civil war refugees. Though Rebmann showed no fear at all, Burton and Speke returned to Rabai in January 1857 "swords in hand to help". They insisted on the evacuation of Mrs. Rebmann and she and her husband did finally retreat to Zanzibar for a period of several months.† They returned to their unspectacular work in 1858, apparently faced with the

---

* J. L. Krapf and J. Rebmann (ed. Thomas Sparshott), *A Nika-English Dictionary* (London, 1887). J. Rebmann (ed. J. L. Krapf), *Dictionary of the Kiniassa Language* (St. Chrischona, 1877). Krapf, *Dictionary of Suahili*, viii. J. Rebmann, *The Gospel of St. Luke translated into the Suaheli Language* (St. Chrischona, 1876 and London, 1881).

† Burton, *Zanzibar*, II, 57, 68–71, 80; CMSA: Rebmann to Venn, 23 March 1857.

task of rebuilding the house at Kisuludini, Burton's sketch of which is reproduced in the present book.*

C.M.S. publications might suggest that Rebmann was forgotten. Yet on three occasions attempts were made to reinforce the mission. Besides the freed slaves, a Mr. Taylor was sent in 1864. He died immediately. Mr. Parnell in 1866 was invalided before his arrival. Sparshott, however, did serve intermittently from 1867 onwards; he found so few opportunities for real work that the C.M.S. considered abandonment again in 1871. Before this time, there had been a scheme to give the Bishop of Mauritius jurisdiction over the mission so that more freed slaves might be introduced from that island. This arrangement was discarded in 1872, but the freed slaves settlement idea was given a great impetus by the recommendations of Sir Bartle Frere following his visit to Zanzibar in 1873. Frere paid a visit to Rebmann whom he found to be blind and alone (Mrs. Rebmann had died in 1866). The potential of the Rabai area for freed slaves impressed Frere and so Sparshott was sent back to East Africa with another missionary in November 1873. But the new era for Rabai really began with the coming of William S. Price in 1874. His arrival "infused new life" into Rebmann, said Price; in fact, Rebmann opposed being sent home. But he also opposed the new initiative over the freed slaves just as he had opposed Krapf's ideas twenty years before. He now believed that it was necessary to teach the whole of Old Testament history to catechumens before any conversions could be made.† Returned to Europe in 1875, Rebmann was treated unsuccessfully in both England and Germany for his blindness. He retired to Kornthal in Württemberg where Krapf found him a suitable widow to marry so that he could be looked after. Rebmann died in October 1876.‡

---

* See plate, 12.

† Stock, *History*, II, 433; III, 83–84. *Intelligencer*, 2nd series, XI (1875), p. 312ff. Norman R. Bennett, "The C.M.S. at Mombasa, 1873–1894" in Jeffrey Butler (ed.), *Boston University Papers in African History*, I (Boston, 1964), 163–165.

‡ *Intelligencer*, 3rd Series, I (1876), 697.

VII   KRAPF'S LATER LIFE: RETURN VISITS TO EAST AFRICA
AND ETHIOPIA

Kornthal was the place where Krapf himself had lived since
1855. It was a pietist settlement near Stuttgart originally
founded in 1819 in reaction against what were regarded as
increasingly rationalist tendencies in the Lutheran Church.
The members accepted the Augsburg Confession but they were
strongly influenced by millenarianism. Their privileges included
exemption from military service or from taking oaths. In
return, they provided some important charitable services in the
fields of education and social relief. Krapf himself, for example,
at one time served as the superintendent of an asylum. His
decision to settle in Kornthal marks something like a return to
the spiritual atmosphere of his youth and he appears to have
found the general development of Europe outside Kornthal not
altogether to his taste. He had deplored the popular commo-
tions of the 1848 revolutions and disliked what he saw as
analagous republican tendencies among East African tribes.
Later, the German Empire was an unwelcome development
since it meant the loss of Kornthal's special privileges.† Life in
Kornthal was made pleasant for him by his second marriage in
1856 to Charlotte, daughter of Senator Pelargus of Stuttgart.
Thomas Wakefield stayed with the couple in 1861 and speaks
of Mrs. Krapf as "pious and devoted" and her husband as "one
of the excellent of the earth; not only learned, but also very
meek and heavenly minded."*

Yet Krapf was not entirely content. In the first place,
Wilhelm Hoffmann, the distinguished university professor and
court preacher who had been Inspector of Missions at Basle,
insisted that Krapf write a book about his life as a missionary.
This task, comprising the German edition of 1858 and the
present shorter English version, took him until 1860 and
inevitably kept alive his concern with Africa. He said in his
work of 1858 that the longer he stayed in Europe, the more

* CMSA: Krapf to Venn, 9 February 1859. Zanzibar Archives, Arc 1:
Krapf to Hamerton, 1 July 1848. E. S. Wakefield, *Thomas Wakefield*
(London, 1904), 112–114.

† W. Claus, *Dr. Ludwig Krapf* (Basel, 1882), 175; Wakefield, *Wakefield*,
20–22.

homesick he became for Africa. He still hoped to have a part in founding missionary stations in the East African lakes region and among the Galla.*

With no immediate prospect of gratifying his wish to return to Africa, Krapf did what he could in Europe to promote the missionary interest. Most notably, he tried to raise support for Bishop Gobat's Ethiopian venture. The number of Christian mechanics sent to work with Theodore increased although only Flad had any real evangelistic success—in his case among the Jewish Felasha. These mechanics came from a teaching institute set up on the Chrischonaberg near Basle, by Friedrich Spittler, a local philanthropist, in 1840. The products of the Institute worked for various other missionary societies, ran an orphanage in Jerusalem and worked in the home field. But the most ambitious project developed as a result of Krapf's association with this St. Chrischona Institute. Having failed to set up a chain of missionary stations from east to west across Africa in 1851, Krapf now wished to have one running up the Nile valley to Abyssinia. The chain would branch east and west from there. It was to be the task of the institute to forge this chain, known because there were to be twelve stations, as the "Apostles' Street". In 1860, Krapf became for a time secretary of the "Pilgrim Mission" committee charged to implement the Apostles' Street idea. St. Matthew at Alexandria, St. Mark at Cairo, St. Peter at Aswan, St. Thomas at Khartoum, and St. Paul at Matamma did eventually get past the planning stage although only the first two became effective creations. The whole scheme had to be abandoned in 1880 because of lack of funds. By this time, in any case, other missionary initiatives in places like Buganda rendered it less necessary.†

The Galla had not been forgotten during the period when Krapf was working for the Chrischona Institute. As early as 1849, Louis Harms of Hermannsburg in Hanover had formed a mission designed to follow up Krapf's suggestions about the Galla. Eight missionaries and eight practical colonists arrived in East Africa in 1854 only to find Krapf away, Rebmann

---

* Krapf, *Reisen* (1858), xxvi, xxviii.

† Warneck, *Outline*, 119, 239. Groves, *Planting*, II, 111. *Intelligencer*, 3rd Series, VII (1882), **142**.

discouraging, and the Zanzibar authorities, backed up by Hamerton, hostile because of their fears of Europeans usurping their position in East Africa—an attitude for which Krapf was still being blamed. The Hermannsburg Mission made a second attempt to reach the Galla in 1858. It was no more successful than the first one but eventually the missionaries found a profitable field in Natal. At about this time, too, a Swedish Evangelical Missionary Society was founded under the influence of Krapf's work. Its attempts in the 1860's to find a foothold in Ethiopia met with limited success, but there was expansion from Massawa after 1889. Interest in the Galla was also maintained in Württemberg by the conversion there and pious death of a Galla slave girl in 1856.*

Krapf's concern with the Galla was to be one of the main reasons for his return to the active missionary field, yet again under the aegis of a British missionary society. The opportunity came in 1860. Charles Cheetham, treasurer of the Missionary Committee of the United Methodist Free Churches, read the present book and was impressed by what he learned, especially about the Galla. He noted also that Krapf had said he was willing "to reach down once more my pilgrim's staff".† Cheetham arranged for Krapf to meet the committee to advise them on the best way of conducting a mission to East Africa. November 1860 thus saw Krapf in Manchester offering to spend two years personally directing the mission. The following year he returned to Kornthal with Thomas Wakefield and J. Woolner, the two men selected by the Methodists for East Africa. Krapf taught them some of the more useful of the dozen languages at his command and also arranged for two Swiss mechanics—Elliker and Graf—to join them from St. Chrischona. The five men then left for East Africa and arrived in Zanzibar in January 1862.

Krapf planned that the two Englishmen should prospect in Usambara after he had assured himself that Arab hostility would not still prove a barrier to reaching that kingdom.

---

* Groves, *Planting*, II, 114–116, 292. C. W. Ledderhose, (trans. J. L. Krapf), *Pauline Fatme; First Fruits of the Galla to Christ Jesus* (London, 1857).

† Below, li.

Meanwhile he and the two Swiss would establish themselves near Malindi as a base for penetration towards Galla land. These plans went awry since Wakefield and Woolner did encounter Arab suspicion and, even when this was overcome, they were unable to find a suitable site. The two Swiss mechanics had stayed with Rebmann and found themselves so dispirited by the local Nyika, the slave wars they saw, the prospect of illness and, one supposes, by Rebmann's lack of enthusiasm, that in April 1862, Krapf had to send them home. Wakefield and Woolner now came north with Krapf and they set up a station at Ribe, fifteen miles north of Mombasa. Krapf was no builder: a house he constructed at Ribe fell down within a few months. More seriously, the physical effort brought on spinal trouble which necessitated his leaving in October 1862 before the agreed two years were up. Woolner also soon left because of illness and Wakefield, feeling rather deserted, left Ribe for a time and fell back on the company of Rebmann.

Rebmann had initially been opposed to both Methodism and "poaching" in his territory, but Krapf's reconciliation with him at this time overcame the difficulty. Wakefield was joined by another recruit, Charles New, who arrived in May 1863. A third man joined them only to die in 1864, but Wakefield and New, two remarkable and today little appreciated men, remained to till the difficult Nyika field. They also made notable journeys of geographical exploration in the tradition established by Krapf. Not only was the snow line of Kilimanjaro reached, but contact made with the Galla tribes to the north.*

Krapf's own final venture in Africa was to be a return to the scene of his first labours. He was engaged to accompany Napier's famous assault on Magdala. Given his pietist background, it is perhaps strange to find him willing to serve in a military expedition. On the other hand, many of the Europeans Theodore had imprisoned were connected with him through the various Württemberg and Swiss missionary institutions. When the British government at last decided in August 1867 to do something about Theodore, they naturally became interested

---

* Charles New, *Life, Wanderings and Labours in Eastern Africa* (London, 1874), 6–22. Wakefield, *Wakefield*, 16–45. CMSA: Krapf to Venn, 17 April 1862, 6 December 1864.

in those with experience of Ethiopia. Krapf and Isenberg's *Journals* of 1843 were consulted while the Indian authorities charged with the conduct of the operation turned up their records of Harris' mission of 1842 and noted the favourable references to Krapf. Sir Robert Napier thereupon suggested that he be engaged as an interpreter for the expedition, "if not too old" and if he promised "to refrain from all missionary efforts".* Krapf received the request early in September 1867 and agreed to go if he were paid and if he were promised friendly treatment like that which he had received from Harris. These conditions being accepted, there arose the difficulty over Napier's stipulation, which was now communicated to Krapf, that there should be no proselytizing.

The old missionary was almost pathetically anxious to be given the opportunity to revisit Ethiopia, even at the cost of leaving his "sickly wife and uneducated offspring", but he felt he must jib at this condition. A rather ridiculous correspondence followed with Krapf pointing out that he could not stop Africans asking questions about religion which he would feel bound to answer. Eventually the India Office told him he could talk on religious matters with the natives as long as he did not initiate the discussion. Krapf left for Abyssinia in October 1867 accompanied by Mr. Haussman, another Lutheran missionary with Ethiopian experience who had been engaged at his suggestion.†

After reaching Annesley Bay, Krapf was attached to Colonel (later Sir) William Lockyer Merewether who was reconnoitering the best route inland from the coast. For a time, Krapf was left in the interior to gather intelligence on Theodore's activities. Merewether rejoined him and they penetrated further, at one period marching thirty-seven miles in three days over very difficult terrain. Krapf dispróved rumours that Theodore had been defeated by Menelik of Shoa. But all of this activity was proving too much for a man of 56, as Henry Morton Stanley noted on his arrival to report the campaign.

---

* *Papers Connected with the Abyssinian Expedition*, 4260 (1867), 56, 234, 261–266.

† *Ibid.*, 134–141, 162, 175–176, 192–194, 208, 210–211, 216–217, 227, 298, 316, 323.

In February, 1868, Krapf was certified medically unfit to continue with his duties. He was now less indispensible following the arrival of Captain C. Speedy, who was better qualified as a military interpreter, and so Napier agreed to his being retired. Krapf had evidently once again attracted favourable notice from British officers, for Napier praised his work in more than conventional terms and recommended that, despite his having served for only three months, he should receive the full amount of the £600 salary which had earlier been agreed upon.*

For the rest of his life, Krapf remained in Württemberg concentrating most of his energies on linguistic work, although he continued to take a close interest in missionary projects, particularly those of the C.M.S. A list of Krapf's dictionaries and translations would include about 25 titles. In his last years, his two main preoccupations seem to have been the completion of his Swahili-English dictionary—which is valuable enough to have been recently re-published—and the editing of the 9,359 pages of the text of an Amharic Bible. The original translation from the Ge'ez had been made by an Abyssinian monk earlier in the century and the British and Foreign Bible Society had now asked Krapf to arrange the publication.†

Krapf did not live long enough to see his Swahili dictionary through the press. On the 25th November 1881, after talking with his old friend Flad, he retired to bed in apparently good health. On the following morning, however, his bedroom window had to be forced open to reveal him kneeling by his bed in an attitude of prayer, but quite dead. It is said that 3,000 mourners attended as his body was laid to rest in a grave beside Rebmann's.‡

---

* *Further Papers Connected with the Abyssinian Expedition*, 4664 (1868), 3–4, 23, 85. Henry Morton Stanley, *Coomassie and Magdala*, (London 1874), 285, 361. Trevenen J. Holland and Henry M. Hozier, *Record of an Expedition to Abyssinia* (London, 1870), I, 312–320, 339–341.

† Krapf, *Dictionary of Suahili* (Farnborough, 1965). Stock, *History*, I, 227–228, III, 102. Stock's date of 1879 for the completion of the Amharic bible is certainly wrong. See bibliography, 70–71.

‡ Beck, in Krapf, *Reisen* (1964), IX. *Intelligencer*, 3rd Series, VII (1882), 51. Claus, *Krapf*, 142, mentions only hundreds of mourners.

VIII KRAPF'S INFLUENCE IN EAST AFRICA AND EUROPE: MISSIONARY STRATEGY, POLITICS AND ECONOMICS

When Krapf died, a new age had begun in Africa. The number and scale of missions had increased and the "scramble" by Europeans for political control was beginning. But this new age and the modern Africa it was to produce cannot be understood without reference to the preceding one, which might be called one of informal European influence. Krapf was one of the dominant figures of this period; by his active work as a missionary and explorer, and no less by his scholarship, he brought Africa and Europe closer together.

It is true that the direct impact of Krapf's mission on East Africa was relatively slight.* In the course of their travels, Krapf and Rebmann did, on some occasions, become involved in inter-tribal politics although they were often unaware of this fact. They were sometimes "used" in a situation where rival chiefs wanted the prestige of having a European and European goods at court. Rebmann's failure to penetrate beyond Machame in 1849 was probably because of Chief Mamkinga's desire to monopolise the stranger and prevent him from associating with rivals like the ruler of Kibosho.†

Kivoi of the Kamba tribe presumably hoped to gain some benefit from his association with Krapf. In the case of his contacts with Usambara, Krapf certainly was aware of the political impact of his dealings with Kimweri although, here again, it seems likely that the King may have been using the missionary as a pawn in a dispute with Zanzibar. At any rate, Krapf was the unfortunate means of bringing the dispute to a head. As we have seen, the French also became involved. Nevertheless, the issues between Zanzibar and Usambara and the French had arisen anyway; they were not a direct result of Krapf's presence in East Africa.

Even at Rabai itself, it is difficult to see that the mission made any considerable difference to the lives of the vast majority of the surrounding Nyika peoples. Although there was a handful of converts, it was not until freed slave settlements

---

* Coupland could find little more than "the influence of personal conduct on the native mind". *Invaders*, 419.
† Below 260–261. Stahl, *Chagga*, 158.

were established in the 1870s that a real impact was made. Perhaps all that can be said is that the existence of Rabai meánt that the C.M.S. went on working in the same area.

In the long run, Krapf's influence on the European powers who were currently or later to be concerned with East Africa was more important than his direct impact on the region itself. Britain, Germany, and France were the countries most involved.

British enterprise in Africa was directly affected, of course by the very fact that, on his own initiative, Krapf had introduced the C.M.S. to East African work. The Methodist mission was another direct result of his stimulus. It was not only missionary societies in Britain who felt his influence. On his 1850 visit, he was a minor celebrity and had audiences with Prince Albert, Lord Palmerston, the Archbishop of Canterbury, and other important figures.* Scholars, particularly those interested in geography and languages, now began to pay attention to his work. He did not, it is true, figure in person at any meetings of the Royal Geographical Society and was certainly never lionised as Livingstone was in 1856 and 1857. Yet Krapf's geographical reports were to have their importance in stimulating the exploration of East Africa, undertaken, as it was, largely by British travellers in the mid-Victorian period.

In Germany, Krapf's influence was even more seminal to the development of interests in Africa. He introduced the work of Livingstone to German readers, for example, but there were also several practical German endeavours in Africa which owed their origin to him. Most notable were the Hermannsburg Mission and the activities of the Chrischona Institute which have already been described. Later on, as interest in East Africa advanced, other missions looked back to Krapf's work for their inspiration. Formed in response to the news of his death, the Bavarian Evangelical Lutheran Society went on in 1886 to institute a mission among the Kamba. The three stations they had founded were taken over by the Leipzig Evangelical Lutheran Mission in 1893. In 1886, Carl Peters and others who were inclined to cast Krapf in the role of a hero of German imperialism called on Germans to respond to Krapf's example by forming a mission to work for the fatherland as

* *Allgemeine Deutsche Biographie* (Leipzig, 1883), XVII, 52.

well as God in East Africa. The Berlin Evangelical Missionary Society, which began work in German East Africa, was the result. The Faith Mission of Pastor L. Doll also owed something to Krapf.*

In the development of German missionary endeavour, Krapf was obviously a key figure. His scientific work, too, had considerable impact in Germany. As early as 1844 his scholarship in Ethiopian languages earned him a Ph.D. degree from Tübingen University. On his return to Europe in 1850, he was invited to Berlin where the geographer, Carl Ritter, took him to meet the most outstanding of Germany's scientists, Baron Alexander von Humboldt, who showed great interest in the East African snow-capped mountains. The King invited them all to dinner and was apparently much impressed with the missionary. Krapf contributed to learned journals, Ritter used his material, and Humboldt mentioned his work in the *Cosmos*. At the practical level, the journeys of the German explorers Albrecht Röscher and Baron Carl Claus von der Decken were, to a large extent, inspired by the example of Krapf and Rebmann, while later travellers like Johann Maria Hildebrandt were also to recognize their debt to the missionaries.†

In France the adventures of Krapf and Rebmann were followed with considerable interest and the Paris Geographical Society, for example, gave the work of the two men much better coverage than did the Royal Geographical Society in London. In 1852, together with Livingstone and William Cotton Oswell, Krapf and Rebmann were each awarded the Society's Silver Medal. Krapf threatened to send his back after his difficulties following the interview with Belligny, but he was nevertheless probably gratified to receive this scientific recognition.‡

Thus Krapf's East African activities came to have implications for Britain, Germany, and France. The nature of these activities makes him more than ordinarily important in the story of the growth of European concern with East Africa. Because of his own breadth of interests, his prediliction for

* Groves, *Planting*, III, 73–76.

† Stock, *History*, I, 130. Beck in Krapf, *Reisen* (1964), VII. *Geographische Mittheilungen*, IV (1858), 396.

‡ *Bulletin de la Societé de Géographie de Paris*, 4th Series, III (1852), 307–330; CMSA: Krapf to Venn, 3 April 1853.

travel, and because of the ideas he developed on a strategy for
the introduction of Christianity, his work had much greater
scope than that of the conventional missionary. Krapf's own
interest in the Gallas, his love of travel, and his belief that the
imminence of the Second Coming made the rapid conversion of
all pagans urgent, help to explain the development of his ideas.
Perhaps, however, it was largely because he did not find it to be
his lot. to make many direct conversions that he turned
increasingly to the promotion of wider schemes as a means of
preparing the way for evangelization.

Like many other early missionaries, Krapf found that making
real contact with potential converts posed a very great problem.
Given a "normal" tribal ethos, Christianity must often have
seemed as irrelevant as it does in Krapf's description of his
experiences among the Nyika people; their "indifference and
dulness" depressed him.* What was to be done in this situation?
In some way, of course, the tribal ethos must be changed.
Many missionaries saw themselves as best able to promote such
a change by choosing to work among peoples who had powerful
chiefs and who could thus be reached by the manipulation of
the chief's influence. Krapf was affected by this thought when
he wrote enthusiastically of the monarchy in Usambara, in
comparison with the "republicanism" of the Nyika. Had he
been able to work in Usambara, it has been suggested,† there
would have been the possibility of a result like that in the
Anglo-Saxon kingdoms of the seventh century. Yet Krapf, it
should be noted, did not really believe in this easy way out of
the dilemma; in the case of Usambara he specifically rejected
the idea of a "political" approach through the king, and
emphasized that Christianity must develop by means of
individual conversions.‡

For similar reasons, Krapf rejected the other way out of the
dilemma in which, as we have seen, Rebmann and Erhardt
apparently believed—the imposition of European civil rule.
Nevertheless, the fact that Krapf turned to travel and discovery
as a means of opening the way for the Gospel made it impossible

* Below, 157–158, 163, 190–191.
† Oliver, *Missionary Factor*, 7–8.
‡ Below, 407.

for him completely to disregard the question of a secular basis
for the introduction of Christianity. Indeed, Krapf had written
in 1845:

> All geographical discovery and other temporal benefits
> and improvements are under God's special direction as
> history proves convincingly. They may and must in part,
> precede as they must prepare the way of the fulfillment of
> higher objects.*

This was written, it might be noted, ten years before
Livingstone's oft quoted remark "The end of the geographical
feat is the beginning of the missionary enterprise". Krapf's
commitment to an unorthodox strategy was less sure and less
convincing than Livingstone's. What made it more difficult for
Krapf to abandon the idea of individual conversions and to
concentrate on preliminary "temporal benefits and improvements" was his theological outlook. Professor Roland Oliver
succinctly explains the contrast with Livingstone when he
writes that the Rabai missionaries, "saw the negro primarily
as a 'fallen man'. Livingstone saw him as primarily as
'suffering'."†

It follows that Krapf was, for example, less concerned with
promoting measures to abolish the slave trade than Livingstone.
The trade was not, in any case, as obtrusive in the regions
where he worked as in the Lake Nyasa area farther south where
Livingstone was to observe the horrors of the march to the
coast. Krapf thought, too, that sensivity on the part of the
Arabs over this question could lead to their making his work
impossible if he made a great issue of slavery. But he certainly
lacked neither compassion for slaves nor interest in the
problem; he sent a long report to the C.M.S. on the subject in
1853 and his suggested remedies were very similar to those
which Livingstone was to popularise a few years later. "You
must get scientific men to explore the interior and to cultivate
new resources to replace the slave trade", he wrote. Yet there
remains a gap between his attitude and Livingstone's; the

---

* Krapf to Graham, 1 May 1845, in *East and West Review*, III (1937),
265.

† Oliver, *Missionary Factor*, 9.

Gospel must, he believed, come first and abolition was "a secondary object of the missionary".*

In the last analysis, then, Krapf was not as revolutionary as Livingstone in his attitude to missionary strategy because he did not carry his ideas as far; he was unable altogether to abandon his concern with individual salvation. Despite this inhibition, however, and despite his advice that nothing should be expected from political changes, there was implicit in the whole tenor of his thinking the idea that Europe must eventually come to have a major influence on East African peoples. The "descendants of Japheth" must steer the East African vessel "by the might of Christianity". Krapf also said that Africans should learn to conform to European customs rather than *vice-versa;* like many other missionaries, he was unable to dissociate Christianity from the European culture that he knew.†

At the time, however, Krapf's work had few immediate political implications for Europe. Possibly his discoveries increased French interest in East Africa—as the Belligny affair shows—but they were not a major factor. Krapf, like Rebmann, regarded himself as a British subject and wanted British rule. He pointed out what was later to become conventional in British strategic thinking—that "the fate of India will someday have to be decided in . . . Africa."‡ Yet he wanted British rule as much as anything to prevent French Roman Catholics from supplanting Protestants in East Africa as they had in Ethiopia.

Probably Krapf never thoroughly thought out all of the implications of his pronouncements or, indeed, of his plans. The chain of missionary stations, for example, seems to have been an end in itself; the precise function of each station in the African society concerned and its relationship, if any, to European power were matters left rather vague. The presence of lay mechanics in the schemes, though, indicates that

---

* CMSA: Krapf to Venn, 26 August 1845; Memoir on East African Slave Trade, 1853; *Church Missionary Record*, XVIII (1847), 16 and below, 134–135.

† Below, 393; *Isenberg and Krapf*, 389.

‡ Below, xlvii.

important attempts to introduce temporal as well as spiritual
benefits were envisaged.

The introduction of temporal benefits implied European
economic enterprise and it is clear that Krapf believed this
enterprise to be necessary in East Africa, although again the
implications of his pronouncements were not clearly thought
out. He presumably believed that European intervention
would pay for itself, for he wrote of East Africa as being "rich
and fertile, overflowing with milk and honey."* This is an odd
comment from one who suffered acutely from hunger and
thirst on his journey to Ukambani in 1851. Erhardt's contribution to the present book on the resources of the Nyika country
is similarly misleading. In fact, in the parts of East Africa
which the missionaries knew, natural conditions force two-
thirds of the population to live in one-tenth of the available
area. The "vast tract of fine country" left unused, which
Krapf noted, was probably, in fact, unusable. In this respect,
Krapf was no worse than the majority of other early visitors
to the region who were all deceived by the apparent luxuriance
of vegetable and animal life into making the naive assumption
that great returns could result from the application of European
capital and enterprise. In promoting the legend of Africa's
potential wealth, Krapf doubtless played his part in attracting
European interests to the continent. He was at least more
practical than some in his realization that no considerable
economic progress would be made until a railway was built.†

His implicit assumption that temporal and spiritual benefits
must reach East Africa as a result of European intervention in
the region makes Krapf one of the precursors of imperialism,
although his precise influence in this respect is difficult to
gauge. But in a much more tangible way, he and his companions are important figures in the story of the process which
culminated in European partition. They promoted a direct
concern with the geographical, scientific, linguistic, and
missionary problems of East Africa rather than with the
specifically political and economic problems. This concern led
to an increase in the scale and tempo of various kinds of

* Below, xlvi.
† CMSA: Krapf to Venn, 26 August 1845. *Intelligencer*, I (1850), 40.

European exploratory and missionary activities—activities which were to create interests in the region for the powers who partitioned it in the 1880's. Indirectly, therefore, Krapf's work was to have a considerable effect on East Africa's future development.

Apart from the spur he gave to missionary activity, Krapf's influence was felt most in the fields of language study, ethnography, and geography. Scholars and travellers from Europe became anxious to test or elaborate on the results that Krapf had obtained in East Africa.

IX LANGUAGES AND ETHNOGRAPHY

Krapf's work on languages and translations was notable both during his active missionary period and his retirement. The results of this scholarship were of practical use to himself and to the missionaries who were to follow him into various parts of Africa. Secondly, they were a major contribution to knowledge in the field of language studies. They were also, thirdly, most useful to the developing discipline of ethnography which increasingly used language as a basis for racial classification. Krapf's contributions were made more than ordinarily important by the wide range of his acquaintance with hitherto little-known tongues. His major studies and translations were derived from his work among Swahili, Nyika, Galla, and Amharic speakers, but individuals he met furnished the means of providing him with new material on the languages of the Kamba, Yao, Teita, and Shambala among Bantu peoples and of the Masai and Somali among others.

In East Africa, the most important spoken language is Swahili and the missionary's work on this language was of fundamental importance. For his own use or for later publication, Krapf translated parts of the Prayer Book and the Bible into Swahili, including the whole of the New Testament. As early as 1846, he completed an outline of the elements of the language which was published four years later and formed both a practical handbook for those who wished to learn the language and a text for scholars of languages. There was little enough existing information on Swahili at this period; a few lists, like that of the twenty-eight words compiled by Henry Salt on his visit to Mozambique in 1812, constituted the extent of recorded European knowledge. It is nevertheless true that those who followed Krapf in the field of Swahili studies found his work unsatisfactory in many respects. The "Kimvita" dialect he used was confined to the Mombasa region and the Zanzibar "Kiunguja" dialect was the more generally employed version. Bishop Edward Steere strongly criticised Krapf over the dialect question, and also disputed his orthography. But even he, together with other scholars like Bleek and Cust, acknowledged his great debt to Krapf.*

In the course of his activities, Krapf realised that Swahili was the key to other languages of East Africa and he soon demonstrated that it was part of the great family of tongues which he proposed initially to call "Nilotic" and then "Orphno-Hamitic" but to which Wilhelm Heinrich Immanuel Bleek was later to give the accepted and less confusing title of "Bantu". The relationship of the languages of Southern Africa was not an entirely unknown fact but Krapf's comparisons greatly advanced knowledge of this language family. Non-Bantu languages spoken in East Africa were clearly distinguished and he was able to give some specimens of them including a vocabulary of the Masai tongue—certainly the first to be compiled.

These linguistic classifications led Krapf into the field of ethnography and he matched the observations that he made on linguistic affinities and contrasts with attempts to delineate the corresponding racial types. There is no point in following Krapf's rather tortuous changes in nomenclature, but it is remarkable that, working from the limited extent of his own knowledge, he was able to arrive at a result in broad accordance with the conventional (if not entirely acceptable) classification later set out by C. G. Seligman on the basis of twentieth century studies.†

* See 69 and 555 below. J. L. Krapf, *Outline of the Elements of the Kisuaheli Language* (Tübingen, 1850). C. N. Frank, "Steere and Kiswahili", *Tanganyika Notes and Records*, 32 (1952), 38–39.

† J. L. Krapf, *Vocabulary of Six East African Languages* (Tübingen 1850). *Intelligencer*, II (1851), 56. J. L. Krapf, *Vocabulary of the Engutuk Eloikob* (Tübingen, 1854) 10–11, 128–129. Robert N. Cust, *A Sketch of the Modern Languages of Africa* (London, 1883), I, 54–56, 149; II, 292, 346–348; Charles Gabriel Seligman, *Races of Africa* (London, 1957), 6, 10, 140–209.

In justifying his ethnographical divisions and in the course of describing his adventures, Krapf published a great deal of valuable information on the peoples he encountered. Much of this material is unsystematically handled but in the present book he does provide connected accounts of the Kamba and Masai peoples while the prefaces to some of his linguistic works contain ethnological descriptions. Naturally Krapf did not write such accounts with the detachment of a modern anthropologist, but in nearly all respects his observations, if not always his social and political interpretations, are in broad agreement with those of modern investigators. Thus his material can now often be used to give historical depth to the description of a people. For example, the missionary's information on the Masai makes it possible to trace the way in which the age grade system operated a hundred years ago.*

Krapf's observations were sometimes inhibited by repugnance: "Their practices of incontinence I blush to transcribe as they are too abominable" he wrote early on in his East African career. His general picture was one of considerable degradation —a degradation increasing with the breakdown into the "republics" which he erroneously deduced. Yet Krapf schooled himself to be charitable and reminded himself that the Gospel gave hope; people were not incapable of improvement. Indeed, Krapf looked forward to the time when there would be a black bishop and clergy. He was not, as far as can be judged, affected by feelings of racial superiority, although he once said he doubted whether Africans would ever "perform considerable atchievements [sic] in philosophy, or in the theoretical branches of science."†

X GEOGRAPHY

For many who read the present book in 1860, Krapf's views on the East African peoples had rather less interest than his geographical material. Although the Ethiopian journeys added

* H. A. Fosbrooke, "The Masai Social System", *Tanganyika Notes and Records*, 26 (1948), 11, 25. Much of the material in *Missionary Labours* refers to the agricultural Masai (Kwavi). Unlike his contemporaries, Krapf often correctly distiguished between the agricultural and pastoral Masai.

† *Church Missionary Record*, XVI (1845), 41. Krapf, *Outline of Kisuaheli*, 7.

to knowledge, it was East Africa which fascinated contemporary readers; here was news of large inland seas, snow-covered mountains on the equator and a problem that had baffled even the ancients—the whereabouts of the sources of the Nile. It was to be the lot of Krapf and Rebmann to give direct information only about the snow mountains; as with other explorers, a great part of what they reported was based on secondhand information. Thus the thirty-four distinct voyages on which visits were made to various points along the coast and the hours in the mission house spent with Africans who had travelled from the interior are almost as important as the major journeys themselves. These major journeys in East Africa are Krapf's two visits to Usambara in 1848 and 1852 and his two ventures o Ukambani of 1849 and 1851. To these must be added Rebmann's visit to Teita in October 1847 followed by his three separate trips to the Kilimanjaro region between April 1848 and June 1849, while Erhardt's experience of the interior came in 1853 when he went to Usambara.

These journeys constituted the first successful modern European ventures into the interior of eastern Africa. Although undertaken in furtherance of a missionary strategy, the expeditions were of great importance to geographers and none of the three men who made them was indifferent to this fact. Krapf, in particular, seems to have been attracted by travel through the unknown for its own sake. He also took some pride in being a "scientific traveller" and both he and Rebmann provide accurate descriptions of what they saw. Yet neither man was scientific in quite the way that the mid-nineteenth century geographers wanted them to be.

In the 1850's, pundits of the Royal Geographical Society laid emphasis on the accurate determination of latitude, longitude, distance, and direction rather than on general geographical description. The Bombay Geographical Society had sent Krapf some observing instruments but even had he known how to use them, which seems doubtful, it was, he claimed, impossible to do so in front of curious and acquisitive Africans. The telescope and compass he did carry had to be kept carefully hidden. There is no indication that Krapf knew how to make a compass traverse in any case, and his distances and directions are nearly all wrong, as the contemporary maps in this volume demonstrate. This fact explains what one scholar, at least, has found puzzling—why the Royal Geographical Society did not award one of its medals to Krapf or Rebmann.* It also partly explains why Krapf and Rebmann did not have sufficient authority for their reports of snow-covered mountains to be readily accepted. Krapf's reputation pales before that of Livingstone here because, while both men saw the importance of geographical exploration in missionary strategy, it was only Livingstone who made himself into a thoroughly "scientific" traveller.

In order to understand the reception of their geographical material, it is necessary also to realise that the missionaries were not writing for a completely uninformed and open-minded audience. From about 1835 onwards, East Africa had been the subject of a considerable amount of geographical deduction on the part of theoretical scholars—the so-called "armchair geographers". In Britain the most notable, or perhaps notorious, was William Desborough Cooley. He was diligent in gleaning information from classical, medieval, Arab, and Portuguese sources. To what he acquired in this way, he added what little contemporary testimony there was, including some from a Zanzibari Arab and his servant who had visited Britain. As a result he was able to produce two major articles on East African geography in 1835 and 1845 while in 1852 and 1854 there followed two books on the subject. Briefly, Cooley deduced that Ptolemy's "Mountains of the Moon" were not in East Africa, that Kilimanjaro and Kenya were isolated mountains on a fifth of the scale required to sustain snow and that there existed one large lake in the interior. The latter seems to have been Lakes Nyasa and Tanganyika run together. Cooley was unprepared to modify his views in the face of evidence from skilled observers, let alone Krapf and Rebmann, and ultimately became discredited. But in the early 1850's, he was still regarded as the leading geographical expert on East Africa. Krapf heard of the severe strictures on his work in

---

* CMSA: Krapf, Journal, 7 August 1851; Krapf to Venn, 3 April 1853. Coupland, *Invaders* 401n. Beck, in Krapf, *Reisen* (1964), VII takes a more kindly view of Krapf's scientific skills.

Cooley's *Inner Africa* just at the time when the crisis over the information he had given Belligny blew up. This double blow temporarily disillusioned him: "why should I endanger my mission for the sake of science" he wrote, "Let Geography perish".*

Another armchair expert was James MacQueen, who had made his geographical reputation by correctly deducing the course and termination of the Niger. He was much better disposed towards the missionaries than Cooley and had contributed a memoir to the 1843 *Journals*. But he had strong views on the sources of the Nile and believed that there were two major East African lakes. A third scholar who may be mentioned among several others was Dr. C. T. Beke, who had practical experience as a traveller in Ethiopia, where he had met Krapf. He believed that Kilimanjaro and Kenya were parts of the "Mountains of the Moon" and that the feeders of the Nile would be found on their slopes. So certain was he of this view that he attempted to have it proved by an odd and unsuitable character from Hanover, called Dr. Bialloblotsky, for whom he collected £249 before packing him off to East Africa in 1849. In consultation with Krapf, Hamerton prevented Bialloblotsky from trying to go inland by refusing to recommend to the Sultan that the necessary letters should be issued asking the coastal governors to help the traveller. †

The effect of the reports of the missionaries was to stimulate further argument among the armchair geographers. As this book shows, Krapf had the scholastic equipment to play the theoretical scholars on their own ground and, for example, to reconcile his views on the sources of the Nile with Speke's discovery of 1858. Immediately more important than his views on the Nile, however were the direct testimonies about the snow mountains. It was in the first issue of the *Church Missionary*

* *Edinburgh Review*, LXI (1835), 346. *The Journal of the Royal Geographical Society*, XV (1845), 185. William Desborough Cooley, *Inner Africa Laid Open* (London, 1852). W. D. Cooley, *Ptolemy and the Nile* (London, 1854). CMSA: Krapf to Venn, 3 April 1853.

† *The Journal of the Royal Geographical Society*, XXVI (1856) 109. Charles Tilstone Beke, *On the Sources of the Nile* (London, 1849). FO 54/13: Bialloblotsky to Palmerston, 27 August 1849, Public Record Office.

Intelligencer that the news of Rebmann's 1848 sighting of the summit of Kilimanjaro was announced in the form that it is reproduced in this book. Krapf, too, later saw the summit and, on 3 December 1849, the snow cap on Mount Kenya. First reactions from the Royal Geographical Society and Beke, for example, expressed no disbelief but in May 1849, Cooley wrote to the *Athenaeum* challenging the authenticity of Rebmann's "ocular testimony". Battle was now joined in various periodicals with Cooley maintaining, "I deny altogether the existence of snow on Kilimanjaro" and elaborating his attack in his book of 1852. Cooley's reputation was great enough for his arguments to implant considerable doubts in the minds of many other geographers including Livingstone and the influential man who dominated the Royal Geographical Society at this time, Sir Roderick Murchison.* The details of the dispute over the snow mountains are no longer of vital interest, but the existence of the controversy is important for it highlighted East African geographical problems and promoted a determination, especially on the part of the Fellows of the Geographical Society, to send out expeditions to investigate such enigmas. In the event, Burton and Speke were unable to visit the mountains in 1857 but Von der Decken finally confirmed the existence of snow on Kilimanjaro in 1861.

In a similar way, great interest was created by the dialogue between the missionaries and the scholars over the question of East Africa's lakes. As early as 1844, Krapf was distinguishing between Lakes Nyasa and Tanganyika, as did Rebmann later. Krapf also heard of what must have been Victoria Nyanza and reports of some of the Rift Valley lakes. It is ironic that Krapf, whose name is so often incorrectly linked with the idea of a single large lake as in the "slug map", should be severely criticised by Cooley for saying there was more than one major lake in East Africa. The "slug map" was the creation of Erhardt and Rebmann and was the result of Erhardt's collecting information whilst he was at Tanga in 1854. Since everyone told him of great waters to the westward, he assumed that there

---

* *Intelligencer*, I (1850), 17, 53–54, 470; III (1852), 219ff. *Athenaeum*, 1119 (1849), 357; 1125, 516–517, *The Proceedings of the Royal Geographical Society*, I (1855–1857), 450.

was water at every point and ran the three major lakes into one enormous inland sea. As Burton said, "He thus brought a second deluge upon sundry provinces and kingdoms thoroughly well known for the last half century." Having returned to Rabai and convinced Rebmann of the interpretation, he drew up and elaborated his map and then sent it to a Württemberg missionary magazine, the *Calwer Missionblatt*, where it appeared later in 1855. Krapf obviously accepted Erhardt's interpretation with reluctance, but he did eventually include it in his book of 1858—the German version of his travels.* Naturally he omitted it from the present book since Burton's results were then known. From Calwer, Dr. Barth had sent the "slug map" to the German geographical scholar, August Petermann, together with three letters written by Rebmann at about the same time and in the same vein as the one Krapf prints in this book (486ff). Petermann submitted a report on these letters to the *Athenaeum* in London in September and another controversy began. Meanwhile the map itself was forwarded to the Royal Geographical Society by the C.M.S. in August 1855, discussed in November, and published early in the following year.†

In London, the map caused intense interest with Beke, Cooley, MacQueen and many others dashing off intemperate letters to the *Athenaeum* and making almost passionate statements of their own interpretations of East Africa's relief and drainage. Within a few months, an expedition was planned and Burton and Speke were setting off for East Africa. Nevertheless, the importance of the "slug map" should not be misunderstood. It is in the first place misleading to regard it as the culmination of the Rabai Mission's geographical work for the crudity of the lake interpretation conceals the rather more accurate knowledge that had been gained and it certainly does not represent Krapf's real views on the conformation of the interior. In the second place, it did not in itself "cause" the Burton and Speke expedition to be sent to East Africa. Speke's testimony, which is accepted in Ravenstein's introduction and

---

* *Intelligencer*, I (1850), pp. 384–385; Cooley, *Inner Africa*, 73. Burton, *Lake Regions*, I, 4. *Das Calwer Missionblatt*, 19 (October 1855), 77–83.

† *Athenaeum*, 1457 (1855), 1116. *The Proceedings of the Royal Geographical Society*, I (1855–1857), 8–13.

which Krapf himself, with a mistaken effacement, quotes in this book,* is misleading in this respect. The interest in East Africa was already great enough at the Royal Geographical Society and on Burton's part for an expedition to be contemplated. But the map did bring to a head this great concern with East African geography; in the discussions at the Royal Geographical Society in 1856 (later Sir) Francis Galton drew attention to the glaring dissimilarities between the maps of Cooley, MacQueen, and Erhardt and said that these disparities demonstrated everyone's "exceeding ignorance" of the region.†

XI KRAPF AND HIS BOOK

Krapf and his companions made the first major contribution towards dispelling Europe's "exceeding ignorance" of East Africa. This book sums up their work and is an impressive memorial to Krapf. At the time when it was first published, it was received kindly and even enthusiastically. The *Quarterly Review* discussed it mainly in terms of the missionaries' place in geographical discovery with some rather unperceptive remarks on Krapf's missionary outlook thrown in. The *Athenaeum* reviewer still doubted the existence of snow but recommended Krapf for providing "vivacious, picturesque and obviously faithful" narrative, for affording "glimpses through the veil" still shrouding so much of Africa and, above all, for describing "adventures as might have worn out the endurance of Sinbad in the Land of Beasts". Yet Krapf's work never won the fame that this praise might lead one to expect. It was to suffer direct competition in the same year when Burton's *Lake Regions* appeared. Burton's was the more recent information on East Africa and it was the work of an accomplished writer. Moreover, where Krapf concealed his disputes with his companions, Burton opened up his own dispute with J. H. Speke and thus further enlivened his narrative. A hundred years later, however, we can see both books in better perspective and agree with the *Athenaeum* reviewer that Krapf has a "permanent rank among discoverers".‡ In the long run, it was

* Below, xxvii, xlix–l.
† *The Proceedings of the Royal Geographical Society*, I (1855–1857), 93.
‡ *Quarterly Review*, CIX (1861), 496–530. *Athenaeum*, 1699 (1860), 677–678.

Livingstone's *Missionary Travels* of 1857 and the fame of Livingstone himself which overshadowed Krapf.

Comparisons between Livingstone and Krapf are frequently made in any consideration of pioneer missionary work in Eastern Africa. Undoubtedly, Krapf was the lesser figure but he was by no means completely outshone. Although Livingstone's was the more important influence both men had an impact in religious, humanitarian, scientific, and official circles. And if Livingstone was unquestionably the greater geographical observer, Krapf was equally unquestionably the greater linguistic pioneer. There are similarities in their personal careers: both nearly missed going to Africa, both lost wives in Africa, both turned to exploration rather than conventional missionary work, both suffered from disputes with their companions, and both were found dead at their bedsides, kneeling in prayer. Perhaps, however, Krapf lacked the total commitment or obsession which meant that Livingstone's bedside was among the Lake Bangweulu swamps. Perhaps, also, he lacked some of the saintly qualities which made Livingstone's numerous failings seem unimportant. Nevertheless Krapf was a remarkable pioneer, a good man, and a notable figure in the history of nineteenth century Africa.

*   *   *   *

The bulk of the present book consists of journals which Krapf sent to the C.M.S. in the course of his work in Africa. Much of this material was published *verbatim* in either the *Church Missionary Record* or the *Intelligencer*. Krapf's English seems to have been good although there are signs that it needed to be polished up by editors on occasions. His style does seem to have deteriorated later in his life. Presumably he kept his original records in German and on these based the publication, in 1858, of the two massive, 500-page long volumes of the German edition of his travels. The English version is not simply a translation of the German. It is much shorter for one thing, partly because Krapf had less need to write up his Ethiopian adventures for English readers, his journals in English having been published in 1843; in this volume there are general accounts of his work in Ethiopia rather than the more detailed journals of the German version. The records of life at Rabai are also much shorter than in the German edition and have been edited more. The selections cover mainly the period 1847–1849 in both cases but it seems to have been assumed that the English reader had less of a stomach for long religious musings.

Part I of this book corresponds roughly with Volume I of the 1858 work, but the latter also has descriptions of the voyages of Rebmann and Erhardt to East Africa. The reader of the English edition will notice, incidentally, that the numbering of the chapters seems to have gone astray in Part I since there is no Chapter XI. Part II, the journals of the interior journeys, is equivalent to Volume II in the German, although again the amount of material is cut down. Part III has the journal of the coasting voyage as in the 1858 volume II, but most of the material here is freshly prepared for English readers. The appendices dealing with the geographical questions are especially notable; indeed the whole book appears to have been produced more for the benefit of the general reader of travels and the geographers than for those specifically interested in missions. The historical chapter was the result of a perusal of Admiral Guillain's work of 1856.*

Another feature of this publication is the introduction by Ernst Georg Ravenstein (1839–1913). A German, from Frankfurt, who had five years before come to Britain to be employed in the War Office Topographical Department, and who had already taken some part in the debates about East African geography, he was the ideal person to introduce Krapf's work to the British public.† The first part of the introduction is, in fact, an exercise in "armchair geography" while the second reflects on the commercial and political situation in East Africa. Together they provide an excellent picture of the region and its problems as seen through the eyes of an intelligent European observer in 1860. There are some minor mistakes which he need not have made as in the dates he

---

* Charles Guillain, *Documents sur l'Histoire, la Géographie, et le Commerce de L'Afrique Orientale* (Paris, 1856), 3 vols.

† Margery Perham, *The Diaries of Lord Lugard* (London, 1959), III, 418–419. *Athenaeum* 1458 (1855), 1153.

gives for Rebmann's journeys and for Dr. Francisco José Maria Lacerda's mission (it should be 1798). As might be expected, the misleading statements in his speculative geography are much more numerous. Ravenstein's discussion on commerce suffers from his lack of quantitative information on East African trade and he fails to foresee the importance of the Suez Canal. Political events are dominated for him by the prospects of the French advances and so, like others, he makes himself doubt the feasibility of the Canal. He would probably have been even more concerned had he known of the French activities in Zanzibar at the time he was writing. But French schemes for influence in East Africa were to be abandoned in 1862 when a joint declaration was made with Britain. guaranteeing Zanzibar's independence.

The two original maps of the 1860 edition have been retained in the present one. What the publishers described as Dr. Krapf's original map is an adequate commentary on his lack of real skill as a geographer and cartographer. Yet it remains an extremely interesting piece of work showing, for example, the rough relationships of various tribes to one another in the 1840's and 1850's. The material seems to be an amalgam of that gathered by Rebmann and Erhardt as well as Krapf and much of the useful detail in the Mombasa region is derived from a map by Rebmann published in the *Church Missionary Intelligencer* for May, 1849. Presumably Krapf supervised the drawing of his map before the full results of Burton and Speke were to hand. Yet it is different from the version in his German edition of 1858, for there Erhardt's slug-shaped lake appears. It is replaced here by two separated lakes, Tanganyika and Nyasa, and by some rather indeterminate shading in the approximate position of Lake Victoria. Krapf must have known by the time that this map was prepared that Burton and Speke had definitely learned of the separation of the lakes but their discovery after all, only confirmed his original opinions. Consequently, this map roughly represents his own conception of the map of eastern Africa at the time when he completed his labours in 1855.

Ravenstein's map is an attempt to relate Krapf's work to the latest information available in mid-1860. This includes John

Petherick's optimistic but erroneous estimates of how far south he had reached in his travels west of the Nile and two conflicting versions of what constituted the "Mountains of the Moon"—one north of Lake Tanganyika following Speke, and the other in Beke's version embracing the snow mountains that the missionaries had discovered. Most notable, however, is the attempt to draw the source of the Nile; a dotted line indicates Speke's guess of 1858 that Lake Victoria was the source but, partly on Krapf's even slenderer evidence, Ravenstein seems to have made Lake Baringo the main source—despite the fact that it was also assumed to feed the Tana river. Ravenstein's map is a useful reminder that only a hundred years ago, even the most basic information about Africa had not been obtained.

A modern map showing the approximate routes of Krapf and Rebmann in East Africa has been added. The drainage pattern may be compared with that deduced by Ravenstein. Inset is a representation of Erhardt's "Slug map."

---

* John Petherick was a Welsh ivory trader in the Upper Nile regions who achieved some notoriety in 1864 as the result of a dispute with J. H. Speke over the conduct of the latter's Nile expedition.

Chronological List of Published Work
by or about Krapf

This list is not comprehensive and does not include, for example, the extensive extracts from Krapf's journals published in the Church Missionary Society's periodicals, the *Record* and the *Intelligencer*, the similar material in the *Bulletin de la Société de Géographie de Paris*, and in German missionary periodicals. Nor does it include articles concerned with Krapf's work in other French and German periodicals such as *Nouvelles Annales de Géographie* and Petermann's *Geographische Mittheilungen*.

An Imperfect Outline of Galla (London, 1840).

Tentamen Imbecillum translationis Evangelii Johannis in Linguam Gallarum (London, 1841).

Evangelium Matthei translatum in Linguam Gallarum (no imprint, [Ankober] 1841).

Vocabulary of the Galla Language, edited by C. W. Isenberg, (London, 1842).

Journals of the Rev. Messrs. Isenberg and Krapf . . . in the years 1839, 1840, 1841 and 1842. With a Geographical Memoir by James McQueen. (London, 1843).

The Beginning of a Spelling Book of Kinika, with J. Rebmann (Bombay, 1848).

Evangelio za Avioandika Lukas, (St Luke in Kinika), (Bombay, 1848).

Outline of the Elements of the Ki-Suahili Language, with a general introduction, (Tübingen, 1850).

Evangelio ta Yunaolete Malkosi, (St Mark in Kikamba) (Tübingen, 1850).

Vocabulary of Six East African Languages, with remarks on Geography and Ethnography (Tübingen, 1850) (Reprinted, Farnborough, 1966).

Sala sa Sabuci na Jioni . . . (C. of E. Morning and Evening Prayers in Swahili) (Tübingen, 1854).

Vocabulary of the Engutuk Eloikob, (Kwavi Language, with an introduction on the tribe) (Tübingen, 1854).

J. Erhardt, *Vocabulary of Enguduk Iloigob* (Masai Language), edited, with a preface, by J. L. Krapf, (Ludwigsburg, 1857).

(Carl Friedrich Ledderhose), *Pauline Fatme; First Fruits of the Galla to Christ Jesus*, translated from the German, with an introduction by J. L. Krapf, ed. J. E. Dalton (London, 1857).

Reisen in Ost-Afrika, 2 vols. (Stuttgart, 1858). Reprinted in one vol. with a new introduction by Hanno Beck, (Stuttgart, 1964).

Travels, Researches and Missionary Labours (London, 1860).

Travels, Researches and Missionary Labours (Boston, 1860). (Identical text but different pagination and no illustrations.)

The Four Gospels, translated into the Tigré language by Debtera Matteos, revised by C. W. Isenberg, ed. by J. L. Krapf (St. Chrischona, 1866).

Johann M. Flad, *The Falashas of Abyssinia*, with a preface by J. L. Krapf (London, 1869).

Theophil Waldmeier, *Erlebnisse in Abessinien* . . . *1858–68*, with a foreword by J. L. Krapf (Basel, 1869).

The Gospel of St. Luke, translated into the Galla language, (St. Chrischona, 1870).

The Gospel of St. John, translated into the Galla language (St. Chrischona, 1871).

Abba Rukh, *The Old Testament*, translated into Amharic. Improved by J. L. Krapf, ed. Thomas Platt (St. Chrischona, 1871–3).

The Psalms, translated into the Galla language, (St. Chrischona, 1872).

The First Book of Moses . . ., translated into the Galla language, (St. Chrischona, 1872).

The New Testament, translated into the Galla language, 4 parts, (St. Chrischona, 1876).

The Second Book of Exodus, translated into the Central Galla dialect, (St. Chrischona, 1877).

J. Rebmann, *Dictionary of the Kiniassa Language*, ed. with an introduction by J. L. Krapf (St. Chrischona, 1877), (Reprinted, Farnborough, 1966).

Johannes Mayer, *Kurze Worte-Sammlung*, ed. with a foreword by J. L. Krapf. (English, German, Amharic, Galla, Gurague) (Basel, 1878).

W. Claus, *Dr. Ludwig Krapf, Weil Missionar in Ostafrika* (Basel, 1882).

The Career of Dr. Krapf, Reprinted from the *Church Missionary Intelligencer*, (London, 1882).

Dictionary of the Suahili Language ed. R.N. Cust (London, 1882), Revised and re-arranged London, 1925, (Reprinted, Farnborough, 1965).

"Some Letters of Krapf", *Proc, Royal Geographical Society* new series, IV (1882) 747–753.

K. F. Ledderhose, "J. L. Krapf" *Allgemeine Deutsche Biographie*, vol. 17, (Leipzig, 1883) 49–53.

Abba Rukh, *The Holy Bible in Amharic*, revised by J. M. Flad (St. Chrischona, 1886).

J. L. Krapf and J. Rebmann, *A Nika-English Dictionary*, ed. Thomas Sparshott. (London, 1887).

"Krapf of East Africa" (Letter to Capt. Graham of 1845) *East and West Review*, III (1937) 259–269.

C. G. Richards, *Krapf, Missionary and Explorer*, (East African Literature Bureau, 1950). Reprinted with corrections, 1958, translated into Swahili, 1963).

N. R. Bennett, "Some Letters of J. L. Krapf" *Boston University Graduate Journal*, IX (1960) 45–58.

R. C. Bridges, "Krapf and the Strategy of the Mission to East Africa" *Makerere Journal*, 5, (1961) 37–50.

CHRONOLOGY

This includes only major events and journeys. Between the principal journeys in East Africa, for example, the missionaries made numerous short excursions by land or sea to various areas near Mombasa.

1810 Jan. 11	Birth of Krapf.
1820 Jan. 16	Birth of Rebmann.
1827–29	Krapf at Basle Mission School.
1834	Completes theological studies at Tübingen.
1834–6	Vicar of Wolfenhausen etc. and returns to Basle.
1837 Feb.	Leaves Basle for Abyssinia.

ABYSSINIA

1837 Dec.	Arrival in Massawa; to Adowa in Tigré.
1838 May	Leaves Tigré, visits Mocha.
1838 Sept.	Arrival in Cairo.
1839 April	Arrival in Tajurra.
1839 May	Arrival in Shoa.
1840 Jan.–March	Journey to S.W. of Shoa.
1842 March	Leaves Shoa.
1842 March–May	JOURNEY OVERLAND TO MASSAWA.
1842 Oct.	Arrival in Cairo and first marriage.
1842 Nov.	Return to Tajurra—refused entry to Shoa.
1843 May–June	To Massawa, attempt to return to Tigré fails and death of daughter.

1843 Nov.   Leaves Aden for Zanzibar.

EAST AFRICA

1844 Jan.	Arrives in Zanzibar.
1844 May	Takes up residence in Mombasa.
1844 July	Death of wife and daughter.
1844 July–1845 Sept.	Numerous short journeys inland including meeting with Kamba people 1845 Jan.
1845 Dec.	Arrives Zanzibar.
1846 Feb.	Return to Mombasa.
1846 June	Arrival of Rebmann.
1846 Sept.	Beginning of residence at Rabai.
1847 March	Visit to Zanzibar.
1847 Oct.	REBMANN'S JOURNEY TO KADIARO IN TEITA.
1848 April–June	REBMANN'S FIRST JOURNEY TO KILIMANJARO AND SIGHT OF SNOW CAP MAY 11TH.
1848 July–Sept.	FIRST JOURNEY TO USAMBARA.
1848 Nov.–1849, Feb.	REBMANN'S SECOND JOURNEY TO KILIMANJARO.
1849 June	Arrival of Erhardt and Wagner.
1849 April–June	REBMANN'S THIRD JOURNEY TO KILIMANJARO.
1849 Aug.	Death of Wagner.
1849 Nov.–Dec.	FIRST JOURNEY TO UKAMBANI, AND SIGHT OF PEAK OF MT. KENYA DEC. 3RD.
1850 Feb.–March	COAST VOYAGE TO CAPE DELGADO WITH ERHARDT.
1850 April	Leaves Rabai for Europe.
1851 April	Return to Rabai.
1851 May	Death of Pfefferle.
1851 July–Sept.	SECOND JOURNEY TO UKAMBANI.
1851 Oct.–1852 March	Rebmann's visit to Cairo and marriage.
1852 Feb.–April	SECOND JOURNEY TO USAMBARA.
1853 March	Erhardt to Pangani.
1853 Aug.–Dec.	ERHARDT'S JOURNEY TO USAMBARA.

1853 Sept.   Krapf leaves Rabai.
1854 March–Oct.   Erhardt in Tanga.

EUROPE, ABYSSINIA AND EAST AFRICA

1854 Nov.–Dec.   To Jerusalem from London.
1855 Feb.–Aug.   JOURNEY MASSAWA — KHARTOUM —
                          CAIRO.
1855 April   Erhardt leaves Rabai.
1855 Sept.   Krapf's return to Württemberg.
1855 Oct.   The "Slug Map" published.
1856   Second marriage.
1857–1858   Rebmann in Zanzibar.
1860 Nov.   Krapf's visit to Manchester.
1861 June–Dec.   Return to Kornthal with Wakefield.
1862 Jan.–Oct.   With the U.M.F.C. Mission to East
                          Africa.
1867 Oct.–1868 Feb.   With Napier's expedition to Abyssinia.
1875 March   Rebmann leaves Rabai.
1876 Oct.   Death of Rebmann.
1881 Nov.   Death of Krapf.
1901 Aug.   Death of Erhardt.

TRAVELS,

RESEARCHES, AND MISSIONARY LABOURS,

DURING AN

EIGHTEEN YEARS' RESIDENCE IN EASTERN AFRICA.

TOGETHER WITH

JOURNEYS TO JAGGA, USAMBARA, UKAMBANI, SHOA, ABESSINIA,
AND KHARTUM; AND A COASTING VOYAGE FROM
MOMBAZ TO CAPE DELGADO.

BY THE REV. DR. J. LEWIS KRAPF,

SECRETARY OF THE CRISHONA INSTITUTE AT BASEL, AND LATE MISSIONARY IN THE SERVICE OF
THE CHURCH MISSIONARY SOCIETY IN EASTERN AND EQUATORIAL AFRICA, ETC. ETC.

𝔚𝔦𝔱𝔥 𝔞𝔫 𝔄𝔭𝔭𝔢𝔫𝔡𝔦𝔵

RESPECTING THE SNOW-CAPPED MOUNTAINS OF EASTERN AFRICA; THE SOURCES
OF THE NILE; THE LANGUAGES AND LITERATURE OF ABESSINIA
AND EASTERN AFRICA, ETC. ETC.

AND

A CONCISE ACCOUNT OF GEOGRAPHICAL RESEARCHES IN EASTERN AFRICA UP TO THE
DISCOVERY OF THE UYENYESI BY DR. LIVINGSTONE IN SEPTEMBER LAST,

BY E. G. RAVENSTEIN, F.R.G.S.

WITH PORTRAIT, MAPS, AND ILLUSTRATIONS OF SCENERY AND COSTUME.

LONDON:
TRÜBNER AND CO., PATERNOSTER ROW.
1860.

CONTENTS.

PART I.

RESEARCHES AND MISSIONARY LABOURS.

EXTRACTS FROM JOURNALS.

CHAP. I.

AUTOBIOGRAPHICAL.

CHAP. II.

TO ADOWA AND ANKOBER.

CHAP. III.

RESIDENCE IN SHOA.

CHAP. IV.

SHOA AND THE SHOANS.

CHAP. V.

THE UNEXPLORED COUNTRIES TO THE SOUTH OF SHOA.

CHAP. VI.

ORMANIA AND THE GALLAS.

CHAP. VII.

FROM ANKOBER TO MASSOWA.

CHAP. VIII.

FROM ADEN TO ZANZIBAR.

CHAP. IX.

MOMBAZ—EXCURSIONS ON THE MAIN-LAND.

CHAP. X.

RABBAI MPIA—EXTRACTS FROM JOURNALS.

CHAP. XII.

EXTRACTS FROM JOURNALS CONTINUED.

CHAP. XIII.

CLOSE OF RESIDENCE IN EASTERN AFRICA:—RETURN HOME.

PART II.

TRAVELS IN EASTERN AFRICA.
KADIARO—JAGGA—USAMBARA—UKAMBANI.

CHAP. I.

REBMANN'S JOURNEY TO KADIARO.

CHAP. II.

REBMANN'S FIRST JOURNEY TO JAGGA.

CHAP. III.

REBMANN'S SECOND JOURNEY TO JAGGA.

CHAP. IV.

REBMANN'S THIRD JOURNEY TO JAGGA.

CHAP. V.

THE AUTHOR'S FIRST JOURNEY TO USAMBARA.

CHAP. VI.

FIRST JOURNEY TO UKAMBANI.

CHAP. VII.

SECOND JOURNEY TO UKAMBANI.

CHAP. VIII.

SECOND JOURNEY TO UKAMBANI CONTINUED.

CHAP. IX.

SECOND JOURNEY TO USAMBARA.

PART III.

GEOGRAPHY, TOPOGRAPHY, AND HISTORY.

THE SOUTH SUAHILI COAST.

CHAP. I.

VOYAGE FROM MOMBAZ TO CAPE DELGADO.

CHAP. II.

FROM JERUSALEM TO GONDAR.

CHAP. III.

FROM GONDAR TO CAIRO.

CHAP. IV.

CONCLUSION.

SUPPLEMENTARY CHAPTER.

SUMMARY OF EAST-AFRICAN HISTORY.

APPENDIX.

GEOGRAPHICAL AND LITERARY.

The Snow-capped Mountains of Eastern Africa—The Sources of the Bar-el-Abiad, the White River, or Nile—The Present Literature of Abessinia, and Languages of Eastern Africa.

List of Plates.

INTRODUCTION.

I. A CONCISE ACCOUNT OF GEOGRAPHICAL DISCOVERY IN EASTERN
AFRICA; with a few Remarks upon the Commerce of Africa,
and the Influence which the proposed Suez Canal is likely to
exercise upon its development; and a Sketch of Recent Political Events in Abessinia and Madagascar.

BY E. G. RAVENSTEIN, F.R.G.S.,
CORRESP. F.G.S. FRANKFORT.

AT no time has discovery taken such rapid strides towards unfolding
the geography of inner Africa as within the last few years. Livingstone, Barth, Galton, Andersson, and many others, have not only
traversed large tracts of country previously left blank on our maps,
or at the most filled up by rivers, lakes, and mountain-chains laid
down from imperfect native reports, but have embodied their results
in maps, based upon astronomical observations, or a careful estimate
of distances.

Eastern Africa has taken its due share in the general progress, and
from the peculiar interest attaching to its geographical features, and
the comparative safety with which travellers may proceed inland, we
may confidently expect it soon to be one of those portions of the
continent most accurately known to us. Its coastline had been surveyed between the years 1822-6, by Capt. W. F. Owen and his
officers, a survey to which but immaterial additions were made by
the French expedition under M. Guillain, (1847-8). Lieutenant Cris-
topher, in 1844, visited Giredi and some other places on the lower
Haines river, but M. Maizan, a French officer, who in the same year

attempted to penetrate into the interior, was slain by the natives at three days' journey from the coast.*

The inland exploration of that part of Eastern Africa may be dated from the time when Dr. Krapf, of the Church Missionary Society, established himself at Rabba Mpia, near Mombaz (1844), a place which subsequently became the starting-point for several journeys into the interior, undertaken by himself and fellow labourers. Dr. Krapf visited thus Ukambani twice, in 1849 and 1851, and Fuga, the capital of Usambara, in 1848 and 1852. The Rev. J. Rebmann undertook three journeys to Jaga in 1848 and 1852, and the Rev. J. Erdhardt in 1853 proceded to Fuga. In addition to this, Dr. Krapf explored the whole of the coast from Cape Guardafui to Cape Delgado, for objects connected with the mission. The most remarkable result obtained by these journeys is the discovery of several mountains covered with perennial snow, a discovery which can only be denied if we assume the missionaries capable of deliberately advancing false statements.† True, no astronomical observations were taken, and the routes explored have not been laid down with all desirable accuracy; nevertheless, the accounts of the missionaries, from their long residence in the country and close intercourse with the natives, with whom they were able to converse in their own language, give to their accounts quite an independent value. On our small map we have laid down the routes to Ukambani and Jagga approximately, and in doing so were under the necessity of greatly reducing the distances as given on the missionary maps. Dr. Krapf, in his original map, places Yata in Ukambani, at a distance

---

* Henry C. Arc Angelo in 1847, and Captain Short in 1849, claim to have ascended the River Jub for a considerable distance. M. Guillain, who in 1847 lodged in the very room at Merka previously occupied by Angelo, heard from his host that that traveller ascended the river for a few miles merely. In fact, the lower Jub is not considered navigable at all by the Arab merchants, who carry their merchandise overland to Ganana, above which the river is navigable for a considerable distance. (See Guillain, " Documents sur l'Afrique Orientale," II. 181).

† In an Itinerary to Kikuyu, by way of Ukambani, given by M. Guillain (II. 289), we find a very high mountain in Kikuyu described as " being of a white colour, wooded at the foot, but entirely barren near its summit." This is undoubtedly Krapf's Kenia, Kegnia or Kirenia. We refer to p. 544 of this volume for further remarks, by Dr. Krapf, on the " Snow-covered Mountains of Eastern Africa."

of 270 miles from the coast. He spent fifteen days on the average in travelling to or from that place, and on his return journey in 1851 only ten days. In the latter he would consequently have travelled at the rate of twenty-seven miles a-day, or at least thirty-five miles of actual travelling, the above distance being given in a direct line. Assuming Dr. Krapf to have travelled at the rate of ten miles a day (on his last journey fifteen miles), Yata would be 150 miles distant from the coast, and this we have adopted on our map. At Kitui, a village four days in a northerly direction from Yata, the snow mountain Kenia could be seen from an eminence during clear weather, and its distance would appear to be at least 100 miles; the Kilimanjaro could be seen from the same locality, towards the S.W. The approximate position of these two mountains we believe to be as follows :—

Kenia.	1° 45' S. lat.	36° E. long.
Kilimanjaro	3° 30' ,,	37° ,,

In addition to the valuable information afforded by the Missionaries with regard to the countries which came under their personal observation, we are indebted to them for a mass of information about the interior, collected from native sources, which the Rev. J. Rebmann and Rev. J. Erhardt incorporated in a map, first published in the Proceedings of the Royal Geographical Society (1856), and the most striking feature of which is a vast lake of a curious shape, extending through twelve degrees of latitude. Dr. Krapf has now published some further information with respect to the countries east of Ukambani, in his work on Eastern Africa, here presented to the public.

The maps of the Missionaries, though open to criticism, as are more or less all compilations of this kind, at once attracted the attention of geographers, and the Royal Geographical Society, aided by government, resolved to send out an expedition to test the accuracy of the data furnished. Major R. Burton, a man well experienced in Eastern travel, and favourably known by his "Pilgrimage to Medina and Mekka," and a visit to Harar, was intrusted with its direction, and, having been joined by Captain Speke, his former companion, set out for Zanzibar, where he arrived on the 20th of December, 1857. After a visit to the Rev. J. Rebmann, at his missionary station at Kisuludini, and a preparatory journey to Fuga, the capital of Usambara, they set out for the interior on the 26th June, 1858. Traversing a mountainous tract, which begins about a hundred miles from the coast, and nowhere exceeds 6000 feet in height, they reached the great inner plateau of Uniamesi, which at Kazeh, an Arab trading post, has an elevation of 3400 feet. Thence westward the country forms a declined plane, and the elevation of the lake of Takanyika, or Uniamesi, which our travellers reached the 3rd of March, is 1843 feet. The lake extends for about 300 miles to the north of Ujiji, as ascertained by actual examination, and is inclosed there by a crescent-shaped chain of mountains, which Captain Speke looks upon as identical with the *Lunæ Montes*, Ptolemy's Mountains of the Moon. This assumption we believe, however, to be premature; Ptolemy had no personal knowledge of the countries of the Upper Nile, and can scarcely be supposed to have been acquainted with the crescent-like shape of the mountains in question. We would therefore rather, with Dr. Beke, claim this appellation for the snow-capped Kenia and Kilimanjaro, as far as we know the highest mountains in that part of Africa. According to native information, the lake extends towards the south to 8° of latitude, where it terminates, communicating perhaps, during the rainy season, with the Rukwe lake.* The information obtained by Dr. Livingstone from an Arab merchant, whom he met on the Liambye, tallies satisfactorily with that obtained by Captains Burton and Speke. That merchant skirted the southern shore of the lake on coming from the coast, and places Cazembe's Town† at ten days' journey to the S. W. of it. A Suaheli whom Dr. Beke had interrogated at Mauritius (*vide* " Athenæum," 12th July, 1856), gave similar information, and describes the Taganyika as being distinct from the more southerly Niassa. In spite of this apparently conclusive evidence regarding the disconnection of the two lakes, Mr. W. Desborough Cooley, than whom no one has done more for the elucidation of the geography of Central South Africa,

* Perhaps identical with the Kalagwe mentioned by Livingstone as communicating with the Taganyika.

† The approximate position of Cazembe's Town (Lunda or Lucenda) is known from the expeditions of Lacerda (1792) and Monteiro and Gamitto (1832, see page 564). The former made astronomical observations at Chama (Moiro Achinto) a village 150 miles to the S.E. of it. The Roapura river, which passes close to it, according to Dr. Livingstone, enters the Liambye, and the elevation of Cazembe's Town could not therefore be assumed at less than 5000 feet, or more than 3000 feet above the Taganyika.

still adheres to his opinion regarding their connection. To our knowledge, however, not a single instance of either Arab or native having
navigated such a lake lengthways has been adduced in support of
this assumption.

On their return from the Taganyika, Captain Burton remained at
Kazeh, to recruit his failing health, whilst Captain Speke proceeded
northward to explore the Victoria Nyanza, Lake Victoria, or lake
of Ukerewe, which he reached on the 3rd of August, and ascertained
to be 3738 feet above the sea. A river is said to debouch from its
northern extremity, and to flow into the Nile. Assuming the lake
to extend to 1° north latitude, and the development of the river to
be equal to twice the direct distance to Gondokoro, the altitude of
which is 1606 feet,* such a river would have a fall of five and a half
feet per mile, a current which would render it quite impracticable
for navigation.

The first information regarding the Upper Nile, or Bahr el Abiad,
is due to the three expeditions sent out by the Egyptian government,
between 1839 and 1842. Private travellers, such as MM. Brun
Rollet, Malzac, and Vayssiéres, but especially the Roman Catholic
missionaries at Gondokoro since 1849, have considerably added to
our knowledge. The visit of a traveller capable of making reliable
astronomical observations is, however, urgently required to clear up
the doubts regarding the true position of the Upper Nile. The
position of Janker Island is variously stated by different observers :—

Selim Bimbashi, Commander of
   second Egyptian Expedition .   4° 35′ N. lat.   32° 25′ E. long.
M. d'Arnaud, Member of two
   Egyptian Expeditions .   .   4° 42′ N. lat.   31° 38′ E. long.
M. Knoblecher, Roman Catholic
   Missionary .   .   .   .   4° 37′ N. lat.   28° 40′ E. long.

Unfortunately, the final results alone of M. Knoblecher's observations
have been given, and we are not, therefore, in a position to judge of
the degree of confidence to be attached to them. The information

---

* The altitude of Gondokoro has been deduced from barometrical observations by Dovyak, continued during thirteen months. The same observer
makes Khartum 882 feet above the sea; according to Russeger it is 1525
feet, and according to Captain Peel 1286 feet.

obtained by Captain Speke regarding the Kibiri river (the Bahr el
Abiad, above Janker Island, is called Tibiri, spelt Tubiri by the
French), which is said to flow towards the north-west on leaving
the Nyanza, would speak in favour of the greater accuracy of
M. Knoblecher's observations.

[For proceedings of the Roman Catholic Missionaries on the Upper
Nile, see the "Annual Reports of the Society of Mary for Promoting
Catholic Missions in Central Africa," Vienna, since 1851. MM. Dov-
yak's and Knoblecher's observations have been reprinted from the
"Annals of. the I. R. Institute for Meteorology and Terrestrial
Magnetism," Vienna, 1859. Other Missionaries established in
Abessinia (as Léon des Avanchers and Miani) have published some
information in the Journal of the Paris Geographical Society.]

After Captain Speke's return from the Nyanza both travellers
went back to Zanzibar, whence they embarked for Europe in March,
1859. Captain Speke is about to proceed again to the scene of his
late discoveries, accompanied by Captain Grant.*

In the mean time a German traveller, Dr. A. Roscher, has made
several attempts to penetrate into the interior, but hitherto his
endeavours have been foiled by almost constant illness. In February
1859 he made a journey by land along the coast from opposite Zanzibar to Kiloa, examining on the way the lower course of the Lufiji.
It was his intention to proceed from Kiloa to Lake Niassi, but in
October he had not yet left the coast, and the Arabs refused to take
him inland, fearing he might die.

The Niassi or Nyanja, by older authorities called Lake of the
Maravi, from a tribe occupying its western shore, was laid down on
Portuguese maps as early as 1546 and 1623. In 1518, even, a
large lake in the interior is mentioned by the Spaniard Fernandez
de Enciso. Manoel Godinho, in his travels to India, in 1663, gives
some more precise information, obtained from a Portuguese who had
actually visited the country. He places the southern extremity of
the lake under 15° 50' S. lat., and the River Zachaf (Shire) connects
it with the Zambezi below Sena.

* Major Burton's account of the expedition is in the press. In the mean
time we refer for further details to "Blackwood's Magazine" (Feb. to May 1858,
and Sept. to Nov. 1859), and to vol. XVIII. of the "Journal of the Royal
Geographical Society."

Gamitto (1831) states the lake to have a breadth of eighteen Portuguese miles, (thirty-three English,) but owing to the strong current it took two to three days to cross it, the canoes being pushed along by poles. According to him, the Shire or Little Nyanja had no communication with the lake. Dr. Livingstone, in his "Missionary Travels in Southern Africa," tells us of a Senhor Candido, long a resident of Tete, who had visited the Nyanja lake. Travelling through the country of the Maravi, that gentleman came upon the lake in the country of the Chiva. It took thirty-six hours to cross the lake to the country of the Mujao (Wahiao). In the middle of its southern end is a mountain island, called Murombo or Murombola, _i. e._ "where the waters divide." Of two rivers which leave the lake, one is the Shire, and enters the Zambezi, the other, he says, flows towards the sea under another name.* Similar information was given to Captain Bedingfield (1858) by Colonel Nunes, at Quillimane, who considered, however, the Nyanja as a chain of lakes.

From native sources we have obtained a number of routes leading to the lake, from Kiloa, Kisanga, and Mozambique. From Kiloa the distance is stated at from thirty to sixty days' journey, from Mozambique at thirty days. All routes agree in traversing near the lake the country of the Mujao or Wahiao (Hiao), and several pass through Lukelingo (Keringo), the capital of that country. At the southernmost ferry persons on opposite sides can speak with each other, and it was probably here where Silva Porto crossed in 1854. At Mjenga, a little further north, the opposite shore can just be seen. Opposite to Moalo is a mountain-island, called Mbaazura on Erhardt and Rebmann's map, possibly the Murombo Island of Senhor Candido. At Gnombo (Ngombo) the opposite shore only appears after three hours' rowing, and still further north the passage of the lake requires from two to three days. Nothing reliable is known regarding the extent of the lake further north : the Missionaries and Mr. Cooley believe it to communicate with the Taganyika or Lake of Uniamesi; Captain Burton and Speke think that it terminates at about 10 S. lat., and Mr. MacQueen ("Proceed.

---

* Both Léon des Avanchers and Dr. Krapf were told that the river Ruvuma took its rise from the large inland lake. See p. 419.

R. G. S.," Vol. IV., No. 1) looks upon the Nyanja as a large river, the head stream of which is a river passing near Cazembe's town.

These various conjectures we may confidently expect to see cleared up at an early date, by the labours of that indefatigable traveller Dr. Livingstone. That gentleman returned in 1858 to the Zambezi in the character of British Consul, and after a minute examination of the river up to the Kabrabesa rapids, he ascended the Shire, and, leaving the steamer at 16° 2' S. lat., continued his journey by land to the Shirwa lake, the existence of which had not hitherto been known to Europeans. This lake has an elevation of 2000 feet; it is surrounded by mountains, and said to be separated from the Nyanja or Nyenyesi (Star Lake) by a narrow strip of land, only six miles wide; its waters are bitter, but drinkable. Later in the year Dr. Livingstone traced the Shire river to the point where it flows from the Lake Nyenyesi (Nyanja or Niasse), 14° 23' S. lat., 35° 30' E. long. From that point the lake appeared to stretch towards the N.N.W., and upon its horizon appeared an island, which may be identical with the mountain island mentioned above. According to native testimony the lake subsequently turns towards the sea.*

COMMERCE OF AFRICA.

THE geographical configuration of Africa is not favourable to the development of commerce. Few rivers are navigable from the coast, and even those which are, are only so during part of the year. There are not many good harbours; the climate along the coast is inimical to European constitutions; and moreover, the continent is split up into innumerable independent communities, almost constantly at war with each other, and offering little security to the acquisition of property or encouragement to enterprise.

We need not, therefore, be surprised to find that the whole commerce of that vast continent does not exceed in amount that carried on by Hamburg alone. In the following table we have attempted

---

* Dr. Krapf was told at Kiloa that the lake might be reached in ten days, thus corroborating the information obtained by Livingstone; for, in order to reach its southern extremity in that time, a daily journey of some forty miles in a direct line would be required.

to give a statement of this commerce, as far as the Custom House returns of the various sea-faring nations enable us to do this.

To	Imports from				
	Northern Africa.*	African Islands.	Cape and Natal.	East and West Coasts.	Total.
	£	£	£	£	£
United Kingdom . .	6,300,000	1,600,000	1,463,000	1,900,000	11,263,000
France	2,742,000	1,300,000	—	900,000	4,942,000
Spain, Portugal, and } Medit. Countries . }	1,600,000	45,000	—	56,000	1,701,000
Remainder of Europe .	43,000	92,000	149,000	161,000	445,000
America . . .	10,000	52,000	185,000	305,000	552,000
British India . . .	—	156,000	51,000	225,000	432,000
Remainder of Asia .	—	100,000	6,000	300,000	406,000
Australasia (British) .	—	500,000	12,000	—	512,000
Total . .	10,695,000	3,845,000	1,866,000	3,847,000	20,253,000

From	Exports to				
	Northern Africa.*	African Islands.	Cape and Natal.	East and West Coasts.	Total.
	£	£	£	£	£
United Kingdom . .	2,104,000	900,000	2,041,000	970,000	6,015,000
France	5,212,000*	1,000,000	—	786,000	6,998,000
Spain, Portugal, and } Medit. Countries . }	1,100,000	16,000	8,000	152,000	1,276,000
Remainder of Europe .	63,000	43,000	84,000	46,000	236,000
America . . .	80,000	95,000	305,000	580,000	1,060,000
British India . . .	—	210,000	77,000	120,000	407,000
Remainder of Asia .	—	700,000	61,000	300,000	1,061,000
Australasia (British) .	—	400,000	15,000	—	415,000
Total . .	8,559,000	3,364,000	2,591,000	2,954,000	17,468,000

Assuming the population of Africa to be 150,000,000, the exports would average 2s. 8d. per head; in Great Britain they amount to 86s., in the United States to 54s., in France to 41s., and in Russia to 7s. But even this amount of 2s., small though it be, would give an exaggerated idea of the proportionate exports of Africa. For Northern Africa the exports amount to 8s. per head of the population, for the African Islands to 96s., for Cape Colony and Natal to 75s., but for the whole west and east coast, including Madagascar, to 9d. only.

The materials at our disposition have not enabled us to separate the commerce of the west coast from that of the east; one third, perhaps, of the total may appertain to the latter. At all events, the direct exports to Europe are trifling; France and the Hanse towns take the largest share; the Americans carry on a considerable trade,

* Transit viâ Suez (chiefly specie) not included. The French exports to Northern Africa include £4,620,000 to Algeria.

and Great Britain indirectly takes part in the commercial movement through British India. The east coast of Africa in many respects is preferable to the west coast: the climate is superior, and fevers scarcely ever prove fatal; there are many good harbours, and a great part of the coast is in the hands of regular governments. The chief drawback, however, is to be looked for in the greater distance from Europe; for, while a sailing vessel may reach the coast of Guinea in fifty days from Liverpool, it takes ninety days to get to Zanzibar. Nor would the opening of the Suez Canal, supposing that scheme capable of being carried out, materially shorten the passage to Zanzibar as regards sailing vessels. The following table shows the average passage in days from Southampton, by way of the Isthmus of Suez and round the Cape of Good Hope.

To or from Southampton.	Round the Cape.			By way of Suez.		
	Distance in Miles.	Average Passage		Distance in Miles.	Average Passage	
		In Screw Steamer.	In Sailing Vessels. Out.	Home.		In Screw Steamer.	In Sailing Vessels. Out.	Home.
		Days.	Days.	Days.		Days.	Days.	Days.
Aden . . .	10,300	*56	*99 [70]	*108	4,100	19	*57	*67
Bombay . . .	10,300	*56	107 [76]	104 [83]	6,000	26	*76	*85
Calcutta . . .	11,200	*60	110 [83]	112 [82]	7,600	36	*93	*103
Hong Kong . .	12,800	*68	134 [114]	120 [99]	9,800	42	*124	*122
Melbourne . .	11,500	59	82 [61]	83 [61]	11,000	53	*112	*114
Mauritius . .	8,100	*48	79 [60]	88 [61]	6,700	30	*80	*90
Natal . . .	6,700	39	63 [48]	72 [46]	8,000	*36	*92	*102
Zanzibar . .	8,500	*48	81 [66]	90 [64]	6,200	*28	*74	*84

The above table has been compiled chiefly from the "passage table" in the "Meteorological Papers," published by authority of the Board of Trade, No. 2, 1858. The average passage to Alexandria (2960 miles) takes 35 days: the quickest has been made in 23 days; the passage home requires on an average 45 days, or at the least 31 days. We have allowed one day for steamers, and two days for sailing vessels, to reach Suez from Alexandria. The navigation of the Red Sea being rather difficult for sailing vessels, we have assumed the voyage from Suez to Aden (1300 miles) to occupy 20 days, but believe this to be rather below what would be required ordinarily. The passage from Kossier to Jedda, for instance requires from 10 to 20 days, and considerably more in Arab boats. Beyond Aden we assumed 90 to 100 miles as the daily

* Based partly on estimates. The figures in brackets [ ] indicate the quickest passage on record.

progress of a sailing vessel, an estimate entirely in favour of the Suez route.   With regard to steam vessels, the saving in point of time is very considerable; but on account of their small stowage room, and the expense of fuel, their use is restricted to the carrying of mails, of passengers, specie, and of few articles of merchandise of small bulk, and for that purpose the railway between Suez and Alexandria suffices. In the trade with Aden, Bombay, and Calcutta, sailing vessels by the canal *in nubibus* would have an advantage of 40, 20, or 12 days respectively; but we doubt whether this would enable them to pay the proposed passage dues, of 10 francs per ton.   Hong Kong, (and the whole of Eastern Asia), Mauritius, and Zanzibar would not gain in point of time; Melbourne and Natal would actually lose.

Mr. MacLeod, late H. B. M. Consul at Mozambique, proposes the establishment of a line of steamers in connection with Aden, and touching at the principal places along the east coast, down to Natal. The time required to reach Natal, either by way of Suez or the Cape, being nearly alike (36 and 39 days respectively), the present line to the Cape, extended to Natal, might be profitably maintained.   Simultaneously, consular officers would have to be appointed to the principal ports.   The facilities for postal intercourse with Europe, thus offered to merchants settled at Zanzibar and elsewhere, could not fail to be highly conducive to the growth of legitimate commerce, and the slave-trade, which is still being carried on actively, might thus be gradually and effectually checked.

Our space will not permit us to enter into details regarding imports and exports, and we refer regarding these to the work of M. Guillain, and to Mr. MacLeod's "Travels in Eastern Africa." The latter gentleman most kindly volunteers to supply merchants with any particulars they may require regarding suitable cargoes, &c.

POLITICAL EVENTS IN ABESSINIA, AND MADAGASCAR.

EASTERN AFRICA, unlike the West Coast, is for the greater part occupied or claimed by foreign powers, and the native states, excepting Abessinia and Madagascar, are of little or no importance.   The Turks occupy several places on the Red Sea, the principal of which is Massowa, and appoint the governor of Zeila.   The dominions of the Imam of Zanzibar include the whole of the coast and neighbouring islands, from about 5° N. latitude to beyond Cape Delgado; many parts of the coast are, however, virtually independent. The Portuguese claim extends from Cape Delgado to Delagoa Bay; but they occupy in reality only the country along the lower Zambezi, and some isolated towns along the coast. Great Britain possesses Perim, a small island at the entrance of the Red Sea; the island Musha, opposite Tajurra, the natural outlet for the commerce of Shoa and Southern Abessinia; the island of Socotra, not at present occupied; the southern half of Delagoa Bay, and the Bay of Santa Lucia, on the coast of Kaffraria; and lastly, Natal, a country destined, from its favourable position and climate, to eclipse Cape Colony as an agricultural settlement. The French have lately acquired the port of Zula, south of Massowa; they also claim the whole of Madagascar, but at present hold but a few insignificant islands on its shore, and Mayotte, one of the Comoros.

Of Massowa, Abessinia, and Madagascar we shall speak more in detail under separate headings; but, before doing so, we would refer in a few words to the political bearings of the Suez Canal scheme. Engineers of eminence and respectability* have pronounced against the practicability of such a canal. Nevertheless, the enterprise is being persevered in under the auspices of the French government, or rather, the isthmus has been occupied within the last few weeks by a party of armed ouvriers. It is the avowed design of France to found in the eastern sea an empire to rival, if not to eclipse, British India, of which empire Madagascar is to be the centre. Across the Isthmus of Suez leads the shortest route from southern France to Madagascar (and India); its possession by a power desirous to extend her dominions in that quarter, and capable of availing herself of its advantages, would therefore be of the utmost consequence. The mere fact of the isthmus being part of the Turkish empire, or of Egypt, would not deter France from occupying it; for scruples of conscience are not allowed by that nation to interfere with political "ideas." Zula has been chosen as the second station on the route to Madagascar, and while the occupation of Suez may at will furnish

---

* We say "respectability" advisedly. No doubt many supporters of the scheme are sincere in believing it feasible. Such, however, can scarcely be the opinion of its actual promoters, otherwise they would have been more conscientious with regard to statements made, or facts omitted.

a pretext for seizing upon Egypt, that of Zula may open Abessinia to French conquest. Fortunately there is a power which can put a veto upon those plans of aggrandizement in North-eastern Africa, and that power is Great Britain. Gibraltar, Malta, Perim,* and Aden, form a magnificent line of military and naval stations on the route to India, and perfectly command it. Only after having converted the last three into French strongholds, and thus striking a decisive blow at the naval supremacy of Great Britain, could France ever hope to carry out her designs.

1.—Massowa and Abessinia.

Massowa in former times constituted part of the Abessinian Empire, and was governed by the Baharnagash, or Prince of the Sea, who had his residence at Dixan. It was occupied at the commencement of the 17th century by the Turks, in whose possession it has remained ever since. The Belaw, who inhabit the island and neighbouring coast, were the first to embrace Islamism, and from amongst them the pasha of Jidda nominated as vice-governor of the mainland, the "naib," *i. e.* substitute, a dignity since confined to the members of one family. The naibs, by stratagem or force, acquired a considerable influence over the neighbouring tribes, and their authority was recognized by the Shoho, Beduan, and Habab. The two former, being the earliest subjects, merely promised a contingent in time of war. The naibs also successfully restricted the commerce of Abessinia to Massowa; and when, about fifty years ago, caravans were known to frequent Ait, a port situated further south, war was made upon that place, and its chief compelled to swear upon the Koran not to receive any more caravans.

Repeated complaints of the arbitrary conduct of the naib at last induced the pasha of Jidda to give orders for his deposition. The governor of Massowa with his Turkish troops crossed over to Arkiko, the residence of the naib, destroyed that place, and built a fort which he garrisoned with 200 men. The naibs subsequently might have

---

* Perim at present is destined merely to bear a light-house. Properly fortified, it would command the entrance to the Red Sea even more effectually than Gibraltar does that to the Mediterranean.

regained their former influence, for the governor's conduct towards the Sohos and Belaw, from whom he demanded taxes, was by no means judicious; family disputes, however, prevented this. In 1853 the Shohos and Belaw were in open rebellion, but they at once returned to their former allegiance when, towards the close of 1854, a new naib arrived from Jidda, where he had successfully prosecuted the claims of his branch of the family to that dignity. He was invested with plenary powers as far as the mainland was concerned, and thus rendered almost independent of the Turkish pasha, who has since 1850 resided at Massowa.

At the present time the Turks have a garrison of 250 Regulars and 150 Bashi-bozuks at Massowa; fifty Bashi-bozuks occupy the fort at Arkiko, and, since July 1857, twenty-seven have occupied Ait.

The claim of Turkey to the west coast of the Red Sea, and specially to that part of the coast extending between Massowa and Ait, however slight her authority, appears to us to be clearly established by the mere fact of her nominating the naibs, and this for a period of nearly 300 years. Abessinia still prefers a claim to these territories, but has never been able to expel the Turks, and as late as 1848, when Ubie, the Regent of Tigre, attempted to do so and sent an army of 20,000 men against Arkiko, he was compelled to retire after having burnt a few villages and made a raid upon some cattle. Still, the claim of Abessinia to the coast offering the sole maritime outlet to her commerce, and formerly part of her territory, might be allowed, were she in a position to enforce it. It must, however, cause surprise to hear of France, a European power, at amity with Turkey, purchasing from the Regent of Tigre, who never held the slightest authority there, the port of Ait, and subsequently that of Zula.

The endeavours of France to gain a footing upon the Red Sea may be traced back for a number of years. M. Combes, who in 1835 visited Adoa, purchased from Ubie, the regent of Tigre, the port of Ait for £300, obviously for the purpose of attracting to it the commerce of Abessinia, then, as now, carried on through Massowa. A French vessel sent there by a Bordeaux house was not, however, able to open commercial intercourse; they neither found purchasers for their ill-assorted wares, nor the expected caravans with ivory and gold-dust. For a long time afterwards French interests in Abessinia were intrusted to the Romish missionaries, and to a consul, who took his residence at Massowa, a port with which France had no inter-course whatever. In 1840 the naib ceded to the consul a small plot of ground at Mokullu, close to Massowa, upon which the Missionaries built a chapel in 1848, and they also extended their operations to a Christian tribe of the Shohos, dwelling above Zula, and to the Bogos to the north of Abessinia. The consul gave the Turkish governor much trouble, and has of late insisted upon considering the mainland as independent. When Kassai had succeeded in making himself master of Abessinia, and a prospect of a stable government was at hand, France, who in this most probably saw the downfall of her own schemes, sowed disunion by rendering her support to Ubie, and subsequently to Yeh, the opponents of Kassai in Tigre. At the close of 1857, the French consul, accompanied by a priest, travelled to Adoa for the purpose of inducing Yeh to occupy the coast. The result of this journey has perhaps been the so-called cession of Zula, a port situated upon Annesley Bay, and only about twenty-five miles south of Massowa.* Zula formerly was a place of great commercial importance; its trade, however, has been removed to Massowa, which is more favourably situated, and at the present day it merely consists of a few huts of fishermen and camel-drivers. Its importance as a naval station is but slight, and the assertion of French writers that it commands the route to Aden is absurd, cut off, as the place would be, from receiving any support whatever in case of hostilities with a naval power like Great Britain, holding in Aden and Perim the keys to the Red Sea. It might, however, serve as a stepping-stone to further conquests in Abessinia; but is France in a position to find funds for the conquest of a second Algeria?†

Abessinia has for a number of years been a prey to intestine wars; which we had hoped to see terminated by the usurpation of the throne by Kassai whose energy may even now enable him to gain the object of his desires—the re-establishment of the Abessinian

---

* According to French papers this cession was made by Ubie (Oubieh) Our information regarding late political events in Abessinia is very fragmen-tary; we nevertheless have reason to suppose that Ubie has left the field of political action.

† The revenues Algeria at the present day covers the expenses of the civil administration (£8 to 900,000); the maintenance of the military esta-blishment requires, however, an outlay of above £2,000,000 more.

Empire. Kassai is a native of Kuara, a small province of Western Abessinia, the limits of which had been extended by his father and elder brother, Komfu, to the Abai and Lake Tsana. He wrested by conquest the province of Dembia from the mother of Ras Ali, Governor of Gondar, thus carrying his boundary to within a few miles of the capital. His desire of independence, and refusal to pay the customary tribute, soon brought him into hostile collision with the Ras, and the latter, in 1850, conferred the greater part of the provinces held by Kassai upon Buru Goshu, Prince of Gojam, a more loyal satrap. Kassai, with his scattered forces, retired before the large army sent against him, to Kuara, where he made active preparations to reconquer his lost territories. When his adversary had quietly settled down in Dembea, he broke forth from his mountains and defeated him in a sanguinary battle near the lake, Buru Goshu himself being amongst the slain. Ras Ali fled from Gondar, but, aided by Ubie of Tigre, and other Abessinian princes, collected a large force ; but he was also defeated in 1853 near Gorada, and obliged to seek safety amongst his Mohammedan relations. Kassai next turned his victorious arms against Ubie, whom he defeated and took prisoner in 1855 ;* he then appointed a relation of Sabagadis, the former rightful sovereign of Tigre, as vice-governor : and by consenting to expel the Romish priests, who had greatly interfered with the internal management of the church, he induced the Abuna to remove from Adoa to Gondar, and to anoint him as Theodore (Tadruss), Negus or Emperor of the Abessinian Empire. In 1856, Shoa was added to the dominions of Kassai. He was not, however, long to enjoy his conquests.

We glean from disjointed information obtained subsequently, that fresh opponents arose against Kassai in Tigre, and at the close of 1858, the fate of the empire had not yet been decided by battle. It is, however, to be hoped in the interests of humanity, that Kassai, who is still a young man, may triumph over his enemies, and thus carry out the reforms he contemplated.†

* Ubie subsequently appears to have been liberated on payment of a ransom of £10,000.

† Compare Dr. Krapf's Travels, p. 440.

2.—MADAGASCAR.

MADAGASCAR first attracted the attention of the French in 1642, when Louis XIII. granted the island to the Companie de l'Orient. Their first vessels arrived in 1643, and possession was taken of the island Ste. Marie and of Antongil Bay, and a small colony established at Ste. Luce, which soon afterwards was removed to Fort Dauphin. The new settlement was but badly supported by France; the governors treated the natives with execrable cruelty, and even sold them to Dutch slave-dealers, conduct which brought about the massacre of the French colonists when celebrating a midnight mass on Christmas eve, 1672. Only a few made their escape to the island of Bourbon.

The next attempt at settlement was directed towards the island Ste. Marie in 1750, but conduct similar to that pursued at Fort Dauphin caused a second massacre, four years after the arrival of the colonists.

Fort Dauphin was again temporarily occupied in 1768, but up to 1774, when Count Benyovski arrived with his expedition in Antongil Bay, France was represented on the island merely by a few independent traders. The count, having lost most of his people in battle or by disease, returned to France to vindicate his conduct. The Government did not, however, think fit to intrust him with the conduct of a second expedition, and, stung with disappointment, he went to the United States, where he collected a band of adventurers, with whom he landed in Madagascar with a view of conquering that island on his own account, but fell in defence of a small fort in 1786, against a French force sent against him from Mauritius.

In 1810, when Great Britain took possession of Mauritius, French agents were found established at Tamatave and Foulepointe, and surrendered to the British squadron. By the treaty of Paris, of 1814, Mauritius with its dependencies was ceded to Great Britain, including, of course, any settlement which might have been made in Madagascar; France, however, subsequently refused to acknowledge this claim. In 1815, a tract of land was purchased from native chiefs at Port Luquez, and a small settlement founded, which was,

however, finally abandoned in 1817, when Great Britain acknowledged the claim of Radama to the whole island.

The French, however, continued their efforts at colonization; in
1819 they reoccupied Ste. Marie and Tintingue, and sent a few men
to garrison Fort Dauphin; native chiefs in 1821 ceded the coast
between Fenerife and Antongil Bay. Radama protested against
this aggression, and in 1822 expelled the French from the main
land, and occupied Fort Dauphin in 1825.

In 1829, another expedition was sent to Madagascar; the French
occupied Tintingue, burnt Tamatave, but were ingloriously defeated
by a much inferior number of Hovas at Foulepointe. The former
place was again evacuated in 1831, and up to the present day the
French settlements on the east coast have been restricted to the
small island of Ste. Marie.

Seeing their efforts in this quarter unavailing, they now directed
their attention to the west coast. In 1840 they procured from
native chiefs the "cession" of Nossibé and some neighbouring
islands, together with the main land facing them; they were not,
however, able to prevent the Hovas from occupying the latter, nor
did they resent their destroying, in 1856, a French fort built near
Bavatuka Bay, thirty miles from Nossibé, where a French company
worked some coal-mines, and from which they carried away five
guns as trophies of victory. The superintendent of the coal-mine,
and others, were killed, and the labourers, about 100 in number,
taken prisoners to Tananarivo.

In 1841 the French also took possession of Mayotte, one of the
Comoro Islands, a position equally useless as a naval station or
commercial entrepôt.*

A more daring attempt upon Madagascar has been made recently,
and reflects little credit upon the government which sanctioned it.
M. Lambert, in 1855, visited Tananarivo avowedly for commercial
purposes, but obviously with the object of organizing a conspiracy
in conjunction with Laborde and several native chiefs. This
Laborde was formerly a slave-dealer, and, at the time, Great
Chamberlain at the court of Emirné. His preliminary arrangements

---

* This island was not " ceded " by the native prince, but occupied under
protest. Vide " Madagascar Past and Present, by a Resident : London 1847,"
p. 222.

being made, M. Lambert started for France, and after two interviews with the emperor returned to Madagascar, taking with him presents to the amount of £2000, and accompanied by Pére Jean, Apostolic Vicar of Madagascar, disguised as a trader, and by Madame Ida Pfeifer, who, we hope, was ignorant of the purport of the mission. The conspirators arrived at Tananarivo in 1857. It was their intention to depose the queen, and place upon the throne a native prince, who, in case of success, promised to acknowledge himself a vassal of France, and to introduce the Roman Catholic religion. The plot, however, was discovered, and the chief conspirators were expelled the island; and many others are supposed to have suffered death in consequence of their participation in it.*

Still more recent is the acquisition of a large tract of land near Bali Bay. A French vessel, the "Marie Angelique," engaged in the so-called Free Immigration Scheme, had been plundered there by the natives, and the government agent on board of her killed. On the news of this disaster reaching Bourbon, the frigate "La Cordelière," was at once sent to the spot; the villages in which the culpable parties were supposed to reside were destroyed; the chief of the territory, a female, was deposed, and her lands given to a neighbouring chief, who, "recognizing the ancient rights of France to the territories occupied," made a cession of the whole. We do not know whether the territory thus acquired has actually been settled, but believe not.

The present state of the French settlements near Madagascar is not at all commensurate with the pains taken in their formation during the two last centuries. Ste. Marie, in 1856, had a population of 5743 souls. The population of Nossi Be, and the smaller islands in its vicinity, was 22,577 in 1856; the imports amounted to £24,000, the exports to only £5400. Mayotte, in 1853, had 6829 inhabitants, and its exports and imports amounted, in 1856, to £30,740. The island of Bourbon, or Réunion, in 1858, had 143,600 inhabitants,

---

* Vide " MacLeod's Travels in Eastern Africa." Barbié de Bocage, in his work on Madagascar (Paris 1859), makes no mention of M. Lambert's share in this conspiracy. He merely gives an extract from the "Patrie" newspaper (p. 276), according to which a " Catholic " party had been formed in opposition to the queen's government, and the discovery of which led to the massacre of 2000 individuals.

amongst whom were 93,000 immigrant labourers. The imports of the island amounted to £1,133,000, in 1856, the exports to £1,187,000.

Réunion has a garrison of 1200 European troops, a company of native Sappers and Miners, 150 men strong, besides an organized militia of 5000 men. The other possessions mentioned are garrisoned by some 200 Europeans and 250 Africans. None of these possess a harbour desirable as a naval station, and the loss of Mauritius, with its safe and well-defended anchorage, and unique position at almost equal distance from Aden, British India, and the Cape, could never be adequately compensated, even by their occupying the whole of Madagascar. Nor are these settlements calculated to become of importance as commercial entrepôts; the French can never hope to see Mayotte the rival of Zanzibar, though no doubt these colonies may become important by the establishment of sugar and coffee plantations. Mauritius, at the present day, depends for its supply of cattle almost exclusively upon Madagascar; for out of 8711 head imported in 1857, 485 only came from other countries. Besides these, 6584 cwt. of rice and a little tobacco were imported from that island, the total imports amounting to only £43,000. During the same period the value of cereals and flour imported from British India and others of our colonies amounted to £494,000. Should the French at some future period be able to stop the export trade of Madagascar, which they could only do by subjecting the whole of that island to their sway, Mauritius might draw the whole of her supply of cattle from our fast-growing colony of Natal,‡ and as long as Great Britain maintains her naval superiority, no fear need be entertained of that island being ever reduced by famine.

In fact, the designs of France upon Madagascar need cause no apprehension; in case of war, that island would prove a source of embarrassment rather than of strength. No doubt commercial operations might be extended, and this without prejudice to British enterprise, which will find much more profitable employment in the colonization of Natal, and ultimately of the whole of Kaffraria.

London, May, 1860.

* The distance from Mauritius to Natal is about 1740 miles. Occasionally cargoes of cattle have been imported from Mombaz or Brava, a much greater distance. Hitherto Natal has not exported any cattle.

II.—THE AUTHOR'S REASONS FOR PUBLICATION—DESIGN AND PLAN.

SOON after my return from East Africa in 1855, I was urged by many of my friends to publish a connected account of my travels in that region; but it was not until I had prepared a brief sketch of Dr. Livingstone's researches in South Africa for the German reader in 1857, that the idea of acceding to their wishes occurred to me, as upon a review of Dr. Livingstone's travels, I was led to believe that my own might form a useful supplementary volume upon the geography of Africa. Dr. Livingstone's travels, commencing at the south and west, terminated on the coast of Mozambique, to which I had penetrated from the north as far as Cape Delgado, and a comparison of my map with that of Dr. Livingstone will show the relative positions in which our researches stand to each other.

After a diligent perusal of my manuscript journals and papers, written on the spot during my residence in Abessinia and Equatorial Africa, I published in German the result of those labours which, in consequence of the publication of Dr. Livingstone's long promised narrative of his discoveries, it has been deemed advisable to present to the English reader in a somewhat new and altered form, and with numerous important additions and pictorial illustrations of the regions described.

My calling, in which through all perils I have been so mercifully preserved and upheld, enables me to set forth in their true light the moral misery and degradation to which the heathen nations of East Africa have fallen, and to point out the various routes by which these benighted populations may be approached, and the means for their elevation to Christian truth and Christian civilization be conveyed to them. A vast area of country has been explored by myself, as well as by my esteemed colleagues Messrs. Rebmann and Erhardt; hitherto unwritten languages have been reduced to writing, and the way prepared for the establishment of missions; the geographical portion of our task in East Africa has been, as it were, all but accomplished; but, in the memorable words of Dr. Livingstone, "the end of the geographical feat is but the commencement of missionary operations."

To some extent the labours of a missionary pioneer must ever form a contribution to geographical and ethnological science, if as should always be the case, those missionaries who enter unexplored wilds become at the same time promoters of geographical knowledge by carefully investigating their relative positions, the course of rivers, the altitude of mountains, climate, and other essential peculiarities, and more especially those which appertain to natural science and the development of the human race.

In the case of East Africa such investigations cannot fail to be the forerunners of the most important changes, both in a commercial and political point of view; and at the present moment there is scarcely any section of the less frequented portions of the globe so full of interest as that to which these pages are devoted, abounding as it does in natural resources infinitely beyond those of other countries into which European commerce and immigration have carried civilization and the arts of peace. It is true that the precious metals may be more abundant elsewhere; but what has the discovery of the gold fields of Australia and America produced to make us regret that, instead of these East Africa produces iron and coal, the surest and most productive of mines in any country; is rich and fertile, overflowing with milk and honey; produces with but little toil rich cereal crops; has cattle, poultry, eggs, in abundance; and coffee, sugar, and tropical fruits—all almost for the gathering.

The great naval powers of the world are the first to recognise the importance of these discoveries as connected with the Eastern coast of Africa. At present the surface is tranquil, and peace prevails. Will it remain so? A French squadron is talked of for Jedda or Sonakin, and a line of transport steamers for the Red Sea has long been building. Egypt swarms with Frenchmen; every branch of the Administration is full of them; and French influence, consequently, preponderates. The *Bombay Gazette* reports—evidently upon sufficient authority—that a French mission is on its way to Gondar, and is even now in the Tigre country, to establish the claims of France to the territory around Annesley Bay, or the Bay of Adulis, said to have been ceded to her, if with no other and less obvious object.

It was an opinion among the ancients that the coast of East Africa was connected with that of India. Erroneous as this was, there is certainly a great political truth involved in the supposition, inasmuch

as the possessor of East Africa will have gained a first step towards
the dominion of India. Any further knowledge, therefore, obtained
respecting East Africa, cannot fail to interest Englishmen, as it may
be that the fate of India itself will some day have to be decided in the
burning solitudes of Africa, no less than in the rich plains of Asia.
No true Englishman can henceforth be an indifferent spectator of
what is passing upon the eastern coast of Africa, from the Isthmus
of Suez to the Cape of Good Hope.

It would be quite preposterous to urge that there is no real political
danger to be apprehended from the possession of these regions, because East Africa presents for the most part, nothing but a barren,
harbourless, and savage coast, not to be invaded with prudence by any
government of Europe. It is true that Africa wears on all her coasts
a forbidding aspect, Providence having furnished her weak nations
by this grim physiognomy with the only weapon of strength which
they can oppose to the dominant Japhetic and Semetic races. But
we may be sure that no coast-barrier will ultimately prevent the
former from possessing the inland regions, in many places not inferior
in fertility, beauty, and healthfulness to any country upon the face of
the globe.

In claiming the reader's indulgence as to the style in which the
work is written, it may only be necessary to state that my journals
and diaries were composed entirely for my own eye, in order to
enable me to place before the Church Missionary Society with which
I was then connected, such details of the progress of the mission at
Rabbai Mpia as could not fail to interest the large and influential
class of persons who, to England's glory, are to be numbered throughout the land amongst the supporters of missionary endeavour to convert the heathen. I believe, in eschewing all desire to shine solely
as a literary man, to which I here make no pretence, my narrative
will gain in accuracy what it may thus lack in word painting,
that plastic elegance of diction which has of late distinguished the
writings of modern travellers.

In a former work,* published some years ago, a full account was

---

* Journals of the Rev. Messrs. Isenberg and Krapf, detailing their Proceedings in the Kingdom of Shoa, and Journeys in other parts of Abyssinia,
in the years 1839—42, with a Geographical Memoir of Abyssinia and South-
eastern Africa, by James M'Queen, Esq. London, 1843. Pp. 529.

given of the missionary labours of my dear friend and fellow-labourer
Missionary Isenberg and myself in Abessinia, to which Mr. McQueen
prefixed a geographical essay, which enables me to devote the more
space in the present volume to such facts as afterwards fell under my
own observation in Equatorial Africa, in regions previously untrodden
by any European. In doing this I have not deemed it necessary
to confirm, correct, or enlarge upon what has been brought together
by the Portuguese, who occupied the immediate sea-shore from lat.
2° N. to lat. 20° S., any more than upon what has been recorded by
Captain Owen, who surveyed the East African waters in 1824 by order
of Government, or upon what has been communicated by M. Guillain,
who has described many parts of the eastern coast with great diligence and accuracy. M. Guillain surveyed the east coast of Africa
in 1846—1848, by order of the French Government, and published
the results of his survey in 1857-1858, in which he brought forward a vast amount of historical facts connected with the ancient
history of the East African continent, of which I have availed myself in the concise historical essay given by way of appendix.

Whilst these sheets were passing through the press news reached
me of the return of Major Burton and Captain Speke from the interior of Africa to Europe, and some intelligence of their most interesting discoveries will be found in " Blackwood's Magazine," and in
the " Proceedings of the Royal Geographical Society of London,"
preparatory to the publication of the entire narrative in a separate
form. The accounts of these courageous, persevering, and scientific
travellers bear in some important points very materially upon the
statements which I obtained in 1851 from the natives at Ukambani.
It is very remarkable that Captain Speke should have seen the great
lake which Rumu wa Kikandi, a native of Uemba, near the snow-
capped mountain Kegnia, mentioned to me under the name "Baringu,"
the end of which cannot be found, "even if you travel a hundred
days' distance along its shores," as my informant expressed himself.
Is is further remarkable that Captain Speke very properly named it
Victoria Nyanza, in honour of Her Majesty, after the mountain in
Mberre which, as will be found by subsequent travellers, presents
the nearest approach from the coast of Mombaz to that lake, had been
called by me " Mount Albert," or Albertino, in honour of His Royal
Highness the Prince Consort. Thus, the one may be said to mark

the spot, the other the nearest way by which it can be reached, on which the greatest geographical problem of Africa, the discovery of the sources of the Nile, will probably be solved under the auspices of the English Government.

It is most satisfactory to find that the reports of the natives made to my fellow-labourers Rebmann and Erhardt, as to the existence of a large inland " bahari" or sea, are fully confirmed by the discovery of the Victoria Nyanza, or Ukerewe; and although there is not alone one " bahari," or lake, but several, in Central South Africa— the Tanganyika, the Niassa, and the Shirwa, the latter discovered by Dr. Livingstone—the presence of these great lakes proves the value of the information thus obtained, even though, to the less critical observation of the natives, all these waters may have appeared as forming one great and connected whole, as represented in Erhardt's chart. In reference to this fact I cannot do better than quote the words of Captain Speke; not a mere theorist, and drawer of maps, carried away by some one cherished idea, but a man of practical experience :—

" I must call attention to the marked fact that the Church missionaries residing for many years at Zanzibar are the prime and first promoters of this discovery. They have been for years past doing their utmost with simple sincerity to Christianize this negro land, and promote a civilized and happy state of existence for these benighted beings. During their sojourn among these blackamoors, they heard from Arabs and others of many of the facts I have now stated; but only in a confused way, such as might be expected in information derived from an uneducated people. Amongst the more important disclosures made by the Arabs was the constant reference to a large lake or inland sea, which their caravans were in the habit of visiting. It was a singular thing that at whatever part of the coast the missionaries arrived, on inquiring from the travelling merchants where they went to, they one and all stated to an inland sea, the dimensions of which were such, that nobody could give any estimate of its length or width. The directions they travelled in pointed north-west, west, and south-west, and their accounts seemed to indicate a single sheet of water extending from the Line down to 14° S. lat., a sea of about 840 miles in length, with an assumed breadth of 200 to 300 miles. In fact, from this great combination of testimony that water lay generally in a continuous line from the Equator up to 14° S. lat., and from not being able to gain information of there being any territorial separations to the said water, they naturally and, I may add, fortunately, created that monster slug of an inland sea which so much attracted the attention of the geographical world in 1855-1856, and caused our being sent out to Africa. The good that may result from this little but happy accident will, I trust, prove proportionately as large and fruitful as the produce from the symbolical grain of mustard seed; and nobody knows or believes in this more fully than one of the chief promoters of this exciting investigation, Mr. Rebmann."

In concluding these remarks I may be permitted to record several wishes which I have much at heart, in the first place expressing my warmest thanks to the Church Missionary Society, and especially to its excellent secretary, the Rev. Mr. Venn. As long as I was connected with that Society, from 1837 to 1855, its committee treated me most kindly and liberally, and with the greatest sympathy, under all circumstances. I also wish to offer my sincerest thanks to Charles Young, Esq. of London, for the assistance he has given to the East African Mission in various ways, and particularly do I publicly thank the Reverend Mr. Olive of St. Lawrence Rectory, Welwyn, for the handsome provision he made for me during a period of six years.

I would recommend my dear colleague, Mr. Rebmann, who, with his noble-hearted wife, continues labouring in solitude among the crooked and perverse generation of Wanika, at Rabbai Mpia, to the prayers and sympathies of missionary friends in England. According to the latest intelligence received from him, his missionary hopes and prospects are more reassuring than they were some years since; his labours of faith, love, and patience, cannot be lost, and He who has asked of the Father to give him the heathen for an inheritance, and who died once unto sin an offering for the whole world, and now liveth unto God, the Mediator for all, will in due time lay the Wanika also prostrate before His cross by the instrumentality of the Gospel, unceasingly preached to the heathen.

I would strenuously recommend Bishop Gobat's Mission in Abessinia, as well as the objects of the so called Apostles' Street, which I have specified in pages 133 and 214. But last, and above all, I would urge the searching out of the numerous Christian remnants, scattered over several countries in the south of Abessinia, as in Gurague, Kambat, Wolamo, Kaffa, and other places.   I am indeed so much interested in this great object, that, had I a sufficiency of private means, or were I supported by a private individual, or a Missionary Society, I would to-morrow give up the comforts of home and the duties of my new and agreeable office, would reach down once more my pilgrim's staff, and return again to the wilds of Eastern Africa.   Having the advantage of a knowledge of the Abessinian language and those of Equatorial East Africa, and knowing the habits and condition of the people, as well as the various routes leading to those scattered Christian tribes, I have not the least doubt that, with the blessing of Providence, success would attend the undertaking.   What a glorious object would it be, if those un-fortunate and benighted fellow Christians, who are closed in in their mountains by barbarous tribes, could be sought out, revived by the pure Word of God, and be rendered the centre of light to the surround-ing heathen.   Would not these revived tribes become spiritual rivers to irrigate the arid wastes of surrounding heathenism?   Who among the wealthy Christians and among the friends of missions and science will take this special object to heart?   Who will stretch out his helping hand to rekindle the dying lamp of the faith of our fellow Christians in the interior of Africa?   Who will lay down his sub-stance, not to say his life, for our brethren perishing from want of the saving knowledge of the Gospel?

With a fervent prayer for the spread of the Gospel throughout the world, I bid the reader God speed.

THE AUTHOR.

RIHEN, NEAR BASEL,
1st *May*, 1860.

PART I.

RESEARCHES AND MISSIONARY LABOURS.

EXTRACTS FROM JOURNALS, ETC.

RESEARCHES AND MISSIONARY LABOURS

EXTRACTS FROM JOURNALS.

CHAPTER I.

AUTOBIOGRAPHICAL.

A PROVIDENTIAL GUIDANCE IN THE LIFE OF MAN.

WE trace, it is said, the impressions, views, and teachings of the child in the after-career of the man influencing his pursuits and giving them a fixed direction. In my case, at least, this was no paradox, and by way of illustration I would place before the reader a short sketch of my early life before I became attached to the East African Mission.

My father, whose circumstances were easy, followed farming and lived in the village of Derendingen, near Tübingen, where I was born on the 11th of January 1810, and baptized by the name of Ludwig, the wrestler, no inapt appellation for one who was destined to become a soldier of the Cross. Many were my providential escapes in childhood from dangers which beset my path, from falling into the mill-stream which flowed through the village, from accidents with fire-arms, or falls from trees in the eager pursuit of birds' nests. The inborn evil nature of the child was somewhat held in check by a nervous susceptibility, and the consequent dread I experienced in witnessing the contest of the elements in storms, or which shook my frame at the sight of the dead and the grave, or even when reading or listening to the narratives of the torments of the wicked in hell. On these occasions I secretly vowed to lead a pious life for the future; though, childlike, I soon forgot the promise when the exciting cause had passed away, as is ever the case throughout life with the natural, unregenerated heart of man. Thus, but for an apparently trivial event in my boyhood, though in it I gratefully recognise the chastening Hand of the great Teacher, the evil of my nature might have choked the good seed with its tares, or destroyed it altogether. When eleven years old I was so severely beaten by a neighbour for a fault which I had not committed, that it brought on a serious illness of six months' duration. Left to myself my thoughts dwelt much upon eternity; and the reading of the Bible and devotional books became my delight, particularly such portions of the Old Testament as recorded the history of the patriarchs and their intercourse with the Creator; and when I read of Abraham conversing with the Almighty, an earnest desire arose in my breast that I too might be permitted to listen to the voice of the Most High, even as did the prophets and apostles of old. If this reading resulted in nothing better, at all events it made me desirous to master the historical portions of the Bible. Nor was this knowledge thrown away; for in the autumn of 1822, during the period of my convalescence, I was in the habit of repeating to the reapers many of the stories of the Bible, so earnestly and vividly, that more than one of them would say to my parents, " Mark my words, Ludwig will some day be a parson." Chance, some might suggest, soon led the bias of my mind in that direction, if it were possible for a moment to deny a Providential guidance in the events of our lives, quite compatible with man's free-will; and in my career this guidance is the more evident, because just such trifling and seemingly unimportant circumstances have governed its whole course. In the early part of the year 1823, on going to Tübingen to buy a new almanack, my sister, mistaking the house, instead of that to which she had been directed for the purpose, called at the dwelling of the widow of a former vicar, whose son attended the grammar-school of the city. Of kindly disposition, and having no false pride the lady entered into conversation with her lowly visitor, and amongst other things inquired if she had any brothers and sisters ; and learning that besides two elder brothers she had one younger, then in his thirteenth year, she asked if he had any knowledge of arithmetic. To this my sister could reply with a safe conscience in the affirmative; upon which the widow said at once,

"I should very much like to see the lad; he may be able to teach my son arithmetic, go to the grammar-school, and perhaps in time study for the Church." My sister replied that she would bring me to see the lady, but added, "We are only simple farmers; so as to grammar-school, and studying for the Church, I think there will be but little chance of that." "Never mind," said the lady, "farmer or no farmer, Adam himself was a farmer; let me see your brother and talk to him myself." Full of the bright prospect which she saw opening for her young brother my sister returned home, and after a while the consent of the whole family was obtained to the proposition; whilst in the joy of the moment I promised to labour night and day with zeal and industry, and prove to them all that I was not unworthy of so much love and affection. Accordingly, a day or two afterwards, I accompanied my sister to the house of the clergyman's widow who, pleased with my boyish answers to her questions, urged again strongly the importance of my being sent at once to the grammar-school. My father, involved in some law proceedings, saw as it were in his mind's eye, in his son a rising lawyer capable of bringing these suits to a successful issue. With that ambition he took me with him to Tübingen in order to be examined by the rector of the Anatolian School. The rector Kaufmann gave me a Latin book to read, to test my familiarity with the characters of the language, which I had taught myself during my six months'

illness, and pleased with the performance promised
to place me at the bottom of the school, adding by
way of encouragement that something might be
made of me, if my father would countenance the
scheme of my going to college. "Let him come to
school at eight o'clock to-morrow morning," he
said, "and bring with him a Latin grammar and
the other books put down on this list, and we will
make a beginning." The books were bought before
we left Tübingen that day, and as a proof of earnest
zeal, after our return home I learnt the first declen-
sion, *mensa*, and rose as early as three o'clock in the
morning to master the second, reaching the school
long before eight o'clock, and was placed by the
under-master on the lowest form, along with boys
but nine years old, which to a great boy of thirteen,
as I then was, could not fail to make me feel a little
abashed and to experience a morbid shame at my
ignorance. But this very shame stood me in good
stead by making me the more desirous to learn, to
be placed in the class above me with boys of my
own age. The early morning always found me on
my road to Tübingen with satchel on my back, in
which besides my books were a bottle of sweet
must and a great hunch of bread, which were to
constitute my simple mid-day's meal, and which
I quickly consumed between twelve and one o'clock,
under the willows on the banks of the Neckar, in
order more leisurely to devour my Latin grammar
and Scheller's vocabulary, which I soon learnt by
heart. In doing this, I was impelled by a desire to

imprint as many words as possible on my memory; and in after-times, when I wished to acquire any new and hitherto unknown tongue, I found this by far the most desirable method of proceeding. For a time this was my daily course; but such a frugal way of life could not long endure without injury to my health, and it was then arranged that I should return home daily to a hot dinner. This necessitated a threefold journey, morning, noon, and evening, from Derendingen and back again, but it laid the foundation of that strong health which during my career as a Missionary I enjoyed for so many years.

My diligence met its reward, and at the end of six months I was at the head of my class; and before the close of the year was placed on the third form, the rector not considering it necessary that I should remain longer in the lower school. I was becoming a good Latin scholar, and speedily removed to the fourth form, where I became a Grecian, and rose to be top boy of the class, my teachers expressing themselves well pleased with my general conduct and progress. Yet even while everything on the surface seemed bright and full of promise, how joyless, how void of peace the heart! Such perishable knowledge ill sufficed to hold my self-love, vain glory, and ambition in check; to yield true peace, or to regenerate a heart whose chief craving was after the imperishable—after its long-cherished desire of immediate intercourse with God! His countenance was still obscured and kept

from me notwithstanding all my resolutions, as I
wandered daily backwards and forwards between
Derendingen and Tübingen, always to walk spotless
in His sight, and to keep His image ever before me!

Whilst I was still on the lowest form, my father
bought me an atlas of the world, and well do I
recollect wondering why there should be so few
names of places put down in the districts of Adal
and Somali in the map of Eastern Africa, and I
said to myself, " Is there then so great a desert
yonder, still untrodden by the foot of any European ?
What, too, if it is full of hyænas ?" for of these I
had just been reading in an odd volume of Bruce's
Travels, which had been lent me by a bookseller in the
town.   How curious that such a thought should have
been instilled into the mind of a child, who in manhood was to be the means of expanding the knowledge of those very regions of which then so little
was known!   My desire for travel was greatly
fostered by the study of geography, and by reading
voyages and travels, and when in my fourteenth
year my future course of life was discussed in the
family circle, I expressed an ardent desire to
become " the captain of a ship, and to visit foreign
lands."   Much as my father would have preferred
my being either a lawyer or a clergyman, he
respected the evident bias of his child, and made
the necessary inquiries as to the cost of apprentice-
ship and outfit, only giving up the scheme upon
finding that the expense would be greatly beyond
his means.   This was a great disappointment to me.
Neither law nor physic were to my mind ; divinity

was less objectionable ; but I dreaded the learning of
Hebrew with its repulsive-looking characters and
unfamiliar sounds. I still continued zealously the
study of Greek and Latin and of general knowledge, adding to these also the commencement of
French and Italian.

Whilst so engaged again a seemingly unimportant
circumstance helped to fix my future career. When
I was in my fifteenth year the rector read an essay
to the whole school on the spread of Christianity
amongst the heathen, in which it was explained what
missions were, how they were conducted, and what
great good they had achieved in various parts of the
world since the beginning of the present century.
It was the first time I had heard of missions amongst
the heathen, and the idea assumed a definite form in
my mind, so that, boy-like, I asked myself, " Why
not become a missionary, and go and convert the
heathen ?" But then quickly arose the inquiry,
" How can he preach the Gospel to the heathen, upon
whose heart its seeds have fallen as upon stony places?"
Oft and oft would the words of the parable of the
sower pass through my mind, impelling me to read the
Bible with greater earnestness, and to pray for a quickening knowledge of it. It was the earnest prayer of
one who knew not yet how to pray, but it was not
uttered in vain. The Easter holidays of 1825 were
at hand, and as I walked homewards from Tübingen
the thought arose in my mind with the force of a command, " to go to Basel and announce myself willing
to devote my life to the labours of a missionary."
The matter was discussed at home and met with the

ready approval of my mother and sister, and, furnished by the former with a letter of introduction to Missionary Inspector Blumhardt, whom she had known and respected when he was vicar of Derendingen, I made the journey to Basel by way of Schaffhausen on foot, and returned home in the same manner taking the road through Freiburg. The Inspector kindly recognised my zeal; but pointed out to me the first requisite for the calling of an evangelist, the renewal of the heart, as still wanting; yet added, by way of encouragement, that as I was yet too young to be received into the Missionary College, I should return home for the present, continue my studies, and cultivate the acquaintance of Christian friends in Tübingen and its neighbourhood; and above all, let the search after gospel truth and a knowledge of my own heart be my chief care, waiting patiently till I should receive a call to enter the Missionary Institute as a labourer in the Lord's vineyard. I resolved to be guided by this sage counsel; but previous to my return home I obtained permission to spend a week at the Institute, and here it was that for the first time in my life I became acquainted with true Christians, who upon their knees prayed beside me, and some of whom became my special friends, in whose subsequent correspondence with me after my return to Tübingen I found the greatest solace and blessing.

In 1826 I entered the fifth and highest form of the Anatolian School, and privately devoted myself to the study of Hebrew with such diligence that before long I had read the greater portion of the Old Testament in the original. During that period I made the acquaintance of a dear friend and thorough Christian, to whose intercourse I perhaps owe it, that after my return from Basel I did not become a backslider from the earnest desire I had to render myself worthy to be a missionary. It is a true saying that "man can only become man amongst his fellows;" but it is also no less true that "a Christian can only be formed amongst Christians." It is amongst them that a young Christian first becomes conscious of his own spiritual wants by witnessing the faith, patience, and constancy of aged persons in the various trials of life; and to such society I was introduced by the friend to whom I owe so much, and by that intercourse I was in a manner better qualified to accept the summons to the Missionary College at Basel, which when it reached me in 1827 filled me with inexpressible joy. At first my father was opposed to his son "being buried alive," as he said, "in a foreign land;" but he gave way at length to my earnest pleading, backed as it was by my mother and sister, who plainly saw in all the finger of God pointing out the course I was to pursue, and he himself accompanied me to Basel. There I remained for two years, during which I made a stealthy acquaintance with the forbidden writings of such mystics as Madame Guion and Jacob Behmen, which took such a hold upon my excited imagination and so imbued me with their fanatic enthusiasm, that I abandoned the idea of becoming a missionary and returned home, intending to give up study, and to labour with my hands as more conducive to happiness and a truly religious life, according to the pernicious doctrines I had imbibed. My parents and family combated the notion, not on religious grounds, of which they were incapable of judging, but on account of the cost of my education and the disgrace it would be to the whole family, if having been brought up with reference to a learned profession, I were to sink again to the level of a mere tiller of the soil. Much against my will I returned to college, completed my studies, and was ordained; then entered upon the curacy of Wolfenhausen, but which in consequence of a sermon, in which I had represented the world to be in the last quarter of its twelfth and final hour, giving umbrage to the Consistory, I resigned for a private tutorship. So it is, gold is purified by fire; and those were years of severe and painful struggle; but they brought with them at its close the restoration of my former healthy tone of mind, and the dismissal from it of the doubts which had so long threatened its peace.

It was about this period that I again met my friend the missionary Fjelstädt, with whom I had been intimate at Basel, and who was but just returned from Smyrna, where he had been stationed as a missionary. He pleaded the cause of the missions, urging me to accept that at Smyrna, and enter again upon the course of life which I had abandoned in 1829. I took time to reflect, calling prayer to my aid, and arrived at the joyful conviction that I ought again to dedicate myself to the service of missions, and find in the starting-point of my career its goal and resting-place. Fjelstädt was delighted with my decision, and brought me into communication with the English Church Missionary Society with which he was himself connected. The wish of the Society was that I should remain for a time in the Missionary College, and await the further orders of the committee. In the autumn of 1836 Mr. Coates, the secretary, came to Basel, and during his stay at the Mission-house tidings were received that Missionary Knoth, who was to have accompanied Blumhardt to Abessinia, had died suddenly at Cairo. The vacant post was offered to me, and having accepted it I gave up the study of Turkish and modern Greek, which I had commenced during my second residence in Basel with a view to Smyrna, which Fjelstädt had originally indicated as my destination, and applied myself to Æthiopic and Amharic, and above all to the perusal of the history of Æthiopia by Ludolf, who has not inaptly been called the Strabo of Abessinia. In February 1837 I set out on my long and difficult journey to Abessinia, the land of my youthful dreams and aspirations; yet it was not without tears at parting, and with fear and trembling, that I took up my pilgrim's staff, and bid adieu to many and dear friends and to the home of my childhood.

CHAPTER II.

TO ADOWA AND ANKOBER.

Commencement of the journey—Storm off Candia—Alexandria and
Cairo—The Red Sea and its navigation—The Canal of the Isthmus
of Suez — Jidda — Arab navigation — Massowa — The Shohos—
Initiation into the dangers of African travel—Rescue—Entry
into Abessinia—Arrival at Adowa, the capital of Tigre and seat
of the Abessinian mission—Interview with the Prince of Tigre—
Native hostility to the mission—Arrival of Roman Catholic priests
and its consequences—The author and his companions have to quit
Tigre—Return of the missionaries to Cairo—The author resolves
to penetrate to Shoa—Return to Cairo—A missionary sheikh and
his slaves—Tajurra—The "Afer" and Ophir—Re-entry into
Abessinia—The Desert of Adal—Narrow escape from a hyæna—
Arrival at Ankober, the capital of Shoa.

My ultimate destination was Adowa, the capital of
Tigre, and seat of the Abessinian mission conducted
by my friends Isenberg and Blumhardt. Reaching
Malta from Marseilles I embarked in an Austrian sailing vessel for Alexandria, and when off Candia a storm
arose of greater violence than our captain declared
he had experienced for forty years. Unaccustomed as
I was to the sea I consoled myself with the thought
that the greatest of all missionaries, the apostle
Paul, had been exposed to similar peril in those
waters and had been preserved by the mercy of

God. I cast myself on His protecting power with child-like and trusting prayer, which so strengthened me that I was enabled to sustain my terrified fellow-voyagers, among whom was a French actress, greatly by reading aloud the narrative of the prophet Jonah, and of the disciples of our Lord when they were in danger on the Sea of Galilee. The impression produced by the Word of God in the hour of need on one of my fellow-voyagers was first made known to me thirteen years afterwards. When I was residing in London in 1850 after my first return from Africa, a gentleman one day entered my room and addressing me, said: " Do you remember that storm on our way to Alexandria, and your reading out of the Word of God to your fellow-voyagers ?" I answered in the affirmative, and the stranger, who had been a doctor of laws at Malta, then told me that after his return from Egypt he had procured a Bible, and feeling the power of the gospel on his heart, he had been impelled to hold prayer-meetings in Malta, which had brought upon him persecution at the hands of the Romish priests, and forced him to leave that island, from whence he had come to England.

Proceeding from Alexandria to Cairo I was hospitably received at the latter place by the missionaries Kruse and Lieder, with whom I remained until September, preparing for my Abessinian journey chiefly by the study of colloquial Arabic, in which I made such progress during those few months that in the autumn I was able to continue my journey to Habesh* without an interpreter. What most gratified me even among the many sights in Egypt, was the flourishing missionary school at Cairo in which many Coptic, Armenian, and Mohammedan children were receiving instruction. From Cairo to Suez there was in those days neither road, public conveyance, nor railway, and I travelled Arab fashion on a camel. Striking, too, is the contrast between the Suez of fifteen years later with those days when steam communication with Bombay was yet in its infancy.

No navigable river flows into the Red Sea, which is full of sunken rocks and sand-banks, that are increasing through the growth of coral reefs. The navigation is difficult and dangerous, and of the many harbours but few are safe, so that in most cases ships of large burden must anchor far out at sea. I do not think, therefore, that the Red Sea will attain more importance, even through the much-talked-of canal across the Isthmus of Suez. In my opinion the great advantage to be derived from the success of this scheme will not be so much in the acquisitions which commerce may derive from the Red Sea and the countries on its shores, as in the extension of European polity and civilization to Arabia, Abessinia, and the whole of South-Eastern Africa. It will weaken Mohammedanism in the land of its birth, Arabia, and on the African coast; tend to suppress the Arabian slave-trade, and subjugate East-African heathenism by Christianity and its civilization; and finally, open up immense and noble regions

* Abessinia.

in southern Abessinia and among the Gallas to thousands of European emigrants when America, Australia, and Tasmania cease to attract them.

From Suez I sailed in an Arabian vessel to Jidda, one of the most flourishing ports of the Red Sea, with large, lofty and solid houses, and many rich inhabitants, which since the English occupation of Aden, has thriven by the Arabian and Indian trade, while Mokha has declined. I was at first much struck by the Arabian practice of halting on the voyage during the night, and laying-to in some haven or anchoring place; but was soon convinced of the necessity of the step, which is caused partly by the many rocks in the Red Sea, partly and chiefly by the unskilfulness of the Arab sailors, which is, indeed, so great, that it is always hazardous to trust one's self in an Arabian vessel. I have had good reason to note that fact in my many voyages during eighteen years on both shores of the Red Sea, as well as on the south coast of Arabia, and on the east shores of Africa, as far as the tenth degree of southern latitude, for often have I been in danger of shipwreck and destruction! On the other hand, the Arabian mode of voyaging has, it must be confessed, its advantages, the chief of which is that the traveller can continually visit and become acquainted with new regions. Reaching Jidda in twenty-two days, I embarked thence for Massowa, an island and chief sea-port of the Abessinian coast, where I arrived in December, 1837. Before prosecuting my journey into Abessinia I had, according to

the usual custom, to repair to Harkiko or Dohono,
the chief place of the Mohammedan Shohos of the
main-land, whose Naib required the propitiation of
a present before leave was granted to traverse his
dominions. The Naib is appointed by the Governor of
Massowa and rules the nomadic and pastoral Shohos,
nominally as the representative of the Porte. A bargain was struck and I received an escort of four
soldiers to conduct me through the Shoho country
to the foot of the mountain Shumfeito. At first all
went well; but when the camels which had carried
my baggage˙had set out on their return to Harkiko I was obliged to hire thirty-one oxen from
the Shohos of the mountain to transport my
effects over the Shumfeito, six thousand feet in
height. Then began the tumult which was to initiate
me into the mysteries of African travel; the savage
Shohos demanded a much larger than the stipulated
sum, and when I refused to pay it they withdrew
with the chiefs to their mountains, reckoning on
my helpless plight. On the third day a terrible
war-shout was heard from the heights, and the
Shohos, descending in great numbers, ranged themselves in battle array a hundred paces in front
of our tents. I was rather alarmed, and the soldiers
of the Naib showed the white feather, and asked for
powder and ball. A couple of shots in the air kept
the enemy from approaching nearer our extempore
fortifications of piled-up chests, behind which we
calmly awaited their onslaught. At the moment
of the greatest danger, however, there suddenly

appeared upon the scene a Würtemberg officer, Herr Kielmaier, with sixty Abessinians sent by my dear fellow-labourer, Missionary Isenberg, to meet me at the foot of the Shumfeito, and to bring my baggage to Adowa. Having struck a bargain with the Shohos, at length we reached Halai, the first Christian village on the Abessinian frontier. The entry into Abessinia had a singular effect on me; the bracing air which I was breathing on a height 6000 feet above the sea, the noble prospect eastward and westward, the consciousness of being again in a country, Christian, it may be only in name, the thought that I should soon be at the end of my long and toilsome journey, and reach the place in which I was to labour for the kingdom of God, all combined to raise my spirits in an extraordinary degree. On the way from Halai, indeed, all was not smooth, obstructions being thrown in our path by the enemies of the Protestant mission at Adowa, who were annoyed by the arrival of another Protestant missionary. But I escaped these troubles in some measure by having hastened forward in advance of my party to greet as soon as possible my fellow-labourers, Isenberg and Blumhardt.

Soon after my arrival in Adowa I accompanied my friends Isenberg and Blumhardt to pay a visit to Ubie, the Prince of Tigre, who received me very kindly, and gave me promises of protection, which were not kept. The priests and chief men of Tigre disliked the Protestant mission, partly from bigotry, partly from unsatisfied greed. Before my arrival

Isenberg, the senior of the mission, had begun to build a new house which he thought necessary. In digging for the foundation and for building materials a deep excavation was made, and the enemies of the mission asserted that we were making a subterranean passage, through which English soldiers and guns were to be brought for the conquest of Abessinia. But the ultimate cause of our expulsion was the arrival of two Frenchmen, the brothers D'Abbadie,* accompanied by two Roman Catholic priests. The hostility of the latter strengthened the hands of the chief priest of Adowa, who requested from Ubie the expulsion of the Protestant missionaries, and the retention of the Roman Catholics, these having asserted that they were of the same family of Christians as the Abessinians themselves. We might have remained had we chosen to offer the prince a present greater than that which he had received from the Roman Catholics; but such a course we deemed an unworthy one, and after a residence of scarcely two months, I had to quit the land in which I would so willingly have striven to spread the Gospel. Many of the Bibles which I had brought to Adowa were destroyed by the Abessinian priests, undoubtedly at the instigation of the Roman Catholics; but many which had been distributed among the other provinces of Abessinia, it was out of their power to destroy. The new mission-house remained unfinished, and gradually

* MM. D'Abbadie were personally obliging and friendly toward the missionaries, who highly valued and readily acknowledged their intellectual gifts and zeal for African discovery.

fell into decay; but its habitable portion was taken possession of by the Alaka, or chief priest, who had long regarded it with a covetous eye.

It was in the March of 1838, that we quitted Adowa, reaching Massowa in safety. There we took counsel as to our future movements, and Isenberg and Blumhardt resolved on returning to Cairo to await the decision of the committee in London. I determined on penetrating to the Christian kingdom of Shoa, whose friendly ruler, Sahela Selassie, had formerly sent a messenger to Isenberg inviting him to visit his dominions. My original intention was to journey from Zeila, a town on the Somali coast, to Shoa; but circumstances led me to modify my plan. Proceeding with my friends to Jidda, I sailed thence in a Persian ship to Mokha. On board this Persian vessel I had ample opportunities of studying the mode in which the Mohammedans force on their new slaves the religion of their prophet. A sheikh kept showing some Galla boys the bowings and genuflexions of Mohammedan prayer, and, in fact, the whole mechanism of his worship. When the poor slaves, who scarcely understood a word of Arabic, did not ape to his satisfaction the forms shown them the sheikh broke out in abusive language, or boxed their ears. At Mokha I found that the proper landing-place from which to penetrate to Shoa was Tajurra on the Adal coast. Severe illness, however, compelled my return to Cairo, and it was not until the early spring of 1839 that I reached, in the company of my fellow-labourer, Isenberg,

THE RIVER HAWASH

my new starting-point, Tajurra, or Tagurrä, which lies in a great plain on the shore of a beautiful bay stretching inward from the village itself, and separating the countries of the Somali and the Adal. Since Aden has been occupied by the English the inhabitants have added a slight timber trade to their traffic with Arabia and Shoa. Till very lately, this was a place whence many slaves, especially Gallas and Christians from Gurague, were sold and shipped to Arabia. The old Sultan of Tajurra who, after consultation with his vizier, had given us permission to land, affected to be the king of all the Adal tribes, but his sovereignty was at the best of a mere nominal kind. The Adal call themselves in their own language "Afer," reminding us of the Hebrew Ophir. Adal is the Abessinian name, and Danakil, the Arabic designation for the Afer nation.

I was detained nearly four weeks at Tajurra, negotiating the cost of transport with the natives. At last on the 27th of April 1839 we set forth, and I was about to become personally acquainted with the country which I had found so barren and empty in the map in my boyhood. As we penetrated the Adal desert we suffered much from heat and want of water, and saw few human beings or habitations. Besides gazelles and ostriches there were few wild animals; yet once we were disturbed by elephants, of which camels are dreadfully afraid. On the 29th of May we crossed the river Hawash and bivouacked in the open air on its woody bank where there are many wild beasts. While we were all asleep, even the watchers, a hyæna glided so near our resting-places that we might have grasped it with our hands. It was in the morning we first noticed that it had been there by the foot-prints left in the sand, and we thanked God for His remarkable mercy. On the 31st of May we reached Dinomali on the frontier, where the customs officers and frontier governors inspected our luggage. A report was forthwith despatched to the king of Shoa announcing that the two "Gypzis," as Europeans are called in Abessinia, had arrived. No foreigner is allowed either to enter or to quit Shoa without the permission of the king; so, until it came we remained in Ferri at the foot of the mountain-land. When the requisite permission had arrived we began to traverse the hill-region of Shoa on the 2nd of June, and on the 3rd we ascended the lofty mountain on which lies the capital, Ankober.

WOMEN OF SHOA.

CHAPTER III.

RESIDENCE IN SHOA.

Reception by the King of Shoa—His promises and character—The missionaries open school—Departure of Isenberg—The Gallas —The sources of the Hawash, and M. Rochet's veracity—The author's participation in the king's expeditions against the Gallas, and its fruits—The rebellious Gallas and their country—Journey to Debra Libanos and geographical notes—Arrival of Major Harris and the English mission—The author's relations with the king and the envoy—Success and failure of the mission—Major Harris's "Highlands of Æthiopia"—The advantages of a connection between England and Shoa—The king, and his father's dream—What might have been and may yet be.

ON the 7th of June we had an audience of the king, Sahela Selassie, who gave us a very friendly reception, and to whom we explained the purely religious purpose of our mission, and on the 6th of July accompanied him by his own express desire to Angolala, the second capital of Shoa, which lies in the immediate neighbourhood of the Galla tribes. He promised to give us in accordance with our request six boys to educate; but afterwards retracted his word, on the pretext that he did not need spiritual teachers so much as doctors, masons, smiths, &c. He was so fond of artisans that he often visited the workshops of the weavers, gun-makers, and smiths, to watch their operations, which had to be altered if not pleasing to him. In July we repaired by the king's command to Ankober, where we were to take up our abode. After we had long vainly entreated Sahela Selassie for boys to educate, we determined to receive any one who should voluntarily offer himself. Several boys soon presented themselves, and amongst them one, Guebra Georgis by name, who had capacity and took delight in learning. I read with him the Amharic Bible and instructed him besides in Geography and History to his great delight. On the 12th of November Isenberg left us with the intention of returning to Cairo and Europe, to prepare Amharic works for the press, and to superintend the printing of them in London. His departure made a very sad impression on me, then the only surviving missionary in Shoa. Shortly before his departure M. Rochet arrived in Shoa and brought with him a powder-mill and other valuable presents, which made his visit very acceptable to the king. Of this gentleman more hereafter.

On the 13th of November the king returned from his campaign against the Gallas in Muger. On a mountain he had found Christians and Churches, severed by the Gallas in the lowlands from the Church of Shoa. Christian remnants of the kind are to be met with here and there in the Galla countries. After the departure of Isenberg I began to learn the Galla language in the hope of visiting as soon as possible a people so widely spread in Africa, and of founding a mission among them. As the Romanist missionary said, "Give us China and Asia is ours;" so may we say, "Give us the Gallas and Central Africa is ours." In translating the New Testament into the Galla language I made use of the Roman alphabet, which gave great displeasure to the Abessinians, 'who would have preferred my selection of the Æthiopic. From the commencement of my residence in Shoa I made particular inquiries respecting everything connected with the Gallas, their religious notions, manners, and customs, their geographical extension, &c., and I accompanied the king on several military expeditions against the tribes in the South. The first campaign which I thus made in January and February 1840 led me into the territories of the tribes of the Abeju, Woberi, Gelan, Dembichu, Finfini, where there are hot springs with much sulphur in them, and of the Mulofalada, Metta Robi, Wogidi, Metta and Kuttai, all Gallas.

In the country of the last-named tribe, M. Rochet and I who accompanied the expedition made inquiries of the king respecting the source of the river Hawash, asking whether he would not extend the expedition to that point. The king answered, that so far as he knew, there was between the Galla tribes Soddo, Becho, Woreb, and Mecha, a boggy country in which the river takes its rise; but that his men would not on 'that occasion press so far forward. And, indeed, on the very same day the king gave orders for a return to Angolala by another route, so that M. Rochet and I were deprived of the satisfaction of making an important discovery. In spite of this, in the book of travels which he afterwards published M. Rochet asserted that he had seen the sources of the Hawash, and that the king had sent an escort to accompany him thither. Both assertions are completely false. Alas! such unconscientious statements are too common on the part of travellers, who huddle up a book and obtain honours and emoluments at the expense of geographical truth. M. Rochet once said to me in the course of that expedition, "M. Krapf, we must assert that we have seen the sources of the Hawash." When I replied that that would not be true, and that we had not seen them, he rejoined with a smile, "Oh! we must be *philosophes!*"

Our participation in these expeditions of the king, which lasted from two to three weeks, and thus did not cause me to be long absent from my school at Ankober, was useful in various ways, as I became more intimately acquainted with the Southern Gallas, and formed a friendship with some of them—for instance, with the brave Chara, son of the queen of the tribe Mulofalada, and specially noted three places where a Galla mission might be founded;—one, on the mountain Yerrer, on the road between Angolala and Gurague; a second, among the tribe Mulofalada with Chamie, the mother of Chara; and a third, in Muger in the vicinity of Debra Libanos not far from the Blue River. Beyond this, during these expeditions I became acquainted with high and low in Shoa and Efat, and often addressed large numbers of men touching the Word of God and other edifying matters, besides obtaining great practice in the Amharic language, and being able to observe closely the ways of the Shoan population. Finally, my health was benefited, and the friendly demeanour of the king to me was manifested to all his subjects. Of course, my connection with the king's expeditions did not arise out of a hostile or martial spirit, but simply from a wish to become acquainted with regions partly unknown, and mainly to promulgate the Gospel among the thousands of soldiers whom the king takes with him in these expeditions, which he is in the habit of undertaking in January, June, and October, to levy the tribute due by the Gallas, and to make further conquests. Widespread devastations follow the frequent refusals to pay the tribute by the Galla tribes, who are very foolish in provoking these calamities, as they might secure themselves by moderate payments in cattle and grain, were it not that their pride and passion for freedom lead to continual revolts and defeats. Pity that those beautiful countries are not turned to better account! The Gallas possess regions so fruitful, so rich in water and pasturage, and suitable both for tillage and for cattle, that Europeans can scarcely imagine their beauty. The climate, too, is as mild and healthy as that of Italy or Greece. The districts of Mulofalada, Adaberga, Metta, and Mecha, are particularly so, where, moreover, there are many and noble trees, among which the juniper deserves particular mention.

In the May of 1840, I made a tour to Debra
Libanos, the most sacred place of the Shoans, four
days' journey to the north-west of Ankober. The
greatest saint of Abessinia, the famous Tekla Haimanot, is said to have lived there in the twelfth
century and to have raised up a miracle-healing
well by his prayers. In the neighbourhood of
Angolala I crossed the river Chacha, which flows
from the province of Bulga and from Angolala
in a deep glen towards the north-west, and which,
near Kum Dengai, in the province Shoa Meda,
unites with the Beresa and some other rivers and
forms the Adabai, flowing at last under the name
of the Jamma into the Blue River, the so-called
Abai, or Abessinian Nile. The Chacha, Adabai,
and Jamma, form a natural dyke against the incursions of the Gallas from the south, who, therefore,
can never entirely subdue or even overrun the
kingdom of Shoa, especially since King Sahela
Selassie founded Angolala at a point where the
Gallas might otherwise have been able to break in.
On the road to Debra Libanos I also passed Sena
Markos, the second most holy locality of Shoa and
which lies on a very steep rock, easily defensi-
ble. From this place you can overlook the whole
north and west of Shoa. Before you ascend the
mountain on which Debra Libanos lies you must
cross the river Segawadam ("Flesh and Blood")
in which the pilgrims bathe and purify themselves. I returned home towards the end of May,
and devoted myself again to the instruction of my

pupils of whom there were ten in the house, without reckoning the others who came and went irregularly. A scholar asked me for instruction in Hebrew, which many of the Abessinian priests are fond of, as they fancy that they can discover deep secrets in the Hebrew words and names. The boys I instructed chiefly in biblical, universal, and natural history, in geography and arithmetic, delivering to them and my household on Sundays a short discourse. There came daily, too, many persons, priests and laymen, to whom I had thus an opportunity of proclaiming the Gospel.

At this time Sahela Selassie conceived the notion of sending letters and presents to the East India Company, in order to bring about friendly relations with them. On the 6th of July 1840 he despatched a messenger with letters to Aden to be delivered to the governor, Captain Haines. A year elapsed, however, before the letters and presents were reciprocated by the mission of Major Harris, who, on the 15th of July 1841 arrived at Dinomali, on the frontier of Shoa, and with his suite and presents was received and treated by the Shoans with a great deal of mistrust. It was mainly the bigoted priests and monks who tried to inspire the king with a distrust of foreigners. The priests were angry with me especially, because they thought that I had induced the king to allow the admission of the English and their presents, although it was the king's own decision to send a messenger to Aden, as he knew, among other things, that since the occu-

pation of Aden the power of England was nearer
to him than that of France, which M. Rochet had
lately represented in Shoa. I kept aloof from all
political relations, and only when the king or Major
Harris asked for advice or aid did I express my
opinions; for it was natural that I should be desired to act as interpreter for the English envoy,
at least in important negotiations, as Major Harris
and his suite did not understand Amharic. The
king, too, had said to me from the very commencement: "You know the customs of my country and of
your own; you must advise me in my dealings with
Major Harris, that I may not offend him and Queen
Victoria of England. If things go wrong, I shall
hold you responsible." In this way, I was obliged
often to express myself openly against the king, as
well as against the English envoy, Major Harris, who,
from the first, treated me in the most friendly manner,
as, indeed, did all the members of the mission,
Captain Graham, Dr. Kirk, Dr. Roth, Herr Bernatz,
&c. Major Harris in his dealings with the king
showed himself intent on accomplishing the object of
his mission, which was by the establishment of a
friendly connection between England and Shoa to
pave the way for an increase of their commercial
intercourse, for the due protection of travellers, and
for the abolition of slavery—an object which, to say
the truth, was attained only upon paper, but not in
reality, by the signature of a treaty, or convention,
consisting of fifteen articles.

The English envoy soon discovered that there

were not in Shoa any important articles of commerce, and that consequently there could not be a profitable trade between it and Aden. The difficulties attending the transit of commodities through the sandy Adal country were very evident, and the envoy soon gave up caring for the execution of the fifteen articles, content to have them to show when he returned home, as a proof at least of the nominal success of the mission, and he openly avowed to me his conviction of all this, and that he should now look to his own interests, as little was to be gained for his government. And, in truth, the envoy acted in this spirit, endeavouring to gain the best possible acquaintance with the country and its inhabitants in order afterwards to be able to write a voluminous book on both. I myself was entreated by him to communicate every notice which my experience and knowledge could furnish, and willingly gratified this desire, and Major Harris interwove these communications into the text of his well-known work of three volumes, " The Highlands of Æthiopia." I gave up much time and thought to the cause of the embassy, and wished for its prosperity and success, as likely to promote the spread of the Gospel, as well as the prosperity of Shoa itself. To Shoa the connection with a Christian power could only exercise a wholesome influence, which from thence would be extended to the unknown countries of the South. I was convinced that there could be no permanence in the mission to the Gallas, in Gurague and Kambat, so long as Shoa was not connected with the coast. On that account

I wished heartily for the establishment of friendly relations between that country and England, and so far
as I could with propriety I did my utmost to forward
them. Sahela Selassie seemed favourable to such relations, perhaps because he still remembered the dream
of his father who had predicted that in the time of
his son, Sahela Selassie, red people (so the whites are
called in Abessinia when the term gypzi—that is,
Egyptians—is not applied to them) would arrive
and teach the Abessinians all arts and knowledge.
Now, since 1836, Europeans, Combes and Tamisier,
Martin, Dufey, Isenberg, and myself, Rochet,
Airston, Dr. Beke, and finally, the English envoy
had rapidly followed each other, and Sahela Selassie
was naturally led to see in this the fulfilment of
the dream, and being, to a certain extent, enlightened and eager for improvement, he could not
but feel it desirable to form a connection with such
a nation as the English of whom he had heard so
much from the Danakil. It is only a pity that the
connection established was not a closer one, and
more productive of blessings to Africa. Yet it has
had the effect of making this and the neighbouring regions better known to geographers at least.
This knowledge will bear fruit in the future when
Shoa shall have a wiser ruler than Sahela Selassie.
He had, indeed, great good nature, delighted in improvement, and possessed a sense of justice, and many
good qualities; but he was too much led away by
the superstition of the priests, the narrow prejudices
of his chiefs, the desire for personal enrichment,

and the oriental habit of accumulating dead treasures. Had he rightly understood and employed
the opportunity which was afforded him of establishing a connection with England, he might have become sovereign not only of Abessinia, but of the
whole of Inner Africa. But such is man. In his
ignorance, he casts away the greatest treasures
for this world and the next—treasures, which, if
he knew how to use them, would secure him temporal no less than his eternal well-being.

CHAPTER IV.

SHOA AND THE SHOANS.

Shoa, in its widest sense, includes the whole of the
Æthiopian highlands which are bounded on the east
by the Adal desert, on the south by the Hawash,
on the west by the Abai (Blue River), and on the
north by the tribes of the Mohammedan Gallas.   In
a more limited sense, it comprises the western portion of those highlands, which eastward in the direction of the Adal desert has received the name of
Efat.   This eastern section of the mountain-land
comprises the provinces Bulga, Fatigar, Menchar in
the south, Argobba in the east, and Geddem and
Efra in the north.   Argobba includes the low lands,
which spread themselves out towards the Adal
desert, and are inhabited by Mohammedans, partly
under Shoan rule, partly as in the north, under
that of the Wollo-Gallas.   Shoa (or the western high-

ANKOBER

lands) in its narrower sense, comprises the provinces and districts of Tegulet, Shoa Meda, Mora-
bietie, Mans and Geshe.   It seems that this division
into Shoa and Efat takes its rise from the mountain
chain which stretches from Fatigar through Bulga
to Ankober and as far as Geshe, and thence still
further into the interior of Abessinia.

Both these sections of the country are tolerably
populous, a circumstance which is aided by the
fertility of the soil, the excellence of the climate, and
the external tranquillity of the country, which for a
long time has seen no enemy within its boundaries.
The population of the kingdom of Shoa may be estimated at upwards of a million if the subjugated
Gallas of the south are included: in extent from
west to east, from the Adal desert to the Blue
River, it is nearly two degrees, and about the same
length from south to north, from the river Hawash to the fortress Dair.   The country is rich
in springs, brooks, and rivers, and lakes are not
wanting.   There are none of the nobler metals in
abundance, but in one locality (in the vicinity of
Debra Berhan) the existence of a gold field is suspected.   There is plenty of iron, sulphur, and pit-
coal; the latter being chiefly found in the eastern
part of Shoa, but the inhabitants have not yet learned
to turn it to account.

The form of government in Shoa is an absolute
monarchy.   The king is the only lord and master of
the country, to whom belong the bodies, lives, and
possessions of his subjects.   He has no standing army,

but only a few hundred body-guards, armed with muskets.   When war breaks out every district-governor
must supply a contingent.   The whole army may
muster from 30,000 to 50,000 men, of whom about
1000 are armed with muskets, the rest being
equipped with spears, shields, and swords.   The
soldiers are mostly cavalry, mounted on horses or
mules.   Art and science are still in a state of infancy
in Shoa.

The mass of the population is Christian after
the form of the Coptic church in Egypt, on which,
as is well known, the Abessinian church is dependent.   In the east, however, there are many
Mohammedans, and in the south, tribes of heathen
Gallas, subject to the ruler of Shoa.   In ecclesias-
tical constitution Shoa, as also Abessinia in general, is
episcopal.   The Coptic patriarch in Egypt has been
since about A.D. 1280 in the habit of nominating
the chief bishop of Abessinia, who is styled Abuna,
" Our father."   This prelate ordains all priests and
deacons; he also consecrates the king and governs the
church by the aid of the Echege, the supreme head
of the monks, who are very numerous and influential.
Those who wish to be ordained must be able to read
and to repeat the Nicene Creed, whereupon the Abuna
breathes on the candidate, laying on hands blesses
him, and bestows on him the sign of the cross,
receiving then two pieces of salt as ordination fees.
After ordination deacons and priests cannot marry,
but must not part with the wives whom they may
have married before ordination.   The duties of

MEN OF SHOA

the priest are to baptize, to administer the Eucharist, and on Sundays to read and sing the long litanies for three or four hours. They must also know by rote all the psalms and the book of hymns—a task which occupies many years. Preaching is not commanded and is seldom heard in Abessinia. There is no ordination of the Debtera, who form the literary class, instruct in reading and writing, copy books upon parchment, and assist, too, in the churches. Unordained, also, are the Alakas, the superintendents of churches, who exercise a control over them, and are intermediate between church and state. They enjoy great power and emoluments, and are often the most influential of persons, before whom the priests themselves must bow.

The literature of the Abessinians comprises from one hundred and thirty to one hundred and fifty books, of which many are only translations of the Greek fathers. These books are divided into four sections or "gabaioch." The first consists of the Old Testament, and the second of the New;—the third, of the books of the Liks, or perfect masters (Chrysostom, Fethanegest, Abushaker, &c.); and the fourth comprises the writings of the monks and saints. ·The Abessinians possess the Old and New Testament in the old Æthiopic, and in the Amharic or popular idiom as well; the former version being ascribed to Frumentius, who was ordained bishop of Æthiopia by St. Athanasius in 331, and is said to have first preached the gospel in the city of Axum.

The Abessinians place the Apocrypha on the same footing with the canonical books, and deem the traditions of the church of equal authority with that of the apostles and prophets. The reading of the Old and New Testaments is not forbidden to the laity, only most of the priests desire that the Scriptures should be read in Æthiopic, which they consider the primeval language—not in Amharic, which they regard merely as a Targum, or translation—just as if the favoured text were not also a translation from the Greek, with which they are not acquainted. One scholar in Shoa maintained that the Jews had falsified the Hebrew Scriptures, which had remained uncorrupted only till the time of Abraham.

In a general way, the Abessinians are acquainted with the chief truths of the Bible, with the Trinity, and the nature and the attributes of God; with the creation, the fall of man and his redemption by Christ; with the Holy Ghost, the angels, the church, the sacraments, the resurrection and the last judgment; with rewards and punishments, and everlasting life and torment; but all these articles are so blended with, and obscured by merely human notions that they exert little influence on the heart and life. The mediatorial function of Christ, for instance, is darkened and limited by a belief in the many saints who, as in the Romish and Greek churches, must mediate between the Mediator and man. Especially a great office is assigned to the Virgin Mary, of whom it is maintained by many

that she died for the sins of the world and saved
144,000 souls! In the Abessinian point of view
the means to expiate sin are alms-giving, fasting,
monastic vows, and reading, or rather gabbling, the
Psalms, &c. The Holy Ghost they consider proceeds only from the Father, not from the Son, who,
in the presence of the Father recedes into the background, just as before the Father and the Son the
Holy Ghost almost dwindles into nothingness.

As regards the doctrine of the two natures of Christ
the Abessinians are extreme Monophysites, for they
admit only one nature and one will in him. For sixty
years the Abessinian church has been rent by great
controversies arising out of the dogma of the three
births of Christ, broached by a monk at Gondar, and
which consists in the assertion that the baptism or
consecration of Christ with the Holy Spirit in Jordan
constituted his third birth. According to some the Son
of God, begotten of the Father before all worlds (first
birth), became man in time (second birth) and was baptized in Jordan (third birth); but according to others,
Christ in the Virgin's womb was already anointed,
prayed, fasted, and so forth, and that they call his
third birth. After a long war with the opposite
party, which acknowledges only two births of Christ,
this doctrine, which evidently harmonises with the
rigid monophysitism of the Abessinians, was elevated
into a dogma of the National Church by the decision
of the king, Sahela Selassie, who had received it from
a priest many years before. Although in the year
1840 a royal ordinance had deposed all priests who

did not believe in the three births, yet it was only on the 24th November 1841 that the victorious party was able to put the ordinance in execution against its rivals. Amid song and acclamation the zealots rushed into the churches and purified them from the presence of the heretics, among whom were many upright men, such as Alaka Melat, Wolda Hanna, and others, with whom I had been on the friendliest footing. The victorious party pressed for a more rigid veneration of the Virgin Mary and of the Saints. Generally, its members departed on many points further from the Scriptures than did the conquered party, which now turned to the Abuna in Gondar, who took them under his protection and summoned the king to drive out the triumphant party, and to re-instate all the expelled priests who believed in the two births, as this was the genuine doctrine of St. Mark of Alexandria. (They believe that their church was founded by the Evangelist Mark.) As Sahela Selassie would not submit, the Abuna menaced him with war—a menace which he has been able to carry into execution against Shoa only since Theodorus has become King of Abessinia. This prince invaded Shoa and some years ago made it subject to himself, and obedient to the Abuna. For the present, therefore, the doctrine of the two births seems to be the ruling one throughout the whole of Abessinia; but it is nevertheless branded with the nickname, "Karra Haimanot," i. e., Knife-faith, because this faith has cut off the third birth of Christ.

No Christian people upon earth are so rigid in their fasting as the Abessinians. They fast, in all, nine months out of the twelve; every Friday and Wednesday throughout the year, then again forty days before Easter, twenty-five days after Trinity, fourteen days in August, twenty-five days before Advent, and on other occasions. Yet, in spite of this, and of a close conformity to the outward observances of a severe ritual, the woeful departure from the pure teaching of the Gospel and a complete absence of culture and knowledge have produced, generally and individually, a sad social condition in Abessinia. Immorality is the order of the day, and even priests and monks break the seventh commandment. Monogamy, it is true, is established by the Church, but concubinage is habitual and general, the king and his five hundred wives leading the way with a bad example; for whenever a beautiful woman was pointed out to him he sent for her. The daughters of many grandees must in this way serve to effect political alliances, and Sahela Selassie actually wished for an English princess to consolidate his alliance with Great Britain! In Abessinia marriage is seldom consecrated by the Church; it is simply a civil contract between the parents and relations of the bride and bridegroom, with the sanction of the local governor or any other personage of position, and can be at any time dissolved. Slavery, too, has done much to demoralize the Christians of Shoa. Christians, indeed, are not allowed to export slaves, but they may import them for their own use. In this, the king's example leads the way, and he has many thousands of slaves employed as hewers of wood, drawers of water, bearers of burdens, cowherds, agricultural labourers, &c., and the free subjects must do feudal task-work.

The superstition of the Abessinians is immeasurably great, and its workings pervade every act of their daily life. Very noticeable and peculiar are the means employed in Shoa for the detection of thieves. The Lebashi (thief-catcher) is much feared, and belongs to the servants of the state. When a theft has been committed the sufferer gives information to this official, upon which he sends his servant a certain dose of black meal, compounded with milk, on which he makes him smoke tobacco. The servant is thrown into a state of frenzy, in which state he goes from house to house, crawling on his hands and feet like one out of his mind. After he has smelt about at a number of houses, the Lebashi all the time holding him tight by a cord fastened round the body, he goes at last into a house, lays on its owner's bed, and sleeps for some time. His master then rouses him with blows, and he awakes and arrests the owner of the house, who is forthwith dragged before the priests, and they make the victim of the robbery swear that he will not assess at more than the real value the articles stolen. The person into whose house the entry was made is regarded as the thief, and is forced to pay, whether he be innocent or guilty.

No wonder that the population trembles when the Lebashi is seen in the street, and that everybody tries to be on good terms with him, as there is no saying when he may make his appearance in a house. The King of Shoa is said to have convinced himself of the truth of this matter by ordering one of his pages to steal a garment of his own, and to conceal it in the house of an inhabitant of Ankober, where the Lebashi is reported to have discovered it. On the 31st of July 1841 I had an opportunity of watching closely this operation of thief-catching in the streets of Ankober.

44

CHAPTER V.

THE UNEXPLORED COUNTRIES TO THE SOUTH OF SHOA.

Christian remnants—Gurague and the slave trade—Kambat—
Wolamo—Kucha—The Golda negroes—Susa—Junction of the
Gojob and Omo—Reported snow-mountain —Traces of Christianity in Susa—Curious transfer of episcopal breath for consecration—Dilbo on the Dokos, a nation of pigmies—Account
of the Dokos—Are they the pigmies of Herodotus?—An alleged
Doko seen by the author—Concurrent testimony to the existence of a nation of pigmies—Kaffa and its Queen, Balli—Abundance of cotton and cotton clothing—Salt and its value—Herodotus and the early Troglodytes—The Gojob and Dilbo's
account of it—Identity of the Gojob and the Jub—River
system of those countries—Enarea, its king, religion, &c.; value
as a coffee-producing country—Its commercial importance if
the Gojob should be found navigable—The civet-cat, &c.—
Senjero—Female slavery and its origin—Human sacrifices—
Evidences of an early civilization in the regions watered by the
Gojob.

HAVING given a slight general sketch of Shoa and
the Shoans, I proceed to speak of the hitherto unexplored regions to the south; and firstly, of the scattered remnants of Christians severed by the Gallas
from Abessinia. Four days' journey from Angolala
through the Galla land subject to the princes of
Shoa, you come to the river Hawash, which flows
round Shoa in an easterly direction and into the

Adal country. With the south bank of this stream begins the country of Gurague, which lies under the eighth degree of north latitude and is mostly inhabited by Christians, who preserve from olden times some connection with Abessinia, and have maintained themselves on their mountains against the Gallas. The name of this country signifies " to the left—on the left hand," and was given it when the Abessinian kings had still their head-quarters on the lofty mountain Endoto, to the left of which Gurague lay when they looked westwards. Formerly the whole country round the Hawash was inhabited by Christians, and even now a Christian remnant is said to survive in the district of Korchass to the south of the Soddo-Gallas. The first Christian village reached after the passage of the Hawash is Aimellele, which is in some measure dependent on Shoa, and the priests of this place often visited me and begged me to come to them. South-east of Aimellele is the large lake Zuai, called by the people of Gurague " Jilalu," and by the Gallas, " Lagi." In this lake are said to be five islands, tenanted by Christian monks, and on one of which it is reported, are many Æthiopic books, which in the time of Gragne, who invaded Shoa from the Adal country, were sent thither by King Nebla Dengel as to a place of security. A Shoan, named Aito Osman, told me that he had seen these books. In Gurague itself the monks do not live in monasteries as in Shoa and the rest of Abessinia, but in their own houses, holding life in common to be hurtful. Gurague is not governed by a single prince, but every town and village has an independent *status*; the cause of many convulsions and civil wars, most of the districts being at war with one another. This state of things has made travelling here very insecure, and has much encouraged the slave-trade; the vanquished in these civil wars being sold to the Mohammedan merchants, and by them despatched to the Adal-land and Arabia. Hence it has come to pass that many of the Guraguans have repeatedly entreated the King of Shoa to take possession of their country; but he has refused the invitation, because, according to his own avowal, he would be deprived of the supply of slaves from that quarter; for in a country belonging to him he would be obliged to prohibit the making of slaves, though he and the Shoans cannot do without them. It may be estimated that annually about three thousand slaves, mostly Christians, are exported from Gurague. Many on their way from one village to another are stolen and sold by their own relations, and houses are frequently set on fire at night and the inmates, in endeavouring to escape, are seized and sold into slavery. Sometimes children are stolen at night from their homes, while their parents are asleep, and, as a precaution against this, many parents lay thick stakes over their children. In the south Gurague appears to be inhabited chiefly by Mohammedans.

Leaving Gurague and proceeding southward you come to the territory of the Adia-Gallas, and thence into the little mountain-land of Kambat, where a small nation of Christians with fifteen churches and monasteries, is said to have retained its existence. It is sometimes visited by the Christian priests of Gurague, who undergo many perils exposed as they are to the Adia and Alaba-Gallas, during the seven days' journey which is necessary to be made, for the most part by night when the moon affords her light. The language of Kambat appears to be very different from that of Gurague, which latter again differs in important respects from the Amharic, and with that of Tigre greatly resembles the old Æthiopic. I regret that a little vocabulary which I composed of the Gurague language has been lost. The capital of Kambat is Karemsa, the residence of King Degoie, a worthy and powerful chief, very well affected to strangers.

To the south-east of Kambat lies Wolamo, a small and very mountainous independent Christian state. The slave-dealers bring many slaves from this country to Shoa, who have a handsome appearance, and speak a language which is not understood there. The capital of Wolamo is said to be called Wofana, and the great river Omo appears to flow through the country, which is surrounded by the districts Senjero, Dumbaro, Mager, Mugo, Kullu, Worata, Jimma and Asu. From Wolamo you come into the kingdom of Kucha, which is inhabited by negro-like Gallas, who have many horses. The king of this hot but fruitful country is

said to be very powerful, and to live in considerable
state.   White people, which must mean Arabs and
Somalis from the east coast of Barawa and Marka,
are said to come here in boats, bringing blue
cloths, pepper, tobacco, copper, &c., and carrying
back in return slaves, ivory, and spices, to the coast,
which lies thirty days' journey distant.   From the
information which I received at Barawa respecting
the interior I am led to conclude that the people of
that place penetrate as far as Kucha, not however
up the river Jub from its mouth, but from Barawa through the Somali country as far as Bardera
and Ganana, and thence into the country of Liven;
where they first take boat, and reach Kucha, where
the Jub which, in its upper course is called the
Gojob receives the stream Torikh.

To the west of Kucha lies the country of the
Golda negroes, who are said to go naked—a circumstance which clearly indicates that they approximate to those African populations whom I
became acquainted with in my journeys to Ukambani, and who also go almost in that state, as we
shall see afterwards.

Westward from the Goldas, between the fourth
and fifth degrees of north latitude, and to the south
of Kaffa, lies the powerful kingdom of Susa, where
the Omo has its source.   The Gojob, which
appears to rise in a vast wilderness, between Kaffa
and Enarea, receives a large volume of water from
the Omo at Dumbaro, at which point the united

streams form a cataract which is heard from afar.
The rainy season in Susa is said to be very severe,
the air very cold, and the land very high; nay,
beyond this country there are reported to be mountains covered with eternal snow, a report which
I can easily believe, as I saw from Ukambani a
snow-mountain in the vicinity of the equator.   The
inhabitants of Susa are said still to retain something of Abessinian Christianity; they are reported not to work on the Sabbath, to observe the
festivals of Michael, George, and Gabriel, and to
have churches and priests, and a written language,
which, however, is neither Amharic nor Æthiopic.

The reader will remember that the priests of
Shoa are ordained by the Abuna, or chief bishop of
Abessinia, who breathes on the candidate for ordination.   They have a tradition that when Cyril was
Abuna in Gondar certain priests came from Susa with
a leathern bag, which the Abuna inflated for them
with his breath, in order that they might ordain
priests with it in their own country, Susa being so
distant from Gondar, and the journey by Kaffa and
Enarea both difficult and dangerous.   I told this
circumstance to a friend on my return to Europe in
1853, who smilingly remarked that such ordination
was very like a bottle of smoke.   The present King of
Susa I heard, was called Beddu, and is the brother
of Bali, the Queen of Kaffa.   The capital, it is said, is
Bonga, where Beddu reigns after the fashion of the
Abessinian kings.   By the marriage of his daughter
Shash to the King Abba Bogibo of Enarea he is re-

ported to have established friendly relations with
the latter, and so to have made possible a connection with Gondar. Mohammedan merchants are said
to arrive from a distance, which is very possible
when the position of the river Maro or Pokomoni is
considered, as it flows into the Indian Ocean above
Malindi, and on it the Suahilis and Pokomos journey
far into the interior in their boats. It would, therefore, be easy to accept as a fact that travellers might
reach from this river the Christians in Susa; and
that it would also be possible to journey from
Barawa to Kucha, and to the Christian remnants in
Wolamo and Kambat. Had there been an energetic
government on the Suahili coast these East-African
countries, still so unknown and yet so important to
Christianity, would long ago have been opened up
to Christian civilization and commerce; but while
power is left in the hands of the lazy and jealous
Arabs a knowledge of these countries will long have
to be waited for. In any case a good distance far
in the interior may be traversed by water, even
though it cannot be employed directly from the
coast, since the rivers of those regions are not deep
at their mouths.

Noteworthy are the reports which in the year
1840 were communicated to me by a slave from
Enarea, who, by order of the King of Shoa, was
charged with the care of my house in Angolala
during my residence in Ankober. His name was
Dilbo, and he was a native of Sabba in Enarea. As
a youth he had made caravan-journeys to Kaffa

and accompanied the slave-hunters from Kaffa to Tuffte, in a ten days' expedition, where he crossed the Omo some sixty feet wide, by means of a wooden bridge; reaching from thence Kullu, in seven days, which is but a few days' journey from the Dokos, a pigmy race of whom Dilbo told almost fabulous stories. Afterwards when in his eighteenth year during an attack on Sabba he was made a prisoner, and passed from Enarea into slavery at Nono, whence he was taken by the slave-dealers to Migra, and thence to Agabja where he was sold for forty pieces of salt. From Agabja he was taken to Gonan in the country of the Soddo-Gallas where he was sold again for sixty pieces of salt. From Gonan he was conveyed to Roggie where his value was raised to eighty pieces of salt, and he was then marched to Golba in the Galla district of Abeju, and there sold for one hundred pieces. At last he reached Aliwamba where a Mohammedan bought him for twelve dollars. Next a widow in Ankober purchased him for fourteen dollars, and at her death he passed into the hands of her brother who, however, was disinherited by the King of Shoa for some offence, and in this way Dilbo became the property of the king. He told me that to the south of Kaffa and Susa there is a very sultry and humid country with many bamboo woods, inhabited by the race called Dokos, who are no bigger than boys of ten years old; that is, only four feet high. They have a dark, olive-coloured complexion, and live in a completely savage state, like the beasts; having neither houses, temples, nor holy trees, like the Gallas, yet possessing something like an idea of a higher being called Yer, to whom in moments of wretchedness and anxiety they pray—not in an erect posture, but reversed with the head on the ground, and the feet supported upright against a tree or stone. In prayer they say: " Yer, if thou really dost exist, why dost thou allow us thus to be slain? We do not ask thee for food and clothing, for we live on serpents, ants, and mice. Thou hast made us, why dost thou permit us to be trodden underfoot?" The Dokos have no chief, no laws, no weapons; they do not hunt, nor till the ground, but live solely on fruits, roots, mice, serpents, ants, honey, and the like, climbing trees and gathering the fruits like monkeys, and both sexes go completely naked. They have thick, protruding lips, flat noses, and small eyes; the hair is not woolly, and is worn by the women over the shoulders. The nails on the hands and feet are allowed to grow like the talons of vultures, and are used in digging for ants, and in tearing to pieces the serpents which they devour raw, for they are unacquainted with fire. The spine of the snake is the only ornament worn round the neck, but they pierce the ears with a sharp-pointed piece of wood.

The Dokos multiply very rapidly, but have no regular marriages, the intercourse of the sexes leading to no settled home, each in perfect independence going whither fancy leads. The mother nurses her child only for a short time, accustoming it as soon as possible to the eating of ants and serpents; and as soon as the child can help itself, the mother lets it depart whither it pleases. Although these people live in thick woods, and conceal themselves amongst the trees, yet they become the prey of the slave-hunters of Susa, Kaffa, Dumbaro, and Kulla; for whole regions of their woods are encircled by the hunters, so that the Dokos cannot easily escape. When the slave-hunters come in sight of the poor creatures they hold up clothes of bright colours, singing and dancing, upon which the Dokos allow themselves to be captured, without resistance, knowing from experience that such resistance is fruitless and can lead only to their destruction. In this way thousands can be captured by a small band of hunters; and once captured they become quite docile. In slavery the Dokos retain their predilection for feeding on mice, serpents, and ants, although often on that account punished by their masters, who in other respects are attached to them, as they are docile and obedient, have few wants, and enjoy good health, for which reasons they are never sold as slaves beyond Enarea. As diseases are unknown among them, they die only of old age, or through the assaults of their enemies.

It cannot be decided whether these Dokos are the pigmies who, according to Herodotus, were discovered near a great river in the vicinity of Central Africa by two youths despatched by Etearch, king of the Oasis of Ammon; yet I can bear witness that I heard of these little people not only in Shoa, but

.also in Ukambani two degrees to the south, and in
Barava a degree and a half to the north of the
Equator. In Barava a slave was shown to me who
accorded completely with the description of Dilbo.
He was four feet high, very thick-set, dark-com-
plexioned, and lively, and the people of the place
assured me that he was of the pigmy race of the
interior. It is not impossible, too, that circumstances, such as continual rains from May to January
and other means, may contribute to produce a di-
minutive people of stunted development in the
interior of Africa. *A priori*, therefore, the reports
collected from different and mutually independent
points of Africa cannot be directly contradicted;
only care must be taken to examine with caution
the fabulous element mixed up with what may be
true by native reporters. In the Suahili dialect
"dogo" means small, and in the language of
Enarea, "doko" is indicative of an ignorant and
stupid person.

To the north of the land of the Dokos, and to the
north-east of the kingdom of Susa, lies the important
region of Kaffa, a name which has figured in the
maps ever since the Portuguese priest Fernandez
and his companions vainly attempted to penetrate
from Abessinia through Enarea and Kaffa to the
coast of Malindi, which formerly belonged to the
crown of Portugal. Incontestably it must have been
reported in Malindi that there was thence a way to
Abessinia, and into the interior of Africa. Had that
attempt succeeded, and had a way been opened

from Malindi into the interior the African travels of discovery in the nineteenth century would have shaped themselves otherwise, and the sources of the Nile would have been long ago discovered, not in the forest of Babia in Enarea under the eleventh degree of north latitude, as M. D'Abbadie will have it, but in the regions of the Equator somewhere about the latitude of Malindi.

According to the fabulous etymology of the Mohammedans the name "Kaffa" is derived from the Arabic word "Yekaffi," it is enough.   A priest, Mahomed Nur by name, is said to have conceived the design of wandering from the East toward Western Africa in order to extend the religion of the prophet, and when he came into the regions where Kaffa lies, Allah is reported to have appeared to him and to have said :—" It is now enough ; go no further."   Since that time according to tradition the country has been called Kaffa.   Just as little can assent be given to the notion of those who believe that the country takes its name from Kahava, or Kahoa, which in Arabic means, prepared coffee ; for the raw coffee, the coffee-bean, is called bun, in the Galla language, bunna.   According to the Arabian tradition the civet-cat brought the coffee-bean to the mountains of the Arusi and Itta-Gallas where it grew and was long cultivated, till an enterprising merchant carried the coffee-plant, five hundred years ago, to Arabia where it soon became acclimatised.

The capital of Kaffa is called Suni and lies on a

mountain of the same name, and it is said not to be
so large as Ankober.   The houses, too, are not so
good as those in Abessinia, where they are mostly
round and built of wood, the roofs being thatched
with a grass called Guasa.   Other important
places, where the king sometimes resides are Nagoa,
Gobi Bura, Alexa Sehija, and Sunge Woda.   In
extent this country is thought to be larger than
Shoa, and the king endeavours to extend his rule
even further to the south, west, and east.   Though
Kaffa lies between the fifth and seventh degrees
of north latitude its influence probably reaches to
the countries lying between the third and fourth
degrees.   It does not lie so high as Enarea, but has
several high mountains; and in the villages the heat
is so great that the traders from Enarea always
desire to return to their own cooler country.

Queen Balli was sovereign when Dilbo, my informant, was in Kaffa.   After the death of her
husband, King Halalo, she seized the rebellious
chiefs and proclaimed herself ruler of the kingdom
to the sound of the state-herald's drum.   Foreign
affairs she left to be managed by her brave son
Gomarra, who leads the army to battle while the
queen remains at home discharging judicial and
other civil functions.   She seldom appears out
of the capital; but when she does so her subjects
are bound to spread clothes in her path.   Gomarra
always returns victorious from his campaigns, laden
with male and female trophies.   The enemy's men
are killed or mutilated, and the women either

killed or savagely disfigured. When I expressed
some doubts as to the accuracy of Dilbo's statement respecting the spreading out of clothes on
Queen Balli's path he observed, that owing to
the quantity of cotton in Kaffa clothes are extremely cheap, and the natives do not care much
about losing them if thereby they can do honour
to their queen. The chief articles brought from
Kaffa by the traders of Enarea are slaves and
cotton cloths. In return they take thither pieces
of salt, copper, horses, cows, coloured clothing,
stuffs, and in general everything that is sold in the
Gondar market. Horned cattle are rare in Kaffa,
on which account in cultivating the fields the
inhabitants do not employ the plough, but break up
the soil with staves, a custom which reminded me
of the tribes in the interior, to the south of the
Equator, who prepare the ground by means of
pointed pieces of wood. The internal portion of
the kingdom is orderly; but on the frontiers there
is always a great deal of fighting going on with
the neighbouring tribes, which the valiant Gomarra,
however, soon sets to rights. Strangers who visit this
kingdom for trading purposes are much esteemed and
their persons and property protected. The people of
Kaffa are partly Christian, though after a very superficial and degenerate fashion, and they practise circumcision, do not work on Fridays and Sundays,
and observe the festivals of Saints. Incredible
and fabulous appears the statement which Dilbo
made to me respecting the relation between husband

and wife, which was to the effect that there is a public resort set apart for the husband, where no woman is permitted to appear, and where no wife must eat or drink with her husband under penalty of three years' imprisonment. Husband and wife see each other only at night, never meeting during the day. The wife remains in the inmost portion of the house, the husband occupying the other part. Such a separation of the sexes is unknown in Abessinia, and would presuppose that the inhabitants of Kaffa are Mohammedans, with whom the isolation of their women is the rule.

Salt is very dear in Kaffa, and five pieces have the same value as twenty pieces (one dollar) in Shoa. The salt comes from Senjero and Enarea, and those countries receive it from Abessinia. The language of Kaffa is neither Æthiopic nor Amharic, nor Galla; it is allied, however, to those of Gobo, Tuffte, and Dambaro. The Kaffans have a tradition according to which the primeval father of their race was called Busase and lived in a cave. The same thing is also told of the first of the population of Enarea; and from this it would seem as if the earliest inhabitants of those countries lived in caves, and thus were Troglodytes as Herodotus reports, until through contact with other tribes they became acquainted with house-building. There are said to be many caves in both these places.

Proceeding from Kaffa to the north it is necessary to cross the great river Gojob, of which something has to be said, before we pursue our course to the northern countries, Mancho, Jimma, Senjero and Enarea.

It was in the October of 1840 that I journeyed from Ankober to Angolala in order to pay my respects to the King of Shoa, and to express to him my wish to be allowed to accompany him in his expedition into the Galla land. The king acceded to my request; but at the same time commanded me to remain for a few days in Angolala until the forces of Shoa were collected. During this time of expectation I often conversed with Dilbo, the Enarean already referred to. Among other things, I asked him whether there were rivers in his country and what information he could give respecting the countries to the south. Later (on the 29th of May 1841) I was in Angolala again along with Dr. Beke; and in the company of that gifted traveller, whose knowledge of Amharic however was then scanty, I again conversed with Dilbo, who reiterated and enlarged upon his former statements. Thus, when I inquired whether there was any river in Enarea like the Hawash, on the southern frontier of Shoa, Dilbo replied at once:—"In Enarea and beyond Enarea there are more than one river; there are the Kibbe, or Gibbe, the Dambese, the Dirdesa, and the Gojob. This last is the largest of them all, and neither rises in Enarea nor flows through that country; but comes from the great desert Gobi which lies to the south-west of Enarea. The Gojob flows between Kaffa and

Mancho to Senjero, and past it towards the rising
of the sun." This was, almost word for word, the
statement of Dilbo in the years 1840 and 1841;
but it was only in 1841, that I attached importance to it, when Dr. Beke pointed attention to its
harmony with Herodotus, who had heard from a
priest of the Temple of Minerva in Thebes, that one
half of the Nile flowed towards the North and the
other half towards the South. This remark of Dr.
Beke made me inquire minutely respecting this
river which is quite distinct from the Kibbe, the
latter having its source in the forest of Babia, near
Kossa and Genna in Enarea, whence it unites with
the Dirdesa which rises near Jeresa in Jimma;
when uniting with the Dambese, which comes from
Wosager in Enarea, it empties itself into the Blue
River, or Abessinian Nile. To the question, whether
he had ever seen the Gojob Dilbo replied that
he had twice crossed it with a relative, who was in
the habit of making every year the journey from
Enarea to Kaffa, in company of other traders.
From his birthplace Sabba, he had journeyed
always in a south-westerly direction, through
Jimma and Mancho, Galla districts, dependent
on Enarea, and had then come to a great desert
where the Mancho people waylay travellers, till
at last he reached the bank of the great river
Gojob, the volume of whose waters so terrified
him that he wished to return to Enarea, fearing
that while crossing the river, he should lose his life
either through the many crocodiles which he saw

in the water, or through the great waves which he
thought would sink rafts made of the trunks of trees.
To the further question how broad the river was, he
said, "the Gojob is, from one bank to another
as far as Angolala to the Gallas village Cherkos,"
the distance between the two latter places being
about two English miles. They had to search the
forest for the terrified Dilbo and bind him with
cords to prevent him from running away in a
fright. Sometimes travellers take time to hollow
out the trunk of some huge tree; but generally they
bind six or seven trunks together, and thus transport over the river from thirty to fifty people, with
horses, mules, asses, cows, &c. As I fancied that
Dilbo had no right notion of either a boat or a
raft I made him construct them by way of illustration
with reeds in my house; when he made a perfect
raft with rudders, so that I could no longer be
sceptical. The Shoans do not know anything either
of boats or rafts, so that Sahela Selassie got a model
of one made for the British envoy, when he was
about to proceed in the direction of Gurague to the
Lake Suai (Zwai).

As it was difficult to ascertain the geographical
positions of the countries spoken of by Dilbo, I made
him attempt a map in sand, which showed the source
of the river towards the west, to the north of Enarea.
In the desert of Gobo there are, it seems, many
elephants, giraffes, and wild beasts generally, and
beyond the desert there are black people. To a
question respecting the mouth of the river Dilbo
replied:—"I know that it flows towards the rising

sun; but I do not know its end. I only know that
I have heard the Mohammedans say, that on this
river they go into the country of the Arabs." At
the time I could not rightly understand this statement of Dilbo; but it all became clear to me when,
in 1843 I became acquainted with the mouth of the
Jub and with the general relations of the eastern
coast under the Equator, and I am convinced
that the Gojob is no other river than the Jub, as
it is called by the Arabs.

After the Gojob, as Dilbo reported, has flowed
onward with great rapidity to Kaffa it takes its way
through a lake, and then further to the east receives
the large river Omo, which rises in the south-west
of Susa. Near the confluence of the two rivers the
Gojob appears to have a cataract, which Dilbo
called Dumbaro, and which he said makes so tre-
mendous a noise that it is heard at a very great
distance. Probably the river here is barred by
rocks, which arrest its flow and make its waters
furious. Now, as regards the origin of the two
rivers, the Gojob and the Omo, it may perhaps be simply explained by the supposition that
those of the mountains of Enarea which seem to
run from south to north contribute their eastern
waters to the Kibbe, whilst the south-western
ranges send theirs into the Gojob. In Enarea
therefore there would be a separation of the streams
running eastward and westward. So likewise may
the south-eastern streams of Kaffa and Susa form
the Omo, whose original source however may be
in snow-mountains and marshes, which certainly

could exist to the north of the Equator, as well
as those seen by me to the south of it. How important it would be if the explorations of future
travellers were directed to the regions of the equator, that one section of them should proceed through
Enarea and Kaffa to Susa, while another section
should pursue the same goal onwards from Barava
or Malindi. The western waters of Susa and Kaffa
flow beyond doubt into the Bahr-el-Abiad; from
which, after all, the interior of Africa both eastward
and westward can more easily be explored, as travelling from the western and eastern coasts of Africa is
extremely difficult, expensive, and dangerous; while
the passage of the Nile is practicable with tolerable
security to the fourth degree of north latitude; and
even the bars of rock there may be surmounted at the
right time of the year when the water is high. The
countries of Kaffa and Susa can be scarcely three
degrees of latitude distant from the Bahr-el-Abiad;
and it ought therefore to be possible to reach the
vicinity of Kaffa by the Sobat, which comes from the
east and flows into the Bahr-el-Abiad, without any
necessity for a considerable journey by land. I cannot doubt that all these problems will be solved by the
next expedition which may penetrate into the regions
of the upper course of the Bahr-el-Abiad, and that
every contributory stream as far as navigable will
be explored. But this is an enterprise which will
require several years to be satisfactorily conducted to
its close.

I now proceed with the further description of

the southern countries of Abessinia. When the
traveller has crossed the Gojob, and proceeds
through the country of the Mancho and Jimma
Gallas, in from twelve to fifteen days he will
reach Enarea, which lies much higher than Kaffa.
Dilbo spoke of five lofty mountains in Enarea the
names of which are, Menjillo, in the centre of
Enarea, Sasala, Gabana, Mutekossa, and Jejilla.
The capital of Enarea is Saka with a population
of about 12,000, where the Sappera, or king, generally resides and where the caravans coming from
Gondar stop for trading purposes. According to
Dilbo there are also the following cities and vil-
lages:—Santo, Lako, Genna, Kossa, Geruke, Affate,
Sabba, Sigaro.

Dilbo informed me that the reigning King of
Enarea is Abba Bogibo, a brave warrior and good ruler,
who administers justice publicly in his capital, and to
whom every one has easy access. On such occasions
he sits on a wooden throne over which a skin is
spread. His people do not bow the upper portions of
the body, nor prostrate themselves to the ground,
as is the custom of the Abessinians in their intercourse with kings and great men; they simply kiss
his hand after the fashion of the Mohammedans.
The sons of the king are not imprisoned either, as
at one time was the case with the sons of the
kings of Abessinia, that they might not stir up in-
surrections against their fathers. In Enarea the
son of the king's chief wife generally becomes
his successor, and he then nominates his brothers to

the governorships of provinces. The king places himself at the head of his troops in the expeditions which he undertakes annually against the Gallas of Gama, Nono, and Limmu, to the north-east of Enarea. The Guderu tribes, too, in the north, as well as the Jimmas and Manchos in the south, and the Shankalas in the north-west, are sometimes visited. The king's influence extends from Enarea as far as the Mächa and Soddo Gallas. The campaigns last at the most from ten to fifteen days, and are carried on by troops in single divisions operating in different directions; and the king, acting in the centre, has cognizance of their movements by the smoke of the villages they set on fire. Children and women are neither slain nor mutilated, but sold into slavery to Gondar and Shoa; this practice however may have ceased since the slave trade was forbidden by Theodorus, the new and energetic King of Abessinia, some years ago.

The King of Enarea possesses a small number of matchlocks which he obtained from the merchants in Gondar, and from Goshu, the former governor of Gojam. Abba Bogibo is a Mohammedan, his father, Bofu Boku, having accepted that creed from his uncle Mutar, and from the Mohammedan traders from Gondar, who with trading always combine religious objects, and with that view take Mohammedan priests with them. A large section of the people of Enarea have been converted to Islamism, and the language is Galla, but differs somewhat from the dialects of the other Gallas.

The necessaries of life are cheap in Enarea; for a piece of salt, worth not more than a groat, you may buy from sixty to seventy pounds of coffee-berries, and at the same price three great pitchers of honey, or several sacks of wheat are procurable. Pieces of salt are however rare. Like the Abessinians the Enareans drink beer and mead. The coffee-tree grows wild in the woods to the height of from twelve to fourteen feet, and its wood is used for fuel in the cold parts of the country; and in Enarea there is said to be more coffee than in Kaffa. What a pity that there should be so much difficulty in communicating with countries like these, from which so valuable an article of commerce could be procured! What results would arise if the Gojob were found to be navigable, or if the river Sobat should conduct to these coffee countries! And how much more important still would this be for the extension of Christianity in Inner Africa! The traders from Gondar carry to Enarea the following articles of commerce:—pieces of salt, glass-beads of various colours and sizes; coloured stuffs, especially blue calico; copper, knives, scissors, nails; weapons, cooking-ware, black pepper, &c.; and receive in exchange coffee, civet, slaves, horses and the skins of lions and leopards, especially of the black leopard (*Gessela*).

Civet is dear, even in Enarea, as it is considered a good medicine for the head-ache and other maladies; and is procured from the civet-cat which is as large as a young dog. This cat lives in the woods, where it is caught in traps, and is then kept in cages in front of which a fire is burnt daily to make it perspire. It has in its hinder parts a little sack or bladder in which the precious material collects, and this is emptied with a spoon from time to time, and put into a horn which with its valuable contents is sold to the traders.

Among the animals of Enarea is the Worsamesa, which from the description appears to be the giraffe, and is found in great numbers in the wilderness of Bakko in the west of Enarea, whence you go into the land of the Blacks. This wilderness is full of wild animals, and is the hunting-ground of hunters of Enarea. Elephants are particularly numerous in it; and amongst these the white elephant, whose hide is like that of a leper; but it must not be killed; for it is considered an " Adbar," that is, a protector of man, and has religious honours paid to it. Any one who should happen to kill a white elephant, which is smaller than the common one, would have to atone for the act with his life; for so their heathen superstition decrees; and here I may take the opportunity to note, that white elephants are said to be extant in the interior also on the coast of Lamu, as Bana Kheri, my Suahili caravan-conductor, assured me. In Enarea there are said to be white buffaloes too, which are likewise sacred and may not be attacked; and indeed in general the white colour is sacred.

The original founder of the race which inhabits Enarea is called Limmu, and like the founder of Kaffa is said to have been a troglodyte and to have dwelt in caves.

To the south-east of Enarea lies the powerful kingdom of Senjero, which formerly consisted of sixteen provinces, but is now, it appears, dependent on Enarea, as Abba Bogibo in conjunction with Limmu and Jimma, is said to have invaded it and made it tributary. A slave from Senjero with whom I became acquainted at Ankober gave me the following information respecting this unknown country. The capital of Senjero which stands upon a hill is called Anger. The name of the king of the country is Amo, and he is a great friend to his soldiers, but not to the poor people. The succession to the throne is hereditary, and not dependent on the flight of a vulture or a bee, as according to the report of a priest of Gurague I had been led to imagine. It was the custom in Senjero after the death of a king, he said, for the chief men of the kingdom to assemble outside the city in an open field, and wait till a vulture or an insect settled on one of the assembly; and he to whom this happened was unanimously elected king. As these African races attach great importance to birds and their cries, such a custom would have been within the limits of possibility. The people of Senjero have to fight on all sides, with Wolamo, Enarea, Goma, and with the Gallas. The river Kibbe is said to mark the boundary, and to be even larger than the Hawash. The natives do not eat the flesh of goats and fowls; for like the Gallas and other South African tribes, they look upon the latter as a species of the vulture tribe. Traders from Gurague repair to Senjero, and during their stay are allowed " dirgo," or daily rations from the king, just as is the custom in Shoa. The population is said to have been Christian, but to have relapsed into heathenism. Sunday is a day of rest, and they keep the feasts of Kidana Meherat and St. Michael, but they have no fast-days, and circumcision prevails.

In Senjero only females are sold into slavery, because once a wife cruelly murdered her husband at the request of the king of the country. At first the king is said to have desired the husband, who was of high rank, to kill his wife and bring him a piece of her flesh, which had been indicated by the soothsayers as a sure cure for the sick monarch. The husband, fascinated by the beauty of his wife, was unwilling to obey the royal command. The king therefore commanded the wife to murder her husband which she did without hesitation. Since that time it has been the custom to sell women into slavery into other countries ; but when male slaves are transported beyond Senjero, they are said generally to commit suicide by hanging themselves.

The people of Senjero offer up human beings as sacrifice to their gods. The slave-dealers always throw a beautiful female slave into the lake Umo, when they leave Senjero with their human wares; and many families, too, must offer up their firstborn sons as sacrifices, because once upon a time, when summer and winter were jumbled together in a bad season, and the fruits of the field would not ripen, the soothsayers enjoined it. At that time a great pillar of iron is said to have stood at the entrance of the capital, which by the advice of the soothsayers was broken down by order of the king, upon which the seasons became regular again. To avert the recurrence of such a confusion of the seasons the soothsayers are reported to have enjoined the king to pour human blood once a-year on the base of the broken shaft of the pillar, and also upon the throne. Since then certain families are obliged to deliver up their first-born sons, who are sacrificed at an appointed time. Although the existence of an iron pillar, the broken shaft of which however is said to be still extant, may be doubted, the statement just given will not be wondered at by those acquainted with the gross superstition of the Africans, especially as it is manifested in seasons of calamity; or by those who consider the craft of the influential magicians and soothsayers, who often give the most inhuman counsel in order to preserve intact their own importance. In the interior I myself was once in great danger of being sacrificed, because it had not rained for a long time, and the absence of rain was ascribed to me, as if I could have hindered it from falling; and again with no less haste, I was all but deified, when after a long drought there was a sudden fall of rain, which was ascribed to my walking on the soil. Salt, which generally passes current in all the countries south of Abessinia, is also the small currency of Senjero. Only in Abessinia do we still find the Maria Theresa dollar which, however, must have a peculiar stamp to be accepted in payment. The seven dots at top, the star in the middle, and the S. F. below, must be distinctly impressed if the dollar is to be considered a female and not a male one, which is a few pieces of salt less valuable than the other.

In Senjero there are said to be good smiths and other artisans. Very probably the countries along the Gojob possessed in earlier times a higher state of civilization, which they received from Arabia or India, by means of the water-communication afforded by the river. The iron pillar and the existence of artisans, may be sufficient warrant for this supposition. The Medinat-el-Nahas, too, that is, the copper city, or city with walls of copper, of which I heard on the Suahili coast, leads one to infer a higher state of civilization, as having existed in the countries watered by the Gojob.

CHAPTER VI.

ORMANIA AND THE GALLAS.

Position, number and migration of the Gallas—Their probable mission in the providential scheme—Their appearance, dress, &c.—The true Galla type to be found near the Equator—Country, climate, and occupation—Field for European emigration—Their priests, prayers, and exorcists—Ideas of a future life—Theories as to their notions of Christianity—Characteristics of their religion—No idols in Eastern Africa—Their notions of a divinity and subordinate deities—Days of rest—The Wollo-Gallas—The "Wodaja"—Mohammedanism of the Wollo-Gallas—Power of Mohammedanism in Eastern Africa—Coming conflict between Christianity and Mohammedanism.

I CONCLUDE my notices of the southern countries of Abessinia with a brief description of the Gallas, a nation to which during my residence in Shoa I paid particular attention, as I consider them destined by Providence after their conversion to Christianity to attain the importance and fulfil the mission which Heaven has pointed out to the Germans in Europe.

In the course of time the Gallas have taken possession of a large section of Eastern Africa. Separated into many tribes independent of each other they extend, so to say, from the eighth degree of north to the third degree of south latitude, numbering, in the whole, from six to eight millions, an amount of which scarcely any other African race can boast. When in the sixteenth century Mohammed Graga overran and destroyed the land, coming from the south with their innumerable horsemen the Gallas seized on some of the finest portions of Abessinia. This movement may have been part of a more general one in the centre of Africa, which drove the tribes of the interior towards the coast, the Gallas migrating towards the north and east; and it would seem to have been providentially ordained by this migration of the Gallas to oppose a barrier to the onward rush of the Mohammedans from Arabia, and so at one and the same time to punish the abominable heresies of Christian Abessinia, and the wild fanaticism of the Mohammedans. Had not Providence brought the Portuguese by sea to the eastern coast in the fifteenth century, and afterwards impelled the Gallas forward from the interior, the fiery and proselytizing Islams would probably have overrun equatorial Africa from east to west, as they once threatened to overrun Europe. The name " Gallas " in their own language means immigrants, and has been given them by the Arabs and Abessinians. They call themselves " Orma," or " Oroma," strong, or brave men ; and their language they call " Afan Orma," the mouth of the Ormas; so as the Gallas have no general name to indicate their nationality or its seat, I propose to include both under the designation of Ormania.

I have heard several very different accounts given of the origin of the Gallas, or, as I would call them, the Ormas; but, whatever it may have been, it is certain that on their first appearance in Abessinia they were a very wild and warlike people, who united under one head might have conquered not only Abessinia, but the whole of Africa. After having occupied, however, the finest provinces of Abessinia, they began to make war upon each other, which checked their further progress, and made it easy for the Abessinians to subjugate one tribe after another. With their horsemen, notwithstanding their numbers, the Gallas found it difficult to conquer the mountainous highlands of Abessinia.

In general the Gallas have a manly appearance; are large and powerfully built, but with savage features, made still more savage-looking and fierce by their long hair, worn like a mane over the shoulders. They are principally of a dark-brown colour, by which, no less than by intellectual capacity and teachableness, they are so advantageously distinguished from all other East-Africans, that the Galla slaves, especially the young women, are much sought after by the slave-dealers, and in Arabia fetch from 100 to 150 dollars each. Their bodies, and long upper-garment in form like the Roman toga are besmeared with a thick crust of butter, giving an unpleasant odour, which strangers scent from afar. The women wear a short gown of leather fastened round their loins by a girdle, on the skirt of which a number of pieces of coral are hung by way of ornament. The more wealthy wear also a large upper-garment over this gown, which gives them the appearance of European women. The weapons of the Gallas are a spear, sword, and shield, and they all ride on horseback; even the women

gallop beside or behind their husbands; for among
them it is considered degrading to go on foot.

The Galla horses are very small, but beautiful in
colour, and extremely swift, though horse-shoes are
unknown. The Gallas in the neighbourhood of
Abessinia are tillers of the soil as well as breeders
of cattle, while their brethren under the Equator are
merely pastoral and lead a nomadic life. Those of
the Equator, moreover, have no horses and are altogether far behind the others, presenting the genuine
type of the original Gallas, especially in their religious notions. Where the Gallas follow agriculture,
the men plough, sow, and reap, while the women look
after the oxen, cows, horses, sheep, and goats, and
take care of the house and its concerns. Rye, wheat,
barley and Indian corn, grow in such great abundance
in the Galla countries, that for a dollar you may buy
almost more barley or rye than a camel can manage
to carry. The climate of most of these countries
is remarkably beautiful and healthy ; the average
temperature being 56 deg. Fahrenheit—the highest 70 deg., and the lowest, 46 deg. The Gallas
occupy vast and noble plains which are verdant
almost all the year round, and afford nourishment
to immense herds of cattle. Their houses or huts
are round and cone-shaped, covered with roofs
of grass and mostly inclosed by a low stone wall
for security against sudden attack. The villages
or hamlets are for the most part in groves or
woods, on heights, or on the sides of mountains and
rivers. The land is rich in springs and brooks, well

supplied by the tropical rains which last for three months; besides which there is a second short rainy season. Wooded mountains and hills also abound, which serve for places of refuge to the inhabitants in time of war; and the tall juniper is among the most remarkable of the trees which adorn these forests. What a noble land would Ormania be if it were under the influence of Christianity and European culture! What a pity that the course of our emigration is not directed to those regions! No doubt the time will come, when the stream of European enterprise which now flows towards America and Australia shall be exhausted. Abessinia will then attain the cosmopolitan standing to which it is entitled by its geographical position.

Like most savage tribes the Gallas are great talkers, and for hours together they can make speeches, with an expression and play of gesture which are very amusing to a European. The language is very harmonious and reminds one of Italian. On the whole, five chief dialects may be distinguished in Ormania, although the difference between them is not so great that the most southern Galla cannot pretty easily understand his most northern brother.

The Gallas have priests, called Lubas, as distinguished from the Kalijas, who are their magicians, exorcists, and medicine-men. As in the case of most heathens, so with these people, a tree has an important place in their religious ceremonies. Under the shadow of the Woda sacrifices and prayers are offered up; a higher spirit even is supposed to dwell within it, on which account the Woda is esteemed holy, and no one dare fell or harm it without losing his life. Of the greatest sanctity is the tree Worka (*Ficus sycamorus*), Woda Nabi, by the river Hawash, where the Gallas every year offer up a great sacrifice, and pray to their highest deity, Waka, sacrificing oxen and sheep to him, and drinking plenty of beer and smoking tobacco. In their prayers, which have no fixed formula, they say, " O Wak, give us children, tobacco, corn, cows, oxen, and sheep. Preserve us from sickness, and help us to slay our enemies who make war upon us, the Sidama (Christians), and the Islama (Mohammedans). O Wak, take us to thee, lead us into the garden, lead us not to Setani, and not into the fire." On this occasion, the Lubas, or priests, augur from the entrails of goats whether victory or defeat is to accompany the Gallas in the coming year. The Luba lets his hair float wildly, carries a bell in his hand, and a copper frontlet encircles his brows when he performs this rite, which reminds one of that of the ancient Romans. If the entrails are very red the Gallas are to be conquered by the Sidama. The Kalijas cast out spirits and devils from the sick, every malady being ascribed to an evil spirit. The number of evil spirits is eighty-eight, which are governed by two chiefs, each of whom has forty-three under his orders. An evil spirit is called Sar. The Kalija hangs dried entrails of the goat round his neck, carries a bell and a whip in his hand, offers a sacrifice to a serpent which is being fed in the house on milk, rubs grease on the sick man, smokes him with aromatic herbs, cries aloud with a horrible noise, gives him at the same time some smart strokes with the whip, and thus endeavours to cast out the evil spirit and to cure the patient.

Like the Abessinians the Gallas live on meat and bread, and drink beer and mead as much as they choose. They do not eat fish nor fowls, considering the former to be of the serpent, and the latter of the vulture species. The serpent, as already mentioned, is considered sacred by the Gallas, and milk is set before it. The Gallas have honey in superabundance; and when the bees swarm the people set up a shout to make them settle; and the interior of the hive is smeared with fragrant substances that the bees may be enticed not to abandon it.

If a Galla kills a man of his own tribe the man-slayer must pay a fine of one thousand oxen; if a woman is killed, the penalty is only fifty oxen, an ox being estimated at from one to two dollars. As respects the abode of the dead the Gallas believe that Christians, Mohammedans and Ormas go to separate places in the lower world, where each is rewarded by Waka or punished by fire. They consider Waka to be an invisible and beautiful being. It is, however, difficult to discover the original religious notions of the Gallas, as in the neighbourhood of Abessinia they have heard many scriptural conceptions, so that a laborious inquirer like Dr. Beke is inclined to consider them degenerate Christians, a theory to which I cannot assent. Even the most degenerate of the Christians of Abessinia retain baptism and the Lord's Supper, religious services in church and elsewhere, the Holy Scriptures and many ordinances and blessings founded on the Bible, all which are entirely wanting to the Gallas. Dr. Beke bases his opinion on information received from a Guderu Galla, to the effect that the Gallas are acquainted with the Abessinian names of saints, &c., and pay them great veneration; for instance, Maremma (Maria), Balawold (Jesus Christ), Sanbata (Sunday), Kedami (Saturday), Maddin (Saviour of the world) Selassie (the Trinity), Girgis (St. George), Dablos (the Devil) who torments the possessed, Sintan or Setani (Satan), who brings death, disease, and misfortune, &c. &c. The Virgin Mary they call Wakaiu, the Mother of God. It is certainly true that the Gallas who live in the neighbourhood of Abessinia are acquainted with these names, at least with some of them; but it by no means follows that we are to consider the Gallas as Christians, even of the most degenerate kind. Among the southern or equatorial Gallas there is no trace of these names and ideas; at most, therefore, it can be only the Gallas bordering on Abessinia who deserve to be regarded as degenerate Christians, and not the Gallas in general.

Great care must be taken to avoid any attempt to identify the peculiar and genuine religious conceptions of the race with those of the Galla-slaves residing in Mohammedan countries, whose stock of

ideas is already so Mohammedanized, that if we were
to consider their notions as of Ormaic origin, a
great error would be committed.   The true Ormaic faith is to be discovered only where (as in the
interior of the equatorial regions) the heathen Gallas
have no intercourse but with heathens, the Wanika,
for example; but not with Mohammedans or Christians, and where they are not subjected to a foreign
yoke.   This much is certain, that the Ormas have
far more expanded and purer ideas of religion
than other heathen tribes of Eastern Africa; and it
is also certain that they, like the others, have no
visible idols; for throughout the whole of Eastern
Africa such are unknown.   This circumstance, on
the one hand, presupposes a very ancient paganism,
and on the other, shows that the East-Africans
are more occupied with temporal than with spiritual
wants and interests.   They are so devoted to the
service of the belly, as not to trouble themselves
much about gods and their worship.   The fear
of evil spirits is not wanting among these heathen
nations; and this has led them to the idea of
the necessity for an atonement, and to the ceremonial of sacrifice.   It is certain, also, that these
nations in general maintain the idea of a Supreme
Being, whom they universally distinguish by the
name " Heaven" (Waka, Mulungu), since by their
own conceptions and without a higher revelation
they cannot ascend beyond the sky, the loftiest
and most exalted of created objects, nor lift up
their eyes to contemplate the One almighty and

living God. They made an approach, it is true, towards such a conception; but stopped short of it when they halted at a material heaven, and could at most only dimly foreshadow the existence of a Supreme Being. So certain is it that man, left to himself without the aid of revelation, can never attain to the knowledge of the One true God.

It has already been noticed, that the Gallas pay great reverence to the serpent, which they regard as the mother of the human race. Now, since the worship of the serpent was a prominent feature in the old Æthiopian idolatry, as we find from the statement of the Abessinians, that before their conversion they worshipped a large serpent, it may be conjectured that the religious conceptions of the Ormas are connected with those of the ancient Æthiopians; and thus the faith of the Gallas may throw some light upon that older creed. Under Wak, as the Most Supreme Being, stand two subordinate divinities, a masculine, Oglie, and a feminine, Atetie. They sacrifice cows and sheep to Oglie between the months of June and July; to Atetie, they sacrifice in September. She is the goddess of fecundity, and women are her especial votaries. At these festivities they ask for numerous progeny, good harvests and victory over their enemies; in other respects, giving themselves over entirely to that sensual enjoyment, which is generally inseparable from heathenism. It is evident that the procreative and fructifying power of nature is expressed by the idea of these two divinities, as was the case with the ancient Egyptians who had similar notions. At the beginning of the rainy season nature germinates, and brings fruit at its close. I mentioned formerly that many of the Galla tribes show great respect for Saturday and Sunday on which days they do not work in the fields. They call Sunday " Sanbata gudda" (greater Sabbath), in contrast to the " Sanbata kenna" (lesser Sabbath). I could detect nothing of this distinction among the Gallas of the Equator; but I satisfied myself as to the non-existence of it by the fact, that the Gallas of the Equator are mostly nomads, for whom there is no necessity to single out certain days for rest, since they can rest any and every day, while it is quite otherwise with the agricultural tribes. A similar circumstance is remarked among the Wanika, the Masai, and Wakuafi. The Wanika rest from their labours every fourth day, whilst the nomadic Masai and Wakuafi know no distinction of days, solely because from their point of view they do not think that any particular day of rest is required.

The Wollo-Gallas, composed of seven tribes and occupying the countries between the north and south of Abessinia, are very fanatical Mohammedans, and the Moslem creed has still more corrupted the originally corrupt nature of the Gallas. In faithlessness and lust of plunder scarcely any nation exceeds the Wollos, despite their external show of friendliness and civility. But they are not given to slaying strangers, although they plunder them without compunction. The heathen

Gallas, on the contrary, murder every one who has not become a "Mogasa," that is, a favourite of their Heyu, or chief, whose term of office is for seven years, another being then chosen in his place by one or more of the Galla tribes. The Heyu commands in time of war, and is judge in time of peace.

It is the custom among the Wollo-Gallas for their chief men to meet early on Thursday and Friday mornings for prayer, when they have coffee and Chat, a sort of tea, and smoke tobacco; and their priests must not absent themselves on these occasions, which are called "Wodaja," Unions, or preservatives of friendship. They believe that at the Wodaja they receive spiritual revelations in reference to military expeditions and other matters, and at it they pray especially that they may be blessed with increase of cows, clothes, &c., and that Allah will bestow gold and silver on their chief, and increase his power and dominion. It was at such a Wodaja that a priest attached to Adara Bille, the chief of Lagga Gora, pretended in 1842 to receive a revelation that I ought to be plundered of everything in my journey through the Wollo-land, a scheme which, as will be hereafter seen, was really carried out, and nearly cost me my life.

The Wollos are said to have been converted to Mohammedanism by an Arab, named Debelo. Since the time of the great Guksa this tribe has possessed considerable influence in the politics of Abessinia. Guksa was the son of the chief Merso, and father of Ali Allula, who was the father of Ras Ali,

Ras Ali for a long time governed western Abessinia, and inclined towards Mohammedanism; but in 1853 he was vanquished in battle by King Theodorus, and obliged to seek refuge among his Mohammedan relatives, with whom it would appear he is still resident, waiting for an opportunity to dislodge the conqueror. Should he succeed Christianity in Abessinia will be in great danger; for the Mohammedans who nourish a strong hatred to King Theodorus, on account of his abolition of the slave trade, would be sure to take signal vengeance on the Christians. Indeed Mohammedanism is still most powerful in Eastern Africa, and it is even very doubtful whether before long it will not become still stronger, and the heathen and Christian populations be involved in a mighty conflict with it.

CHAPTER VII.

FROM ANKOBER TO MASSOWA.

Success of the author's missionary efforts in Shoa—Reasons for repairing to the coast—The king's farewell and offer of an official post—Departure from Angolala—Interesting interview with the King's mother—Feelings on entering the Wollo country—Adara Bille and his apparent friendliness—A young Imam—English drill, and lucifer matches—Alarm on the road—Retreat to Adara Bille—His treachery—Imprisonment and robbery of the author—Subsequent adventures and liberation—Toilsome pilgrimage to the Shoho frontier—Singular offer of vengeance — Arrival at Massowa—Arrival at Harkiko—Kindness of the French consul—To Aden—Marriage in Egypt—Return to Aden—The author's and his fellow-labourers' Abessinian projects.

By the beginning of 1842 I found that my missionary residence in Ankober had been far from unfruitful; for I had distributed 1000 copies of the Scriptures, and many of the priests of Shoa had been awakened to a knowledge of the truth, and to a consciousness of the corrupt state of their church. My little school of ten boys, whom I fed, clothed, and educated at home, was prospering. The king had bestowed on me a silver sword which gave me the rank of a governor. At the period mentioned I had thoughts of no longer confining my activity to the Christians of Shoa; but of establishing several missions among the heathen Gallas, and one in Gurague, with its perishing church, priests of which had often visited me in Ankober. This scheme was baffled, partly by an insurrection of the Gallas in Yerrer, rendering the road to Gurague unsafe, and occasioning a hostile expedition of the king against the rebels; but chiefly by the receipt of intelligence that my new fellow-labourers, Mühleisen-Arnold* and Müller had arrived at Tajurra, and found great difficulties thrown by the Adals in the way of their further progress to Shoa, which induced me therefore to proceed to the coast rather than to the interior, in order to facilitate the journey of my friends through the Adal-land. I had besides a personal interest which impelled me to this journey, the intention of marrying Rosine Dietrich, a maiden lady of Basel, who had been betrothed to missionary Kühnlein, who died in 1837 at Marseilles. In leaving Europe I had not harboured the slightest idea of marriage, but my experiences in Abessinia convinced me that an unmarried missionary could not eventually prosper. There were other inducements, too, which led me to choose the route by Massowa and Gondar, instead of the direct way to Tajurra, one of which was to make the acquaintance of the new Archbishop, or Abuna, who had arrived in Abes-

---

* My former colleague, Dr. Mühleisen-Arnold, is the author of " Ishmael; or, A natural History of Islamism, and its Relation to Christianity." Every lover of general knowledge, but more especially every missionary proceeding to Mohammedan countries, should possess this most valuable book, the entire proceeds of the publication of which will be given towards founding " a Society for propagating the Gospel among the Mohammedans."

sinia in 1841, and to ascertain his sentiments towards the Protestant missionaries; whilst another was to investigate the state of things in Adowa, and see if it might not be possible to re-establish the missionary station, given up in 1838; and a third, to become acquainted with the new route, in case that through the Adal-land should hereafter be interrupted. I thought I might undertake the journey with safety as the treaty of 1841 between England and Shoa provided for the security of British subjects during their sojourn in Abessinia, but how greatly I was mistaken will appear in the sequel.

On the 10th of March 1842 I bid farewell to my household, after prayer and scriptural meditation, and provided with a considerable number of Æthiopic and Amharic Bibles I proceeded from Ankober to Angolala to take leave both of the king and of the British envoy. On the 11th the king bade me a hearty farewell, and presented me with a mule and other most useful things for the journey, and even offered me an official situation, for which the presentation of the silver sword had paved the way. When I had declined it as altogether inconsistent with my missionary calling, he expressed his regret that in negotiations with the British agent, he should no longer have an adviser who understood the customs of England as well as those of Shoa. On the 12th of March I left Angolala and journeying in a north-easterly direction passed through Debra Berhan where the king resides during some part of the year, and so to Bollo Workie where every week a great market is held, to which the Gallas bring their horses, asses, grain, &c. resting at night in the village Logeita, near the famous monastery of St. Abbo, the monks of which used at one time to convert many Gallas to Christianity. My retinue, I may add, consisted of ten armed servants, partly to wait on me, and partly for protection on the road.

In the afternoon of the following day, the 13th, we reached Salla Dengai, the capital and residence of Senama-Work, the mother of King Sahela Selassie. We were hospitably received, and the next day I was presented to the king's mother, who, next to the king, is the most powerful personage in the country, as she rules in comparative independence nearly half of Shoa in the name of her son. She is an elderly and venerable woman, apparently more than sixty years of age, and wore a large white Abessinian dress. She received me in a pleasant little room, where she was seated on an Abessinian bedstead, covered by a piece of carpet, surrounded by a number of female attendants, whilst her male ones, with several priests and counsellors, stood at some distance. Both men and women were well dressed, and when I entered all were talking familiarly with their mistress, who had a lively and a youthful appearance for her years, and seemed to be at once an intelligent and energetic personage, and easy of access. She received my presents—a shawl of many colours, a pair of fine English scissors, a looking-glass, an Æthiopic New Testament, and a complete Amharic Bible, in a very friendly way, often repeating the words "God reward you," and the books appeared to give especial delight. She asked me many questions,—among others, how my countrymen had come to be able to invent and manufacture such wonderful things? I replied, that God had promised in His Word not only spiritual but temporal rewards to those who obeyed His commandments; that the English, Germans, and Europeans in general, had once been as rude and ignorant as the Gallas, but after their acceptance of the Gospel God had given them with science and arts wondrous blessings of an earthly kind; and that if Sahela Selassie went on imitating the enlightened princes of Europe, and above all improving the moral condition of his subjects, Shoa would be able to produce the wonderful things which now surprised her. Upon my taking leave she wished me a prosperous journey, and promised to send one of her servants to introduce me to the Governor of Geshe, on the northern frontier of Shoa, and bid him promote my further journey.

On the 14th March I left Salla Dengai where it was tolerably cold. Crossing the river Mofer, which, joining the Kaskash, flows into the Jumma, after forming the boundary between the provinces Tegulet and Mans, we had to ascend a very steep mountain, where the temperature was much colder, taking the direction to north-north-west. Mans is the largest province in Shoa, and is considered by the king's widow as her dower. The inhabitants try to preserve their ancient independence, yet live in a state

of feud with each other for want of the strong hand
of authority to keep them in check. I found them
most inhospitable, so much so indeed, that though I
had a servant of the king and also one of his mother
with me, the head man of the most insignificant village would give me neither a night's shelter in his
dwelling, nor the most trifling assistance. The climate
harmonizes with their disposition; for when the east
wind blows it is so cold that one can scarcely fancy
one's self in the interior of Eastern Africa.

In the afternoon we crossed the rivers Gurmengne,
and Sanafilasfakh, putting up for the night in the
hamlet of Wokan, and next day crossing the rivers
Retmat, Igum, and Aftanat, all flowing westward
into the Nile. Further on we crossed the rivers
Hulladeha, Gedambo, and Aganja, and on the way
our caravan was joined by a number of Shoans,
young lads and youths, from eight years old to four-
and-twenty, going up to the new Abuna, for ordination, and who hoped under our protection to arrive
more safely at Gondar. On the 16th, we quitted
the village of Amad-Washa, where we had slept,
and distributed a number of Amharic books in a
district of Shoa, to which as yet none of the publications of the Mission had found their way. From
the heights of Amad-Washa we had now to descend
some 3000 feet into the defile, through which flows
the river Kacheni, separating Mans from the province
of Geshe. The place where we crossed often exposes
the traveller to danger from the attacks of the Wollo-
Gallas who live on the other side of the river. Into

the province of Mans itself they cannot penetrate;
for it is impossible to ascend those steep heights so
long as the governor of Geshe is faithful to the King
of Shoa, and so long as they are defended by a
handful of soldiers, who by rolling down stones can
bar the passage of a whole army.   The governorship
is intrusted only to a most devoted subject of the
king, and yet all his actions are narrowly watched
and reported on by paid spies.

From the ravine of the Kacheni the road still
ascends until the foot of the hill of Dair is reached, on
which is the hill fort of the governor of Geshe.   I
stayed a few days in Dair to prepare myself for my
passage through the country of the Wollo-Gallas by re-
packing my effects; and here the Shoans who wished
to travel to Gondar with our caravan left me.   Their
road lay through the country of the Wollo chief Abie,
with whom the King of Shoa was at war; mine through
the district of Lagga Gora, with whose chief, Adara
Bille, the king was on friendly terms, and to whom
by the king's orders the governor of Geshe was
to send a soldier with me recommending me to his
protection.   On the 18th of March I quitted Dair
with sensations, more readily experienced than described; for a difficult and dangerous journey lay
before me, and had I not been powerfully strengthened by perusing the 91st Psalm, I should perhaps have returned to Ankober.   On the 19th of
March the little caravan crossed the boundary of
Shoa and the Wollo country, and entered the district of the Wollo tribe, Lagga Gora.   The same

day we arrived at Gatira, the residence of Adara
Bille, who received me hospitably and at our interview asked several questions, which, believing in
the friendliness he expressed, I answered fearlessly.
He appeared pleased with my presents, and provided
a guide as far as the district of Worra Himano.
Very different was his treatment on my second visit!

On the 20th of March I left Gatira, and after two
threatened attacks from which I was preserved only
through the fear inspired by the bayonets of my servants, reached Tanta, the residence of the Imam
Liban, the ruler of Worra Himano, and to whom I
was recommended by Adara Bille, on the 22nd. He
was a youth of fifteen and received me in a friendly
manner; both he and his guardians putting an infinite
number of questions about the men and things of
Europe. At his request I made my people go through
the military exercise which they had learned from the
English artillerymen at Ankober. The men shoul-
dered arms, loaded and fired quickly and with regu-
larity, so that the youthful prince was greatly
astonished, covered his face with his garment and
exclaimed, "No Abessinian army can stand against
a few hundred soldiers of the Franks." He stated
however to my great regret, that the road to Gondar was made very unsafe by numerous predatory
bands, who were hovering about the river Checheho
and plundering travellers; but kindly added, that
he would order the governor of Daunt to secure me
a safe passage over the river; and as the son of this
personage was in the room the friendly Imam di-

rected him to repair next morning to his father, and give the necessary orders for my safe transit. On March 23, I took leave of the young Imam, offering some presents, among which was a box of lucifer-matches, with which he was particularly delighted.

As my little caravan could not keep pace with the son of the governor of Daunt, he went forward to deliver the message as soon as possible. In the evening we bivouacked supperless on the bank of the river Bashilo, and ascended a steep mountain, on the top of which lies the great plain Dalanta, in the morning, whence the road runs in a south-westerly direction into a lower-lying region in which is the town of Daunt. On a sudden cries of wailing were heard from that quarter, and fugitives brought the alarming tidings that the governor had that morning been killed, and his son taken prisoner by Berru Aligas, the chief of Wadela, who had made an incursion into the territory of the Imam Liban. I was proceeding, notwithstanding, when a few hundred paces further on we were met by a tall lady, a relation of the Imam, who confirmed the news and begged us to accompany her to him. Whilst I was speaking to her there came other fugitives, warning us against proceeding further; so a retreat was decided on, and we passed the night in a village near Dalanta, expecting to hear further tidings on the morrow. The population of the whole plain was in the greatest consternation, every one removing his property to a place of safety. In the morning came the news that the enemy was

approaching, so the best plan seemed to be to return
to the Imam and ask his advice. He advised me to
go back to Shoa, or to take refuge in a fortress
defended by his vizier Yusuf, but it was fortunate
that I did not follow this latter piece of advice; for
that very stronghold was afterwards assaulted and
taken by Berru Aligas. I decided on returning to
the friendly Adara Bille, taking my way through the
territory of the Worra Himano, and at its southern
frontier had a magnificent view over almost all
the countries of the Wollo-Gallas. Mountain ranges
stretch from the south or south-east towards the
north and north-west; every mountain range being
separated from the others by a plain, river, or
stream, and inhabited by a different Wollo tribe, just
as is the case in the Galla-land to the south of Shoa,
where rivers form the boundaries of the tribes.

On the 28th of March, we reached Gatira again,
and I was received by Adara Bille not only with
friendliness, but with emphatic expressions of sympathy with my disappointment, and congratulations
upon my escape and safe return to Gatira; yet when
two days afterwards I wished to leave, he desired
me to remain until he received permission from
the governor in Dair to send me back to Shoa,
as the King of Shoa had only ordered him to
send me forward to Gondar, but not back. Vain
were protests. Meanwhile, however, I was plentifully supplied with meat and drink, and sent a messenger and a letter to Dair; but, as I afterwards
heard, neither reached their destination, as my

messenger was thrown into prison at the frontier. I made several presents to Adara Bille, thinking that perhaps this was what he wanted, which were accepted; but when on the 31st of March I again sought permission to leave Gatira, he replied that I was not to say another word upon the subject until the return of his messenger. The next day the chief held a Wodaja, at which as I learned afterwards the priest Tahir pretended to have received a revelation that the traveller had much gold, which the chief ought to take.

Adara Bille, who had removed my mules and horses into his own stables, now set a watch upon me; and wherever I went, a soldier dogged me, and when I was going to buy anything would ask, "Why this extravagance?" A beggar asked for a dollar, and when I refused it rejoined, "You do not know whether you will leave this place a happy man, or a beggar like myself." I began to have my suspicions, thought of flying by night, and consulted with some of my Abessinian servants, who treated my fears as groundless. It appeared afterwards that Adara Bille had received from one of them a hint of my intentions, and gave me in consequence more marked demonstrations of friendship to lull my suspicions, by sending every hour to ask if I wanted anything, and supplying provisions in abundance.

On the following day the blow long threatened was struck. In the forenoon the messenger returned from Dair, but without definite instructions respecting my return. I was surprised to learn that my messenger had been imprisoned, and to hear one of Adara Bille's counsellors say: "You have no friend or kinsman here, save God." I packed up all my valuables, and resolved to steal quietly out of the house at midnight, and if possible to reach the frontier of Shoa by daybreak. During the day I explored the roads in the environs of Gatira. Through my faithless servant, probably, Adara Bille received information of our intended flight, and sent for me, telling me that the governor of Dair had nothing to object to my return to Shoa, and that I might depart next morning early. I was led away by this apparent friendliness, and remembered, too, that my servant who was imprisoned at the frontier was ill. Scarcely had I quitted the Chief's house, when he cunningly sent a fresh supply of provisions for the journey to Shoa, to strengthen me in the belief of my approaching departure. I went soon to bed that I might rise very early in the morning, and was already asleep when I was suddenly awakened by a servant of the Chief, with the command to repair immediately to Adara Bille, who wished to bid me farewell. This late invitation rather startled me; but I complied without delay hoping to have done, once for all, with the annoyance. At the same time, all my servants, including the treacherous one,* who was

---

* This treacherous servant, who accompanied the British envoy to Aden, afterwards went mad, and there tried to cut his own throat with a razor.

THE AUTHOR MADE PRISONER BY ORDER OF ADARA BILLE

to take care of the baggage, were summoned to the Chief's. When Adara Bille saw me enter his chamber he bowed, and said that he was very glad that I had complied with the invitation. He had summoned me so late, he said, only because on the morrow he should have a great deal of business on hand, and thus could not personally bid farewell to his departing friend, whose conversation, too, he desired once more to enjoy. He then wanted to try on my spectacles; but could not see with them, as his sight was good. The cunning rascal, too, wished to know what was in my boots, and asked me to draw off one, which I did, not to offend him by a refusal. The conversation was then prolonged, and meat and bread set before us. At last I grew tired of the farce and was rising to say "good night," when Adara Bille rejoined: "Go not yet, my Father, I have not yet sufficiently enjoyed your conversation; nor have you eaten and drank enough." After a brief interval I stood up, determined to go home. The chief, too, now rose, went into a little closet behind his bedstead upon which he had been sitting, and that very moment the soldiers fell upon me and my people. One seized me by the arm and said: "You are a prisoner; give security that you will not escape!" At first I thought that it was a practical joke of Adara Bille to test my courage; but I soon saw that the Wollo-chief was in earnest. I was taken into the little room beside the dwelling of the Chief, and my servants were thrust into a small

separate hut, which I could see for a moment. In
the prison all my clothes and the contents of my
pockets were demanded. As I hesitated, the guards
declared that they had orders to kill me forthwith, and my Abessinian cloak was torn from off my
back. Upon appealing to Adara Bille's justice
and friendship I was answered derisively with the
exclamation: "Out with your treasures! Death
if you conceal the smallest of your goods!" The
female slaves, who were grinding corn in a corner
of the room, began to shriek, thinking that the
foreign man was about to be murdered. I had to
submit to an examination of my pockets. A single
dollar, a trunk-key, and a knife were found, and immediately taken away; and an English Testament
and my note-book were also wrested from me. As
it was very cold and the little fire in the room
diffused but a small amount of warmth, I ventured
to ask for the return of my cloak. A soldier communicated the request to the Chief, and he had
pity enough left to send it back. From the
corn-grinding female slaves, who were not allowed
to speak with me, I learned this at least, that
neither I nor my servants were to be murdered.
Wearied out and full of the saddest thoughts I
lay down on the ground to sleep, but sleep fled
my eyelids until after midnight. Out of the
depths of my soul I called on the Good Shepherd, the God of all help, who knows the cares
and sorrows of his servants, and who had ever
been my trust and support! After the soldiers had

conveyed the stolen baggage into safe custody, they came again into the prison and lay down on both sides on the ends of my cloak to prevent my escape; on the outside, too, the prison was surrounded.

On the 3rd of April I awoke with the consciousness of being a prisoner, yet still one whose life had been preserved by the mercy of Providence. As I was being led from the prison to my former dwelling many of the villagers came to greet me, and to express sympathy. Even the soldiers, who had treated me so barbarously the night before, expressed their disapproval of Adara Bille's conduct, and his chief wife, Fatima, herself sent consolatory messages. I was told that Adara Bille had set off in the morning to visit the governor of Dair, and upon his return in the evening I was taken back to my prison. The next day I requested an interview, as also leave to depart and necessaries for the journey; but he would neither see me, nor grant anything; sending me word that he did not care if I had to beg my daily bread. At length, however, he sent me three dollars and my worst mule, which I had to dispose of on the road to purchase food and shelter. So, too, my manuscripts—an Amharic dictionary and my diary—as well as my English Testament, were restored. The paper which was not written upon was retained by him, along with 140 dollars, five mules, several pistols, ten muskets furnished with bayonets, a rifle, my watch, the compass, and many other valuable things, which I had received from the British envoy.

On the morning of the 5th of April I was told
that I and my servants were to be conducted beyond
the frontier by six soldiers of the chief; but the route
and the direction were not mentioned. In silence
and unarmed we followed the men, who had spears,
shields, and swords. Almost the whole population
of Gatira was collected; some wept, others wished
us a happy journey, nobody said a word for the
Chief, and not a few predicted that Heaven would
punish the country where the stranger had been so
wronged.

I and my people followed the soldiers at as quick
a pace as permitted; for in my fear lest I should
be recalled I would have flown if I could out of
Gatira. From the position of the sun—for I had
no compass left to guide me, the route seemed to
be north-eastward in the direction of Tehuladere;
but whatever the way it was a matter of indifference to me, as I had nothing more to lose, and in any
case, had to journey by a route never before traversed
by European. I consoled myself with the thought
of Abraham, to whom God had promised to show
the way that he should go, and to be his shield.
In the afternoon by whom should we be accosted
but by the very priest Tahir, who had pretended
that a revelation from heaven ordered me to be
plundered. He greeted me with smiles, and invited me to his village and house, where he would
give me something to eat. I accepted the invitation, and certainly the godless priest behaved with
a friendliness which I had not expected, lighted

a fire as it was cold and rainy, and brought me
food and drink, which were very acceptable. When
leaving on the 6th I thanked him for his hospitality;
but remarked that I had nothing then with which to
recompense him; upon which Tahir answered, " It
does not matter, I have already had my share;"
and laughing, went his ways.

Leaving Adara Bille's country, but still closely
guarded by the soldiers, we entered the noble
valley of Totola intersected by the river Gerado,
where a famous market is held which is visited by
traders from all parts of Abessinia. On both sides of
the valley are mountain-ranges covered with juniper-
trees; and on these hills you see villages and hamlets.
There is scarcely to be found a lovelier district in all
Abessinia, and I wished to stop several times to contemplate the beautiful scene, but the soldiers drove
me forward with the words, " You are our cattle, we
can do with you what we please." About noon,
before we reached the river Berkona which flows
eastward into the Hawash, we met by Providential
guidance a merchant coming from Totola, who was
surprised to see a white man on foot and without
baggage. I told him what I had suffered at the
hands of Adara Bille, adding that I had heard the
orders of the soldiers were to take me to Ali Gongul,
the governor under Amade, chief of the Wollo tribe
Tehuladere, whose territory began on this side of
the Berkona. It struck the merchant as singular
that Adara Bille should send us to the governor
and not to the chief, Amade, himself. He therefore

advised us not to go with the soldiers to Ali Gongul, who had no right to dispose of strangers without the knowledge of his master. If the soldiers would not take us to Amade, he advised us to set up a loud cry, on which the people in the fields would come to our aid, and conduct us themselves to their prince, who lived in Mofa on a high hill, from which the lake Haik could be seen. We followed this excellent advice; and when we were about half a league from Mofa, observing from the way some country people in a field, we sat down and told the soldiers that we wished to be taken to Amade, and not to Ali Gongul. The soldiers were furious and brandished their swords; but we called the peasants, and told them the story of our robbery by Adara Bille, and after some resistance the soldiers were obliged to give in, and, with the peasants, we all repaired to Amade. After listening to our story he was angry that Adara Bille should send soldiers through his territory, and ordered them to turn back immediately, or he would throw them into prison. Amade gave us permission to go whithersoever we chose, and we were immediately set free. From Mofa the path which we took had a steep descent, and at nightfall we reached a Christian village, where a Christian merchant from Gondar gave us a friendly reception and hospitable shelter.

Journeying in a north-easterly direction as far as Antalo, and thence in a north-westerly direction, seventeen days elapsed before we reached Tekunda,

the frontier village of Tigre, on the borders of the
Shoho land, and from which the route proceeds to
Massowa. The way lay through every description
of country; fruitful valleys and plains, mountain
heights, past desert wildernesses; sometimes amid
dense populations, sometimes where no human soul
was to be found; and for the most part, we had to beg
for food and shelter. Occasionally a Mohammedan
would receive us hospitably, occasionally a Christian; in the latter case the motive frequently was
to receive an amulet against illness, or some magical
cure from the white man; for it is a common belief
in Abessinia that all white men come from Jerusalem, where they think there is no sickness, and all
is plenty and splendour. When I contradicted these
superstitious notions, we would sometimes be hus-
tled out of the Christian's house, as Mussulmans in
disguise, sent to sleep in the open air and the cold,
and ordered to depart before break of day. A few
horse-beans grudgingly given were often all that we
had to subsist on, and once, even to procure them I
had to sell the girdle of my chief servant. In the
province of Tigre especially the grudging inhospi-
tality of the Abessinians reached its acme, and we
longed, day after day, for our arrival at the coast.

At last, on the 29th of April, after unspeakable
perils, sufferings and fatigues, we reached Tekunda,
where my miserable and beggarly condition made no
very favourable impression on the Governor. On
hearing, however, that I was an English subject,
and acquainted with Bishop Gobat, he became a

little more friendly, bringing me and my people some bread and horse-beans. He listened with great apparent sympathy to the recital of our robbery by Adara Bille, and when it was concluded, he showed me some Mohammedan pilgrims who had come from Mecca, and who were subjects of Adara Bille: "Take these," he said; "revenge yourself on them, and spoil them of their clothes." But I declared that as a Christian and a messenger of the Gospel, I could not repay evil with evil, especially on that day, Good Friday, which reminds the Christian that Christ, the Son of God, died for all—the unjust no less than the just, in order to reconcile them to God, and to bestow on them the spirit of love and peace. The Governor assigned to me a spacious dwelling and provisions, so that after long suffering, privation, and severe exertion, I enjoyed a little repose, and could solemnise the holy day in tranquillity. After considerable difficulties on the score of payment which I could not make, but only promise, we quitted Tekunda under the care of a Shoho guide; for, as mentioned in a former chapter, the Shohos do not allow any traveller to proceed through their country without a guide. In about three hours after leaving Tekunda, we arrived at the spot where the road joins that from Halai. I immediately remembered the place as that where, four years ago, I had to chaffer and dispute for three days with the savage Shohos. At last, after intense fatigue and several menaces from the surrounding savages, we arrived at Harkiko about nine o'clock on the morning of the 2nd of May.

Although half lame with the march, I hastened to the house of the Naib, whom I met in the street. When I had told him my adventures he ordered his servants " to give the weary traveller an apartment, and to make everything comfortable for him." With joyful and grateful feelings towards God for his manifold and wonderful protection, preservation, and aid, during this toilsome and difficult journey, I laid myself down on a bed in the house of the Naib Hassan. After I had rested for some time, I inquired whether there was not an English ship bound for Aden, lying at anchor in the harbour of Massowa, and was told that an English schooner which had brought a Mr. Coffin from Aden had left the harbour three days before. When I heard the name of Coffin and was informed that he was staying in Harkiko, I immediately went to him and received all sorts of interesting news from Europe and Egypt. I was particularly sorry to hear that my friends, who were to have penetrated from Tajurra to Ankober in order to strengthen the missionary establishment there, had returned to Egypt because of the impossibility of travelling safely through the Adal-land.

On the 4th of May I set out for Massowa along the coast, till I approached near the island upon which it stands. My feet were swollen, so I adopted the Abessinian fashion of going barefooted. At Massowa I went to the house of the agent of Mr. Coffin, but left it when the French consul, M. de Goutin, gave me a friendly invitation to stay at the Consular House. Without having seen me and without asking to what nation I belonged, or knowing whether he could trust me, he offered me as much money as I needed for my journey to Aden. It is true, however, that the Consul had heard of me from a Frenchman, who had been plundered in Sokota, and who afterwards had gone to Shoa, where he received much kindness from me, and he wished, therefore, by friendly treatment to reciprocate the kindness shown to his countryman. Our subsequent voyage from Massowa to Aden lasted fifteen days; and from Aden I proceeded to Suez by the next steam-boat, in which I received a free passage, on account of the services rendered by me to Major Harris in Shoa. I remained in Egypt up to the time of my marriage with my wife, Rosine Dietrich, in the autumn of 1842, when I returned with my colleagues, Isenberg and Mühleisen-Arnold, to Aden. Our purpose was then to penetrate through the Adal Desert to Shoa, and thence to commence missionary operations among the Gallas, and to visit the dispersed Christian remnants in Gurague, Kambat, and Kaffa, spreading among them the Bible, of which we had thirty chests full, having plentifully supplied ourselves with the sacred volume in Cairo.

TAJURRA.

CHAPTER VIII.

FROM ADEN TO ZANZIBAR.

Prohibition of the Abessinian mission—French intrigue : M. Rochet and his book—Final attempt and its failure—The Abessinian mission abandoned—The author resolves to proceed to the south-eastern coast of Africa, and found a mission among the Gallas—Departure from Aden and forced return—Second voyage—The Somali coast—Mukdisha—Breach of Slave Trade treaty with England—Barava —The Jub—Christmas day spent on the Galla coast—Stay in Takaungu—Native complaints of the abandonment of Mombaz by the English—The Southern Gallas—The Dana—The disappointment of the first voyage providential—Mombaz and its recent history—The Wanika—Tanga—The Pangani and its mouth—The Waseguas and the Slave Trade—Arrival at Zanzibar—The importance of a Galla mission—Presentation to the Sultan—Extent of his rule—Brief description of Zanzibar.

On my arrival at Tajurra with my wife and colleagues on the 20th of November 1842 with the intention of proceeding to Shoa, we were informed by the Sultan of Tajurra that he had received written orders from the King of Shoa to grant no European an entrance into the interior. All our protests were in vain and we repaired to Zeila, thinking to attempt a new route to Shoa through the country of the Somalis. Up to the March of 1843 we were negotiating the terms of transit with the Somali chiefs, when I received a letter from Major Harris announcing the departure of the British mission from Shoa.

and the decided refusal of the king to allow us to return. Major Harris ascribed the king's new mood to the fanaticism of the Abessinian priesthood; but it was mainly due, I believe, to M. Rochet, the Frenchman, who had succeeded in prejudicing the Queen of Shoa against me and the Protestant missionaries generally. Since 1854, when he died as French consul at Jidda, M. Rochet has been removed from all human tribunals, and it is not, therefore, for me to pronounce a verdict on one to whom while he was in Shoa I showed great kindness, and gave much information, which he embodied in his book on Abessinia, but in such a way that what I contributed is ignored. M. Rochet once told me, that when he became king of Abessinia he would make me minister of public worship : perhaps, if this was more than a joke, he may have disliked the presence of a European in the country who could not but disdain to be the minister of a rebel. The King of Shoa, too, no longer needed me, as what he had coveted from the English mission was now obtained; and besides it would not have been pleasant for him to be conscious of ·the presence of a European, who could observe and report on his breaches of the treaty with England. Under these circumstances the question arose, "What were we to do?" Isenberg and Mühleisen-Arnold resolved to proceed through Tigre to Gondar, and see whether nothing could be done in the west of Abessinia, since failure had attended our efforts in the east and south. On the other hand, I wished as in the year 1838, to betake myself

to the south, having heard that the Gallas, whose
conversion I had had at heart since the commencement of my residence in Shoa, extended as far as
the Equator. Yet I had many scruples respecting
the prosecution of missionary enterprise in the south,
especially as I had not received the sanction of the
London Committee of the Church Missionary Society; nor could I bring myself to take a final farewell of Abessinia before a last experiment had been
tried in the west. At Aden I resolved, therefore, to
proceed to Massowa to rejoin my colleagues, and
arrived there on the 14th of May 1843, and had
forthwith to receive the painful intelligence of the obstacles which had opposed themselves to their efforts
in Adowa. Our old enemy, Kidana Mariam, still
lived in Adowa, and laboured hard to influence Ubie
whose favourite he was against the Protestant missionaries, and not only to prevent them from
proceeding to Gondar and the Abuna, but to force
them to quit Tigre at once and to return to Massowa. I did not allow myself to be daunted by the
bad news which I had heard in Massowa; but proceeded with my wife through the Shoho land to the
frontier of Tigre, with a large supply of Amharic
and Æthiopic Bibles and testaments. On the way,
we had to submit to the probation of a severe trial;
for in the Shoho wilderness my beloved wife was
prematurely delivered of a little daughter, whom I
christened "Eneba," a tear. I had to bury the
dear child, for she lived only a few hours, under
a tree by the wayside, and her mourning mother

was obliged to prosecute her journey on the third day after her confinement, as the Shohos would not wait any longer, and there was no village in the neighbourhood where she could have enjoyed repose. We arrived safely at the frontier of Tigre, and busied ourselves distributing the Bibles, which were much sought after in the circumjacent villages of Hamassien, until we were joined by our friend Mühleisen-Arnold, and later by Isenberg; when we returned together to Massowa. The last attempt to work in Abessinia had also failed through the hostility of the priesthood of Adowa, led on beyond doubt by our European foes already mentioned. It is true the Abuna in Gondar had written to Ubie not to molest the Protestant missionaries, but they had already begun the return journey, when the Abuna's letter arrived. The Abuna's opposition to our enemies was, moreover, so feeble, and his intervention on our behalf so timid, that we could not reckon on him with certainty. Ubie worked so strenuously in the interest of Rome, that the Abuna could not prevail upon the Prince even to cherish the Abessinian church to which he belonged. It was therefore evident that the Protestant mission must entirely abandon Abessinia and seek elsewhere for a sphere of labour; and such was the result. Isenberg and Mühleisen-Arnold journeyed to Egypt, whence they were afterwards sent by the committee to the East Indies; but my wife and I returned to Aden, and thence, with the approbation of my superiors, undertook the voyage to the south-east of

Africa. In any case, the missionaries had the consolation of knowing that, during their last attempt in Abessinia, they had distributed nearly 2000 copies of the Scriptures, and from first to last, nearly 8000.

Having sought preparation for the long sea-voyage by prayer and meditation, I set sail with my wife from Aden on the 11th of November 1843, our destination being Zanzibar. After being nearly shipwrecked we landed at Aden again on the 15th, and sailed once more from it on the 23rd in another ship, the captain of which was a native of Mombaz, and knew the Suahili coast well. I could not but see that the disaster of the first voyage was under Providence made serviceable to me; for had I made the voyage with the Arab captain of the first ship, he would have sailed direct from Arabia to Zanzibar, after the manner of his countrymen, without running into any port, and I should have lost the opportunity of personally exploring the places on the coast from Mukdisha to Zanzibar.

Skirting the Arabian coast very slowly, partly because the winds were against us, partly because we were often becalmed, we arrived on the 5th of December at Makalla, and on the 13th at Sihut, whence we steered for the East-African coast in the direction of Socotra, and on the 18th sighted Cape Guardafui, the Ras Gerdaf of the Arabs. From this point to the Equator the coast is inhabited by the Somalis, who, as far as Mukdisha, are much dreaded, as they plunder the crews of shipwrecked vessels, and sell them for slaves into the interior.

The Somali coast from Cape Guardafui southwards, is designated by the Arabs "Dar Ajam" not "Ajan," as the maps wrongly have it—because no Arabic is spoken in it. So, too, they designate the Abessinian and Persian coasts; for the word "ajam," or "ayam," corresponds to the Greek "barbaros," applied to every person not a Greek. On the 23rd we passed the towns Mukdisha, the Magadoxo of the maps, and Marka, each of which has some 5000 inhabitants, who trade with the Galla countries in the interior, fetching from them chiefly gum, ivory, horses, slaves and hides. From Mukdisha, southward, the appearance of the coast improves; and you see, here and there, trees and bushes, which is not the case to the north, where mere sand, red earth, and rocks, offer themselves to the eye. It must be confessed that this barren and sultry coast is much healthier than that south of the Equator, where the vegetation is very rich, but the climate unhealthy, especially after the rainy season. Since 1847 the slave-trade is forbidden to the north of Barava, England having concluded a treaty with the Sultan Said-Said at Zanzibar, in virtue of which no slaves are to be exported beyond the tenth degree of south, and the second of north latitude; the traffic to be tolerated, however, within the twelve degrees of the Suahili coast. But in spite of this prohibition, on my second visit to Mukdisha in the year 1853, I saw twenty Arabian ships employed in smuggling slaves to Arabia.

On the 24th of December I visited Barava, an important town on the Suahili coast, and which was long in the possession of the Portuguese. The population amounts to something like 3000, among whom are many slaves brought from the interior and the Suahili coast. The people of Barava go northwards as far as Adari or Harrar, and make trading journeys also to the Galla tribes, Wardai, Korei, Rendille, Boren and Liban. On the other side of the territory of the Boren-Gallas is said to be a country named Gonsi, inhabited by Amhara, that is, by Christians. Whether this be Kambat or Wolamo, or whether it be some other Christian country of which I had heard nothing in Shoa, is uncertain. Ten days' journey to the north-west of Barawa lies the town of Bardera on the Jub, whence caravans proceed along the river to the important trading town of Ganana or Ganali. The district round Barava is composed of red sand and clay, turned to account in the manufacture of pottery; and journeys from here into the interior are made upon camels or asses. The people of this place grow cotton, Durra, pumpkins, &c., and provisions are cheap, a cow costing from three to five dollars, and a score of fowls a dollar; twenty raw hides are sold for thirteen dollars.

Respecting the river Jub, as it is called by the Arabs—the Somalis call it Govin, and the Suahilis Wumbu—I heard from the Barava chief Dera, that it is a branch of a great inland river from which the Osi and the Pangani take their rise. The Arabs believe that this great inland river is an arm of the

Nile, as I often heard them repeat along the Suahili coast. On the 25th of December we sailed past the mouth of the Jub, which colours the sea for the distance of a league with its reddish water; and the river is there but a few feet deep, so that it is only at high tide that boats of any size can run into it; but further up it is said to be deeper; whilst from the number of trees and bushes, the breadth of the mouth can scarcely be calculated. In the afternoon we anchored in the harbour of the island of Kiama, which lies a few hundred paces from the main-land, and is some eight leagues distant from the Jub. The people of Kiama are Suahilis and trade with the Gallas, who bring rhinoceros-horns, tusks of elephants, hippopotamus-hides, and cattle, receiving in Kiama clothes, copper-wire, beads, &c.; and here I saw and spoke to some Gallas. The thought that exactly on Christmas-day we had arrived at the Galla coast upheld and strengthened us, and we prayed fervently to the Lord that He would open up to us a way to convert these heathen whom we had journeyed to this distant shore to bring into His fold.

On the 28th of December we landed at Takaungu, as our captain had to return home with the ship in which we had come, and we were to proceed in a smaller one to Zanzibar. Accordingly we remained at Takaungu until the 3rd of January, 1844. The inhabitants were most hospitable to my wife and myself, giving us the only stone house in the village to lodge in. Takaungu is fruitful, and being beautifully situated, it forms one among many localities admirably suited for the residence of Europeans. The inhabitants of Takaungu complained to me that the English had left the Masrue in Mombaz in the lurch, and not protected them against the Imam of Muscat; of whom and his conduct to these people, I shall have to speak again. They inveighed bitterly against him for his treacherous behaviour to their chief men, averring that the English had done wrong in giving over the people of Mombaz to his rule, as they had voluntarily become the subjects of England, and been mildly governed by the English for three years. I was vexed to have to listen at my first arrival to such complaints, and could only reply that I had nothing to do with political matters, and recommend them to submit to the dispensations of Providence. At Takaungu I saw some Gallas, between whom and the people of the place there is friendly intercourse as they come at certain periods into the neighbourhood to sell ivory, cattle, &c.; and I found that these southern Gallas differed from those of the north in their political system, no less than in their religion, not worshiping the serpent, the Atetie, nor the Oglie, and knowing nothing of the Maremma (Virgin Mary), a proof that the northern Gallas have imbibed many notions from the Abessinians. But Kalija and Wato, priests and exorcists, exist among the southern as well as among the northern Gallas. In cruelty and inhumanity those of the south exceed the northern, murdering every stranger whom they meet by the way;

a characteristic which their wandering life contri-
butes to strengthen; however all the Gallas of the
south are not nomadic. I have not hitherto mentioned
that to the south of the Osi there is another important river, the Dana, flowing into the bay of Formosa,
called by the Gallas, Maro, and by the heathen
Pokomo tribes who dwell upon its banks, the
Pokomoni. Its mouth is not deep, and can only be
entered at high tide by boats of large size; but
inland the stream is said to have a depth of
from twelve to twenty feet. Along its banks dwell
Gallas, Pokomos, and other tribes who are not so
savage as the nomadic Gallas, being both agriculturists and traders. The Dana has its source
in the snow-mountain Kegnia, or Kenia, in the
north-west of Ukambani, where in the year 1851 I
drank of its waters as will afterwards be seen. On
the maps this river figures as the Quilimansi, a
name with which the natives are acquainted only in
so far as it designates a mountain-stream, or a mountain with streams.

At Takaungu I was told for the first time of the
heathen Wanika of whom I there saw several belonging to the tribe Kauma, and heard with great
interest that they were accessible to strangers,
were agriculturists and traders, and that a stranger
might travel among them without any special danger,
provided he were furnished with a guide and companion from the Suahilis of the coast. Here,
too, I met with the first mention of the country
Jagga in the interior, to the south-west of

Mombaz, as well as of the country of Usambara, and the inner African tribes of Uniamesi, in whose territory there is a great lake. In short I acquired during my residence in Takaungu a brief know-ledge of East-African geography and ethnography, as far as Mozambique and Madagascar. These geo-graphical data were, it is true, rather confused; but they were extremely useful as points of departure in subsequent journeys and inquiries. I could not help feeling that it was under the guidance of Providence that I had not been permitted to proceed at once to Zanzibar, but had been carried in the second ship to Takaungu. In Zanzibar I could not have learned, heard, or seen nearly so much; and my movements on the coast would have shaped themselves quite differently; nor would the establishment of the mission station have had Mombaz for its starting point.

On the 3rd of January 1844 I left the hospitable village of Takaungu in a small boat, called a "Daw" by the Suahilis, which is the smallest sea-going vessel. In it you are but a few feet above the water; but have the advantage of being able to sail over rocks and sand-banks, and always close to the shore. From Takaungu southward the coast is very low, as, indeed, it is almost continuously from the Jub to the Malindi, lying in general only from twenty to thirty feet above the sea, and stretching some leagues back into the interior, where there are chains of moun-tains, 800 to 1200 feet in height. The undercliff is, for the most part, in the hands of the Mohammedan

Suahilis, who cultivate rice, Indian corn, millet, cassia, red pepper, &c., but the higher regions are in the occupation of heathen tribes, likewise agriculturists. From Takaungu to the islands Wassin and Tanga extend the Wanika, who may number from 50,000 to 60,000, and are divided into twelve tribes. South from these are the Wasegechu, Washinsi, and Wasegua, and to the west of the Washinsi are the Wasamba, or Wasambara, who are governed by King Kmeri, or Kimeri. From Takaungu we reached the isle of Mombaz, which has a harbour capable of containing ships of a tolerably large size. This island is several leagues in circumference, but is only very partially cultivated; yet mangoes and cocoa-nuts, oranges and limes, and in parts, the cinnamon-tree, are indigenous, whilst wild swine, introduced by the Portuguese, abound. I soon found out that the people here were well acquainted with the English, and it was at once apparent that the governors of the Suahili coast were dependent on a ruler, who, as was the case with Said-Said, Sultan of Zanzibar or Imam of Muscat, was well affected towards Europeans, a disposition which of course was reflected by the conduct of his subordinates, as I experienced from the governor of the fortress, whose guest I was. The capital of the island contains from 8,000 to 10,000 inhabitants, who are mostly Suahilis; but there are also many Arabs, and some thirty or forty Banians, who have in their hands the chief trade of the place. There are houses of stone, but the majority are wooden huts. A tolerably large fortress commands

THE FORT OF MOMBAZ.

the harbour and the town, and is garrisoned by 400 Beluches, who are in the pay of the Sultan of Zanzibar. The fortress exhibits a Portuguese inscription, put up by Xeixas de Cabreira, the governor, in 1639, giving the date of 1635 as that of its erection, at which time Mombaz, as well as Malindi, was in the hands of the Portuguese, who were driven out of the island by Sheikh Sef, the Imam of Muscat. When Sef died the ancestors of Said-Said took possession of Muscat and the island of Zanzibar; while the Masrue family, which was of Persian origin, kept possession of Mombaz up to the year 1823, when they delivered it over to the English, fearing that it would otherwise fall into the hands of the Imam of Muscat. The Imam claimed it as having belonged to his forefathers, upon which the English withdrew, when he sent a fleet, bombarded the town, and brought it under his rule. Had England recognised the importance of the place, she would not have parted with it so easily; but the trade with the Suahili coast had not then received its present development, and she wished to oblige the Imam who was devoted to her, and whom she recognised as ruler of the whole coast, from Mukdisha to Mozambique, in order to prevent foreign powers from taking up a position on the East-African coast. The unhealthy climate of the place and of the coast in general, may also have made her less disposed to retain the island; so she contented herself with the stipulations respecting the slave-trade already alluded to. The people of Mombaz trade with the Wanika and Wakamba of the surrounding country, and sometimes their caravans go even as far as the mountain-land of Jagga, bringing thence chiefly ivory and slaves. The Wanika tribes are nominally dependent upon Mombaz, and are governed by four Suahili sheikhs who live in Mombaz; but the connection between the town and these tribes is extremely loose and undefined; rendered more so, indeed, by the barbarous conduct of the people of Mombaz towards these heathen tribes, especially in time of famine, when they purchase the children of the Wanika, or make off with them as slaves in return for provisions furnished to the parents. Things will never progress on this coast so long as the Arabian rule is maintained in its present state, as it not only makes no improvements, but often destroys what good has descended from the olden time.

On the 4th of January we quitted the island of Mombaz, which is only a few hundred yards distant from the main-land, and next day reached the little island of Tanga, where there was an abundance of cocoa-nut trees, rice plantations, beans, red pepper, millet, bananas, oranges, limes, pine-apples, figs, &c. I could not refrain from the thought that this spot was well suited for a preliminary missionary station, whence progress might ·be made into the interior; but the reflection that my missionary efforts must begin with the Gallas nipped that idea in the bud. On the 6th, we reached the mouth of the Pangani river, which has its main source in the snow mountain Kilimanjaro, in Jagga, recalling to us

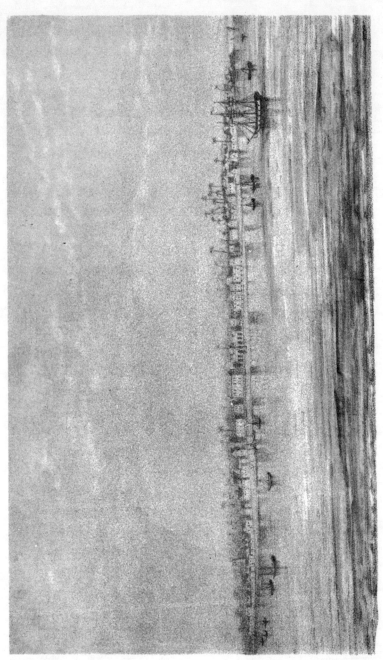

ZANZIBAR.

the burning of his ship by Vasco de Gama, in the Bay
of Tangata, into which it flows, when after doubling
the Cape in 1497, his crew fell a prey to disease on
the east coast of Africa on his return from Calicut.
To the south of the Pangani is the territory of the
heathen Wasegua tribes, the great centre of the slave
trade. The Arabs on the island of Zanzibar come
here and promise the Wasegua chiefs a number of
muskets, with powder and shot, for a certain number
of slaves; so when a chief has entered into the contract he suddenly falls upon a hostile village, sets
it on fire, carries off the inhabitants, and thus is
enabled to fulfil the terms of the agreement. The
Waseguas being Kofar, *i. e.*, unbelievers, the Moslems
think that they are acting mercifully in selling them
into slavery, in which state they must become
Mohammedans. The river Pangani, I may add, is
at its mouth some hundred and fifty yards broad,
from twelve to fifteen feet deep, and is navigable
into the interior for small boats, for several days'
journey. From its mouth there is a good view of
the mountain-land Usambara, which I visited in the
years 1848 and 1852, as will be noticed hereafter.

At two in the afternoon of the 7th of January we
dropped anchor in the safe and spacious harbour of
the capital of the island of Zanzibar, where we were
to repose for a time, after our long and fatiguing
voyage, while I deliberated on my further plans
and consulted my friends respecting them. We
were hospitably received by Major Hamerton, the
English consul, and until we could erect a dwell-

ing we lived in the house of Mr. Waters, the American consul, who was a zealous friend to the mission. He wished me to remain in Zanzibar, preaching on Sundays to its few Europeans; working amongst the Banians from India, of whom there are seven hundred in Zanzibar; founding schools for the instruction of the native Suahilis and Arabs; and preparing books in the languages of the main-land for future missionaries; but I could not abandon my original design of founding a mission in the Galla land, which, so far as I know at present, extends to the fourth degree of south latitude. I felt that their conversion would produce the greatest impression on the whole of Eastern Africa, although it might be more difficult to found missions among them than among the Wanika, Wakamba, and Waseguas. To my mind Ormania is the Germany of Africa. If the Gallas were not gathered into the Christian Church, it seemed to me they would fall into Islamism, (which has made great progress among them on the borders of Abessinia) and must in that case form a strong bulwark against the introduction of Christianity and true morality into Africa; for the Gallas when once they have embraced it hold very firmly to Islamism, as is seen in the case of the Wollos.

On the second day after my arrival in Zanzibar I was presented by the English Consul to the Sultan Said-Said, commonly called by Europeans by his other title, the Imam of Muscat. His palace lies outside the city, and its exterior reminds the visitor of a German or Swiss manufactory. When the consul appeared with me at the entrance of the palace, the Sultan accompanied by one of his sons and several grandees came forth to meet us, displaying a condescension and courtesy which I had not before met with at the hands of any oriental ruler. He conducted us into the audience-chamber, which is pretty large and paved with marble slabs; American chairs lined the walls, and a stately chandelier hung in the middle of the room. The Sultan bade us be seated, and I described to him in Arabic, his native language, my Abessinian adventures, and plans for converting the Gallas. He listened with attention and promised every assistance, at the same time pointing out the dangers to which I might be exposed. Although advanced in years he looked very well, and was most friendly and communicative. Sultan Said-Said ascended the throne in 1807, and lived at Muscat up to the year 1840, when he removed the seat of government to Zanzibar, chiefly on account of its trade. He was early brought into connection with the English, who in 1819 helped him against the fanatical Wahabis, in Arabia, and the pirates of its waters; hence his devotion to that people. He claims in Arabia the whole coast from Aden to Muscat, and from Muscat to the Persian Gulf, with its islands; and, in Africa, asserts supremacy over the coast from Cape Guardafui to Cape Delgado, in the proximity of the Portuguese possessions of Mozambique. Hitherto no foreign power has contested the right to these enormous possessions; whilst the Arabs and Africans submit to his nominal pretensions, so long as their own old arrangements are not too stringently interfered with. They receive the Sultan's governors and pay the dues which he levies from their ports; but beyond that Said-Said seems to have no hope of their further obedience and subjection.

The island of Zanzibar lies under the 6th degree of south latitude, is from six to seven leagues distant from the main-land, and has a length of six to seven leagues from north to south, and a breadth of about six. The climate is not so unhealthy as on the main-land; but every one who arrives for the first time must, sooner or later, submit to a period of often dangerous fever. The capital, which lies, $6°\ 10''$ south on the western shore, is somewhat healthier than the interior. The population of the island amounts to about 100,000, the greater number of whom live in the capital. The majority are Suahilis, the richer and more influential classes are Arabs, and about twenty Europeans mostly engaged in trade have established themselves here. The chief European exports from Zanzibar are ivory, copal-gum, cloves, hides, cocoa-nuts and cocoa-oil, semsem (an oil plant), aloes, &c. The imports consist mainly of a white calico, called by the natives Americano, glass beads of every kind, fire-arms, brass and copper· wire, glass and pottery, cutlery, swords, and all articles suitable for the markets of uncivilized nations. Zanzibar is completely Mohammedan with the exception of the

Banians from India and the Europeans. On the whole it will be not going far wrong to estimate the Moslem population of the Suahili coast, including that of Zanzibar, at half a million. All religions are, however, tolerated; and the intercourse of the Mohammedans with the heathen tribes, their general prosperity, and other causes, hold in check the usual fanaticism of the Arabs.

CHAPTER IX.

MOMBAZ—EXCURSIONS ON THE MAIN-LAND.

Lamu—Mombaz—Study of the native languages—Sea trip—Hindu
and Mohammedan fellow passengers—Astronomy of the Koran—
Translation of the Bible into Suahili—Death of the author's
wife and daughter—Visions of missionary enterprise—Excursion
to Old Rabbai—Makarunge—The houses of the Wanika—Kamba
and its chief—The Mohammedans and their proselytism—The
animal and vegetable worlds: elephants and ivory—Wanika
Atheism—Abdallah and his friendship—A Wakamba village—
Relations of the Wanika and Wakamba—Characteristics of the
Wakamba—Preaching in a Wanika village; failure and its
causes—Rabbai Mpia, its situation and suitability for a missionary station—Missionary interview with the elders of the village—First sight of the snow-mountain Kadiaro—The ensuing
twelvemonth, voyages, journeys, and illnesses—Arrival of Rebmann—Visit to Rabbai Mpia and selection of it for a missionary
station—The chiefs—Our removal to Rabbai Mpia—Fever and
house-building difficulties—Public worship and discouragements
—The Wanika.

I REMAINED in Zanzibar from the 7th of January to
the beginning of March 1844, hearing, seeing, and
learning much. On Sundays I preached to the
English and American residents, and during the
whole period of my stay cultivated the acquaintance of Arabs, Banians, and Suahilis, gathering from
them information respecting the coast and the interior. At the period named I resolved to leave my

dear wife at Zanzibar, and to proceed to the island of Lamu, and thence to penetrate among the Gallas and found a missionary station. I took with me a letter of recommendation from Sultan Said-Said addressed to the governors of the coast, and couched in the following terms:—" This comes from Said-Said Sultan; greeting all our subjects, friends, and governors. This letter is written in behalf of Dr. Krapf, the German, a good man who wishes to convert the world to God. Behave well to him, and be everywhere serviceable to him." We touched at the island of Pemba, which lies five degrees south of the Equator, where the governor received me kindly, and warned me not to proceed to Lamu, as now the Kus, the south wind, was beginning to blow and would prevent my returning to Zanzibar before the end of November. He asked me many questions concerning the politics and religion of Europe, and expressed a wish for an Arabic Bible. This I sent him afterwards through Mr. Waters, the only European who before my arrival had given Bibles and tracts to the natives. In accordance with the advice of the friendly governor I gave up the idea of proceeding to Lamu, but wished before returning to Zanzibar to make a little sea trip along the coast, and accordingly arranged with a skipper for a passage to Tanga. The voyage was a very slow one through the ignorance and unskilfulness of the captain and the laziness and indifference of the crew, who were slaves and would not obey him. The more he rated them, the more they laughed at

him. It is very sad to see how obstructively slavery
influences all the activity of the natives, and so long
as that evil remains in those countries, there is
no hope of improving their social condition. There
slaves must do everything; they till the fields,
conduct trade, sail vessels, and bring up the children
of the house; while the free people eat, drink, and
are idle, run into the mosques to pray, or enjoy
themselves with their many wives. No wonder that
a curse rests on all they undertake. The slaves perform whatever they have to do under compulsion,
lazily, unwillingly, and mechanically. On the 11th
of March I arrived at Tanga. The hut which the
friendly governor gave me for a lodging was soon
surrounded by hundreds of men, but alas! I could
not speak to them not having then mastered the
Suahili language.

On the 13th of March I arrived at Mombaz,
where I was hospitably received by the governor of
the city, Ali ben Nasser, who had been twice in
London as representative of the Sultan of Zanzibar, on
a political mission to the English government. In
the streets of Mombaz I saw some heathen Wanika,
who had come from the neighbouring mountains.
The inhabitants of Mombaz, too, visited me in great
numbers and were very friendly. Then, all at
once, the thought came upon me that Mombaz
would be best suited for the establishment of a missionary station, especially as the Gallas are to be
met with a few days' journey to the north of it,
when they go to the market of Emberria, a village

of the Wanika. The longer I remained in Mombaz, the more evident it became to me that it seemed the will of God to make the Gallas acquainted with the Gospel through the Wanika; and that, therefore, the first missionary station on this coast should be established among the Wanika whom I could easily reach from Mombaz. The Imam was at war with Patta, so that I had to forego the intention of establishing myself at Lamu. I was strengthened in my growing conviction by the friendliness of the people and officials of Mombaz towards Europeans, especially the English; by the proximity of this place to the neighbouring pagan tribes, a proximity so close that a missionary can visit their villages during the day and return to Mombaz at night; and by its healthiness and the conveniences which it offered in the way of living and residence. I resolved, therefore, to return to Zanzibar for my dear wife, and then to take up my abode in Mombaz, studying the Suahili language, making excursions among the pagan Wanika, and becoming acquainted with the condition of the interior, where I intended to preach the Gospel as soon as I was master of the language.

After I had engaged a teacher of the Suahili and Kinika languages I quitted Mombaz on the 18th of March, some of my fellow-passengers being natives of Arabia and India, and among them a Hindu of the Rajpoot caste who had attended a missionary school at Bombay. The acquaintance of this person convinced me that a great influence is exerted on

the characters of heathens by attendance at our
schools, even although it may last but a short time
and they do not at once become Christian. When
I spoke to him about the idol-worship of the Indians
he said: " There is only one Creator of heaven and
earth, who is everywhere present, and sees and knows
everything, even the thoughts of the human heart."
An Arab chief from Lamu who saw me reading the
Psalms asked me for the book, and being . much
pleased with it begged for a complete Bible.
Arabic tracts would have been eagerly welcomed by
these people, especially such as treat of geography
and history. When I explained to a Mohammedan
sheikh from Lamu the round shape of the earth and
its motion round the sun, he became very indignant,
and warned the passengers against doctrines like
these, which contradicted the Koran. The Hindu
already referred to, who had learned something of
geography at Bombay, took my part and said to the
sheikh: " The Frank can prove his statements, but
your only confutation of them is that they contradict
the Koran." The sheikh then turned to the passengers and treated them to some of the fables of Mohammedan cosmography and geography.

I reached Zanzibar on the 24th of March, and
returned to Mombaz with my wife at the beginning of May, where I had to put up with several personal annoyances more or less trying. My
greatest difficulty, however, lay in my want of
a knowledge of the Suahili language, and in the
absence of any help in the study, neither a gram-

mar nor a dictionary of it having yet been compiled by any European. With the aid of Arabic,
I surmounted this hinderance by degrees; but found
in it, however, peculiarities which at first gave me
immense trouble, but which also were converted into
a source of delight, when I was at length able to
cry " Eureka !" Now that I had settled down at
Mombaz engaged in the study of the Suahili and
Kinika languages, I sought the acquaintance of
the Wanika chiefs who came to the island. On the
8th of June, 1844, I began the translation of the
First Book of Moses with the aid of Sheikh Ali
Ben, Mueddin of Barava, who was the Kadi (Judge)
of Mombaz. I always considered this day as one of
the most important of my life; but scarcely had I
commenced this important work, and began to con-
gratulate myself on the progress of my missionary
labours, when myself and family were subjected to
a very severe trial. The rainy season at Mombaz
had been one of unusual severity, and the native
inhabitants had been afflicted by all sorts of sickness,
especially with fever and headache. On the 1st of
July I was attacked by the fever ; on the 4th I was
somewhat better again, but the next day, my wife
was attacked by it severely, and the attack was all the
more serious that she was every day expecting her
confinement, which happened on the 6th, when she
gave birth to a healthy daughter. But on the 9th
of July after midnight she became delirious, and
when she recovered her senses was fully convinced
that she would soon be removed from my side. So

strong was this conviction that she took farewell of
me and the servants in touching accents, especially recommending them (they were Mohammedans) to place their trust in Christ, not in Mohammed, as neither in life nor death could he bestow
help, whereas Christ, the Son of God, gave her
now indescribable peace.   One of her last and most
pressing requests was that I should not praise her
in my report, but merely say to her friends at home
that the Saviour had been merciful to her as to a
poor sinner.   In these trying moments I lay on
my couch beside her death-bed, so prostrated by
fever that only with the greatest effort could I rise
up to convince myself that she was really dead.
Lying in agony I could not rightly, at the moment,
estimate the extent of this great loss.   She was buried opposite to Mombaz on the main-land, in the presence of the Governor, the Kadi, and some Suahilis,
by the way-side leading into the Wanika territory.
Afterwards Mr. Waters and his friends in Bombay
erected a stone monument over the grave, so that it
might always remind the wandering Suahilis and
Wanika, that here rested a Christian woman who
had left father, mother, and home, to labour for the
salvation of Africa.   It was only with great exertion
that I managed to be present at the funeral, and had
scarcely returned home when symptoms of the malady
were shown by the dear child.   They became fatal
on the 15th, and I was obliged by the climate to
conduct this second victim of the king of terrors to
the grave of my beloved Rosine as soon as possible.

After several weeks my health was restored and
I betook myself with fresh zeal to the study of
Suahili, and planned frequent excursions to the
Wanika-land. In those days in my zeal for the
conversion of Africa I used to calculate how many
missionaries and how much money would be required
to connect Eastern and Western Africa by a chain
of missionary stations.* I estimated at some 900
leagues the distance from Mombaz to the river
Gabun in Western Africa, where the Americans,
before the occupation of the French, had founded a

* The reader may like to be informed, that since this was written,
I have been appointed the secretary of a special committee (connected with the Missionary Institution at Chrishona, near Bâsel)
for the purpose of locating twelve mission-stations along the banks
of the Nile from Alexandria to Gondar, the capital of Abessinia,
whence other stations will be hereafter established toward the south,
east, and west of Africa, as it shall please Providence to show the way,
and point out the requisite means. This line of twelve stations will
be termed the "Apostles' Street," as each station, which is to be fifty
leagues distant from the other, will be called by the name of an
apostle—for instance, the station at Alexandria will be named that
of St. Matthew; the station at Cairo, of St. Mark; at Assuan, St.
Luke; and so on. Thus the African continental mission chain will
be started from the north instead of from east to west, as I had
originally contemplated. I may also remark, that a Christian lady
in England has on learning of this scheme kindly promised the gift
of £100 for every station, in each case of its actual commencement; that
his Majesty the King of Würtemberg has graciously released from
military service the first missionary, whom (in connection with two
others) the committee have chosen to commence the first station at
Cairo. The missionaries are requested, as much as their direct
missionary labour will allow, to devote themselves to agricultural
and commercial pursuits, to support themselves in a measure, and to
enable the committee to establish the whole mission chain within the
shortest period of time. Knowing what a glorious field this will

mission and laboured successfully. Now, if stations with four missionaries were established at intervals of 100 leagues, nine stations and thirty-six missionaries would be needed, probably at an annual expense of from £4000 to £5000. If every year progress were made both from west and east, I calculated that the chain of missions would be completed in from four to five years. I thought then of Dafeta (in Jagga) as the locality where the first eastern station in the interior should be established. After I had forgotten these ideas, they were re-awakened in the years 1849 and 1850 during my visit to England, when the committee listened attentively to my statements on this subject, and sought to realize them by strengthening the East-African mission. I had already, too, begun to think that England might profitably establish on the east coast a colony for liberated slaves like Sierra Leone on the western coast, and that they might be employed as aids in the conversion of the Inner-African races. For such a colony, Malindi, or Mombaz and its environs, would be the best site. If more attention were given to the formation of a chain of such missions through Africa, the fall of slavery and of the slave-trade with America and Arabia would be quickly and thoroughly effected. Till Christianity becomes the ruling faith in Africa, however great and noble may be the exertions of the Government of Great Britain, open, I would urge all Christian friends of Africa to give effectual aid to this important undertaking, which aims at bringing about the scriptural promise, Psalm lxviii. 31: "Ethiopia shall soon stretch out her hands unto God."

and however liberal its expenditure in sending out
squadrons to intercept slave-ships, the slave-trade
will continue to flourish.   Christianity and civilization ever go hand in hand; brother will not sell
brother; and when the colour of a man's skin no
longer excludes him from the office of an evangelist,
the traffic in slaves will have had its knell.   A black
bishop and black clergy of the Protestant Church
may, ere long, become a necessity in the civilization
of Africa.

On the 19th of August, I made an excursion to
the village Rabbai Ku, Great Rabbai, or Old
Rabbai, partly to see whether the locality was
suited for a missionary station.   When we landed
at four in the afternoon I was received by a crowd
of heathen Wanika, who lifted me out of the
boat and bore me on their shoulders to the land
with singing, dancing, brandishing of arrows, and
every other possible mode of rejoicing.   Ascending
from the shore across a grassy soil we arrived at a
wood of lofty trees.   The narrow footpath in the
wood led to three entrances in a triple palisade which
encircled the village ; which with its wretched cone-
shaped huts lies quite in the wood.   We saw only two
men, who beat upon great drums in honour of the
visit, and I was sorry not to have seen the chief and
people of the village.   In the evening I returned
to the house of Abdalla-Ben-Pisila, who gave me
shelter for the night, the chief sending a message
that he would visit me early in the morning, to
which I replied that my departure would be early

on account of the tide. The Wanika had made a
favourable impression on me; for they were both
quick and well behaved, but wore extremely little
in the way of clothes, even the women not being
sufficiently clad; yet on leaving Rabbai I was not
quite convinced of its suitability for a missionary
station.

On the 3rd of September I left Mombaz with a
guide, and after a sea-trip of a couple of hours or
so we anchored before the hamlet of Makarunge,
where I was very kindly received by the Mohammedan Sheikh, Ibrahim, who offered me a bed for
the night and sent off a messenger to the neighbouring Wanika, to announce the arrival of a
Msungu, or European. With sunrise I left Makarunge accompanied by the sheikh, and towards
noon reached the outermost gate of the village
of Ribe, where we were to await the chiefs and
their retinue.   They arrived, welcomed me, and
conducted us through three entrances in the palisades
into the village, amid cries of rejoicing, dancing, and
brandishing of swords and bows.   In the village the noise was still greater as young and old,
men and women, streamed forth to pay the European
the same honours which are paid to a great man
from Mombaz, when he visits the Wanika; whenever
any one only stood and looked on, he was driven
by the chiefs into the crowd, to dance and shriek
with his neighbours.   As I entered the house of the
first chief the people, especially the younger ones,
cleared the way.   The houses of the Wanika look

like haycocks in Europe. Stakes are thrust into
the ground, and from top to bottom there is a complete covering of grass, so that wind and light
cannot enter; in the centre there is a thick stake,
which supports and strengthens the whole structure.
Through the low door you can only enter by stoop-
ing very much; and if you wish for light a fire must
be kindled. At night, the inhabitants of the hut
lie round the fire on cow-hides, and do not trouble
themselves about the smoke, the heat, and ver-
min, such as fleas, lice, and bugs, being only afraid
of serpents. These huts stand so close together,
that when one takes fire, the whole village is soon
in flames. Lofty cocoa-palms surround them and
serve, so to speak, as their immediate wine cellars,
whence the Wanika fetch their favourite drink, the
Uji (in Suahili, Tembo) and cocoa-nuts. In the
trees they hew a kind of steps by which they can
ascend quickly and readily.

Whilst I remained in the hut of the chief the
crowd dispersed, only the elders and the boys remaining, who behaved decorously and respectfully.
Some looked very intelligent, had clear complexions,
and were not so black and ugly as the Wanika,
whom I had seen at Takaungu. When I declared to the chiefs that I was not a soldier, nor
a merchant who had come there to trade, but
a Christian teacher who wished to instruct the
Wanika and the Galla in the true knowledge of
God, they looked at me with something of a
stupefied expression, and could not rightly under-

stand, but assured me of their friendly disposition.
They gave me some cocoa-nuts, after which I went
out and inspected the village, estimating the population at about 600 to 700 souls. After I had
taken leave of the elders of the village of Ribe,
and of Sheikh Ibrahim, who was returning home,
I journeyed further eastward on the chain of hills,
and on the way saw some fine fields of rice and
maize; and when I had gone some little distance I
was met by the chief of Kambe and his people,
come out to escort me into the village. The chief
had on his holiday clothes, and ostrich feathers on his
head. In shaking hands he first grasped my hand
and pressed his thumb against mine, as is the custom of the Wanika on such occasions; he was
stately, but received and treated me very respectfully, speaking a little Galla; but the tumult of the
joyful reception given was still noisier in the village of Kambe than in Ribe. I soon formed the
idea that this large village was very suitable
for a missionary station. I did not, however,
remain long in it being desirous of spending the
night in the house of my guide who had a plantation in the village of Magombani, which lies at
the foot of the mountain Jibana, and is inhabited by Mohammedans, who here have a monopoly
of the copal-gum trade, cultivate rice and maize,
and out of the noble forest-trees get planking for
ships, which they sell to the Arab ship-builders.
These people craftily possess themselves by degrees of the lowlands of the Wanika, and con-

structing small villages, here and there, along the mountain range, people them with their slaves, gain over the Wanika by trifling presents, and purchase their produce very cheaply. In the course of time new settlers arrive and bring a sheikh, who deals with the religious wants of the heathen. Thus they combine missionary-work with trading speculations, and when soft words are of no avail they use force, or try to excite one tribe against another, so that they may be called on to act as mediators. In times of famine, which often occur, many Wanika are glad to become Mohammedans in order to save themselves from starvation; but throw off their new creed as soon as they have enough to eat. From this it may be seen how religion, politics, and trade are combined in the case of the followers of Mahomet.

From Magombani I had to continue the ascent a league and a half, until I reached the village Jibana. The road was very steep and rough, and led through woods of sumach, the copal-tree, which reached a height of from sixty to seventy feet, with thin and small leaves and a white bark. I saw many trees with incisions in them made by the natives, that the sap might flow to the ground and crystallize by mixing with the earth, and the Mohammedans make yearly a great deal of money by this valuable varnish, which is sent to India and Europe. There are few wild beasts in these woods, but they abound with beautiful birds. There are said to be elephants in the Galla land, in the neighbourhood of Emberria; but in the Wanika territories there are no longer any of these animals to be found, as they recede more and more into the large forests, and to the rivers of the interior, owing to their being so much molested since European commerce with Zanzibar has produced so great a demand for ivory. If it be true that yearly about 6000 elephants' tusks are brought to the Suahili coast, it can easily be understood how quickly these animals diminish, and why they recede ever further into the interior of Africa.

On the 7th of September I arrived again at Mombaz, being on the whole well pleased with my journey, having only to regret that the Wanika villages were so remote from the bay, as in consequence many difficulties must arise for the transport of baggage to the missionary station.   Most of all, however, I was grieved in witnessing the drunkenness and sensuality, the dulness and indifference, which I had observed among the Wanika ; the chief of Kambe said openly, " There is no God since he is not to be seen.   The Wanika need trouble themselves about nothing except Tembo (cocoa-wine), corn, rice, Indian corn (Mahindi), and clothes ;—these are their heaven.   The Watsumba" (Mohammedans)he added, "were fools to pray and fast so much."   Meanwhile, with the view of settling down among the Wanika I remained in Mombaz, prosecuting with great zeal the study of the Suahili language, into which by degrees I translated the whole of the New Testament, and composing a short grammar and a dictionary, continuing likewise my geographical and

ethnographical studies in the certain conviction
that the time would come when Eastern Africa, too,
would be drawn into European intercourse, and
these introductory studies would be made available,
even if for the present no great missionary result
were to be attained.

In my next excursion I derived great advantage
from the acquaintance of Abdalla Ben-Pisila, whose
devotion I had secured by a loan of ten dollars,
which rescued him from prison in Mombaz.   He
offered voluntarily to accompany me to the Wanika and Wakamba with whom he was a great
favourite, having received from the chiefs of Old
Rabbai a piece of ground by the creek, where he
had settled down to traffic with both these tribes.
The friendship of such a man was of great consequence for the commencement of a mission, and
I gladly accepted his invitation to make a temporary
home of his house in the vicinity of Great Rabbai.
On the 30th of January 1845 I set out in Abdalla's
company from his plantation for Endila, to make
the acquaintance of the Wakamba of whom I had
heard much in Mombaz.   After a three hours' walk
we reached the village of Endila, which consists of
only some eight or ten huts.   The elders were sitting under a tree, and I felt rather strange on behold-
ing these naked savages, who said scarcely anything when I appeared, and did not even stand up,
but looked sadly and gloomily on the ground, often
gazing at me as if I were a higher being.   The
chief went at last into his hut and fetched a bowl of

milk, mixed with blood as I afterwards found; for they believe that thus taken, blood helps to nourish their natural strength. Like most savages they are very fond of ornaments, especially of beads and copper wire. Their legs and arms, necks and hair, were covered with white and blue beads, which in combination with their nudity gave them a striking and singular appearance; for many of the men were perfectly naked, whilst others wore a mere rag in imitation of the fig-leaf of sculptors, and even the women had a very scant covering below the waist, being otherwise completely naked from head to foot. Behind, a kind of leather caudal appendage was worn, fastened round the loins with a thong. No wonder then that people say "there are people with tails in the interior of Africa!" In general, the Wakamba appear to be a finer and more powerful race than the Wanika, but their huts are more wretched than theirs. The Wakamba in the vicinity of the coast are immigrants who since the great famine of 1836 have settled down on the territory of the Wanika, being driven by hunger from the interior and receiving permission from the original possessors of the land to pasture their cattle on the grassy plains. By degrees, they acquired wealth by the breeding of cattle, and the ivory trade with the interior, and soon began to till the ground.

The Wanika liked them at first, because they derived many advantages from their presence; but the Wakamba threatened to take the upper hand and broils and feuds arose. These were

always however amicably settled, as the Wakamba accustomed to the cocoa-wine and other
luxuries of the coast did not care to return to their
own country in the interior, and the Wanika imbibed
too great a liking for their cows, sheep, &c. to let
them depart. For all this the Wakamba and the
Wanika do not in a general way blend with each
other, but retain each their aboriginal habits. The
Wakamba do not intermarry with the Wanika, yet
the intercourse of the former with the coast has
produced changes among them. Thus, for instance,
the Wakamba of the interior do not bury their dead,
but throw them into fields or woods and cover them
with stones and grass, yet those on the coast allow
the dead to be buried by the Wanika, who make the
grave, and charge a cow for their trouble. The Wakamba, too, put on a little clothing when they go
to Mombaz, or to a Wanika village. But with a
little good they have likewise learned from the
Wanika much that is bad. They are ardently fond
of Tembo (cocoa-wine), and as they have the means
of indulgence they go to still greater lengths than
their teachers. With their carousals they combine
dancing, which they have learned from the Wanika.
Uganga and Utawi, too (exorcism and incantation),
they have adopted from the Wanika and Watsumba
(Suahilis). No less have these latter tribes acquired
much that is bad from the former, particularly the
habit of going naked, at least when not observed
by the inhabitants of the country, especially on
journeys.

The Wakamba go in caravans of from 200 to 300 persons into the interior to fetch ivory, and form in a general way the commercial medium between the coast and the interior, into which they journey a distance of from 200 to 250 leagues. I therefore regarded this people as an important element in relation to future missionary designs in Eastern Africa. On these journeys the Wakamba are often attacked by the tribes of the interior, especially by the Galla, who, however, are as often stoutly repelled and beaten. As with most East-African tribes circumcision is prevalent with the Wakamba. Their language belongs to the great South-African division,* extending from the Equator to the Kaffers in South Africa, and which I have named the Orphno-Hamitic (dark-brown Hamitic, as distinguished from the negro Hamitic). The Wakamba live chiefly on milk and animal food, and cultivate maize, are not nomads, but have fixed dwelling-places. I may observe, by the way, that the prefix " wa" denotes the concrete plurality of a tribe or race, while the prefix "m," or " mu," denotes the singular, and " u" the tribe or race in the abstract. Thus, "Wakamba" means " the Wakamba race;" " Mkamba," " one of the Wakamba;" "Ukamba," or " Ukambani," the land of the Wakamba; " Wanika," the Wanika; " Mnika," one of the tribe; and " Unika," the domain of the Wanika.

From Endila I wended my way towards Old Rab-

---

* For much curious information on the languages of South Africa, the reader is referred to the introduction and notes to Sir George Grey's valuable catalogue, published by Trübner and Co.

bai by a route hitherto unknown to me. On entering
the first gate I saw a few huts from three to four
feet high, and on asking for what purpose they
served, was told that this was the Jumba ja Mulungu
—that is, the house of Mulungu, which stands in the
front of every village, and where the Wanika perform
religious services, sacrifice, exorcise evil spirits, and
where, too, they lay whatever they do not wish to
bring into the village, fancying that it is secure in
that sanctuary and will not be stolen; and the graves
of the Wanika are generally in the vicinity of
this place, and there, too, the living eat, drink, and
dance at burials and on other occasions. Over
the last gate of the village, I saw a cocoa-nut
hanging, an Uganga (a charm) which at the instance of the Waganga (magicians) was hung up,
that the cocoa-nuts might not be stolen while the
people were away on their plantations. This charm
is supposed to be effectual in keeping thieves and
robbers at a distance from the trees and the village,
and many Wanika suspend a similar Uganga before
the doors of their huts; it is a kind of " cave canem;"
for nobody dares to enter so long as it is not removed.

When I had arrived at Abdallah's I received a
visit from the elders of Rabbai, to whom I explained
that I was neither a soldier nor a merchant, nor an
official employed by the Arabian or English governments, nor a traveller, nor a Mganga nor Mtawi,
physician, exorcist, or enchanter; but was a
teacher, a book-man, who wished to show the Wanika, the Wakamba, the Galla, and even the Wat-

sumba (Mohammedans) the right way to salvation in
the world to come, and was answered, "Our land,
our trees, houses, our sons and daughters, are all
thine." How far they kept their word the sequel will
show. The next morning I sailed back to Mombaz.

The ensuing few weeks were spent partly in
excursions, partly at my residence in Mombaz. On
the 17th of March I made an excursion to Likoni
and some villages to the south of it. It happened to
be a market-day in the place and the Wanika
women were purchasing meat from a Mohammedan,
who had slaughtered a cow. As the people paid no
great attention to my words respecting eternity
and the life to come, I went into another hamlet
further south where the whole population were
dancing round a Mohammedan, who was beating a
drum, and wished to work Uganga (magic). When
they saw me they became suddenly silent, and young
and old listened to the discourse. But, after a time,
one after another slipped away until only a few men
and women remained. Perhaps they did not rightly
understand my Suahili, or perhaps I failed to express myself with sufficient imagery, and spoke too
plainly; for abstract notions are not understood by
savages, and everything must be expressed in tropes
and figures, and then rendered into the intelligible
language of daily life. The Wanika, and many
other East-African tribes, have a custom of repeating the last words of the speaker, or at least of
uttering an assenting sound. It is a kind of wild
response, which is certainly troublesome to Euro-

peans, but has its advantage, and shows him whether he is understood or not.   After I had spoken of the love of God to man in sending His only begotten Son into the world, in my address, I asked the chief of the place to show me the way to the scattered villages.   He was quite ready to do so, but warned me not to visit the village Yumbo, because the Wanika were celebrating their Ugnaro there.   This is a horrible sport, practised from time to time by the young people when they have reached a certain age.   They smear the body, especially the face, with white and grey earth, so that they cannot be recognised, being also almost in a complete state of nudity; upon which they remain in the woods until they have killed a man, after which they wash themselves and return home, where they then feast and carouse to their hearts' content.   It is not therefore advisable to journey at such times through these places, as solitary travellers, especially slaves, are their favourite prey.   A wise government in Mombaz would long ago have suppressed this abomination.   Before quitting the scene I may add, another reason for the want of attention of the people to my address, that they mistook me for a Mohammedan, not having as yet become acquainted with any other religion; and that they are very hostile to Mohammedanism; as also that their drunkenness and materialism have completely blunted their perception of everything connected with spiritual religion.

On the 25th of March I made an excursion from

Abdallah's plantation to Rabbai Mpia (New or Little Rabbai) a village consisting of some twenty to twenty-five huts. The sun was very hot when we left the plantation, but the sky presently clouded over, and a heavy thunderstorm followed soon after. At first our way lay through a wood, upwards, by means of the bed of a mountain stream, then along a well-trodden footpath, to the right and left of which the ground was covered by thorn-bushes and tall grass; till having ascended for several hundred yards, we came to the hill itself on which the village of New Rabbai is built, and where the more abrupt ascent really began; for the village, with the cocoa-nut wood in which it stands, seemed to lie straight up above our heads, so steep was the rock which we had to mount upwards and upwards till we found ourselves in the cocoa-nut wood in which Rabbai Mpia lies. Before the rain came on we had found shelter in a hut, and it was a favourable circumstance that it rained just when the white man entered the village for the first time. The Wanika imagined that it was my foot which brought the welcome rain; and, against my wishes, for I would never turn superstition to account, Abdallah strengthened them in that conviction. Eastward there was a magnificent view of the sea, of Mombaz, and the level country; and to the north and west stretched far away the plains of the Wanika and the Wakamba; whilst to the south was wood connecting this peninsular hill, as it were, with the level country; and right and left a deep ravine, forming the hill itself into a noble natural fortress, which art might greatly improve. I felt at once the impression that this would be just the place for a missionary station.

During the rain the elders were convoked in the house of Jindoa, who is regarded as the Sheha (Sheikh) of Rabbai Mpia, and who happened to be somewhat unwell. The elders were very friendly and, what pleased me very much, did not beg. I explained to them that the object of my visit was to teach them the words of the book (the Bible) which I held in my hand. One of the elders asked whether I was an enchanter, who could tell him out of the book how long he was to live; or whether I could heal the sick chief by a prayer from it. I answered that this book could make them live in everlasting joy, if they accepted and believed what was read to them; that they would be cured of the worst of maladies, sin, if they believed in the Son of God. I then narrated to them some of the chief facts in the life of Christ, and pointed out in conclusion that God so loved the world, that He gave his only begotten Son, that whosoever believeth in Him should not perish, but have everlasting life. One of the elders said that it was really true that God loved men, for He gave the Wanika rain, tembo, and clothes. I rejoined that these were certainly great proofs of Divine love, but that, after all, they were only earthly gifts, and would not avail them, if God had not taken care for their souls, and had not sent his Son to free them from sin and Satan. Another elder, who seemed to understand me better, repeated my whole address, and that with tolerable accuracy. After the rain had ceased they all dispersed quickly, to go and sow their rice, but heartily shook me by the hand and offered me a goat by way of gift. I refused it, however, being determined to hold aloof from the system of giving and taking, the receipt of a present among these people always entailing the bestowal of one. On the whole, I could not avoid seeing that the people were somewhat shy of me for fear that I should convert them to Mohammedanism; for they could not draw any distinction between Christianity and Islamism. Mothers removed their children as soon as they saw me in the streets of the village, a practice not uncommon among the Wanika, arising out of the apprehension that strangers merely come to steal the children to sell them into slavery.

From Rabbai Mpia I went in a south-westerly direction towards the Wakamba-land. Close to Mutsi Muvia, New Rabbai, I passed some graves, and saw an empty cocoa-nut shell lying on one of them. On asking the meaning of it, I was told that from time to time it was filled with tembo, because the Wanika believe that after death the Koma or shade of the dead person cannot exist without that drink; and for a similar reason, rice and maize are laid upon the graves; all which proves, at least, a belief in a continued existence after death. In another Wakamba village which we traversed, the women and children again ran away when they saw me, and even the men appeared to be frightened. Especially were my shoes, which they took for

iron, my hair, which seemed to them like the hair
of the ape, and my spectacles, objects of astonishment and ridicule. I read to them some passages
out of my translation of the Gospel of St. John into
Wakamba, but they could not understand me, nor
could I express myself sufficiently in their own language, and they did not understand Suahili. The
women were half-naked, but partly covered with
beads and copper-wire.

On my way back I had the pleasure of seeing for
the first time the mountain Kadiaro, which is distant
about thirty-six leagues from Rabbai Mpia, and
rises some 4000 feet above the level of the sea.
The sight of this mountain gave me great delight,
and in imagination I already saw a missionary-
station established in that cool climate for the
spiritual subjection of the countries of the interior.
On the whole, these first visits to the Wanika-land
stimulated and quickened my missionary yearnings;
the vicinity of the Wakamba, the level country,
with its scattered hamlets, the high and healthy
situation of Rabbai Mpia, the friendly disposition of
the inhabitants, the proximity of an arm of the sea,
Abdallah's plantation, and, last not least, Kadiaro,
all led me to think of Rabbai Mpia as a most suitable missionary station.

The ensuing twelvemonth was a period of varied
experience and suffering. After the rainy season,
in March 1845, I left Mombaz on a trip to Takaungu, exploring the coast and its immediate interior

at the same time, visiting Emberria in August, and Kambe and Jibana in September. At the beginning of October I had a violent attack of fever, brought on by exposure to the sun, while I was engaged on the flat roof of my house at Mombaz in superintending the construction of a room destined for my colleague, the missionary Rebmann, whose arrival from England was daily expected. On the 1st of December, being a little recovered, and having formerly felt the good effects of the sea air, I took a trip to Zanzibar, where I received much kindness from the English consul, Major Hamerton. Three months later I took another sea trip, and explored among other places the ruined and deserted town of Malindi, which might again be a populous and flourishing port, serving as an important missionary centre, were the English to occupy it as they have done Aden. At last on the 10th of June 1846 my dear and long-expected fellow-labourer, Rebmann, arrived at Mombaz. A native of Gerlingen, in Würtemberg, he had gone through the preparatory studies for the missionary vocation. After a few days he, too, was attacked by fever, but soon recovered sufficiently to accompany me to Rabbai Mpia, to receive the assent of the elders to the establishment of a missionary-station there.

When we arrived at Rabbai Mpia twelve chiefs were immediately summoned to a Maneno or palaver. They seated themselves on the ground, as did Rebmann and myself, along with Abdallah; and

I then introduced my beloved fellow-labourer to the chiefs, and asked for the same friendly reception for him which had been given to myself, which was promised with pleasure. I then explained the object of the mission, remarking that I had now visited the whole of the Wanika-land, and was convinced that we should be welcomed in every village. To this they assented. But, I continued, Rabbai Mpia seemed to me the place best suited for our object; and that as here I had met with more kindness than anywhere else I asked them whether they would consent to our establishing ourselves among them. Immediately and without any stipulation, even without asking after African fashion for a present, they responded, "Yes!" and truly with one heart and mouth. They gave us the strongest assurances of friendship; the whole country should be open to us; we might journey whithersoever we pleased; they would defend us to the uttermost; we should be the kings of the land, &c. When we then spoke of dwelling-places, they replied: "The birds have nests, and the Wasungu (Europeans) too, must have houses." I mentioned to them two huts, which at that very time were uninhabited, and asked them to repair and improve them, until we were ready to remove from Mombaz to Rabbai, and this was assented to most willingly. "It was wonderful," says Rebmann, in a letter to the committee, "to see how Krapf's labours have not been in vain; for this willingness, though little less than a direct manifestation of God in the wilderness, must also, in some measure, be considered as the fruit of his exertions."

Scarcely had we returned to Mombaz, when we were both attacked by fever, and a whole month elapsed before Rebmann was cónvalescent. In the interval I visited the chiefs of Rabbai Mpia to see how they were getting on with the house; no progress, however, had been made, the chiefs excusing themselves on account of the labours of the field. At last on the 22nd of August I sailed with my dear fellow-labourer for Abdallah's plantation, but was immediately on my arrival attacked by fever. The chiefs of Rabbai Mpia visited us in the evening, and fixed on the 25th as the day of our entry into the village. On the morning of that day, I had another severe attack of fever, but it did not keep me from journeying thither. Whether the result be life or death, I said to myself, the mission must be begun; and with this resolve, and an inward prayer for succour, I tottered along by the side of Rebmann, who was likewise very weak and could scarcely walk. We therefore determined to ride by turns on our single ass, but after some time I was quite unable to go on foot and obliged to monopolize the beast. With much pain I ascended the steep hill, which even without a rider the ass could scarcely have mounted, and Rebmann, also, could only clamber up by the most painful exertion. Scarcely ever was a mission begun in such weakness; but so it was to be, that we might neither boast of our own strength, nor our successors forget that in working out His

purposes, God sanctifies even our human infirmities
to the fulfilment of His ends.

It was surprising how my physical strength increased the higher I ascended. The cool air was a
genuine stimulant. Arrived at the summit, I felt myself, nevertheless, quite exhausted, and was obliged
at once to lie down on a cow-hide in the house of
the chief Jindoa, where I slept for several hours.
The sleep was so refreshing that I awoke with the
consciousness and strength of convalescence. The
chiefs then came in a body to greet us and to fix
the day for the commencement of the building.
They wished themselves to build, and we were to
give in return a present of fixed amount. Some
days afterwards, they brought building materials,
but the business went on so slowly that they had
to be reminded of the promise; for the house in
which we remained during the interval was so damp
and small, that we feared we should not be able to
make a long residence in it. At last on the 16th of September the new house was roofed in, and thus the work
of the Wanika ended. We were now obliged to do
the rest of it mostly with our own hands. The Wanika
indeed removed the bushes and grass from the
ground; but they merely wished to stick the stakes of
the walls only in a superficial manner into the soil,
which by no means suited our views, and so we had
ourselves first to dig a foundation, breaking up the
ground for nearly two feet, that we might fix the
poles more firmly. As in places there were blocks
of stone under the slight soil, these had first

to be dug out or broken into pieces, and in the heat
of the sun, in our weak state of health, this was no
slight toil. The house was twenty-four feet long,
and eighteen feet in width and height; the walls
were plastered with mud within and without, the
roof being covered with Makuti, *i.e.*, the plaited
leaves of the cocoa-nut tree. Our new home lay in
a grove of these trees, from 800 to 1000 feet above
the sea, and from which the fortress of Mombaz and
the ships in the harbour are visible. The excellent
air, as well as the healthful work of breaking the
stones and felling and hewing the trees, had a good
effect on the feverish health of both of us, and so far
it was well that we were obliged to take the labour
of building into our own hands; for all that the
Wanika would have done would have been done
wretchedly and superficially. If any one had seen
us then and there in dirty and tattered clothes,
bleeding from wounds caused by the thorns and
stones, flinging mud on the walls in the native fashion
and plastering it with the palm of our hands,
he would scarcely have looked upon us as clergy-
men. But a missionary must not let trifles put
him out; he must learn to be high and to be lowly
for the sake of his Master's work; and with all this
toil our hearts were made glad, even more so than
in quiet times, before and afterwards. During every
interval of rest, I persevered with the translation
which I had begun, though often during the renewed
attacks of fever, the thought would arise that even
before the commencement of my proper missionary

RABBAI MPIA

labours I might be summoned into eternity. At such times I consoled myself with the reflection, that the Lord, even if it should please Him to take me hence, had given me a faithful fellow-labourer by whom the good work would be continued. Meanwhile, I often prayed fervently for the preservation of my life in Africa, at least until one soul should be saved; for I was certain that if once a single stone of the spiritual temple were laid in any country, the Lord would bless the work, and continue the structure, by the conversion of those who were now sitting in darkness and in the shadow of death, and to whom our missionary labours were but as the dawn of the day-star from on High.*

After the erection of the house we had to attend to many other little building matters—kitchen, stable, store-house, oven, and especially a hut for public worship, were all to be provided. All this went on slowly; for the elders were very dilatory in bringing the building materials, although well paid. On the first Sunday after the erection of the hut for public worship some twelve to fifteen Wanika assembled in it, and I explained to them the purpose for which it had been built and invited them to come again every Sunday, and listen to God's holy word. When I had finished my address a

---

* That I was not mistaken or disappointed in this fervent hope and belief will be seen from a communication of my friend Rebmann dated Zanzibar, December 15, 1858, in which he writes to the committee, that on his return to Rabbai Mpia six Wanika were ready to become Christians through the instrumentality of Abbe Gunya, the first convert.—*Vide* the Church Missionary Record, July, 1859, pp. 213-217.

Mnika, Abbe Kondi by name, from Jembeni, asked what we would give the Wanika to eat, if they were to come here every Siku ku (great day, Sunday). If the Wanika received rice and a cow, they would always come; but if not, they would stay away; for no Mnika went to a maneno (palaver) without eating and drinking. This was rather a humbling experience for the day of our little church's consecration; but we consoled ourselves with the thought that the Jews preferred to look upon our Divine Master rather as upon an earthly king, than as upon the King eternal, the only wise God. I therefore found it necessary to make house-to-house visits to prepare the Wanika for public worship, and to announce to them the day on which Christians keep their Sabbath. Every Sunday morning, I gave a signal by firing off a gun once or twice, and afterwards by ringing a small bell which had been sent us from London to Rabbai Mpia. Besides this, we tried to familiarize the people with the Christian Sunday by buying nothing on that day; by not allowing our servants to do any work on it; and by wearing holiday clothes on it to enhance the significance of the day. In this way the Wanika attained by degrees a notion of Sunday, and an insight into the fact that Christians do not pass that holy day in eating and drinking like Mohammedans and heathens, but with prayer and meditation on the word of God in peaceful quiet and simplicity.

After the work of building was over I began to

visit the neighbouring hamlets and plantations of the Wanika to speak to them about the salvation of their souls, and to open up to them the kingdom of Heaven. My dear fellow-labourer Rebmann had to learn the language, and to look after much that was needful in the house arrangements ; on which account it was only later that he could enter upon the sphere of direct missionary labour. When he could speak the language tolerably he undertook the instruction of some boys, among whom was the son of our chief, Jindoa, a lad of ten, who learned to read fairly, and to write a little. But, alas! he gave up learning as he grew older because we would or could not satisfy his desire for clothing and other visible and material things. In my own excursions from Rabbai Mpia among the Rabbai tribe, which altogether does not amount to more than 4000 souls, I was in the habit of visiting hamlets and plantations with a collective population of perhaps about 3000. The number of all the Wanika, forming twelve tribes, may amount to about 50,000, in which are included some 30,000, composing the Wadigo tribes to the south of Mombaz. In the course of time it became ever more evident to us, impressing itself upon us with all the force of a positive command, that it was our duty not to limit our missionary labours to the coast tribes of the Suahili and Wanika, but to keep in mind as well the spiritual darkness of the tribes and nations of Inner Africa. This consideration induced us to take those important journeys into the interior, a detailed narrative of which will be found in the second portion of the present volume. But before I conclude this first part, I would give some extracts from my journals as calculated to throw light partly on the district of Rabbai Mpia and the surrounding country, and partly on the manners and customs of the Wanika and Suahili.

CHAPTER X.

RABBAI MPIA—EXTRACTS FROM JOURNALS.

Retrospect of the past year, and hopes for the future—The women's Muansa—Wanika self-conceit—The Muansa; nature of the imposture and its political uses—Trip to Zanzibar and interview with the Sultan—Liverpool speculation on the East coast—Antimony mines and their tipsy owners—Wanika and Zulus—Gardening begun — The god of the Wanika—Remonstrant chiefs and the author's successful protest against their superstition—Rain-making and rain-makers—A Wanika Dream-woman—Stories of cannibals and pigmies in the interior—Theory of their origin, and comparison with Abessinian fables—View of Kilibassi and Kadiaro—A Kinika Primer—Trial by ordeal among the Wanika—Curious details—The begging habits of the Wanika and savages in general —The author's advice to missionaries—The Koma : Wanika belief in a continuance of being after death—Attack on a Mnika by a Mkamba : condolence-custom of the Wanika—Retrospect of a year at Rabbai Mpia—Mercies and achievements—Projected visit to Kadiaro—Suahili notion of the end of the world and its probable origin—An intelligent Mohammedan : his request for wine refused—Rebmann's journey to and return from Kadiaro— Public worship and Kinika hymn—Results of civilization "pure and simple"—Retrospect of another year : difficulties and hopes.

January, 1847. — AT the beginning of this year, I find the following remarks in my diary :—

During the past twelvemonth I have suffered much, and have been often and dangerously ill. On the other hand, I have had much to be grateful for in the arrival of my beloved fellow-labourer, the missionary

Rebmann, and in the establishment of a missionary-
station at Rabbai Mpia, which I pray and hope may
become a Zion, whence the law of the Lord will
dawn on the benighted African.   May the Lord,
during the new year, enable us to increase the number of souls sincerely seeking after Christ!   Above
all, may my communion with God be quickening
and inmost, so that I may not, like those we are told
of in Scripture, be building a Noah's ark for others,
while I myself perish.   Amen.

To-day there were many Wanika here, especially
of the tribe Kiriama.   I devote particular attention to
strangers, and endeavour to implant in them a knowledge of the Word of God as comprehensive as possible, because they are in a position to publish in distant regions what they hear from the missionaries.

15th January.—Last night heathenism showed itself
again and strikingly in its most gloomy and im-
moral colours.   The women of Rabbai Mpia and
its environs assembled towards evening in the village; went in procession along the roads and sang,
danced, and played on the women's Muansa the
livelong night, so that the noise was over only with
daybreak.   The women presented themselves before
each house and asked for a present; but when they
came before our door, I told them that if they
were doing any good work we would gladly give
something; but it went against our conscience, and
the object of our settlement among them, to reward
the works of darkness; adding, that they knew full
well that we should recompense them if they would

clear the village of the withered grass which might cause a conflagration.

Nominally, no men are allowed to be present at these festivals of the women, but the immoralities and abominations practised on such occasions in the neighbouring wood are well known to every one. Among the Wanika every age and sex has, at appointed times, certain festivities which begin and end with gluttony and drunkenness. First, the chiefs have their feasts, then the young men, and, lastly, the boys; and it is the same with the women, old and young. It would seem that these festivities bind the people together; for no one may be absent from these festive meetings but at the risk of being fined a goat or a cow; and thus they form strong bulwarks against missionary labour.

17th January. — To-day I had a visit from a Mnika, whom I reproved for saying that he had done a good work in pouring some palm wine over the grave of his father. When I spoke of sins and transgressions he said, "We are good people, who is it has been defaming us to you?" I read Romans i., and showed him that most of the sins mentioned there are rife among the Wanika, a position which he could not deny.

2nd February.—To-day the chief and some other Wanika advised us to close the doors of our house, as the Muansa was to roar. I reproved them for their superstition, and their deceit in leading the people to believe that the Muansa is a wild beast making a noise in the wood, whereas it is in reality nothing but the stem of a tree hollowed out, which is made to give forth a frightful sound by rubbing. I could not, I told them, be silent at such sinful doings, and would leave my house-door open to show that I was not afraid of their superstitions and evil spirits.

4th February.—In the afternoon after the women had cleared the grass, &c. from the pathways of the village the elders made their appearance with strange musical instruments, which gave out a sound very similar to that of a weaver's spool thrown backwards and forwards. We left the doors of our house open; so when the procession of the elders came near, one of them suddenly approached and shut the door to, which I immediately re-opened, protesting against their works of darkness; upon which they then betook themselves to the Moroni, or council-house, where the Muansa-wa-Kurri had already begun to play, or rather to bellow. At nightfall the shrieking, dancing, singing, and shouting of the elders, with the bellowing of the Muansa, made up a frightful noise; and this wild tumult lasted all night, so that we were often awakened from our sleep, when the blind and mad servants of the Muansa passed the house. As may be expected, they fortified themselves, from time to time, with large draughts of palm-wine, which rekindled their flagging powers, and rendered them more uproarious.

On my asking what the Muansa really was and what it meant a Mnika answered, that he could not say; for no one not an elder was allowed to see the instrument. If children or women were to see it they would immediately fall down dead, or the women, at least, would not bear any more children. As soon, therefore, as those who are not summoned hear the bellow of the Muansa, which is always played in the forest, even from a distance, they must hide in the wood or in a house, and whoever neglects to do so has to pay the penalty of a cow or a couple of oxen. It is evident that the elders use this instrument to retain the people in fear or subjection; for the Muansa forms the centre of their civic and religious life; and when the Wanika sacrifice and pray for rain, or are going to strangle a mis-shapen child in the wood, or promulgate any new laws, it is always brought into play. Only certain individuals are initiated into the mystery of the Muansa, and the initiation is accompanied by a plentiful donation of rice, palm-wine, meat, &c., made by the person who wishes to be initiated. The instrument itself can be purchased by any Mnika who is willing to be at the expense for the sum of from three to four dollars; or he may get a carpenter to make one for that sum. The possessor of it enjoys the privilege of participating in all carousals, and altogether becomes a person of import-ance and influence among his republican fellow-countrymen, with whom those alone rank high who are distinguished by wealth, generosity, the power of eloquence, or by some deed or other of self-sacrifice. The Muansa is said to have been introduced by the southern Wanika, the so-called Wadigo; and the Wakamba, Wateita, Wajagga, and other tribes, are not acquainted with it and its solemnities.

11*th March*.—On the 5th, we had received letters from Europe, India, and Zanzibar, by the arrival of the ship Anne from Liverpool, commanded by Captain Parker, and on the 7th, we set sail from Mombaz in an Arabian vessel for the latter place; my friend, Rebmann, and I thinking that the voyage would do good to our health, which was still impaired by recent attacks of fever. We reached Zanzibar on the 9th, and to-day we waited upon the Sultan, who, as usual, was very friendly. He said that the Wanika were bad people, and that we ought, therefore, to reside in Mombaz rather than in the Wanika-land. I remarked that the inhabitants of the South Sea islands had been still worse than the Wanika, who were not cannibals, like them. European teachers had gone to these cannibals, had taught them out of the Word of God, and they were now quite different men. The Sultan rejoined: "If that be so, it is all right; you may stay among the Wanika as long as you choose, and do whatever you please."

15*th March*.—As Captain Pain, of the Prince of Wales, of Liverpool, offered us a passage in his ship to Mombaz, we availed ourselves of the opportunity to return home to Rabbai Mpia. On the voyage we met Captain Parker in the ship Ann, and he induced Captain Pain to return to Zanzibar. (Captain Parker was the agent of a commercial company in Liverpool with a capital of £70,000, which wished to trade with Eastern Africa, but was soon obliged to give up the enterprise with loss as quite unprofitable, which information was given me by Europeans at Zanzibar some time after.)

19th March.—Yesterday, after Captain Parker had finished his business in Zanzibar he came to us on board the "Prince of Wales," just as Captain Pain was about to sail to Mombaz; and to-day, we arrived at the island. Captain Parker wished me to accompany him to the Wanika and Duruma, where he intended to purchase from the chiefs the mines of antimony which exist there, and to pave the way for working them; but as I foresaw that the enterprise would displease the Sultan of Zanzibar; that the Wanika chiefs would suspect the missionaries of wishing to sell their country to the Europeans; and also that the powder and shot which he thought of disposing of to the Suahilis would do no good, I declined his proposal.

23rd March.—Mr. P. paid a visit to the Duruma chiefs, but found them so tipsy that he could do nothing with them. He was so frightened by their demeanour and savage appearance, that he gave them at once the presents which he had brought for them, and then quitted them without further parley. He said that he thought the Wanika were fifty times worse than the Zulus in South Africa, with whom he had become acquainted; and certainly as regards drunkenness, this opinion may be the true one, but in every other respect the Wanika are far superior to the Zulus.

31st March.—After our return to Rabbai we began to lay out a garden, in doing which we had to burn a great many weeds, and this gave me occasion to show to our Wanika visitors, how the weeds of the heart, too, must be destroyed, if the heart is to become a garden and fitting abode for God's Spirit.

14th April.—To-day my fellow-labourer, Rebmann, planted a number of potatoes, and sowed seeds of different kinds received from Europe and India.

22nd April.—The Wanika offered to-day a Sadaka or sacrifice, partly to obtain rain, and partly for the sake of a man who had died. A black sheep was slaughtered; the blood was spilt on the grave, whilst the spiller ejaculated:—"May there soon be rain; may the dead man enjoy repose; may the sick be healed," &c.

To the question, what precise meaning the Wanika attach to the word Mulungu? one said that Mulungu was thunder; some thought it meant heaven, the visible sky; some, again, were of opinion that Mulungu was the being who caused diseases; whilst others, however, still held fast to a feeble notion of a Supreme Being as expressed by that word. Some, too, believe that every man becomes a Mulungu after death.

30th April.—To-day, several chiefs came to ask us why we did not shut our doors when the Muansa passed our house; even the Mohammedans shut their doors, why did we not act like they did? We replied that we are not Mohammedans who, like the Wanika, love the works of darkness; that we have

come to the Wanika-land to give a testimony against
the works of darkness, and to exhort the Wanika to
turn to the living God; that we are not afraid of the
Muansa, because we know that it is only a piece of
wood, which the sooner they burn the better; and
that it would be more pleasing to God,
if after burning the Muansa, they were to build a
school-house, and admonish the children to come to
us to be taught. Further, that the chiefs ought to
be the first to set a good example, and allow themselves to be instructed in the gospel; their doing
which would bring a blessing upon the country, so
that they would no longer find it necessary to rule
over the people by means of deception. Whoso
honours God, God will honour; and the people would
obey them better and more sincerely than now, when
they are obliged to compel obedience by superstitious and sensual practices. Whilst speaking thus
earnestly and solemnly, one of the chiefs said to me:
"You are a true magician," by which he meant,
"We cannot resist your eloquence." The chiefs
then announced, repeatedly, that they would make
an exception in our case and would not punish us
when we looked at the Muansa, but the Wanika
should be punished if they did not shut up their
huts when it passed by.

10th May.—* * * Noteworthy is the faith of
the Wakamba in rain-makers, who every where play
a prominent part in Eastern Africa. Among the
Wanika there are certain families which lay claim to
a power of causing it to rain, and maintain that

this great secret can be transmitted from father to
son. This hereditary dignity of rain-making gives
them great importance among the people, which
naturally leads them to do their utmost to encourage
the belief. Observing carefully the state of the
weather, and knowing from long experience about
the time when the earliest rain is to fall, they forthwith call upon the chiefs to offer up a sacrifice.
These again command the people to make a Zansi,
i. e., to contribute to the purchase of a cow or a
sheep for the rain-sacrifice. If the rain comes, it is
of course ascribed to the power of the rain-maker;
but if it does not, the cunning rain-maker manages
to get up another sacrifice; but fixes on such a
colour for the sacrificial animal, that some time must
elapse before a suitable one can be found. Meanwhile the rain comes down, and the cheat has got
out of the difficulty. The rain-makers seem, too, to
have a kind of thermometer made of a peculiar wood,
which they place in the water; and observe, moreover,
the course of the clouds, which are generally drawn to
the summits of the mountains. There are, however,
many Wanika who look upon rain-making as mere
Mateso, or artifice; and as a tradition without the
least foundation in reality. The Wanika attach great
importance to the song and flight of birds, and
undertake or neglect much in accordance with both,
paying special attention to birds when undertaking a journey. The medicine men (Waganga) dili-
gently observe the nature of grasses, plants, &c., but
envelope the healing art in superstitious ceremonies.

11*th May.*—I went into the plantations of the Wanika to read the Word and to preach, but found only a few persons there. I heard from a woman of the name of Amehari Pegue, that she often ordained sacrifices for the dead, and for other events requiring them. She is said suddenly to set up a cry at night, and tell the people that the Koma, or spirit, of this or that dead person has appeared to her in a dream and ordered the offering up of a sacrifice for some certain individual, or for some threatened calamity coming upon the land. Those present ask the dreamer of what the sacrifice is to consist, and she replies, perhaps, that it must be a red or black sheep, or a cow. The order is communicated next morning to the chiefs, or to the relations of the deceased, and the sacrifice must forthwith be made. As a matter of course the dreamer, the Alosaye, receives, as well as the chiefs, her share of the sacrificial meat. The woman, who is probably hysterical, is said to eat and drink but seldom; but no doubt there is a great deal of deception in the background. The chiefs have not power enough to procure respect for the laws, and, therefore, put into the mouth of the dreamer what she is to announce to the people as the revelations of a Koma. The chiefs are often hungry and long for a feast, and then the holy woman must come to their aid, and help to levy a sacrifice on the people.

13*th May.*—* * * Our servant Amri told us some fabulous tales of the Wabilikimo, that is, of the pigmies, and cannibals in the interior. There is said to be a tribe in the interior by whom human beings are fattened for slaughter. A Mnika, it appears, once escaped from a house, where he was to have been slaughtered for dinner. The Wabilikimo in the interior, it would seem, place low seats for their stranger-guests, which by the pressure fix themselves to the seat of honour, and hinder them from rising. I conjecture that these stories have been invented by the Wakamba and the caravan leaders, in order to deter the inhabitants of the coast from journeying into the interior, so that their monopoly of the trade with the interior may not be interfered with. In Abessinia, too, I used to hear similar stories of cannibals, invented by the slave dealers, to terrify the slaves with the fear of being eaten up if they were to loiter on the road or run away.

22nd May.—To-day, Rebmann and I made an excursion to the Wakamba in the neighbourhood. We saw quite distinctly the mountains, Kilibassi and Kadiaro, which rise out of the plain towards the south-west, some four days' journey from this. The Wakamba carry on a trade in cattle, and a lucrative one in ivory with the interior, and have begun, too, to cultivate the soil and to grow rice, Indian corn, cassia, &c.

24th May.—I began to prepare a primer in the Kinika language. Many Wanika looked in to speak to us, and we discoursed with them on the one thing necessary for salvation.

26th June.—To-day, we received the following details respecting the oaths and ordeals in use among the Wanika :—

1. *Kirapo ja Zoka*, the ordeal of the hatchet. The magician who administers the oath, and performs the other ceremonies in connection with it, takes the hand of the supposed thief, or criminal, and makes him repeat as follows: "If I have stolen the property of —— (naming the person), or committed this crime, let Mulungu (Heaven) respond for me; but if I have not stolen, nor done this wickedness, may he save me." After these words, the magician passes the red hot iron four times over the flat hand of the accused; and the Wakamba believe that if he is guilty, his hand will be burnt, but if innocent, that he will suffer no injury. In the former case, the accused must undergo the punishment for the alleged crime, whether he confess it himself, or not, Mulungu having responded by means of the ordeal.

2. *Kirapo ja jungu ja Gnandu*, the ordeal of the copper kettle. The magician takes an empty copper kettle, makes it red hot, and casts into it a stone called Mango, which emits sparks. He then adds the "Raha ya Gnonsi," a portion of a slaughtered goat, saying to the accused, "Heia lomborera," come, say thy prayer; to which the latter responds: "May God let me have justice." Then the suppliant reaches with his hand into the kettle, and takes out the glowing stone; and, if guilty, his hand and face are burnt; if innocent, no harm happens to him.

3. *Kirapo ja Sumba*, the ordeal of the needle. The magician takes a thick needle, makes it red hot, and draws it through the lips of the alleged

criminal. If guilty, a quantity of blood will flow from the wound, but none if innocent.

4. *Kirapo ja Kikahe*, the ordeal of the piece of bread. The accused has to eat a piece of bread which has been poisoned. If innocent he will swallow it without trouble : if guilty, it will stick in his throat, and can only be ejected with considerable pain and loss of blood. Instead of bread, rice is often used.

On such occasions, the magician receives a piece of clothing from the accused and from the accuser by way of recompense.

29th June.—In the course of the day, we learned that the chiefs had punished a boy for not hiding himself as the Muansa passed by. I told our chief, who made me a call, that they had condemned an innocent person, and that the lad had done nothing wrong. The chief replied that the young people would take to our "Ada," or customs, but that the others were too old. Furthermore he observed that he would call together the other chiefs and put an end to the Muansa if they were willing to do so; but of himself he could do nothing. I regarded these remarks simply as complimentary, though I believe he would abrogate these feasts and much more if he had the power, or if the other chiefs would aid him. I censured his nephew for his laziness and drunkenness, as well as for the constant habit of begging, which made him extremely burdensome to us; for no one who has not personally experienced it, can imagine what annoyance is caused to missionaries by

these begging propensities of the heathen, who beg
every thing they see. If a Mnika, or Mkamba,
or Suahili, wants anything, he says: " I am going
to the Msungu (European) and will ask it of him;
he will not refuse it me." So it often came about
that our house was like a shop where there are
customers in abundance, except that in our case they
were customers who wished to have every thing for
nothing. One wanted a hatchet, another a garment,
a third needles, a fourth a dollar, a fifth salt or
pepper, a sixth physic, and so in one day we sometimes had fifteen or twenty applicants, all begging,
and often after a very cunning fashion. How is one
to act in such a case ? A missionary cannot give to
all, but neither can he refuse all. Were he to be
guided only by a sense of what is right, there would
be an end to his usefulness; for the heathen would say:
" He does not himself practise what he preaches to
us; he preaches love and self-denial, and he does not
practise them; let the Msungu show us a good life,
then we may believe that his doctrine is good also."
As the result of many years' experience, I would
advise every missionary, no less for the sake of his calling than for his own, to bear this persecution patiently,
and to give as much as he can, letting wisdom and
prudence be his guide. What is given is not lost
if it be given from love, and for his Master's sake.
A missionary has not the gift of miracles like the
apostles; but love, humility, patience, and self-
denial all work wonders, which, even in our day,
have a mighty power of attraction for the heathen.

They ask themselves and each other : " How comes
it that this man denies himself so much for our sake,
and does us so much good ?   His book, which
teaches him thus to act must be good ; let us therefore also seek to become acquainted with it."

4th August.—* * * It is clear that the Wanika ascribe a higher nature and power to the
Koma, the spirits or shades of the dead, just as the
Romanists do to the saints; but the Wanika have no
image or idol of the Koma, nor indeed of any kind
whatsoever.   The Koma, they say, is at one time
in the grave, then above the earth, or in thunder
and lightning as it lists; it cannot, however, be seen,
although it receives the gifts which are offered to
it, and is appeased by them and rendered friendly
to the living.   The chief resting-place of the Koma
is in or about the Kaya, the central point or chief
town of the tribe, where a hut is erected for its
habitation; and in that hut, all property deposited
by the people is safe, for a Kirapo, talisman, is sus-
pended in it, which prevents the approach of thieves.
As the Koma dwells in preference at the Kaya, the
people often bring their dead from a great distance
thither; and even disinter them in distant localities,
and transport them for reinterment to the grave-
yard at the Kaya, thinking that they find there
greater repose—so great is the longing of man's
nature for rest after death.   It is clear from this
faith in the Koma, that the Wanika have some idea
of a future state after death, and that idea gives a
missionary a common point to start from; whilst

heathenism which affords none such would be a very difficult one for missionaries to contend with; but there is none of that sort in Eastern Africa.

11th August.—Last night our store-room was entered by thieves, and a quantity of victuals, along with tools, nails, &c., stolen; for as the Wanika had never yet robbed us of even the smallest article, we had not thought it necessary to lock it up. The Wanika have many bad habits, but are seldom or never thieves; and, indeed, whatever we have happened to leave out of doors, has always been honestly returned to us by the finder. (It turned out afterwards, that the robbery had been committed by Suahili.)

22nd August.—To-day a circumstance happened which might easily have led to very serious consequences. A Mkamba had for a long time been on terms of hostility with the son of one of our chiefs of Rabbai Mpia. This morning the Mkamba saw the latter in his plantation, when he rushed upon him and gave him a sabre-stroke over the head, ears, and shoulders. As soon as the young men of Rabbai heard the news, they seized their arms and proposed to attack the neighbouring village of the Wakamba, the inhabitants of which were already beginning to fly; but the Rabbai chiefs interposed, and pacified the young warriors, by telling them that the Kaya, or chief-town of Rabbai, ought first to be placed in a state of defence, and the fruits of the field brought home, before war was waged on the Wakamba; and this produced the desired effect.

It was a lucky thing that the wounded man was not killed; for now, as soon as he is well again, the matter will be peacefully arranged by the payment of four or five coins to the wounded man by the Mkamba. For the present, he has sent a sheep, whose blood was poured out in the presence of the wounded Mnika, which is a preliminary act of reconciliation, and a token that the culprit seeks the pardon of his victim, and is ready to pay such a fine as will restore peace between them.

25th August.—It is a year to-day since we arrived here. How much grace and mercy has the Lord shown to His servants during this year! How mightily has He preserved us within and without! By His aid we have had access to this people; have built a habitation to dwell in, and above all, have raised a humble fane, though but a poor hut, for worship; have laid out a small garden, and opened a school. We have made tolerable proficiency in the language, prepared books for the people, preached the Gospel to many Wanika, Wakamba, and Suahili, and become acquainted with the manners and customs, the prejudices, and, in short, with the good and evil qualities, as well as the geographical relations of these tribes, by which means our allotted task in Eastern Africa has become clearer to us, and in our hearts, too, we have had many blessed experiences. Viewing all these things, we are full of thankfulness, and take courage for the future!

In the afternoon, we were visited by five men from the mountain Kadiaro, in Teita, who brought some Mtungu or Hanja, as the Suahili call it, a resin which the Wanika mix with castor-oil, and use as a scent of which the people of Barava are said to be very fond.   The five men gave us some information respecting the people of Teita.   When they had left, I told our chief that we wished to visit Kadiaro ; upon which he inquired at once, what we wanted to buy there ?   I expressed my surprise at such a question, and asked if he did not know us better, and had not yet discovered that we were not traders, but preachers of the Word, who desired to spread the Gospel throughout the whole of Africa; adding that we had, indeed, settled down in the Wanika-land and made it our head-quarters; but still desired to see other tribes to show them the way to everlasting life.

29th August.—As the Wanika live scattered about on their plantations, and take but little pleasure in listening to the words of the preacher, we had few hearers to-day, Sunday ; but many came into the village, not so much for our sake as to visit the wounded Mnika, the son of our neighbour.   It is a custom with this people for the relations, friends, and in general the men of the same tribe, to come from a great distance to visit a sick person and condole with him ; and to neglect to offer such condolence would be a great breach of good manners in the eye of a Wanika. Most of the visitors came afterwards to us, and so it was ordered that the very event which might have plunged the country in war, served to make several Wanika acquainted with the Gospel.

16th September.—According to our servant, Amri, the Suahili have the following curious notion of the end of the earth. They believe that the earth finishes in a great morass in the west of Africa, that it is, as it were, buried there, and that is the end of the world; so they call it " Usiko wa nti "— burial of the earth. Probably this idea has arisen from the spectacle of a great marshy lake, or boggy country, seen by the fathers of the present race during journeys into the interior. Before the Galla and Wakuafi had shut out all ingress to the interior the people of the coast were certainly better acquainted with Inner and Western Africa than they are at present; but their descendants have only traditions from which, in all probability, the above-mentioned notion has taken its rise.

23rd September.—To-day, we made arrangements respecting the journey to Kadiaro, whither we had been invited by the Teita people who recently visited us. Brother Rebmann is to undertake the journey whilst I remain behind at our head-quarters in Rabbai; and we have hired six Wanika to accompany him and carry his things, each man to receive three dollars, the sum asked and agreed upon.

26th September.—Rebmann intended to set off to-morrow, and I was to accompany him a part of the way; but unexpectedly, at nightfall, two chiefs of Great Rabbai called upon us, and declared that the house of every Mnika who went to Kadiaro should be burnt. I rejoined, in few words, that I would lay the whole matter before the Governor of Mombaz, who would find out the author of the prohibition. (I deemed it necessary to have this matter examined into by the proper authorities, to secure ourselves against similar vexation and annoyance in future, by showing the Wanika and Suahili that we are protected by the government of Mombaz. *Obsta principiis* is my motto.)

28th September.—We went to the Mohammedan village of Jumfu yesterday, whence we reached Mombaz by boat, and to-day complained of the conduct of the chiefs of Great Rabbai to the Governor, and asked him to remove the obstacles thrown in the way of our journey. He promised to grant the request and gave us a letter, and soldiers who are to communicate his orders to the chiefs. He wrote also to Bana Kheri, the Suahili leader of a caravan, which was on the point of leaving for Jagga.

30th September.—We discovered to-day the author of the opposition which had been formed against us in Rabbai to be Emshande, one of the chiefs of the village of Jumfu, who considers himself the king of the Wanika, and who for the gratification of his greed sought to interpose between us and the Wanika, so that we might employ him as a middleman and give him a handsome present. He had incited the Wanika not to allow us to depart until we had made a present to him and to the chiefs of Great Rabbai.

4th October.—There was a party of Wanika with us, to whom we narrated and expounded the parable of the rich man (Luke xvi.). Another party arrived

afterwards, and with them we discoursed on the
prodigal son.

11*th October.*—We received a visit from Bana
Hamade, an intelligent and influential Suahili, chief
of Mombaz, who gave us a great deal of important
information respecting the geography and history of
this coast. According to him, Shunguaya, now a
decayed place on the coast of Patta, was the original
home of the Suahili, who driven thence by the
Galla fled to Malindi. After being driven from
Malindi they fled to the Bight of Kilefi, and finally
to Mombaz. The Galla, it seems, formerly ruled as
far as Tanga and Usambara, and the Wanika came
from Rombo in Jagga; but the fierce Masai and
Wakuafi are now the ruling population of the interior.
The forefathers of the Wanika-tribe, Kiriama, are
said to have lived in Mangea on the river Sabaki,
and to have been driven thence by the Galla.

Bana Hamade afterwards sent his slave to ask for
some bottles of wine, which we refused, because as a
Mohammedan he was not permitted to drink wine,
and we did not, like some Europeans, deem it meritorious to seek to convert Mohammedans by making
them acquainted with wine and brandy. If Bana
Hamade, we said, were to give up not only a bit, but
the whole of his Mohammedan doctrine, and drink
wine not merely in secret but freely and openly, then
we might give him a bottle or two, but we would not
encourage him to be a hypocrite, doing in secret
what he would not do in public. We had a small
store of wine which we husbanded for the benefit

of our own health.   It is singular how the Arabs
and Suahili have begun to relish wine and brandy,
since they have become acquainted with Europeans
in Zanzibar and other places.   It will produce at
last a reaction of the rigid Mohammedans against all
that is European, and resuscitate the old fanaticism.

13*th October*.—Bana Kheri paid us a visit, to put
himself right with us respecting the opposition of
the Wanika, as well as to make our friendship,
and to offer his services on the journey to Jagga;
here again it was so ordered that the opposition of
Emshande resulted in good; for Bana Kheri is the
very man to be useful as a guide in our contemplated
journeys into the interior.   He said, that to the west
of Uniamesi there were Mohammedans, and to the
west of them again, Europeans, which may very probably refer to the Portuguese on the west coast.

14*th October*.—*   *   * This evening Rebmann
set forth on his journey to Kadiaro.   We read Isaiah
xlix., and prayed together, asking a blessing upon
our work, and beseeching that this journey might be
made effectual towards the extension of the Gospel
in the interior.

25*th October*.—I had the pleasure of welcoming
the return of my beloved fellow-labourer Rebmann
from Kadiaro in good health.   He was the bearer of
much valuable information, and stated that the Teita
people in Maquasini, the first village on the mountain
Kadiaro, had given him a friendly reception with
permission to dwell among them, and to preach the
Gospel in their land.

28th October.—My dear brother Rebmann's reports of his journey so powerfully raised my spirits to-day, that I thought earnestly and deeply upon the extension of our missionary labours. There ought to be a missionary settled among the northern Wanika in Kambe or Jogni, another on the mountain Kadiaro, a third in Jagga, a fourth in Usambara, and a fifth in Ukambani. Oh, that we had men and means enough for the noble field which is opening upon us! A missionary often shares in common the desires and aspirations of a great conqueror, only of a very different kind; for he wrestles not against flesh and blood, but against principalities, against powers, against the rulers of the darkness of this world, against spiritual wickedness in high places.

14th November.—At the commencement of public worship to-day, there were some twenty persons present, who left us, however, as soon as we had finished the singing, which Rebmann accompanied on the flageolet. The harvest is small, yet we will not despond, but trust to Him who can animate the dead and awaken them to a new and better life! Rebmann had also composed a hymn in the Kinika language, which we sang during the service. The following is one of the verses:—

Jesus Christos, fania	Jesus Christ, make
Moyowangu muvia;	My heart new;
Uwe muokosi wangu,	Thou art my Saviour,
Uzi ussa maigangu	Thou hast forgiven me my sin.
Jesus Christos, fania	Jesus Christ, make
Moyowangu muvia.	My heart new.

21st December.—* * * * What horrors and
sins would be made manifest if ivory, copal, and
articles of commerce generally, imported from Africa
into Europe, could speak! How many slaves, how
many women, how much palm-wine, how many
objects for the gratification of lust and vanity, are
purchased by the Galla, Wanika, Wakamba, and
Suahili, with the ivory which they bring to the
coast! In truth, these tribes could not bear greater
affluence and prosperity; they would sink to the level
of mere beasts of the field, and the luxuries which
civilization brings with it would soon make them
extinct, unless the misuse of them were to be
controlled by the spread of Christianity!

31st December.—In a retrospect of the past year I
am specially grieved by the indifference of the Wanika to the means of salvation through the Saviour,
which have been so often offered to them during
the last twelve months. How joyfully would we
have assembled them to hear the Word; and how
gladly would we have instructed the young; but
the darkened and worldly-minded people remain
deaf to all exhortation! My dear fellow-labourer
Rebmann had at one time collected a flock of children at Bunni, a hamlet in the vicinity of Rabbai
Mpia, and begun to teach them; but they soon dispersed. We have often exhorted the chiefs and
parents to allow the children to be taught, and though
they approve of our proposal, they let the matter rest
there, and never seriously exhort the young to come
to school; fearing that the Ada or customs of the

Wanika will be destroyed, that the young people will conform to the Ada of Europeans, and that the Koma or spirits of the dead will be angry, withhold the rain, and send diseases. Nevertheless, we will seek to imitate David, who strengthened himself in his God, and patiently and trustingly continued to bear his sorrows, until God should be pleased to help him to the promised kingship. We will seek comfort in the promise that His Word, wherever it is preached, shall never come back empty; and so we look forward with courage and confidence to continue in the new year the work which we have begun, casting the bread of life upon the waters, hoping still to find it again after many days!

Let every thing that hath breath praise the Lord!

CHAPTER XII.

EXTRACTS FROM JOURNALS CONTINUED.

Completion of Suahili and Kinika Dictionary—A Wanika-exorcism
—Undue denunciation—Rebmann's journey to Jagga; the author
left alone—Mringe the cripple awakened to the Gospel—Tre-
mendous storm, and Wanika infanticide—Appearance of two
French naval officers—Rebmann's safe return from Jagga—Main
results of his journey—Comparison of the East-African and West-
African missions—The sea-serpent—Fanciful origin of the Galla,
Wakamba, and Wakuafi—Mringe's new hut and persecutions—
Wanika name-giving—A neighbour of Mringe's awakened—
Mringe's reception of the Gospel—Glories of the missionary
state—Wanika belief in metempsychosis—A Portuguese image
converted into a pagan idol—The "free and independent" Wanika—Boso-festival—Arrival of Erhardt and Wagner—Illness
and recovery of Erhardt; Wagner's death—His funeral a striking lesson to the Wanika—Journey to Ukambani, and return to
Rabbai Mpia.

1st January, 1848.—THE promise, "Fear not, Abram,
I am thy shield, and thy exceeding great reward,"
has been very consolatory to me at the beginning of
this year.   I spoke with our chief on these words to-
day, and read with his son, Shehe, Luke ii. 42, and
following verses, exhorting him with the new year
to increase in wisdom and grace.   In the afternoon
there arrived the other boys who had formerly refused to come, fancying that we ought to pay them

for coming to school, just as we pay our servants for their services; so that we had to make it known that we would give nothing to any one for attending the school, and that those who sought such a recompense, had better stay away.

3rd January. — I continued the translation of Dr. Barth's "Bible Stories" into the Kinika language.

5th January.—Our neighbour was busy with Uganga for the supposed benefit of his daughter, whose painful boils, he imagined, were caused by an evil spirit. It was of no use to denounce the magical ceremony; no one would listen to me, even for a minute; but one and all clapped their hands, drummed, danced about in a circle, and worked themselves into such a state of excitement that like furies they alternately bellowed, shouted, groaned, and laughed.

11th January.—To-day the completion of my English-Suahili and Kinika Dictionary closes a long and troublesome labour. My task will now be, (1) to make a copy of this dictionary; (2) to continue my translation of the New Testament, and of Dr. Barth's "Bible Stories;" (3) to make, daily, an excursion to the plantations of the Wanika, and preach to them; (4) to instruct such Wanika children as wish for instruction; (5) to address the Wanika of the district, and to devote myself to those who visit us at our home from far and near; and (6) from time to time to make journeys into the interior, in order to become acquainted with its

geographical and ethnological peculiarities and languages, preaching the Gospel as far as can be done
on these journeys, and thus pave the way for the
mission in the interior, when we shall have received
more fellow-labourers from Europe.

28th January.—We visited to-day a Wakamba
hamlet. On our homeward way, we came upon a
band of Wanika, who informed us that they were
bent on expelling an evil spirit from a sick person.
In the centre of the throng stood a wooden mortar
filled with water ; near the mortar stuck into the
ground was a staff, which they call Moroi, about
three feet long, and of the thickness of a man's
finger, painted black and ornamented with white
and blue glass beads and a red feather. The
Wanika believe that the evil spirit loves these
beads, and that his attention becomes gradually
drawn to them, until he at last completely forsakes
the sick person and fastens upon the beads. From
time to time a boy kept dipping twigs into the
water, and sprinkling the head of the sick man, while
the throng danced about him, drumming and making
a frightful noise. It was impossible for me to
attempt a word of warning to the maddened crowd ;
even when they were obliged at last to rest for very
weariness, they tried to recruit themselves by drinking palm-wine, and then the shrieking, dancing,
and drumming began anew, completely drowning
every expostulation I essayed to make.

20th February.—In the evening I received a visit
from the mfiere (eldest) Sahu, one of those Wanika

who will not so much as listen to the Word of Promise. It is he, too, who presses and drives the Wanika to offer sacrifices, and to get up carousals, so that we have called him, not inappropriately, the Master of the Ceremonies for Rabbai. I exhorted him earnestly, to think of the salvation of his soul, when he said, that he would first drink palm-wine and have a sleep; to-morrow he would come and speak to me about these matters. When told that he ought to speak now about the salvation of his soul; for he did not know whether God would not this night require it of him, and place him at the bar of judgment, he went away, saying, "God will not punish me." It is astonishing what a power of darkness rests upon the heathen who have become the leaders and teachers of heathen customs and ceremonies to others. I lately heard from Rebmann, that this stiff-necked scoffer was massacred by the Masai in the spring of 1857, when those wild robbers fell upon and decimated the Rabbai tribe.

9th March.—This morning, two old Wanika women, as self-righteous as any persons in Europe can be, paid me a visit. When I spoke of the evil heart of man one of the women said: "Who has been slandering me to you? I have a good heart, and know of no sin." The other woman said: "I came to you to ask for a garment, and not to listen to your Manens (discourse)." A Mnika said: "If I am to be always praying to your Lord, how can I look after my plantation?"

17th March.—It was inwardly made manifest to me

to-day, that for some time past I have attacked too
fiercely the heathen customs and superstitions of the
Wanika, the sight of the abominations moving me
to indignation; and that I ought to preach more the
love of the Redeemer for His sheep lost, and gone
astray, or taken captive by Satan. I must bring
them closer to the cross of Christ; show more compassion, and let my words be full of commiseration
and pity; looking forward earnestly and prayerfully
for the conversion of this hard people more from
God's blessing upon the work than from my own
activity. It is neither the gifts nor the works,
neither the words nor the prayers and feelings of
the missionary, but the Lord Jesus alone who can
convert a human being! It is He who must say:
"Lazarus, come forth," and though bound hand and
foot, the dead man will come forth from the grave
of sin and death, and live!

I completed the Kinika version of the "Bible
Stories" of Dr. Barth.

The indifference and dulness of the Wanika towards the Gospel often depress me.

14*th April.*—We spoke with Bana Kheri about the
journey to Jagga.

19*th to* 21*st April.*—I went to Mombaz to forward
Rebmann's journey to Jagga, and to purchase
necessaries for it. The governor of the fortress
was somewhat dubious on the subject, and was
unwilling that Rebmann should undertake the journey, on the ground that it was exposed to many
dangers from Galla, Wakuafi, Masai, as well as wild

beasts. In any case, said he, he must not ascend the mountain Kilimanjaro, because it is full of evil spirits (Jins). For, said he, people who have ascended the mountain have been slain by the spirits, their feet and hands have been stiffened, their powder has hung fire, and all kinds of disasters have befallen them. I did not then know that there was snow upon the mountain, and therefore merely said, that Rebmann would take care not to go too near the fine sand, which, as I then supposed, must have caused the destruction of the people.

27th April.—To-day, my dear brother Rebmann began his journey to Jagga, and I accompanied him a short way, committing him to the protection of Almighty God. The feelings which overpowered me at parting are not easily to be described to friends at home. To have been for several years bound up with a beloved fellow-labourer, and now all at once to see him depart and enter upon an unknown and dangerous route into the midst of the heathen world of Africa, with mere liars and knaves for his companions, who are destitute of any thought but of self, is no small pain to him who undertakes the journey, no less than to him who remains behind. Rebmann turned his face towards the south-west, while I returned to the lonely hut to bear him in my prayerful heart, and wish him God speed!

29th April.—A letter from Rebmann, written from Engoni, at the entrance into the great wilderness which leads to Jagga and Ukambani, was a welcome sight to me to-day.

8th May.—I began. to read aloud to the Wanika who visited me the "Bible Stories" which I had translated into Kinika.

11th May.—In Muihani I came upon some ten persons to whom I discoursed upon John iii. A cripple named Mringe wondered, like Nicodemus, when I said, that man must be born again. He asked, how that could be? He thought that God ought to do something special for him, as he had to suffer so much in this life.

21st May.—After midnight there arose a tempest with thunder and lightning, such as I had not witnessed since my residence on the Suahili coast. It seemed as if the wrath of God were to be manifested on the abominations which the Wanika were to transact this morning, and as if the Almighty wished to show the hardened and merciless sinners that He could and would destroy them, because they showed no mercy to a poor creature of their own kind. A woman in Muelle, as it happened, had given birth to two children, one of whom had six fingers but neither nose nor lips. In conformity with the custom of the Wanika the parents took the mis-shapen child to the chiefs, declaring the while, that as it was a Rogo, or a mis-birth, and would therefore be a criminal, they refused to nurture it, and brought it to the chiefs that it might be strangled and buried in the wood. In conformity with this declaration the chiefs pressed its neck until it was suffocated; then burying it, and making the Muansa play, they offered up a Sadaka (sacrifice) that no harm might come upon the land because a Rogo was born. This I learnt afterwards from the chief's brother; for though I had heard the Muansa play in the midst of the storm, I did not understand what was meant. In a general way many horrors happen among the heathen of which a missionary hears nothing, or only by the merest chance, and he is therefore often disposed to think better of them than he otherwise might be led to do. Thus, the Wanika often try to conceal from us a great deal of what is going on, because they know well that we should condemn it out of the Word of God.

As soon as it was day and the rain had ceased I went into the plantations, and made the abomination of child-murder by the Wanika the chief subject of my discourse.

22nd May.—I spoke against child-murder on every occasion, and to all the Wanika who came to me.

23rd May.—I was in Kijembeni and spoke against infanticide. A woman set up a great shout of laughter when I touched upon this point; but another, on the contrary, showed more sensibility, and said: "It is true, the strangling of mis-shapen children is a bad practice;" though another rejoined: "We will adhere to our Ada (custom)."

24th May.—Whilst engaged in breaking stones near my hut two Europeans approached, and I found that they were officers from a French ship of war which was exploring the haven of Mombaz. One of them was a good botanist, and both were very friendly.

27th May.—* * * I heard with much sorrow
that a French sailor had entered the house of a
Mnika, and had attempted to take liberties with his
wife. The Mnika wanted to lodge a complaint
with me, but desisted when he heard that the
French did not belong to my Kabila, my tribe or
people.

31st May.—The cripple Mringe called upon me
to-day in Rabbai-Mpia for the first time. I told him
that we must acknowledge and worship God, as
Father, Son, and Holy Ghost. These were memorable words to him, and made an extraordinary impression.

6th June.—The cripple Mringe called again upon
me, and I explained to him a portion of the history of
the passion of Christ, whilst another Mnika listened
with attention to the discourse. I sometimes think
that there will soon be a change among these people,
though I am so often disappointed in this anticipation;
for I seem but to sow the seed upon stony places;
yet have I joy in hope, hope in believing, and work
on with trust; fervent in spirit, serving the Lord to
the best of my ability, and patiently waiting His
own time for the blessing!

8th June.—The savage Masai are occupying the
route to Jagga, so that Rebmann will be obliged
to go to the coast from the Pangani, or wait in
Jagga until the way is clear again. When I
consulted with the elders about the despatch of a
messenger to Kadiaro or Jagga, they said that
I must wait for three or four days more. I took

this opportunity to protest earnestly against infanticide, and implore the chiefs to abolish that horrible custom. They said that they would not repeat it; but the future alone can show whether they will keep their word.

9th June.—To-night I was very anxious respecting my fellow-labourer, Rebmann, and could do nothing but commend him to the protection of the Almighty. If any calamity should befall him, the heathen would say, "Where is now thy God?"

10th June.—While explaining Matthew x. to the chief we heard suddenly sounds of rejoicing and piping, and soon received from the men who had returned from Jagga tidings that Rebmann had arrived safely at Kadiaro from Jagga, and that he intended to return thence by Shimba to Mombaz. A portion of his diary was delivered to me.

11th June.—Rebmann's diary makes it clear that there is a noble country in the interior, well fitted for cultivation; that as Mount Kilimanjaro is covered with perpetual snow Jagga has plenty of water; and as the climate is good the whole land can be made use of for the growth of vegetable productions. Slavery is a great curse in Jagga; the chiefs and tribes wage war with each other, and sell their prisoners to the coast. He adds that the Arabs and Suahili have described us Europeans as cannibals; that the power of the chiefs is absolute and despotic; and that they and the people are great beggars. The route, it would seem, is at present free from Wakuafi, but may at any moment be endangered by Masai and Galla; and that the chiefs will allow a missionary to dwell among them.

12th June.—I went to Mombaz, to greet my dear fellow-labourer upon his return from Jagga, and to hear the details of his journey.

13th June.—We returned to Rabbai. Abdallah, who came to see us, said that the Wanika had been incensed against the French, because the latter, on visiting them, had asked at once where the boundary of the country was. " What boundary?" said the Wanika, " give us first a heshima," (a present.) It is unwise in a stranger to begin with geographical questions, as he is then sure to be taken for a spy sent by the king of his country.

20th June.—We wandered to the Wakamba hamlet, Endenge wa Kingodo, where we wished to make the acquaintance of the famous Wakamba chief, Kivoi of Kitui in Ukambani; but he was not at home. I visited, too, the Mnika Heba whom I wished to engage as a guide for my journey to Usambara to visit king Kmeri.

26th June.—I thought to-day a great deal on the question whether it would not be possible to obtain a number of missionaries who could support themselves by the labour of their own hands.

2nd September.—I began my translation of the Gospel of St. John into the Kinika language. The following is a comparison of the East-African with the West-African mission :—Our brothers in Western Africa can labour in compact hamlets and large towns, whilst we in the east, live amid a dispersed population. They have a difficult struggle to maintain with slavery, and the evil influence of the white people, but find the heathen inquisitive respecting the Gospel of Christ, which is not the case among the Wanika on this coast, as the people here are entirely worldly, and do not trouble themselves about spiritual matters. It is not easy, either, to find a large number of them together, and the establishment of schools is especially difficult.

21st September.—I completed the translation of the Gospel of St. John into the Kinika language.

5th November.—Mringe came to me and remained till the evening, giving me some information respecting several customs of the Wanika. When eating or drinking they place a little meat or drink on the ground, as a gift to the Koma, a custom which I had observed on several occasions, but did not understand its meaning till now. The heathen in Polynesia do the same. The Wanika believe that every tree, especially every cocoa-nut tree, and every spring or marsh where water is found, has its Shetani Mugo, its good Satan, or good spirit. They distinguish between Shetani Mudzo and Mui, good or bad spirits. The destruction of a cocoa-nut tree is regarded as equivalent to matricide, because that tree gives them life and nourishment, as a mother does her child.

10th November.—The chief told me of a great serpent which is sometimes seen out at sea, reaching from the sea to the sky, and which appears especially during heavy rain. I told him this was no serpent, but a water-spout, which corresponded to the whirlwind on dry land. I conversed with Mringe on Romans ii.

16*th November.*—According to the mythology of the Wanika, the Galla, Wakamba, and Wakuafi, had one common father whose eldest son was called Galla, who plundered another tribe of its cattle; upon which his brothers, Mkuafi and Mkamba, asked for a share of the booty; but were refused by their brother, Galla; whereupon Mkuafi robbed Galla, and he, again, was robbed by Mkamba, and *vice versâ;* and from that time arose a deadly enmity among the three brothers which has had no end.

19*th November.* (Sunday.)—I visited Muihani; and wherever I found people at work I spoke on the observance of the Sabbath.

Mringe said he wished to buy a hut, in which he might be alone and gather people round him; so I gave him half a dollar, and with this he got a hut built, in which I visited him. It was impossible for this sick and suffering, but God-seeking man longer to remain in the confined hut of his mother, who had begun to hate him as soon as he commenced to love the Word. His relations, too, despise him, and yet this poor man cannot work and earn his bread.

27*th November.*—On my way to Muihani I met many Wanika, to whom I discoursed. Afterwards I visited the eldest Abbe Mamkale, who has a great deal of wit and intelligence, but is a sad toper, going from him straight to Mringe, who is evidently upheld by grace from Above. Afterwards I went to the hut of a Mnika who shortly before had lost a little child by death. He said, that when next a child was born him he would call it "Rebmann;" for the Wanika have a custom of giving their children names in accordance with the circumstances or events of the time at which they are born. Because Rebmann was just then on his way to Jagga the parents wished to choose his name; and in like manner a Mnika-mother once bestowed on a child the name "Msungu," European, because it was born during my stay in Kambe.

28th November.—In Muihani Mringe made me acquainted with his neighbour Ndune who in sickness had listened attentively to Mringe's discourse respecting the gospel of Christ. His superstitious mother had wished the sick man to rely upon the Uganga, but he protested against such foolish practices.

Mringe's mother asked me whether a man must be always sitting over his book and reading. I replied, a Christian reads his Bible in the morning, says his prayers, and then goes to his daily labour; in the evening, he does the same, and while working, thinks on God and upon that which he has read.

29th November.—Mringe was with me during the night. We discoursed towards midnight about the world to come and the City of God; about the occupations of the blessed, and the incorruptible body of

our future state, and many other things. My poor
cripple devoured the words as they fell from my
lips; and I saw that they made an impression on
him, and felt happy, indeed, for it is at moments like
these that one feels the importance of a missionary's
calling. A missionary who feels the working of the
Spirit within him, and is upheld in its manifestation
to others, is the happiest being upon earth. In his
sight what are royal and imperial honours compared
with the office of a preacher in the bush or lonely
hut? And sure it is, that unless a missionary feels
ennobled by his calling, he will forsake his post, or
become an unprofitable labourer in the vineyard.

1st December.—Mringe told me that the Wanika believe that the spirit of a dying person goes into a
child unborn, and that thus every one is born a
second time. This was the first time that I had
heard of the transmigration of souls as a belief
among the Wanika, and I think that only a few
of them are acquainted with the idea, which, perhaps, has been learned from the Banians in
Mombaz, or from the Mohammedans, who may have
heard of it in their intercourse with the Hindoos.
As children tolerably resemble their parents the
Wanika believe that one of the deceased forefathers
of the family has entered into the child, and that,
therefore, this child resembles him (Utsihalanah).
Probably it is this idea of transmigration which
has decided the Wanika to kill misshapen children,
in the belief that they can only become criminals,
because they have been so in a former state.

Whilst I was speaking about Christ with the young Endaro who had often listened to me, he asked, " Who is Christ?" The question came upon my heart like a thunder-bolt; for I had thought that Endaro had long known whom I meant by Christ. My feelings were like those of Dr. Carey in India, when told by a native who had often listened to him, that he did not understand his discourse, while the speaker had fancied that after so long a residence in India he was perfectly understood by the natives.

15th December.—* * * In Great Rabbai there is said to be a Kisuka, a little devil, *i. e.*, an image probably of a saint which the Portuguese left behind them after their expulsion from Mombaz, which is now reverenced by the Wanika as a kind of war-god, and is borne round in procession before the outbreak of a war to rouse the warriors to heroic deeds. This is the only idol I have heard of in Eastern Africa, and it remarkably enough comes from an idolatrous Christian church.

25th December.—A number of Wanika collected in the Kaya, to call the chief to account, for having permitted the Sheikh Gabiri of Mombaz to cut down more trees for ship-building than had been allowed by the elders. The powerless chief was obliged to buy himself off by giving his people a cow. Such is the liberty and equality prevalent here, and indeed, in a general way, these African republics have long ago completely possessed what is still struggled for by those of Europe and America.

Among the Wanika and Wakamba every one is " free and independent" and yet, so controlled by his neighbour that freedom and dependence go hand in hand. In fact, our own civilized republics have still much to learn from those of uncivilized Africa.

28th December.—I visited Mringe and Ndune. The latter as well as the former begins to love the truth, though still much afraid of his drunken comrades, who threaten to get him punished if he abandons them altogether.

Mringe told me, that several chiefs had said to him, he might follow me if he pleased. There are now only wanting some to make a beginning, when many Wanika would be converted by the Word, so I urged Mringe, that he and Ndune should take the lead.

16th February, 1849.—Rebmann returned to-day from his second journey to Jagga; it appears desirable to extend our journeys of exploration by way of Jagga to Uniamesi, and thence to the western coast of Africa; and Rebmann resolved to enter on the long, difficult, and dangerous journey with thirty men, at the commencement of next April, after I have paid a preliminary visit to Zanzibar to purchase the necessaries for the expedition.

18th February.—To-day the Wanika celebrated their Boso festival, or the festival of the young people, who come to the Kaya to dance, shout, eat, and carouse. This time, however, not many children came; and several visited me just when the old Saha happened to be with me. When I was going to speak to the children about Christ, and to show them the folly of the feast, that hardened sinner who tries on all occasions to keep the Wanika back from the gospel said to them: " Go on with your dancing, that is your business." I had great difficulty in restraining myself from being angry with him, and could not help telling him that the Saviour had said that " whoso shall offend one of these little ones that believe in me, it were better for him that a millstone were hanged about his neck, and that he were drowned in the depth of the sea." The obdurate chief replied : " We Wanika will not quit our own ways; let you talk to us of Christ as you please." He was afterwards killed by the Masai; and similar, too, was the end of another Mnika who once said to me : " As little as you can make my finger when cut off grow again to my hand, just so little will we abandon our customs." This man, in a state of drunkenness set fire to a quantity of powder which burnt him dreadfully, so that he died in great pain.

5th April.—Rebmann entered on the journey to Uniamesi accompanied by me to the foot of the mountain Kadiaro, whence I returned on the 15th to Rabbai with five men.

16th to 18th April.—I rested from the toils of the journey; the heavy marches had terribly fatigued me.

28th April.—I planned to-day a journey to Ukambani, so that the north-east, too, might be explored, and preparations made for the erection of future missionary-stations; for the missionaries in Rabbai-Mpia must be the pioneers of Eastern Africa.

Since the beginning of this month it has been raining steadily, and I do not remember such a wet season on this coast. This and other reasons induced me to give up the journey to Lake Niassa, which is, it seems, full ten days' journey from Kiloa. The Suahili make the journey when the south wind begins to blow at the commencement of the rainy season, that they may meet with water on the way.

This afternoon I spoke seriously with the chief respecting the indifference of the Wanika, who will not learn even now, after we have procured them books at a great cost; for some time ago we received 500 printed copies each of my Kinika version of the Gospel of Luke, of the Heidelberg Catechism, and of a primer from Bombay, where they had been printed at the expense of the Church Missionary Society.

Read and expounded to the Wanika Abbe Sindo, Abbe Kunde, Muandoro, and Jwaha, the parable of the sower.

10th June.—I received intelligence of the arrival of our brothers Erhardt and Wagner in Mombaz.

11th June.—I went to Mombaz to welcome my brethren, and found Erhardt very ill, and advised him to proceed to Rabbai as quickly as possible, that he might benefit by the cooler climate.

15th June.—Poor Erhardt came to Rabbai in quite an exhausted state, and I feared that the fever would terminate fatally; for he was in a much worse plight than Rebmann and myself in 1846.

20th June.—Erhardt is still very ill. I com-

menced with our servant Amri the study of the
Kikamba language. Wagner has also been attacked by fever; against my advice, he would clothe
himself too lightly, and caught cold in the cool air
of Rabbai; for the rainy season is not over, and
the winds from the sea in this direction are high
and cold. I had hoped to find my burden lightened
by the arrival of new fellow-labourers, but the care
of the sick produces quite a contrary result. Our
Portuguese servant, Anthony, whom Erhardt has
brought with him from Bombay, is also unwell, and
my house has become a complete hospital.

27th June.—To-day Rebmann came back from
Jagga. The Lord has preserved him from many
and great dangers.

1st July.—The crisis of Erhardt's fever is over,
and he is progressing towards convalescence; Wagner, on the contrary, is worse.

3rd July.—It seems to me necessary, for the sake
of future missionaries, that I must learn the Kikamba,
Kiteita, Jagga, and Kisambara languages.

1st August.—Our dear brother Johannes Wagner
ended his sufferings yesterday, and was summoned
into a better world by the Lord and Giver of life,
who in the midst of life hath placed us in death!
Incomprehensible at first appeared to us this guidance which so quickly took from us our newly-
arrived fellow-labourer; but his very death has
brought a blessing to the Wanika, and although
dead, he still speaks to them; for they have now,
for the first time, seen the death and burial of a

Christian, whose joyful hope is in Christ, the life and the resurrection. After I had read the funeral service of the English liturgy, translating it into the Kinika language, I spoke to those present and those who had dug the grave, on 1 Thessalonians iv. 13, and finally we sang some verses of a hymn. From all this the natives were enabled to recognize the marked distinction between Christianity and the horrible wailing and other dark practices of heathenism; and so in this way, our departed friend did not come in vain into this benighted land.

18th September.—To-day I arranged with a troop of Wanika for my journey to Ukambani, promising each eight dollars for the journey to Kakunda, the village of Kivoi, the chief of the Wakamba tribe Kitui.

31st October.—The second chapter of Haggai strengthened me greatly, as regards my impending journey.

The chiefs of Duruma came to-day and demanded a present, so that I might be allowed a passage through their territory; asking, too, that I would take half of my baggage-bearers from Duruma, and only half from the Rabbai tribe. Everywhere nothing but greed and mendicancy opposed themselves to my journey! Our friends in Europe can scarcely conceive what obstacles a missionary has to meet and to overcome who wishes to travel into the interior, independent of the difficulties in the interior itself, before he can set forth from the coast.

1st November to 21st December, 1849.—Journey to

Ukambani, and thence back to Rabbai. After my return from Ukambani I continued for a few weeks, as formerly, my daily wanderings among the Wanika in the neighbourhood of Rabbai, preaching the gospel, and bidding all to the feast prepared, even the kingdom of Heaven; scattering the seed, not disheartened though so little had fallen upon good ground, and in Mringe alone has sprung up with a promise of bearing fruit an hundredfold, hopeful and trustful to the end!

CHAPTER XIII.

CLOSE OF RESIDENCE IN EASTERN AFRICA :—RETURN HOME.

First return to Europe—The Church Missionary Society re-inforces the East-African Mission—Return to Rabbai Mpia—Death and sickness among the missionary band—Mringe and his successor —Colonizing aspects of the Mission—The author's journeys into the interior—Second return to Europe—Bishop Gobat's Abessinian scheme—The author's latest visit to Abessinia—The way to Shoa closed : Return to Egypt—Farewell to Africa—Return home—Sympathy and offers of the Church Missionary Society.

PARTLY for the improvement of my health, and partly for the welfare of the East-African mission, I decided in the spring of 1850 on returning to Europe, which I had not seen since 1837. I was unwilling, however, to leave Africa without executing a project which I have cherished for years, which was to inspect the whole coast southward from Zanzibar as far as Cape Delgado, where the possessions of the Sultan of Zanzibar cease and those of the Portuguese commence, and in the company of my fellow-labourer, J. Erhardt, the voyage was performed in the February and March of 1850. After my return from this exploration I began in

April of the same year, my homeward journey by way of Aden and Egypt, reaching Europe in June.

After a short stay in Bâsel and Würtemberg, I proceeded to London, to advocate in person with the Committee of the Church Missionary Society, my scheme of an African chain of missions to be established through the whole breadth of the land, from east to west, in the direction of the Equator, and to obtain their consent to the printing of my Suahili grammar, and a comparative vocabulary of six East-African languages. This latter was assented to with the utmost readiness, and the Committee entered so far into the scheme of the chain of missions, as to resolve on founding without delay two new stations—one in the kingdom of Usambara, and the other in Ukambani, or in Jagga. With that object, two missionaries, Pfefferle and Dihlmann, were to be despatched with myself to Eastern Africa, accompanied by three lay brothers, Hagemann, Kaiser, and Metzler, of whom the first was a carpenter, the second an agriculturist, and the third a smith, so that with the Gospel the Africans might be offered the blessings of Christian civilization. Improved in health and with fresh courage and faith, and renewed strength for missionary work, I started on my return journey at the beginning of 1851, by way of Trieste, Smyrna, and Alexandria, and reached Mombaz in April. Scarcely had our new fellow-labourers (with the exception of Dihlmann, who left us at Aden, and returned to Europe) been fourteen days at Rabbai Mpia, when they were one after another attacked by fever. Missionary Pfefferle, who during the tedious voyage had endeared himself to all of us by his devotion and humility, and by his hearty faith and prayerful spirit, no less than by his determined zeal and purpose, was promising much for the East-African mission, we had to bear to the grave before long, whilst the speediest possible return to Europe seemed the most desirable course for our two brothers, Kaiser and Metzler, unless they, too, were destined to a like fate. On my return from Europe I found the mission much as I had left it, with the exception that poor Mringe had departed in peace, in faith in Christ, and had been baptized by Rebmann before his death. His place, however, was filled by another Mnika of the name of Abbe Gunja, with whom I had become slightly acquainted before my departure in the April of 1850, through the introduction of Mringe, as one who wished to learn the book of the Europeans. After my departure, he was instructed by Rebmann, and has since given gratifying proofs of a renewed heart.

Another change, too, had been effected by the purchase made by my two fellow-labourers, Rebmann and Erhardt, of a considerable piece of land in Kisuludini, on which they had begun to build a new house for two missionary families. It was purchased from the chiefs of Rabbai Mpia for thirty dollars, and was to serve partly as a place of settlement for the converted Wanika, and partly by cultivation to render invitingly apparent to the Wanika, Wa-

kamba, and Suahili, the blessings of agriculture and
home life, or, in other words, the benefits of civilization. My instructions from the Committee were to
proceed with Pfefferle to Ukambani, and to found
a new station there; but as Pfefferle was dead I
undertook the journey to Ukambani by myself on
the 11th of July, 1851. On the heights of Yata,
some 110 leagues from Mombaz, I intended to establish a missionary station, but the attempt failed, as
will be seen hereafter, in the narrative of this
difficult and dangerous journey. After my return
on the 30th September 1851 to Rabbai from my
Ukambani journey I continued, as formerly, to visit
the scattered Wanika and to preach the Gospel to
them. In October of that year Rebmann went to
Egypt, to marry an amiable English lady, who had
already proved her aptitude for missionary life
amongst the heathen whilst residing with the wife of
missionary Lieder at Cairo. Soon afterwards I
resolved to visit Usambara a second time, being
desirous of knowing whether king Kmeri was
disposed to fulfil the promise made by him in the
year 1848, and at what place he would allow the
station to be established. This second expedition
was carried out in the period between the 10th of
February and the 14th of April, 1852. On my
return from Usambara I had the pleasure of greeting my dear fellow-labourer Rebmann and his
wife. Erhardt had meanwhile pretty well finished
the building in Kisuludini, so that the two missionaries could now occupy their pretty residence

MISSIONARY HOUSE AT KISULUTINI.
(MISSIONARY REBMANN PREACHING)
SKETCHED ON THE SPOT BY CAPTAIN RICHARD BURTON.

there, while I remained in the old hut in the Kaya, making from it daily excursions to the Wanika. I endeavoured, moreover, to organize in the Kaya itself a regular congregation, which was joined every morning by some neighbouring families and my servants, when after prayers I explained to them the gospels according to the order in which they are to be read in the Church.

It was late in the autumn of 1853 that I was compelled to leave Rabbai, and to return to Europe for the restoration of my health. Rebmann and his wife were now alone at the station, as Erhardt was in Usambara, and on the 25th of September I took leave of my dear friends from whom I had experienced so much love. Leaving Mombaz in October I sailed to Aden, thence to Suez, and from Alexandria, in an Austrian steamer, to Trieste. Travelling thence by Vienna and Dresden, I reached the dear fatherland, Würtemberg, about Christmas, but in a very enfeebled condition. As soon as my health permitted it I proceeded in the year 1854 to make my report to the Committee on the Rabbai-mission, and to receive further instructions. It was resolved to reinforce the mission by a new missionary in the person of our dear Brother Deimler from Bavaria. About the same time the Bishop of Jerusalem had formed the plan of sending to Abessinia a number of brethren, brought up as mechanics, who had received some missionary instruction at the Institute of St. Chrishona,* his object being, if possible, to revive

* The Missionary Institute at St. Chrishona, near Basel, was

the mission to that country which had fallen through
in the year 1843. I accordingly offered to visit Abessinia on my way back to Rabbai, and in the company of one of these brothers to pave the way for the
contemplated mission. The Committee approved of
my plan, and in the November of 1854 I left
Trieste, after having published at Tübingen my
Wakuafi Dictionary, and the English Liturgy in
the Suahili language. On my arrival at Jerusalem
I waited upon Bishop Gobat respecting the Abessinian mission, and received from him the necessary
instructions, with which early in 1855 I paid my
last visit to Abessinia, an account of which is given
in Part III. Arrived at Gondar, the capital of
Abessinia, we found the road to Shoa completely

founded in 1840 by Herr Spittler, the well-known Christian philanthropist, and originator of most of the Christian institutions,
which have flourished in and near Basel, since the beginning of the
present century. The purpose of the Missionary Institution at St.
Chrishona is to combine theological instruction with agricultural
and mechanical training, in order to enable the missionaries to
support themselves by their own hands in cases of necessity. The
fixed number of the students will in future amount to thirty; and
these, having finished their theological course of four years, are to be
transferred to any missionary society that may ask the committee
for any number of missionaries. The committee of the St. Chrishona
Institution has, up to the present time, selected no mission-field abroad,
except Abessinia and Egypt, where it is about to found the Apostles'
Street, as it is to be called, mentioned at page 133, a chain of twelve
stations connecting Gondar with Jerusalem. Most of the missionaries
from St. Chrishona have been sent to North America for the German
immigrants, to Western Africa, Turkey, Russia, Abessinia, and one
to Patagonia. The Chrishona Institution must not be confounded
with the great missionary seminary which was founded in 1816, in the
town of Basel, and which aims at a more extensive theological training.

closed by the war which the new king, Theodorus, was waging against that country; so it seemed the best plan under the circumstances, to return to Egypt, forward a report to Bishop Gobat, and then, by way of Cairo and Aden proceed to Rabbai by sea. Fever, sun-stroke, and fatigue on the return journey nearly killed me, and I quite expected to have found a grave in the Nubian Desert. On my arrival at Cairo it became clear to me that I could not go on to Rabbai in this suffering condition, nor indeed any longer endure the climate of Africa or present way of life, and that therefore my work in Africa was at an end. So, with deep sorrow in August 1855, I bade farewell to the land where I had suffered so much, journeyed so much, and experienced so many proofs of the protecting and sustaining hand of God; where, too, I had been permitted to administer to many souls the Word of Life, and to name the Name of Jesus Christ in places where it had never before been uttered and known. God grant, that the seed so broad-cast may not have fallen only on stony places, but may spring up in due season, and bear fruit an hundredfold !

In the September of 1855 I reached Stuttgardt, and resided for a time at Kornthal till my future career of usefulness should develop itself. The Committee of the Church Missionary Society in London manifested a kind sympathy with my sufferings, and expressing a hope that I might soon be so far recovered as to be able to continue my labours in Africa in a better climate, proposed

to me to go to the Mauritius, and seek out such
natives of Eastern Africa as had formerly been thence
sold into slavery, but were now residing in the island
as free men, who might be willing to learn; and to
instruct them sufficiently to become catechists, with
a view of ultimately sending them back to Africa in
that capacity, a plan which had been attended with
much success at Sierra Leone in Western Africa. At
the Cape of Good Hope, too, the Committee was of
opinion that such persons were also to be met with.
Agreeable and inviting as was this proposal, much
as I approved of it, having regard to its important
results, I could not persuade myself to return to
Africa for some years to come, as I wished first for
the complete restoration of my health, and for time
to review my whole life, especially my missionary
life in Africa; an occupation for which, out there,
I had never yet found sufficient time or leisure.

Our merciful Father, who hath hitherto so wonderfully upheld me, and rendered my path in life pleasant to me, even amidst care and toil, hath been
pleased to bestow upon His servant an helpmeet for
him in the daughter of senator Pelargus, of Stuttgardt, my beloved wife Charlotte, whose Christian
experiences, joined to a perfect disregard of self and
an affectionate nature, have been my greatest support,
both in the calling in which I labour, and in the
shattered state of my health; for, indeed, she has
proved herself to me the best and truest human support, alike for body and soul!

Full of trust in His hands do I leave the future of

my life on earth, whether of activity at home, or in
the former field of my labour amongst the heathen
of Africa!   To Him would I render, as is most due,
all honour and praise, worshipping Him in time and
eternity, being thankful to Him, and blessing His
Name for all His mercies bestowed upon me from my
youth upwards, especially in the trials and perils of
my sojourn amongst the benighted tribes of Eastern
Africa!

END OF PART I.

PART II.

———

TRAVELS IN EASTERN AFRICA.

———

KADIARO—JAGGA—USAMBARA—UKAMBANI.

CHAPTER I.

REBMANN'S JOURNEY TO KADIARO.

Departure by moonlight—Endunga : the wilderness—The magic
staves and missionary resistance—Flora and fauna of the wilderness
—The Baschi ; pig and ass—Sunday evening in the wilderness;
missionary discourse—Kadiaro—Maguasini—First greeting of a
Teita family; comparison with a Wanika reception—Fears of the
Teita people—The missionary fortress—Pare people and native
tobacco-pipes—Dress and ornaments in Teita—Its geography and
population—Mission prospects—Return journey to Rabbai Mpia
—European shoes and native sandals—Burden-bearing—Africa
and her children.

Before I attempt to describe my more extended travels in Eastern
Africa, I would introduce some narratives of travel by my former fellow-
labourer, Missionary Rebmann. It was he who inaugurated the commencement of our journeys of exploration; first, by his excursion to the mountain
Kadiaro, in the Teita-country, some thirty-six leagues from the sea-coast of
Mombaz; and then by his journeys to Jagga, about one hundred leagues
in the interior of the African main-land. My dear friend describes his
journey to Kadiaro in the following pleasing manner.

ON the night of the 14th of October 1847 just as
the moon was appearing above the horizon I began
my journey being accompanied by six Wanika
and two Mohammedans. During that night I proceeded about one league and a half; and in the
morning after daybreak we journeyed through a
tolerably level and rich pasture country for about a
league and a half, till we came to a tract more undu-

lating in appearance, covered with bushes and a few
stunted trees rather than grass, and nowhere cultivated, yet serving the Wanika for grazing-land.
We bivouacked under a tree in the forest near the
Wanika village of Engoni; and the next day, after
a march of more than four leagues over stony ground,
with little vegetation and completely uncultivated,
we reached Endungu, the name of the whole eastern
boundary of the wilderness, which stretches westward
from hence to Teita, for a breadth of full twenty
leagues; and which forms a great plain, which is
somewhat undulating in its eastern half, while the
western half presents a dead level. As Endungu
stands some hundred feet above the outstretched
plain, it afforded me a splendid view over its whole
extent from west to east, with the mountains of Teita
rising to a height of from 4000 to 5000 feet in the
background.

This desert, or more properly speaking, this
wilderness, has of late years become infested with
Wakuafi and Galla, and consequently it cannot be
traversed in safety, which has led both Mohammedans and heathen to invoke the supposed superior
protection of the powers of darkness in many ways,
of which superstition my own people were about to
give me a specimen. As we descended the slope
from Endunguni we found two magic-staves stuck
in the ground by the way-side, about two feet long,
burnt black, and wreathed round at the top with
the bark of a tree. My people wished these to be
carried with us through the wilderness, nor would they

stir at my command without them, so I tore the bark
off one of them and threw them away as far as I
could ; but they still demurred, and wanted to turn
back and search for them, and only after a long controversy would they consent to proceed without
them ; for they told me what my Bible was to me
the staves would be to them, a preservative against
wild beasts and robbers.   My caravan-driver, too,
held back, evidently determined to recover the one
from which I had not torn the talismanic bark ; but
I was determined that whilst the men served me
they should use none of these magic Uganga, and
told him so, stating that on arriving at Teita, whither
we were then journeying, the first thing I should
do would be to teach the Teita the Gospel, and by
its means destroy their Uganga, telling them that
magic was sinful in the sight of Him who had sent
His only Son, Jesus Christ, into the world to save all
sinners, Europeans and Africans, Suahili, Wanika,
Galla, and Wakuafi, if they would only believe and
be baptized.

Descending into the wilderness, our narrow footpath soon wound, for a short way, through a thicket,
in which many sorts of Euphorbia were to be seen.
The circumstance that even where no path has been
made, the wilderness is at once easily permeable and
affords bush enough to conceal an enemy, has made
the journey of the caravans very insecure.   The soil
appeared to me in many places very favourable for
culture.   Among the wild animals which are very
numerous, gazelles, antelopes, and giraffes, are par-

ticularly observable. Another species of animal which we often met with, and which the natives called Baschi, I was not acquainted with. The young are very like swine, on which account the Mohammedans do not eat them, while the old ones have more the form of an ass and are of a grey colour. Late in the evening of the 16th of October we reached Kurundu, and spent the night in the bush a little further on. Next morning we recommenced our journey, and continued it until the setting of the sun, when my people again looked about for a place suitable for a bivouac, which must always be in some measure surrounded by bush. It was Sunday evening; some of my people named the Name of Christ, and I profited by the opportunity once more to bear testimony to Him. I told them of His miracles; spoke especially of His atoning death, and that He had died to discharge us of our sins; mine as well as theirs. On the third day, on Sunday, the first day of the week, He had risen again; therefore, in the land of my home, Sunday was kept holy. He who believed in Christ, received forgiveness of his sins, with life and blessedness. I told them that they must seek to obtain new hearts, and then all would go right; their country too, would become new. Our fathers and countrymen had once been like them and theirs, and our country like theirs, bog and wilderness; but since we had believed in Christ, our land had been transformed into a garden of God. They asked, "Who, then, told you of Christ?" I replied: People who came

to us from other countries, as now we come to you,
and brought with them the book of God ; our fathers
received it, and since then everything has gone well
with us.   Such a statement always makes some impression upon them.   Already at the commencement
of this conversation the leader of our little caravan
had said, they had given up their magic staves, and
would like now to become acquainted with my book.
When they became acquainted with the Bible, I
rejoined, they would see for themselves in what
estimation to hold their magicians and their spells.

Next day at noon, after a march of between three
and four hours we reached Kadimu, which is an out-
post of the mountains of Teita, consisting of enormous
masses of rock, towering more than 100 feet above
each other, and almost destitute of vegetation.   Here
is it, above all, that the Galla and Wakuafi lie in wait
for the caravans, and surprise them all the more
easily as the passes through these ranges are rather
narrow.   After bivouacking for the last time in
the wilderness we reached next morning, the 19th of
October, that part of Teita which is called Kadiaro.
It is a solitary mountain-mass, stretching about one
league and a half from south to north, and near
its centre reaching its highest summit which consists
of an enormous mass of rock and is, for the most
part, completely perpendicular.   After ascending
the mountain for more than a league we reached
the village Maguasini, containing about fifty huts,
which are built among enormous rocks protruding
from the mountain, with broken masses lying scat-

tered around. On such a rock it was that I greeted one of the elders of the village with his large family, as the first assemblage of Teita people which I had met. The quiet and more earnest character of this mountain people prevented them from making a great deal of fuss in the reception of the first European whom they had seen in their midst, as is the custom of the Wanika, who always, when you come for the first time into one of their villages, set up dancing and singing in honour of the stranger. Here there was nothing of the kind; but on the other hand, they immediately asked whether I had come to build a fortress on their mountain? a question which, as it seemed to me, had been put into their heads by my own people. I answered that the only fortress which I had come to build for them, was one in which they might escape the wrath of God; for I had come to preach to them Christ, who had released all men from the power of sin, and from the wrath of God, and who had become our Saviour. In this and other ways I sought to sow the seed of the Divine Word in their hearts, and the manner in which they listened to me induced me to believe that I had not laboured in vain.

At Maguasini I saw also two men of the tribe of Pare, which lies two days' journey to the south-west of Teita. They were clothed in skins, and used perfectly formed tobacco-pipes manufactured by themselves. The bowls were of clay and the sticks of a kind of bamboo, ornamented with wire. From

the Teita people I heard that their ancestors had
come thirty days' journey from the North, and the
structure of their huts quite coincides with this
tradition, which after the fashion of Abessinia have
mostly a circular, and here and there, too, an oval
form; nor do the roofs, like those of the Wanika,
reach down to the floor, but spring at a rise of
four feet above the ground. The clothing of the
men is very simple; they only throw a piece of
cloth round them, the arms and ears being more
or less hung with brass wire. By their strange
adornment the females are completely disfigured,
encircling as they do the neck with whole
loads of beads, such as the Romanists use for their
rosaries, and winding them round the feet. Then
they wear two leather aprons, one in front and one
behind, which with garnish of beads they gird
round their loins, covering even the edges with
similar ornaments. It rarely happens, and when it
does merely on account of the cold, that they throw
a piece of cloth round the upper part of their bodies
and their bosoms, the latter being generally bare.
On their arms, like the men and even more so, they
wear brass wire, which is the ornament in use among
all the tribes of these regions. Amongst the natural
productions is the sugar-cane of good quality, from
which the people of Teita prepare a favourite beverage, which perhaps may resemble that of Pompey's
dark followers mentioned by Lucan.

The Teita-land forms a Delta, or triangle, the
southerly point of which is the mountain Kadiaro,

already described, and the northerly and north-westerly points are formed by the mountain chains of Endara and Bura, which both stretch in one direction from south-west to north-east for a length amounting to about three days' journey. Endara itself, to the east of Bura, is a day's journey, some ten leagues, and Bura two days' journey from Kadiaro. With the Teita-land I had hoped to ascend a second terrace of the African highlands; but in place of this between the Kadiaro and the two northern mountain chains of Teita the same table-land extends, to which the ascent is formed by the downs which run along the coast, and which constitute the plain inhabited by the Wanika tribes. As to population, there seem to be in Kadiaro, the southern section of the Teita-land, only eight villages, with a population, including that of the village of Maguasini, of about 2000 souls. The Bura mountains, sometimes called Kilima Kibomu, may contain 500, and the Endara 100 villages; an estimate which, if not exaggerated, would give a population of about 152,000 for the whole Teita-land.

As regards a mission to this people, up to this date we can only say that it is very feasible and very desirable. The way is clear; but when it shall take place cannot be foretold. Let us hope that the time is not far distant when the messengers of peace, proceeding from east and west, will make their voices heard, until they meet together in the centre of the African continent.

On the morning of the third day after my arrival

in Teita (22nd of October) I began my return-journey through the wilderness. We passed again the same stations as on the journey to Teita, and after a tough march of three days, during which I walked mostly only in my stockings, as my shoes hurt me, I reached our missionary-station at Rabbai Mpia, safely, on the morning of the 25th of October. I bore up tolerably against the heat of the sun, although during the day its rays fell perpendicularly on our heads; and my only trouble arose from my shoes, on which account I was often tempted to envy the natives, who go barefoot; and if on a long journey that manner of walking becomes painful, or the thorns compel them to change it, they wear a simple sort of sandal, which every one makes for himself out of a little piece of leather. During a journey they carry their loads on their heads, not as we do, across the shoulders. If the load is heavy they are obliged to bend forward to some extent, that it may rest as much as possible on the back. Singularly enough they then present a figure precisely like that of the massive and monotonous continent of Africa whose children they are, and which, as if in strict harmony with its painful history, wears the appearance of a huge monster-slave bent down by his burden, and looking despondingly towards America.

CHAPTER II.

To Bura—Forced residence near Jawia—Timidity of the Teita, and its causes—Beautiful scenery; reminiscences of home—The Chief Muina—Onward again—Astonishment of the guide—The trap-pits of the Teita—First view of Kilimanjaro, the snow-mountain — The country between Teita and Jagga—Arrival in Kilema—Distinct view of Kilimanjaro; contrasts of scenery—King Masaki—The Kishogno—Mutual present-giving—Visit from the king—His appearance—Strange use of a fork—The king's cordiality—Ascent of a mountain; extensive prospect—The return—NOTES ON JAGGA AND MISSIONS—Geographical conformation, and civil economy—Politics and society in Jagga—Its habitations—Substitute for salt—Native expedition to Kilimanjaro—Advantages of Jagga as a mission-station —Argument for the establishment of missionary colonies in Eastern Africa.

ABOUT noon on the 27th of April 1848, having commended ourselves to the guidance of Providence, I began my journey with nine men to carry the baggage, necessary for a passage through such great wastes; and for seven days our way lay through a wilderness, for the most part perfectly level. From Kadiaro we struck north-westward, reaching Bugada, a mountain covered with wood, but having no inhabitants, on the 1st of May. To make way was very difficult, on account of the thick and thorny jungle, through which our guide had missed the path. On

SUAHILI & WOMEN OF KAMBA & JAGGA.

the 3rd of May we passed the little river Madade, which flows from the east foot of the Bura from north to south, gathering in its course the other waters of the Bura, when, after assuming the name of Gnaro, it absorbs the river Jiarbo, and finally empties itself into the sea at Wassin. When we had crossed the river we were in the Bura territory, and encamped at a spot on its bank in the forest, sending at once three men to Mbosa, the chief of the nearest village, Jawia, which lies on the top of the mountain, to announce our arrival and to summon him to us. But before they returned, several Teita arrived from the neighbouring plantations, bringing sugar-cane, bananas, and Indian corn, which my people enjoyed very much, our own provisions having come to an end.

Constant rain, and the illness of one of my servants, kept me in the neighbourhood of the village Jawia until the 6th of May. The inhabitants and their chiefs appeared so stupid and fearful, that it would have required a long stay on my part to have gained their confidence, so as to induce them to hearken to the glad tidings of the Gospel. The women and children were especially afraid of me, so much indeed that in one of the villages I felt compelled to say, " Why are you afraid of me ? You are many, and at home ; I am not afraid, although I am alone, and a stranger among you." The causes of this timidity are twofold ; the poor people, with their faith in magic, look upon Europeans as magicians ; and the lying Mohammedan traders for purposes of their own seek to alienate the natives of the interior from Europeans, by ascribing to the latter all sorts of crimes, and cannibalism among the rest.

On the 7th of May we took our way westward through the most luxuriant grass and undergrowth, alternating with noble trees, first ascending and then descending the mountain, at the foot of which we had encamped, till after an hour's journey we descended into a narrow valley, through which a clear brook murmured on its way, and on whose banks sugar-cane sprang up indigenously. Some Teita came; but, stupid as the rest of their race, they scarcely looked at us. How different from the Wakamba, those nomads and traders of all Eastern Africa, who, when they see a European crowd from all sides and wonder at everything they see! From the valley we ascended again, and had a noble prospect, particularly towards the south and south-west. How splendid the whole landscape, with its rich variety of mountain, hill, and dale, covered by the most luxurious vegetation! I could have fancied myself on the Jura mountains, near Basel, or in the region about Cannstatt in the dear fatherland, so beautiful was the country, so delightful the climate. Our way was across the bed of a mountain stream, over hill and dale, through plantations of Indian corn and beans, past small herds of cattle belonging to the Teita, then along fields of sugar-cane and banana, till we descended into the valley, with its rich pasture-lands. What a pity that this luxuriant growth of grass year after year must perish unused! An immeasurable tract of the richest land stands here open

to the church of Christ.   " The meek shall inherit the
earth."   The destiny of these noble regions must be
a great one.   We halted in the vicinity of the village
Muasagnombe, where I had again to give some presents, American calico and beads, to two chiefs,
through whose country I had wandered, and had
still to pass.   The people here showed rather more
curiosity, and I explained to the Chief Maina and
his brother Lugo, as well as to some other people,
the reason for my journey.

May 7th (Sunday).—A lovely morning.   It seemed
to me as if Nature were celebrating with me the
Sabbath.   Mountains and all hills ; fruitful trees ;
beasts and all cattle ; creeping things, and flying
fowl with the varied melody of their song, praised
their Creator with me.   In the morning I had again
an opportunity to explain to some people the great
object of my journey.   I generally do this by showing them my Bible, and telling them that it is the
Word of God, which points out to us the way to
heaven ; that I would translate this book into their
language, and by and by seek to make old and young
acquainted with its contents.   Our fathers, I tell
them, were made happy by this book.   Little, however, is to be done with these people during short
visits ; if they are to become really acquainted with
the Gospel we must dwell among them.

May 8.—After a short excursion I found the
chief, Maina, with another Teita, sitting under a
tree.   He asked me some questions, and a Mnika
who was with me, translated for him my statement

of the chief articles of our faith. He did not
encourage my wish to converse on religious matters
with him; yet the more serious character of the
Teita showed itself however in this, that Maina
did not laugh, as the Wanika are in the habit of
doing, when he heard of the resurrection.   On
the 9th of May, when I was to take leave of Maina,
to continue my journey to Jagga, he first presented me with Jofi, a beverage which is prepared from sugar-cane, the " tenera duleis ab arun-
dine succus" of the poet of Cordova, and the half of
a heifer, which he ordered to be slaughtered. The
libations and semi-religious ceremonies with which
he accompanied the leave-taking I refused to par-
ticipate in, although he assured me that there was
no question of Uganga.   After my people had
prepared the flesh of the heifer for the journey by
smoking it, we departed about four o'clock in the
afternoon, and bivouacked by the river Gnaro.
After another day's journey through thick jungle
and the forest we bivouacked under a large tree,
a little after sunset.   Here my guide looked at me
with astonishment, saying: " You are here with
nothing but an umbrella, and formerly we needed
five hundred muskets, so dangerous was the spot
where we are; for this was one of the chief encamp-
ments of the plundering Wakuafi." I replied: " It
is the work of God; He has opened a way for his
Gospel." As my people had a good deal of meat
with them, in the night we heard several hyenas
quite close to us, attracted by the scent.

On the 10th of May we left the Gnaro at daybreak and proceeded through a pathless wilderness,
as my guide had quarrelled with the king of Dufeta,
and was afraid to cross his country, although it is
the ordinary route from Teita to Jagga.   This
circumstance made the journey more painful, as
the kind of grass over which we went was full
of pointed leaves and burs that wounded my
feet severely, as I did not wear boots, but only
shoes.   After we had travelled some leagues, we
came to a place where the Teita had prepared
a number of pits in which to catch elephants,
buffaloes, and all sorts of wild animals.   The
wilderness between Teita and Jagga appears
to be richer in elephants, than that to the east
of Teita, whence these animals have mostly
disappeared and withdrawn into the interior.   In
the course of the day we saw many herds of
giraffes and zebras, and in the evening a rhinoceros.
There is great uniformity in the characteristic gran-
deur of this country; always repeating itself—great
plains, then suddenly, again, high monotonous
mountain-masses.

May 11.—In the midst of a great wilderness, full
of wild beasts, such as rhinoceroses, buffaloes, and
elephants, we slept beneath thorn-bushes, quietly
and securely under God's gracious protection ! This
morning we discerned the mountains of Jagga more
distinctly than ever; and about ten o'clock, I fancied
I saw the summit of one of them covered with
a dazzlingly white cloud.   My guide called the

white which I saw, merely " Beredi," cold; it was
perfectly clear to me, however, that it could be
nothing else but snow. Resting for a while soon
afterwards under a tree, I read in the English Bible
the cxith Psalm, to which I came in the order
of my reading. The promise made a lasting impression upon me, in sight of the magnificent snow-
mountain; for the sixth verse expresses so majestically and clearly that of which I had only noted
down the presentiment in my journal on Saturday
last.*

The whole country round between Teita and
Jagga has a sublime character. To the west, was
the lofty Mount Kilimanjaro with its perpetual snow;
to the south-west was the massive and monotonous
Ugano; to the north-west, the extended mountain-chain of Kikumbulia; and to the east, the
chains of the Teita-mountains with their highest
summit, called Veruga, which (with the exception
of Kilimanjaro) rise 4000 to 6000 feet above the
plain surrounding them. In the course of the day
I had also a faint view towards Kaptei (or Kaftei),
as the country proper of the Wakuafi is called,
lying to the north of Jagga.

May 12.—We crossed the river Lumi or Lomi
at seven in the morning. The nearer we approached
the mountains of Jagga the richer was the vegetation; here and there we met with large and
magnificent trees, such as I had not seen since I left

---

* " He hath shewed his people the power of his works, that he
may give them the heritage of the heathen."

the coast, till at last we entered a noble valley,
thickly grown over with grass which reached up to
our middle. Abundant pasture-land for thousands
of cattle! Oh, what a noble country has God reserved
for his people! Between four and five in the afternoon we reached the beautiful and sparkling river
Gona, which has its source in the snowy summit of
Kilimanjaro. A great tree served as a most unsatisfactory bridge over it, and upon reaching the
opposite bank I enjoyed a refreshing bath, the
extreme coldness of the water plainly showing that
its source can only be in the snow-mountain. The
coast portion of the journey to the river had been
very stony, and much obstructed by jungle.

May 13.—After bivouacking on the bank of the
Gona for the night, we recommenced our journey at
eight o'clock this morning, and after a painful march
of many hours through thick jungle, reached the first
trench which surrounds the little kingdom of Kilema.
Crossing the ditch on a very shaky bridge, consisting of a slim tree, we were again on pasture-
land, where we could see the plantations of Kilema,
but not the dwellings hidden in them. About a
quarter of an hour afterwards we were met by a
number of soldiers of Masaki, the King of Kilema,
whose only clothing was some fringed hides, hanging very loosely about them. We sat down for a
while under the shadow of a large tree, where we
had to wait for about an hour. I gazed on the
lovely country, which seemed to be bursting with
plenteousness, and presented in a comparatively

small extent the most striking contrasts. In our immediate vicinity was the beautiful river Gona; and on its banks, as well as on the foot of the mountains around, the richest vegetation of a perfect dark green of perpetual summer; and when I raised my eyes I beheld, apparently only a few leagues distant, but in reality from one to two days' journey, Kilimanjaro, covered with perpetual snow and ice. When I was summoned to Masaki my guide put grass into my hand after the custom of the country, that I might so greet the king, who had, likewise, some in his. In conformity with their usage I gave my hand to him and to his ministers. There was nothing to distinguish him, while some of his chief men wore caps made out of skins, and long garments. Our salutations over a sheep was slaughtered in order to present me with the Kishogno, token of friendship, which consists of a little bit of skin, from the forehead of the animal, which the king fastened on my middle finger. In a little hut, in the midst of a whole forest of bananas, and which completely shut out any view, I afterwards delivered to the young king my presents, consisting chiefly of calico and beads, a knife, fork, scissors, needles, and thread, and some other trifles, worth, altogether, from ten to twelve dollars; receiving in return, as provisions for myself and my little caravan, a cow and several sheep and goats.

The wounds on my feet prevented me from leaving my hut until the 20th of May. The king's vizier and other chief men of the land visited me

several times almost every day. On the 14th I
was asked by some of them, with the aid of what
weapons I had come thither ? To which my guide
at once replied, that I had nothing with me but my
umbrella ; but I added, pointing to Heaven, that
" I had come, trusting in God, the Christians'
' Eruwa,' alone !"* They rejoined : " In Eruwa
alone ! " " Yes," I said, " for He alone is all and
everything, and wild beasts, as well as wicked men,
are in His hand." They could scarcely believe,
much less understand, how I could have made so
long a journey without spear and shield, or without the use of powerful enchantments.

On the 16th the king himself visited me, accompanied by his vizier and brother-in-law. Everything I had on and with me attracted his attention,
even the buttons on my trousers. When his curiosity
was a little satisfied I took my Bible in my hand,
and said to him that we Europeans had to thank this
book for everything that he had just seen. To visit
his country was of small moment to me ; but to teach
him and his people the contents of this book was
what I desired above all. Our fathers had once lived
on as ignorant as all the people in these countries,
until they had obtained this book. On this Masaki
took my Bible boldly into his hands, and amused
himself by turning over the leaves. He is a lively
young man, with a bearing no less intelligent

---

* All the time of my residence in Jagga it rained in torrents
almost every night, on which account the sun is welcome to the
inhabitants, and is their god ;—Eruwa = sun, heaven, god.

than worthy of a king; so that, without wearing any external mark of his rank, he is easily distinguishable from his subjects. He visited me again on the 19th for a few minutes, having a fork, (which along with a knife I had presented to him), in his hair as an ornament! I explained to him the use of it; he laughed, but did not seem to understand.

May 24.—The king visited me once more with some of his chiefs. I assured them again, and earnestly, that I had no other aim and occupation than to teach what was written in my book. This, and a great deal more about my mission and myself was excellently interpreted to them by my guide, Bana Kheri, so that they understood me very well. By and by they went out of the little hut and consulted with my guide, who then told me that the king would receive me or my brother as a teacher, and that we were to go into no other country. Before returning to the coast I was to stay for three days longer, having full permission to make excursions when and whither I chose, the best possible sign of the king's confidence in me.

May 25.—I ascended to-day a mountain about two thousand feet high, from which I had a most extensive view in almost every direction. To the south-east, there was an open prospect almost to the sea-coast, and I could clearly distinguish the summit of the lofty mountain Yombo in the Wanika-land, in the neighbourhood of Wassin; and on that mountain, as my guide told me, you can see, at one and the same time, Zanzibar and the Kilimanjaro, an interesting geographical fact. To-day Kilimanjaro was veiled in clouds, otherwise I might have seen it invested with the silver crown, by which it seems to claim the title of king of the mountains of Eastern Africa. Before I descended from the noble mountain on which I had enjoyed so grand a view, I prayed from the depths of my heart, as regards all the populations around,—" Thy kingdom come." On the way back to my gloomy hut we visited several of the king's residences, which were, however, nothing more than the usual African huts covered with withered grass and impenetrable to light and air. This evening I heard that the people of Jagga, too, pray to the souls of the dead, which they call Warumu; but instead of rice and palm-wine, like the Wanika, they place milk on the graves. This custom, diffused far and wide in Eastern Africa, proves a strong yearning after life in a future state.

On the 26th of May Rehani, the king's vizier, came to me early, and asked me all sorts of questions respecting my supposed supernatural gifts; and as the rain kept him with me, I had time to lay before him the chief articles of our faith, so that the name of Christ has at least been named in this country, and the people know that I am His servant, and not a trafficker or dealer in magic and lies. At noon on the 29th, Rehani with the king's uncle and one of his brothers came to bid me farewell in the king's name, as he himself, it appeared, could not come on account of

the sickness of a child. They brought a goat as provisions for the three days' march through th wilderness to Teita, after which we could again procure
food. In taking leave of me, they asked me to return
soon again to their country and reside in it, and not
go to any other.

In the evening I began at last my journey back.
At first, walking was painful, for the wounds on my
feet were not yet healed, and the vegetable world of
the wilderness seems to have conspired to make the
way difficult for us poor wanderers. The journey
back to Bura was accomplished safely in three days'
hard walking. During it, we found a fine antelope
in one of the pits dug by the Teita to trap elephants
and other animals. We reached Kadiaro on the 7th
of June. As I had already travelled three times the
route from Kadiaro to Rabbai, I took that by Shimba
to Mombaz. Shimba is the southern continuation of
the mountains on the coast inhabited by the Wanika,
and is a day's journey distant from Rabbai. Immediately to the west of it I saw a most magnificent
country, intersected by numerous streams, and bearing on its face every proof of fertility, but lying
almost wholly unused ;—land enough for thousands
of families, while the spacious and lofty plateau of
the Shimba itself offers to the settler the finest and
healthiest situation, with an extended view over the
Indian Ocean, and with continuous enjoyment of
the fresh sea-air ! On the 10th of June, I camped
out for the last time on my return-journey ; and on
the 11th I reached Mombaz, safely ending under

God's protection and blessing my six weeks' life of
wandering.

NOTES ON JAGGA AND MISSIONS.

It is their form of government which chiefly dis-
tinguishes the inhabitants of Jagga from the
Wateita, Wakamba, and Wanika.   It seems as if
there were a harmony between the physical con-
formations of those countries and their political constitutions.   Among the Wakamba in their plains,
there is a uniform level, so that scarcely any individual is clothed with any degree of authority and
mastership.   The Jaggas go to the other extreme;
they exalt a single individual to such a political
height above themselves, that they are almost slaves,
just as their snow-crowned Kilimanjaro lifts its
head so high above the clouds, that the other mountains around it are almost reduced to comparative
insignificance.

The greatest delight of the Mangi lies in the birth of
a Msoro.   As soon as they can do without a mother's
care all male children are compelled to live together,
to be trained early to serve the king as guards, and
their country as engineers, in the construction of
water-courses and in keeping up the trenches of
defence.   The greater part of domestic and field-
labour devolves upon the women, whose toil is much
increased by the useful practice of stall-feeding.
The Wasoro work very little, their business being to
guard their king and country, for which purpose
they almost always carry spears and shields, the

latter prettily elaborated out of elephants' and buffaloes' hides. In spite of the richness of the soil, from their ignorance of agriculture and want of markets for their produce, the inhabitants are extremely poor. They share their dwellings with their cattle, yet they must not be accused of want of cleanliness, for they wash and bathe frequently, and the Jagga are a very robust and powerful race, which is partly to be attributed to the healthiness of the climate.

There are in Jagga no compact villages or towns, but only isolated inclosures, separated from each other by open spaces extending about the eighth of a mile, and always covered with banana-trees. Each yard is occupied by a single family, in several huts, protected by hedgerows of growing bushes, or of dried branches, which serve as a defence against wild beasts, more especially hyenas. Here again on a small scale the Jagga typify the habits of the entire races of East Africa, which never commingle with one another, but, as it is with the families of Jagga, are separated from each other by interstices. But just as traffic brings many of the powerful tribes into frequent contact, so do the Jagga often meet together at their Sangaras, or marketplaces, with their nearest neighbours, the Dafeta, the Ugono, and the Kahe, which cannot but afford a missionary excellent opportunities of preaching the Gospel. A peculiar article of trade with them is Emballa, which is found in the Kahe-land to the south of Jagga, and is a kind of earth which they dissolve in water, using the liquor for admixture with their food instead of salt, which they have not. The taste of this water is brackish, and reminded me immediately of the mineral water of Bahlingen. They give it also as a beverage to their sick cattle, and every way its bitter seems to be advantageous to health. The Jagga are apt workmen in the manufacture of implements of war and of articles for domestic use, and the women by means of knitting ornament their leather clothing with small beads.

Rungua, king of Majame, the father of Mamkinga, once sent a large expedition to investigate the nature of snow. He hoped it might prove to be silver, or something of the kind; but only one of the party survived, and with frozen hands and feet announced to the king the melancholy fate of his companions, who had been destroyed not only by the cold, but by fear and terror; for in their ignorance they ascribed the effects of the cold to evil spirits, and fled away, only to meet with destruction in severer frost and cold. My guide told me that he had seen the poor man, whose frost-bitten hands and feet were bent inwards by the cold, and that he had heard from his own lips the story of his adventures.

One great obstacle to the establishment of a mission in Jagga exists in the shocking state of the route which leads to it. In other respects a mis-

sionary will find there facilities denied him among
the Wakamba, Wanika, and Wateita. Let him once
secure the friendship of the king, and all else will
quickly follow; for the king will then provide both
dwelling-place and school, and call the people
together to hear the gospel preached. To sustain
the friendly feeling of the king, he should be accompanied by a good doctor and some useful
mechanics, whose presence would be profitable to
the king. Indeed, in a general way, a missionary
to Eastern Africa should always be similarly accompanied, and by married men and their families
in preference to unmarried ones. These tribes, at
once sensual and destitute of all the conveniences of
life, should have Christianity presented to them not
only in sermons and teaching, but realized and
embodied; exercising its influence on every-day life,
especially in the married state and in the bringing
up of children. People out here do not believe us,
or at least not rightly, when we tell them that in
our country the land is so much better cultivated
than theirs, that their cultivation of it appears by
contrast a mere nothing. When we tell them that
with us oxen and cattle are used in the tillage of the
soil, they know not what to make of it. They must
be led to see with their own eyes that the people
who follow the Christ whom we preach to them,
really understand better than they how to cultivate
the soil, and can do a great deal else that is not less
desirable for them to know. Families, families—
Christian families, really converted fathers and

mothers, with well-nurtured children, are the tools which are chiefly needed for missionary work in Eastern Africa. Once surround the missionary with families who present in living and visible reality "muscular" Christianity in life and death, in labour and repose, in marriage and education, in public worship, in common prayer and psalmody, in devout listening to the Word of God,—then will our poor and careless Wanika easily and clearly understand to what a blessed condition out of their present destitution, to what life out of death, to what light out of darkness, to what joy in the Holy Spirit out of present dread of evil spirits, to what love out of selfishness, to what genuine peace out of worldly security, we are helping them. The problem solved by such Christian communities would be to render not only themselves, but missionaries independent of society at home in regard to outward support; but, to effect this, these little communities must be prepared to sacrifice all that they possess; for in the service of Christ we must be content with food and raiment, which will never fail us, if first we seek the kingdom of God and His righteousness; for He has promised that then all these things shall be added unto us.

CHAPTER III.

REBMANN'S SECOND JOURNEY TO JAGGA.

Change of plan—Arrival at Kilema—Detention by Masaki, and its motive—Arrival of escort from the king Mamkinga—Journey to Majame — Strange ceremony — The sorcerers and the production of rain — Interview with the king — His friendly reception and disinterestedness—Invitation to remain—Journey homeward—The mountains of Jagga — Kilimanjaro and its meaning—Snow, and the natives of Jagga—Snow demonstrated to the Suahili mind—Arrival at Rabbai.

WITH Bana Kheri once more for my guide and fifteen other Suahili to carry my baggage, armed partly with muskets and partly with bows and arrows, I started from Mombaz on the 14th of November 1848, and reached Bura on the 26th. My original plan of a visit to Kikuyu and Mbelete was altered by circumstances, so I resolved to content myself with a journey to Kilema and Majame in Jagga. On the 4th of December I started again for Jagga, and after three days' march of about 80 English miles through the wilderness arrived safely in Kilema, and met with a friendly reception from Masaki. By and by, however, when he found that I was bent on prosecuting my journey and visiting the king of Majame, he began to throw difficulties in the way. He did not

wish the calico and beads, which I had with me for
my further journey, to take their departure and
become the property of another than himself.   Probably I should not have succeeded in getting far
from Kilema, westward to Majame, had there not
been fortunately for me with Masaki some soldiers
of King Mamkinga, who is the greatest of the
kings of the Jagga-land.   I told them of my
plan, and Masaki could not now altogether thwart
it without provoking the anger of Mamkinga,
on whom he is virtually dependent.   The soldiers
of Mamkinga told me, that I should be well received
by their master, who had lately thought of sending
to the coast for some European to remain with him
as one of his sorcerers, a class of whom he is
extremely fond.   At last, Masaki sent messengers to
Mamkinga to inform him of my wish, and to request
an escort for me if he desired a visit from me.   He
did send a troop of soldiers under the command of
his brother Kilewo, in whose company on the 4th
January 1849 I began my journey towards Majame, much impoverished by the shameless mendicancy of Masaki and his relatives.   We traversed
an often undulating country, ascending as we went
for some two or three leagues north-westward right
towards Kilimanjaro, to which we came so near
that I could distinctly see, even by night, in the
light of the moon, its majestic snow-clad summit.
It was as cold as in Germany in November, and we
were very glad to sleep in a hut warmed by a good
fire.   Further upward the country was uninhabited,

and unfit for the cultivation of the banana, the chief food of the population of Jagga.   On the 5th of January we continued our journey for some leagues north-westward, till we had reached a height of about a thousand feet above the place where we had slept.   Thence descending for some five or six leagues we reached again the inhabited country, and the region of the banana.   At noon we halted, and received some bananas and honey sent us by Mawishe, who rules over a portion of the little territory of Uru.   Next day, we continued our journey westward, crossing some very deep valleys and descending always towards Majame.   From Uru I had a good view westwards towards Majame, which lies considerably lower, stretching between the south-western foot of Kilimanjaro and the north-eastern foot of Shira, which is also some-times covered with snow.   On the 6th, our way led us first into a deep valley, from which, after a steep ascent we reached a table-land.   After a march of twenty minutes we had to descend into a still deeper valley, ascending from the other side of which we reached a large elevated plain, ex-tending some three or four miles from east to west. Here we crossed the river which separates Uru from the district of Lambongo, and leaving it behind us, we proceeded onward for several leagues, the ground covered with banana-trees, the fruit of which was rotting, for there was no one to gather it, and to such an extent that the very air was fœtid.   After crossing two other rivers our route led us downward into the level country, which stretches through the southern part of Jagga, and which appeared never to have been cultivated, being covered with impenetrable jungle. Here I found some raspberries, of which I ate. Journeying some four or six English miles further, crossing several rivers, which at this time of the year would have been dried up had not their sources been in the region of perpetual snow, we reached the little territory of Kimdi, separated by a small river from the district of Kimbo. From Kimbo we had still to travel through a fine open champaign for about three miles, till at length we reached the river Veriveri about four in the afternoon. This fine river which serves as a barrier against every enemy forms the eastern boundary of Majame, where we had now arrived. I was obliged to remain on the bank of the river until a goat had been brought, and the Kishogno ceremony gone through, without which no stranger can enter the country of Jagga. After the ceremony Kilemo conducted me to one of his huts.

Next day, and again on the 8th of January I received visits from Muigno Wessiri, a Suahili, who has lived in Jagga for six years, and has been appointed by the king his medicine-man and sorcerer, personages identical in savage countries. He came to inspect the presents which I was to offer to the king, who had heard that most of my things had been given away during my long residence at Kilema ; yet the king sent me a hearty welcome, as it was myself, not my goods, he desired. For a per-

sonal interview with the king I had to wait until
the 12th of January. The sorcerers were the cause
of this delay. I was told, that on the arrival of a
stranger a medicine must be compounded out of a
certain plant, or a tree fetched from a distance,
mixed with the blood of the sheep or the goat, from
which the king himself makes the Kishogno for his
guest. And what is done with this mixture? The
stranger is besmeared or besprinkled with it, before
he is allowed to come into the presence of the king.
So it happened, when, on the evening of that day,
the king appeared with a great retinue, that, instead
of receiving at once the long-wished-for audience,
I was commanded to remain in my dark hut, whilst
out of doors the victim was being strangled, not only
for my behoof, but to serve in the production of rain.
And in very deed it so fell out that the sorcerer had
scarcely completed his ceremonial, when amid thunder the rain began to fall in torrents, and the
deluded spectators were excited to honour the
fortunate magician with the words: "Hei muanga
wa Mangi! hei muanga wa Mangi!"—Well done,
O sorcerer of the king! Muanga (sorcerer) is a title
of honour in Jagga. That the rain would fall just
at the right moment, had no doubt been calculated on
by the crafty and practised sorcerer, for these muangas
usually combine a knowledge of natural phenomena
with their delusive art. In no country can the fall of
rain be known beforehand more easily than in Jagga,
where the whole process of cloud-formation can be
daily perceived. As soon as the sun begins to be a

little hot, thin vapours are seen floating hither and
thither over the snow, and these by degrees form
thin clouds, so that about noon thunder is mostly
heard. With a little practice in daily observation,
and with the study of the seasons, the muanga is
soon enabled to predict rain an hour before its fall.
When the rain began to fall I was summoned to
leave my hut, and while I stood beneath its lower
opening, the sorcerer without asking my permission bespattered my face and the front part of my
body with his filthy mixture, using a cow's tail for
the purpose. It was as well that my leave had
not been asked, for I should have absolutely refused
it. After the rain was over I was summoned to the
king, as he wished to present me with the Kishogno
in person. Upon this I had to return once more to
my hut, whither the king and his chiefs followed
me to receive his presents, and to hear what I had
to say; but it was evident that he cared more about
myself than about my presents. I stretched out my
Bible towards him, and told him my only business
was with this book, which contained the word of
God, and which we wished to teach to all nations.
The design of my journey was not to buy slaves nor
ivory, but to form a friendship with him, and to ask
him whether he did not wish persons like ourselves
in his country. If this were the case I would communicate in writing his wish to those who had sent
me, and who would take care that it should be gratified; but I could not say how long a delay might
elapse, as our country was very distant. The king was

very much pleased, and said, " How can I refuse this man's wish ?" He then examined the few things which I had still to give him, and among them a certain kind of bead, and a white flask, appeared to please him particularly. After he had ordered me during my stay in Majame to reside with Muigno Wessin, who stood nearer him than his brother Kilemo, he retired to his hut. The following day, the 13th of January, he made me a present of a sheep, and promised to forward my speedy return. Again on the 16th I had an audience of the king, who would not allow me to depart until the 29th. Although disappointed of finding a sorcerer in me, he assured me frequently of his great affection for me, and would have kept me much longer with him, had I not entreated him to allow me to return. Indeed, he would have been well pleased if I had at once settled down at Majame, in which event he would have given me his own son for a pupil.

During the return-journey, which was performed in the hot season, when the mountains are not enveloped in clouds as in the rainy season, I was able for the first time to see distinctly the lofty summits of the mountains of Jagga and the outline of their connection and separation. There are two principal summits placed upon a basis some ten leagues long and as many broad, so that the space between them forms as it were, a saddle, which extends three or four leagues from east to west. The eastern summit is lower, and pointed, whilst the western and higher

one presents a fine crown, which, even in the hot
season, when its western and lowlier neighbour can
no longer support its snowy roof, remains covered
by a mass of snow. The snow of Kilimanjaro is
not only the perpetual source of the many rivers
(twenty, at least) which proceed from it, but even
in the hot season, and indeed then more particularly,
it is a continual source of rain, as may be daily observed, and as I have already described in alluding
to the use made of the phenomenon by the sorcerers.
The Suahili of the coast call the snow-mountain
Kilimanjaro, "mountain of greatness;" it may
also mean "mountain of caravans" (Kilima, mountain,—Jaro, caravans), a landmark for the caravans
seen everywhere from afar; but the inhabitants of
Jagga call it Kibo, snow. On my first journey
my guide had misinformed me, when he said that
the people of Jagga had no word for snow; but
when I asked the natives of Jagga themselves,
their various statements,—for example, that the
Kibo when put into the fire turns into water,—convinced me that they not only knew it as " Kibo,"
but knew no less well its nature and properties.
They assented, too, when I told them that the
river flowing by had its source in Kibo. I showed
the Suahili that the white covering could not be
silver, as they could see with their own eyes that
on the one mountain it appeared and disappeared
with the seasons, while on the other it increased and
decreased, which could not be the case if it were
silver. I pointed also to the many rivers which

descend from the mountain as a testimony of the fact that the white covering is only another form of water. My guide was completely convinced, and said that the people of Jagga would not buy from the Suahili the armlets of lead worn by the latter as ornaments, if they had in their territory such a mass of silver. This much is known, moreover, that at times people ascend the mountain, and descend again in safety, if they but choose the right season; of which, indeed, they are mostly ignorant, and hence many have perished in the attempt.

Journeying by way of Kilema, Bura, and Kadiaro, I arrived at Rabbai in safety on the 16th of February.

CHAPTER IV.

REBMANN'S THIRD JOURNEY TO JAGGA.

Journeying in the rainy season—Encounter with a rhinoceros—
Masaki once more—Rain-making and rain-preventing—Extemporized hut—Obstinacy of the bearers—Necessity pulls down
the hut—Agreeable disappointment—Arrival at Majame—
Altered demeanour of King Mamkinga—Extortion and persecution—Missionary-tears misinterpreted—King Mamkinga's ivory—
Heathen hypocrisy—Ceremonial of leave-taking—Mercenary farewell—Speedy departure—Masaki evaded—The native axe in
the jungle—Extemporized bridges and their dangers—Entrance
into the Wilderness—A feast of fledglings—Nearing home—
Arrival at Rabbai—Concluding reflections.

KING MAMKINGA had as mentioned in the previous
chapter shown himself friendly, and promised to
aid me in prosecuting further journeys from his
country. Accordingly, after my return from my
second journey to Jagga, it was resolved, upon
mature deliberation, that I should return again to
Jagga and endeavour to penetrate to Uniamesi at
least. We considered it to be our duty to make
Christians at home acquainted with the unknown
countries of the African interior, that they might be
stimulated to promote the Gospel more energetically
than hitherto in that part of the world. In any
case, we wished to pave the way for evangelizing

Eastern Africa by making ourselves acquainted with
its unexplored countries, their manners, modes of
thought, languages, government, &c., by at least
naming the name of Christ where it had never been
named before, and by explaining to the natives the
general character of our objects.

On the 6th of April 1849 I started once more,
well provided with articles of various kinds for
presents, and having hired thirty men, chiefly
Wanika, as the meditated journey to Uniamesi was
a long one. The rainy season had just commenced,
which made my journey from Jagga to Kadiaro
very difficult; for it often rained the livelong night,
with myself and people lying in the open air, without any other shelter than that of my solitary umbrella. The rivers of Jagga, too, were swollen.
On the 19th of April we crossed the Lumi, close to
which, at a distance of from ten to fifteen paces, we
came upon a rhinoceros which had been concealed
by the bushes. Only one of my people was in advance of me; the rest, who were all behind me, threw
down their loads and ran away, while the one in front
retreated to my rear. As I was so near I wished
now to see distinctly the animal, and therefore only
retreated slowly a few paces. The mighty creature
seemed to have the same wish; for it stood motion-
less for about a minute, staring at us; when all at
once as if terror-stricken by the number of people,
it sprang away at a quick trot. In their superstition my bearers believed that the Bible which
I carried in my pocket had put the beast to

flight, and considered this a proof that my book had
magical power.

I would willingly have avoided Kilema and gone
on straight to Majame; but want of provisions
and the continual rain forced me into the lion's den
once more.   After experiencing from Masaki the
annoyances which I had expected, I succeeded in
being allowed to continue my journey, his kingship
previously to my departure causing his troops, consisting of some four or five hundred men, to defile
past me, doubtless by way of convincing me that
he, too, was a great king.   On the 15th we were
overtaken by night when within a league of Majame, and then I had to pass a rainy night indeed,
although among the Jagga people who were with
us there was a rain-maker, who now wished to show
off as a rain-preventer also.   He had himself announced that during our journey he would control the
rain; but the poor fellow was now fairly disgraced.
The Jagga erected a hut of banana-leaves; but it
would contain only ten persons, and with some others
I passed the night in the rain, sheltering myself a little
by the aid of my umbrella.   At break of day I wished
to push forward, as I knew that a league further on
we should find our best shelter from the rain in
the huts of Majame; but such of my people as
were in the hut wished to wait till the rain was over.
The rain increased rather than decreased, and in
spite of my repeated summons, they still would
not go forward, but continued their wild chanting,
so that I saw nothing for it but to knock down their

hut and let them find a damper in the rain, in order to force them to go on. Instead of being angry they laughed, for they knew that I was in the right in desiring to go forward, and thus get shelter from the rain, and so we went onward, and crossing the Weri-weri reached Majame, where huts were immediately placed at our disposal.

It was on the 25th of May that king Mamkinga first came to see me, and to receive the presents intended for him. From this time forward he began to develope his treacherous character promising, in the hope of presents, to promote my journey to Uniamesi, while all the while he had resolved to prevent it. Extortion, too, followed upon extortion, his magician, Muigni Wessiri, speaking and acting in the king's name. I saw the stock of goods which I had intended for Uniamesi gradually melting away, and when by order of the king I was obliged to part with piece after piece of the calico which I had reserved for my further journey, I could not suppress my tears. The king observed them and asked the cause; Muigni Wessiri replied that I wept because of the loss of my goods; when I rejoined, that I was not weeping on that account, but because the things had been given me by good people at home, who wished to send the Book of Life to all Africans, with which object I had made the journey; whereas I was now deprived of my property and the good design of my friends was defeated. The king replied that he was not robbing me, as he would give me ivory in exchange, a promise which

naturally was not very consolatory to me.   Other
persecutions were added to robbery, and my health as
well as my spirits gave way under the influence
of the cold and wet weather, and the smoke with
which my miserable hut was filled.   I was attacked
both by fever and dysentery; so now wished, of
course, to return to the coast as soon as possible,
a wish which my people shared with me; for they
as well as myself were plundered and threatened.
We could not depart, however, without a formal
leave-taking of the king or his representative, and
this was put off from day to day.   Of course the
promise of ivory proved to be a delusion; I had been
told at first, that the king would give me three great
elephants' tusks, which if sold at Mombaz for about
120 dollars, might have met the cost of my com-
pulsory presents.   But when at last on the 6th of
June I received from the king leave to depart, his
brother said, that as Manajuoni, *i. e.*, son of the
book, or teacher of the Word of God, I ought not to
wish for ivory.   I was further told that the king
desired very much to have his children instructed,
and that, therefore, I should be welcomed by him at
any time; but if I wished for ivory, of which the
king had plenty, I was to come again and bring
another stock of goods to exchange for it.   An old
tusk of little worth, however, was given me, that I
might buy food on the road.   I replied: " It is all
right now, I have no other wish than to return.'
Their greed was displayed even at the moment of
our leave-taking, which was accompanied by the

usual ceremony of expectorating upon the departing stranger, and repeating the words "Go in peace." For this dirty expectoration with which, first the Wanika, then the Suahili, and last of all myself, were favoured, a special payment was exacted from each. My Wanika had nothing but a handful of beads, which I had given them for the purchase of their daily food; but one of the Suahili wore a rather better garment, as is the custom of the Mohammedans, and this was demanded of him in the rudest manner, and so he was obliged to take it off, and pay with it the price of the saliva of peace. After the leave-taking my Wanika could no longer be restrained, and would not even wait for the Jagga soldiers who, at my desire, were to have accompanied us to Kilema. They broke up in the greatest haste on the 7th of June, so I was obliged to follow; and in truth, I was right glad to exchange the company of such people, for the wilderness itself.

Out of fear of Masaki we resolved to avoid all chance of contact with him, and to return through the wilderness, which stretches along the south of Jagga. Crossing the Weri-weri, we were shown by a native a footpath in the desired direction; but it soon led us into thick jungle, and after several hours it seemed to be taking us back to Jagga. We quitted it accordingly, and resolved to hew our way through the jungle with our axes, an operation which lasted for several days. The first night in the forest was dark and rainy, and we had neither fire nor water; for our water-carriers, calculating upon the vicinity of the river, had brought none with them.   Next night we reached a brook, and cooked some beans which we had brought from Majame. During the next two days we had to cross unfordable streams by means of trees which we felled, and formed into extempore bridges for the purpose, and falling from one of them I was nearly carried away by the stream; so that the next, I straddled, instead of walking across it.   At length on the 17th of June we reached the Lomi after a seven days' journey from Majame, which with a tolerable path we might have performed in three.   From this point the wilderness was all but a desert, no rivers flowing through it.   On the first day of our journey in it we found wild honey and many nests of young birds, and the latter were much relished by my Wanika; many of the trees were almost covered with nests, which hung apparently loosely, but securely from the smallest twigs.   I thanked God for this food, our store of beans being almost exhausted, while a journey of two or three days through the desert was still before us.   In the night of the 15th we had no water in which to boil our beans, and could only roast them.   While praying amongst the brushwood of the wilderness my heart melted within me at the remembrance of how I had experienced on this journey the depravity of these heathen Africans no less than that of my own heart.   Although I was deprived of all the comforts of this life, I have seldom felt so happy as when this outburst had soothed the repinings of my heart.

On the morning of the 17th we entered the district of Maina, chief of Bura, and rested till the 19th. On the 21st, we reached Kadiaro, where we rested again, and purchased beans and Indian corn, starting on the 23rd to perform the last section of our difficult journey. For want of proper nourishment my strength, owing to the continued toils of the journey, began to fail me. I wrote therefore on the 26th to Dr. Krapf, to send me a bottle of wine and some biscuits; and I ordered the greater portion of my people to precede me to Rabbai, while I followed slowly with a couple of attendants. Contrary to my expectation I reached on the same day the end of the wilderness, and arrived at the Duruma territory, where I passed the night in the village Ngoni. My host provided me with better food than I had enjoyed for a long time, and I felt myself strong enough next day to continue my journey without waiting for the restoratives, which my dear fellow-labourer was to send from Rabbai. In a short time, however, I met our servant Amri, whom Dr. Krapf had sent to meet me with supplies, and after a further march of three or four leagues, I reached our hut in Rabbai safely. I found our family increased by two new members, Missionaries Erhardt and Johann Wagner. They had arrived a few weeks before from Europe, and immediately on their arrival had been attacked by fever, which in the case of Wagner assumed a fatal character, and ended in his death on the 1st of August.

As a specimen of the languages of Eastern Africa,

in which the words always end with a vowel, I have chosen a portion of the petition or prayer of Maina, which he uttered upon my taking leave of him on the 9th of May, when he presented me with the sweet beverage called Jofi, as mentioned at page 234. There is so much natural piety and simplicity in the words, that it cannot fail to strike the reader as hopeful, that when Christianity shall have taken root amongst these benighted people, it will be upheld and cherished by them.

Mgeni hu atoka kuao, adsha kuangu : "Maina,
Stranger this went out from his, came to me: "Maina,

tugore, tupatane!" Mimi nai : "tuseme tukizeka;
let us talk, let us unite!" I to him: "let us speak (as) joyous friends;

tu soye Mulungu pamenga nti ipoe!" Ukongo*
*let us pray (to) Heaven together the land to bless!" Sickness**

usume muzi wangu! Mgeni hu huko aënendako
depart from village mine! Stranger this whereunto he goes

asione kindu endiani; asikomoe na
(may) he not see anything in the way; not kept back by

miba; asikomoe na kisiki; asionane na enzosu;
thorns; not kept back by long grass; meet not with elephants;

asionane na mbea; asionane na emmessa!
meet not with rhinoceroses; meet not with enemies!

Akisika Kirima Wa-Kirima wa-m-zeke! Mimi
When he reaches Jagga People of Jagga pleasure him! I

natereva Koma endeo-wangu, na sa mayo-
pray the Spirit of father mine, and of the mother

wangu m-fisheni! Mundu hu, tudshe, tuonane
mine him to let arrive! Man this, may he come, may we meet

mimi nai tuzeke!
I with him to rejoice!

* There was sickness in the place at the time.

CHAPTER V.

THE AUTHOR'S FIRST JOURNEY TO USAMBARA.

Inducements to the journey—King Kmeri—Mtongwe—Lunguma—
Plain of Shimba—Kwale—Pipes and tobacco—Bundini—Musket-
firing and evil spirits—Teaching Wadigo boys their A, B, C—
At home in the wilderness—Description of the country—Flora and
Fauna—Wild beasts and their *habitats*—Gonja—Kusi—Way-
side sermon—Mohammedan haughtiness rebuked—King Kmeri's
daughter—The Washinsi—Trustfulness of the people : democracy
and despotism—Forward towards Fuga—Mountain-scenery : the
one thing wanting—Fuga—Salla—Interview with king Kmeri—
Attitude of the people—Kmeri's harem—Interview with the
king—Return-journey—Astonishment of the Suahili—Prayer and
thanksgiving—Zanzibar, the Sultan and Kilimanjaro—Arrival at
Rabbai.

AFTER Rebmann's return from his first journey to
Jagga, extending to some hundred leagues or more
into the interior, it was determined between us that
I should visit the countries to the south and south-west
of Mombaz, to preach the Gospel in a region near to
Zanzibar, and to explore its capabilities for being
made the seat of missionary-stations. As regarded
Kmeri, or Kimeri, king of Usambara, I knew well that
he would soon learn to respect any European missionary, and give him leave to reside in his country;
adopting such measures for his protection, that he
would always have access to him by way of Tanga

and Pangani, both in his dominions, without fear of
molestation from the Suahili, an object of the greatest
importance for spreading the Gospel in East Africa.
Accordingly on the 12th of July 1848 I left Mombaz having engaged Bana Kheri, Rebmann's guide
to Jagga, for the sum of fifteen dollars, as guide
on my journey to Usambara, and seven Suahili as
baggage-bearers at the rate of five dollars per man.
I had with me also the needful articles: calico, beads,
knives, &c. for presents, and for the purchase of
provisions. We left the harbour of Mombaz at 9 A.M.
and landed at the Mohammedan village of Mtongwe,
to the south of Mombaz. Ascending the higher
ground we reached the hamlet Lunguma, inhabited
by the Lungo tribe, a branch of the Wadigo tribes
of the Wanika. The Wanika, who live to the south
of Mombaz, are called, as formerly mentioned,
Wadigo, and their country Udigo; those to the
north-west and north-east are called Walupanga.
Muaje Kuku, the chief of Lunguma, gave us a
friendly reception and presented us with fresh cocoa-
nuts, the pleasant milk of which revived me much.
Next day, we presented the chief with twenty ells of
American calico manufactured at Lowell, in return for his hospitality; and proceeded on our
way, gradually ascending as we went. Our road
became now steeper and more difficult for the ass
which I had brought with me from Mombaz. After
continuing the ascent for about three leagues we
reached the fine plain of Shimba, where I felt so
cold that I longed for warmer clothing. The pro-

spect towards the lowlands, towards Mombaz and its
bays, and towards the western mountain-chain of the
Wanika-land, was magnificent.   After a march of
two leagues over the plain we came to the jungle in
which the village Kwale lies, the chief of which,
Mualuahu, gave us a very friendly reception.   The village contains about seventy huts, of which very few
are inhabited, as the people generally reside upon
their plantations.   At Kwale I was not a little astonished to see men and women, old and young, smoking tobacco and making use of a pipe not unlike our
European ones, the bowl being neatly constructed out
of clay and fastened to a stick some feet in length.
Not only do the Wadigo grow a great deal of tobacco,
but also buy it in quantities in Usambara, in small,
round, dried cakes, which they dispose of in Kiriama
and Emberria, to be sold to the Galla.   As regards
religion the Wadigo appear to be as indifferent and
dull as the Walupangu, and to this their intercourse
with the deceptive Mohammedans has much contributed.   Nevertheless, I had sometimes interesting
conversations with Wadigo people, who at first took
me for a Mohammedan.

July 14*th.*—Our direction was at first to the south-
west, and when in the Pemba district, about half
a league from Kwale, we began to descend into
the Wakuafi wilderness, which from the coast, from
Wassin to Tanga as well as from the Wanika-land,
stretches as an immeasurable plain into the interior
of the African continent, with only here and there
an isolated mountain, or a mountain-mass, where

you meet with human inhabitants to whom the Gospel has still to be preached. At ten we passed the little Mto wa Pemba (river of Pemba), and about noon saw distinctly the mountains Kadiaro and Kilibasse. At one in the afternoon we arrived at the village Bundini, whose chief, Guedden, gave us a friendly reception, and forthwith called upon one of my musket-men to fire off his gun by way of expelling evil spirits from the village. I spoke against this superstition, indicating to him the right mode of expelling evil spirits from the human heart, not by the application of powder and shot, but by true repentance of our sins, and by faith in the Lord Jesus, proclaimed in the book, the Bible which I held in my hand. When I told the chief, that in Rabbai we instructed young people according to our book, he said, " Then take these boys," of whom five or six sat beside him, " and instruct them." I wrote down immediately on a little bit of paper a Kinika alphabet, and began to teach them the letters one by one. The boys did not seem to be either dull or unsusceptible, but capable of receiving instruction.

July 15*th.*—This morning my people prepared sandals for the thorny journey through the wilderness out of the skin of a jackal, and when they had purchased the necessary provisions for the journey we started about ten from Bundini. The right direction would have been south by east, by which we should have arrived at Usambara, in the vicinity of Daluni ; but instead of that we went almost

continuously eastward towards the coast of Wassin
and Tanga, a route which was very circuitous.

The country which we traversed to-day was for
the most part level, covered with grass, acacias, and
other trees and shrubs. I soon felt myself at my
ease in the wilderness, as there I always travel with
pleasure, because I meet with no greedy and bicker-
ing begging kings or chiefs; because the air is so
wholesome and strengthening; because the stillness
and quiet of the night beside a blazing fire does
one the greatest good; and because, no less perhaps,
I can give myself up undisturbed to my reflections
on religious and geographical subjects, and find a
Bethel under every tree or bush. The constant
experience of Divine protection against wild beasts
and savages is also most encouraging. In short, in
spite of all the sufferings of hunger and thirst;
in spite of weariness and the relentless thorns,
which destroyed my clothes; in spite of dangers
from robbers from within and without, in the
wilderness, I have always felt as happy as few kings
and princes can feel in the midst of all their glory
and splendour. The one disadvantage is that,
except one's own attendants, there is no one in the
wilderness with whom one can commune, no one to
bring into the way of truth!

July 17th.—Our night-fire was fed with ebony,
of which the wilderness is full. The country continued level during this day's march, excepting here
and there where it was slightly undulating, being
also sometimes covered with high grass and thick

wood, whilst at many places were pools, much
frequented by wild elephants, and in places the soil
was of red sand and pebbles. This is the general
character of the wilderness through which we travelled; the tall grass and the thick wood increasing as we proceeded, and the soil becoming
moister, and therefore more fitted for cultivation.
I do not doubt that a botanist who might investigate
the flora of the Wakuafi-wilderness, would be richly
rewarded and discover much that is new.

In the afternoon, the way was so impeded by
euphorbia, or spurge, and wild aloe, that I was
unable to ride my ass. As before nightfall we could
not emerge from the thicket, we hewed away the
wood and made ready our encampment, kindling a
great fire as protection against wild beasts, traces of
whom, especially of the rhinoceros, we had observed
in the thick jungle. The rhinoceros frequents
places covered with euphorbia, aloe, and acacia, and
thus rendered impassable; whilst the elephant prefers
more marshy ground, where there is plenty of tall
grass, and forest at hand into which he can retreat.
The buffalo chooses more open ground, where he can
have tender grass for provender, and thin acacia-
bushes, behind which he can conceal himself.
Thus, every beast has his own locality assigned
to him; and I could always tell my people before
hand, from the nature of the ground what kind
of wild beasts we should probably meet with;
and, *vice versâ*, I could define the character of the
country from the animals inhabiting it. Thus, the

wilderness is extremely instructive to the thoughtful traveller.

July 18.—To-day, in the midst of an alarm caused by the appearance of a rhinoceros, I lost my ass; for whilst I stood with gun presented should the enemy approach, Bana Kheri fired at random, and startled the poor beast, who set off saddled and bridled, and was lost in the wilderness. In the course of the day we emerged from the jungle and came upon meadow-land, where we saw giraffes (tia or tiga, in Suahili) in groups of from eight to ten. They allowed us to come within about three hundred paces of them, when they started off with the speed of the wind. As we had marched the whole day without interruption I felt quite wearied, and I would now have been gladly mounted on my ass; but I was to experience the hardships of the wilderness on foot, and not merely on the back of a beast.

July 19.—At noon we came to the river Leni, and on its bank we cooked our mid-day meal. I cut a great cross and the date of the year on a tree near the spot ere we crossed the river; we next came to a Wadigo hamlet, whence for a few beads a native conducted us to the chief of Gonja, a Wadigo village on the river Umba.

July 20.—Mua Muiri, the chief of Gonja, in return for a gift of eight ells of American calico accompanied us to the large village of Nugniri, where a daughter of king Kmeri rules a portion of the Washinsi-land. The soil of Gonja is very fruitful, and the natives cultivate Indian corn, rice, cassave, beans, &c.

July 21.—Before I left Gonja this morning a native asked me seriously whether the Europeans were cannibals. If nothing more our journeys serve to dissipate the prejudices of the natives and the slanders of the Mohammedans.

After crossing the Umba, we soon came to the brook Jubba. On the way a Mnika asked me among other things, whether we, too, had slaves. When I told him that Europeans had no slaves, neither buying nor selling them, he turned to the Suahilis, and said, "Why do you then make slaves?" He was very much pleased to learn that Europeans had abolished slavery, and hospitably gave us a good dish of boiled cassave, which we enjoyed heartily in the midst of a pouring rain.

22nd July.—After we had crossed several streams and passed through several villages, we reached, about noon, the great village Kusi, where the Wadigo chief Muhensano gave me a friendly reception, presenting me with a sheep for which I paid him a dollar. Scarcely had I seated myself under a tree, when a crowd of old and young Wadigo assembled round me, who behaved themselves very decorously and respectfully and never once so much as begged. I narrated to them the fall of Adam, and spoke of the atonement through Jesus Christ, the Son of God. When they asked me whether we ate pork and the flesh of beasts slaughtered by the Wanika I was obliged to answer in the affirmative; upon which Bana Kheri was so provoked that he called me a Mkafiri, unbeliever, like the Wanika, so by way of reproof of this and his attempts to ride rough-shod over my Wanika, I told him that in many respects the Suahili were worse than the heathen. I then showed him that Mohammed was an impostor, who had stolen from the Bible of the Christians everything good taught in the Koran, and who had spread his religion by the sword. The Wanika, who listened attentively were delighted that I had thus driven the proud Mohammedan into a corner.

July 23.—We passed several large villages, and crossed the river Engambu, sleeping in the village Muhesa at the house of our guide's brother, Mua Muiri.

July 24.—With the village Fumoni we entered the territory of the king of Usambara, and after passing through several other villages of the Washinsi, we arrived before the gate of the large village Nugniri, the residence, as already mentioned, of a daughter of king Kmeri. We were conducted to a hut in the vicinity of the one she inhabited, whither her slaves brought us water, wood, and provisions. Late in the evening, she came with her husband, Bana Emsangasi, to greet us. There is little to distinguish her from other women of the Washinsi, as she works with her own hands and herself prepares the food for her family, although she has many female slaves around her.

The tranquillity and respect with which the people accosted me, not one of them begging anything, soon showed me that in the territory of king Kmeri there must reign such order as is sought for in vain among the republican communities of the Wanika and Wakamba.

July 25.—* * * By their brown colour the Washinsi are easily to be distinguished from the Suahili and Wanika, who are much darker. They cultivate rice, Indian corn, millet, cassave, &c., and as they have no cocoa-nut trees, they cannot give themselves up to drunkenness like the Wanika. Tobacco-smoking is universal among the Washinsi and Wasambara.

By degrees the people of Nugniri became so trustful that they often called me out of my hut to talk with them; and when I went in again they would say, "O, there, he is going in again!" As already indicated, I found no begging among them; but whether in the course of a longer residence this would have always remained the same, is another question; yet my belief is, that missionaries have less to suffer from that system in a despotic than in a republican country, it being presupposed that they have somewhat appeased at their first coming, those greatest of beggars, their kings and chiefs.

The number of Washinsi subject to king Kmeri may amount in the plain to 30,000, and in the mountains to 60,000, souls; but his whole empire includes, at least, half a million of subjects, from the coast to the Pare mountains, some six or eight good days' journey from east to west. The boundaries of Usambara are, to the south the river Pangani, to the north the Wakuafi wilderness and the Wadigoland.

July 26.—To-day I delivered to the king's daughter and her husband my presents of clothes and beads, worth about two dollars, which they hid very cleverly under their clothes, so that no one might see and inform the king what they had received from me; for otherwise, as they told me, they would lose their heads as everything belonged to him. From this time all the mistrust ceased of which I had observed some symptoms before, and both she and her husband now visited me frequently, and sent me provisions for my caravan of seven men.

July 28.—Yesterday evening a messenger arrived from Fuga, the residence of the king, with orders that I should proceed forthwith to the capital.

We started, therefore, and journeyed for some leagues over a plain to the foot of the mountain Pambire, which rises 2000 feet above the level of the sea. I would recommend this mountain as the first missionary-station in Ushinsi and Usambara, as it is distant from the coast only from fifteen to seventeen leagues.

July 30.—Our way lay westward of Pambire, with a slight inclination towards the south, up hill and down dale continually, which was very fatiguing. Scarcely had we reached the top of a hill, when we had to descend on the other side, and to cross, at a depth equivalent to its height, some stream or glen. In this East-African alpine land mountain succeeds to mountain, stream to stream, glen to glen. The marsh-land at the foot of the mountains is used as rice-plantations, the hills are covered with excellent sugar-cane and banana-trees, and the woods contain superior available timber. It will be a noble land, when Christian culture shall hallow it! Crossing the river Emgambo we soon found ourselves in a deep valley, from which our way lay up Mount Makueri, which is at least 3000 feet high, and the higher we went, the cooler and more pleasant was the air. The cool water trickling from the granite rocks, the little hamlets rising above the mountain-ridges, the many patches of Indian corn, rice, bananas, and sugar-cane, the numerous cascades, the murmur of the river Emgambo, the mountain masses in the distance,—all tend greatly to elevate the spirits of the wanderer.

July 31.—We saw many dogs, something of the jackal species, reddish-brown and white, which the Wasambara make food of. Bana Kheri told me that he had journeyed through the land of Wasegua to Engu, Fuju, Karaguë, Kinalomegera, Usagarra, and Kuiwa, the way being from Jagga across Usuma, Kahe, Arusha, Donio Nerok, Koyo, Jajuru, Itandu, Ramba, and hence through Ukimbu to Yoggo where Uniamesi commences. He took shipping, if it may so be termed, and sailed for eight days on the waters of the great inland sea Uniamesi, laying to every night and landing upon some island. On the western shore is Usambiro, the territory of king Lebue. He says that wild asses and iron are plentiful in Koyo.

August 7.—After one day of rest, and five of

weary pilgrimage up hill and down dale and across
rivers, we reached yesterday afternoon the foot of
the mountain on which lies Fuga, the chief capital of
king Kmeri; and to-day I was questioned as to the
object of my journey by the king's representative,
king Kmeri being absent in Salla, his second capital,
when my replies and presents were deemed satisfactory.

August 9.—To-day I reached Salla, which I
entered with a heavy heart, as I did not know how
the Simba wa Muene, " the independent lion," or
" the only true lion," as Kmeri is called by his subjects, would receive me. If he takes me for a spy
and a magician my life will be in danger. Yet at
the beginning of the journey I had the words of
1 Peter, iii. 22,* to strengthen me, why should I be
afraid, knowing whose servant I am?

August 10.—The king sent for me to-day to ascertain the object of my journey, and to receive my
presents. His abode was guarded by soldiers. When
I stepped into the audience-chamber he raised himself a little from the bedstead on which he was
lying, with a fire burning before it, round which
his chief men were seated, and I was bidden to sit
upon a bedstead opposite the king.

I told him first that I had been in Abessinia and
among the Gallas to teach them my book, which
contained the revealed Word of God; that I had
afterwards come to Rabbai, and had there built a

---

* " Who is gone into heaven, and is on the right hand of God;
angels and authorities and powers being made subject unto him."

house and begun to instruct the Wanika from it.
With the same object, my Brother Rebmann, had
been to Jagga, and the kings there had received
him kindly and invited him to remain in their
country, and to instruct their people. With this
view, I, too, had come to Usambara to ask the king
whether he wished for teachers of the glad tidings,
which that book made known? In the event of his
wishing for them, I, or one of my friends, would
come and remain in his country. The king at
once expressed his desire for such teachers, and observed that he would afterwards talk with me on
that matter. He then said he wished to receive the
presents; and having inspected them all, he sent them
to his treasury. He would have been glad if I had
given him more beads, cloth-stuffs, and writing-
paper for despatches, and as he cannot himself write,
he has always Suahili about him who write his
letters for him. He has two sons, also, who have
become Mohammedans, and have learned to read
and write. Their father threw no obstacle in their
way, when they resolved on abandoning heathenism.

When the people of Salla saw that the king had
received me graciously they came to visit me; but
previously no one would come near me, or speak to
me. Even the king's wives, of whom Kmeri is said
to have several hundred, now peeped from behind
their inclosures to see the strange man. Each of
them has her own hut, her own plantation, and her
own female slaves. Their dwellings are on a hill,
where no one is allowed to set foot, and they are

veiled like the Mohammedan women. This large
harem swallows up a large portion of the king's
revenues.

August 11.—As I had expressed a wish to return
as soon as possible to Rabbai the king sent for me
to bid me farewell. I told him once more of the
object which had led me to him, and tried to familiarize him with the chief doctrines of Scripture,
describing the fall of man, and then showing the
necessity of the atonement by Jesus Christ, both
God and man. When the Mohammedans were
about to interrupt me, the king said : " I see what
his words are ; they are words of the Book." He
then asked me whether I would accept ivory, slaves,
and cattle, as he had nothing else to give me. I
replied, that I should wish him to let me have five
boys, whom I could instruct at Rabbai. To this he
rejoined, that his people did not understand these
things and that parents would think their children
were to be made slaves of and sold ; but if I would
return to his country he would intrust me with
young persons to instruct; but he could not send
them out of the country. He wished, too, for skilled
people, especially a good medical man. Then he
asked repeatedly whether I would return in three
or four months ? but I could not answer this question
definitively, as I had first to consult with my
brother at Rabbai, and to write to my friends in
Europe, which would require a long time. He also
told me that in future I was to perform my journey
to him from the Pangani, and he ordered a Mo-

hammedan who was in attendance to accompany me, and finally gave me five goats for the return journey, because I would accept neither ivory nor slaves.

On the whole I had reason to be very well satisfied with the king, especially when I considered the pains taken by the Mohammedans to injure me in his estimation. They advised him, it would seem, not to allow me to come into his presence, and at once to send me back to the coast: but to this, I was told, he replied, that I was his guest whom he would protect. It is obviously his wish to enter into closer relations with Europeans; when he has once become acquainted with them, the intriguing Suahili will soon fall into disgrace.

August 13.—At leave-taking the king asked me again how soon I would return? He then gave me two soldiers who were to accompany me to the Pangani and protect me. At the close of the interview, he said: " Kua heri, Baba !"—" Fare thee well, father !"

I returned homeward by Bumbarri, and on the 19th of August reached the Pangani village, where I was kindly received by a friendly Banian. The Suahili marvelled greatly when they heard that I had reached Usambara from Mombaz by land, and could scarcely believe that my journey was a *fait accompli*. I sought out a solitary place where I could undisturbed give hearty thanks to my God and Saviour for all the protection and help which He had so bounteously vouchsafed me on this toilsome journey.

On the 20th of August I dismissed my Wasambara attendants, and sailed to Zanzibar where, owing to the light winds, I did not arrive till the 22nd, and met with a friendly reception and hospitable shelter from the English consul, Major Hamerton. On the 24th, I had the pleasure of seeing the Sultan of Zanzibar, and of thanking him for the kindness which he had formerly showed to my dear colleague, Rebmann, and myself. He asked me a great deal about the mountain Kilimanjaro, which Rebmann had been the first to visit. I told him that the white crown which the Suahili took to be silver, was nothing but snow, and that the evil spirits at whom they were terrified, were merely the frost and cold consequent on the great height of the mountain. On the 29th I set sail for Mombaz; and on the 1st of September I rejoined Rebmann at Rabbai. We encouraged each other anew to pray and to labour for the conversion of Eastern Africa, where in so many places the portals stood open for us to begin the blessed work.

CHAPTER VI.

FIRST JOURNEY TO UKAMBANI.

FROM the first establishment of our missionary station at Rabbai Mpia it had been our wish to visit in
the interior those Wakamba tribes who, traversing
as they do for trading purposes a large section of
East Africa, may well claim the most serious attention of a missionary. After Rebmann's third journey
to Jagga, and Erhardt's arrival from Europe, it
was our unanimous decision that I should visit the
Wakamba in the interior, some 100 leagues from
Rabbai, make the Gospel known among them, and
inquire whether there might not be a route from
Ukambani to Uniamesi, to the sources of the Nile,

and to those still surviving Christian remnants at the equator of whom I had heard in Shoa.

Accordingly I hired some Suahili as attendants and baggage-bearers for the distant and, perhaps too, dangerous journey, the immediate aim of which was to penetrate as far as Kitui and the Wakamba chief, Kivoi, with whom we had become acquainted at Rabbai in the July of 1848, whence I purposed, with Kivoi's help to reach the river Dana. I promised each bearer eight dollars as far as Kitui, and two dollars further to the Dana, which as I already knew separates Ukambani on the north and east from the other tribes of the interior. After we had commended each other in prayer to the mercy and protection of Heaven, I started with eleven bearers from Rabbai on the 1st of November 1849. Rebmann accompanied me for about a league, as far as the plantation of the Mnika, Mana Zahu, whom I had selected as the leader of my little caravan. Early next morning he returned to Rabbai, whilst I continued my further journey in a westerly direction. After our leave-taking I was depressed at heart for several hours, until I was strengthened by the 91st Psalm:—"I will say of the Lord, *he* is my refuge and my fortress: my God; in him will I trust," and could go on my way rejoicing. Crossing the river Muaje we proceeded over a sandy and rocky country covered for the most part with acacia, and spent the night at the little village of Abbe Gome, where we remained during the whole of the next day. The day

after we recommenced our march; and I had to
yield to the importunities of my people, and give
them a cow; when scarcely had it been slaughtered,
partly divided, partly eaten, and partly prepared for
the journey through the desert, when we heard all at
once the sound of a war-horn, and from twenty-five
to thirty fellows marched in martial array towards
us, remaining, however, at a distance from us of
about a hundred paces. As I knew the cowardice of
the Wanika I remained quietly sitting on the ground
for some time, and watched their manœuvres. My
leader went up to them and spoke to them; but
their mutual shrieks were so violent and so blended,
that I could not understand the purport of their
wild converse, yet deduced this much, that it had
reference to a Heshima, or present. As my leader
seemed unsuccessful I went up to them alone and
unarmed, and quietly observed that I wished to
travel in peace through their country, and had paid
such and such chiefs handsomely for leave to journey
onward without molestation, upon which they became somewhat more quiet, but still asked for a
present. I then told them that I would return to
Rabbài and abandon the journey, and ordered my
bearers to take up their loads, and return again.
When the Durumas saw this, they held a council.
At the same time the village people begged me not
to turn about, but to wait for the appearance of
the head men of the place, who were then absent.
At last one of the hostile party came to us and
stated that they would be content with a piece of

cloth of the value of half a dollar, and would let us proceed. I gratified their wish, after which they became friendly and allowed us to pursue our way in peace. We bivouacked for the night in the forest of Kumbulu from which we should soon have to enter the wilderness.

November 6.—The leader of a little Wakamba caravan which had joined our party, sang songs in honour of his tribe in the interior, and prayed to Mulungu (Heaven) to protect his person, his beads, and the other property which he had with him. Throughout the day we had a good level path to travel on, the ground on both sides being covered with wood.

November 7.—To-day we frequently progressed through Zakka—woods of acacia, euphorbia, and other trees, the boughs of which obstructed our progress and tore our clothes, so that we had often to creep on hands and feet through the thicket, and a beast of burden would have been here quite useless.

November 8.—About noon we reached the plain of Kadidza which travellers are always afraid of, as the Gallas hide themselves in the neighbouring wood, in order to waylay and plunder them. After crossing the plain we entered the forest again, and encamped at a place called Muangeni, very much wearied, for we had marched at least eleven hours under a hot sun.

November 9.—After we had started from Muangeni we presently crossed a good and broad path, run-

ning from north, southward or south-westward, made
by the Galla and Wakuafi on their plundering and
devastating expeditions.   We had scarcely passed
it when we met with some Wakamba, who gave us
the unwelcome tidings that three days before the
Masai had been seen near the river Tzawo; that
they had killed several Wakamba, and had made an
incursion into the Galla-land.   Towards noon we
reached the foot of the mountain Maungu, an important point for travellers, as between Ukambani
and the coast, the mountain Ndara excepted, there
is no other place where provisions can be obtained.
From Maungu the view was magnificent; to the east,
lay the Galla-land ; to the north-west and west, the
Endara and Bura ; to the south-east, Kadiaro and
the mountains of Pare.   Our direction was north-
by-west, and the road up the mountain was in some
places very steep.

November 10.—This morning we had a beautiful
distant view of the snow-mountain Kilimanjaro,
in Jagga.   It was high above Endara and Bura,
yet even at this distance I could discern that its
white crown must be snow.   All the arguments
which Mr. Cooley has adduced against the existence
of such a snow-mountain, and against the accuracy
of Rebmann's report, dwindle into nothing when
one has the evidence of one's own eyes of the fact
before one ; so that they are scarcely worth refuting.
At two o'clock we left Maungu, and afterwards encamped at the foot of the Wa, where we found water
in the rock, and tarried for the Wakamba caravan

which had remained behind, looking after a bearer who had run away.

November 11—13.—Two days of weary wandering, the fatigue of which was aggravated by the want of water. On the night of the 13th we encamped at the foot of the Kangongo in a thicket; some of our party ascending it to fetch water, whilst I with five men guarded the encampment.

November 14.— At sunrise the water-seekers returned, but without a drop of water! Our perplexity was great, for our stock of water was nearly exhausted, and the river Tzawo was fourteen leagues off. We started, therefore, in haste and journeyed as fast as we could; though the sun soon became burning hot. At noon, whilst we were resting a little under the shade of a tree, one of my Mohammedan bearers became so fretful over the annoyances of the journey, that he exclaimed angrily : " Am I to receive only eight dollars for this journey ? " and became so frantic that he levelled his gun at a Wanika, who endeavoured to quiet him.

Towards two in the afternoon the heat became almost unbearable, and the more so, as we were still without water, and far from the Tzawo. The Mohammedan already mentioned was again the first to turn restive, declaring that he was not in a condition to continue the journey. I now exhorted the others to put forth all their strength to reach the river before nightfall, and as they hesitated, I called upon all who would volunteer to accompany me; when six men offered themselves for the arduous expedition; for we were all extremely weary and thirsty, and the river was still distant. The sun was just setting when we perceived some trees of the palm family, called Mikoma, in the Wanika language. I redoubled my pace in the sure conviction that the trees seen must be on the bank of the Tzawo; and so it proved; for after a brief interval, we were standing on the bank of that noble river, and refreshing ourselves with its cool water. On the soft soil we observed fresh footprints of men and goats, and also the remains of fires, which my people took to be the traces of the savage Masai, who shortly before our arrival had been at the river. The delay at the Maungu occasioned by the fugitive Mkamba had been, in the hands of Providence the means of preserving us from a meeting with the Masai; and from this apparently trifling circumstance I derived the important lesson, to be patient in every conjuncture which we cannot alter; for God may have so ordered it for our preservation, although at the moment, we cannot comprehend His ways. At the time I had been very discontented and impatient, and would have started earlier from Maungu, if my people would have followed me; now I saw my folly, and was grateful for our preservation!

November 16.—A hard day's march yesterday; yet we started again early this morning. As the air became clear we could see quite distinctly the whole of the eastern side of the Jagga-land and its enormous mountain mass; as well as the transparent

white crown on the dome-like summit of Kilimanjaro.

November 17.—When we reached Kikumbuliu
the Wakamba soon surrounded me, and looked at
me as if I were a being from another world. Hair,
hat, shoes, and umbrella, excited their liveliest attention, and they hopped about me like children. They
often asked if rain would fall, and whether I could
not make it come, as I was a "mundu wa mansi
manene," a man of the great water (the sea-coast),
and had with me "niumba ya mbua," an umbrella.

November 19.—As we rested yesterday and to-day
by the reservoirs in Idumuo many Wakamba came
to see me. From morning to evening I was surrounded by them, and every one wished to converse
with me, and to touch my clothes; and some even
wished us to fire off our guns. I narrated to them
stories from the Bible, especially the history of the
Saviour, and also told them many things about the
customs of my country.

November 20.—To-day the first rain fell in Kikumbulia, which placed me in great favour with the
Wakamba, although I tried to counteract their
superstitious notions, and to ascribe all to God.
My people would have gladly made the Wakamba
believe that they had brought a European rain-
maker into the country, as they hoped, in return, to
receive a sheep or an elephant's tusk. After we
had left Idumuo, after a league we came to the little
river Majijio ma Anduku, encamping at night at
Maveni.

November 21.—After a very rainy and uncomfortable night, which we had passed under the open canopy of heaven, we started at dawn, and marched some six leagues mostly through woody country, until we had descended gently to the bed of the river Adi, which forms the south-western boundary of Ukambani proper. We now began to ascend the mountain-chain which stretches from Endunguni along the Gallaland to Ukambani, and then on to Kikuyu. The whole district is called Yata, and when we had arrived at the top, we had a splendid view in every direction. To the north and north-west we saw the serpent-like windings of the Adi, and the hills and plains of the Wakuafi; to the south and south-west, the mountains Julu, Engolia, Theuka; and to the east, the mountains of Mudumoni, which separate Ukambani from the Gallas. The banks of the river Adi rising to upwards of twenty feet, are covered with noble trees, and the stream which is somewhat sluggish is one hundred and seventy feet wide; but at this time the bed was dried up till within sixty feet, and the water was little more than eighteen inches deep.

We took up our quarters for the night in one of the many little villages of the Wakamba, who were very friendly towards us, and offered us the meat of giraffes and elephants, as well as fowls for sale. I enjoyed my giraffe steak very much; but I found the flesh of the elephant too hard and tough, and although roasted, it had a peculiar and unpalatable flavour. My Mohammedans were most indignant at this meat of the "unbelievers," as they called it, and asked for beads to buy fowls with, which for the sake of peace I did not refuse them.

November 22.—We journeyed on for a league across the plain of Yata, and then ascended into the extensive wilderness of Tangai which is totally uninhabited, and stretches as far as the Mudumoni mountains and the Galla-land towards the east and south-east. After we had left the Tangai wilderness behind us our route lay through Ukambani proper, and we had no longer to traverse thick jungle, as between the coast and Kikumbuliu. About three o'clock, we reached the river Tiva which is said to rise in Ulu, the north-western province of Ukambani; but which is dried up in the hot season, and it is only on removing the surface sand that water can be obtained.

November 23.—About ten o'clock we rested at Mbo, a water-station, after traversing a red and sometimes black soil, and at four o'clock we encamped in Mbandi under a large tree. To-day Kilimanjaro was seen frequently; indeed we were constantly in view of the snow-mountain, wherever the ground was somewhat elevated and afforded a lookout into the distance.

November 24.—We halted in the afternoon at Nsou, and in the evening encamped at Ilangilo. The whole of this district is more beautiful and richer in grass and trees, than any we had yet seen during our journey. We were now in Ukambani itself, which at the coast I had often heard described as a beautiful country.

November 25.—I passed a night of trouble. As

my people knew that to-day we would reach Kivoi and that our journey was drawing to its close, they asked with the greatest insolence for an increase of pay; and now demanded thirteen instead of the eight dollars which had been agreed upon at Rabbai. They said that three dollars had been already consumed by their wives and children, and had been received in advance before leaving Rabbai; and now they insisted on receiving ten dollars more. Besides this they demanded all the ivory which Kivoi might give me in return for my presents. Should I refuse compliance, they threatened to abandon me forthwith; and throughout they were so furious, that had I used the slightest offensive word in reply, they would infallibly have killed me on the spot. I therefore remained quiet all the night through, and allowed them to shriek and bawl. At length I promised them the ten dollars without more ado, and even the thirteen dollars "if the demand were recognized as a just one by the authorities at the coast; but here, in the wilderness, there was no proper tribunal to judge between us." This declaration appeased them at last, so that they departed from Ilangilo and proceeded to the village of Kivoi.

November 26—On reaching Kivoi's village we seated ourselves under a tree and waited till he should come to us. He came at last out of his little village, accompanied by his chief wife who carried in her hand a magic-staff which was coloured black. The chief gave me a friendly greeting, and said that when I spoke to him at Rabbai about a journey to Ukambani, he had thought I was not speaking the truth, as he could not imagine that I should ever perform so distant a journey; but now he saw that I had spoken the truth I was very welcome to his country. He then ordered a lodging to be prepared for me in the hut of one of his wives, who was forced to leave it, whilst the Wakamba ran together in crowds to see and to wonder at the Musungu, European.

After I was somewhat settled in my new abode I visited the chief, and spoke to him respecting the object of my journey, which was to learn whether the Wakamba would receive Christian instructors, who would teach them the way to true happiness through the knowledge of God and His Son Jesus Christ. I told him further that I wished to extend my journey as far as the river Dana, and would therefore ask him for an escort for the execution of my plan. I did not ask for any ivory in return for my presents; I asked for nothing more than my daily sustenance so long as I remained with him. The chief replied: "I understand your object, and you shall receive all that you desire. You will remain with me till next month, when I am going to Muea, in the Wandurobo country, and also to Kikuyu, to fetch ivory thence, and you can go with me to all these districts. After my return I shall make a journey to the coast to sell my ivory, in some four or five months, when you can go with me; but you must send away your Wanika, for I do not like them, because they rob me of my ivory when

I go through their country." Upon this he brought
a cow, which was slaughtered by my Mohammedans,
and divided between me and Kivoi's family. He
would not give anything to the Wanika, especially
when he heard that they had behaved badly to
me at Ilangilo. In another conversation Kivoi expressed the wish that the governor of Mombaz would
send boats up the river Dana, always navigable, to
bring away his ivory by water, as its transport to
Mombaz by land was very difficult. This and
other communications on the same subject, pleased
me very much, for I had long wished to see set on
foot the navigation of the so-called Quilimancy,
which may be, probably, equivalent to Kilimansi,
or Kilima ja mansi—mountain of the water. This
Quilimancy is, therefore, nothing else than the river
Dana, which is formed by the snow-water of Kegnia,
and in its further course receives many rivers, for
instance, the Dida, Kingaji, and Ludi.

November 27.—This morning Kivoi introduced
me to his chiefs and relatives. He made use of
my presence to raise himself up in their eyes. He
said: "Did I not tell you that I would bring a
Musungu to you? Now he is here; am I not a man
of note since a Musungu has come to me into my
country?" They all cried out with one voice:
"Truly, Kivoi is a great man, and has spoken to us
the truth!" They then looked courteously at me,
and took delight in inspecting my shoes, hair, hat,
clothes, and especially my umbrella, which was often
opened and shut up. They then began to quaff uki,

a drink prepared out of sugar-cane. Kivoi repeated his former promise to accompany me wheresoever I wished, although I had already resolved to return to the coast. I felt unwell, having had no proper food since I left Kikumbuliu, and the rain now prevented my journey to the Dana. If I sent away my Wanika, I should be entirely dependent on Kivoi for my return to Rabbai, and I had reason to trust the Wakamba even less than the Wanika. These were among my reasons for wishing to return. After I had passed some time with the Wakamba chiefs, who sat perfectly naked on their little stools, I returned to my hut, where a number of people assembled again, to whom I endeavoured to proclaim the Gospel, even though I was not yet master of the Wakamba language. Kivoi arrived afterwards and asked me for the presents I had brought for him, and which I then gave to him.

November 28.—Kivoi mentioned the existence of a volcano in the vicinity and to the north-west of Kegnia, the fire-plains of which are dreaded by the hunters as dangerous ground. During my stay in the village a dance was performed by some natives of Kikuyu, which consisted in each person springing as high as possible into the air, and upon his reaching the ground again, stamping with all his might with his feet and shouting out "Yolle! Yolle!" when after moving backwards a little the whole body of dancers came forwards in a ring; upon which the dance was several times repeated. These Kikuyu were by no means repulsive-looking, indeed they were handsomer than even the dwellers along the coast, and their language is evidently a mixture of Kikamba and Kikaufi, as indeed is that of the tribes of Mbe and Uimbu, which also dwell in the vicinity of Kegnia, and like them their chief articles of trade are ivory and tobacco.

December 3.—The wives of the chief prepared meat for our journey to the coast.

In the afternoon, we took leave of Kivoi, who delivered the following long address to me and to my people :—" I wished the Musungu (European) to remain with me, and go next month with me to Kikuyu, where the river Dana can be crossed ; but the Musungu wishes to return to the coast. He can go if he pleases ; I will not prevent him. I wished to bestow upon him one elephant's tusk four feet long, another three feet and a half in length ; for what he has is mine, and what I have is his ; but here I have no ivory, it is at Kikuyu. I will go and fetch it, and then I will travel to the coast, and bring with me two elephants' tusks for the Musungu ; and if his brother at Rabbai will go with me to Ukambani, he may go with me, but ivory here have I none. I will go to Kikuyu and to the Andulobbo and fetch it next month. I am a man of note ; I do not use many words, but I will keep my promise. And you Wanika, listen to me ; I have a word to say to you also. You are not to give any annoyance on the road to the Musungu ; for he is my friend. You are to take him in safety to his house at Rabbai, that my anger may not be provoked against you. And now here are 170 strings of beads and a "doti" (four yards) of calico; this will suffice you to buy food in Kikumbuliu, and to reach the coast. And now I have told you my whole heart. Salute Tangai, the governor of the fortress of Mombaz."

Tangai was personally known to the chief, as he is in the habit of buying ivory of him when Kivoi goes to Mombaz. After this address we started accompanied by Kivoi, who went with us a few hundred paces. In the evening we bivouacked in the village of one of his relatives.

December 11.—Yesterday we reached the first place in Kikumbuliu, our route having lain by Nsambani (on the 4th), Ilangilo (the 5th), Nsou (the 6th), Mbo (the 7th), the river Tiwa (the 8th), and the Adi (the 9th).

On our homeward journey we met with no particular adventures, only we were often troubled for want of water and by the fear of enemies. On the 20th of December we reached Mount Ndungani, whence we looked back once more on the great wilderness which we had traversed. I thought of the toils, privations, and dangers which we had survived in the days just past. They were all over now; but the many proofs of the protecting power, mercy, and compassion of my God can never be forgotten by me, but must be a continual stimulus to gratitude and to zeal in prayer and in labour for the furtherance of His kingdom in the darkened regions with which I have become acquainted. This looking back into the wilderness reminded me, too, of the dying Christian standing upon the hill of death, looking for the last time backwards upon the wilderness of this world, contemplating his conflicts with sin and the world, and after a well-fought battle approaching the repose which his God and Saviour has mercifully prepared for him in heaven. Strengthened by this thought, I recommenced my march once more and journeyed the whole day, until in the evening we reached the dwelling of our guide, Mana Zahu, where (only a league from Rabbai) I spent the night, his wife providing me with wholesome food in abundance. On the morning of the 21st I had the pleasure of rejoining once more my dear fellow-labourers, Rebmann and Erhardt, and of telling them what I had seen and heard in the past fifty-one days, and what the Father of all mercies had done for me.

CHAPTER VII.

SECOND JOURNEY TO UKAMBANI.

Contemplated missionary-station at Yata—Advantages of the locality—Departure—The wilderness: "silence!"—Robbers ahead—
No water—Forward towards the Tzawo—Onslaught of the robbers
—Fortunate deliverance—A false alarm—Arrival at Yata—
Friendly reception from the chiefs—No house, and its incon-
veniences—Threatened desertion of the Wanika, and flight of the
author's only servant—House-building operations: unsatisfactory
results—Annoyances from the Wakamba—Visit to Kivoi resolved
on—Departure—Sickness—Too swift an escort—Arrival at Kivoi's
—Uki—War with the Atua—The deserted village—Kivoi's
return and promises—Peace-rejoicings—Expedition to the Dana—
Under way again—Poison-wood, its commerce and manipulation—
Unexpected venison—Nearing the Dana.

THE immediate object of my second journey to
Ukambani was, in accordance with the decision of
the Committee of the Church Missionary Society,
to found a missionary-station in Ukambani, and thus
actually to commence the chain of missions through
Africa formerly spoken of. If the Ukambani-mission
succeeded, it was hoped that then a further missionary-station might be established in the neighbourhood of the snow-mountain situated on the
high ground of Yata, some 110 leagues from Rabbai
in the village of a Mkamba, Mtangi wa Nsuki, a
man of great influence in the district of Yata, and

which being visited by all the caravans which journey either from Ukambani to the seacoast, or from the latter to Ukambani, a missionary stationed there would have frequent opportunities of corresponding with his brethren at Rabbai. The village lies in a plain, which is at least 2000 feet above the level of the sea and contains many Wakamba villages. As the Wakamba-land proper begins with Yata a missionary stationed there could make excursions in every direction, and as at the same time many Wakamba from Yata were settled at Rabbai Mpia, in constant intercourse with their friends and relations in the interior, the Yata people would be obliged to be careful in their treatment of the stranger. If they maltreated him the authorities of the coast would in accordance with the East-African custom, retaliate on the settlers from the interior in their power.

I engaged thirty Wanika as burden-bearers and escort, Mana Zahu being the leader of the little caravan, which was joined on the way by about 100 Wakamba, who were returning to their homes. Our departure from Rabbai took place on the 11th of July. The disorder, insane chatter, drunkenness, gluttony, and disobedience of my people were great, and gave me much pain, until on the 14th of July we left behind us the inhabited country and reached, the great wilderness at Ndunguni, when the Wanika were obliged to be quiet and silent. On the 15th we were met by a caravan of Wakamba coming from the interior with ivory to the coast, and to some of them, who seated themselves on the ground beside me, I explained the object of my journey; after which, a Mkamba told me that in his youth he had travelled to Mbellete, and had then proceeded into the country of the Wabilikimo, or "little people" (pigmies). The distance between Ukambani and Ubilikimoni was greater than that between the former and Mombaz; the Wabilikimo had long feet, but short bodies, and on their backs a kind of hump; and nobody understood their language. The Wakamba made friends with them by offering copper rings, for which honey was presented in return; they were good, harmless people, and there were many elephants in their country. At our night bivouac the Wanika and Wakamba were quarrelling over the division of a slaughtered goat, whereupon a Mkamba made a long speech in which he exhorted the people thenceforth to observe silence, and on the march not to leave the caravan, as the way was dangerous. After a very fatiguing march of two days we reached Mount Maungu, where we met a number of Wanika of the Kiriama tribe, waiting for ivory caravans from Ukambani. They gave us the unwelcome intelligence that the day before a large band of Gallas had been seen in the neighbourhood of Kadiza, evidently with the design of attacking and plundering the ivory-caravans of the Wakamba. On the 18th of July we determined to rest for a little at Maungu. The Kiriama people surrounded me almost the whole day putting questions, or trying to inspect the things which I was taking to Ukambani. With a few of them I had some talk upon religious matters, and they asked who was Jesus Christ, and what had He done ? To-day the leaders of the Wakamba caravans made their people swear, that in case of an attack by the Gallas or Masai, they would not run away but would defend themselves. My leader, too, was obliged to be present at the oath-taking. I took no notice of the circumstance, but in the course of the journey I found that the caravan-leaders had shown very proper forethought. A European ought not altogether to despise the reports and fears of the natives; but because the people had babbled so much about the dangers of the journey to Ukambani, and I had performed my last journey thither in safety, I looked on their tales and terrors as fanciful. However I was later forced to acknowledge that the natives had good ground for their anxieties and precautions.

We started again on the morning of the 19th of July, our route lying more to the north and our path being level and sandy. Leaving Mount Ndara on the left we marched some six leagues till we reached the river Woi, where we bivouacked. On the 20th we crossed the Woi, and noticed on the bank fresh traces of elephants; and upon entering the noble prairie, free of thorns and jungle, with which the eastern range of the Bura mountains terminates, we saw here and there a shy zebra, or a giraffe, which my people vainly endeavoured to capture. At noon we reached Kangongo; but, as had been the case two

years ago, we found no water there, and so pushed
forward to reach the Tzawo. On the 21st we started
before dawn to reach the Tzawo as soon as possible, as
our stock of water was nearly exhausted, and about
nine we ascended a small hill, and sat down in the
vicinity of a thick wood. How little did I suspect
that lurking enemies were surrounding and watching
us ! During the march, I had been ruminating upon
the various petitions of the Lord's Prayer, and
almost every word of it had impressed itself as
a blessing to me. Till now the Wakamba caravan
which kept company with us, had preceded us during
the whole journey, but when we resumed our march
it remained, I know not why or how, behind my
people. Just as I had entered with my Wanika
a large thicket where it was difficult to move to the
right or to the left, we heard suddenly a loud cry
which proceeded from the Wakamba, who formed the
rearguard. They cried "Aendi! Aendi! Acndi!"—
Robbers! Robbers! Robbers! (literally hunters). A
frightful confusion now arose among my people ; they
threw down their loads, and would have fled into the
wood, but found it difficult to penetrate the bushes.
One called out this, another that ; several shouted,
"Fire off the guns, fire off the guns !" I wished to
do so, but the man who carried my double-barrelled
one had fled, and I was quite unarmed. I got
hold of him and it at last and fired in the air,
on which the Wanika set up a dreadful war-cry, and
the others who had guns then fired three or four
shots in succession. Whilst this firing was going on

at our front, the Wakamba were discharging their poisoned arrows at the Aendi, who had shot theirs at them, from the hill I have mentioned. The Wakamba who were furthest behind, threw down their loads at the sight of the enemy, allowing them to come and put them on their shoulders, whereupon the Wakamba fired and shot three of the robbers dead; and we had one Mkamba wounded. When the enemy saw that the Wakamba made a stand and heard our firing, they retreated to their hiding-place, upon which my scattered Wanika collected again, took courage, and joined the Wakamba, who had been exposed to the greatest danger. Had the conflict lasted longer we should have been in a very perilous plight, as in the confusion I lost my powder-horn, and one of my people burst the barrel of his gun by putting too large a charge into it. The ramrod of another was broken, through his being knocked over by a Mnika in the confusion, just as he was going to load; whilst the gun of another missed fire altogether. I saw clearly that it was God who preserved us, and not our own sword and bow. After the rearguard of the Wakamba had got up to us, we hurried on to escape from the inhospitable thickets; but we had not gone far, when those in front cried, "Aendi! Aendi!" "Robbers! Robbers!" We fired at once in the air; but we soon discovered our mistake, and got off with the mere alarm; as it turned out to be the caravan expected at Maungu, consisting of three to four hundred Wakamba, who were coming from the interior with a number of elephants' tusks, and whom our vanguard had taken for robbers. Fortunately the travellers at once recognized our Wanika, and cried to us, " Do not fire, we are trading people !" Some of these Wakamba came from one side through the thicket, and as I still took them to be robbers I pointed my gun at them, but waited a moment, till they should begin the attack. Fortunately the Wanika called out to me : " Do not fire, they are friends !" Fear was succeeded by sudden joy; evidently the robbers had intended to attack the expected caravan, but on the principle of a bird in the bush, thought it better to plunder us as first comers, and we had thus prepared the way for the large caravan. It was fortunate for me that the first attack had been made on the Wakamba, for they defended their property, while my people cared neither for me nor for my baggage, but were anxious about their own lives alone.

We reached the Tzawo in safety, and, continuing our journey on the 22nd, arrived on the 24th after a two days' very toilsome march at Kikumbuliu, where we rested for a day. At last, on the afternoon of the 26th, we crossed the Adi and began to ascend the high land of Yata, my destination as a missionary. On the way, I besought earnestly in my heart the Father of all mercies to guide and help me to make a commencement of missionary work in this country. Arrived at the plain on the top we proceeded to the nearest village, and inquired after the Mkamba, Muilu wa Kiwui, with whom I was first to reside. We were told that he had quitted the village, in consequence of a famine from which the country was suffering through want of rain. We then betook ourselves to Mtangi wa Nsuki, another Wakamba chief, who gave us a friendly reception; and in a short time there was an assemblage of the other chiefs to whom I explained the object of my journey. They declared that they would willingly permit me to reside among them, build a hut, and do whatever I pleased, assuring me of their protection. After this declaration I delivered to them my present which consisted of eight ells of calico and some four pounds of beads; for which they presented me in return with a goat. I made a special present to Mtangi wa Nsuki, as it was within his enclosure that I was to erect my hut, and as he had offered me his particular protection. Thus far at starting everything had gone satisfactorily, so that I took courage and thanked God for His powerful protection and assistance.

July 27.—In the course of the day I was visited by many Wakamba, who wished to see me and my baggage, which I was obliged to leave lying in the open air, whilst for want of a proper dwelling-place I too was forced to camp out, with no other shelter than that which my umbrella afforded me against the heat of the sun during the day; whilst at night a cold wind was blowing from the south from Kilimanjaro and Yulu; and even in the morning at 10 o'clock the glass stood at 68°, and did not reach beyond 72° at midday. It was most unpleasant to me to have no habitation, however small, in which

I could rest from the fatigues of the journey and be sheltered from the intrusion of the Wakamba. I felt, consequently, rather low spirited, and this mood was somewhat aggravated by the declaration of my Wanika, that next day they intended to return to Rabbai with a Wakamba caravan which was journeying towards the coast. I reminded them of their undertaking to build me a dwelling-place before they returned to the coast, which they did not deny, and at once set to work with it. In a few hours they had put together, with stakes fetched from the wood, a miserable hencoop, scarcely six feet high, and about as many feet broad and long, but with which I was fain to be content as my things were lying in the open air, and I had neither shelter by day from the heat of the sun, nor by night from the cold of the bitter blast sweeping in from the southern mountains.

July 28.—My Wanika started this morning without finishing the roofing in of the hut with grass; and the single servant whom I had brought from Rabbai ran away, although I had always treated him with particular affection and kindness. I could not trust the Wakamba; my conscience forbade me to buy a slave; and yet I was obliged to have some one who could look after my things, and to whose care I could entrust my hut, and I saw that I must have a tolerable servant and a better dwelling-place, if I was to settle in Yata. In my hencoop I could neither write, nor read, nor sleep, and was continually besieged by the Wakamba, who by day, even before dawn, did not leave me a moment alone. If I wished to read, they asked if I was trying to spy into their hearts, or whether I was looking for rain and inquiring after diseases; when I wrote, they wanted to know what I had written, and whether it contained sorcery. Every one of my movements was sharply observed. Many came to beg this or that, to see new things, or to buy wares, as they took me for a merchant; others brought a few eggs or a little meal, and then asked for twice or three times as much as their presents were worth; whilst others, again, wished merely to be amused. My hut had not even a door, so that I could not close it, and by night I was safe neither from thieves nor from wild beasts.

July 30.—Meditating this morning on my painful position, I came to the conclusion, on the one hand, that I ought not to abandon Yata, as the people, on the whole, were friendly, and part of them listened with attention when I strove to make them acquainted with the Word of God; on the other hand, it was clear to me that I could not remain if my two Wanika were to forsake me now, or at the close of two months; for on the flight of my servant (who was afraid to stay in Ukambani by himself), these two had offered their services, very highly paid, for two months only, at the end of which I was either to return with them to the coast, or remain by myself in Yata. I therefore resolved to make use of the interval in visiting the interior of Ukambani as far as the river Dana, and first of all to repair to my old friend

Kivoi, with whose help I might attain my object. If I were then obliged to quit Ukambani I should, at least, have added to my knowledge of the country, and have promulgated the gospel in it, here and there. After I had decided on journeying to Kivoi I asked Mtangi wa Nsuki for a small escort, which he readily granted, giving me, however, to understand that I was to return to him, and remain with him.

August 1.—I awoke this morning in a very feverish state, caused partly by the cold at night, partly by the unwholesome air of my hut; but, nevertheless set out on the journey to Kivoi, accompanied by four Wakamba and one of my two Mnika servants, leaving the other to look after my things. The Wakamba moved on so swiftly that I could not keep pace with them; it was more like jumping than walking. In the villages which we passed through, I had often to stop and allow myself to be gaped at by the people like an ape or bear in Europe. In the evening we reached the river Tiwa.

August 2.—On waking this morning I was so unwell that I would have returned to Yata, if my servant and the Wakamba would have allowed me. My servant hoped to receive a piece of ivory from Kivoi, which was the reason why he would not return to Yata. So on we went, the Wakamba running so fast that I could not keep up with them, and our way lay through an uninhabited and uncultivated country.

August 4.—About noon we reached the village of the chief, Kivoi, who was absent. When he came home he greeted me in a friendly manner, and observed that he should have taken it very ill, if I had not come to him. He told me, among other things, that he had at present a feud with the Wakamba-tribe Atua, which had destroyed the house of his relative, Ngumbau, because the wife of the latter, who is reputed a witch, had been suspected of casting a spell upon the cattle of the Atua.

August 5.—To-day Kivoi introduced me to Rumu. wa Kikandi, a native of the tribe Uembu, whose territory lies five or six days' journey to the north-west of Kitui, quite close to the snow-mountain Kirenia (Kenia). He told me that he had frequently been to the mountain, but had not ascended it, because it contained Kirira, a white substance, producing very great cold. What the Jagga people call Kibo, snow, is called by the natives of Uembu, Kirira, which brings to mind the Ethiopic word kur, or kuir (coldness). The white substance, he added, produced continually a quantity of water, which descended the mountain and formed a large lake, from which the river Dana took its rise.

August 7.—* * * * In Kivoi's hut, I saw a quantity of Magaddi, a dried earth of whitish hue, which has a sour but aromatic odour, and is found in Jagga as well as in Udeizu and in the north-eastern Wakamba-land. It is made into a powder by the Wakamba and Wanika, and mixed with snuff, of which the East-Africans are passionately fond.

August 9.—To-day, Kivoi had a quantity of Uki prepared for the banquet which he was to give to his tribe to induce them to accompany him on an expedition against the Atua, if a reconciliation with the latter turned out to be impossible. This beverage is thus prepared from sugar-cane: first, the bark of the cane is cut away; then the cane is cut into small pieces and put into a wooden mortar, which is made firm in the earth; after it has been pounded into a pulp it is put into a pit, when being covered over with a cowhide and pressed down, the juice rises through to the top. The expressed juice, which is very sweet, is then poured into calabashes, and these are placed near a fire, to be made hot. When this process is over, the beverage is ready for use.

August 13.—Many Wakamba were here to-day; they sat in groups in Kivoi's yard, where I had an opportunity of becoming acquainted with many of them, and of speaking to them respecting the salvation of their souls.

August 14.—To-day, about 200 men appeared in Kivoi's village. They came singing, dancing, and piping, and seated themselves in a semi-circle on the ground outside the village. Kivoi asked me to accompany him, with my telescope in my hand; which I did, and when perfect quiet was restored, Kivoi marched up and down within the semi-circle, and delivered a long address. On his head he wore a kind of hat decorated with ostrich-feathers; in his hand he carried a club, and by his side hung his sword and powder-horn; his body was perfectly naked, with the exception of a scanty piece of cloth. He stated in his address that he wished to recover from the Atua the cattle of which his relative had been robbed. If they would not assist him he should depart out of the land, and then they would never again see a stranger like me. After the people had promised obedience and assistance, they started on the expedition with Kivoi at their head.

The population of the village was now reduced to females only; it did not contain a single male, except myself, my servant, and Ngumbau, whose wife was said to have bewitched and destroyed the cattle of the Atua. The people were in great terror of an attack of the Atua by night, who might easily have taken and burned the village. Ngumbau came during the night trembling into my hut, and asked me to look through my telescope and see whether friends or foes were coming; my servant, too, was in great terror, and wished to return immediately to Yata and the seacoast; I commended myself to the protection of Almighty God, and laid down in tranquillity on my bed.

August 17.—Kivoi returned after having peacefully arranged his quarrel with the Atua, the latter having promised to restore the cattle which had been stolen. Both parties had slaughtered an animal, eaten certain portions of it, and sworn to observe the treaty of peace. I spoke to Kivoi respecting that true peace which the world cannot give nor take away.

August 18.—When I informed the chief to-day of my wish to return to Yata, he said I was not to do so as he would soon accompany me to the river Dana and to Mbe. He would afterwards go with me to Mombaz; there I was to hire some Suahili, who could build me a substantial dwelling in Ukambani; he would then help me to visit all the countries round about, and I might do with him what I pleased. I had no doubt that Kivoi could and might execute all these intentions, yet I feared his great greed, which would lead him to try to make capital out of me. He was well acquainted with Europeans, Suahili, and Arabs; he possessed great influence, too, on the coast and in the interior; but I felt no impulse to throw myself into his arms, and to enter into his schemes. I was still of the opinion that Yata was the best place for a missionary-station.

August 19.—Kivoi's whole village rejoiced and danced in consequence of the restoration of peace. The chief had a quantity of uki prepared for our approaching journey to the river Dana. Early in the morning, whilst walking up and down in his enclosure, he gave each of his female slaves a quantity of Indian corn to grind.

August 20.—A little caravan arrived yesterday from Mbe with tobacco, which the Mbe people wished to sell in Ukambani.

August 24.—We started on our much-talked-of expedition yesterday evening, our route being to the north and north-west, mostly through very fine country, well suited for tillage and grazing. In the evening we bivouacked by a brook which flows towards Kitui. In the open and grassy wilderness, through which we wandered, there was here and there an acacia-tree to be seen; but otherwise the country was completely without wood.

August 25.—We broke up early, and after a short march we came upon four rhinoceroses grazing; but as we did not disturb them they remained quietly where they were. I used to have a great dread of those ugly and clumsy creatures, but by degrees I grew accustomed to them. All day we were gradually ascending; there was not a single tree to be seen, nothing but grass. We observed great herds of antelopes; and at one time we saw a flock of vultures flying upwards and then descending to the ground again; upon which the Wakamba immediately threw down their loads, and ran to the spot, where to their joy they found a great piece of the flesh of Ngundi, a kind of large antelope. Everywhere on our road Kivoi set fire to the grass, which did us mischief subsequently, as the fire informed the enemy of our onward march. We passed soon afterwards the brook Andilai, the water of which was very salt, on the banks of which I remarked a stratum of crystallized salt, which, however, was mixed with earth; but Kivoi's wives collected a quantity of it for our use on the road.

August 26.—We started very early. The little caravan of Uembu people, whose leader was my friend Rumu wa Kikandi, carried a quantity of the wood of the poison-tree which grows in Kikambuliu, Mberria, and Teita, in pieces of from three to four inches thick. The wood is pounded, and then boiled, and the point of the arrow is besmeared with the black, thick paste, which is the result of the operation, the strength of the poison being first

tested on animals. The people on the other side of
the river Dana exchange tobacco and ivory for this
wood, which does not grow in those regions, and in
Kikumbuliu I saw whole caravans conveying heavy
loads of this wood to Ukambani. Our way led us first
up and then over a hill, a continuation of the Data,
from the top of which there is a magnificent view
towards Kikuyu and the valley of the Dana. To
the south-west are Mounts Iweti and Nsao Wi, and
beyond them the lofty Muka Mku and the Kanjallo,
which mark the beginning of the highlands of Kikuyu.
It seems probable that the chain of mountains which
stretches from Ndungnai to Yata, and so on to Kanjallo, may lose itself in Kirenia. When we had
descended it on the other side, we halted by a
brook, and while we were resting, the Wakamba
saw again a number of vultures flying upward and
downward. My servant ran immediately to the
spot and found a great piece of a fallow-deer, which
had been seized and partly devoured in the morning
by a lion, whose footprints were apparent. I was
glad of this roasting-joint, as Kivoi had but indif-
ferently fulfilled his promise of furnishing us with
provisions during the journey, and on the first day
we had had nothing but bananas. After we had
enjoyed our venison, we continued our journey.
Again we saw the high mountain Muka Mku, past the
eastern foot of which the river Dika is said to flow,
falling in Muea into the Dana, the Dana itself flowing to the west of Muka Mku.

CHAPTER VIII.

August 27.—LAST night we had encamped in a
grassy wilderness; I felt much disquieted, and
awoke several times. Once the wind drove the fire
to our encampment; another time, I thought I heard
people running about. In the morning, we had no
water for cooking purposes, so that there was but
little enjoyment of our meal. When we reached the
isolated Mount Kense, which rises up out of the great
plain leading to the Dana, some twenty-five of
Kivoi's people who had left Kitui after us joined our
caravan, which now comprised from fifty to fifty-five
persons. Not far from Kense, where we had halted,
Kivoi lost the handle of my umbrella, which I had

given him. After an hour and a half, he first discovered the loss, when he immediately commanded a
halt, and returned with a troop of people to look for
the missing article. This unimportant circumstance
irritated me not a little, as I was hungry and
thirsty, and wished to reach the river as soon as possible; and being thus discontented with the behaviour
of Kivoi, who troubled himself about such a trifle as
the loss of an umbrella-handle, I went forward alone
hoping that five or six Wakamba would follow me, and
hasten onward to the river. But not one of them
moved an inch because, as they said, Kivoi had
not ordered them to break up the encampment, and
was still a good way from us; so I had to stomach
my ire as best I might, and was after all obliged to
remain for several hours with the caravan, till Kivoi
returned with the recovered umbrella-handle. As
soon as he had arrived, we broke up and journeyed
onward; when after a short march, one of Kivoi's
wives found in the grass a quantity of ostrich-feathers,
upon which he again commanded a halt to make a
search for more feathers. He seated himself on the
ground, and had the feathers found brought to him,
not allowing any one to share them with him.
When we were again in motion, and were within
a good league of the Dana, Kivoi's slaves on a
sudden pointed towards the forest towards which
we were marching from the grassy and treeless
plain. I ran to Kivoi's side, and saw a party of
about ten men emerging from the forest, and soon
afterwards came other and larger parties from

another side, evidently with the object of surrounding us. Our whole caravan was panic-stricken, and the cry, " Meida," they are robbers, ran through our ranks, upon which Kivoi fired off his gun, and bade me do the same. After we had fired thrice the robbers began to relax their pace, probably because they had heard the whistling of our bullets through the air. In the confusion and the hurry of loading I had left my ramrod in the barrel of my gun and fired it off, so that I could not load again. Whilst we were firing and our caravan was preparing for a conflict, Kivoi ordered one of his wives to open my umbrella, when the robbers immediately slackened their speed. They were also obstructed by the grass, which Kivoi had set on fire that the wind might blow the flames in their faces. When at last they had come within bow-shot of us Kivoi called to them to stop, and not to approach nearer. He then ran towards them, and invited them to a parley upon which they ran up and down, brandishing their swords and raising a shout of triumph. After a few minutes, Kivoi succeeded in persuading three of them to come into our encampment, where we had seated ourselves in rank and file upon the ground. The enemy likewise seated themselves. Kivoi now made a speech, telling them who he was and whither he was going; and after he had finished his address the spokesman of the opposite party laughed and said: " You need not be afraid ; we have no hostile design ; we saw the grass on fire, and only wished to know who the travellers were that had set it on fire.

You can now go forward to the river; we will follow at once, and yonder settle our business with you." The robbers then remained seated, and took counsel with each other, while we continued our journey.

On the way Kivoi was much troubled, and said that the interview had been unsatisfactory, and that the people were robbers. At last we entered the forest, the pathway on either side being inclosed by trees and bushes. Whenever our caravan rested for a little the robbers were seen following us from the plain, so I took advantage of one such interval to cut myself in haste a ramrod, and to load my gun. Meanwhile some five robbers came to us and said: "This is the way to the river; follow us." We followed them, I marching with the Uembu people, the front men of our caravan, while Kivoi remained behind. Suddenly the robbers in front wheeled round, set up a war-shout, and began to discharge their arrows at us, and the robbers in the rear surrounded Kivoi. A great confusion arose; our people threw away their burdens, and discharged their arrows at the enemy, begging me imploringly to fire as quickly as I could. I fired twice, but in the air; for I could not bring myself to shed the blood of man. Whilst I was reloading a Mkamba rushed past me wounded in the hip, a stream of blood flowing from him. Right and left fell the arrows at my feet, but without touching me. When our people saw that they could not cope with an enemy 120 strong they took to flight. Rumu wa

FLIGHT FROM SAVAGES SUDDENLY INTERRUPTED

Kikandi and his people ran away and left me quite alone.

I deemed it now time to think of flight, especially as in the confusion I could not distinguish friend from foe; so I set off at a run in the direction taken by Rumu and his people; but scarcely had I gone some sixty paces, when I came to a trench or rather the dried-up bed of a brook, some ten feet deep, and from four to five in width. The Uembu-people had thrown their loads into it, and leapt over the trench; but when I made the attempt I fell into it, breaking the butt-end of my gun and wounding my haunches in the fall; and as I could not climb up the steep bank of the brook I ran on along its bed until I came to a place where I could emerge from it. When I had gained the bank I ran on as fast as I could after the Uembu-people, pursued by the arrows of the robbers which reached the brook; but as I could not come up with the former, my gun and the heavy ammunition in my pockets impeding my progress, I remained behind all alone in the forest; all my people had disappeared from before my face, and not one of them was to be seen. I may mention, that when I first took to flight, and before I reached the trench, I heard a heavy fall on the ground, and at once it occurred to me that Kivoi must have fallen, and this as I afterwards found out was really the case. I now ran on as quickly as I could by the side of the brook into the forest. All at once I came to a glade where I saw a number of men, some 300 paces in front of me. Thinking

them to be my people, recovered from their terror
and collected again, I crossed the brook to reach
them. Suddenly it came into my head that they
might be the robbers, so I took my telescope, looked
through it, and discovered to my horror that they
were indeed the robbers, who were carrying off the
booty plundered from our caravan. I noticed particularly one man with ostrich-feathers on his head,
whom I recognized as one of the band when we first
met with it; so I retreated immediately across the
brook again, without being observed by the Meida,
although I could see them with the naked eye. As I
was re-entering the wood two large rhinoceroses met
my view, which were standing quietly in front of me,
some fifteen to twenty paces from me, but they soon
turned aside and disappeared in the forest. For eight
or ten minutes I resumed my flight at a run, till I
thought I was out of the robbers' track, and emerged
again into an open and grassy plain where I laid down
beneath a tree, first of all giving thanks to the Father
of mercy who had preserved me through so great a
danger. I then reflected on my critical situation
and the possibility of returning to Kivoi's village;
then thought that I would repair to Mberre and
seek our people there, to accompany me back
again. But how was I to pay them and buy
food, my servants having thrown away àll that
belonged to me, and fled towards the Wakamba-
land? Besides, I was not certain whether I might
not meet again with the robbers, or even whether
I might not be murdered by the people of Mberre,

to which a portion of the robbers belonged,
added to which I was quite alone, and had but
a slight acquaintance with the dialect of Mberre.
On the other hand, how was I without a guide,
without food, and without a knowledge of the
water-stations, to make a return-journey of thirty-
five or thirty-six leagues to Kivoi's village? In
this difficulty I remembered that Heaven had yesterday caused a lion to furnish me with food; I was
now one of God's poor, for whom he could and would
provide; "man's extremity is God's opportunity!"
Most of all was I strengthened and comforted
by the previous day's experience of the lion
sent to provide us with food in the wilderness.
My most pressing and immediate want was water;
for I was extremely thirsty, and had not had anything
to drink all day. I knew that the Dana was near at
hand, and seeing at some distance very lofty trees, I
conjectured that the bed of the river was there.
I saw, too, the mountain past the foot of which, as
Kivoi told me yesterday, the river flows, and so I
determined to press forward to the river, towards
which I was not now impelled by geographical
curiosity, but by extreme thirst. As the country
through which I was wending my way was without
either trees or brushwood, I was afraid of being seen
by the robbers; yet the river had to be reached at any
cost. After a short march I came to a trodden pathway which I followed, and soon saw the surface of the
river gleaming through the trees and bushes on its
banks with a pleasure which no pen can describe,

and which none but those who have been similarly placed can realize. The path led me over the high bank down to the water's edge; " Praise and thanks be to God," I exclaimed, " now I can slake my thirst and have water in plenty for the return-journey!" The water was cool and pleasant; for the banks were steep and lofty; and when I reached the river there was a pool, which led me to think that the river had an ebb and flow. After my thirst was satisfied, for want of water-bottles I filled the leather case of my telescope as well as the barrels of my gun, which was now useless to me; and I stopped up the mouths of the gun-barrels with grass, and with bits of cloth cut off my trousers.

After I had attended sufficiently to my animal wants I made a slight exploration of the river which was about 150 feet in width, and from six to seven feet deep. But this cannot be its normal depth during the hot season, for Kivoi, and Ruma wa Kikandi, both told me distinctly that then it only reached to the neck; and this was the reason why Kivoi had fixed on the hot season for his journey, in order to cross the Dana when its water was low; for in the rainy season the Wakamba cross the river on rafts. Its course, so far as I could see, is serpentine, running towards the east; but I do not doubt that it makes great detours before it arrives at the Indian Ocean. If its source in the lake at Kirenia is 6000 feet above the level of the sea, it must certainly take a very circuitous course, or we must suppose it to form lofty cataracts before it reaches the level

of the sea. Important results might be attained if
Europeans would explore this river more fully, and
discover whether it is navigable, and if so, to what
distance. In the Mberre-land on the other side of
the river, I saw a lofty mountain, which I named
Mount Albert, in honour of the audience accorded to
me by the Prince Consort at Windsor, in 1850.

Revived by the water of the Dana, I began again
to think of my return-journey, and as it was still
day it did not appear advisable to proceed any
further at present, so I concealed myself behind the
bushes, and waited for nightfall; and then as may
be supposed, I could not see the path in the deep
darkness, but followed as much as possible the course
of the wind; for as it was in our backs when we
came, I judged rightly that returning I should
always have it in my face. I wended on my way
through thick and thin, often tumbling into little
pits, or over stones and trunks of trees; but the
thorns and the tall grass impeded me most of all,
and I was troubled, too, by thoughts of the many
wild beasts known to be in the neighbourhood of the
Dana. I was so impeded and wearied by the tall
grass that I determined to lie down and sleep, even
if I were to die here in the wilderness; for it seemed
as if I never should reach the coast again; but then
I thought, straightway, that in no situation should
man despair, but do the utmost for self-preservation
and put his trust in God as to the issue. I called to
mind Mungo Park who had been in a similar strait
in Western Africa. So, taking courage I marched

forward again as swiftly as I could, and in due course emerged from the jungle and reached the great plain in which Kivoi had set fire to the grass. I now felt in better spirits, as I could proceed more quickly and with fewer obstructions. About midnight I came to a mountain which we had noticed in the course of our journey hither. As it had no name, I called it Mount William, in memory of the audience granted me in 1850, by his Majesty Frederick William IV. of Prussia. This mountain commands a view of the whole region of the Dana, and serves as a landmark for the caravans which journey towards Ukambani, or towards Kikuyu and Mberre. Believing myself on the right track, I lay down behind a bush; for I was so wearied out that I could scarcely keep my feet, and for protection against the keen wind which blew over the plain, I cut some dry grass and spread it over and under my body. Awaking after a few hours I saw to the east a hill, as it were on fire, the flames lighting up the whole country round. It occurred to me immediately to bend my steps towards that hill, fearing at daybreak to be met or noticed in the plain by the robbers, while I hoped to pursue my course unobserved in the mountain-jungle, which I should be sure to find there. The result proved that I was in the right; for as I afterwards heard the robbers kept up the pursuit of the flying Wakamba during the ensuing day.

After I had started again, I felt the pangs of hunger and thirst; the water in my telescope-case

had run out, and that in the barrels of my gun which
I had not drunk, had been lost on my way to
Mount William, as the bushes had torn out the grass
stoppers, and so I lost a portion of the invaluable fluid
which, in spite of the gunpowder-flavour imparted to
it by the barrels, thirst had rendered delicious. My
hunger was so great that I tried to chew leaves, roots,
and elephant's excrement to stay it, and when day
broke to break my fast on ants. The roar of a lion
would have been music in my ears, trusting he would
provide me with a meal. A little before daybreak
I did hear a lion roar, and immediately afterwards
the cry of an animal which, however, soon ceased;
for no doubt, the lion had seized his prey; but the
direction from which the cry came was too distant
for me to risk leaving my route and to descend into
the plain. For some time I marched along the
barrier formed by the burning grass. It was a
grand sight, and the warmth was very acceptable
in the coolness of the night.

August 28.—When day dawned I saw that I was
a good way from the Dana. I thanked God for his
preservation of me during the night just gone by,
and commended myself to his protection for the
coming day. I found that I was taking the right
direction, although not on the same track which we
had travelled when coming hither. Indeed, it often
seemed as if an invisible hand guided my steps; for
I had invariably a strong sensation that I was going
wrong, whenever, by chance, I deviated from the
right direction. Soon after daybreak I saw four

immense rhinoceroses feeding behind some bushes
ahead; they stared at me but did not move, and I
naturally made no attempt to disturb them. On
the whole I was no longer afraid of wild beasts, and
the only thought that occupied me was how to reach
Kitui as soon as possible. Coming to a sand-pit with
a somewhat moistish surface, like a hart panting for
the waterbrooks, I anticipated the existence of the
precious fluid, and dug in the sand for it, but only to
meet with disappointment; so I put some of the moist
sand into my mouth, but this only increased my thirst.
About ten o'clock A.M. I quite lost sight of the Dana-
district and began to descend the mountain reaching
a deep valley about noon, when I came upon the
dry and sandy bed of the river, which we must
have crossed more to the south-west a few days
before. Scarcely had I entered its bed, when I
heard the chattering of monkeys, a most joyful
sound, for I knew that there must be water wherever monkeys appear in a low-lying place. I followed the course of the bed and soon came to a pit
dug by monkeys in the sand, in which I found the
priceless water. I thanked God for this great gift, and
having quenched my thirst I first filled my powder-
horn, tying up the powder in my handkerchief, and
then my telescope-case, and the barrels of my gun.
To still the pangs of hunger I took a handful of
powder and ate with it some young shoots of a tree,
which grew near the water; but they were bitter,
and I soon felt severe pain in my stomach. After
climbing the mountain for some way, all of a sudden

I observed a man and woman standing on a rock
which projected from it, and tried to conceal myself
behind a bush, but they had seen me and came towards me. By aid of my telescope, I discovered
that these people were Wakamba. They called me
by my name, and I came out of my hiding-place and
went towards them, recognizing Ngumbau and his
wife, who had been accused of witchcraft by the
Atua, and doomed to death. Both had been afraid
to remain behind during Kivoi's absence, and on
that account had accompanied us to the Dana; but
on the onslaught of the robbers they had fled and,
like myself, been journeying through the night. We
were heartily glad to see each other, and they inquired anxiously about Kivoi and our caravan, but I
could only tell them of what had befallen myself. The
woman who saw at once that I was famished gave
me a bit of dried cassave about the size of my
thumb. Reaching the more open and less wooded
portion of the mountain we came upon three rhinoceroses, which frightened the Wakamba terribly,
while I, for my part, had lost all fear of them not
having found them by any means so dangerous and
such enemies to man as they are described to be
in books. To escape observation we journeyed as
much as possible over ground covered with trees or
bush and about three in the afternoon we reached
the foot of the Data, where we took shelter in the
bush to avoid crossing the open plain by daylight.
I soon fell asleep, and when I awoke, the Wakamba
wanted to start again; but I thought it too early

and wished first to search for water in the sandy bed of the river, so we waited till the approach of night when after a search of half an hour without finding water, we continued our journey over the plain. Every now and then the views of the Wakamba were opposed to mine, so that I often wished to be alone again and allowed to follow my own judgment. I wanted to go more to the south, while they insisted on taking an easterly direction; they wished to sleep by night and to travel by day, while I preferred the very contrary. After we had journeyed till midnight I felt so tired out that I implored the Wakamba to rest for a while and we slept for a few hours; but when I wished to start, they said the wind was so cold that they could not bear it, so I entreated them to leave me to go on alone, but they would not separate from me. About eight in the morning we saw in the distant open and bushless plain some people in a south-easterly direction. Taking them for robbers we lay down on the ground and concealed ourselves in the grass; but seeing that they did not come towards us we proceeded onward. In this wilderness a man who is not swift of foot cannot easily escape, and I walked literally in agony, but was to experience the keeping of the God of Israel. My Wakamba ran on so fast that I could not keep pace with them. The pangs of hunger and thirst returned, and my tongue cleaved to the roof of my mouth so that I could not articulate. How great was the relief when at last, about noon, we came to a brook, where we found deliciously cool water! After a few hours we reached the brook on the bank of which we had bivouacked on the first day of our journey with Kivoi; so now, for the first time, we cheered up and considered ourselves safe. After a short march we met two men of Ulu, who told us they had heard that Kivoi and the Musungu, as they called me, had been killed. In the evening we reached the plantations of the Wakamba and with nightfall arrived at the village of Umama, a relation of Kivoi's. I was now so weary, that after I had eaten a few bananas I fell asleep immediately in spite of the cold, which was here more penetrating than in the wilderness, as for covering I had nothing but the tattered clothes I wore. From Umama we heard that many fugitives had already returned, but that four Wakamba, with Kivoi and one of his wives, had been killed. I heard, too, that my Mnika servant had returned in safety.

August 30.—The Wakamba have been extremely cold in their demeanour towards me. One or two bananas and a few beans were all that they gave me for breakfast although I was very hungry; and some of them visited Umama, and said openly, "The Musungu is a Munde Muduku," the European is a wicked man, for not having protected Kivoi and his caravan, whilst several were of opinion that I ought to be punished by death. Knowing the superstitious and capricious character of the people, I had little doubt of some homicidal attempt and, therefore, resolved to escape the following night.

August 31.—In the afternoon two Wakamba made

their appearance, and carried me off to the village of Kitetu, before mentioned, and on the way, I was forced to halt in the middle of a village because the whole population wanted to stare at me. In the evening Kitetu slaughtered a cow to entertain the villagers; first the feet, then the mouth of the beast, were bound; the nostrils were stopped up, and so the poor animal was suffocated. I had not known that this was the usual way in which the Wakamba slaughtered their cattle. The people waited for about a quarter of an hour, when they cut off the head and collected the blood in a great calabash.

September 1.—The people kept coming the live-long day to look at me; my little English New Testament, my paper, pencil, and telescope, were all regarded as connected with sorcery. When I heard that my Mnika servant was in the neighbourhood, I sent for him; but he would not come, fearing lest the Wakamba should kill both of us.

September 2.—Kitetu would not allow me to start either for Yata or for Kivoi's village, and I heard from some Wakamba that Kivoi's relations intended to kill me, asking why I had gone to the Dana, since, as a magician, for which they took me, I ought to have known that the robbers were there. In any case, they said, I ought to have died along with Kivoi; so it was now clear to me why Kitetu detained me so long in his house.

September 4.—I was yesterday convinced of the murderous designs harboured against me by Kivoi's relatives, and resolved to escape by night from

Kitetu's house. Yesterday, too, I had heard that the fifteen trading-people, who arrived at Kivoi's village before our Dana journey, had been slain by his relatives merely because they were from Mbe, to which country our robbers were said to have belonged. In the same way a few years before a caravan of Kikuyu people had been put to death in Ukambani, because some Wakamba people had been murdered in Kikuyu, on which occasion as soon as the news reached Ukambani, a search was made for Kikuyu people and they were put to death. Such is sanguinary revenge in Inner Africa.

Remembering that I let slip the best time for flight, when in 1842 I was amused from day to day by Adara Bille, the Wollo-Galla chief, I resolved to put my purpose in execution without a moment's delay. Designing to escape this very night, before I lay down in the evening I put some food and a calabash with water all ready for my flight. After midnight, about two in the morning, I rose from my hard couch and not without a beating of the heart opened the door of the hut. It consisted of heavy billets of wood, the Wakamba having no regular doors but piling up logs above each other in the aperture of the habitation. Kitetu and his family did not hear the noise necessarily made by the displacement of this primitive door, and after I had made an opening in it sufficient to creep out I gained the exterior of the hut and hung the cowhide, on which I had been sleeping, over the aperture, lest the cold wind, blowing into the hut

should awaken its inmates before the usual hour,
and fortunately there were no dogs in the inclosure.
After leaving Kitetu's hut behind me I had to
pass another in which a woman was nursing her
child before a fire; but she did not notice me. I came
then to two thorn-hedges over which I jumped with
difficulty. Meanwhile the moon was disappearing
behind the mountains of Kikuyu, as I now bent my
steps in a south-westerly direction towards a village
which I had noticed the day before; as for several days
previously, I had been inquiring after the route preparatory to my flight to Yata. When I had reached
the village in question I saw a fire in an inclosure
and heard the people talking and the dogs barking,
upon which I struck immediately aside into the fields
and ran on as fast as I could along the grassy
plain. When day dawned I sought concealment upon
the slope of a hill, which was covered with grass
and bushes, and though my hiding-place was not far
from a village, for I could hear the Wakamba talking, I lay the whole day hidden in the grass.

September 5.—At nightfall I quitted my hiding-
place and continued my journey towards Yata. I
had an additional reason to reach it as quickly as
possible, in the fear that my people might have
seized upon my property, on hearing as was
very probable that I had been killed. The tall
grass and the thorns sadly obstructed my path, and
made my progress slower than I could have wished.
Often in the darkness I fell into pits or over
stones, and the thorns, those relentless tyrants of the

wilderness, made sad havoc with my clothes. Wishing to husband my little stock of provisions I plucked as I passed through the plantations of the Wakamba green Mbellasi, a kind of bean and thrust them into my pockets. About midnight I stumbled on the sandy bed of a forest brook, and became hopeful of finding water, so I followed its course, and was overjoyed to meet with it in a sandpit, which, no doubt, had been dug by wild beasts. Thanking God for this mercy I drank plentifully, and then filled my calabash. On leaving the bed of the brook I re-entered thorny and grassy land, full of holes which the grass prevented me from seeing, and so, wearied out by my exhausting night-journey I laid me down under a tree and slept for about an hour. On waking I ran on, forgetting to take my gun with me; but after some time, I noticed my oversight, and returned; though in the darkness I could not discover the place where I had slept, so I did not care to waste precious time in further search, especially as the weapon was broken and might have been only a burden to me on the journey; and continued my onward course. My treasure of food and water was of more importance than the gun. After a while I came to marshy ground, where I noticed a quantity of sugar-cane, a most welcome discovery. I immediately cut off a number of canes and, after peeling them chewed some of them, taking the remainder with me. The horizon began soon to blush with the crimson of morning, and warned me to look out again for a hiding-place; so as I saw at a little distance a huge tree, the large branches of which drooped till they touched the grassy ground beneath, I concealed myself under it at daybreak. When it was quite day I climbed the tree to ascertain my whereabouts; and great was my astonishment to find myself so near Mount Kidimui; so that there were yet thirty-six leagues to be traversed before I could reach Yata.

Towards noon I was very nearly discovered by some women who were gathering wood only thirty paces from my hiding-place; for one of them was making straight for the tree under which I was lying, when her child which she had put on the ground some sixty paces off of it, began to cry bitterly, which made her retrace her steps to quiet it. After I had been kept in suspense for an hour, oscillating between fear and hope, the women took their loads of wood upon their backs and made haste to their village. My flight from the Dana to Kidimui was very different from the present one; then I traversed a country both level and uninhabited, and could journey by day as well as by night; but now I could progress only by night, and in a region full of thorns, holes, and villages, liable to be discovered at any moment and to be put to death as a magician, or detained in captivity until a ransom came from the coast.

September 6.—Hearing throughout the day the croak of frogs I anticipated the vicinity of water. With nightfall I recommenced my journey, and soon came to a bog where I procured water, and at a little dis-

tance from it I came again upon sugar-cane, which
I relished with a gusto which only such an outcast
as I then was can understand. But as I proceeded
I found myself so entangled in the high grass, and
obstructed by thorns, pits, and brushwood, that I
began to despair of ever reaching the goal of my
journey. Throughout the night I kept losing my
course, having to go out of my way to avoid bogs
and holes, and the darkness made my compass of
no avail. About midnight, I came to a tolerable
path, which seemed to run in a south-westerly
direction, and followed it until I came to a ravine,
round which I had to wind. After I had hurried
round it I came upon a large plantation, where I
suddenly saw a fire only a few paces in front of me,
upon which I immediately retreated, and had scarcely
concealed myself in the bush, when the Wakamba set
up a loud cry, thinking, no doubt, that a wild hog
had broken into the plantation. I waited till all was
quiet, and then leaving the plantation behind me, I
got upon a good path which I followed as quickly
as I could, fearing to be shot down by the watchers
of the plantation, who might suppose that I was a
wild hog, with felonious designs on the cassave
and other crops. The path conducted me at last
to a flowing brook, out of which I drank and
filled my calabash ; but having crossed it, found
on the other side so many footpaths, that I was
fairly puzzled which to follow, and so went straight
on. At last I felt so utterly weary that I lay down
under a tree, and slept till about three in the morn-

ing, when I awoke and recommenced my journey,
finding myself anew in the meshes of the forest-
jungle. The day dawned, and I was still uncertain
as to my course, and seeing the rock Nsambani some
three or four leagues to the east of the place where I
was, I felt at once the impossibility of reaching Yata
by night-marches; for in the course of three nights
of hard walking I had scarcely gone six leagues
forward; and so thought it best, at any risk,
to surrender myself to Kivoi's kinsfolk, and place
myself at their mercy. I did not, however,
choose to return to Kitetu, but selected as my
destination Kivoi's village where I had left some of
my things. Early in the morning I met a Mkamba,
who knew of my flight from Kitetu's hut, and
I asked him to show me the way to Kivoi's village,
which he did at once.

On my way thither it occurred to me to visit and
to inform Kaduku, an influential Mkamba whose
son had settled in the district of Rabbai on the
coast, of my position. Thus, I thought, if Kivoi's
kinsfolk put me to death the news would at least
reach Rabbai, that I had not been murdered by the
robbers at the Dana, but that I had returned in
safety to Ukambani, and then and there been
slain by Kivoi's relations. Kaduku gave me a
friendly reception and told me that my servant,
Muambawa, had arrived in the neighbourhood, and
intended to journey to Rabbai with a small caravan
of Wanika, intelligence which was truly gratifying.
Kaduku's wife gave me something to eat, upon

which I proceeded in the company of a Mkamba
to the village where my servant was reported to be.
On our way a Mkamba accosted me and strove to
hinder me from going any further, because, he said,
I intended to fly out of the country. My companion, however, pleaded energetically in my behalf,
and I was allowed to proceed. On reaching the
village we were told that my servant and the
Wanika had left, and when I wished to return again
to Kaduku, the Wakamba refused permission, so
there was no alternative but to proceed to Kivoi's
village, which was close at hand. I was obliged to
wait before the gate until Kivoi's brother was informed of my arrival; but he soon came out to meet
me, in the company of Kivoi's chief wife who, like
all his deceased brother's wives, now belonged to him,
and he showed much apparent compassion for the
disaster which had befallen me at the Dana. I then
told him the whole story from the beginning, and
mentioned my flight from Kitetu's house, a step
taken, I said, because I had been prevented from
going straight to Kivoi's village. I made, likewise,
the remark that I had heard Kivoi's relations
wished to put me to death; so if they harboured that
design, I was now in their hands; they could do
with me what they pleased, but, I added, they would
have to take the consequences which would affect
all their tribe; for the Governor at the coast would
certainly not allow my violent death to go un-
punished. If on the other hand they would remain
my friends and escort me to Yata, I would present

them with a portion of the things which I had left
there. Muinda, Kivoi's eldest brother, replied that
they had formed no design to kill me, and that it was
an arbitrary act of Kitetu's to detain me, induced
by his desire to appropriate to himself alone my
property at Yata; so seeing that they were disposed
to allow me to proceed to Yata, I held my peace. I
felt in a very feverish state, and was glad, therefore,
to get hold of a cowhide on which I could lay me
down and enjoy a few hours' repose, although the
unfeeling Wakamba at first allowed me no rest by
surrounding me, and tormenting me with their in-
quisitiveness. Woman is always kind and compas-
sionate in sickness! Kivoi's chief wife gave me some
milk, which refreshed me so greatly that I fell asleep,
when it induced a perspiration, so that upon my awaking, the feverishness was gone. I was now in a painful
plight; one, so to speak, rejected of men, and forced
to be content if I escaped with my life, and had to
ask for every thing like a mendicant. Nobody
would procure me any food, or even fetch me water,
or kindle me a fire. When I asked for the things
which I had left behind on setting out for the Dana,
only my shoes, my air-bed, and a little rice, were
restored to me; all the more important articles were
kept back; and when I inquired after the thief
Kivoi's wives bade them tell me, that if I laid any
stress on the discovery of the author of the robbery
they would have me murdered; and so I thought it
best to say no more on the subject.

September 7.—This morning I felt again feverish;

and suffered much from my left foot, which had
been injured in one of my night-journeys by my
falling over the trunk of a tree, and from a wound in
the middle finger of my right hand which had been
almost torn off by the thorns in the darkness.
The Wakamba watched all my movements, and this
roused my suspicions anew.

September 8.—I felt very weak from the consequences of my last flight, and still more from want of
proper nourishment, and therefore asked Muinda very
pressingly for an escort to Yata, threatening him with
secret flight if he prevented my departure. He said
that to-morrow he and Kitetu would go with me and
take some of their people to fetch the articles which I
had promised to Kivoi. It was now clear that Kivoi's
kinsfolk had given up all intention of murdering me
but, on the other hand, had resolved to get out of me
as much of my property at Yata as possible.

September 9.—Kitetu having arrived, I was allowed
to set forth. Muinda himself did not go with
us; but sent some of his people, who, however,
took with them but a scanty stock of food for the
journey.

10*th*-11*th September.*—I suffered much from thirst,
as the Wakamba were too lazy to carry water in
their calabashes, and at several stations the reservoirs
were dried up; Kitetu too, had given me nothing
to eat but some hard grains of Indian corn, which
I could not masticate. When I complained the
Wakamba only laughed at me, and spoke of my
property at Yata, with which I could there pur-

chase food for myself. The people whom we met on the way were surprised to see me still alive, the general impression being that I was dead.

13th September.—We reached Yata in safety, and the whole population of the village was in a state of excitement and came forth to see and greet me, some Wakamba who had come from Kitui, having spread the news that I had been killed along with Kivoi.

I was very glad to find in Yata the Wanika of whom I had heard, but had at once to receive the unsatisfactory tidings that the Wakamba of Mudu-moni had plundered them of their ivory and goats, and even of their very water-jugs.

Entering my hut I found my servant Muambawa busy opening a bag containing beads, which he intended for the purchase of food for himself and the eleven Wanika who had been plundered. He did not seem rejoiced at my safe return to Yata, having thought me slain and himself the inheritor of my property. Kitetu now saw that I had not without reason, pressed for a speedy return to Yata to prevent the misappropriation of my goods.

14th September.—To-day, I handed over to Kivoi's kinsmen a portion of my things, as a reward for their escort of me to Yata; but they were not content and would have liked to have had the whole, though in the end they were obliged to depart with what they had got, as they could not use force in a district not their own.

16th September.—As both my servants insisted on

returning with the Wanika to Rabbai, and I could
not trust the Wakamba either as servants or burden-
bearers on a journey, no choice was left me but to
return in the company of the Wanika, if I did not
desire to place myself entirely in the hands of the
capricious and uncertain Wakamba. Kivoi, the only
influential Mkamba who had been my friend, was
dead; Mtangi wa Nsuki of Yata had not yet been
tested; my knowledge of the Wakamba dialect was
very defective; I could not dwell in a straw-hut
without injury to my health; and what was to become of me in sickness without a faithful servant?
Can I be blamed if I renounced for the time the
Ukambani mission, and returned to the coast, whilst
an opportunity was still afforded me? The Wanika
needed my aid for their support during the journey,
and I needed their assistance in the way of escort,
and for transporting my effects to the coast.

The people of Yata, and especially Mtangi wa
Nsuki made objections at first to my return, wishing,
as they did, that I should remain among them longer.
At length, however, they gave in, and let me depart
not only in peace, but with honour, the head men of
Yata presenting me with a goat as a symbol of their
friendly feeling towards me. From Mtangi and his
family, too, I parted in friendship and peace, and they
promised to take good care of the things which I had
left behind until my return. At parting, the chiefs
took some water in their mouths, and ejected it
upwards, with the words:—" We wish thee a prosperous journey—may Mulungu protect thee, and may

rain soon fall upon our land!" My servant Muambawa, without my sanction, also took water in his
mouth, ejected it towards the elders, and wished
them happiness and prosperity. I gave to them and
to Mtangi my farewell-present, and then all was ready
for the journey.

17*th September.*—I quitted Yata with painful feelings. It grieved me not to have been privileged to
make a longer missionary experiment in Ukambani,
as I could not feel satisfied that a mission in this
country would not succeed, as the people of Yata
had behaved with friendliness towards me; yet, situated as I was, my further stay was impossible.

Crossing the river Adi, at the foot of Yata, I
found its volume of water much smaller than in
July, it being now the rainy season neither in Kikuyu
nor in Ukambani.

19*th September.*—We encamped in the inclosure of
Ndunda, a chief in Kikumbuliu, in whose village we
purchased provisions for the journey. The people
kept asking me if I did not know whether it was
going to rain, and if I could not make the rain fall.
I replied, that if I had that power I should not buy
calabashes for the transport of water on the journey;
but their questioning gave me the opportunity to
speak to them of the Creator of all things, whose
will it was to bestow on us through His Son Jesus
Christ the most precious of gifts for time and for
eternity.

20*th September.*—To-day, we left Kikumbuliu,
and on the way met some children from Mount

Ngolia carrying the flesh of giraffes, which their parents had hunted down. We procured a quantity of it in exchange for salt which is valuable in Ukambani. The children took us at first for robbers, and were running away after throwing down their loads; so I made them a present of some salt to give them confidence. At night we encamped in Mdido wa Andei.

21st September.—Onward for several.hours through a well-wooded country; then as we were resting at noon under a tree we were joined by three Wakamba carrying a huge elephant's tusk, who reached us just at the right time, as we had resolved to pursue our journey through the forest to avoid the robbers of Kilima-Kibomu, and as my people did not know the way well the Wakamba served us as guides. I thanked God heartily for this gracious providence. What truth in the English saying, "Man's extremity is God's opportunity!" Truly, it is no pleasure-trip to wend one's way, or rather to crawl through an African "Tzakka," thorn-wood, when, besides hunger and thirst, perils from wild beasts and savage men menace the traveller, let alone the weary fatigue of the journey on foot!

22nd September.—Onwards again through the dense and thorny wood, and as our stock of water was consumed, and the great heat had made us very thirsty, we exerted ourselves to the utmost to reach the river Tzavo. At noon, we came to the red hills which separate the Galla-land from the wilderness, and which are a continuation of the

Ndungani-range. This time I crossed the noble river much more to the east than on former occasions, and at a place where the banks were not very steep; and though at a time when there had been no rain either in Jagga or in the surrounding country, its stream was as deep as on these occasions; but I could explain this phenomenon by my knowledge of the fact that the eternal snows of Kilimanjaro form its source. After we had crossed the Tzavo we entered a still larger wood, where my people would have lost their way completely had they not climbed tall trees, from which they could discern the summits of the Kilima-Kibomu and Ndara.

23rd September.—As we were journeying this morning through a somewhat open wood my people all at once threw down their loads and fled in all directions, without telling me the cause of their hasty flight; so I speeded after them thinking they might have seen robbers, for I could not suppose that they would run away from wild beasts. After they had got about 300 paces a Mnika stopped and said, "Stop! they must be gone now." I asked, "who must be gone?" and he replied, "the elephants." "How absurd and silly!" I said, "to run away for such a cause; had I but known what it was I should not have troubled myself to run after you." In running I lost the bullets for my gun and my pocket-knife; my water-jug, too, fell from my hand, and the calabash of my servant Muambawa was broken. I recovered the bullets, but the knife was not to be found;

it was the loss of the water, however, which vexed me most. The Wakamba were much more courageous than the cowardly Wanika; for the former merely went on one side and allowed the animals to pass by. I did not see the elephants at all. In running a sharp piece of wood pierced through the soles of my shoe and entered my foot, giving me great pain and forcing me to limp as I proceeded. At night we reared a thorn-fence round our encampment, and having cooked our suppers, put out the fire to avoid being noticed by robbers. We were then about five leagues distant from Kilima-Kibomu, but quite close to the Galla-land.

24th September.—Our path lay this morning over a rich black soil only slightly clothed with trees and shrubs, so that we might have been easily seen by robbers, the consciousness of which made us march in the greatest haste. About ten, we entered the large forest, which surrounds the river Woi; and finding no water in the sandy bed of the river, we resolved to send a party to Mbuyuni, at the foot of the mountain Ndara, where there is water all the year round; but it was first necessary for us to discover the beaten track (so to speak) to Ukambani. In quest of it we traversed a wood which would have been quite impenetrable by man, had not elephants and rhinoceroses made a way for us. How useful are these large animals in such places! Their total destruction or removal would be a pity; for they are the true path-makers of these forest wildernesses! After we had found the track and drawn water we

continued our journey in the hope of reaching
Mount Kamlingo before nightfall, which however was
impossible. Towards four in the afternoon the sky
was covered by dark clouds, and soon afterwards rain
fell heavily forcing us to encamp for the night, when
fortunately, we found a large dschengo, thorn-inclo-
sure, close by which must have been recently formed
by a caravan. We had no longer to regret the want
of water; the kindling a fire was our difficulty, all the
wood and grass being wet; but at last we found
some dry elephant's dung, with the aid of which we
soon lighted a fire.

27th September.—Hunger and thirst drove us forward on our journey at a very early hour. When
day had fairly dawned my people saw a buffalo,
which so terrified them that they hastily threw down
their loads and climbed up trees; but this time I did
not allow myself to be hurried away by their idle
panic, and merely went on one side of the path. For
a long time after the buffalo had disappeared the
people remained in the trees, and would not descend
until I went forward by myself, on which they followed me; the cowardice of the Wanika on any sudden
alarm is astonishing. About eleven we reached the
water-station, Nsekano, where we cooked our forenoon meal, which consisted of a kind of bean. The
district round about Nsekano was fresh with verdure,
as rain had fallen some time before; but the rains from
the coast extend only to Nsekano, or at furthest to
Maungu and Ndara. This district may, therefore, be
fresh and green, whilst in the interior it is quite dry

and parched; and, on the other hand also, verdure may cover the interior while aridity reigns on the coast. On the coast the second rainy season, which however is very irregular, is in September and October; in the interior its period is the months of November and December; the first or chief rainy season begins at Mombaz usually in April; in the interior, in May or June.

In the evening we reached Ndunguni where we bivouacked. I was now so exhausted and ill from the forced marches that, in truth, I must have succumbed had the journey lasted a few days more. The Wakamba quitted us here, fearing to be robbed of their elephant's tusk if they went openly through the Duruma district. They would have been plundered ere this by my Wanika, if the latter had not been in my service, because the Wakamba in Mudumoni had robbed the Wanika, as already mentioned. Every outrage that the Wakamba perpetrate in the interior is revenged on the coast in this way, and *vice versá*, the Wakamba in the interior revenge themselves on the Wanika, when the latter harm their countrymen on the coast.

28th September.—We broke up early from Ndunguni and journeyed eastward through a part of the Duruma country which hitherto no missionary had trodden. It is a noble district, formerly cultivated by the Duruma tribe, but afterwards abandoned by them. We crossed a brook the water of which was as salt as that of the sea, and whence the Wanika could furnish themselves with salt without being obliged to buy it from the Arabs. At ten, we reached Mufumba, the first inhabited village which we had seen since we quitted Kikumbuliu; when the chief of the place gave me a large calabash of milk, and a "sima," porridge, made of water and Indian corn-flour; and as I partook rather too heartily of these dainties, my stomach suffered in consequence.

In the evening, weary and worn, I reached my hut in Rabbai Mpia where I found my friends well with the exception of Kaiser and Metzler, who were still ill with fever, as I had left them in July. It had long been given out on the coast that I was dead, so the joy of my friends, as well as of the Wanika, was proportionately great when they saw me arrive alive.

The facts and results of this journey to Ukambani, in its relation to the missionaries and their operations, may be summed up as follows:—As the route to Ukambani is an extremely dangerous one, partly on account of the Gallas and partly and chiefly on account of the robbers of Kilima-Kibomu, and as the gross superstition and, still more, the lawlessness and anarchy, the faithlessness, capriciousness, and greed, of the Wakamba are very great, a permanent residence among them must be a very unsafe and doubtful enterprise. Further, as the distance from the coast to Yata is at least 110 leagues, and thus the keeping up a communication with Rabbai in the absence of an intermediate station would be rather difficult, it seems that an intermediate station should be established in Kadiaro or in Ndara, or on Mount Buru, before a Ukambani mission is undertaken.

This mission, so long at least as there are not more missionaries in Rabbai, ought to be postponed, but not given up; since the Wakamba are connected with very many tribes in the interior, who are only to be come at through Ukambani. It is true that there is no direct route from Ukambani to Uniamesi as I had formerly thought there was, but Ukambani opens to us the route to many other tribes, and, it seems probable, precisely to those which inhabit the regions about the sources of the Nile. There appears to be a possibility, too, in Kikuyu, whither the route through Ukambani leads, of coming into contact with the Wakuafi, as in many localities in that region the Kikuyuans appear to live in companionship with the Wakuafi. No doubt, a journey to Ukambani and still more a residence in it, involve painful and trying self-denial on the part of a missionary; but let us bear in mind the great daring of the Wakamba, and the dangers to which they expose themselves on their journeys and hunting expeditions, merely for the sake of earthly gain. Shall their love of lucre be allowed to put to shame the zeal of a missionary who has the highest of all objects at heart—the greatest of all gain—the regeneration of the heathen! I would add that he should be able to take with him into the interior trusty servants from the coast, and, if possible, some native Christian catechists, and if the latter could be found in Rabbai, so much the better. If they are to be trained, however, for their functions at Bombay or at the Mauritius, among the many East Africans to be found there, use must be made of their instrumentality, should the other alternative fail.

In concluding the narrative of my journey to Ukambani, I would here throw together the most interesting facts which I have gathered respecting the manners and customs of the Wakamba, and of the Wakuafi and Masai, to whom I have so often had occasion to refer.

THE WAKAMBA.

As regards the origin of the Wakamba called by the Suahili, Waumanguo, they are said to have come from the south-east in the vicinity of Jagga. Probably they were driven forward by the advance of the Wakuafi and Masai towards the north and east, where there stood open to them land more mountainous, which those savages continue to esteem lightly, as they look out solely for grass-plains where they can pasture their numerous herds, and expel weaker tribes from such localities. At first the country which they now inhabit was taken possession of by small parties of Wakamba; but by degrees came larger hordes. Here the Wakamba could not live an exclusively pastoral life, and were forced to cultivate the soil; yet, although they relinquished their nomadic habits, and accustomed themselves to permanent locations, they did not give up their intercourse with those tribes with whom they had stood on a friendly footing before their expulsion, but visited them from time to time as traders, offering such commodities as were acceptable to them. In a general way they sought intercourse with all tribes who were not so savage as the Masai and Galla, and so at last they found access to the coast of Mombaz, where they settled down in the territory of the Wanika, devoting themselves to agriculture and the breeding of cattle, and, above all, engaging in trade with the coast as well as the interior, by which they have attained considerable opulence, as the commerce in ivory is chiefly in their hands. Their horned cattle, sheep, goats, and grease, are purchased by the Suahili and the Wanika; the latter tribes having a liking for the Wakamba, and the Wakamba also recognizing the advantages of their connection with the coast. The Suahili purvey to the Wakamba cotton-fabrics (Americano), blue calico, glass beads, copper and brass wire, ruddle, black pepper, salt, luaha, blue vitriol (zinc), &c., and receive in exchange, chiefly cattle and ivory.

The features of the Wakamba are not what can be called ugly, and in no case do they belong to the Negro race. Their lips are somewhat protruding, their eyes tolerably large, the chin rather pointed, the beard scanty or altogether wanting, the teeth white and artificially pointed, the skin smooth and blackish; the forms, both of men and women, are slender; and their hair is either shaved off, or curled with wire.

The Wakamba go almost completely naked, having, it is true, clothes, but do not usually dress themselves, contenting themselves with a single rag wound round their loins. The women wear pieces of peltry, which are profusely decorated with beads, by way of aprons, while the upper part of their bodies and their feet are left in a state of complete nudity. The Wakamba smear their bodies with butter and ruddle, by which their natural colour is disguised, and to their hair which they twist like small twine, they often attach a quantity of white beads. On their necks, and on their loins and ankles, they wear small copper chains, or strings of beads of different colours. These chains are very small, and neatly made by the Wakamba smiths. In general, they suspend from their bodies every object which delights them; they even pierce dollars through with this design; for there is a strong love of ornament among all the African natives I have seen, as indeed generally amongst all savages.

The Wakamba marry as soon as youths and maidens come to maturity. The bridegroom must give the parents of the bride a number of cows, and must then carry off the bride by force or stratagem, the parents and kinsfolk not surrendering her without a struggle; so he has often to lie in wait for the bride in the fields, or to pounce upon her when she goes to draw water. The Wakamba marry, if so disposed, more than one wife; but she who is distinguished by beauty, intelligence, experience, and attachment to her husband, or who has most replenished her husband's quiver with Heaven's best heritage, is considered the chief amongst them. The wives have to grind corn, fetch wood, cultivate the soil, and attend to all household duties.

The Wakamba are very talkative, noisy, treacherous, and greedy; on the coast they have the reputation of being thieves; in any case they are great beggars and great liars; but, on the other hand, they can often act with magnanimity. On their hunting expeditions and on journeys they are courageous and enterprising, and can bear great hardships; in general, they are very lively and amusing, gaping at strangers, and dancing about them like children; but, although they appear harmless, it takes but little to excite them, and in such a mood they do not hesitate to fight other tribes even to the slaying and murdering of their enemy. The consciousness of their wealth and their independence makes them proud and vehement, and they hold poorer tribes than themselves in great contempt.

In number they amount to about 70,000 souls, and have no king or chief recognised as such by the whole nation; nor have they any laws universally binding. In connection with the elders of the place the head of every family village rules the people who belong to him, in accordance with the old customs and usages of the country. Wealth, a ready flow of language, an imposing personal appearance, and, above all, the reputation of being a magician and rain-maker, are the surest means by which a Mkamba can attain power and importance, and secure the obedience of his countrymen. Kivoi possessed all these qualities in a high degree; hence his great influence in Ukambani.

The gross superstition of the Wakamba is evi-

denced chiefly in their sorcery, whereby some pre-
tend to be able to injure others by destroying their
cattle and other property, or even their health; in
their rain-making, the magician claiming power over
winds and clouds; in their "Kilito," the wearing of
rams-horns, in which a rare and secret spell is supposed to be concealed, affording protection against
enemies on a journey; in their belief in bird-augury,
by consulting of which enterprises are undertaken
or stayed; and, finally, in their dread of evil spirits,
to whom they offer sacrifices. Like the other East-
African tribes the Wakamba have a feeble idea of
a Supreme Being, whom they call Mulungu, and like
those other tribes, too, they have no idols, and are
not degraded to Fetish-worship; but as they have
no religious requirements they are wholly sunk in
materialism, and have but few notions of religion
itself. In this, as in so many other respects, the
nations of Western Africa are much superior to those
of Eastern Africa; and for the fact that the East-
African heathen have not completely lost their feeble
conception of a Supreme Being, the Mulungu, they
have to thank Mohammedanism, with which commercial intercourse has brought them in contact for
centuries.

The food of the Wakamba consists chiefly of milk
and meat, and of a thick porridge which they make
out of Indian corn-flour by boiling it in water.
They prepare their beverage partly from the juice of
the sugar-cane, and partly from millet. Whilst the
women look after the house and field, the men

squat idly in little knots drinking, laughing, and talking together.

The houses or huts of the Wakamba are built of wood, short stakes being thrust into the ground so as to form a circular wall, and over these a circular roof of poles is fastened, which is covered with grass, and made firm by a thick post in the centre, and as the door of the hut is very low and narrow, you have almost to crawl into it. In this hut they keep their scanty furniture and implements, such as earthen pots and calabashes for water; their corn, which they grind between two stones on which the pot is placed; their bedstead of bamboos, or wooden poles, resting on two posts above and below; their sacks, which they make out of the fibres of the bark of trees; their hatchets or axes, used by them in hewing wood, and which they construct out of hard iron; their knives and long swords, which they forge themselves; their tobacco-pipes and tobacco; their staves of hard wood, with which they break up the ground before they put the seed-corn into it; and finally, their bows and poisoned arrows, their drums and war-horns, which they use for summoning the warriors together.

Recently slavery has made great way among the Wakamba. In the interior they buy slaves in Mbe, and on the coast from the Suahili, who give slaves in exchange for cows, goats, ivory, &c., the slaves from the interior being mostly prisoners of war. It is much to be feared that the growing prosperity of the Wakamba will increase slavery, as the Suahili can sell slaves at a low price now, as they are no longer allowed to export them to Arabia.

The more precious metals have not yet been found in Ukambani; but there is an abundance of iron of excellent quality, which is preferred by the people of Mombaz to that which comes from India, as they deem it equal to the " Suez" iron (which probably refers to that of Sweden), and is indeed little inferior to it in hardness.

THE WAKUAFI AND MASAI TRIBES.

The Wakuafi and Masai, who call themselves " Orloikob," or " Loikob," " loigob " (in the singular, " Orloiksbani), that is, possessors of the land, similar to the Greek word *autochthonos*, aborigines, primeval inhabitants, occupy large plains in the interior of Eastern Africa, which extend from about two degrees north of the Equator to about four degrees south of it. The names " Wakuafi" and " Masai" are given them by the tribes of the coast. Their language differs widely from that of the great South-African section, which I have called the Orphno-Hamitic, but has, on the contrary, regarded linguistically, some affinity to a very ancient Arabic termed the Cushite Arabic. Their manner of life is nomadic, and where they find water and grass, there they encamp often for months together. They live entirely on milk, butter, honey, and the meat of black cattle, goats, and sheep, and on game which they hunt down; having a great distaste for agriculture, believing that the nourishment afforded by cereals enfeebles,

and is only suited to the despised tribes of the
mountains; while to feed on meat and milk gives
strength and courage. When cattle fail them they
make raids on the tribes which they know to be
in possession of herds. They say that Engai
(Heaven) gave them all that exists in the way of
cattle, and that no other nation ought to possess any.
Wherever there is a herd of cattle, thither it is the
call of the Wakuafi and Masai to proceed and seize it.
Agreeably with this maxim they undertake expeditions for hundreds of leagues to attain their object,
and make forays into the territories of the Wakamba,
the Galla, the Wajagga, and even of the Wanika
on the sea-coast. They are dreaded as warriors,
laying all waste with fire and sword, so that the
weaker tribes do not venture to resist them in the
open field, but leave them in possession of their
herds, and seek only to save themselves by the
quickest possible flight.

The weapons of the Masai and Wakuafi consist of
a spear, a large oblong shield, and a club round and
thick at the top, hurling which with the greatest
precision, at a distance of from fifty to seventy
paces they can dash out the brains of an enemy;
and it is this weapon above all, which strikes terror
into the East-Africans, the Suahili with their muskets not excepted. The Wakuafi shelter themselves
behind their long shields until they come close
enough to the enemy to make good use of their
clubs. They conquer or die, death having no
terrors for them.

As to the origin of these truculent savages, they have a tradition that Engai—Heaven, or Rain—placed in the beginning of time a man named Neiterkob, or Neiternkob, on the Oredoinio-eibor (White Mountain, Snow Mountain, the Kegnia of the Wakamba) who was a kind of demi-god; for he was exalted above men and yet not equal to Engai. Tidings of this extraordinary being dwelling on the White Mountain reached a man named Njemasi Enauner, inhabiting with his wife Samba the lofty mountain Samba which lies to the south-west of Oredoinio-eibor, but is now covered with perpetual snow. Through the intercession of Neiterkob the woman Samba gave birth to a number of children, the progenitors of the Wakuafi and Masai. Neiter-kob taught Njemasi Enauner among other things, how to tame the wild cattle and buffaloes which roamed in countless numbers round the foot of the White Mountain. Thus was implanted in the Wa-kuafi the habit of that pastoral and nomadic life, which is retained by them to this day. Neiterkob suddenly disappearing. from the White Mountain, Njemasi returned again to the mountain Samba, which became thenceforward the chief seat of the Masai. The Wakuafi, the brothers of the Masai, on the other hand, look upon the White Mountain as their primeval home, and to this day wend their way to it from a far distance, when they wish to bring sacrifices to Engai, and to pray for rain, health, cattle, and so forth. The broad, level, pasture land which stretches to the south-east of the White Mountain, is called Kaptei or Kaputei, and there the primeval Wakuafi tribes abide. They thus possess the entire country which lies between Kilimanjaro and Kegnia, in the midst of which are the sources of the White River, just as the savage Ayans wander round the sources of the Blue River. Nevertheless, the two kindred tribes, the Wakuafi and Masai, hate each other mortally, which is, however, a fortunate circumstance for the weaker African tribes; since, were they united and ruled by one supreme head, there would soon be an end to the existence of the other East-African tribes, who could not possibly resist them, the savage Gallas themselves not excepted; for the latter fly before the Wakuafi and Masai, and at the most only prove dangerous enemies to them by stratagem and cunning, but never cope with them in a fair and open field.

As regards the physical conformation of the Masai and Wakuafi, their forms are tall and slender, with handsome and rather light-complexioned features. Their greatest resemblance is to the Somali, who are considered Mohammedanized Gallas, and who, divided into many tribes, inhabit the eastern coast of Africa from the river Jub northward, to the Bay of Tajurra. From their beauty of form the Masai and Wakuafi slaves, especially the young females, are much sought after by the Arabs and Suahilis of the coast; and they become much attached to their Mohammedan masters, provided always that the latter do not require from them any kind of labour which is repugnant to their habits, such as tilling the soil and similar occupations.

The Wakuafi and Masai as pastoral tribes consider themselves the exclusive possessors of the plains and wildernesses with their springs and rivers, and they do not attack the inhabitants of the mountains, so long as they confine themselves to their mountains, and refrain from descending into the level country to turn it to agricultural or pastoral purposes. It is said, however, that very recently they have resolved to take possession of the mountain Kadiaro to facilitate their freebooting expeditions against the Galla, Wanika, and Suahili, and to exclude these tribes of the coast from access to the interior.

Where the Masai and Wakuafi abide for any length of time, they build a large town or Orlma-mara—a smaller is called Engany, and a settlement which promises to be important and is large, is styled Enganassa—in which they construct huts, covered with cow-hides or grass, and surrounded by thorn hedges and ditches for protection against an enemy's attack. The town is guarded by the Elmoran, the young men of from twenty to twenty-five, who form a standing army, as it were, ever ready to ward off the attack of an enemy, and to make incursions into the territories of stranger-tribes. At their head stands the Oilkibroni, or chief, who must be distinguished by wisdom, fluency of speech, valour, pastoral riches, &c., and in conjunction with the Oilebon, magician, medicine-man, soothsayer, and augur, he conducts the affairs of the Wakuafi and Masai republics; but his dignity is not hereditary, for he can be deposed, and even put to death, if he is often defeated by the enemy.

The subdivisions of age are more numerous with the Wakuafi and Masai than among the Wanika and other tribes. The children, Engera, remain with their mothers and old people, who tend the cattle and do the household work; the youths, Leiok, from fourteen to twenty, devote themselves to the national games and the pursuits of the chase; the young men, Elmoran, from twenty to twenty-five, who among the Wanika form the association of the Kambe, are the warriors; those older who are married and are designated Khieko, partly engage in war, partly in hunting elephants, buffaloes, &c.; whilst the aged men, who are termed Eekiilsharo or Eekiminsho, remain at home, and with their wisdom and experience enlighten their juniors, who pay them great respect. Maidens only marry when they have come completely to maturity, and the women are clad in dresses of leather, which descend below their knees. The Wakuafi and Masai marry several wives, whom the bridegroom purchases from the parents by the payment of a number of black cattle. Each family recognises its herd by particular marks with which the cattle are branded.

Like all East-Africans the Wakuafi and Masai are passionately fond of tobacco, but use it more as snuff than for smoking, and procure it principally from Kikuyu, Jagga, and Usambara, countries with which they have some connection. They also obtain tobacco, as well as clothes, glass beads, copper wire, &c. from the Suahili traders, who, in caravans from 600 to 1000 men, strong, and mostly armed with muskets, venture into the countries of the Wakuafi and Masai to fetch ivory, but are often nearly all slain.

Olmarua, hydromel, or honey-water, is a favourite beverage of the Wakuafi and Masai, who have honey in abundance. Their household-gear consists chiefly of calabashes, leather-bags, baskets, and pots, which are carried by the women, or borne on asses when the tribe wanders from one place to another.

In the countries of the Masai and Wakuafi, there are many lions, elephants, buffaloes, rhinoceroses, leopards, hyænas, wild boars and swine, giraffes, jackals, zebras, monkeys, many varieties of the antelope, crocodile, and hippopotamus.

Towards beggars, blind men, and strangers of their own nation, the Wakuafi are said to act very liberally and kindly; but towards " Olmagnati," people of other races, they evince at once suspicion and hostility; the Suahili traders therefore when they go near them have both to exercise caution, and to appear in superior force. The Wakuafi and Masai do not make slaves of their prisoners, but kill men and women alike in cold blood, sparing only very young girls, and consequently do not traffic in slaves; but there are tribes in the interior, such as the Wandmoho, Elkonono, and Waman, who stand in the same relation to the Masai and Wakuafi, as the Dahalo do to the Galla on the coast of Malindi, who are forced to hunt elephants for the Masai and Wakuafi, and to perform other labour, such as the manufacture of spears, swords, and knives.

In burying the dead the Masai and Wakuafi do not appear to get up the howling, tumult, and dancing as is the custom of the agricultural tribes of Eastern Africa; nor have they, it is said, any special days of rest like the Wanika for instance, who do no work upon every fourth day, but spend it in feasting and carousing. Circumcision appears to be practised among the Wakuafi and Masai, as among the other tribes of Eastern Africa, where it has become the universal custom.

As regards the religious notions of the Masai and Wakuafi they appear, like other East-Africans, to have a vague idea of a Supreme Being, whom they call Engai, as mentioned at page 359. This Supreme Being dwells on the White Mountain, whence comes the water or the rain, which is so indispensable to their meadows and herds. But, according to the notion of the Wakuafi, there is an intermediary being between Engai and themselves, the Neiterkob, who is, as it were, the mediator between Engai and man; and it is, therefore, to him that the Wakuafi first turn to gain a hearing from Engai, when, as we have seen, they pray for rain, health, victory, or cattle. What notions they entertain of evil spirits, and how far their souls are subjugated by a fear of these, I have not been able to learn, though probably they do not differ much from other

Africans in this respect; for the dread of evil spirits is the invariable accompaniment of the worship of Baal, and of fallen man, as long as he does not learn to recognise a reconciled God and Father through Christ. Man must fear and serve the evil one as long as he does not strive to become an habitation of God through the Spirit. May it soon be granted to our Protestant Church, to send missionaries to the millions of Wakuafi and Masai, to proclaim to them the Word which preaches reconciliation, so that these worst of heathen, "a nation scattered and peeled, a people terrible from their beginning hitherto," may be brought as an acceptable offering in the sight of the Lord God of Sabaoth to Mount Zion, and taught to know, to love, and to honour the true Neiterkob, "the shining light of the world," and cease to murder and to extirpate their fellow-men. The Wakuafi may be reached by missionaries most easily and expeditiously from Usambara, where they are in communication with the tribes of the coast in the district of Masinde.*

* Those desirous of further information respecting the Masai and Wakuafi, will find a more elaborate description of them in the article which I contributed in 1857 to the "Ausland."

CHAPTER IX.

SECOND JOURNEY TO USAMBARA.

Motives for the Journey—Comparison between Shoa and Usambara
—The Pangani district—Forward towards Fuga—A daughter of
king Kmeri's—The mountain-land of Usambara—Kmeri and his
dynasty—The European trade in fire-arms and its consequences—
Arrival at Fuga—The capital—Kmeri's friendly messages—The
cannibal Wadoe—Interview with Kmeri—Anti-missionary intrigues of the king's sorcerers—Kmeri receives his presents—
The Ala-African aborigines—The king consents to the establishment of a missionary station—Interview with a son of Kmeri—
Departure from Fuga—A new route to the coast—The Pangani
people and their Mohammedanism—Punishment and pardon of a
young thief—Results of the journey—Exposition of missionary
policy—Advantages of Usambara as a mission-field—The climate.

HAVING remained at Rabbai Mpia for a few months
after my return from Ukambani, I determined on a
second journey to Usambara to procure a renewal
and confirmation of the permission given me by its
king in 1848 to found a missionary settlement in
his territories. My last journey to Ukambani had
convinced me that it led to Uniamesi as little as
Jagga, the true route to which must be found in
Usambara, and the countries to the south of it.
If a chain of missions were to be established
throughout Southern Africa, and the two ends of the
chain were to meet in Uniamesi, Usambara then
must be the spot in which the first station should

be founded. Resolving this time to penetrate to Usambara from the mouth of the river Pangani, not as on the last occasion through the Wakuafi wilderness, I hired a boat in Mombaz, and made straight for Tanga to obtain the governor's permission for the journey; but as he declined to grant it without written orders of the Sultan Said-Said, I told the skipper to put the ship about and to proceed at once to the mouth of the river Pangani, which we reached on the evening of the 11th of February. I landed without delay to visit my friend Minjie-Minjie, and after I had found him I requested him to further the progress of my messengers to Fuga, bearing an Arabic letter in which I explained the object of my journey; and as Minjie-Minjie was himself about to proceed to the king he willingly took my people with him. In the interim I purposed to proceed to Zanzibar, and to return to the Pangani in ten or twelve days, by which time my messengers would have returned. On the 13th I reached Zanzibar; but as Major Hamerton had left for Muscat, where there were political differences to be adjusted, I was in some perplexity as to a lodging; but was however soon relieved from it by the harbour-master, Jeran, who handed me the keys of the British consular residence.

M. de Belligny, the French consul, also kindly invited me to take up my abode in the French consulate during my stay, and I experienced likewise much civility from his wife and from Mr. Kuhlmann, his secretary. This gentleman had a love, kindred to my own, for all that is in any way connected with the geography and history of Eastern Africa, which made my stay at Zanzibar a pleasant little episode in my life's history.

As I did not wish to spend my time idly in the island till I should be able to journey to the river Pangani, I made a little trip by sea to the village Kipumbui in the country of the Wasegua, which lies right over against the island of Zanzibar upon an arm of the sea which stretches inland to the mountain Gendagenda, upon which are the chief dwelling-places of the Wasegua, and which is well adapted for a missionary station.

On the 20th of February I returned again to the Pangani, and had at once the satisfaction of finding my messengers waiting for me on its banks. They told me that in the course of their journey to Fuga, they had been stopped on the 13th of February in the hamlet of Jumbi by the Governor Muigni Hatubu, who informed them that along with the Mdoe, or royal vizier, and the Mboki, or military chief, he was himself about to proceed to the village of Pangani to collect tribute, and to escort in person the European who purposed to journey to Kmeri. Minjie-Minjie who came on board our vessel confirmed this intelligence. As it was now dark I did not care to land, but sent my salutations to the Mdoe, as well as to Muigni Hatubu and to Abdallah, the governor of Dofa. The two latter are the sons of Kmeri, who have embraced the Mohammedan religion without hinderance from their royal parent, as previously noticed.

21st February.—Accompanied by Minjie-Minjie, I paid a visit to these three dignitaries and met with a most friendly reception from them, the Mdoe at once assuring me that he would accompany me to Kmeri, who was at Fuga. Never before had a journey been made so easy for me; the whole matter was settled in five minutes; I had no trouble either with the chiefs of the Pangani village, or about baggage-bearers; the Mdoe of his own accord promising to have my luggage transported by his soldiers. I saw at once, that I was in a country where much better order reigns than in the lawless republics of the Wanika and Wakamba. Only in the kingdom of Shoa had I seen anything similar; and indeed, physically and politically, Shoa offers many points of resemblance to Usambara. In both countries the king is the only lord of the land and its inhabitants, and a foreigner who enjoys his favour need never be at a loss for the transport of his effects. In both, the movements of the stranger must be made in accordance solely with the will of the king, and he can neither enter nor leave the land without the permission of the sovereign. In both, moreover, it is expected that the traveller should offer the king a present. In Shoa, as in Usambara, all property of the people is subject to the king, "Gieta," in Amharic, "Bana," in Suahili, for he is the soul of the whole country. The very women belong to him, and a woman regards it as a gracious condescension when her beauty so attracts the king that he prizes her and takes her to himself. " Why," say the Africans, " is he king, if he is not absolute and a kind of ' Mulungu ? " " True he does not always exercise his power to the utmost, just as the lion is not always fierce and seeking whom he may devour, but rests in his den when his appetite is sated. So is it with the Usambaric Simba wa Muene, the only true lion, as he is called by way of contrast to the governors of districts, who as smaller lions dwell on the mountains of Usambara. He mostly demeans himself gently towards his subjects, but only to make them bear with his despotism all the more patiently.

I have not done with the comparison between Shoa and Usambara yet. Both countries are very mountainous, though the formations of their mountains are very different. The mountains of Shoa are much higher, and have extensive plains on their summits, which yield plenteous crops of wheat and other cereals, whilst the mountains of Usambara are steep and gable-shaped, and their summits do not afford room for many inhabitants or for much cultivation, and only small villages, groves, and at most, on their summits plantain-plantations are to be found.

As regards civilization. Christian Shoa has certainly made greater progress than heathen Usambara ; still it may be doubted whether much has been gained for true Christian civilization. At all events the calling of a missionary is much more arduous in Shoa than in Usambara, inasmuch as in the

former country he has to cope with a fanatical priesthood, whilst in Usambara his only opponents are
the magicians, who, however, as counsellors of the
king may do him great injury, especially if they
are Mohammedans. In Usambara, as elsewhere, the
kingdom of God can be established only amidst much
affliction; and missionaries, no less than future Christians of that country, must be content to attain the
goal by a painful road. I had something like a presentiment of this this morning before I went on shore.
After midnight I had slept but little, and was subjected to a severe mental struggle in considering
the question: " Shall I proceed to Usambara or not?
Is or is not the time ripe for a mission to that
country? Ought I not to go elsewhere?" It was
not till the words of our Lord, " The Son of man
is come to save that which was lost," spoke to my
spirit, that I felt tranquillized and received courage, and determined to land. In the life of an apostle of peace there are often experiences like those
recorded in Genesis xxxii. 24,* and xv. 12; † for
the opening of a new mission is often only brought
about amidst great agony and conflict in the soul of
a missionary!

23rd February.—There was a heavy fall of rain to-
day, although the proper rainy season is not looked
for until towards the end of March. The people

---

* " And Jacob was left alone; and there wrestled a man with
him until the breaking of the day."

† " And when the sun was going down, a deep sleep fell upon
Abram; and lo, an horror of great darkness fell upon him."

kept asking me the cause of my journey to Usambara, and I told them explicitly that I desired
to spread Christianity throughout the land. The
Pangani villages are inhabited altogether by Mohammedans, who, however, are not fanatics, because,
in the first place, they are ruled by a pagan prince;
in the second, because they are very ignorant and
understand little or nothing of the Koran; and
lastly, because, by means of their many slaves and
in their trade they are closely connected with heathen
men. They procure their slaves from Uniamesi,
from Ngu, from the Wasegua, and other tribes, who
dwell to the south of the river Pangani. The population of the four villages at the mouth of the Pangani
amounts to about 4000 persons, and they are in rather
ill odour from their sensuality, their idleness, and
their propensity to deal in slaves. The Pangani
people, who are now subjects of the King of Usambara, have constructed little villages along the river
and brought the very fruitful soil into cultivation, by
which they have obtained great influence among the
heathen in this district; indeed, to such an extent
that they have compelled the Mkafiri (heathen) to
dispose of their produce, rice, Indian corn, horned
cattle, sheep, goats, ivory, slaves, &c., to Mohammedans only, and not to trade direct with Zanzibar,
the course preferred by the tribes of the interior,
to whom the Suahili sell clothes, copper-wire, beads,
guns, &c. A large quantity of rice and Indian
corn is thus yearly exported from the Pangani
district; and the ivory which is brought into that

market, comes from the land of the Masai and Wakuafi, from Pare, Ugono, Kisungu, Ngu, and generally from the countries lying to the west and south of Usambara.

The Pangani villages are only a little above the level of the river, so that during the heavy rain season they are inundated and the inhabitants suffer severely. The whole of the level country, forming the lowlands, a kind of undercliff from the coast to the foot of the mountain-ranges, extends some twelve to eighteen leagues from east to west. Although naturally very fertile the greater portion of these lowlands is a perfect wilderness, partly in consequence of the incursions of the Wasegua, partly from the indolence of the inhabitants. The mountain which lies nearest to the coast, and to the northern bank of the Pangani, is Tongue, the district round which is said to be extremely fertile. Twelve years ago, it seems, there were about and on this mountain numerous villages and plantations, which, however, were destroyed by the Wasegua, and the inhabitants consequently retreated more to the north, to the mountains Mringa and Pambire. The Wasegua appear to have procured fire-arms in Zanzibar, where newly opened European and American commerce had introduced them in large numbers, and to have surprised the Wasambara, ignorant until then of such weapons. Abandoned, this district of Tongue soon became a forest and the abode of elephants and buffaloes; but its old inhabitants meanwhile have not forgotten their fertile plains,

and abide their time when they may with safety
return again to Tongue.   A large wood with noble
trees, as well as supplies of water, are to be found
on the mountain.   No wonder that Minjie-Minjie
recommended it to me for a missionary settlement,
where for the greatest part water was attainable.

23rd February.—At break of day the war-horn
sounded, and a soldier ran up and down the village shouting with a loud voice, " Get ready, ye
Wasambara soldiers, the Mazumbe the kings (the
vizier and the two governors), are about to depart."
The whole village was at once in motion; for the
people were glad of their departure, the soldiers having behaved to them with violence, and robbed
them of poultry and other things, and the owner
of the house in which I was had buried his valuables
out of fear of the soldiery.   The tribute paid on this
occasion by the Pangani people to king Kmeri was
not very large, consisting of 200 yards of Americano,
Lowel calico, of the value of from fifty to sixty
dollars.   This tribute is exacted only once in every
two or three years, when the vizier comes to the
coast.

Ere the departure of the Mazumbe I was informed
that they were about to proceed to Madanga, a village
some three leagues from the coast, there to levy
tribute, and that the day after to-morrow they
would proceed to Fuga; and I was therefore asked to
meet them at Madanga.   After their departure numbers of people came to visit me, to put questions
about my journey, to talk over religious matters, to

quarrel, and to beg all sorts of things. My Mnika, Abbegunja, who takes delight in the Word of God, was a great help to me. Under such circumstances, it is a priceless blessing to have even a single person who can understand the missionary, and pursue the same object as he does. The Mohammedans were angry, and would not believe that a Mkafiri, heathen, had embraced the Engil (Gospel); yet now they saw us pray together, and read and expound the Bible together in our dwelling.

25th February.—* * * Late in the evening, I reached Madanga, where the Mazumbe gave me a friendly reception, and made every arrangement for my comfort in the way of food and lodging. Certainly a monarchy is thrice as good as a republic, whether it be savage or civilized!

26th February.—With dawn of day the war-horn announced the marching orders of the Mdoe, who was about to quit Madanga. We journeyed at first through a flat, grazing, and well-wooded country, along a well-trodden path, and at 10 o'clock the heat of the sun became almost unendurable. At five in the afternoon we reached the large village of Jumbi, the residence of Muigni Hattibu, the governor of Pambire, where a number of people collected to see me; but their demeanour was so courteous, modest, and quiet, that I was agreeably surprised; for not one of them made himself offensive by begging, or by touching my clothes or my person. The governor killed a cow for myself and the vizier, who was still behind me on his way. The great differ-

ence between monarchical Usambara and the un-
bridled republicanisms of the Wanika and Wakamba
struck even my two Wanika servants, who could not
sufficiently extol the order prevailing in the land.

27th February.—The large ants tormented me
sadly last night. Many Washinsi came to-day to
inquire about the object of my journey. Abbegunja prayed aloud in the presence of the Mohammedans, of whom there are many in Jumbi.
It is fortunate for the Washinsi that they have very
few cocoa-nut trees, if any, so that they cannot get
intoxicated like the Wanika.

28th February.—I set off from Jumbi without
the Mdoe, who had fallen ill; and keeping to the north
of the lofty mountain Mringa we crossed a brook
called Mruka, which flows into the river Mgambo.
While we were sitting on its bank we were joined
by a son of Kmeri, who holds a small official post
in the neighbourhood, and who asked me to give
him a flint for his gun. The request was so modest
that I gave him two, and he was extremely satisfied
with the present. " What a difference," I thought
to myself, "between this country and Abessinia,
where the most trumpery village official is a mendicant, and is scarcely content with a donation of five
or six dollars!" Never have I travelled anywhere
so comfortably as in Usambara; for here I am not
tormented by the monster mendicancy; or, at least,
it assumes a very modest form; whilst as regards
security, I do not believe that one could be safer in
any European country than in Usambara, provided

the country is not in a state of war. Round about the Mruka it is extremely romantic, and reminded me of many parts of Switzerland and the Black Forest, the river flowing through a deep rock-ravine, clad on either side by noble woods. After refreshing ourselves with bananas, meat, and the cool water of the brook, we proceeded through a beautiful wood, in which we rested for a while at noon; when imprudently lying down and going to sleep on the damp ground, without a cowhide or mat beneath me, I awoke with an attack of fever, but soon drove it away by a severe march which threw me into a perspiration. In the evening we reached the village of Kadango, which lies upon a hill, and is ruled by Mbikiri, a daughter of Kmeri, who is so like her father in size and appearance, that there can be no doubt as to her parentage. She gave me forthwith a sheep, and some porridge of Indian corn, in return for which I presented her with an Americano (piece of calico), though she would have much preferred a Bersati (coloured dress) worth half a dollar. As at Jumbi, so at Kadango, the demeanour of the people towards me was very respectful, and nobody attempted to beg. They speak pure Kishinsi, which is the chief dialect of Bondei, or of the district between the sea-coast and the valley of Kerenge in the west, and has most affinity with the language of the Wasegua tribes, while the proper language of Usambara is more allied to that spoken in Pare and Nga. A missionary in this country has a heavy linguistic task before him, as he must learn Kishinsi,

Kisambara, and Kisegua, and then Kipare and
Kingu. It is not possible to compile a truly comprehensive dictionary of the South-African family of
languages, until you have mastered the majority of
their dialects, as one dialect explains and expands
another. For example, I never knew how to explain,
in Suahili, the phrase, "yuna wasinm—he is mad,"
until I learned that in Kisambara, "wasinm"
denotes spirits and, emphatically, evil spirits; therefore, he has evil spirits, he is possessed, is tantamount
to he is mad, he has lost his wits.*

29*th February.*—To-day, we ascended the lofty
Kombora, 4000 feet high, and which is, in fact, a
mountain-range stretching from north to south.
Hitherto, we had crossed only smaller hills, from
600 to 800 feet in height; now we began to ascend
the alpine region of Usambara. At first Kombora
is not very steep, but towards the middle of the
ascent the path became extremely difficult and slippery, so that at every thirty or forty paces I was
fain to lie down on the ground and take a rest, as
my chest and feet gave me great pain, so that I
was inclined to say to myself: "Better two journeys
to Jagga and Ukambani, than one across this precipitous mountain-land." The natives, indeed, think
little of this mountain-climbing, to which they are

---

* On these South-African languages and dialects the very interesting essay by Mr. W. H. J. Bleek, which is prefixed to Sir George
Grey's catalogue of philological books, illustrative of the languages
of Southern Africa, is at once complete and satisfactory. The Catalogue is published by Messrs. Trübner and Co.

accustomed from their childhood; but with their loads upon their heads they climb up the rocks like monkeys, and they make game of the lowlanders, to whom journeying on the heights is laborious and painful.

About six in the evening we reached the summit of the Kombora, where we were rewarded for our exertions by a magnificent view of the sea, and the lofty mountains and valleys in the neighbourhood. I was very glad to find quarters for the night in a half-finished hut in the Washinsi village, Hingo, for I was weary and hungry. The poor people had nothing to give us but a little Indian corn and mahuta, bananas; yet, notwithstanding their hard fare, how simple and tranquil is their life on their lofty, cold, and isolated mountains! You hear no wailing, no quarrelling; you see no drunkenness, no idolatry; each goes his own way quietly, and tends his cattle or tills the soil, seemingly harmless and happy; but seemingly only, for how can we call a man "happy" who passes life away without a knowledge of God, and of his Saviour and Redeemer; without hope of everlasting life, in the darkness and shadow of spiritual death, and in total estrangement from that life which is in Christ? When the gospel reaches these people, it will be seen whether they are as susceptible of truth as their simplicity and harmlessness seem to promise. Perhaps their superstition, and their fear of evil spirits, may throw as great obstacles in the way of the gospel for a time, as does the elaborate idolatry of other nations, till it shall please the Lord by His light to dispel the clouds of darkness from this mountain-population, now sundered as it were from the rest of the world. Then the sound of the Sabbath-bell will be heard from mountain to mountain, and from valley to valley, calling together the inhabitants to praise and worship the living God! Then will first be made manifest the bright destiny and rank of this wonderful alpine land, which will one day bring to light treasures, both animate and inanimate, long hidden from view, from out of the soil itself no less than from the depths of its vast wilderness.

1st March.—We quitted early the village of Hingo, which is inhabited by Wasegeju. In the feud between the Wadigo and the Wasegeju a portion of the latter left the valley of Kerenge, whence some families came to the mountain Kombora, and founded the village Hingo. I always feel great commiseration for the surviving remnants of scattered or worn-out races, and nourish a belief that God in His own time will reveal to such His mercy and His goodness, no less than His justice and judgment. The Wanika, Wakamba, Wandurobbo, Wasegeju, and several other tribes, are fragments of the kind referred to, all driven from their primeval homes by a succession of dominant races.

Ascending and descending we reached at last the village of Kisara, on the top of the lofty mountain, whence a son of Kmeri rules the country around. From its height we had a majestic view of the valley of Kerenge, and the lofty mountains of Usambara. The governor told us that only a

few days before some 800 Masai had passed through
the valley on their way to carry off the cattle of the
Wasegua; for as the Wasegua are enemies of king
Kmeri he does not prevent the Masai from traversing
his country, although I suspect this permission is
given more from fear than policy; for no East-
African nation dares to offer resistance to the Masai
and Wakuafi.

2nd March.—We remained to-day at Kisara, as
my people wished to wait for the sick Mdoe, who
had promised to follow us slowly. For this reason
his soldiers had conducted us through the steepest
and most mountainous regions, in order to gain time
for the recovery of their master, who was to follow
by the best route, as he wished to have the honour
of personally presenting me to Kmeri.

To-day Minjie-Minjie gave me some information respecting the dynasty of king Kmeri, who
is the fourth monarch who has ruled over Usambara since it became a kingdom, it having been
founded by his great-grandfather, who came from the
mountains of Ngu, three or four days to the south-
west of Usambara. The first two kings possessed
Usambara merely as far as Bondei, a district conquered by Kmeri's father. In his younger days
Kmeri himself was a great warrior, who made journeys of inspection through his whole realm as far as
the Pangani. Formerly, his kingdom was more extensive, before he lost a portion of the Wadigo land
and other territories. In the Wasegua land, too, he
lost his influence through European traffic, which

brought fire-arms to Zanzibar, and these the Wasegua were the first to make use of and to turn
against the armies of the king. The East-African
trade in fire-arms will have at least the effect of
making it even more and more difficult for the population of the coast, including of course the Suahili,
to penetrate into the interior; for when the inhabitants of the interior once have fire-arms, travelling
will be much impeded. But, if the Suahili can no
longer fetch ivory from the interior, what will the
Europeans do at Zanzibar? They will discover too
late that they would have done better, if they had
foregone the quick profit made in the traffic in fire-
arms, and had only brought harmless articles of
commerce into the East-African market. Oh! that
the world would but believe that in politics, as in
trade, every crooked and perverse course will in
time bring down its own judgment upon it, and
be punished in the very way in which the sin has
been committed! But the children of this world
do not recognise the unfailing fact; they wish to
be wiser than the Word of God, which teaches the
true principles which ought to guide us in everything, in trade as well as in the government of
nations! God, indeed, allows self-seeking men to
play their own game for a time, and to make a
temporary profit, but He takes care, eventually, to
turn them to mockery and shame; He suffers them to
execute and carry out their principles until by their
own sufferings they are forced to see that God's Word
alone is the only true light for time and eternity!

Oh! how the world's progress will yet justify the revealed Book of God, and put to shame the book of man's vaunted reason, and its selfishness; for history will always be the best apology for the Bible, and for Christianity!

In the course of the day I remarked something that gave me fresh insight into the superstition of the Suahili. My servant Hassein, from Zanzibar, sat on the ground in the house where I lodged and was scraping the sand with his hands like a madman, whilst he uttered some unintelligible words. I allowed him to go on for some time, but at last interrupted him by asking what such folly meant. He replied that he was looking in the sand for a star, from which he could predict whether we should meet with the Masai.

The Wasambara call the Suahili "Waunguana," free people, in contradistinction to themselves. They look upon themselves as slaves* in comparison with the Mohammedans of the coast, who are, indeed, subjects of Kmeri, but are allowed much more freedom than the Washinsi and Wasambara. The latter may ride neither horses nor asses, nor wear costly garments, nor travel into distant countries, while all this is permitted to the Suahili. Kmeri knows perfectly well that the Suahili, through their connection with the Arabs, might become dangerous

---

* I once asked a native Msambara whether in his country there were any liberated slaves? His reply was:—"With us no one can free a slave; for we are all slaves of the Zumbe (king), who is our Mulungu."

to him if he were to treat them with similar rigour. Here, again, we may compare Shoa with Usambara; for whilst the king of Shoa permits his Mohammedan subjects to travel to the coast, he stringently prohibits his Christian subjects from doing so. Nor can the latter without his special permission use silver or gold, or wear costly garments, or even so much as manufacture hydromel or honey-water, which the Mohammedans are not prevented from doing. Like the Shoans the Wasambara do not care to amass riches; for in doing this they would live in constant dread of provoking the jealousy and covetousness of the king and his governors. However the social condition of Usambara would be a critical one, if its inhabitants were not ruled by the iron hand of their monarch; for every petty magistrate or chief would revolt upon his mountain, and strive to be independent; and so all intercourse with the country would become impossible. It were well if those quarrelsome and drunken republicans, the Wanika and the Wakamba, could feel, at least for a time, the power of an African lion-king!

3rd March.—As we were about to leave Kisara there arrived a messenger from the vizier with orders for the soldiers who were with me to return immediately to Jumbi, where their assistance was needed in the subjection of a rebellious Washinsi village. The soldiers obeyed, and started off immediately, for a disobedient soldier in Usambara is sold into slavery. After their departure, we performed a toilsome journey to Utinde, which lies on the summit of one of the loftiest mountains of Bondei, upon a solid block of granite, which rises abruptly like a perpendicular wall, and forms an impregnable natural fortress. From this point I surveyed almost the whole of Kmeri's dominions, and I do not remember to have met with a grander prospect in any African country. I could not approach the edge of this rock without feeling giddy, and had to turn away from it very soon. It is quite otherwise with the natives, who run about the brink of the frightful precipice, and even pasture on it their black cattle, sheep, and goats. The district of Utinde is governed by a son of Kmeri, who by no means resembles his father; and as the " Little Lion " gave us nothing but bananas to eat, we did not care to remain long with him.

4th March.—So sparingly dieted by the governor we left Utinde, but were soon recalled by some people, who told us that the vizier would arrive to-day, and that the governor would increase our rations. Although we had reason to doubt the correctness of the information, yet we resolved to wait until to-morrow, and so returned to the village. * * *

5—6th March.—The vizier not arriving, and the provisions given us being still scanty, we quitted Utinde and reached yèsterday evening the large village of Jairi, where we discovered to our surprise that we might have come from Utinde by a much less mountainous path, but that the soldier of the vizier had purposely led us by a worse route in order to delay us till his master could reach us; so to-day we rested in the hope that the vizier would arrive. The repose was in other respects very welcome, as I suffered much in my feet from the fatigues of the journey. I employed this leisure in reading and meditating with Abbegunja, who has been of great service to me on this journey.

7th March.—After we had left Jairi, we had again to mount upwards, and the rays of the sun, hot even when it rose, considerably aggravated the exertion of climbing the mountain. Day after day I grew more and more weary of this exhausting journey, and longed for its close. My people, too, suffered much from the continual windings and ascents and descents of this singular country. Here we skirted a precipice, there we had only a shrub or some tufts of grass to hold by in clambering up the precipitous path; in ascending the tendons of my ankles, in descending my knees and legs, pained me. Nor could we journey as we pleased, as we had to direct our course in accordance with the distances and the positions of the villages where we might find food and shelter for the night; for in Usambara any one found by night in the woods, or absent from a village, is taken up for a robber; but independent of this the cold and other circumstances would not permit it. We passed to-day several brooks, and plantations of sugar-cane and banana-trees; and at one place I noticed the Mkinda-tree, which resembles the date-tree and bears an edible fruit. Its stem is very straight and long, but not thick.

I often looked on in astonishment at my Wasambara baggage-bearers, who ascended and descended the mountains with the greatest ease. In a few minutes they would shoot far ahead of myself and my Wanika, when they would lie down on the ground and wait till we came up, and then dart forward once more to halt again in the same way. The Wasambara are in general of the middle size, the colour of their skin is yellowish, and their frames strong enough for them to carry burdens. Their mode of life is of the simplest; the banana roasted or boiled is all that they require, and all that in many places they possess beside their herds. The cool mountain-air and the simplicity of their mode of life contribute apparently to the excellent health which they enjoy; for, except in the shape of rheumatism and cutaneous disorders, illness is apparently unknown to them.

The working men have not in an ordinary way more than one wife apiece; not that they are forbidden to have more, but they are too poor to be polygamists. From its mountainous character Usambara is a poor country, much poorer than Bondei and the lowlands, the inhabitants of which would be rich if they were more industrious. Even the Wasambara might be better off, if they knew how to avail themselves of the natural resources of their country. How many mills and factories might be driven by the numerous streams of this region! Wood, indeed, is often scarce, so that in many places dried cowdung has to be used for fuel, as in Abessinia and other parts of Africa.

The sugar-cane which we came upon to-day was particularly excellent, being extremely sweet and juicy. It is found in deep and moist dells, never on the summits or on the roof-shaped mountain-sides. In the evening we reached the village of Pombe, governed by one of Kmeri's daughters; and we were obliged to content ourselves with shelter in a hot, smoky, and filthy hut, where men and beasts herded together, the entrance or door to which was made only for goats and calves, and human beings were forced to crawl in literally on their hands and knees.

8th March.—We started from Pombe and journeyed in great haste, Kmeri's daughter having treated us very shabbily in the matter of provisions. She asked for a cotton-print, which I refused with the remark that my baggage was in the hands of the vizier, and that what I had with me was intended as a present for the king.

The nearer we approached to the capital the less savage was the appearance of the mountains; we had no longer to descend into deep ravines, but could march over tolerably level ground; which however became at the same time barer and more destitute of grass, shrub, and tree. The soil looks quite red, so that here the Wakamba have no need to colour themselves with ruddle; as they have only to squat on the ground to have their clothes and bodies assume its colour; for wherever I sat down my clothes and hands were immediately coloured red. Here and there I saw tobacco, banana, and sugar plan-

tations; otherwise, these mountains are bare, unfruitful, and uncultivated. They are like the yolk
of a hard egg, or the cupola of a tower. On these
cupolas stand the huts of the natives, and it is on
such a cupola-shaped hill that the capital Fuga, itself,
is built.

A large brook flows towards Fuga, whence turning
to the south it runs through the valley of Kerenge. Before we reached the foot of the hill on
which Fuga lies, we passed the hill Muhesa, where
Kmeri has recently begun to build a little village, and
as we passed the place my people fired a salute in
honour of the king, which his musketeers replied to
in a similar fashion. As we reached the foot of
the hill of Fuga we were met by a troop of soldiers,
who fired off their pieces in honour of me, and then
conducted us to one of the many huts, which are constructed in Suahili fashion for the use of strangers.
The door of the hut was tolerably high and wide,
so that there was light enough within; and a bedstead was forthwith procured, and, in a general way,
everything done to lodge me comfortably. Mbereko,
the captain of the king's body-guard, appeared soon
afterwards with a sheep and other provisions, which
were intended for our use; for he adds to his military
functions that of providing foreigners and visitors
with food and drink, whether the king is in Fuga or
absent from it; in which, again, there is a resemblance
between Shoa and Usambara. After some time
we were visited by Bana Osman, a Mohammedan
of Zanzibar, who fills the offices of king's physician,

chief-magician, and court-jester! Several years before, he had been summoned by Kmeri from the island Kisimani on the river Pangani, to compose powerful talismans against Kisuma, the chief of Mafe, who gave the king at that time a great deal of trouble. Osman is an intelligent man, and I had pleasure in his conversation. He comprehended the object of my journey. Usually these magicians are full of pride and pretension, nothing of which I remarked in Osman, high as he stands in favour with the king.

9th March.—Mbereko and Minjie-Minjie went to Muhesa to inform the king of my arrival, and to ask when I could see him. The captain soon came back with word that the king had expressed great pleasure at my return to Usambara, and would gladly permit me to form a settlement at Tongue; the king's physician, Osman, had long before petitioned for Tongue as the site of a hamlet for trade and tillage, but the king would give that mountain to no one but the Musungu (European). This news was very cheering. At the same time, Mbereko informed me that I was to remain where I was until the vizier arrived with my baggage, when the king himself would come to Fuga.

11th March.—Another magician arrived yesterday from Buyeni, a Mohammedan village on the Pangani. These impostors teach the people to write talismans, and employ the opportunity thus afforded them to attempt the conversion of the ignorant heathen to Mohammedanism. Many people came to me to ask

for writing-paper, on which they wished the Mohammedan magicians to scribble magic formulas. I
roundly refused their requests, and declared all
magic to be a sin against God.

I was much interested to-day in hearing something further respecting the Wadoe tribes, who dwell
to the south of the Wasegua land, and who are in
bad odour on account of their cannibalism. The
Wadoe are said to have ruled at one time over all
the country to the south of the Pangani, as far as the
Ngu mountains in the west, at which time, it seems,
the Wakamba inhabited Shikiani, near Sadan, opposite the island of Zanzibar, and waged continual wars
with the Wadoe. But when the Wadoe were found
to drag into the forest the Wakamba whom they
had taken prisoners, and even the bodies of the slain,
and to cook and devour them, the Wakamba conceived such a horror of the Wadoe that they
migrated from their own country, and sought a
new home in the regions abandoned by the Gallas,
who are now in the interior, the neighbours of the
Wakamba. This tradition, I may add, harmonizes
with the information which I received in Ukambani,
—that the Wakamba had come from the south. My
informant remarked that the Wadoe at this day
drink out of the skulls of men whom they sometimes devour.

At the height of their power the Wadoe perpe-
trated great cruelties against the Mohammedans of
the coast, upon which all the Moslems united, and
in a decisive battle so completely vanquished the

cannibals that the latter have never since recovered
their former strength. In warfare they are said to
make use of shields of such size that five or six men
can conceal themselves behind one, a statement to
which I can scarcely give credence. The king of the
Wadoe, I was told, at one time surpassed Kmeri
in power, and his officers were placed in regular
grades, and great order prevailed among them. I do
not doubt that at an earlier period there were
greater monarchies in East Africa than any we find
there at this day. Probably the kingdom of Æthiopia
extended to the Equator, and in its decline gave the
African rulers a model of power and strength. Out
of the ruins of the fallen state some of the chief
families founded monarchies of their own, which
kept their ground for a time, until, becoming more
and more feeble, as no individual of mark again
stepped forth to grasp the sceptre, they sank into the
republics of modern times. In our own day a dis-
integrating process is ever spreading among the
nations of Eastern Africa, and the East-Africans
themselves avow that things went better with them
in their fathers' time; that greater kings and chiefs
existed then than now, and that a new element must
be introduced among them. The descendants of
Ham have outlived themselves; it is, therefore, evident that the descendants of Japheth must steer the
vessel by the might of Christianity, the only safe
rudder for East-Africa, as for all other continents. The
Gospel alone can save Africa from complete destruction. This is the impression which cannot fail of

suggesting itself to others as it did to me in all the countries which I visited.

One of the earlier kings of the Wadoe is said to have formed the design of conquering the realm of Usambara; but when he arrived in the vicinity of the first mountain of the country, he is reported to have observed a dense fog on it, which he took for the smoke of tobacco-pipes. On this he concluded that the number of the enemy must be so large that the Wadoe army could effect nothing, and therefore it would be wiser not to disturb these countless hosts of tobacco-smokers upon their mountains.

13th March.—To-day Kmeri sent a large ox for myself and followers. In a general way we receive daily either a sheep or a goat, so that we have no lack of food. As the vizier has arrived to-day I shall soon be able to see the king; for without a present to offer a stranger may not appear before the Simba wa Muene; and the main portion of my baggage, containing the presents intended for the king, had been left behind at Jumbi in the hands of the vizier.

14th March.—In the course of the afternoon Kmeri came on foot to Fuga, preceded by a number of soldiers who fired off their muskets, which awoke a powerful echo among the hills. I stationed myself by the side of the road to greet the king in passing; and as soon as he saw me he stood still and looked at me without saying a word, and then went into the hut of his chief medicine man, Osman. He wore over his ordinary dress a Boshuti,

or a thick cloak of black cloth, to protect him against
rain and cold, and, like most of the African potentates
whom I have seen, he went barefoot. After he had
seated himself on a bedstead in the hut he took,
without saying a word, a tobacco-pipe, and began to
smoke with great gravity, which in savage life is
unmistakable evidence of monarchical dignity.

A number of people from Fuga and other places
came and addressed their sovereign with the words,
" Simba," or " Shimba wa Muene," Lion of heaven,
or, as the expression may be also translated, Thyself,
thou art the lion; to which his only reply was a
humming " M," and those who had thus saluted him
retired to make room for another party ; so that, after
all, but for the more formal ceremonial, the levee of
a black king bears a strong affinity to that of his
white brother.* This ceremony being over, and only
a few courtiers with the chief medicine man, Osman,
surrounding him, I explained to the king why I had
not been able to fulfil the promise which I had made
in 1848 to return to him at an earlier period. I told
him that I had been twice to Ukambani, that then I
had visited my friends in Europe, and that I had been
prevented by my labours at Rabbai from returning
earlier to Usambara. The king appeared to be satisfied with this explanation, and I retired to my hut.
Kmeri looked much older than in 1848, but he had the
same piercing eye as then. He is a large stout
man, in appearance very like Kivoi, whom I have

* When the king coughed, the courtiers exclaimed, " Muisa."

mentioned in the account of my journey to Ukambani.

15*th March.*—I heard to-day that the Mohammedan
magicians, Osman and Manioka, had advised the
king to refuse me permission to reside in Usambara,
on the pretext that wherever a European once plants
his foot, the whole country must soon fall into his
hands. I gave my informants to understand that if
the Mohammedans continued to intrigue against me, I
would denounce them to the English consul at Zanzibar,
and have them punished in an exemplary manner.

The king sent for me to tell me that he would
arrange every thing to my satisfaction as soon as he
had received the tribute brought by the vizier from
the coast, consisting of 200 pieces Americano, and a
number of oxen and sheep. Of the 200 pieces of cloth
the king retained 100 for himself and his wives,
giving forty-two to the vizier and his soldiers,
thirty-three to the head men of Fuga, and twenty-
five to Mbereko and his servants. After his majesty
had completed this important financial operation he
proceeded to sit in judgment on the relatives of a
criminal who, when the vizier was collecting tribute
in the village of Mringano, had shot three of his
soldiers, and taking to his heels had fled into the
forest, where he had not yet been discovered. His
relatives, however, were apprehended and brought
before the king, who, after hearing the report of the
vizier, pronounced the following sentence :—" The
kinsmen shall be confined in the state-prison until
the criminal is discovered and slain; and his children

who have been apprehended shall be sold as slaves."
When the Simba wa Muene had pronounced this
sentence the soldiers twisted their garments into the
semblance of thick ropes, with which they bound
the prisoners, who were carried off to the state-
dungeon. At the same time messengers were despatched to all the governors, ordering a search to be
made for the criminal, who, when found, was to be
despatched to Fuga.

16*th March.*—The presents which I delivered this
morning to the king consisted chiefly of knives,
beads, Americano, and some coloured articles from
Muscat. The coloured caps pleased him most.
Whilst the presents lay spread out before him a
heavy shower began to fall, penetrating the roof and
forcing the king to get the things hurriedly packed
away. I feel always sad when I am called upon to
bestow merely earthly gifts on a heathen. If the
heathen sought first the kingdom of God and his
righteousness, they would no longer ask a missionary
for earthly gifts; but so long as they only say,
"What shall we eat? What shall we drink? or
Wherewithal shall we be clothed?"—so long as no
higher motives induce them to allow missionaries
ingress to their country,—so long must he accommodate himself to circumstances, until they come to prize
the spiritual treasures which he has to bestow,—and
then their craving for mere earthly gifts will cease of
itself. The great matter in commencing is that
the missionary be admitted into and received in the
country, that he be allowed to dwell among the

heathen, and to begin his spiritual labours. But this can only be attained in a heathen land by his making the friendship of its king or chiefs; and such friendship, in accordance with the notions of an African ruler, cannot exist unless the friend bestows on him a suitable present. A missionary has, therefore, to choose between two courses: either he gives a present and is admitted into the country, or he refuses a present, and is consequently excluded from it, thus closing at once the avenue to his sphere of usefulness; for with the mendicant princes and chiefs of Africa there is no third course.

I was sad at heart as I contemplated the old king, lying on his bedstead, reverenced and flattered by his courtiers and magicians, complacently surveying his presents, or taking them in his hands and turning them over; for I was compelled to note his utter indifference to the message of peace and of eternal happiness which I would so gladly have offered him by bearing testimony to the gospel of reconciliation. Sitting at his feet and sighing inwardly, I waited anxiously for the moment when it might be possible for me to engage the king in a conversation on spiritual matters; but the chattering of the people around him, and his own love for the things of this world, did not allow me to do more than to explain in a general way the chief duties of a missionary. How bowed down and penitent will these poor benighted rulers of this darkened land be when they discover that they have put off the day of salvation, and have despised the offer of the great mercy which God has made them through the least of his servants! During the moments which I passed at Kmeri's feet he might have received what is of more value than his whole kingdom; he might have listened to words of everlasting life, which would have laid the foundation of his true temporal and spiritual happiness. And, besides, he might have been instrumental in procuring the salvation of millions of souls in his own kingdom and in Eastern Africa. I cannot, indeed, say that Kmeri refused me the chief boon directly in question—the establishment of a missionary in his country; but it pained me that he would not enter into any personal relation with the Truth which, as a missionary, I wished to testify to him. The more comforting it was therefore to me when I was visited afterwards by many of the people of Fuga, with whom I could converse more explicitly and impressively than with their prince, respecting the salvation of their souls.

I was much interested by what I heard of the Ala, a dispersed little tribe which inhabit the forests of the wilderness, and live by the chase. The Wasambara call these people Wassi; and the Wakuafi, who look upon them as their slaves, call them Wandurobbo. A number of these Ala are said to dwell in the vicinity of the Wakuafi in Masinde, and the Pangani people repair to them continually to purchase ivory. It seems as if the Ala were a surviving remnant of the aboriginal inhabitants of Eastern Africa; they are found in the interior and on the coast, in Shimba, in the Wanika-land, and at Daluni and Bondei; and are neither agricultural nor

pastoral, but live in the woods on the produce of
the chase; so that wherever they kill an elephant or
other wild beast they remain until it is consumed.
They are said to speak a language which no other
East-Africans understand; and the Arabs maintain
that the Ala came originally from Arabia, and
therefore they will neither buy them nor sell them
as slaves. The Wanika of the Duruma tribe call
the Ala, Masaka, and are reported to have sold
many of them into slavery in the time of scarcity.
It would be interesting to know these people and
their language more closely, and it would be well
if some families of them could be induced to settle
among the missionaries, since history shows that
outcast, despised, and poor races, have accepted the
Gospel sooner than the powerful and wealthy.

17*th March.*—Mbereko, the captain of the king's
body-guard, informed me by command of the king,
that Kmeri had placed my affairs in his hands, and
that I need not doubt the bestowal of Tongue, Mringa,
or Pambire on me by the king, for a missionary
station. I expressed my gratitude for this kindness,
but requested that the king would confirm the assurance with his own lips. Mbereko replied, that this
would be done when Kmeri bade me farewell.

18*th March.*—I repaired this morning to the king,
to take my leave, representing to him that I was
in haste to return before the rainy season set in,
when the rivers could no longer be passed, and
the ground would be extremely slippery. After
a short pause, using a kind of form, the king

said : "I grant the European his request without reservation, and I commission thee, O Mbereko, to carry out my will." Mbereko then took the king's right hand and pressed it against the king's body, which is done to denote a kind of adjuratory assurance. By this act Mbereko became my Mlaw, or guide and intermediary; for every governor, even although he be the son of the king, must have a Mlaw at the court of Fuga to whom he communicates all his affairs, and who lays them before the king. Mbereko is the Mlaw of the Pangani and the Tongue districts. Here, again, there is an affinity between the customs of Usambara and Abessinia, as in the latter country, too, a stranger requires to have a Balderaba, an introducer and intermediary near the king.

After the king had finished the affairs of Tongue, he ordered Mbereko to accompany me to the coast, and then to give me an elephant's tusk and two slaves; and before starting I was to receive three sheep for the journey. I accepted the offer of the sheep, but declined that of the ivory and the slaves. Before I left Fuga the king asked me for a final present in the shape of an emetic, as he felt unwell; so I gave him twenty-seven grains of ipecacuanha, which had the desired effect; but I complied with his wish rather reluctantly, fearing the consequences if anything went wrong with him; for the chief Mabewa put a physician to death whose treatment of his wife had been such that she expired under it.

19*th March*—6*th April.*—To avoid, as much as

possible the mountain-regions of Usambara I returned by a different route, and one which I had never traversed before, keeping to the south and south-east, whilst leaving behind us the last mountain of Usambara, and reaching the valley of Kerenge on the 21st of March. On the 30th we reached the village of Pangani, where I waited for the arrival of Mbereko, which took place to-day. I had daily conversations with the natives of the place, who visited me in considerable numbers. I felt great commiseration for the Pangani people, who are like lost sheep, without any other shepherd than the false teachers of the Koran. Their chief occupations are, gossiping, drumming, feasting, running into the mosques, cheating those of whom they have borrowed money, &c. The degradation of the Mohammedans of this village is very great, and one cannot but admire the long-suffering of God, in permitting such a people still to exist and to sink thus low in the scale of humanity, trusting that in His good time they may in consequence the more readily discern the imposture of the Koran, and become desirous of the truth as it is in Christ, which is now about to be proclaimed to them by a Christian mission. History shows that the Gospel generally reaches a nation when it is on the brink of destruction, a circumstance sometimes ignorantly and maliciously made use of by the enemies of missions, to ascribe to the latter the ruin of the nations where they are planted.

A little occurrence which happened in the house

where I lodged, enabled me to realize, as it were, to the people, the doctrine of Christ's atonement. A boy, who often visited me to receive instruction (so at least he said) stole a fishing-rod which belonged to my servant, and the latter with the consent of the lad's father tied his hands to a post and gave him a sound flogging. I let the servant flog away for a time, being convinced that the boy deserved a severe chastisement for his thievish practices; but at last I ordered him to be set at liberty, promising the servant that I would make good the loss of the fishing-rod. The boy was untied and dismissed in the presence of a number of Mohammedans, who were standing round. "See," I then said, "this boy has been restored to liberty because I mediated for him, and made good the damage which he had done; in a much higher sense has Jesus Christ, the Son of God, borne and made compensation on the cross for your unrighteousness. If you believe in Him, you will be saved from the wrath of God; but if you persist in the rejection of the only Saviour whom God has given you, you will call out in hell for deliverance, but will find no mediator; for Christ, whom I declare unto you, is the only propitiation for our sins; and not for ours only, but also for the sins of the whole world."

On the arrival of Mbereko at the Pangani I accompanied him in a small craft to Zanzibar, where I was at once informed that Brother Rebmann had returned with his wife from Egypt, and had proceeded a fortnight previously to Mombaz, whither I followed him in a few days, arranging before I started for a boat to take the Mbereko back to the Pangani. He was very grateful for all the kindness shown him, and promised to do his utmost for the gratification of my wishes. He had brought with him to Zanzibar some elephants' tusks, but, on account of their small size, did not meet with a purchaser in the French merchant, whom he expected to buy them. As in conformity with Kmeri's orders, he sought to form connections with the European merchants at Zanzibar, so as to obviate the necessity of disposing of the products of Usambara through the agency of the cheating Suahili, I furnished him with the names of some European and American mercantile firms to which he might apply, and forthwith the envy and malice of the Suahili made use of this circumstance to traduce me to the sultan and the English consul at Zanzibar, to whom they represented that I had been conducting political intrigues in Usambara; a calumny for which they could not offer the shadow of a proof. I was naturally a thorn in the side of the Suahili, because I had taken a Mkafiri (unbeliever) to Zanzibar, where he could see with his own eyes things as they were, and report accordingly to his master at Fuga. In this way an exposure was made, once for all, of the deception practised by the Suahili, who do their utmost to prevent the inhabitants of the interior from knowing what is going on at the coast, as well as Europeans from coming personally in contact with the natives of the interior, because they fear that such intercourse would give a blow to their monopoly of the trade with the interior, from which it would never recover.

The following are among the results of this and my former journey to Usambara :—

(1.) It is certain that the king of Usambara is now, as previously, disposed to admit missionaries to his country, and will allow them to select their own locations.

(2.) Usambara is a country with many and large villages, where a missionary can address masses of people when he is once master of the language.

(3.) The natives are accustomed to order and to obey their superiors. They are peaceable, and not without intelligence, or a wish for self-improvement. Drunkenness, mendicancy, and violence, are much less common among them than among the republican tribes.

(4.) In time of peace a missionary can safely roam about the country everywhere if he has but secured the friendship of the king.

(5.) It is, however, indispensable that missionaries should conduct themselves towards the king with all respect, and carefully avoid the slightest semblance of political interference in the affairs of the country. It is also necessary for them to transmit to the king occasionally a suitable present as a token of respect and gratitude for benefits received: the provision, for instance, made by the governors for their food, lodging, the transport of their effects, &c. A missionary must not suppose that because his is a

spiritual vocation, and he preaches the gospel to
the natives gratuitously, he is therefore to accept
the benefactions of the king without rendering
an equivalent.   That were a folly of which he
would have to repent the consequences.   On the
contrary, he must be grateful for everything, even
for the smallest trifle; and he must distinctly show
his gratitude by deeds.   True, he is not to court the
favour and friendship of the great and powerful of
the land; but wherever their friendship falls to his
lot he is not to throw it away by failing in respect
and gratitude.   Europeans often commit the fault
of not paying sufficient respect to a native ruler,
because they find in his demeanour to them that he
is coarse, given to begging, selfish, suspicious, and
unrefined; so that it is, indeed, difficult to pay him
always proper respect; but a missionary must make
it a principle in that case, as in every other, to deny
himself for the sake of the Master whom he serves.
He must resolutely battle with and conquer every
tendency to show, in word or act, anger towards an
African ruler, be he great or small.   And whilst he
must not expect much from the great and powerful
of the land, with regard to the salvation of their
souls and to the rendering by them of genuine
assistance in the promulgation of the gospel—for
"not many wise men after the flesh, not many
mighty, not many noble, are called" (1 Cor. i. 26)
—yet he must not let any opportunity slip of bringing the gospel nigh unto them, as a testimony against
them in the day when the secrets of all hearts shall

be made known.   Our Saviour himself had little
to do with the rulers of his age.   He searched out the
poor, the sick, and sinners, and they yearned towards
him.   Therefore I would advise a missionary in
Usambara not to remain too long in the vicinity of
the king, in the hope or with the design of first converting him and those who surround him.   On the
contrary, he must keep as far as possible from kings
and courts, and rather turn with his glad tidings
to the common people; unless the king should
express a wish for him to instruct himself and his
sons out of the Word of God.   The Jesuits have a
maxim that it is well to work first on the prince of
a country, and through him to influence his subjects.
In his book upon Shoa M. Rochet has urgently
recommended this principle to the Romish missionaries; but a Protestant missionary must act in strict
antagonism to it.   He must appeal to the heart
and conscience of every man as he finds him, in the
conviction that the poorest and most insignificant
when they truly believe in Christ and are born of
God, are more worthy, and contribute more to the
extension of Christianity by their prayers and religious life, than is possible in the case of any ruler
who simulates Christianity from worldly motives, and
seeks by mere force to spread its doctrines.

(6.) As regards the means of transport available
to missionaries in this country, my journey to it
proves that there are no great difficulties to be overcome.   In the first place, the governors are bound
to have the effects of a traveller transported by their

peasants or soldiers; in the second place, even were this not the case, and a missionary should prefer to travel at his own expense, he can always, for half a dollar or a dollar, hire people to go a tolerable distance.

(7.) All personal necessaries required by a missionary, if not to be had in the country, can be procured from Zanzibar, which is nearer than Rabbai and Mombaz to Bondei and Usambara.

(8). No country can be better suited than Usambara for the extension of the gospel in the interior. Missionaries can proceed from it to the Wasegua, to Pare, Jagga, Ngu, Unguenu, Uniamesi, and even, starting from Masinde, to the savage Wakuafi.

(9.) In the Alpine country, the climate cannot be other than favourable to the constitution of Europeans, although they must be prepared for an attack of fever of longer or shorter duration; for as yet, no European in any African country whatever has wholly escaped the attacks of fever, and it is, once for all, an inevitable ingredient in the cup which must be drunk by every missionary in East Africa, who wishes to preach Christ, and him crucified.

END OF PART II.

PART III.

GEOGRAPHY, TOPOGRAPHY, AND HISTORY.

THE SOUTH SUAHILI COAST—ABESSINIA—REBMANN
IN UNIAMESI—ERHARDT ON THE WANIKA LAND—
SKETCH OF THE HISTORY OF EASTERN AFRICA.

CHAPTER I.

VOYAGE FROM MOMBAZ TO CAPE DELGADO.

Importance of the Voyage—Under way—Tiwi—Wanika fisher-
men — Palm wine — Narrow escape from drowning—Magugu
missionaries and Mohammedans—Tanga Bay—View of the Usam-
bara mountains—A travelled Suahili—Tangata and its Divani—
Buyeni—The coast southward and its inhabitants—Msasani—
Mtotana—Caravan from Uniamesi—Maisan and his murder—
Sinda — Jole — The cowrie trade — The Banian's sandbank—
Kiloa Kibenje — Slave-catching in the interior—The Niassa
country — Kiloa Kisiwani — Kisueri—Muania—Mkindani — The
Lufuma—To Zanzibar again—Return to Europe.

BEFORE returning to Europe and re-visiting my
native country, which I had not seen since 1837,
in February 1850 I wished to survey personally the
whole of the coast south from Mombaz as far as the
Portuguese settlements at Mozambique. With the
coast from Mombaz to Zanzibar I had long been
familiar; but from that island to Kila and Cape
Delgado or Tungue, where Arab rule ceases and that
of Portugal begins, the coast had not been visited by
me; and yet it is most important that the friends
of missionary labour, who are seeking to encircle the
whole of Africa with missions in order to bring this
great continent under the rule of the Gospel, should
also obtain some knowledge of this unexplored portion of the East-African coast, and thus become

better acquainted with the various routes by which
messengers of the Gospel may press forward to some
common centre, which in my opinion is Uniamesi,
the great country of the interior, towards which
missionaries from east, west, and south should con-
verge ; as from Uniamesi they can reach the innumerable tribes of Central Africa by water in all directions.

On the 2nd of February I made arrangements at
Mombaz with the skipper of a small Suahili vessel
to take my fellow-labourer Erhardt and myself to
all the important havens and towns, or villages,
south of Mombaz as far as Cape Delgado.   On the
4th of February we sailed with a favourable wind
from the harbour of Mombaz, and in accordance
with our agreement our Suahili captain was to hug
the shore as closely as possible, so that we might
survey the entire line of coast.   Skirting a portion
of the shore of the Wadigo-land, with its abundant
groves, shrubs, and palm-trees, we sighted the
Kinika village Niali, lying almost concealed in a
grove of cocoanut-trees, and made for the haven of
Tiwi, where we were to pass the night.   Seeing on
the shore a number of Wanika of the Wadigo tribe
catching fish, partly with nets, partly with long and
broad pieces of cloth which they dexterously and
quickly drew together in the water by the four
corners, I told our skipper to launch our canoe,
consisting of the trunk of a tree hollowed out which
served as a boat, and to pull me to the natives, while
Erhardt remained on board-ship.   After some diffi-

culty, our frail bark having to contend with a heavy
surf, whilst I had to lie on my back while a Suahili
sailor paddled, we reached land, where I was soon
surrounded by the Wanika, who listened for some
minutes attentively to what I had to say, till I asked
them to conduct me to the chief of their village,
which lies half a league to the west of the shore;
upon which one of them inquired what my presents
for the chief were, and what reward I would give
the guide? I replied that I was the bearer of
heavenly treasures to the chief and his people,
pointing to the Bible, which I held in my hand.
The effect produced by this declaration was, that
some of the people ran away, a few continued to
listen, and others forthwith remarked that it was
now time to drink tembo, palm-wine, and they
must go home. As they would not conduct me to
their village, and finding the tide coming in so as to
render the lagune leading to the village impassable,
I resolved to return to the ship; but wind and waves
were against us, and just when we were nearing her
we were driven back towards the shore, not far from
which the boat capsized, and I fell backwards into
the sea. Fortunately the water was not very deep,
otherwise probably I should have been drowned, as
I cannot swim. We tried again to reach the vessel,
but the rain and the wind and waves drove the
frail bark always back towards the shore; so there
was no help for it but to wait till midnight, when
the wind generally abates. Near the shore lay a
large boat, in which we took refuge to shelter our-

selves from the chills of evening, which I felt all
the more as my clothes were wet. Erhardt, however, who was very anxious about me, got the skipper
to despatch a larger boat for me after dusk, which
entered the haven during the evening, when I got
into it and reached our vessel safely, and gave thanks
to God for my preservation.

On the morning of the 5th of February we set
sail again, hugging the shore as closely as possible.
The coast here is very low and woody, and much
honey-combed by the sea. In general the East-African
coast southward from the Equator has been very much
worn by the sea; whence the many islets and coral-
reefs, which though in some respects commodious for
coasting vessels are at the same time very dangerous.
In the afternoon we ran into the bay of Wassin,
where we saw distinctly Kirugu, Mrima, and Jombo,
all inhabited by Wadigo-Wanika; and our thoughts
naturally led us to people these mountains with
converts to Christianity rejoicing in the truths of
the Gospel. In the evening we anchored in the
little bight of Wanga and Magugu, two Mohammedan villages which are only a few feet above the
level of the sea, and in the morning we paid the
villages a visit. In Magugu we found some relatives
of Bana Kheri, who had formerly been my guide,
and who had accompanied Rebmann more than
once to Jagga, all of whom had heard long before
that Bana Kheri had been killed on his last journey from Jagga. I tried to engage the people of
Magugu in religious conversation; but it was with

them as it is always with Mohammedans; for as soon
as mention was made of the divinity of Christ, they
began to wrangle and to say, "God has no son;
neither is He begotten nor begets." In the vicinity
of Wanga dwell Wasegeju, who are for the most
part at war with the Wadigo-Wanika; and the
people of Wanga have much intercourse with the
interior, with the Wanika, Wasegeju, Waschinsi,
Wasambara, and even go as far as Dafeta and
Jagga to trade and hunt.

On the 7th we weighed anchor very early, and by
noon arrived at the noble bight of Tanga, where we
landed. It was with peculiar thoughts and feelings
that again I trod this soil. It was in the year 1844
that for the first time I saw this coast and the lofty
mountains of Usambara, those ramparts of East-
African heathenism; then it all lay obscure and
unexplored before me; but now I sailed past with
very different sensations. The consciousness that
my feet had penetrated yonder, that my heart had
prayed to the Lord on the heights of Usambara, and
had commended the whole heathen world around to
His mercy; that my lips had been permitted here
and there to announce the message of peace both
elevated and upheld me.

Before we landed we received a visit from a
Suahili soldier who had visited England, and could
thus speak a little English. He had been to London
in a trading vessel belonging to the Sultan of
Zanzibar, and during two years of illness he had
spent a considerable portion in the marine hospital

there, until an Englishman took him to Bombay, whence he had returned to Africa. Whilst we were talking with him we heard a noise of shouting and fire-arms discharged in the villages Kiumbageni and Mkokoani, which at first rather startled us. We soon ascertained, however, that a caravan of traders had arrived from the country of the Masai in the interior; having made a circuit round Usambara, eastward, northward, and westward, journeying to Dafeta, and thence to the mountain Mlozo, which is occupied by the Masai, and in the vicinity of which there are elephants in abundance. From our friend the Suahili sailor we learned that the people of Tanga give the ivory-bearers who go to Mlozo ten dollars for their services, and for this, each bearer carries there and back again a heavy load of fifty-four pounds, and is often absent for six months. At Tanga, too, I heard that king Kmeri was anxiously expecting me.

On the 9th of February, we sailed for Tangata, or Tagnata as it is often called, and on landing met with a friendly reception from the harbour-master. A Banian immediately summoned the Divan, who paid me every respect. Divani (man of the divan) is the title of a head-man or governor, appointed by Kmeri to uphold his influence among the Suahili on the coast, whom he considers to be his subjects. If any one wishes to become a Divani he must make the king a suitable present and, over and above, be recognised and confirmed by the Sultan of Zanzibar, who makes the candidate a present that he may not lose sight of the sultan's interests should they run counter to those of the king of Usambara.   Thus the Divani must receive the assent of the sovereign by sea, as well as of the sovereign by land, when he alone may do what is allowed to no one else, wear a particular kind of sandal, carry a state-umbrella, and have musicians going in procession before him.   At Tangata I was again asked when I intended to return to Kmeri, a question which perplexed me not a little.   We also heard there that the ivory-traders have to pay two dollars by way of duty on every farasala (equivalent to thirty-six pounds weight) that comes from the Wadigo-land; and that if it comes from Jagga and Usambara the duty is four dollars; if from Uniamesi, twelve dollars.   In Mombaz the import-duty levied upon ivory amounts to three dollars per farasala.   These duties go to the Sultan of Zanzibar, who, in a general way, does not trouble himself about this coast except in so far as regards its trade.

On the 10th of February we left Tangata and reached the mouth of the river Pangani at four in the afternoon.   Here, too, I was asked, on landing, when I would return to Kmeri, and what answer I wished taken to the king at Fuga respecting my journey thither.   I sent greetings and a message that I was now journeying to Mgau, and should then proceed to Europe; but that after my return from home my best thoughts should be devoted to him.

In the village of Buyeni to the south of the Pangani, I visited the governor, who asked, among other things, why the English attempted everywhere to put down the slave-trade. I replied, that their prohibition of it was based upon the divine command, "Thou shalt love thy neighbour as thyself." The governor then asked me whether the English consul in Zanzibar protected only Serkali people, that is, his fellow-countrymen, or whether other persons came also within his jurisdiction and under his protection; to which I answered that every consul had to protect all the subjects of his sovereign; and that, therefore, the English consul took under his protection the Banians also, because, though not his own countrymen, they were subjects of the British crown. This reply delighted the Banian who was seated by the governor's side.

On the 11th we sailed from the mouth of the Pangani along a coast with which I had been hitherto unacquainted. The section of it which we were now to skirt is inhabited by the following tribes:— First, there are the heathen Wasegua, who begin at the south bank of the Pangani, and cease with the Suahili village, Sadan, which is opposite to Zanzibar, and form several sub-divisions. Second, south from the Wasegua are the Wadoie, who are said to be cannibals, but this is scarcely credible; third, to the south of the Wadoie follow the Waseramu; then, fourth, the Wakatoa; fifth, the Watumbi; sixth, the Wagnindo; seventh, the Wamuera at Kiloa Kilenje; eighth, the Makonde; and ninth, the Makua, with whom begins the portion of the sea-coast belonging to the Portuguese. With all these tribes the Suahili inhabiting the seaboard maintain friendly relations; all of them are, if not directly, more or less indirectly, subject to the rule of the Sultan of Zanzibar; and heathen and Mohammedan find it their interest to live on peaceful terms with each other. The Wasegua-coast is very low, and does not possess a single good harbour. Among these tribes the slave-trade has flourished hitherto to a frightful extent, chiefly owing to the encouragement of the Arabs of Zanzibar.

12th February.—The violence of the north wind forced us to remain all day in the harbour of Msasami, where we had anchored yesterday evening. Our skipper, who belonged to the Wamuera-tribe and was born at Kiloa, told us that many years ago he had journeyed with a caravan from Kiloa to the country of the Wahiau, near Lake Niassa. The route into the interior was good and level, and from Kiloa he came to Lingabura; then to Kiturika, places in the territory of the Wamuera; then to Jipera, Mbuemkurro, Mkura, Mkarre, Lujanda (a river), and, finally, to Keringo and Ripeta, where the caravan procured slaves and ivory, the latter being brought by the Waniassa from the western side of the lake. The Waniassa construct light but water-tight boats of the bark of trees, in which they cross the lake to buy ivory from the Mawisa-tribes. They make clothes, too, out of the bast of a tree. The river Lufuma or Rufuma is said to have its source in the Niassa, which must mean in the eastern shore of the lake.

13th February.—At four in the afternoon we anchored in the haven of the village Mtotana, where we met a large caravan of people belonging to the tribe Ukimbu in Uniamesi. These people who came with their wives and children from the interior and lived in small huts by the seashore, told me that they had spent three months on the journey; and had brought slaves and ivory. Their figures and features were by no means unsightly; indeed many were of tall stature. I could understand a good deal of what they said, which proves that their language belongs to the great South-African family. One of them said that he had been in Sofala, and brought copper thence; and they seem also to be acquainted with the west coast of Africa. The great lake in Uniamesi, they said, ebbs and flows, a remark which struck me, as it must others, as important. They asked me whether it was true, as they had heard from the Suahili in the interior, that Europeans were cannibals? so I explained to them that the Suahili calumniated Europeans to the tribes of the interior, in order to prevent any direct intercourse between the two, which would tend to destroy the Suahili monopoly of trade. I was anxious and took pains to give the Uniamesi people an accurate notion of Christianity and of Europeans; and told them that one of these days I would visit Uniamesi, when they said I had only to come, and I should be well treated.

At Mtotana I saw a Suahili formerly in the

service of M. Maisan, a Frenchman, who was murdered by the Washinsi some three days' journey from the coast in the year 1847, in the course of an expedition to Uniamesi, whilst proceeding into the interior by way of Buyani. When he had reached the chief of the Washinsi, that petty ruler thought fit to covet the chests of the traveller which he fancied were filled with dollars; so he surrounded by night the house in which M. Maisan lodged, and first attacked his servants. Roused by the cries of the dying M. Maisan discharged his gun at the assailants, but at the same moment fell pierced by their spears. Then the chief set fire to the house, upon which three of the murdered man's servants who survived took to flight. When the Sultan of Zanzibar heard of this atrocious crime he sent 200 soldiers to arrest the chief, who it seems had made his escape, and so one of his kinsmen was seized in his stead and carried to Zanzibar.

14th February.—There was but little wind, so we got no further to-day than to the small island of Sinda, and here we met again with many trading people from Uniamesi who build little huts on the strand, and stay in them until they return homeward. The Uniamesi caravans consist generally of from three to four thousand men, that they may be strong enough to defend themselves on the way from the attacks of hostile tribes. These people had been here for several months; for they leave Uniamesi in September, and arrive in December at the coast; and return home again in March and April.

16th February.—We passed the small islands of Shungimbili and Niovro, probably the same which are called on the maps "Latham's Islands," containing guano, which our skipper told us was most abundant though much spoilt by the rain. The coast opposite is very low, but fertile, the sight of which led one of the sailors to shout, "Hindi Bastani Belad ya Baniani," India is a garden and the land of the Banians. In the afternoon we reached the island Mafia, wrongly named Monfia on the maps, and anchored at Kisiman Mafia.

17th February.—In the harbour of Kisiman Mafia was a ship from Kiloa with thirty slaves, who were being carried to Zanzibar. The captain of the ship wished to buy rice from us, as his slaves had nothing to eat; but we were in the same predicament, and very glad to reach the noble island of Jole, where water-melons, cassave, rice, Indian corn, cocoanuts, and many other good things were procurable. In Jole there has lately sprung up an important trade in cowries, of which there is an abundance on this coast, these shells being bought by traders from Zanzibar, who dispose of them to Europeans there, by whom they are sent to the west coast of Africa where, as is well known, they form the currency. We were told that two measures of cowries were given for one measure of rice.

19th February.—At noon we passed the islands Songosongo and Pumbafu, and then the sandbank called "Fungu ya Baniana," Banian's Sandbank, so named from a Banian who perished there, having been landed on it from an Arabian ship in order to prepare his food, as no one who does not belong to their caste must look on during the preparation of their food by their Banians. The captain, however, set sail during the process and abandoned the unhappy Banian to his fate.

At four in the afternoon we arrived at the harbour of Kiloa Kibenje, the most important town on the coast between Mozambique and Zanzibar, with from twelve to fifteen thousand inhabitants, the centre of the trade of those regions, and the confluence, as it were, of the two streams of wealth flowing from north and south. It drives a very considerable trade in ivory, rice, copal, tobacco, and especially in slaves, which are brought from Uniamesi, and from the regions of the lake Niassa. From ten to twelve thousand slaves are said to pass yearly through Kiloa on their way to the various ports of the Suahili coast and to Arabia, and we saw many gangs of from six to ten slaves chained to each other, and obliged to carry burdens on their heads. In this country the life of a man is of small moment, and one would almost be led to wonder why God in His mercy affixes no limits to such horrors and such violations of the laws of humanity, if in the remembrance of what horrors these slaves would have had to submit to in their own country, we did not see cause to acknowledge, even in this vile traffic, how by human agency, alone, He works out His inscrutable purposes.

The Wahiau, who are in the habit of coming to

Kiloa, are said often treacherously to sell each other to the Suahili. One kinsman will send another to the house of a Suahili, on the pretence that there is something there for him to fetch back, when the Suahili, with whom the bargain has already been struck, closes the door upon the victim and chains him, and keeps him so chained until there is an opportunity of selling him and shipping him to Zanzibar or Arabia. Although the Sultan of Zanzibar has prohibited the slave-trade with Arabia, yet many slave-ships proceed there annually, starting from Kiloa and sailing round Zanzibar on the eastern side of the island, so as to evade the sultan's police; and slaves are often smuggled to Arabia by the aid of a declaration of the captain that they are sailors. Many a Wahiau and Waniassa, returning from Kiloa to his own country, is caught at night in a snare, laid in the way by the Wamueras to entrap travellers after dark, when the captive has a forked-like piece of wood placed round his neck, and his hands bound, and so the poor wretch is taken to Kiloa. The Waniassa are placed on shipboard with their hands bound, nor are they unloosed until the ship is out at sea, far from shore, lest accustomed as they are at home to swimming in their lake Niassa, they might attempt to escape by plunging into the sea. The caravans start in March from Kiloa for the Niassa country, which is still the chief seat of the East-African slave-trade, and they return again in November. They must, however, be strong enough to defend themselves on the way against the various chiefs and tribes. From Kiloa you can reach the lake Niassa, commonly termed on the maps Morawi, it seems in fifteen or twenty days (even in ten days, according to some.) May Heaven soon grant to the friends of missionary teaching opportunities of spreading the Gospel throughout the benighted regions round lake Niassa, and of establishing one missionary station after another! From that central region the Gospel might soon penetrate further, southward, westward, and northward, and for this the navigation of the lake itself cannot but afford great facilities.

On the 21st we left Kiloa Kibenje, and sailed to Kiloa Kisiwani, or Kiloa-island, the other Kiloa being on the mainland, Kiloa Kisiwani rising just above the level of the sea, which is encroaching more and more upon the island. We noticed that a portion of the little fortress had been thrown down by the force of the ocean, and that the fall of one of the towers was hourly threatened, though when the fort was first built the sea must have been a good distance from its foundations, but now the walls, to a height of four or five feet, are splashed by its waves. In Zanzibar, likewise, the encroachment of the sea and the submersion of the dry land are observable. The East-African coast is, as it were, emblematical of the social condition of the people; both are in a state of decadence. A new element must be introduced on it creating a new life and sweeping away the mouldy and rotten old.

I visited the commandant of the fort, an elderly and venerable Beloochee, whose demeanour was very courteous, and who inquired earnestly whether the English had defeated the Sikhs and annexed the Punjaub to their Indian empire. The fort is a good square stone building with a tower at each corner, and room for a considerable garrison; but it is now garrisoned only by a few Beloochees in the service of the Sultan of Zanzibar, who claims this island which belonged formerly to the Portuguese. In 1505 the Portuguese admiral, Francisco d'Almeyda, landed with 700 men and conquered and burnt the town upon the island; and a fort was subsequently built on it by the Portuguese, but not long retained, the unhealthy climate sweeping off its European garrisons. After the departure of the Portuguese the Kiloans had governors of their own until these were supplanted by the Imam of Muscat, who took possession of the island in the course of last century, at the time when the French thought of making Kiloa a slave-depôt.

I wandered for awhile through the ruined city, where I was particularly attracted by the remains of an old and large mosque built in the Egyptian style. In the time of its prosperity the island is said to have contained 300 mosques, which naturally suggests a very numerous population; but in the way of inhabited buildings, it now contains only some huts tenanted by Suahili. This is all that remains of the once great Kiloat-el-Muluk, Kiloa the Mistress, as the Arabs call her. Undoubtedly she had been formerly, like Kiloa Kibenje, a metropolis of the slave-trade, but now she has become herself a slave and dwindled into a wretched place, whose former glories have all departed for ever. The best thing that could be done with Kiloa-island would be to establish on it a colony like that of Sierra Leone; as in such a colony, slaves captured at sea by the English might be settled, instructed, and made useful in aiding the civilization of Eastern Africa.

22nd, 23rd February.—Yesterday we anchored in the fine bay of Kisueri, and to-day in that of Lindi, which is still larger and more romantic than that of Kisueri; in fact, south of Kiloa the coast begins to be altogether very interesting. We anchored facing Muitinge, a village which had been burnt a year before by command of the Imam to punish the inhabitants for having, contrary to the law of 1847, entered into relations with a Portuguese slave-ship, when the governor of Kiloa was commissioned to destroy the village through the instrumentality both of a land and of a sea force. The bights and bays of this coast generally look as if they had been purposely constructed to harbour slave-ships, and formerly they must here have carried on their horrible traffic undisturbed and unseen. But now their occupation, at least in so far as regards European slavers, has been destroyed by the influence of the English, though the Suahili may continue the traffic in slaves without let or hindrance, provided they do not carry it on south or north, in the limits of the jurisdiction of the Sultan of Zanzibar, or with Europeans and Americans, but merely with Africans, according to the provisions of the Anglo-Arabian convention of 1847.

On the 24th we sailed to the bight of Muania where we met numbers of people. Some of them asked us immediately whether we did not wish to visit lake Niassa, as they would be happy to guide us to it. Others asked whether we would not buy cowries. The governor of Muania said, "Remain here; build a house and do whatever you please; you will be welcome to me." I had told him that we were travelling about to announce to the people the Word of God, as we do at Rabbai. The people of Muania had heard of us before, and, indeed, along the whole coast our residence at Mombaz was talked of; so we needed no letters of recommendation to the governors in that quarter.

It was melancholy to notice at all these places the evil influence which the trade with Europe, centred at Zanzibar, had begun to exert on the people. Brandy was everywhere asked for by the natives, even by the governors and their soldiers; for the love of brandy has spread rapidly among these Mohammedans. It is French brandy mainly that is imported into this region. What if this increasing love of ardent spirits should eventually break up the false religion of their prophet, and so great good come out of the evil? On the other hand, European commerce with the coast has done a great deal of good by introducing more life and activity among the Suahili, who at last must arrive at the conclusion, that they have a great deal more to gain by legitimate commerce than by the slave-trade.

On the 25th we reached the great bight of

Mkindani, surrounded on both sides by hamlets. We anchored near the village of Pemba on the north side, which is scarcely above the level of the sea. The people soon gathered round us in large numbers, and I had some religious conversation with them. Those of Mkindani often journey to the lake Niassa, and declared themselves ready to accompany us to it if we would give them brandy.

On the evening of the 26th we reached the bight, which forms the estuary of the river Lufuma. The coast round its mouth lies very low, and there seem to be rocks at the entrance of the river; but as the wind ceased to blow just when we arrived, we could not go closer and run up the mouth of the river. There are no inhabitants in the neighbourhood, which seems to indicate that the river at its mouth is of no importance. In the dry season it is said to be but a few feet deep, but quite impassable in the rainy season. Our skipper assured me repeatedly that this river had its source in Lake Niassa : and if so, it is very desirable that the Lufuma should be explored by a small steam-boat as far as it is navigable. To the south of the river is Cape Delgado, apparently called Suahu by the Suahili in latitude 10° 41′ 2″ south, and longitude 40° 34′ 6″ east. In its vicinity is the village of Tungue which belongs to the jurisdiction of the Sultan of Zanzibar; but the region lying farther south is under the rule of the Portuguese in Mozambique. We had now completed our voyage, the conclusion of which we were heartily glad of, as day after day we had felt more and more the hardships of our life on board ship, as our food became more scanty and poorer, and the increasing rain was a source of continual annoyance. Yet no less heartily did we feel the desire that this first visit of the messengers of Peace, proclaiming here and there but a syllable of the Word of Life, might herald the dawn of a brighter day, so that these regions may become not only better known to the geographer, but gradually more and more lighted up by the truths of the Gospel.

On our return-voyage we saw at Kisueri two ships filled with men. We were told that they were only sailors, but it was clear that they were slaves, who, under this pretext, were to be transported to Mozambique. ' Another Arabian ship had, it was said, forty chests of brandy on board, bought on the coast, to be carried to Mozambique ; but I was told, that at Mozambique slaves were often brought on board ship packed in chests, to escape detection by the police of the harbour.

On the 5th of March we reached again Kiloa Kibenje, where the governor, who tried to make himself agreeable to us in every possible way, gave us a capital dinner in the Arabian fashion. He told us that, even if we arrived at night, the gates of the town would be opened to us, since the English and the Sultan of Zanzibar were the very best of friends. He also told us of a Suahili, who had journeyed from Kiloa to the lake Niassa, and thence to Loango on the western coast of Africa.

In the afternoon of the 12th of March after a tedious passage we arrived at Zanzibar, where Major

Hamerton, the English consul, received us with his usual hospitality. On the 16th we quitted Zanzibar, arriving on the 20th at Mombaz, and on the 23rd at Rabbai, where we found our poor Rebmann suffering from wounds in the feet, caused by the thoughtlessness of a Mnika, who had poured boiling water on them. I then made my preparations for my journey to Europe, and started on the 10th of April, arriving on the 26th safely at Aden, and on the 10th of June I landed at Trieste.

CHAPTER II.

FROM JERUSALEM TO GONDAR.

Bishop Gobat and the Abessinian mission—Jerusalem—Cairo—
Tor — Greek Christians in Arabia — Jidda — Mohammedan pil-
grims—The author's servant, Wolda-Gabriel—Storm and fire—
Massowa—The new king Theodorus—News from Abessinia—
Dohono—Shumfeito—A Romish missionary—Halai—The Za-
ranna wilderness—Adowa—Axum—To Gondar—Jan Meda—
The king's camp—Conference with the Abuna—Interview with
king Theodorus—Back to Gondar—Notes on the city.

It had long been the wish of Bishop Gobat of
Jerusalem, as well as of Mr. Spittler of Basel, to
send some of the pupils of the Chrishona Missionary
Institute to Abessinia, in order to revive missionary
labours in that country which had been interrupted
in the year 1838, and to resume them in such a
way as should lead to very different results from
those that followed that formerly pursued. The new
missionaries were to be laymen and handicraftsmen,
who were to follow their secular callings, but, at the
same time, by their Christian walk and conversation,
to make their light shine before the Abessinians, and
to circulate the Bible among them. Accordingly, in
the year 1854 six of the pupils were sent to Jerusalem, there to be prepared for the office under

Bishop Gobat's superintendence, and in due course to proceed to Habesh; for Bishop Gobat, as is well known, had formerly himself been a missionary in Abessinia, and, in spite of all his painful experiences in it, that country was still dear to him. As it happened that at that very time I was about to return to Eastern Africa and to my home at Rabbai Mpia I offered my services, proposing to proceed first to Jerusalem, and thence to take with me one or more of these missionary pupils, and to investigate the actual state of things in Abessinia; in short to take them to that country, and show them the way, making them acquainted with the condition of Abessinia and the neighbouring states, before the whole of the pupils should proceed to Habesh. After completing this my desire was to penetrate from Gondar to Shoa and thence to Gurague, with the view of making an exploratory visit to the scattered Christian remnants in Kambat, Wolamo, &c., and, if possible, to reach the coast of Marka ar l Barawa in the vicinity of the equator, whence I could proceed by sea to Rabbai.

In conformity with this plan, and accompanied by my fellow-labourer Deimler (from Bavaria), who had been appointed to the Rabbai mission, I set out for Jerusalem, where we arrived in December 1854; and upon Bishop Gobat selecting brother Martin Flad (from Würtemberg) as my companion to Habesh, we proceeded forthwith to Cairo, where we were joined by a young Abessinian, named Maderakal, who had been educated for four years in

the English College at Malta, and wishing to return
to his native country bore us company to Suez,
whence he could take shipping for Abessinia. At
Suez Deimler took the steamer for Bombay, where he
was to study Arabic for a time, and then to cross
over to the East-African coast. On the 20th of
January, 1855, accompanied by Flad, Maderakal,
and my servant Wolda Gabriel (from Shoa), I embarked in an Arabian vessel for Jidda.

On the 21st we reached the port of Tor on the
Arabian coast, where there are some ten or twelve
poor families of Greek Christians, who receive their
priest from Mount Sinai, and live by trade and
fishing. With the exception of the monks on Mount
Sinai, these are the only surviving Christians tolerated in Arabia. Two of them visited us and asked
anxiously after the progress of the war between
Russia and Turkey; their opinion being that the
Czar must be victorious, because he was the protector of the true faith.

23rd January.—We passed with a tolerably fair
wind Cape (Ras) Mahomed, the bight of Akaba,
and the anchorages of Etzbe, Bogos, Shabane,
Yambo, and Jar. During the passage, on the
whole a pleasant one, I read the Amharic New Testament with Flad and our Abessinian, and offered
up our morning and evening prayers mostly in
Amharic, which I had neither heard nor made use of
since 1843.

1st and 2nd February.—We arrived yesterday at
Jidda, where Mr. Cole, the English consul, gave

us a friendly reception, and at once introduced us
to an Arabian captain, who agreed for a small sum
to take us to Massowa, the chief port of the Abessinian coast.   Mr. Cole, who by his prudent and
friendly demeanour has made himself much beloved
by the inhabitants of Jidda, not only entertained
us hospitably in his house, but gave us every assistance in our preparations for the voyage to Massowa.
People at home little know how much good can be
effected by a consul abroad, when he combines true
morality with necessary official abilities and qualifi-
cations.   Notwithstanding their official power im-
moral and incapable persons, occupying a consular
position, do immeasurable mischief.

3rd February.—On board our ship were a great
number of Mohammedan pilgrims coming from Mecca,
and returning to Abessinia.   Some were from Massowa and Tigre; others belonged to the Wollo tribe
Tchuladere, on Lake Haik.   I heard from these
pilgrims that Adara Bille, the chief of Lagga-gora
who plundered me in the year 1842 was dead,
and that his son ruled in his place.   They were
very bigoted, and there soon arose a quarrel between
them and our servant, Wolda Gabriel, who rather
acrimoniously defended Christianity against the
attacks of the Wollo-Galla.   Let me give a brief
history of this Wolda Gabriel.   He was born in
the town of Makhfud in Shoa, and asserts that in
his boyhood he saw me at Ankober.   From Shoa he
went to Gondar with a priest, who had business
with the Abuna; when this was settled the priest

resolved to make a pilgrimage to Jerusalem in the company of Wolda Gabriel and another youth of Shoa. The latter fell ill on their arrival at Jidda, and Wolda Gabriel tended him in his illness. One day Gabriel went to the well to draw water and on his return found his sick companion lying dead upon the ground and the priest away, when on inquiry it turned out that the latter had carried off the effects both of the dead youth and of Gabriel himself, and had sailed from Jidda. The owner of the house, a Mohammedan, seized upon the surviving youth and sold him into slavery to Mecca, where he was sold again as a slave to Medina. The priest, no doubt, had sold the lad to the Mohammedan to raise funds for his journey to Jerusalem. Gabriel was now forced by actual violence to become a Mohammedan. After he had been about a year in Mecca and Medina his new master took him to Jidda, where he became acquainted with a Mohammedan merchant from Massowa, who advised him to make his escape from Jidda and to come on board his ship, where he would appoint him overseer of the slaves, whom he purposed to sell at Suez. Gabriel followed the advice, and reached Suez safely with the slave-dealer, where the lying rascal sold him as a slave to a rich Mohammedan at Cairo, by whom he was sent to school. One day, at Cairo he was accosted in the street by an Abessinian Christian priest who addressed him in Amharic, and asked who he was and whence he came. Gabriel told the priest his story, and by the priest it was repeated to the Coptic patriarch, who brought the matter before the Egyptian authorities and the youth was restored to freedom. He then journeyed with a caravan of Abessinian pilgrims to Jerusalem, where he became an inmate of the Abessinian monastery. Dissatisfied with monastic life he quitted the monastery, and entered the service of missionary Georges in Jerusalem, who was employed in the conversion of the Jews, and through him Gabriel became acquainted with the Bible and the Protestant faith. On my arrival at Jerusalem he heard of my intended journey to Gondar and Ankober, and offered me his services, which I gladly accepted. This youth knew how to read and write, was a clever disputant, and could defend pure Christianity against Mohammedans and bigoted Christians of the Greek, Romish, and Abessinian churches; but, in spite of all his intellectual acquirements, his heart was still unrenewed and unregenerate. He afterwards fell ill at Adowa, and could not accompany us to Gondar.

12th February.—We were overtaken by a terrible storm, with thunder and lightning, wind and rain, and it was with difficulty that we gained the open harbour of Birket, on the Arabian coast. In his dread and alarm our poor skipper kept crying out, "Ya Rabb! Ya Rabb!"—"O God! O God!"

15th, 16th February.—The storm and rain continued. The sailors threw out four anchors to steady the ship. Had we been driven on the coast inhabited by the fanatical Assir Arabs, and there been wrecked, we " dogs of Christians " would have been plundered and killed beyond all doubt. The violent rain falling on the open boat soaked our luggage, and spoilt a portion of the provisions destined for our land-journey, whilst the little cabin, too, was far from impervious to the rain. May I never forget from what dangers the mercy of God has preserved me during the last three days and nights !

18*th February.*—Last night the man at the helm having gone to sleep at his post, the flame of the binnacle light,which was burning in a little wooden box, caught the paper which surrounded the ship's compass. The flame then fastened on the sails which were lying on deck near the sleeper. Luckily he awoke before it reached the powder-bag, which the sailors had foolishly laid just over the cabin in which we slept. This merciful preservation of God showed us anew how necessary it is to commend ourselves with earnestness, day and night, to his mercy and protection.

20*th February.*—To-day we arrived safely at the island of Massowa. Signor Baroni, an Italian, secretary to Mr. Plowden, the English consul, who happened to be absent, hospitably received us into his house, and told us the important news that Ubie, the ruler of Tigre, had been routed by Dejesmaj Kassai. We also had an interview with the young Abessinian, Guebru, who was educated at Bombay with his brother Mirja by Dr. Wilson, and sent to Tigre to open a school in Abessinia. Guebru told us that after his first return from India, he and his brother had opened a school at Adowa, but they had met with great opposition from the Alaka Kidana Mariam who in 1838 had received a hundred dollars from the Romish priests, as a bribe to procure the expulsion of the Protestant missionaries from Abessinia. As the two brothers could not establish the school, they employed a priest from Waldubba, and provided him with the necessary means; but unfortunately the smallpox broke out at Adowa and carried off the priest and some of the scholars, and so the school was shut up.

26th February.—Mr. Plowden, the English consul, returned to-day to Massowa. He thinks that we may proceed with safety to the frontiers of Tigre, but that we should halt there until the government of the new king, Theodorus, (just mentioned by the name of Kassai), shall be consolidated, and to allow of the dispersion of the bands of robbers, which every political revolution in ill-fated Abessinia is sure to call into being; for as soon as the new king is proclaimed in the chief market-places of the country tranquillity will be restored. Mr. Plowden's opinion is, that the condition of Abessinia will be materially improved by the new monarch, whom he knows personally. The Abessinians (according to Bishop Gobat) have a book, called "Fakera Yasus" (Love of Jesus), which declares that a certain Theodorus will arise in Greece and subject the whole world to his rule, and that from his time forward Christianity will prevail throughout the world. The Falasha have also a notion that the Messiah will appear as a great conqueror, under the name of Theodorus, and it is possibly out of regard to this saying, that Kassai adopted his new name.

1st March.—We received to-day, fresh and certain tidings from Abessinia. Ubie has been completely defeated by Theodorus, taken captive, and imprisoned. His brave son, Shetu, fell in battle; his two other sons, Kassai and Gongal, have surrendered to Kassai; and the latter, under the name of Theodorus, has had himself crowned " King of the kings of Æthiopia." Theodorus took 7000 muskets, 60,000 dollars, and many other valuables from Ubie, who has to pay besides 40,000 dollars before he will be set free. Balgadaraia, a relation of Ras Wolda Selassie and Sabagadis, and a friend to Europeans, has been appointed viceroy of Tigre. The Romish missionaries have been expelled from Tigre, and are not to return to it. Upon the receipt of this news the consul encouraged us to prosecute our journey to Abessinia.

6th—10th March.—On the 6th we sailed to Harkiko, or Dohono, and leaving it on the 7th we mounted our camels, and arrived on the 9th at the Shumfeito, whence the camels had to return, and oxen had to carry our baggage up the mountain to Halai, the first Christian village in Tigre, where we arrived on the 10th, and met with a friendly reception from Aito Habtai and his brother Wolda Michael, both friends of the English consul.

12th March. — The Romish missionary, father

Jakobis, arrived to-day from the interior. He had fled from Gondar, and performed the journey in disguise. What a wonderful change in the state of things! When Jakobis and his companions came sixteen years ago to Abessinia, Isenberg, Blumhardt, and I, were obliged to leave the country, while we are now permitted to return to it, and the Romanists must depart. The Romish missionaries have had a long period allowed them for action, and for the promulgation of their doctrines; but no such period was vouchsafed to us to work in. The Romanists made converts in Halai, Dixan, Kaich, Kur, and in other places, on the frontiers of Tigre; as many priests in the interior played into their hands. Then too, to swell the number they re-baptized their Abessinian converts, and ordained priests a second time. They committed our Bibles to the flames, or locked them up in chests, so that nobody should read them.* They did everything in their power to procure the removal of the present Coptic Abuna, or Primate, who is unfavourably disposed towards the Romish faith. They strove earnestly to encourage an exaggerated Mariolatry, and to make the

* A Jesuit missionary told me once that the apostles had not been commanded to write, but only to preach the gospel; and that, consequently, there was no occasion to read what they had written. When I showed him Revelation i. 3 ("Blessed is he that readeth, and they that hear the words of his prophecy, and keep those things which are written therein: for the time is at hand"), and verse 19 of the same chapter ("Write the things which thou hast seen, and the things which are, and the things which shall be hereafter"), he had not a word to say, unless it were to scoff at the Bibliolatry of Protestants.

veneration of the Virgin the chief object of their activity in Abessinia. Ubie, the ruler of Tigre, patronized the Romanists in every way, and they gave him, from time to time, valuable presents to insure his protection against the Abessinian opposition. Indeed, father Jakobis is said even to have promised him the presence and aid of foreign troops, if Ubie would make him patriarch of the whole of Æthiopia. But all these successes and plans were rendered nugatory on the day when Kassai conquered Ubie, and had himself proclaimed sovereign of Abessinia.

13th—18th March.—Many Abessinian priests and others, visited us at Halai, and I had abundant opportunities of bearing testimony to the Word of God at this place. I received the visit of some boys, too, who had received instruction from Father Jakobis, who wore copper crosses round their necks, which had been given them by him as symbols of their Christianity, and they maintained that devils could do them no harm so long as they wore these crosses. Then, too, they insisted that the Virgin Mary must be worshipped as the queen of Heaven, and when I asked them for a proof from the Bible of this idle dogma, they could only appeal to an apocryphal work, "Dersana Mariam" (History of the Virgin Mary), a favourite work in Abessinia, and one which father Jakobis is said to have made a handbook when instructing the people. When I adduced the passage, 1 Timothy ii. 5, "There is one God, and one Mediator between God and men, the man Christ Jesus," they could say nothing in reply, and scampered off. I afterwards heard that Jakobis had forbidden the boys to visit me again. We were visited thrice a day by an Abessinian priest, evidently with the design to spy out whether any Abessinians with Romish tendencies came to see us. His son was a priest in the service of the Romanists. I did not engage in any formal refutation of the Romish doctrines, but simply read and expounded the Bible, the surest refutation of all errors, whether they come from Rome or from any other church.

20th—26th March.—Hearing on the 20th from Mr. Coffin, who had been resident in Abessinia for some forty years, that the way to Adowa was tolerably safe, and that the new sovereign had been proclaimed king in the market-place there, we set forth at once. On the 22nd, we quitted Halai, and, traversing the Tzaranna wilderness (ordinarily infested by robbers), we reached Adowa in the afternoon of the 26th, where we became occupants of the house of Mr. Plowden, whose servants paid us every attention in his absence.

29th March.—In the course of the day, we received a visit from Mirja, the son of Aito Workie, and brother of the two youths, Guebru and Mirja, formerly mentioned. He confirmed the news that the king had prohibited the slave-trade and expelled the Romish missionaries, and we now learned that he had forbidden polygamy among his soldiers, and that he had sent an envoy to the Emperor of Russia to form an alliance with his Imperial Majesty,

probably with a view to the extirpation of the
Mohammedans, whom he had ordered either to
become Christians in two years, or to quit the
country.

In the afternoon, I visited Aito Wolda Rufael, in
whose house Isenberg and Bishop Gobat had formerly lived as missionaries. He and his wife told
me that since our expulsion from Abessinia they
had had a great deal to suffer, and began asking
whether now, after the removal of Ubie and all the
other opponents of our cause the Protestant missionaries would not return again. I inquired after
the Amharic Bibles which we had left behind us in
1838, and Rufael told me that they had been partly
sold, partly given away, and that only fifty copies
remained undisposed of.

From Rufael's house I went to the brook Hassam,
on the bank of which are the buildings which our
sudden expulsion in 1838 prevented us from completing. The little stone house in which Blumhardt
and I used to live, was still in tolerable repair, and
is tenanted by a priest. But Isenberg's unfinished
house and the walls which surround it have fallen
into decay; and some priests of Adowa have built
wretched huts on the site.

On my return I received a visit from Debtera
Matteos, who had assisted Isenberg in translating
the Old and New Testaments into the language
of Tigre. He inquired earnestly whether Isenberg
would not now return to Adowa, as King Theodorus and the viceroy would restore the house

to my missionary friend if he wished for it. I
did not go into the subject, although I believe that
much good might be effected in Tigre by a European missionary, with the aid of the young men
Maderakal, Mirja, Guebru, and Berru (the latter
still in the Institute at Malta), and with the literary
assistance of Debtera Matteos, who knows Æthiopic
well and speaks Arabic. It would, indeed, be a pity
if such Abessinian aids were to be lost to the cause
of Protestant missions.

I advised Maderakal to open a school, and also to
compile a dictionary of the Tigre language, which
might be useful to future missionaries. His mother
is possessed of some property, and is a pious
woman after the Abessinian fashion, praying a
great deal, and behaving liberally to the poor, the
priests, the monks, and the churches. As a boy,
Maderakal himself quitted his native city, Adowa,
and went to France with M. Lefevre, a French naval
officer, and traveller in Abessinia. There he was
presented to M. Guizot, who was then minister,
and by him to the King Louis Philippe, who had
the youth educated with the view of making him
afterwards a French agent in Abessinia. After
he had spent four years in a French school he
intended to return with Lefevre to Abessinia, but
in Cairo they separated, and Maderakal became a
pupil in the school of Missionary Lieder. There
he was made acquainted with the Bible and the
Protestant faith, which had so many attractions for
him, that, to gain a more profound knowledge of the

Word of God, he asked to be admitted into the Protestant College at Malta where he spent four years, until a strong desire awoke in him to return to his native country, and there diffuse a knowledge of the Bible, which he had learned to love.

30th March.—I had a delightful conversation with Salekh, Mr. Plowden's upper servant, or Bellata. He was a thoughtful man, fond of reading the Bible, and of comparing the Æthiopic text with the Amharic. We talked of fasting, the forgiveness of sins, the worship of the saints, and other points of the Abessinian theology. As Salekh was so fond of reading Amharic, I gave him an Amharic Psalter.

In the evening I had a conversation with Pakha Seino on the chief points of Mohammedanism. As he could not contradict me, he cut the discussion short by remarking, "To-morrow I will bring a learned Mohammedan with me, whom you will not be able to confute."

31st March.—Neither Pakha Seino nor the promised learned man made his appearance. We prepared for our journey to Gondar, buying two mules and hiring bearers for the transport of our things.

2nd April.—We left Adowa at eight in the morning, and in about four hours reached Axum, the former capital of Æthiopia. We were hospitably received in the house of Agau Déras, who respects white people, and who personally knew and valued Bishop Gobat. His chief inquiry was as to the reason why the English had prohibited the slave-trade, in which he was formerly engaged. I referred him to the command, "Thou shalt love thy neighbour as thyself," and to the self-sacrifice of the Redeemer on the cross, who became the servant of all that he might save all. In the evening, we went out to see the church and obelisks of Axum,* some of which are still standing, but most of them have fallen; and it seems to me that the largest obelisks have been hewn out of the granite hill which stood to the east of Axum, and the broken stone and rubbish removed, when the pillar naturally remained standing alone. On the base of more than one of the obelisks we saw the figure of a dish distinctly cut, which seems to indicate that sacrifices were here offered to heathen divinities, and that Axum was, perhaps, the central seat of Æthiopic paganism. To the east of the obelisks there is a large pond from which the priests in attendance on the idols procured their water, and in which they performed their lavations. To the present day, the people of Axum fetch their water from this reservoir, which is supplied by rain-fall. In all probability the large stone church in Axum was originally a pagan temple which, when the country was converted to Christianity, was trans-

---

* The Abessinians say that the three sons of Noah separated, and each took up his abode in one of three divisions of the world, setting up a pillar in his own division:—Shem in Asia, Japheth in Europe, and Ham in Africa; the pillar of the last is that at Axum. The common people say that it was made by the devil, as it could not have been the work of a man. According to tradition, Cush, the son of Ham, begat twelve sons in Axum, and one of these was Æthiops, the progenitor of the Abessinians.

formed into a Christian church by the aid of Greek or Egyptian architects of the Byzantine Empire.* Perhaps it is on this account that the Abessinians say this church was built by the devil; wishing thereby to indicate that it was erected in the time of paganism, which is justly regarded in the Bible as the religion of Baal, Beelzebub, or the devil. The Abessinians assert, moreover, that their first kings were serpents; and Sando, i. e. an enormous serpent, formerly ruled over Tigre and Hamassen. This evidently refers to the pagan and despotic kings of Æthiopia. The church of Axum stands in great need of repairs, but no one thinks of restoring it, though it is an inviolable place of refuge.†

There is an enormous Worka, or sycamore-tree, in the vicinity of two of the obelisks, still standing. When the people saw us inspecting the obelisks they asked us whether we had come to search for gold under their bases. The tallest of these obelisks is some sixty-five feet high. Axum must once have been a

* This church is called Hedar Tsion. In it, according to Abessinian tradition, is preserved the ark of the covenant, which Menelek, the son of Solomon by the Queen of Sheba stole when he returned from Jerusalem to Abessinia, where he founded the Solomonic dynasty. The person intrusted with the guardianship of the ark of the covenant at Axum, is called Nabrid. He is governor of Axum and of Tigre proper at the same time.

† The chief places of refuge in Abessinia are Axum, Waldubba, Gundigundi, Debra Damo, Debra Abai. The existence of places of refuge forms another point of resemblance between Abessinia and Usambara. In the latter country, there are four such sanctuaries— Fuga, Manga, Kirrei, and Shierri—where a man-slayer is safe from pursuit. These cities remind one of the six cities of refuge mentioned in the thirty-fifth chapter of the book of Numbers.

great city, and it is a pity that Theodorus has not restored it to the dignity of metropolis. A noble plain
stretches from it, towards the south and south-east.

We saw a number of priests in the city, but they
seemed careless and indifferent as to religious matters; for not one of them came to converse with us,
either out of curiosity or otherwise, on such topics.

3rd—8th April.—We left Axum on the 3rd our
route to Gondar lying through the province of
Shirre. Yesterday evening we arrived at the village
of Heida, where we spent the night, and have remained to-day, as it is the day on which the Abessinians celebrate Easter this year, and upon which
their forty days' fast comes to an end. I tried to
awaken Easter thoughts in my people by reading
and expounding the narrative of the resurrection;
but the worldly-minded men had only thoughts
for their feast of goat's flesh, their beer, and for idle
gossip. It is painful to see the indifference of these
so-called Christians; and yet there is a great difference between them and the Mohammedan and
heathen; for low as is the state of Christianity in
Abessinia, yet a missionary has one thing at least,
a creed in common with the Abessinians, which only
needs a reformation and revivification, whilst the
heathen are greatly removed from him, both in
theory and practice, for they are without all knowledge of God and Christ in the world.

9th—15th April.—From Heida to Gondar our
journey occupied nearly five days, and during it we
were very roughly handled by more than one go-

vernor and customs-officer. On arriving at Gondar
yesterday we proceeded to Kedus Gabriel, as the
part of the city is called in which the Abuna has
his seat; and, after some delay we were admitted
into the archiepiscopal palace. To-day has been
one of the most anxious that I have spent in Abessinia. We heard that the king, with the Abuna and
the army, was approaching the country of the hostile Wollo-Gallas, so that it became necessary for
us to hurry forward to reach him, before he should
come into collision with the enemy. This was a difficult enterprise, as the royal camp was some twenty-
five to thirty leagues distant from the capital. We
required not only a guide, but luggage-bearers for
the journey; and in this dilemma we were aided by
Haji Kher, an Egyptian priest and old acquaintance, who gave us some of his people, as nobody in
Gondar would enter our service; whilst a great man
of Kedas Gabriel offered himself as our guide, who,
as we afterwards discovered, entertained the wish to
proceed to Jerusalem with us on our return.

16th—18th April.—We left Gondar at eight in the
morning, and proceeded in a south-easterly direction
towards Lake Tzana. From Efak, a town of considerable commercial importance, which we reached on the
17th, we journeyed on the 18th through the fertile
valley of Foggara, which might support thousands of
inhabitants. The little province of Foggara is bor-
dered on the east by Lake Tzana; its principal places
are Lamge, Nabaga, Terita, and Efak. Near Nabaga
the river Ereb flows into Lake Tzana, the shores of

which (in the district of Baguesa) are inhabited by
heathen Figen who are held in great horror by the
Abessinians, who accuse them of sorcery and a love
of murder; and on this account they dare not venture
to come to Gondar. They live chiefly by the chase;
selling their ivory to the Agows and to the inhabitants of Dembea and Kuara; and they probably
belong to the savage and nomadic tribe of Fuga,
who are very much dreaded in Gurague, making
use of poisoned arrows, and eating everything that
Christians reject. Perhaps they are a kind of Shan-
kela, under which designation the Abessinians comprehend all the black heathen, who inhabit forests
and marshes. To the Fuga, who are reported to
have horrible customs, and to dwell in caves, belong
also the heathen Woito, who live near Lake Tzana,
as well as the Wato on the Hawash, the source of
which river I may add, appears to be a marsh close
by the mountain Encheti, between the Galla-tribes
Mætscha and Bechoworeb.

19th April.—About ten, we arrived at Debra
Tabor, the residence of Ras Ali, the former ruler of
Western Abessinia. The town, if it deserves the
name, lies upon a hill, at the foot of which spreads a
beautiful meadow, indispensable for an Abessinian
ruler, who has to keep a number of horses.

We made all possible haste to reach the royal
camp at Jan Meda, as it was said that the king
was about to break it up, and move forward.
Reaching the camp at noon we proceeded forthwith
to the tent of the Abuna, and as soon as he heard

who we were, he came to meet us and bade us
heartily welcome upon which I delivered to him the
letters of Bishop Gobat and of Cyrillus, the Coptic
patriarch at Cairo.   After he had made us take our
places on an outspread cow-hide, he ordered his
servant, who had formerly been in the service of
Isenberg at Adowa, to set bread and wine before
us, and in the meantime he perused the letters.

This done, the archbishop entered into conversation with us as heartily and confidentially as if
we had been his equals in rank and importance.
He remembered to have seen me at Missionary
Kruse's school in Cairo in the year 1837, during
my first journey to Abessinia.   We spoke in Arabic
and Amharic.   His chief object seemed to be to give
us a correct notion of the actual state of things in
Abessinia.   He told us that king Theodorus was
one in heart and soul with him; that in every
possible way the king supported the Church, which
had neither been done by Ras Ali nor by Ubie; that
his Majesty's wish was to conquer the territories of
the Mohammedan and heathen Gallas, as well as Shoa;
to re-establish one great Æthiopian empire, as there
was of yore; and to make the Christian religion
the ruling one.   He added, that the king went regularly to church and has partaken as regularly of the
Lord's supper; that he read the Bible in Amharic,
while his Ittegie, or Queen, who is an only daughter
of Ras Ali, read it in Æthiopic; that the king had
prohibited polygamy and the slave-trade, and had
ordered the Mohammedans within a fixed period to

embrace Christianity. When, upon this, I hinted that it was not in harmony with the spirit of the gospel to make people Christians by force, the Abuna replied that the king wished, first of all, to conquer the country of the Gallas, to send priests among them, and to establish churches and schools for the conversion of those who were not Christians. I then told him that Bishop Gobat proposed to send Christian artizans to Abessinia, whose primary occupation would be to work at their trades; but who at the same time would be the means of spreading the gospel both by precept and example. The Abuna rejoined that the king would be glad to receive skilled workmen, and that his Majesty had purposed to write to England, France, and Germany for such persons. He promised to read Bishop Gobat's letter to the king, and to recommend its contents to his Majesty's consideration and approval.

The Abuna then spoke on the subject of the Romish missionaries. "So long as I live," he said "I will not allow them to return to Abessinia; for they have intrigued against me and endeavoured to expel me from Gondar; they have further interfered with my government of the church, by procuring a second baptism and a second ordination of their converts, as if our Abessinian baptism and ordination were of no value. I would not have disturbed them had they been content to teach, or if they had merely converted and baptized the Gallas; for I wish the Gallas to become Christians. The Romish missionaries cannot complain if I dismiss them from

Abessinia; for the Pope would in the twinkling of an eye drive out of his dominions any priest or teacher of another communion found promulgating its dogmas in Rome. The Protestant missionaries do not injure the Abessinian Church; for they circulate the Bible, and that only. I shall be delighted to receive men like Kruse and Lieder; but the Romanists shall never return to Abessinia."

As to-day was the monthly festival of St. Michael on which the king distributes alms, the Abuna could not at once introduce us to the sovereign. I heard afterwards that his Majesty had distributed 3000 dollars, and numbers of mules, asses, horses, and quantities of clothing among the poor, sick, and lame priests, monks, &c. When we quitted the tent of the Abuna, he ordered his servant to give us an ox and some hydromel for our present sustenance.

In the evening we received a visit from Mr. Bell, an intelligent Englishman, who has resided here for many years, and in language and habits has become a complete Abessinian. The king has made him his adjutant and Lika Mankuas, i. e., wearer of regal clothing in battle. There are four Lika Mankuas, who have to clothe themselves exactly like his Majesty, so that the enemy may not be able to distinguish the king. It is an honourable but dangerous post, for filling which Mr. Bell has received considerable estates to support his Abessinian wife and children. The Abuna had commissioned Mr. Bell to tell us that we were not to say anything to the king about the religious vocation of the persons whom Bishop Gobat proposed to send to Abessinia, but to dwell on the known and secular character of the mission, as religious matters belonged to the jurisdiction of the Abuna who was our friend, and would protect and support Bishop Gobat's people so far as he had it in his power. I told Mr. Bell, that Bishop Gobat cared not merely for the temporal weal and civilization of Abessinia, but principally and above all things, for the religious regeneration of the country, by establishing schools, distributing the Bible, and promulgating the pure faith of the Gospel. Mr. Bell replied: " Very true, this is right and good, and the Abuna knows it to be such; but he bids me tell you not to speak about it to the king, but only about the artizans; for the religious aspect of the matter you will have to arrange with the Abuna himself."

20th April.—About eight in the morning we were conducted by the Abuna to the king, whose handsome tent was already struck, as he is about to move forward with the army. When the king saw the Abuna he went to meet him, and led him to a kind of bedstead covered with a beautiful Persian carpet, and bid him place himself on it, while we were motioned to a similar carpet on the floor at his Majesty's feet. His Majesty wore the crown upon his head, and a magnificent upper garment. After the introduction the Abuna read the letters from Bishop Gobat and the Coptic patriarch. The king immediately asked, " Is Gobat well? His letter" his Majesty continued, "pleases me, and I

wish him to send me for the present only three artizans, a gunsmith, a builder, and a letter-press printer
(by which last, however, according to more recent
intelligence received, his Majesty must have meant
a die-sinker or seal-engraver); I will pay them
well, and if they are content with what I give them
and satisfy me, I will ask Gobat for more workmen." When the king had said this, the Abuna
observed : "Your Majesty, however, will not interfere with their religion, but will allow them to live
in their own belief." To this the king replied :
" I will not interfere with matters of belief; that
is your business. In regard to that, I will do whatever you advise me." Upon this, I spoke of our
return-journey through Matamma to Sennar, Khartum and Cairo. I remarked that the rainy season
was now at hand when fever is rife in the low-
lying districts of the country, and that on that account we wished to expedite our return. The king
then said that we could surely remain in Gondar
at least to the close of the rainy season ; but that he
would not interfere with our return to Egypt.
When we took our leave his Majesty ordered an
officer to provide us with two good mules, a soldier,
and by way of food on the journey, with two oxen,
fifty loaves, three pitchers of wine, and other necessaries.

After this audience the king set forth immediately
with his army which was already in motion. It is
said to be 40,000 strong, and to be destined to
receive an addition of from 20 to 30,000 men on its

march towards the Wollo-Galla-country; for the divisions from Gojam and Tigre had not yet arrived. The king is about thirty-five years old (the same age as the Abuna), a handsome man, dark-brown complexion, middle stature, and keen glance. Although friendly and condescending towards those about him he never forgets his kingly dignity. Whatever he does, is done with the greatest quiet and circumspection. His judgment is quick, his replies brief but decisive. He is friendly to Europeans, to whose advice and information he willingly listens. To the poor, the priests, and the churches, he is extremely liberal. In judicial matters he is exact and just, often giving decisions adverse to the opinions of his counsellors learned in the law; and hence he is continually besieged by people from all parts of Abessinia, who have law-suits pending. Passing the night in the camp we heard as early as two in the morning, the people shouting, "Jan hoi! Jan hoi!"*—"O king! O king!" With this cry they were attempting to procure an entrance into the royal tent, to lay their plaints before the king. He at once answered through the Kal Hazie, the Mouth of the King, or State-herald, and from two till eight in the morning, one party after another retired to make way for others,

---

* It was this title, used by the Abessinians in addressing their kings, which, in the fifteenth century, when the Portuguese first came to the Western coast of Africa, led to the report of a great king, Prester John, "Jan", ruling in Eastern Africa. It was afterwards discovered that it referred to the Khan of Tartary.

and each party received an answer and the king's decision. Besides this the king conducts all war-like operations, so that it is incomprehensible how he can endure the labours which he must undergo by night and by day. When his courtiers seek to lessen the toil of this strict dispensing of justice, he is in the habit of saying: "If I do not help the poor, they will complain of me to God; I myself have been a poor man." His mother is said to have been a vender of kosso, the well-known medicine against the tape-worm, at Gondar, while his father, a kinsman of Dejaj Comfu who, as governor of Dembea, several times defeated the Egyptian troops marching forward from Sennar, occupied an official post in the province of Kuara in the west of Abessinia. Kasai, as King Theodorus was formerly called, learned to read and write at Gondar, and became afterwards a soldier in the army of Dejaj Comfu, who recommended him to his master, Ras Ali. The latter soon recognized Kasai's prudence and valour, gave him his daughter in marriage, and an official appointment under the superintendence of the famous Waisoro Mennen, the mother of Ras Ali. Kasai soon quarrelled with Waisoro Mennen, defeated her army, took her prisoner, and conquered her fine province of Dembea on Lake Tzana, which he retained, setting however the lady herself at liberty. Ras Ali recognizing the danger that threatened made over Dembea to the Dejaj Berru Goshu, the governor of Gojam, who drove Kasai back towards Kuara in the year 1850. Kasai, however, with a band of trusty followers made an incursion into Dembea in 1852, surprised the camp of Berru Goshu, shot him dead himself, and defeated his army between Dembea and Jangar close to Lake Tzana. Ras Ali now became uneasy, and marched in 1853 against Kasai, but lost a decisive battle and was obliged to fly to the Gallas, while Kasai remained master of the whole of Amhara, consisting of the whole country west of Takassie as far as the Blue River. After these successes Kasai sent for the Abuna, Abba Salama, who then resided at Adowa in Tigre, his plan being to form an alliance with the head of the church before he attacked Ubie. The Abuna returned for reply that he would not come to Gondar so long as the Romish priests were tolerated there; which led Kasai to expel the priests, and then the Abuna appeared in Gondar, and formed an alliance with him for the restoration of the Abessinian Church and empire. Kasai's next step was to summon Ubie, the ruler of Tigre, to pay tribute as subject to the Prince of Amhara. Ubie refused and rushed to arms, but lost at the battle of Debruski in Semien, both his kingdom and his liberty, for he was taken prisoner. After this victory Kasai, as has been already mentioned, under the name of Theodorus, caused himself to be proclaimed King of the kings of Æthiopia; clearly with a reference to the old Abessinian tradition that a king of the name of Theodorus would arise who should make Abessinia great and prosperous, and destroy Mecca and Medina, the two chief cities of the Mohammedans in Arabia.

24th—28th April.—After we had taken leave of the Abuna we commenced our return-journey to Gondar, which we reached in safety. To-day Mr. Plowden arrived in Gondar. He intended to accompany the king during his campaign against the Gallas, and to give him good advice respecting the improvement of his country. We took leave of Mr. Plowden, who has shown us much kindness and hospitality.

3rd May.—To-day we quitted Gondar, which, with the exception of Axum is the most important city in the whole of Abessinia. It contains some 10 to 12,000 inhabitants, but was formerly much more populous, as may be gathered from the number of houses in ruins which meet the eye on every side. The streets are extremely crooked, narrow, and often very steep and filthy, as the city lies upon a rising ground north and south. The houses are circular, and almost all built of stone, frequently of two stories, and with thatched roofs. The Christians live at the top of the hill, near the royal palace, built by Portuguese architects and builders. There are a number of churches and monasteries, and some places of refuge, as well as a large market-place, in the Christian quarter. The Mohammedans who amount to several thousands, and who live chiefly by trade, inhabit the south-western slope of the city. The Falasha, or Jews, who in Gondar are artizans, most of the smiths, carpenters, and masons, belonging to their fraternity, are settled in a little village in the valley of Gaha, at some distance from Gondar. A market is held weekly, where you can buy lard, salt, honey, corn, cattle, coffee-beans, &c. I may mention that the Abessinians have three kinds of coffee-beans (they call coffee in the berry bun, or bunna; afterwards, when manufactured into the bean, as in Arabic, it is designated kahawa): 1, the coffee-bean, grown near Lake Tzana, of a very inferior quality; 2, a better quality, produced in Harrar, to the east of Shoa; and 3, the best quality of all, which comes from Enarea and Kaffa, probably the native country of the coffee-plant. The last two sorts are exported to Arabia, and frequently sold as genuine Mocha.

During our short residence in Gondar I was particularly struck by the circumstance that so few priests and laymen engaged in religious conversation with us, although it was in this very Gondar that Bishop Gobat, when a missionary in Abessinia, had found his chief field of active utility. The principal cause of this apparent anomaly must have been that the people were afraid that we were Roman Catholic missionaries, who had recently been banished and excommunicated.

CHAPTER III.

FROM GONDAR TO CAIRO.

Departure—Lake Tsamburu—Singular Telegraph—Boch—Custom of eating raw flesh—The Alaka Selat ; controversies with priests —Gunter and the river Kuang—The Western Abessinians less indifferent to religious matters—Romish missionaries at Kaffa —Emmanuel—The Camant—The Salane—Cotton, and the cotton district—Wekhne, and its importance as an emporium— Cotton again—Matamma and its market—Abessinian penitence— Egyptian order and hospitality—Doka—Slave smuggling— Asser, and its hospitality—Sennar—A Roman Catholic priest at Fedasi—Coptic school—General drunkenness—Departure from Sennar—Former diffusion of Christianity—Wasalie—Coptic scribes—The Coptic communities and their possible future—Sufferings in the desert—Khartum—Visit to the Roman Catholic mission, and details respecting it—Fever—Invitation to explore the Sabat—Opening for Protestant missions—Shendi—Egypt's past and present—What Mehemet Ali has done—Berber and the Barabra—The desert again : anticipations of death—The pure air of the desert medicinal—Camel-drivers and camel-driving— Joyful arrival at Korusko—Assuan, the Syene of the ancients : its quarries and obelisks—Cairo—Kindness of Dr. Lieder— Return to Europe—Bishop Gobat's dispatch of missionary pupils to Abessinia ; their arrival, reception, and activity—Latest from Abessinia.

3rd May.—Leaving Gondar behind us we took at first a south-westerly direction to reach the village of Boch, where Aito Engeda, the governor of Dembea, was to receive us, and whence he was to give us an escort to Wekhne. On the way a

Mohammedan who had been in Kaffa joined our little caravan. He told me that on the other side of the country of Worata, which lies to the southeast of Kaffa, there is a large lake called Tsamburie, which is probably the large lake Tsamburu, of which I had heard from the Wakamba in Rabbai Mpia. He mentioned a singular kind of telegraph by means of drums which is used in Kaffa. At given distances drummers are placed near a tall tree, any one of whom upon sighting an enemy immediately climbs the tree, and signals the event by so many beats of the drum, which is taken up by the next drummer also mounting his tree for the purpose, and so on to the end of the line. They have various other signals all well understood. Late in the evening we reached the village of Boch, where we were received in the friendliest manner by Aito Engeda. After a plentiful meal, consisting of raw meat, pepper-soup, bread, beer, and wine, some priests asked religious questions, which I answered conformably to Scripture. The Abessinians call raw flesh Brundo. When they eat it, they take most delight in the Shaluda the double or geminus muscle, of a cow. The practice mentioned by Bruce of the Abessinians cutting a piece of flesh from a living cow, and covering up the place again I never witnessed in any part of the country; but with my own eyes I saw some Christian soldiers of Shoa, on an expedition against the Gallas, cut off the foot of a live sheep, and then leave the animal to its fate. The foot was forthwith devoured raw. It is true

that they were in a great hurry, and had not time
to slaughter the animal in the regular way.

4th May.—Before our departure the governor introduced us to the Alaka Selat who had been personally acquainted with Bishop Gobat, and inquired
earnestly after him. I was charmed by his modest,
enlightened, and tolerant character. The priests,
deacons, and laymen who were about him paid him
great respect. The priests soon began with religious
discussions and I had a long controversy with them,
chiefly on the nature of Christ; they were adherents
of the monophysitic doctrine, and I did my best to
confute them from Scripture. The old Alaka listened
to me patiently and without anger, merely saying:
"though we differ, still let us love one another; for
love is the greatest of all virtues." I have not seen
a more amiable man in Abessinia, more forbearing,
more reflective, and better acquainted with the Bible
than this Alaka, who bade us greet Bishop Gobat
heartily from him.

At five in the afternoon we reached the village of
Gunter near the river Kuang, chiefly inhabited by
priests, monks, and deacons. We were sorry that we
could not give them Amharic Bibles, for which some
of them expressed a desire; for these western Abessinians seem to take more interest in religious matters than the people of Tigre, and more Bibles
should be distributed among them. It was for this
reason chiefly that I selected the route from Gondar
to Sennar for our return-journey, to become personally acquainted with the condition of this part of

Abessinia, where no Protestant missionary had
hitherto travelled.   The Abuna had proposed to procure us an escort to the sources of the Blue River,
in the Agaw-country, said to be twelve days' journey
from Gondar.   When I talked to him of the journey
to Kaffa, he said that the Gallas would not allow
white people to visit it, especially if they were provided with fire-arms.   In spite of this some Romish
missionaries seem to have succeeded in reaching
Kaffa, where they are said to have been very well
received by the king of the country.

5th, 6th May.—Proceeding yesterday morning from
Gunter down into the valley, we passed the river
Kuang, said to have its rise in Dembea near Lake
Tsana and to join the Atbara.   On the western bank
we discovered coal, the use of which is still unknown
to the Abessinians.   We encamped in the evening
at the village of Emmanuel, and to-day we had to
ascend and descend in a mountainous country for
several hours.   We left to the right the country of
the Camante who inhabit the mountainous region
from Enchiet Amba to Mount Waha, which forms,
in the vicinity of Wekhne, an impregnable natural
fortress.   It is the duty of the Camante to guard
the mountain-passes from the lowlands into the highlands, and thus into Abessinia proper; they are
therefore held in some esteem by the Abessinian
rulers.   They are baptized, have priests, and receive
the sacrament of the Lord's supper; but, in spite of
this, the Abessinians look upon them as heathen.
They perform their religious ceremonies in dense

forests, where they are said to pay particular reverence to the Cactus, ascribing to it a reasonable soul, and believing that the human race sprang from it. Here and there we met a family of the heathen Salane, who wander from place to place, leading a pastoral life. They have to pay the sovereign of Abessinia a tribute of oxen, in return for which they are allowed to roam about Western Abessinia. They seem to me to be harmless people, who understand Amharic, indeed, but use among themselves their own Kuara language.

7th May.—Leaving the village of Sebaskie, where we had spent the night, we descended into the deep valley of the Lagnat, and reached the Senkoa at noon. On our way we met many dealers bringing cotton on asses from Wekhne to Gondar and Gojam. The cotton is grown in the province of Kalabat, which forms the western boundary of Abessinia, dividing it from the Egyptian district of Sennar belonging to Soudan. Up hill and down dale, and after many windings through a wild and uninhabited country, we reached the village of Wekhne, consisting of a number of straw huts, erected among groups of noble trees. The inhabitants are mostly Christians and chiefly traders. As all articles imported from Sennar and Khartum, or exported from Abessinia, must pass through Wekhne, the importance of the place is manifest. Cotton, coffee, hides, ivory, slaves (only on the sly, just now, as Theodorus has forbidden the slave-trade), beads, coloured stuffs, and other Egyptian and European, as well as Abessinian products, pass through the village of Wekhne which lies at the foot of a mountain range.

9th May.—We rested at Wekhne and laid in a fresh stock of provisions for our further journey. Several Abessinians begged us to take them with us to Jerusalem, a pilgrimage thither being considered by the priests a meritorious work, bringing rest and peace to the soul. I showed them the true source of peace in Christ, and warned them against being deceived by their own thoughts and ways.

10th May.—We left Wekhne, keeping along the foot of the mountain, and found ourselves in an undulating plain to which we could see no end. On our way we met with bamboo-canes, of which we had seen none since we left the deep defile formed by the river Takassie. These deep defiles with terraces, are called "Kolla" in Amharic, and are from 1000 to 6000 feet above the level of the sea, and 3000 feet is about the level of Wekhne. The higher grounds, called "Daga," comprise all that which is above 6000 feet above the level of the sea, and in some places rise to an altitude of 14,000 feet, as on the Abba Yared, Bewahit, and Amba Hai. In these "Kolla" are found elephants, rhinoceroses, buffaloes, lions, antelopes, and other animals, as well as luxurious vegetation, tamarinds, the terebinth or turpentine-tree, frankincense, bamboo, ebony, cotton, olives, grapes, coffee, &c., besides sycamores, adansonia or sour-gourd, willows, and other trees and shrubs.

It is by no means improbable that the Æthiopian

" vessels of bulrushes," mentioned in the eighteenth
chapter of Isaiah, were made out of bamboo, conveyed to Meroe, the then centre of Æthiopian commerce, by the waters of the Takassie and other
rivers. Before noon, we crossed the Abai (not to
be confounded with the great Abai, the Baher-el-
Azrak, the " Blue river" of the Arabs), and the
Gendoa. In the evening we met 300 camels and 100
asses, carrying cotton from Matamma to Wekhne.

11*th*, 12*th May.*—After a journey yesterday through
a wooded wilderness, with numbers of antelopes and
guinea-fowls we reached a Mohammedan village,
where we stopped for the night. To-day we arrived at
Matamma, where the new Sheik Ibrahim, a governor
appointed by Theodorus, has charge of the frontier
between the territories of Egypt and Abessinia. He
is a Mohammedan, like most of the inhabitants, and
gave us a friendly reception, providing us immediately with a hut to lodge in.

At Matamma we met with people of all nations,
who come here for trading purposes, Abessinians,
Arabs, Tagruri, and others; for it is even more of
a commercial centre than Wekhne. The population
is about 1500, more dependent upon Abessinia than
Egypt, paying, however, tribute to the rulers of
both countries. The inhabitants are partly Dabeina
Arabs, partly Tagruri, who came hither long ago
from Darfur. They cultivate Indian corn, barley,
cotton, tobacco, &c., and have horses, asses, camels,
sheep, and black cattle, whilst honey, wax, musk,
and ivory are plentiful in their markets.

13*th*, 14*th May*.—We rested yesterday waiting for the camels which were to take us to Doka. To-day was market-day in Matamma. We saw in the market, cotton, beads, wax, honey, mirrors, razors, nails, drinking vessels, coffee, coffee-cups, salt, onions, durra, stibium, horns, coloured fabrics, sheep, goats, black cattle, camels, and many other things, which one would scarcely have sought for, or expected to find in the wilderness of Kalabat. Our servant Darangot, who had offended us yesterday and run away in consequence, returned to us to-day with a large stone upon his head, and asked us to forgive him.*

16*th May*.—We started this morning from Matamma, and in the evening reached the village of Etteb, where we were hospitably received. We were at once provided with a hut, bedsteads, water, and food; indeed we met with a similar reception at most places in the course of our journey to Sennar, which gave us a good impression of the order introduced into these distant countries by the Egyptian government. In Abessinia, for the most part, there is a great deal of wrangling and bluster before a lodging and the needful provisions can be obtained, so different from this.

17*th*, 18*th May*.—We travelled yesterday, as the day before, over a level country, frequently covered

---

* Concerning this Abessinian custom in which a person, conscious that he has done wrong and seeking forgiveness, places a stone upon his head or neck, see Bp. Gobat's "Journal of Three Years' Residence in Abessinia," p. 359.

with acacias. At noon to-day we reached the
village of Doka, where we met with a very friendly
reception both from Muallem Saad, the government
official, a Coptic Christian, as well as from the Kashif,
or Judge, Muhammed Kurd-el-Kuttli, though one
would hardly have expected so much friendliness and
order in this out-of-the-way nook of the globe. Doka
was formerly an important centre of the slave-trade,
carried on by the Jibberti between Abessinia and
Sennar. It is now contrary to law, but the
Jibberti nevertheless still transport slaves in disguise
through Doka by night. The slave-dealers can
easily conduct their secret traffic, as there are no
European consuls here to receive information and
make the necessary representations to the authorities.
The Mohammedans of Gondar are said to keep their
slaves concealed in cellars under their houses, whence
they bring them forth at night and send them to
Chelga with their mouths stuffed with rags, so that
the poor wretches cannot cry out and appeal to any
one on the road. From Doka they are conveyed
to Sennar and other places on the Blue River.

20*th*, 21*st May*.—Yesterday we reached Asser, the
chief place of the district El Gadarif, and were hospitably entertained by the son of Muallem Saad.
When we quitted Asser to-day, ·the governor furnished us with a soldier and two camels for which
he himself paid. He seemed to wish us to proceed
to Sennar with favourable impressions. Our Coptic
host provided us with provisions, and accompanied
us with his people a part of the way, giving the kiss

of peace when he bade us farewell. Such cordial hospitality we had never before experienced. Our Abessinians were so touched, that they exclaimed: " These
people are kings and Christians indeed, compared with
our greedy Abessinian countrymen." We promised
to send them Arabic Bibles and tracts from Cairo.

22nd, 28th May.—Eight days of painful progress,
sometimes losing our way, and once narrowly escaping
by night with the loss of a leather bag containing
our cooking utensils, from the clutches of a hyæna.
We slept on the 22nd at the village of Bela, on the
24th at that of Kummer, on the 25th, after crossing
the Rahat, we bivouacked under a tree, on the 26th,
we rested in a village on the Rahat, which we had
reached again, as it has a very winding course, and,
on the 27th, we spent a most uncomfortable night at
Daud in a hut, full of soldiers and their wives,
where there was not room enough for us to spread
out our cow-hides to sleep on. This morning the
chief constable of the place, who had forced us to
accept this wretched lodging, came before our departure to apologize for his treatment of us, fearing
lest we might complain of him to the governor at
Sennar. In about three hours we reached the village of Abbas, on the Blue River. We repaired to
the house of a Coptic Christian, named Georgis, who
is clerk to the resident Egyptian governor. The
privations and difficulties of the Abessinian journey
were over, and we had now to face those of Nubian
travel.

29th May.—To-day we arrived at Sennar, and

took up our abode in the house of the Komos Theodorus—in the Coptic church, Komos is the next
dignitary to the bishop—who officiates as priest and
schoolmaster in his little community of some fifty
souls.   He gave us a friendly reception, and a
chamber where we could repose from the fatigues
of our journey.   Most of the Copts in Sennar are
government officials; others are merchants.

The rectangular houses of Sennar are built of
lime-bricks as there is no stone here, and have flat
roofs with covered balconies. These bricks are simply
dried in the sun, so that the houses often collapse
when the rainy season is unusually severe. The town
occupies a considerable extent of ground, but I doubt
whether the population amounts to more than 12 or
15,000 souls.   The Egyptian garrison consists of
from 4 to 500 disciplined black soldiers.   There is a
weekly market where all sorts of Abessinian, Egyptian,
and European articles are sold.   Caravans proceed
from Sennar in all directions, towards Abessinia,
Fazokli, and the White River in the West.   The
Blue River is navigable as far as the seventh cataract
at Roseres in the province of Fazokli, which is the
limit of the Pacha's sovereignty towards the south.
The rocks at Roseres prevent boats from proceeding
further up than Sennar.

30th May.—Upon calling upon the governor of
Sennar, and asking him for a boat to Khartum, we
learned that the boats had not yet arrived from
Fazokli, so that we must proceed by land to Wad
Medine and Khartum.   This was very disagreeable

news, as we had come to Sennar partly on purpose to journey by water to Khartum. Some time ago an Italian priest is said to have penetrated to Gezan, which is apparently twelve days' journey south of Sennar, and thence to have proceeded to Fadasi, the chief place of the tribe Bene-Shongol. He seems to have purposed to reach Enarea and Kaffa, where there are some Romish missionaries, who went to Kaffa from Abessinia. As the priest could not proceed further than Fadasi, he appears to have remained there for some time, during which he gained the favour of the prince by curing his sick son. The Romish missionaries therefore are about to found a missionary station in Fadasi in connection with Khartum, hoping so to reach Enarea, Kaffa, and the nations of Central Africa, whose conversion they consider to be the goal of the Roman Catholic mission.

The Coptic priest, Theodorus, has a little school in which he educates Coptic boys, who are very quick, attentive, and desirous to learn; more the pity that the mode of instruction is merely mechanical. It is sad for us to see the addiction of the Copts here to brandy drinking; indeed drunkenness is prevalent among both Christians and Mohammedans, and has been greatly spread by the Egyptian soldiers.

1st June.—To-day, we visited the chapel which has been built by the Copts with the consent of the Pasha, at Sennar; but were pained by the noisy and unmeaning ceremonies, which the priests performed in a very mechanical manner, and there seemed to be no end to the bowing, the burning of incense, and the lighting of candles. One part of the lessons was read in Arabic, and the other in Coptic, although they do not understand a word of the latter; but the present Copts wish to restore the use of Coptic, or at least to write Arabic in Coptic characters. Komos Theodorus asked me why we did not establish a school in Sennar, as Missionary Lieder has done in Cairo; and as he had only one Arabic Bible in his school, and that imperfect, we promised to send him Bibles from Cairo.

2nd June.—We left Sennar, where the heat both by day and night is very great. To the south-west of Sennar we saw a hill in the vicinity of the White River, on which the komos told us there are the ruins of a Christian church. Doubtless, Christianity was once diffused over the peninsula between the White and the Blue Rivers, and it is possible that there are still Christian remnants to be found in the south, just as in the Galla-countries, where in many places the Christians withdrew to steep mountains, and have since lived isolated from the whole of Christendom. The conquests made by the Egyptian government along the White and Blue Rivers, may under Providence pave the way for the extension of the Gospel to the heart of Africa.

3rd, 4th June.—Last night we slept at the village of Wasalie, and leaving it this morning, reached at noon the town of Wad Medine, which appears to be larger than Sennar. The houses are built like those of Sennar, and the language of the people is Arabic. We lodged at the house of a Copt, a government official. Coptic clerks are found everywhere at the chief seats of government, which is glad of their services. Wherever such an official is stationed, he soon induces his relatives and friends to settle and trade, and thus, by degrees, there is formed a little community of Coptic Christians, who build a chapel and appoint a priest to it; for they are now allowed to build chapels where they please; and when in Kenne,* in Upper Egypt, the Mohammedans pulled down the Coptic chapel, the Pasha commanded the Cadi to rebuild it at the expense of the Mohammedan population. Who can tell to what importance these little colonies of Copts may yet attain? Supposing there were to be a thorough revival and awakening among these nominal Christians, would not such little communities become noble centres of light, diffusing it amongst the heathen and Mohammedan?

5th—11th June.—We could not find at Wad Medine any boat for Khartum, and so set off again on the 6th, and reached the village of Dengai in the evening, where we lodged in a house, like an Arab Caravansarai, set apart expressly for travellers, the townspeople providing us with water and food. We stopped the

---

* The town of Kenne is famous for the manufacture of a porous kind of terra-cotta vessels, used in Egypt for cooling water. Every year bands of Mohammedan pilgrims centre there on their way from Kossir to Mecca. No wonder that the town has become so fanatical and demoralized.

next night at Mot Ferun. The excessive heat and the simoom-like wind were unbearable. The gale did not last more than a few minutes at a time, but it was as hot as if it came from an oven. Never yet had I experienced any thing of the kind, although I had suffered much from the heat in Arabia and in the Adal-desert. I cannot express what I suffered on this journey, and how I longed for its close: for more than once my sensations were as if fire had passed through my brain, and first maddened and then paralyzed it. Our journey was made at the season of the greatest heat, when even the natives keep as much as possible within doors. Resting at the village Matadib on the evening of the 9th, we slept in the open air; but on the night of the 10th, there arose all at once so cold and violent a sand-wind, that we had not time to roll our bed clothes over us; and the consequence was a cold, laying the foundation of a fever which attacked me at Khartum, where we arrived at noon. We met with a friendly reception and hospitable shelter from Mr. Bender, the Austrian Vice-Consul.

The town of Khartum lies on the Blue River, which joins the White River a little farther to the north. It contains about 20,000 inhabitants. Khartum is the seat of the Governor of Sudan, and all civil and military officers are under his orders. He is the greatest person after the Pasha himself, and is the ruler of Egypt, Nubia, and Sudan.

13*th June.*—We visited Messieurs Kirchner and Gossner, the German Roman Catholic missionaries,

who received us with much courtesy. Mr. Gossner
was prostrate with fever; but Mr. Kirchner had the
kindness to show us the extensive garden, which the
lay missionaries have laid out and planted with all
kinds of tropical plants and trees; it is surrounded
by a wall, and is watered from the Blue River.
Mr. Kirchner showed us, also, their church and
school, in which instruction is imparted to thirty
boys, collected from different tribes in the interior,
most of whom have been liberated from slavery.
When their period of instruction is completed they
will be sent back to their countrymen. He told
us that since the establishment of the mission at
Khartum, no less than ten missionaries had died,
notwithstanding the many European comforts which
they are enabled to procure from Europe and Cairo.
The mission derives great assistance from its lay
brothers, artizans, masons, carpenters, &c., who enjoy better health than the fathers themselves. The
sedentary life of the latter, and their good living
and want of exercise does not quite agree with them
—at least, so one of the lay brothers told us. At
present an extensive and massive two-storied mis-
sionary-house is being built of stone, intended also
to serve as a block-house, in case of an attack by the
tribes which live on the banks of the Blue and
White Rivers. As soon as the large building is
completed there will be an accession of priests and
laymen, accompanied by nuns and sisters of charity.
The mission at Khartum is governed and supported
by the Marien-Verein at Vienna, and the mission-

aries are mostly Germans from the Austrian Tyrol
and Bavaria, with a few Italians.   Khartum is the
central point of their missionary-stations on the
White River; but they have a station in the Bari-
country, four degrees north from the equator, and
another among the Kiks-tribe, seven degrees north
of it.   The chief importance of the station at Khartum is as a central point and connecting link between
Europe, the missions in Central Africa, and that designed for Abessinia, Sennar, and the countries both on
the Blue and White Rivers.   At Khartum itself, the
missionaries can effect little, as the inhabitants are all
Mohammedans, with the exception of a few Coptic
Christians who have a church and bishop of their own.

Mr. Kirchner was good enough to show me a
dictionary of the Bari language, and, also, a vocabulary of twelve languages spoken on the White River,
several of which have a mutual affinity.   As far as I
could perceive, the Bari language does not belong to
the great South-African family; but rather approxi-
mates somewhat to that of the Wakuafi, spoken about
the Equator.

13th January.—A renewed and severe attack of
fever forced me to call to my aid Doctor Kenet, the
French military surgeon, who has already spent
many years at Khartum.

At Khartum, we also became acquainted with
Mr. Petherick, the English consular agent*, who has
a commercial house in Khartum as well as one at

* Mr. Petherick is now Her Majesty's consul for Soudan, and is
interesting himself to promote the exploration of the countries

Kordofan. His boat, some time before, had sailed up the Sobat, which is a tributary of the White River, and seems to have its source in the neighbourhood of Kaffa or Enarea. Mr. Petherick asked me to sail with him up the White River, if possible to its source, in October when the temperature is cool, the White River full, and the winds blow from the north. Gladly as I would have accepted his invitation it was quite impossible for me to entertain it under the circumstances.

19th June.—Taught by experience that there is no better remedy for fever than change of air, I resolved to leave Khartum as soon as possible. Mr. Petherick offered us for 600 piastres a vessel from Khartum to Berber. As I quitted Khartum I reflected how desirable it would be to establish Protestant mission-stations in these countries, now so providentially laid open by the power of Egypt. How easy by means of the White River and its many tributaries to reach the nations of Central Africa, which the friends of Protestant missions will do well to bear in mind.

21st June.—We reached about noon the point where the bed of the Nile becomes narrower, and forces itself along through hills. At the risk of seeming ungrateful, I must say that the change of air and the coolness of the river did me more good than the doctor's medicine.

around Lake Nyanza, the region of the supposed sources of the Nile, about to be undertaken by Captains Speke and Grant, by the employment of boats from Khartum, as I perceive by a letter from him in the "Times" of the 5th of April, in the present year, 1860.

22nd June. — We reached the town of Shendi, where we passed the night. How different the aspect of this region from that which it wore in 1811, when Burkhardt travelled through the regions of the Nile! How great then was the insecurity at Shendi from which he was obliged to return to Cairo, abandoning his plan for the discovery of the Niger! How much reason have travellers to be grateful to Mehemet Ali, by whom the numerous independent little potentates on the banks of the Nile, comporting themselves like sultans, have been removed with iron hand and his own rule substituted for theirs.

25th June.—At noon we reached the town of Berber, whence we could proceed no further, as the water of the Nile was then too low for us to sail safely over its rocks and rapids. The right time is in September and October: Since leaving Khartum we had heard only the language of the Berber, in the plural, Barabra.* They are active, courageous, enterprising, and very different from the timid and slavish Nuba of Sennar.

26th June.—We procured camels for our land journey from Berber to Abu Hamed, and thence through the eastern Nubian desert to the village Korusko on the Nile. As I was suffering severely from fever, and felt extremely weak, I could not conceal from myself and my dear companion Flad,

---

* The language of these Berbers, of which I could not understand a word, is not the *Tema-shirh-t* of the Tarki, or Renegates, of the Arabs, the Berbers more properly so called, which is spoken throughout the greatest part of Western Sahara, &c.

that I feared the most serious results from this long and toilsome journey through the desert; for I expected nothing less than to find a grave in the desert of Atmor.

27th June—4th July.—We left Berber on the 27th. The journey from Khor to Abu Hamed was a painful one to me; as the camel drivers paid no regard to the state of my health, and only wished to finish the journey as quickly as possible. We left Abu Hamed yesterday, the 3rd.

5th—14th July.—For some days we travelled over a level plain, where right and left we saw only here and there hills in the distance. The more we penetrated into the wilderness the purer became the air, so that I felt myself wonderfully strengthened. The dry air of the more elevated desert is evidently more healthful than the atmosphere on the banks of the Nile; and although the heat was great I did not suffer from it so much as between Sennar and Khartum. My greatest sufferings were caused by camel riding, and the sand-wind which inflamed my eyes; our guide often growled and grumbled at the slowness of our progress, but for poor sick me, the pace was always too great.

It was with joy that we greeted our arrival at the little village of Korusko, where we fortunately found at once a boat to take us to Assuan on the 16th. During our river voyage we frequently wondered at the narrow slips of land, which are all that the mountains and the rivers have left the inhabitants

for cultivation, which are often scarcely 60 to 100
feet wide, realizing the words of Isaiah : " A nation
meted out and trodden down, whose land the rivers
have spoiled!" The Berbers or Barabra who inhabit
the banks of the Nile live chiefly on durra and dates;
and we found groves of date-trees everywhere along
the river. Cows and goats are not very numerous
between Korusko and Assuan, the latter being the
Syene of the ancients, and remarkable for the Syenite
terraces, consisting of a reddish granite containing
particles of hornblende. Here are the quarries
from which the obelisks and colossal statues of the
Egyptian temples were dug, and an obelisk partially
formed, and still remaining attached to its native
rock, seems to bear out the conjecture I ventured to
throw out at page 447, whilst also bearing testimony
to the toilsome and persevering efforts of ancient
art. These terraces, shaped into peaks cross the bed
of the Nile, which rolls its mighty waters majestically
over them. It was at Assuan that Eratosthenes made
the first attempt to measure the circumference of the
globe, and it is here likewise that Strabo places the
well which marked the summer solstice; for on the
day when the style of the sun-dial cast no shade at
noon, the vertical sun shot his rays to the bottom of
the well. Our boat could not proceed further than
the island Philæ, from which we had to proceed
by land on asses, for the distance of a league, to
Assuan, where we hired a boat to Cairo.

17th—28th July.—I had hoped that my health
would have been much improved by the river-voyage

from Assuan to Cairo; but this was not the case.
I was, however, glad and grateful to reach Cairo
alive, after seeing before me at Abu Hamed, nothing
but death and the grave. The oft-tried hospitality
and aid of Dr. Lieder, the missionary at Cairo,
essentially contributed to such a partial restoration
of my health, as allowed me soon to undertake
the voyage to Europe, where I arrived in September.
The dear companion of my toils, Martin Flad,
proceeded to Jerusalem, to make his report respecting our journey to our excellent friend, Bishop Gobat.
The bishop felt induced to send four pupils of the
Chrischona Institute at Basel, to Abessinia, where,
after a severe struggle with hardship and sickness,
they arrived in April 1856, and were well received
by king Theodorus. They forthwith set to work to
distribute the Bibles, which they had brought with
them, chiefly in western Abessinia, and particularly
to the Falashe, who are especially desirous to
possess them, and among whom the brothers think
of settling, although they would almost have preferred to have found a settlement among the Gallas.

———

In concluding this chapter devoted to my latest
journey in Abessinia I may add that, according to intelligence recently received by me from that country,
king Theodorus has defeated king Haila Malakot
in Shoa, and has taken possession of his dominions.
Malakot died suddenly, on which the army sub·

mitted to the conqueror, who made the son of
Malakot Governor of Shoa. He is to make him
Viceroy in due time. Several tribes of the Wollo-
Gallas have been completely routed by Theodorus;
and among them that of Adara Bille, whose whole
family was put to the sword, and whose town,
Gatira, was burnt. Mr. Bell, the king's adjutant,
directed in person the burning of the town, on
which occasion he said, he had not forgotten that
there a European had been plundered and his missionary labours interrupted, a crime now so signally
visited upon its perpetrators. In Ankober the king
is reported to have found Amharic Bibles still remaining, which I had left behind in my house; and
to have had them distributed, as for the future he
wishes the Bible to be read only in Amharic, the
language of the people, and no longer in the old
Æthiopic, which the people do not understand.

CHAPTER IV.

CONCLUSION.

IT is pleasant in drawing this volume to a close to be able to announce that the power and mercy of God have revealed themselves anew at Rabbai Mpia. The wife of Abbegunja, whom the reader may probably recollect, begins to pray, and he himself is diffusing Christianity among his countrymen. A single Christian family among a heathen people is of signal value. God allows great things to arise out of small and insignificant beginnings, as He has promised:—" A little one shall become a thousand."

If less important, still no less interesting are the geographical results which have proceeded from our missionary labours in Eastern Africa. The following extract from a communication of my friend Rebmann, dated " Mombaz, 23rd April, 1855," points out the source of some recent expeditions and discoveries, made by English travellers in Eastern Africa, which are just now being brought prominently before the notice of the public.

" During my friend Erhardt's six months' residence at Tanga to study the Kisambara language, he had often *nolens volens* to listen to narratives of journeys, introduced into the conversations held by him with the ivory-traders of that place. They represented to him that the Sea of Uniamesi was simply a continuation of the Lake Niassa, the latter, according to them, striking out westward from its northerly direction, and then spreading itself out even to a greater expanse than hitherto, so as to approach the mountains which pass through the centre of the continent, and form a most important and impenetrable barrier and water-shed. The northern side of this barrier contains the sources of the Nile, of Lake Tsad, and of the river Chadda, while the south side sends its waters partly to the Atlantic Ocean, by the river Congo or Zaire, partly to the Indian Ocean by the Jub, Dana, and Osi, and also, as I think highly probable, to the great lake of the interior itself.

" As we must regard all such accounts of the natives necessarily as very vague and inaccurate, Erhardt was not at first inclined to give unqualified credence to this statement; but one circumstance could not fail to strike him as remarkable, that persons journeying into the interior from very different starting points, such as Uibo, Kiloa, Mbuamaji, Bagamoyo, Pangani, and Tanga, a tract of coast extending some six degrees of latitude, all represent themselves, at very varying points of distance from the coast, as arriving at a Baheri or inland-sea.* This, however, did not necessarily prove to him that the Lake of Uniamesi is a continuation of that of Niassa, and that both thus form but a single large lake, or rather sea, in the centre of the continent.

" After Erhardt's return to Rabbai we naturally

* The chief caravan routes which lead from the Suahili coast to the great inland-sea are the following :—

1. The route from the island of Tanga, upon which the Suahili ivory-traders cross several isolated mountain-masses, and among them the snowy Kilimanjaro and Doinio Engai, and upon which also travellers have to pass through the level pasture-land of the Masai tribes to Burgenej. This journey occupies fifty-five days, and is performed at the rate of about seven leagues a day. From Burgenej the route lies for eight days through the very populous country of the Waniamesi, and then suddenly reaches the inland-sea. The Masai are savages, but breeders of cattle; the Waniamesi, on the contrary, are quiet and well-disposed, and cultivate the soil. Thus the distance from Tanga to the inland-sea would appear to be about 400 or 450 leagues.

2. The second route is from Mbuamaj, south of Zanzibar, to Ujiji, a town in Uniamesi. This route is almost as long as the first, and is used by numerous caravans journeying with beasts of burden, horses, asses, &c., to fetch slaves, ivory, and copper ore. The country through which it passes is quite level with the exception of the Ngu range of hills, which is not far from the coast.

3. The routes from Kiloa or Kirimba to the ferries of Gnombo and Mdenga, which are used partly by the Portuguese slave-dealers, partly by the Arabs.

Ujiji is the point from whence large row-boats cross the lake conversed now and then upon this subject, but could come to no other conclusion than that one of these days a European visiting the localities themselves would alone be able to clear the matter up. Curious enough, however, a man named Salimini had been in my service for a year whose home is but two or three days' journey to the west of Lake Niassa, and who had formerly told me that in his country most of the rivers flow to the north, and that going from his home, Kumpande, at two and a half days' journey eastward, and three days' journey north-ward, you reach Lake Nianja, as it is there called.

" In the meantime Erhardt had begun to mark down all these geographical data, obtained from one source or another, on a large map, and by this process he exhibited the inland-sea, when drawn in accordance with the statements of the ivory-dealers, in that position towards the rivers, all of which an old English map represented as flowing from the south, so that there could then hardly remain a doubt as to their emptying themselves into it. At last it happened that as we were one November day discussing the matter together, and comparing what we knew of it with the physical conformation of Africa in the south and north, and in the east and

to the west.   In five days these boats reach the mountainous island of Kavogo.   It takes another twenty-five days before they reach the western shore, where they purchase copper.   The shores of the sea are low, sandy, and shelving.   Only at its south end are there lofty mountains.   The waves of the lake are often very high ; it consists of fresh-water, and is full of fish.   Its shores are, for the most part, inhabited.

west, at one and the same moment the problem
flashed on both of us as solved by the simple supposition that, where geographical hypotheses had
hitherto supposed an enormous mountain-land, we
must now look for an enormous valley and an inland sea. With this solution the statements of our
African informants completely harmonized, not only
with what had been correctly given on former maps
as previously discovered, but witu what we knew
of the conformation of the country from our own
observation, extending over no small surface. If
the centre of Africa were an elevated mountain-
land, how could there be a flow towards the north
of the whole series of rivers which the Portuguese
cross on their route from east to west? And why
have we not, flowing from the south side of the
so-called Mountains of the Moon, a river similar
to the Congo in the west, and the Dana and Jub
in the east, which could not be much inferior to
the Nile or the Chadda? Both these questions
are completely solved by the supposition of an
inland-sea in Central Africa. The chief features
then of the geographical conformation of Central
Africa would thus be a very decided declivity from
the north-west and south, forming an enormous
basin in the centre; but towards the east an extensive plain upon which, however, there is a very
remarkable series of single and perfectly isolated
mountains and mountain-groups, some of which the
all-wise Creator and Architect of the earth has
crowned with perennial snow, just where it is hottest,

close to the Equator, to cool and refresh the earth, which seem to form the links of a chain running from south to north to join the so-called Mountains of the Moon, just where we have to look for the more eastern sources of the White Nile. Its western sources are probably close together in the neighbourhood of the Shary, which flows into the Tsad, and of the Chadda which joins the Niger. If so the Arabian writers of the middle ages, as well as European geographers up to the middle of the last century, would be quite correct in their assertion that the Niger by means of its tributary, the Chadda, rises near the sources of the Nile, and pursuing a westerly course through the continent pours its waters into the Atlantic Ocean. The mountain-groups referred to, in so far as we ourselves have seen them, from south to north, are chiefly the following :— Ngu, Usambara with Pare, Bura with Ndara and Kadiaro, Kilimanjaro with Shira, Kisongo with Ugono, the snow-mountain Kenia (Kegnia), seen by Dr. Krapf in the distance, along with Kikuyu. That none of these mountains form terraces which lead to more elevated lands, and that Kilimanjaro is not, as Dr. Kiepert figures it in his Atlas, a mountain-range, or part of mountain-chain, but a completely isolated mountain-mass, merely surrounded by smaller and likewise isolated mountains, we have convinced ourselves with our own eyes. The mountain-range, some 1500 feet high, and only some four leagues from the coast which stretches from the bay of Kilefi to Usambara, and is inhabited by the

Wanika, is the only approach to such a terrace. A section of it lying inland from Mombaz is nothing else than our own Rabbai, with Rabbai Mpia and Kisuludini where we are stationed. From Kilefi to Ras Ngome there is also a smaller mountain-ridge in the Galla-land. But thence, as far as Cape Gerdaf the land rises very gently and imperceptibly from the coast towards the interior. In general the country to the south of Usambara as far as Cape Delgado or Mgau presents the same character. It is well worthy of remark that the small elevated land which is borne, as it were, on the shoulders of the Wanika-mountains, rather sinks than rises as you go further inland; indeed at a good day's journey from our station you have to descend a declivity some 150 feet deep, called 'Ndunguni,' which forms a semicircle from Usambara to Ukam-bani, so that, on his journey to Ukambani Dr. Krapf had first to descend, and then at Yata to ascend the heights again. So little do the mountains of Teita form a terrace, that on the journey to Jagga you would leave them altogether on the one side, were it not that you have to purchase food from their inhabitants. Then again, the country slopes gently towards the foot of Kilimanjaro, and in the west of it, as well as round about it, I saw to my surprise the same plain again spreading out no higher than to the east of it, like the smooth surface of the sea. Our African informants, too, who proceed from the various points of the coast already mentioned in a south-westerly, westerly, or north-westerly direction, to the great inland-sea, are all unanimous in declaring that any one who maintains that there are mountains to be traversed in their journeys, is neither more nor less than a liar. Certainly there are mountains, but these are, they say, like houses, which you do not climb over but go round as you proceed. Only in the immediate proximity of the lake, which is called Niassa, the traveller has to cross a pretty high mountain-range stretching along its eastern shore, and the depth of his descent on the western side corresponds with the height of his ascent on the eastern. This mountain-range which is, as it were, a wall and water-shed to the lake, and which, according to my servant from Kumpande has in the west a similar and corresponding elevation, is probably joined in the north by other separate and isolated mountains, mountain-chains, and mountain-groups, where the not unimportant rivers Lufiji and Rufuma have their sources, until we come to the Ngu group, from which the further continuation of the chain as far as the Equator is known to us from personal survey.

"To come to further details respecting this inland-sea shut in on three sides, at first its southern opening, according to our African informants, is so narrow that people on the opposite shores can call to each other; and here seems to be the first ferry, called 'Zandinge,'—come and fetch me. The next ferry, further northward, lies between the village Msauka, on the western shore, and Mjangga on the eastern, between which a boat crosses only twice or thrice a day. The next ferry has an intermediate station, the island of Mount Mbaazuru (height). Passengers stop there the first day of their passage across, spend the night on it, and go on the next day. Still further to the north is the ferry between Zenga on the western, and Gnombo on the eastern shore, where it takes the boat the whole day to make the passage, or according to the African mode of reckoning, from cock-crow to the return of the fowls to their roosts. This passage is considered so dangerous, that it is only attempted when there is not a breath of wind and when, therefore, sails are not necessary, and merely oars are used. Nor do father and son, or two brothers, ever go together in the same boat, in order that they may avoid a common death. To ascertain beforehand the complete absence of wind they drop thrice during the same day meal from their hands upon the earth. If the meal falls every time straight to the ground the passage is undertaken next day. This is called, 'Ku demba Nianja,' examination òf the Niassa. If they return in safety from crossing this ferry, they hold a joyful feast, called Kirosi. Any one who never attempts to cross, is nick-named ' Kiwerenga Masira,' egg-counter—perhaps somewhat equivalent to the English stay-at-home term, ' Mammy's apron-string.'

" The eastern shore of the lake is inhabited by the Wajania, a tribe of Wahiaos, who are spread out for a considerable distance towards the sea-coast, and are called Wanguru by the tribes who live to the west of the lake. Along the western shore we find the Wamaravi first, whose district is called Maravi, whence the lake has been wrongly designated Marovi on some old maps. The Wamaravi (people of Maravi) inhabit partly the plain, which extends for about half a day's journey westward from the lake, and partly also the eastern declivity of the elevated mountain-land, which meets us here. Such of them as live close by the shore of the lake are also called Wanianja (people of Nianja or Niassa). On the elevated mountain-land itself, we find the Wakamdunda, literally highlanders, to whom our servant from Kumpande belongs. Besides these there are Wamuera and Wakumbodo (or Wambodo), that is, south and north countrymen, clearly appellations derived from the Lake Niassa, and the suitability of which becomes more striking, when it is known that where the Wakumbodo begin the lake forsakes its northern direction, bends round to the north-west and west, and so receives the rivers coming from the south, the Roanga, the Zambezi (not to be confounded with the other Zambezi, which flows eastward, and is also called Kilimani), the Murusura, the Roapura, the Mufira, the Guarava, and the Rofoe. The large stream Bua flows some two days' journey northward from the country of my Kumpande servant, and receives the smaller rivers, Zaru, Pfubui, Mde, Mdede, Kakuyu. When the lake, as already mentioned, bends round to the west, it seems to be so broad that no communication takes place between the opposite shores; and on their fishing expeditions the Wakumbodo are said not to go beyond the nearest islands. To what extent westward this collection of waters stretches, before it again bends round to the west; of its extent northward, and the probable breadth of the Ukerewe, as the inland-sea there is called; and, finally, as to the position of the wonderful island, Mount Kavogo, said by the natives to touch the skies, and on which, according to tradition, the deity who owns the Ukerewe dwells, and manifests his mercy and his wrath in various ways; are points to which the reader is referred to the elaborate and admirably executed map of my dear fellow-labourer, Erhardt.*

"My informant, Salimini, told me further that in his country the year has only two divisions, Mu-amfu, the hot, and Zinja, the cold or rainy season. The cold there reaches a point at which the leaves fall from the trees, and all the grass withers; and even the water freezes where it is standing in small quantities. The soil seems to be extremely fer-tile and the inhabitants would live in the greatest comfort, if they had not been induced by the Por-tuguese slave-traders to hunt and sell each other. The Portuguese, who are called Wakogunda, have two settlements in that country in the vicinity of Kumpande, the one called Kubale, the other Kum-koma."

Thus far my friend Rebmann, the chief facts con-

* Erhardt's Map was published in "The Proceedings of the Royal Geographical Society," and "The Church Missionary Intelligencer" of 1856.

tained in whose interesting communication have been confirmed and elucidated by the explorations made by Major Burton and Captain Speke in their expedition from Zanzibar to Uniamesi in 1857.*

As regards myself, so far back as the period of my arrival in Eastern Africa in the year 1844, I heard of an inland-sea in Uniamesi as well as of the Lake Niassa. The inland-sea of Uniamesi was designated to me under the name of Tanganika, the name by which it was known in the part where my informant had seen it. When in Ukambani in 1851 too, I had heard of a mighty inland-sea, the end of which was not to be reached even after a journey of 100 days. Of the existence of an enormous lake in the interior I had long been convinced; but whether the Lake Niassa is connected with that of Uniamesi may be doubtful, more especially as I heard from several African travellers, such as Bana Kheri, that the lakes were completely separated from one another.

I join heartily in the wish expressed by my dear friend Rebmann, and in his longing for the time when the messengers of peace shall sail on the Nile, and that arm of the Niger, the Chadda, from the north, and on the Zambezi or Kilimani from the coast to the Ukerewe sea, and after a longer or shorter land journey in the heart of Africa, proceed to proclaim the merciful year of the Lord and the day of salvation to the teeming millions on its shores.

---

* Another expedition, to explore the sources of the Nile, is at present about to proceed to the countries bordering on Lake Niassa, under Captains Speke and Grant.

I am persuaded that the work which in our great weakness we have commenced in Eastern Africa will not be allowed by the Lord to pass away; but that He will stir up His people to continue it with energy, and to complete it with glory. But our own too sanguine expectations,—the flesh, ever anxious to rejoice in its own achievements, must first perish; so that we may render all the glory not to ourselves, but to the Lord, who at His own appointed season and hour will also establish His kingdom in Eastern Africa.

———

In conclusion, I cannot refrain from adding to Rebmann's important communication, the following interesting memoir from my dear fellow-labourer Erhardt, on

THE RESOURCES AND PRODUCTS OF THE WANIKA-LAND.

" Two things are necessary to the attainment of a correct idea as to the resources of this country, in so far as they serve for the maintenance of the natives or admit of extension, or as the means of promoting a hopeful intercourse with other nations. The first is a thorough investigation of products actually existing, whether they belong to the animal or vegetable systems; the other, a survey of the resources that can be opened up by the increased diligence of the natives, in cultivating these products, as well as by the introduction of foreign animals and plants suited to the climate. Add to this a glance at the means of taxation, in order to render more clearly the nature of the intercourse which may eventually be looked for between Europe and these distant countries.

" That the present period of interference on the part of Said-Said, Sultan of Zanzibar, with the affairs of these coast-tribes is of great importance for our missionary labours is not to be denied; and we must above all things make perfectly clear the mode in which we can best urge on the work confided to us, for the benefit of our Wanika people. No doubt, our great mission is to preach Christ and Him crucified; but as there is no spiritual development possible without a worldly one—as no man after being awakened by the light of the Gospel, can remain in the debased state to which heathenism has confined him, it becomes our duty so to labour that, with its light the temporal blessings of Christianity may be diffused among these uncivilized tribes; or as Mr. Moffat, the missionary, has very forcibly said: ' Instead of sinking to the low stage of existence occupied by the natives, a descent to which there are great temptations, we must always labour to raise our converts to our own level." If riches come without Christianity, they are poison to the soul, instead of a benefit; but if they follow as the result of Christianity, they entwine around the Gospel, and identify themselves with the missionary. From this often proceeds an appeal for the presence of a missionary; the heathen seeing that it brings temporal benefits with it. The influence to be in future exerted on the interior of Africa by an organized mission, will be manifested just as it has been manifested in South and Western Africa. Commercial intercourse, too, will then not only receive a new impulse, for Christian commerce and Christian teaching go hand in hand, but as resulting from the teaching, what is much more important for us, tidings of the Book of the Europeans will be borne into the interior and indirectly pave the way for our missionary labours. But so long as our missions are not embodied into a community, however small, so long will Christianity be unable to reveal itself in its complete form, and produce that impression which has always hitherto attracted the heathen.

"It is very remarkable to observe how of late Mohammedanism has been forced to assume a protecting attitude towards missionary effort in Egypt and the Turkish empire, and as it seems, even now in this land of outer darkness. Under this protection, however feeble, it is clearly our duty to prosecute our work with unceasing diligence. When Christianity has once taken root, though the secular arm is not powerful enough to protect it, there is ever One at hand to watch over it.

" The sources of the food of a people are not only such as it cultivates and maintains, but also those which nature and the peculiar circumstances of the country spontaneously offer to man. Among the former are the breeding of cattle and tillage of the land ; among the latter, wild animals and wild fruits.

" The sources of animal food are sustained by the

breeding of cattle; and by the war man wages with wild animals, or game, by shooting, fowling, hunting, and fishing.

" The animals existing among the Wanika are the following:—

a. Cattle and poultry:—

Gnombe, black cattle; Kondo, sheep; Mbusi, goats; Punda, donkeys; Kuku, fowls; and Bata, ducks.

b. Wild animals:

" If we consider the number of destructive animals found in the vicinity, we may easily picture to ourselves the lazy, listless life in which the natives pass away their days. Nature rules so perfectly uncontrolled, that even land capable of cultivation is surrendered to monkeys, apes, and wild swine, and left to run wild as part of the wilderness.

"In the following list of animals I have confined myself to such as are met within the Rabbais, and their neighbourhood:—

Embawa mke,	Kuro (dog),	Niati (buffalo),
Funo,	Lobe,	Niumbu,
Kemgu mume,	Malu,	Pa (a kind of
Kongoni,	Mburumbu,	antelope),
Kuagna-sa,	Ngawa (civet cat),	Witungule (hares).

" Among the beasts of prey:—Simba (lion), Gala, Tui (leopard), Fisi (hyæna), Kiboko (crocodile) Kiniegere (Fel. Lynx).

" Among birds (besides the birds of prey, which include a great variety of the falcon tribe) are the Kanga, Kororo, Kuinsi, Ninga, and Ndiwa (pigeon).

" The second chief source of nourishment on which man depends is the soil.

"In the Wanika-land is no soil which is absolutely incapable of cultivation, and its products might be increased at least sixty-fold, when there would still remain pasture and forest-land sufficient to provide for all the wants of the inhabitants. The fruits of the field and of trees which we see cultivated are inconsiderable in quantity, because there is an absence of the necessary energy to till the ground, and also because the inhabitants have no markets for the surplus.

" The cereals and edible vegetables are:—

Mpunga (rice),	Mbasi, ⎫	Madango,
Mtama (tufted maize),	Kunde, ⎬ cereals,	Tungudsha,
Mahindi (Indian corn),	Fiwi (beans),	Wimumunia,
Muhogo (cassave),	Fiasi (sweet potatoes),	Nduniasa,
Uwimbi, ⎫ cereals,	Fiasi manga (yam),	Ndu mawe,
Muelle, ⎬	Ndisi (bananas),	Mandano.
	Kimanga,	Mbonó (Thicinus).
	Podsho,	

" The oleaginous plants are the following:— Mbono, Mafuta tanga, Tondo, Kweme, Nasi.

"Resin and gum are contained in:—Handsha, copal.

Amongst the fruits cultivated will be found:—

Mdellasini (cinnamon tree),	Mfenesi (bread-tree),	Mnasi (cocoa-nut tree),
Makuadsha (Tamarinde).	Muembe (mango),	Mjungua (orange-tree),
	Mpera (guava),	
———	Msambarao,	Mlimau (citron-tree),
	Mgandshu,	Mdimu (lime-tree),
Mua (sugar cane),	Mkoma munga,	Mpapaju,
Mbamba (cotton plant),	Mtomoko,	Mgrufu (clove tree),
	Mnanasi (pine-apple),	Msufi.

"Among the many trees growing wild which bear fruit, we may mention: Mkunasi, Mgunga, Mbungo, Vitoria, Vipo, Futu, &c.

"The useful forest trees which produce wood suited for houses and ships, or are adapted for cabinet-makers' work, are: — Mfule (of a reddish colour, and well suited for planks and boards), Mbambakofi, Muafi, Mdshe, Mdshani, Mkoko, Mgnambo, Mtiwa shibili, Mdshje, Mgurure (teak), Mismari, Mkuaju, Mfunda, Mpingo (ebony), Mbawa, Kikuata (*Acacia vera*, producing gum arabic), Mtondo, Msikundasi, Mkomafi, Msandarisi (producing copal : its wood is hard, resinous, and used for the masts of ships).*

"Looking at the multiplicity of the products of the country enumerated above, and at its uncultivated condition, it is clear that there is no necessity for the introduction of foreign products, if an improvement can be made in the cultivation of those which already exist in the country.

"With such a list before us, it is not a difficult matter to answer the obvious question: What can and should be done to benefit the interior of this great continent ?

"The influence which one people exerts upon another is, in general, regulated by its wealth. If

---

* Other forest trees found on the East-coast are: Mkomasi (a red wood), Mgurusi (a very hard wood for beams), Msimbati, Mgniemsu, Mleha, Mnaninga (a hard, yellowish red wood), Mkalambaki (the wood has a pleasant odour, is blackish, and takes a good polish), and Mtata.

a people becomes impoverished, its influence abroad will decrease in proportion to the decrease of its internal prosperity. The social reasons on which such a dogma is based, always presuppose that "worldly prosperity follows in the wake of Christianity." It is, consequently, certain, that if the tribes of the coast are to influence those of the interior, they must first be elevated in the social scale. Our duty and self-proposed labour as missionaries should thus be to rouse the natives to be more diligent in agriculture, and in cattle-breeding; to impress upon them the advantages of both; to point out to them such articles as are most profitable; and finally, to place within their reach such animals and seeds as can be usefully introduced for their benefit.

"The breeding of cattle and poultry should first have attention paid to it, and should be increased in an extraordinary degree. A more extensive breeding of oxen, cows, goats, sheep, asses, fowls, ducks, geese, and turkeys (the two last, as yet, quite unknown), would add to the prosperity of the natives both at home and elsewhere. Peltry, too, including the skins of wild animals, should go hand in hand with the trade in ivory and horns; for example, in the case of buffaloes and rhinoceroses; nor should the profit to be derived from the Ngawa, civet-cat, be overlooked.

"As regards new animals, it might be desirable to introduce the domestic hog and Egyptian sheep, the latter of which would yield not only a very

quick, but a very profitable return. Wool and
cotton are two articles which are in constant demand in England, and which, if cultivated to any
extent, would ultimately contribute to bring these
countries under European protection; and the eastern coast of Africa could almost produce cotton
enough to satisfy the demands of the whole of
England, and thus in promoting the growth of
sheep and cotton a powerful blow would be dealt
to the American slave-trade.

" As regards, in the second place, agriculture and
planting, it is questionable whether this country
could ever be a granary for other lands; however
enough might be produced to meet the demands of
the interior. Of the following productions a sale
might be anticipated abroad:—

" 1. Munga, Mlimau, Mdimu (oranges, limes,
lemons, which, on account of their juice, are used
in great quantities by the English navy).

" 2. Ukuadshu (tamarindes, exported in casks,
after hot syrup has been poured over them).

" 3. Mua (sugar-cane).

" 4. Grafu, Dellasini, Mandano.

" 5. Bamba, cotton, and Sufu—(both of them cultivated and growing wild; the latter growing on
high trees, and used as a substitute for cotton and
feathers in stuffing beds).

" 6. Uwanga (arrow-root, grows wild in large
quantities).

" 7. Kauma (calamus, or sweet-flag).

" 8. Various kinds of oils:—

a. Mbono (*Palma Christi*).

b. Mafuta ya nasi (cocoanut-oil).

c. Mafuta Tanga, which has lately come into use.

d. Tondo and Kweme, only important as being oleaginous.

e. Semsem.

" As regards the products of the interior, all long known, of most importance, are:—

a. Ivory.

b. Horns of the Kifaru (rhinoceros).

c. Horns of the Niati (Buffalo).

d. Tusks of the Mamba (Hippopotamus).

e. Horns of different Antelopes.

f. Ostrich-feathers.

" As these nations rise in the social scale, the mineral productions of the soil will also be made available. Amongst these coal and iron are the most important; the former, the use of which is still unknown to the natives, is met with in many parts, and the latter, more particularly in Ukambani and Jagga. Antimony is found in Daruma; cornelians and other precious stones in Wabilikimo; and the natives manufacture various articles, such as pretty mats, all of which might be made available as means of spreading the Gospel amongst a nation meted out and trodden down.

" As regards taxation, the condition of the people and of their property must be clearly kept in view; from which it is evident that a king would be unable to levy taxes in kind, as to do so would require beforehand an extended and organized administration, which would cost more than could be drawn from the poor Schamba, or plantations, of the Wanika; and consequently such an impost would degenerate into violence and extortion. Taxation of this kind would not only be useless to the king, but directly injurious to the Wanika.

"As all the Wanika individually, in point of wealth, are on a tolerable equality one with another, a poll-tax would suit them best. Ivory might, perhaps, be indirectly taxed as an article of export, and other indirect taxation levied for a time upon all articles exported or imported. After the general productive power of the nation shall have increased, and the Wanika become more removed from one another in point of income, each branch of productive and remunerative industry might be taxed, and the poll-tax abolished; but it is desirable that at first all industry should not be checked by heavy taxation. To tax a marriageable young man two dollars a year would not be too much; for he could easily raise his two dollars without being oppressed, by collecting copal, rearing goats, or from the sale of cocoanuts and palm-wine, Indian-corn, &c. He would, indeed, require to be somewhat more industrious than he usually is, and to be less addicted to drinking; but that is just what is to be wished for in the case of every Wanika of them all."

And now that I have communicated these two most interesting and important contributions of my dear friends Rebmann and Erhardt to the geography, natural history, and social economy of Eastern Africa, my work draws to a close; but I would first impress the following points on the attention of missionaries who are destined to labour in that region of the continent:—

1. Resist with all the power of faith, of prayer and of truth, that mood of despondency and faint-heartedness, which is disposed to say with the men sent to spy out the land of Canaan, "We be not able to go up against the people; for they are stronger than we." The state of the East-African heathen, their indifference towards all that is spiritual, or to any progress in mere human affairs, (they are, as Rebmann rightly says, "profitable in nothing either to God or to the world,") may easily beget in the heart of a missionary a mood of disappointment, in which he would say with Isaiah, "I have laboured in vain; I have spent my strength for nought, and in vain." At times, you may be assailed and tried by this mood, in order that you may be made mindful of your own utter want of power, and of complete dependence on the Lord, lest you should think that the heathen are given to you, and not to Him, as an inheritance. But this casual desponding must not become habitual, otherwise you will be cast down and numbered amongst the faint-hearted who stand without the gates of the city of God. Labour on courageously, faithfully, patiently, and believingly; for "to continue labouring in patience," says our venerated prelate Œttinger, "is in itself vic-

tory." Examine yourself at the same time to discover whether your present want of confidence, and your despondency, do not arise from a foregone self-confidence — an egotistical self-sufficiency, which sought to proceed only according to its own thoughts and plans. Or perhaps you have entered upon the fight without due preparation, and have imagined that you could soon lead a great host of these heathen to the Cross; and because this has not happened you look upon it as too difficult, and deem that nothing is to be done for the great cause. Let your first care be to convert the heathen within your own heart, your self-confidence, your self-love. Be modest, but not faint-hearted, and the Lord will show you His mercy!

2. Seek in East-Africa to root out all longing for a life of ease and comfort, and accommodate yourself to the lowliest.

Many a young missionary when he arrives from Europe, wishes forthwith to make himself stationary in some heathen district, and to settle down comfortably behind bolt and bar at some place on the coast, instead of moving about for five or six years, until the fruits of his labours make it necessary to exchange his provisional arrangement for a more fixed dwelling-place. The wish to settle down as comfortably as possible and to marry entangles a missionary in many external engagements which may lead him away from his Master and his duty. This wish naturally prompts him to trouble himself about irrelevant or subordinate matters, such for instance, as house-building, all sorts of colonizing schemes, and scientific labours; till by degrees he puts the chief matter of all, the promulgation of the Gospel, on the shelf. He goes no more, or less frequently, among the heathen; does not seek them out in their huts; but thinks, "They know where I live; if they care for the salvation of their souls they can come to me to my house, where I have more room than in their narrow, smoky, gloomy, vermin-breeding huts." Do not allow anything to keep you from your true field of action; go and seek the heathen, speak to them respecting the salvation of their souls, and in time there will come a blessing on yourself, upon your labours, and upon them. But at the same time do not become a mere rolling-stone, but choose head-quarters whence you may go forth, and whither you may return to collect your thoughts and refresh your frame.

3. Be not either wearied by or angry at the annoying mendicancy of the natives. Display no unnecessary outward splendour, lest the people regard you as wealthy and consider themselves justified in begging everything they can from you. Deny yourself, that you may be able to give so much the more to the sick, the poor, and the stranger-guest of the people, among whom you live. Do not expect to receive as a matter of course from the bounty of the people and its chiefs such things as water, wood, shelter, &c.; but be grateful for everything, and show that gratitude by plentiful acts of love, which in the sight of God are as acceptable, and no less efficacious

as any miracle worked by the immediate followers of
our Lord.   Let your life be the embodiment of your
teaching, otherwise your teaching among the heathen
will become a burden; you will grow weary and long
to be away from a barren soil, where your self-
idolatry finds neither nourishment nor satisfaction.
Think of the missionaries in Labrador, in Green-
land, and in the islands of the South Seas, who must
toil and deny themselves much more than you have
need to do.   Remember that capital invested in the
conversion of the heathen will be repaid with interest when they are converted.   They will then
give to the Missionary-fund instead of taking from
it.*   But guard yourself from thinking that giving
is an artificial means by which the heathen may be
attracted to Christianity.   That were the Jesuits'
principle of driving out one devil by another.   Whoever thinks to convert the heathen by merely external
means, is himself still a heathen, and knows not the
power of God.   Give yourself up in love daily to
your God and to heathen fellow-men, so shall you
learn the right mode of giving outwardly without
covetousness and without prodigality.

4. Respect an old and experienced missionary,
even although he should take little heed of your
thoughts and suggestions as those of a novice.   But
do not accept unconditionally everything that he
says or does, when either his sayings or his doings

---

* At home, you are every day accosted by beggars and asked for
alms.   And you yourself are a beggar; for men beg for you, that
they may have the means of sending you to convert the heathen.

appear at variance with the revealed Word of God. If, at the commencement of his course, a young missionary can humble himself among others, good will come of him; but if, at starting, he insists on criticising everything, and on having everything done according to his own fancy, he will bring ruin upon himself and the Mission together. No wonder that God arrests many a one in his course by an early death. Better death than a fall, or backsliding, and a slackening of his pace in his spiritual career. This may happen, too, because the person desired to carry out his own wishes exclusively, and would not remain at home in some humbler station, bearing his cross in simplicity and truth, and seeking to convert himself. If you will not uproot your own self-will at home, God may lead you out into the world of the heathen, and there allow you to die, and after death you will vainly repent that you did not pay greater heed to the will of God, but by the obstinacy of your own self-will became your own murderer. Search your heart, therefore, to see whether your own or God's spirit calls you to the heathen. Many a one need not have died, and many a one could have died more blessed, if he could have separated himself from himself, and have committed himself to the mercy and power of God; in one word, if he could have made his *Ego* to disappear so that Christ might have dwelt within him. If any one repairs to the heathen with over-wrought spiritual ideas, ideas, therefore, not conformable to Scripture, he is sure

soon to become carnal and worldly, because he
aimed at being too unworldly. Therefore free yourself more and more from all that is not conformable
to God's truth. If any one has a call to go into the
heathen world, and, from a love of comfort or any
other impure motive, does not go forth, he will lose
his Christianity as certainly as he who has gone forth
only to gratify his self-will. Yet if both become
sobered in time, recognising the error of their ways,
and humbling themselves before God, then all may
have been for the best and may help to further them
on their way; for God is willing to convert our
faults into blessings, if we repent us of the same, and
the very circumstance which made us stumble, can
and will serve to raise us up again, provided we do
not keep ever brooding over the fault, but cast our
care upon the Lamb of God, who careth for us, and
both can and will save and snatch us out of all
trouble. Only do not look merely upon your sin
and sorrow, nor desire to be unaided help to yourself,
but trust to the power, love and mercy of God in
Christ Jesus, who can and is willing to raise up them
that fall, and to blot out every sin.

5. Expect nothing, or very little, from political
changes in Eastern Africa. As soon as you begin to
anticipate much good for missionary labour from
politics, you will be in danger of mixing yourself up
with them. Do not think that because the East-
Africans are " profitable in nothing to God and
the world," they ought to be brought under the
dominion of some European power, in the hope that

they may then bestir themselves more actively and eagerly for what is worldly, and, in consequence, become eventually more awake to what is spiritual and eternal. On the contrary, banish the thought that Europe must spread her protecting wings over Eastern Africa, if missionary work is to prosper in that land of outer darkness. Europe would, no doubt, remove much that is mischievous and obstructive out of the way of missionary work, but she would probably set in its place as many, and perhaps, still greater checks. It is a vital error to make the result of missionary labour dependent on the powers that be. Accept the development and the condition of the heathen as you find them. Be not led away either by the low or high condition of their culture ; by the dulness or the enthusiasm of any heathen people. Assail the heathen only with the sword of the Spirit, with the Word of God, and the right hand of the Lord will vanquish at last, if only at first as with us at Rabbai Mpia, by the conversion of a single soul. The great thing is for you to recognise that the Lord has called you to be a soldier of the Cross. I am assured that it was through the guidance of the Lord that I went to Eastern Africa, and found myself among the Wanika and Wakamba; therefore I am no less certain that the Word of God will be victorious among them, if it is preached to them with energy, without interruption for years. Whether Europeans take possession of Eastern Africa or not, I care very little, if at all; yet I know full well, that missionary labour has its human phase, and that it cannot, as if by magic, without any outward preparation of the people for its reception, grasp the life of a nation. But many persons vastly overrate this human phase of our work and, like the Jew, wish to see the bottom of the water before they cross the river. In Eastern Africa the presence of Europeans, especially of the English in Mombaz, has done quite as much in this way as a missionary can wish. It is not missionaries, but those who are not missionaries, who see impossibilities in the way of the regeneration of Eastern Africa. " Where there is a will," says the English proverb, " there is a way," and this saying is worthy of that self-reliant people, and the key to that indomitable perseverance which is their great characteristic. Prosecute your missionary work along the whole coast from Barava to Cape Delgado, and you will find everywhere an opening; but be not led astray by the heathen materialism of Eastern Africa, nor by human reason, nor by the long apparent barrenness of your labours. Keep in mind that St. Paul, when the Son was revealed within him, " that he might preach among the heathen, conferred not with flesh and blood, but went into Arabia," and, as he did, preach Christ crucified to the Heathen.

SUPPLEMENTARY CHAPTER.

NOTES ON EAST-AFRICAN HISTORY.

The Arabs of the coast and Eastern Africa—The Hamiaritic Kings, Solomon and the Phœnicians—Solomon, the Queen of Sheba, and the Phœnician king, Hiram—The East-African coast, the Ophir of the Bible—Proofs philological and Scriptural—Notices of Eastern Africa in ancient writers—The Periplus of Arrian—Ptolemy—Cosmas—New era in the history of Eastern Africa :—the Mohammedan Arabs—Arab settlements on the coast—Portuguese conquest of Eastern Africa—Decline of the Portuguese power and its causes—The princes of Oman and Eastern Africa—Said-Said and the Msara of Mombaz—Long struggle for supremacy over Mombaz and the East-African coast—Mombaz adopts the Protectorate of England—Refusal of Government to sanction the arrangement—Said-Said's career, character, and death—Europe and Eastern Africa.

AMONG the most important phenomena in the early history of Eastern Africa must have been the intercourse kept up with it by the inhabitants of the Arabian sea-board. The southern coast of Arabia must from the earliest period have been necessarily connected with Eastern Africa by the wants of its inhabitants. From Eastern Africa the Arab of the coast derived his corn, his rice, his Durra, his wood, his ivory, and especially his slaves.

It is so to-day, and it must have been so from immemorial antiquity. Such being the case, it is extremely probable that when the Hamiaritic kings and the Arabs had thus recognised their dependence upon it, and had once established commercial relations with Eastern Africa, and obtained a footing on its coast, they would desire to exclude all other nations, especially the Egyptians, from a share in this commerce; and that with this design, more especially to keep the power of Egypt in check, these South-Arabs would be disposed to form a close connection with the greatest ruler of Western Asia, King Solomon. According to this theory it may have been in part a political connection which was formed between Solomon and the Queen of Sheba, who was at once a South-Arab potentate and sovereign of Abessinia, and ruler of the coast of Eastern Africa lying southward. The policy of the king of commercial Phœnicia would naturally coincide with that of these two great sovereigns. The Phœnicians had probably attempted to establish a direct intercourse with the Red Sea and the Arabs by means of Egypt; but the Egyptians were not fond of the sea; their monarchs were too haughty, self-seeking, and exclusive; nor, had it been otherwise, would the Arabs have been disposed to allow the energetic Phœnicians to compete with them on the seas of the south. All the more welcome then to the Phœnicians must have been the alliance which Solomon contracted with their King Hiram, in accordance with which they received a port in Idumea on the Red Sea, apparently, amongst other things, for the purpose of teaching the Israelites both shipbuilding and navigation. Hence we read in 1 Kings ix. 26—28 : " And king Solomon made a navy of ships in Ezion-Geber, which is beside Eloth, on the shore of the Red Sea, in the land of Edom. And Hiram sent in the navy his servants, shipmen that had knowledge of the sea, with the servants of Solomon. And they came to Ophir, and fetched from thence gold, four hundred and twenty talents, and brought it to King Solomon." And again, in 1 Kings x. 22, we read: "For the king had at sea a navy at Tharshish with the navy of Hiram : once in three years came the navy of Tharshish, bringing gold, and silver, ivory, and apes, and peacocks." That the Ophir of the Bible is to be sought for on the eastern coast of Africa is evident from two circumstances. One is, that right opposite to Arabia Felix there is to be found a people who call themselves " Afer," the Danakil, called by others Adals, or Danakil, from their chief tribe " Ad Alli," but whose designation in their own language is " Afer." In the second place, it must be considered that Ophir beyond a doubt means gold-dust ; for in Job xxviii. 6, the words " dust of gold " in Hebrew are " Ophirot Sahab." Now it was chiefly gold that the Arabs, as well as the Phœnicians and Israelites wished to discover ; so the word Ophir was thus made to comprise two things, the name of a people and of a substance ; and the land of the people called Afer was simply the land where Æfer Sahab, gold-dust, was found. Although the Adal-land was not precisely the gold-dust country, yet it formed the commencement of the line of coast on which, as in Sofala, gold of the purest quality was found in large quantities. That Ophir cannot have been Arabia-Felix,* nor the coast of Malabar, or the island of Ceylon, as has been maintained, is easily demonstrated from the nature of the objects which are said to have been brought from it. Neither in Arabia, nor in India, is there either gold or silver in sufficient quantity for export. As there is scarcely enough for the wants of themselves, how could the Arabs or Indians have been in a position to export gold in the quantities indicated in 1 Kings ix. 28? As to ivory, there is none at all in Arabia; and that of India is much less useful than that of Africa. There are, it is true, apes in abundance, both in Arabia and India; but then the question arises, what kind of ape is alluded to? Very probably Solomon as a naturalist was desirous of obtaining living specimens of the fine ape Guresa† (*Colobus*), of which, as far as I know, no living specimen has hitherto been brought to Europe. This family of the ape is found in Abessinia, chiefly in Shoa, in the vicinity of the Adal or Afer country. It is true that peacocks are

---

* The locality Dafar in Southern Arabia has been fixed on by some as the Ophir of the Bible; but no dangerous voyage of three years would have been needful to reach it, and from it all articles of commerce might have been brought by land on camels; just as the Queen of Sheba, to whom Dafar certainly belonged, went to Jerusalem by land.

† The guresa has fine black hair on its back, and white on its stomach.

not met with in Eastern Africa, but it may be questioned whether the Hebrew word "Tukijim" means precisely peacocks, or whether it may not rather be taken to denote the guinea-hen, which abounds in Eastern Africa and especially in Abessinia.

Passing over the various references in ancient writers to the alleged circumnavigation of Africa, we come to the Periplus of the Erythræan sea, ascribed to Arrian, and the date of which is referred by none to a period posterior to A. D. 210. The account given in the Periplus of the voyage along the East-African coast is most interesting to any one who has a knowledge of the localities; and in reading it, I feel as if the author had lived in our time and been a modern traveller. We find him quitting Egypt in July, sailing in August or September along the Somali coast, and reaching Cape Guardafui in the middle of October. On his way he ran into the chief havens, after the present fashion of the natives. With the aid of the north-east wind he sailed in November from Cape Guardafui along the eastern coast, which he calls A-zanie, and which afterwards (in the sixth century) was called Zingium, or coast of the Sendsch, whence Sendschibar or Sanguebar, Zanzibar, country of the blacks or slaves. From Zanzibar he seems to have reached the mouth of the river Lufidschi, which I take to be meant by the Rhapta of his narrative. The chronicle abounds with details which can be verified by any traveller in our day. In his description of the East-African coast the great geographer, Ptolemy,* falls far short of the author of the Periplus, either, perhaps, because he wrote before the latter, or because he wrote, not as an eye-witness, but as a compiler from the accounts of others. With the decay of the Roman empire the Greeks and Romans ceased from enterprises in distant lands; and we hear consequently little afterwards from them about Eastern Africa. From the description given of it in his "Topographia," by Cosmas, in the sixth century, we see how little the Greeks and Romans knew of it four hundred years after Ptolemy and the Periplus. No wonder then

---

* He tells that "a certain pilot of the name of Dioscorus makes the distance from Rhapta to Cape Prasum about 5000 stadia," which would place Prasum somewhere near our Mosambique. Diogenes, the voyager, was driven by a north wind in twenty-five days to the marshes on which the Nile has its source, and these marshes were to the north of Cape Rhaptum. Ptolemy enumerates the following as the chief places on the East-African coast:—"In the first gulf is the village of Pans, a day's journey from Aromata, and the market town of Opone is six days' beyond the village. Close to Opone is another gulf, just where Azania begins, at the entrance of which are the promontory Zingis and Mount Phalargis, with its triple summit. This gulf is called Apokopes, and it takes two days and two nights to sail across it, when the shore is formed into two divisions, one three days in length and the other five, and adjoining the latter is another gulf, on which is the market town of Essina, which is reached by water in two days and two nights. In twenty-four hours after leaving the gulf of Essina the harbour of Sæarapion is reached, and thence begins another gulf, at the entrance to which is the commercial town of Niki, and by means of which in three days and three nights Rhapta is approached. Into Cape Rhaptum flows a river upon which the capital of the country is situated, both having the same name. Along the coast which stretches from Rhapta to the promontory of Prasum, forming a large shallow gulf, dwell none but savage, naked cannibals."

that the Arabs resumed their original monopoly
without molestation, as barbarism gained the upper
hand in Europe, Egypt, and Asia Minor, upon the fall
of the Roman Empire. Their supremacy became
fixed by the rise and growth of Mohammedanism,
which gave them political unity, and sent them forth
as conquerors in every direction. Of course, so
long as they were pagans they founded no regular
states and kingdoms in Eastern Africa ; nor were its
law-givers conquerors or colonizers, but merely
traders with commercial establishments. The reason
of this lay in the fact that in Arabia itself there was
then no political unity ; the inhabitants being divided
into a number of republican tribes, generally at war
with each other, which rendered it impossible for
them to pursue a career of conquest elsewhere. All
this was altered by the rise of Mohammedanism, and
with it we come to a new era in the history of the
East-African coast; the Arabs re-appear on it, as
disciples of Islam, and founders of small independent states.

It is well known that the Mohammedan Arabs,
during the first period of their history, for 150 years,
overran a large section of Asia, Africa, and Europe,
and that soon after the death of their prophet Mohammed they fell a prey to political and religious
dissensions, and the defeated party resolved to abandon the land of their birth. Where was a better
home to be found than in the fruitful strand of Eastern
Africa ? There they were already known, and would
be safe from the pursuit of their fanatical con-

querors. It seems that the first settlements of the kind were made in various points of the East-African coast in the year 740 by the Emosaids, or adherents of Said, a great-grandson of Ali, the prophet's cousin and son-in-law. Said, proclaimed Caliph by the rebels, was defeated and slain, on which his adherents had to seek safety by flight; and it was in East Africa that they found refuge. In the works of various Arabian historians and geographers for several centuries afterwards we find interesting notices of these Arab settlements. From all these notices it is to be gathered that the Mohammedan Arabs founded political and religious states or towns in Eastern Africa, and that their migration to that region was sometimes voluntary, sometimes forced upon them. Among these Arabian states and towns the most prominent are (1) Mukdisha; (2) Kiloa; (3) Barava, Malindi, and Mombaz. Mukdisha was supreme in the north, while Kiloa was queen of the south, from Zanzibar to Sofala. With the declining power of these two states and towns, Malindi and Mombaz, situated midway between them, appear to have increased in influence and importance. Mukdisha seems to have been founded between A.D. 909 and 951; and Kiloa between A.D. 960 and 1000. It is likely from the narrative of the famous Ibn-Batuta, who visited Mombaz about 1330, that the Wanika had not then settled in the vicinity of the coast. Probably they first migrated from the interior after the disappearance of the savage Zimbos, who devastated the coast in 1588.

These Arabian cities and communities were prosperous and in some degree civilized; but they were deficient in military organization. They had not been founded by conquerors; but by traders, emigrants, and exiles, who behaved peaceably to the natives, and so developed and established their influence and power slowly, but at the same time the more surely. They were pacific colonists, and by the trade and commerce which they originated the natives of the interior could not but recognize the advantages of peaceful intercourse with the strangers, and be glad of their presence. If feuds arose occasionally and the natives of the main-land attacked the settlers, the Arabs could easily protect themselves behind the walls of their towns with the aid of their match-locks and small cannon. But the Arabs were not to remain for ever in exclusive possession of the knowledge, the commerce, and the power of Eastern Africa, a possession which would have ultimately led them to rule and to convert the whole of Southern Africa. Providence interposed, and at the right time led into those waters and to that coast a Christian power, to check the progress and weaken the influence of Mohammedanism.

It was Vasco de Gama's discovery of the route to India by the Cape that led to the establishment of Portuguese and Christian influence on the eastern coast of Africa. During his first voyage he touched at Mozambique, Mombaz, and Malindi, on the whole meeting with a friendly reception. The Portuguese soon saw the advantage of the East-African coast to ships proceeding to India, and in 1500 Pedro Alvarez Cabral was despatched by king Emmanuel of Portugal to extend his influence in that region.

He set sail with eleven ships and fifteen hundred soldiers, but only six of the ships reached Mozambique, the others having been lost or wrecked on the passage. From Mozambique Cabral proceeded to the island of Kiloa, where he entered into a treaty of allegiance with Sheikh Ibrahim, a crafty and intriguing chief, whose dominions extended as far as Sofala; but who, upon the departure of the Portuguese Admiral, threw off his allegiance and attached himself to the interests of the Arabian princes. To punish his perfidy Vasco da Gama was despatched a second time to East Africa in 1502, where, after having reached the coast of Sofala, he proceeded to Mozambique and Kiloa, and compelled Sheikh Ibrahim to acknowledge the supremacy of Portugal, and to pay a yearly tribute. But Vasco da Gama did more than found the sovereignty of Portugal in East Africa; for, proceeding from Kiloa to India, he overtook a ship laden with treasures and pilgrims on its way to Mecca, and, having made himself master of it, he destroyed all on board, except some twenty children, and committed the ship to the flames, thus laying the foundation of that internecine war which afterwards raged so fiercely between Christians and Mohammedans in the Indian Ocean and Arabian sea, and which ultimately stayed the progress of Islamism towards the south, and destroyed the shipping trade of Arabia.

The great naval hero, Alphonso D'Albuquerque, followed Gama and Cabral; and Zanzibar, surrendering to Captain Navasco, whose ship had been separated from the admiral's squadron in a storm, became tributary to Portugal. This was followed by the surrender of Barava, and gradually, after long and protracted struggles, Portuguese supremacy was established along the whole East-African coast. Mombaz was the place that gave the Portuguese the most trouble, and it was only after they had taken and burnt it for the second time under Nuno da Cunha in 1528, that Portugal could rest for a time, and claim undisputed sway over the whole coast from Barava to Cape Corrientes. In 1586 there was a general insurrection along the coast against the Portuguese, promoted by Ali Bey, who suddenly appeared in those waters and claimed the sovereignty for the Turkish sultan, upon which Mukdisha, Lusiwa, Lamu, and Patta soon fell into his hands, and Mombaz and Kalifi joined in the revolt, when the Portuguese commandant, Thomas de Suza Cutinho, arrived with twenty ships before Mombaz, took Ali Bey prisoner, when driven into the sea by the truculent Wasimba, and sent him to Lisbon, where he embraced Christianity and died. While the Portuguese commandant was besieging rebellious Mombaz the savage Wasimba, pressing forward from the south, arrived in the neighbourhood of Mombaz, and promised the islanders that, if they were admitted into the city, they would aid them to shake off the Portuguese yoke. The people of Mombaz opened

their gates to them; but no sooner were the savages
admitted, than they turned indiscriminately upon
friend and foe, and murdered every one they met.
The inhabitants took refuge from their allies in the
sea, where they were massacred by the Portuguese.
The Wasimba came from the banks of the river
Kuama in the interior, spreading northward along
the coast, devouring in their progress man and beast
alike; for they were cannibals, and are said to have
eaten in Kiloa alone no fewer than three thousand
Mohammedans! Mombaz was afterwards burnt, and
the rebellious sheikhs of the coast at Lamu, Patta,
Pasa, and Mandra surrendered, after the Portuguese
had inflicted on those places exemplary punishment.
The sovereignty of the Portuguese was thus re-esta-
blished, and the Turks, completely defeated, did not
venture to return.

The supremacy of Portugal in Eastern Africa
as in other parts of the world, gradually declined,
in spite of the revenues which flowed into her
treasury from every quarter, but which could not but
become exhausted by the numerous fleets and armies
which she had to despatch in every direction. Battles
by sea and by land, and deadly climates swept off
soldiers and officers by thousands; governors and
high officials became more and more unfit for the
discharge of their duties, as their only wish was to
become quickly rich, and to enjoy their ill-gotten
wealth at home; added to which luxury came with
the spoils of other lands into the mother-country,
and gradually enervated and corrupted the Portuguese

as a nation. Those in authority abroad became unjust and tyrannical towards those subjected to their rule, and what wonder then that there grew up a spirit of discontent among subjugated princes and states which was sedulously encouraged by the Moham- medans in Asia and Africa, the fiercest enemies of ·the Portuguese then, as they now are of the English. The original enthusiasm which impelled men of all classes in Portugal to adventure in foreign countries died away, satiated by the immense achievements and acquisitions of the past; whilst the war of succession which broke out between Portugal and Spain in 1580, compelled the government of the former country to recall its troops to Europe, so that her colonial governors had to fall back upon the services of native troops, and thus the great weakness of her rule could no longer be disguised. Nor was it a rule which any friend of humanity could have wished to see perpetuated. In East-Africa, for instance, Portugal enriched herself by levying tribute and taxes, in addition to her enormous gains from the gold-mines of Sofala; but East-Africa received nothing in return. She ruled the East-Africans with a rod of iron, and her pride and cruelty had their reward in the bitter hatred of the natives. In Eastern Africa the Portuguese have left nothing behind them but ruined fortresses, palaces, and eccle- siastical buildings. Nowhere is there to be seen a single trace of any real improvement effected by them. No wonder that the Portuguese rule was of short duration, and that it fell as quickly as it had risen.

John IV. had, indeed, restored independence to
Portugal in 1640 ; but he could no longer save his
colonies.   In 1620 Portugal had already lost the
island of Ormuz in consequence of the alliance
between the Shah of Persia and the English ; and
its loss was the more felt, because it gave the Arabs
in Oman courage and leisure to extend and to
strengthen their influence in the Persian Gulf and
in Eastern Africa.   Portugal had no longer men,
like Albuquerque, capable of restoring the falling
influence of their country in those seas.   All were
now alike corrupt and incapable.   In India and its
waters England and Holland had appeared upon the
stage, and with their appearance the star of Portugal
had to sink to the horizon.

We have still to show how the authority of the
Arabian princes of Oman first arose, and gradually
replaced that of the Portuguese along the East-
African coast.   Oman comprises the north and
south-eastern portions of Arabia, which lay on the
Gulf of Persia and the Indian ocean.   In the year
1624, after great disorders and dissensions Oman
and its inhabitants became subject to the rule of a
sagacious and energetic Imam, Nassar Ben Murjed, the
Yarebite.   After he had established his sovereignty
in Oman he planned the complete expulsion of the
Portuguese from their Arabian and African possessions;
indeed their supremacy had already begun to decline
with the loss of Ormuz, and with the alliance between
England and Persia.   His victories over the Portuguese were continued by his cousin and successor,

Sultan Ben Sef-Ben-Malek, who took Muscat in 1658, leaving the Portuguese then no sea-port of any consequence on the coast of Arabia. His second son, Sultan Sef, who had defeated his brother Belareb and usurped the throne, at the request of the people of Mombaz sent a fleet to Eastern Africa and captured Mombaz, Zanzibar, and Kiloa, and laid siege to Mozambique in 1698. He placed a governor in Mombaz, who was nominally subject to Oman. After the fall of Mombaz the Portuguese on the East-African coast were everywhere massacred or expelled; and there was an end to their sovereignty from Cape Delgado to Cape Guardafui. Even the town of Mukdisha, which had retained its independence during the period of Portuguese rule, placed itself under the protection of the princes of Oman. The subjection of the African coast to the rulers of Oman was, however, rather nominal than real. The princes of Oman found plenty to occupy them in Arabia, and had but little time to devote to the affairs of their African possessions, contenting themselves apparently with having expelled the infidel Christians.

Notwithstanding several declarations of independence to the contrary, we still find this nominal sovereignty of the Imams of Muscat over the East-African coast in existence in the year 1785. In the year 1806 Sultan Said-Said, so often mentioned in this volume, became Imam of Muscat. The governorship of Mombaz had previously become, in some measure, hereditary, and confined to the family of

the Msara; and when the office was assumed in 1814
by Abdallah Ben Akhmed, the son of Akhmed Ben
Muhamed Ben Osman, he formed the design of
rendering Mombaz completely independent of Muscat.
Accordingly on assuming his office he sent Said-Said
a little powder and shot, with a shirt of mail, and
a kebaba, or small measure for corn, instead of the
usual valuable present. Said-Said understood what
was meant, but made no comment; and Abdallah,
knowing very well what he might expect from the
Sultan of Oman, went to Bombay and gained the
friendship of the Anglo-Indian government, by whom
he was well received. He reduced Barava to dependence on Mombaz; but lost it again in 1822, when
Said-Said sent a fleet against it and brought it into
subjection. Abdallah was unsuccessful in his attempts
to support the anti-Muscat party in Patta, and to
preserve the island of Pemba; an expedition to
recover which commanded by his brother, Mbarak,
signally failed. He died in 1822.

In due course Abdallah's brother, Salem, would
have succeeded as governor of Mombaz, but Mbarak
opposed him. To avoid a civil war Soliman Ben
Ali, who had been governor of Pemba, was made
provisionally Sultan of Mombaz; but he was an aged
and feeble man, quite incapable of making head
against Said-Said, who had already.become master of
Patta, Barava, Lamu, Zanzibar, and Pemba, and
now threatened to attack Mombaz itself. In this
emergency Soliman Ben Ali resolved to appeal for
aid to the English, who were then exploring the

waters of the East-African coast under Captain Owen. On the 3rd of December 1823, accompanied by a number of influential persons, Mbarak went on board the English ship of war Baracouta, and requested Captain Vidal to plant the English flag on the fortress and town of Mombaz to which Captain Vidal consented; and when soon afterwards Said-Said's fleet under Abdallah Ben Selim appeared before Mombaz, and was about to blockade the harbour, the inhabitants hoisted the English flag. On the 7th of February 1824 Captain Owen came himself in the frigate Leven; he entered into a convention with the islanders, subject to the approval of the English Government at home, in conformity with which Mombaz and its dependencies, Pemba and the whole of the coast between Malindi and the river Pangani, were to be under the protectorate of Great Britain. The government of the whole was to remain hereditarily vested in the family of the Msara, but an English agent was to reside in Mombaz to look after the execution of the convention. One half of the public revenues was to be paid to the English, the other half to the Msara; and the English were to be entitled to trade with the interior and, finally, the slave-trade was to be abolished in Mombaz.

Abdallah Ben Selim to whom Captain Owen communicated this convention, promised to observe its stipulations, provided his master at Muscat assented, and quitted Mombaz with his fleet. Mbarak forthwith resumed the occupation of Pemba, whither

Captain Owen conveyed fifty soldiers from Mombaz, leaving a lieutenant behind at Mombaz with three sailors and a corporal to train the native soldiery. From Pemba Captain Owen proceeded to Zanzibar to induce the governor, Said Ben Muhamed Ben Akhabiri, to a voluntary surrender of Zanzibar to the Msara; but the governor referred him to Said-Said at Muscat; upon which Captain Owen proceeded to the Mauritius with Mbarak, who was well received by Mr. Cole, the English governor, who sent a report of the whole affair to London, while Mbarak returned to Mombaz, in the hope that the English Government would sanction the convention. In November 1824 Captain Owen returned to Mombaz where in the meantime Lieutenant Emery, as English Agent had been called upon to give an important judicial decision, in the case of an Arab who, contrary to the convention, had smuggled slaves to Mombaz. Lieutenant Emery took the slaves from him, and settled them on a tract of land which had been presented to the English, and which he sent them to cultivate; and the owner of the slaves was transported to the Seychelles, in 1825. Captain Owen proceeded to Mukdisha, the inhabitants of which had been at variance for a year with Said-Said. The English captain hoped that they would voluntarily place themselves under the protection of England, but he was disappointed; the inhabitants of Barava, however, accepted at once the English protectorate, and placing themselves under the government of Mombaz promised to give up the slave-trade.

The people of Mombaz could breathe freely again, and their commerce received anew a fresh impetus; but at the same time with the removal of the pressure from without their internal dissensions revived. Mbarak insisted that the provisional governor, Soliman Ben Ali, should resign in favour of his brother Salem, and when Soliman refused he and his sons were imprisoned, and in 1826 Salem became the ruler of Mombaz, the English agent assenting to the arrangement. And now a new and important event occurred; for this state of things was not destined to last. The English government refused to sanction Captain Owen's convention, declined the protectorate, and withdrew its agents from Mombaz, which was again abandoned to itself.

After the withdrawal of the English permitted Said-Said to take steps against Mombaz, he commenced operations without delay, seeing very clearly that his hold on Eastern Africa would always be a dubious one, as long as Mwita*, the contumacious, was not completely subdued. His first proceeding was to write and summon Governor Salem to submit, which the latter declined to do, but sent envoys to Muscat in 1827 with a view to open negociations, into which Said-Said, however, refused

---

* Mwita is the native name for Mombaz. The Kabila tribe of the Wamwita comprehends the original inhabitants of Mombaz. There are eleven other tribes besides which contribute to the population of Mombaz, many are the remnants of Arabian and native tribes dispersed or destroyed in the course of time, especially during the rule of the Portuguese.

to enter. The following year Said-Said arrived in person before Mombaz with 2000 soldiers, a ship of war, the Liverpool of seventy-four guns, the frigate Shah-Allum of sixty-four guns, two corvettes, and seven smaller vessels. He anchored outside the harbour of Mombaz opposite Serakupa, and sent a negociator to Salem who would not hear of peace; and so, after three days, Said commenced hostilities against the island. The battery Serakupa, and the town, were bombarded first; then Said himself ran his largest vessel into the harbour, and sent for the two Msara, Salem and Mbarak, who, however, declined the invitation until they had received two hostages of the sultan's own family as a pledge for their safety. By a secret compact between them and Said-Said it was settled and sworn to on the Koran, 1. that the fortress should be surrendered to the Sultan, and garrisoned by fifty Henaui soldiers; 2. that Salem and his posterity should govern Mombaz in the name of the Imam of Muscat; and 3. that the revenues should be shared between the two contracting parties, and be sent to Muscat by a collector of the sultan's.

This agreement, however, was broken by the sultan a few days after he had gradually introduced 200 soldiers into the fortress; when he ordered Salem to evacuate it and withdraw into the town. Aware of Said-Said's superior strength the two Msara, Salem and Mbarak, complied, and at the end of three weeks Said-Said departed, leaving a garrison of three hundred soldiers, Belochees, Seidgali, and Arabs, in the fortress. He sailed to Zanzibar where he gave orders for the construction of a palace, intending henceforth to take up his residence in Africa, being wearied of the begging propensities and turbulence of his aristocracy at Muscat. In the course of three months, however, he was obliged to return to Arabia to repress a rebellion which had broken out in his absence; and he was followed thither by his admiral, who on his way to Muscat bombarded Mukdischa, and compelled it to surrender.

Soon after the departure of Said discord arose between Mombaz and Muscat. Nasser Ben Soliman, Governor of Pemba, coveted the governorship of Mombaz, and accused the Msara to Said-Said of a design to rebel against him. Proceeding to Mombaz Nasser demanded in the name of the Imam, that Salem should resign into his hands the government of the island. Salem and Mbarak asked for his written credentials; but Nasser replied that he was his own credentials, whereupon Mbarak ordered him to quit the island in four-and-twenty hours, as a person not entitled to represent even the sandals of Said-Said. Withdrawing into the fortress Nasser opened a cannonade upon the town; but it was unsuccessful. Attacked in turn he and the garrison had to capitulate through want of provisions; and Nasser was thrown into prison and strangled there. Upon this Said-Said sent his admiral with a military force and the frigate Shah-Allum, but they came too late; the people of Mombaz had dissolved their connection with Muscat; and therefore to restore it, he next year headed in person an expedition against the island; but his bombardment of it this time failing in its object, he had to return discomfited to Muscat, where new troubles had broken out. In 1833 he made another unsuccessful attack upon Mombaz and, on its failure, once more returned to Muscat.

At last, however, his ambition was gratified. In 1834 the town of Siwi revolted against him, and the rebel-leader having appealed to Salem at Mombaz for help, the latter went to the aid of the Siwians with a number of soldiers; but on the blockade of Siwi by Said-Said he had to return to Mombaz, where he died in March 1835, the death of his brother Mbarak having occurred some time prevously. Upon this there arose a violent contest in Mombaz respecting the succession to the governorship, which was not ended by the selection of one of the Msara family in the December of 1836. Muallem Shafei, the Sheikh of Kilendini (a crafty personage who often tried to draw me into politics), and many Suahili were altogether disaffected to the family of the Msara, and were not disposed any longer to recognize a member of it as governor. These traitors repaired to Muscat and asked the sultan, who at the very time was preparing an expedition against Mombaz, to aid them against their native city. Said-Said came with a fleet and soldiers, who were disembarked at Kilindini where the traitors welcomed them; and the Suahili of Gavana, or Mji wa Kale or Har-el-Kadama, (Old Town—so called because its site was said to

have been that of the town of Mombaz formerly),
also went over to Said-Said. The Wanika tribes
were likewise won over to him by Muallem Shafei
and the sultan's liberal presents. The Msara seeing
with dismay that they were deserted by their own
people, offered terms to Said-Said, consenting to his
stipulations that they should evacuate the fortress,
settle in the town, and conform to the articles of the
former treaty. Some misunderstanding arising with
them afterwards Said-Said listened willingly to the
insinuations of some Suahili, that the island would
never be tranquil so long as the family of the Msara
remained at the helm, and were thus in a position to
rebel. He sent forthwith one of his sons to Mombaz
with a corvette, to seize secretly the chiefs of the
Msara. The attempt succeeded, and twenty-five of
them were seized in one night, carried on board the
vessel, transported to Zanzibar and thence to Arabia,
where most of them died from the effects of the
severe captivity in iron chains to which they were
subjected. Those who were not captured fled
on the night of the surprise with their wives and
children, leaving behind them all their property,
and took refuge in the Wanika-land, in the north of
which they afterwards settled at Takaunga, near
Malindi, and in the south at Gassi, and there they
still remain. After recovering his sovereignty over
Mombaz Said-Said had along the coast, from Mukdischa to Cape Delgado, no enemies of any importance with the exception of the people of Siwi in
Patta, at whose hands he had suffered several de-

feats, and whom he has never been able thoroughly to subdue.

Thus it happened that Said-Said had attained his long-cherished wish in February 1837—the very month and year in which I started on my journey from Europe to Abessinia. How little could I suppose, when beginning my journey, that in the distant south of Africa an Arabian prince was preparing for me a way to the heathen! Yet, so it was; for without the conquest of Mombaz by a prince as well inclined as the Imam of Muscat to Europeans, and especially to the English, the establishment of a missionary station in the Wanika-land could never have been effected. There are two circumstances which seem likely to secure the Prince of Oman the possession of Eastern Africa; the one, that his Highness imposes but few taxes on his African subjects, least of all on those towns and districts which are most quickly roused to revolt, and the reconquest of which from the nature of the ground would be attended with great difficulty to the ruler; and the other, the fear entertained by the natives of the English, French, and Americans, nations which are on the friendliest footing with the Imam of Muscat, and which would and must support him. In the first place the commercial relations of these nations with Eastern Africa could not allow of any lengthened disturbances, and in the second, it would not suit their policy to permit the disintegration of Eastern Africa into a number of small states, since, in such an event, one of these three powers might be tempted to interfere

and to appropriate to itself a portion of the coast;
while, on the contrary, so long as a single prince is
the recognized sovereign of the coast, any annexation
of the kind is virtually prevented.

The excellent climate of Zanzibar, its increasing
commerce, the wishes of the Europeans, the general
importance of his African possessions, the peculiar
state of Patta and Mombaz, and his desire to escape
from the mendicancy and turbulence of the leading
men of Mascat, constituted the circumstances which
induced Said-Said to transfer his court, and the seat
of his sovereignty from Muscat to Zanzibar in 1840.
After the transfer foreign consuls were appointed at
Zanzibar—the American was the first, the English
followed in 1843, and the French in 1847.   Foreign
commercial houses were also established, and drove
a trade which was extremely lucrative from the first.
It would lead me too far to chronicle the subsequent
history of Said-Said; I shall only add that on his
voyage back from Muscat, towards the close of 1856,
this remarkable man died of dysentery, a disease
to which he had long been subject.   His son
Majed succeeded him in the government of his
African dominions; whilst another of his many sons
has possessed himself of the sovereignty of his Asiatic
provinces, and has his residence at Muscat.

Hitherto, the more recent relations of Europeans
with Eastern Africa have been always of a peaceful
kind, and calculated to efface the bad impressions
which the conduct of the Portuguese in earlier
times had left behind.   The natives are pleased

with, and desirous of European intercourse, and if Europeans deal with them honourably and justly, it will never be otherwise. In Eastern Africa a very great deal depends on the consuls of foreign countries. If these are sagacious, energetic, heedful of the interests of the natives as well as of those of their own countrymen, and most important of all, if they are men of Christian disposition, the respect of the East-Africans will go on increasing, and they will be ever more and more convinced that the Wasungu, Europeans, are really what the name implies, wise and capable people,—"not slothful in business; fervent in spirit, serving the Lord."

END OF PART III.

APPENDIX.

APPENDIX.

I.—THE SNOW-CAPPED MOUNTAINS OF EASTERN AFRICA.

WHEN first the missionaries of the Church Missionary Society at Rabbai Mpia mentioned the existence of snow-capped mountains in Eastern Africa, they were at once attacked by many European geographers, and it was asserted that they had mistaken for snow the calcareous earth, or rocks, covering the summits of the mountains in question, and presenting at a distance the appearance of snow. It may therefore not be out of place to put on record the simple facts of the case.

Mr. Rebmann, on his first journey to Jagga in 1848, saw on the 11th of May for the first time the snowy peak of Mount Kilimanjaro, or Ndsharo, as the Teita people call the mountain, Kilima meaning simply mountain; and on subsequent journeys to Jagga he saw it again. On the 10th November 1849, upon my first journey to Ukambani I also beheld it first near Mount Maungu, thirty-six leagues from Mombaz, and afterwards in Ukambani, whence from every elevation the silver-crowned summit of the lofty mountain was plainly visible. On my second journey to Ukambani in 1851 the mountain Njaro was not only easily discernible with the telescope, but also with the naked eye. In addition to this Mr. Rebmann slept at the base of the mountain, and even by moonlight could distinctly make out snow. He conversed with the natives in reference to the white matter visible upon the dome-like summit of the mountain, and he was told that the silver-like stuff, when brought down in bottles proved to be nothing but water

that many who ascended the mountain perished from extreme cold,
or returned with frozen extremities, which persons unacquainted
with the real cause ascribed to the malignant influence of dshins or
evil spirits.* After all these corroborative circumstances what
doubt could longer remain in our minds respecting the existence of
snow in Eastern Africa?

The second snow-capped mountain bears various names among the
native tribes. The Wacamba call it Kima ja Kegnia, Mount of
Whiteness, Snow-white Libanon; other tribes Kirenia, or Ndur
Kegnia; the Wakuafi, Orldoinio eibor, White Mountain; it has
only been seen by myself. Scarcely had I arrived at Kitui, on the
26th of November 1849 in company with the chief Kivoi, when he
told me that he had been to Jagga, and had seen the Kima ja
Jeu, Mount of Whiteness, the name given by the Wakamba to
the Kilimanjaro, in contradistinction to the Kegnia; and also stated
that there was a still greater mountain six days' journey from Kitui,
which was called Kimaja Kegnia, adding that if I would ascend
the hill a little above his village, if the sky were clear I should be
able to see the mountain. As the rainy season had already set in
the region about the Kegnia was enveloped in clouds, and in addition
to this the Kilimanjaro is usually visible only about 10 A.M. as
the sun's progress envelopes it in clouds during the rest of the
day. However, it happened that on leaving Kitui on the 3rd of
December, 1849 I could see the Kegnia most distinctly, and observed two large horns or pillars, as it were, rising over an enormous

---

* Mr. Cooley, in his "Inner Africa Laid Open," published in 1852, quoting
from the first volume of the "Missionary Intelligencer," in which the
discoveries of the missionaries at Rabbai Mpia were recorded, treats the
statement of Mr. Rebmann respecting snow seen by him on the summit of
Kilimanjaro, as "a most delightful mental recognition only, not supported by
the evidence of his senses," and sneers at the narrative of the natives as to the
frostbitten explorers, noticed above, as a fireside tale. Had Mr. Cooley been
accustomed to weigh and sift evidence more closely, he would have argued
differently from that very fact; for by its own law evidence is always
strengthened by the record of trivial and immaterial circumstances. The
candid reader of Mr. Cooley's objections will not fail to see that in attempting
to prove too much, he has managed to place himself out of court, and the
presence of snow-capped mountains in Equatorial Africa will be credited,
notwithstanding the implied and open discredit which he attempts to cast
upon the narratives of the missionaries of Rabbai Mpia.

mountain to the north-west of the Kilimanjaro, covered with a white substance.

On my second journey to Ukambani in 1851 Kivoi repeated his statement respecting the Kegnia, and the mountain of smoke, volcano, which he said was in the vicinity of the snow-capped mountain. This time I did not see Mount Kegnia owing to the cloudy sky which lay continuously over the region in which I had formerly observed the mountains; but Kivoi's statement was fully borne out by the people from Mbē and Uembu, whom I met with at his village, Rumu wa Kikandi, a native of Uembu, positively stating that the Kegnia was six days' journey from Kitui; that his tribe was near the white mountain; that he had often been at the foot of it, but had not ascended it to any great altitude on account of the intense cold and the white matter which rolled down the mountain with a great noise, which last would seem to indicate the existence of glaciers. The people from Kikuyu confirmed these reports, and a Mnika from Rabbai also, who had been at Kikuyu mentioned to me a mountain, the summit of which was covered with a substance resembling white flour.

From personal observation, therefore, which confirmed the repeated information of the natives of different tribes, I became firmly convinced of the existence of at least two snow-capped mountains one of which, the Kegnia, was larger than the other, the Kilimanjaro, the first having peaks at its summit, while the second possesses a dome-like shape, and is situated to the south-east of the former.

That both mountains are covered with perennial snow is proved by the multitude of rivers rising amidst them. Of these Mr. Rebmann has counted more than twenty flowing from the heights of Mount Kilimanjaro, and among them two considerable ones, the Gona and the Lumi, forming the main streams of the river Lufu, or Pangani. I myself passed the river Zawo, which at the dryest season was two feet and a half deep and flows, I was informed, from the Lake Luaya, the northern receptacle of the waters which descend from the snowy Kilimanjaro. In like manner I visited the river Dana at the dry season and found it six or seven feet deep. Its main source was reported to have its rise from a jyāru, or lake, which was the receptacle of the waters of the snowy Kegnia, and besides the river Dana there are more than fifteen rivers running from the west and north of the Kegnia. One of these, the Tumbiri, is very large and flows, according to the report made to me by Rumu wa Kikandi, in a northerly direction to the great lake Baringu, by which, in the phrase of my informant, you may travel a hundred days along its shores and find no end. To this lake, or chain of lakes, as it has been found to be, I have referred in the introduction. The great river Tumbiri is evidently identical with the river Tubiri, mentioned by Mr. Werne as being a name of the White River, Bahr el Abiad, at four degrees north latitude from the Equator.

How are we to explain the phenomenon of such a multiplicity of rivers flowing from both mountains, unless we are to admit the existence of snow? I have seen the mountains of Usambara, of Pare, Kadiaro, Bura, Theuka, Julu, and Mr. Rebmann has seen the mountains of Agono, Usange, Kisungu, and Mloso, but neither of us found that any river of magnitude flowed from these mountains. The Woi and Madade, rising from the Bura group, are rapidly exhausted after the rains, and although the rivers Mgambo, Umba, Mkulumus, in Usambara are perennial, they are very small and shallow during the dry season, whereas the Gona, Lumi, Zawo, and the Dana, are considerable streams even at the driest season. Snow existing in considerable masses among these mountains can alone explain this hypothesis in a satisfactory manner.

And why should the existence of snow in Equatorial Africa be doubted when there is snow under the Equator in America; when there is snow no less sometimes on the Cameroons of Western Africa; when snow is frequently observed upon the heights of Mount Amba Hai, in Abessinia, being situated 16,000 feet above the level of the sea; and when there is snow in the south of Kaffa, as Bruce has positively stated?* On my first arrival at Mombaz in 1844, I had not the least idea of the "silver matter," as it was called, reported to exist in the interior, being snow. I regarded the silver and the jins or evil spirits of Kilimanjaro as some kind of impalpable white sand which, as the Arabs told me, exists in Southern Arabia, where the sandy baher-el-safi forms a kind of whirl-pit, swallowing up everything that approaches it. I was not then aware that Ptolemy had alluded to a mountainous country, and that these mountains were covered

* Bruce's Travels, Vol. VII. p. 105.

with perennial snow, and considered by him as the real sources of the Nile. The western branch of the White River, according to him, runs from a lake in six degrees of south latitude, and the eastern branch from another lake in seven degrees of south latitude, uniting at two degrees south latitude. All this was unknown to me on my first arrival.

The existence of equatorial snow also will be doubted by no one if it is borne in mind that sandy deserts do not exist under the Equator; but on the other hand that, for hundreds of miles, there extends a region of rich vegetation and forest land, absorbent of the fiery sunbeams, while the north-east and south-west winds are cooling Eastern Africa throughout the year, producing less heat in Equatorial Africa than would naturally be supposed to be the case from the proximity of the Equator.

It may be urged, however, that on the recent journey of Major Burton and Captain Speke to the lakes Tanganyika and Ukerewe, they did not see the snowy mountains mentioned by the missionaries. The reason is obvious. The route of these gentlemen lay far to the south and west of the snow-capped mountains; nor can their summit be observed except when there is a very clear sky. Neither of these travellers object to the existence of such snow-capped mountains; on the contrary, as Dr. Petermann rightly observes, they seem to take them for granted, as though their existence were not a matter of dispute. Major Burton, when engaged at Tanga in very strict researches about Kilimanjaro, admits that the cold upon that mountain must be very intense.

In like manner Dr. Petermann very properly states that the fact of Dr. Livingstone having seen in latitudes 12° and 13° S. mountains covered at the summit with white stones, is no argument against the contemporaneous existence of snowy mountains in the Equatorial region. The same learned authority states that, since the reports of the Missionaries have been confirmed by Messrs. Burton and Speke in their essentials, reliance may be placed upon the accounts of the former relative to the existence of such mountains.

II. The probable Sources of the White River, or Nile.

Whilst correcting these pages for press I received the "Proceedings of the Royal Geographical Society of London," vol. iii., No. iv., 1859, and "Blackwood's Edinburgh Magazine," September, October, and November, 1859.

In both these publications allusion is frequently made to me in connection with the grand problem of the sources of the Nile. Captain Speke, the discoverer of Lakes Tanganyika,* and Ukerewe, which latter he styled Victoria Nyanza, Lake Victoria, remarks that he must be mistaken if the Ukerewe does not ultimately turn out to be the real source of the Nile; whilst Mr. McQueen, the well-known geographer, thinks that the Nile has nothing to do with the lake, or, in fact, with any river or lake south of the Equator, nor with the snow-capped Kilimanjaro; that the swelling of the White River is caused by the tropical rains of the northern torrid zone, as Julius Cæsar was told by the Egyptian priest Arnoreis, two thousand years ago. Captain Speke, on the contrary, asserts that the swelling of the Nile is caused, not indeed by snow-water, but by the tropical rains swelling the Victoria Nyanza, from the *Montes Lunæ,* the Mountains of the Moon, or mountains rising in the west of the lake to the height of 6000 feet, and in part from waters flowing from the snow-capped Mount Kegnia, on the eastern shore of Lake Nyanza.

My own opinion remains the same as that which I recorded in 1854 in my "Wakuafi Vocabulary," p. 128, and in my preface to Mr. Erhardt's "Vocabulary of the Masai language," p. 4 :—" There can be no question but that the opinion of the ancients, who believed the *Caput Nili* to be in Æthiopia, is truly correct; for the Wakuafi, whose language is of Æthiopico-Semetic origin, are in possession of the countries which give rise to that river. The real sources of the Nile appear to me to be traceable partly to the woody and marshy land of the Wamau people, about 2½ or 3° south of the Equator, of whom Rumu wa Kikandi told me in Ukambani, in 1851."

As to the marshy land of theWamau people, the reader may compare Seneca's description, given in his "Quæstiones Naturales," lib. vi.—"Ego quidem centuriones duos, quos Nero Cæsar ad investigandum Caput Nili miserat, audivi narrantes, longum illos iter peregisse, quum a rege Æthiopiæ instructi auxilio, commendatique proximis regibus, penetrassent ad ulteriora. Equidem, aiebant, pervenimus ad immensas paludes, quarum exitum nec incolæ noverant, nec sperare quisquam potest, ita implicitæ aquis herbæ sunt, et aquæ nec pediti eluctabiles, nec navigio, quod nisi parvum et unius capax, limosa et obsita palus non ferat. Ibi, inquit, vidimus duas petras, ex quibus ingens vis fluminis excidebat. Sed sive caput illa, sive accèssio est Nili, sive tunc nascitur, sive in terras ex priore recepta cursu redit : nonne tu credis, illam, quidquid est, ex magno terrarum lacu ascendere? Habeat enim oportet pluribus locis sparsum humorem, et in imo coactum, ut eructare tanto impetu possit."

It may be that the Lake Ukerewe of Captain Speke is identical, either with the bog in Umaū, or with the Baringu, mentioned by Rumu wa Kikandi. In either case, Captain Speke has the honour of having almost solved the great geographical problem of Africa, the discovery of the *Caput Nili*. At all events, he has been nearest to the spot where that *caput* must be sought. Nothing, however, can be definitely determined till some scientific traveller, capable of making reliable astronomical observations, as suggested at page xxix, furnishes accurate data as to the relative level of the countries to the north of the Victoria Nyanza.

Though somewhat figurative and poetical, did not the difficulty in relation to this measurement exist, I should at once recur to Colonel Sykes's view, communicated in the " Proceedings of the Royal Geographical Society of London," in May, 1859, (vol. iii., No. iv., p. 213.) :—" He illustrated his observation by a practical reference to the human hand and arm; supposing the latter to be the main stream, the fingers might form the sources, all converging at the wrist to one great whole, the Victoria Lake. The only question was, which of those branches should be considered the chief source of the river? But each might be equal in size and of equal distance from the point of junction. The fact was, they were all sources."

" Captain Speke described a range of mountains running, not from east to west, but from north to south across the Equator. This range had necessarily a double watershed to the east and to the west. The rivers observed by Dr. Krapf ran down to the eastward, but other rivers mentioned by him ran also down to the westward. Consequently, there were two directions in which the waters ran in exactly the same locality. What, therefore, could be more reasonable than to suppose that the water, parting to the westward, should run into the lake mentioned by Captain Speke? And as this lake was at an elevation of 4000 feet above the sea, and the depression of the country was from the lake towards the north generally, as indicated by the course of the Nile, which had been traced up to $3\frac{1}{2}°$ of the Equator, it is more than probable that the lake was one of the chief sources of the Nile, and that other neighbouring sources would be found in the snow peaks of Kilimanjaro and Kegnia, forming part of the range of mountains spoken of by Captain Speke."

To this statement of the gallant colonel I will only remark, that no river known to me or to Mr. Rebmann runs from Kilimanjaro to the west. We never heard of any, nor can it run in that direction, owing to the very mountainous country of Kikuyu, which lies nearly west of Kilimanjaro. But rivers do run from the north and west of Mount Kegnia, and these doubtless form Lake Victoria, if it is one of the true sources of the Nile, which can in no way flow from a lake alone, no great river ever doing so, but coming from beyond such lake, as the Abai in Abessinia, and the Rhine in Europe clearly prove. Mr. McQueen is therefore quite right in asserting that the Nile has nothing to do with the Kilimanjaro, but in regard to the Kegnia he is undoubtedly wrong. He is also quite correct in maintaining that the swelling of the White River is caused by the tropical rains in the north of the Equator; and, in like manner, Captain Speke is correct in stating that it would be highly erroneous to suppose that the Nile could have any great fluctuations from any other source than periodical rains. Were the Nile supplied by snow alone its perennial volume would ever be the same—there would be no material fluctuations observable in it. In proof of the Nile's inundation not being caused by the tropical rains south of the Equator, as Captain Speke seems to suppose in contradistinction to Mr. McQueen, the latter refers to the expedition of the Pasha of Egypt in 1840, which reached the island of Ianka, in $4\frac{1}{2}°$ N. in the month of January, when the waters of the White Nile were rapidly subsiding, so that the expedition was compelled to return as it could not pass the south cataracts of the Bari land. The rains south of the Equator begin in November; consequently, if they produced the inundation, the water would not have subsided in January, and the expedition would not have been compelled to return. Mr. McQueen is therefore quite right in this respect, but he goes too far in asserting that, in consequence of this phenomenon, the sources of the Nile do not exist south of the Equator, as Captain Speke and myself argue. His assertion does not mark the distinction between *sources* and *inundation* of the river; for why should not the source of the Nile be situated south of the Equator, and yet the inundation of the river be caused by the tropical rains in the north, where they begin in May and June, so that the Nile begins to rise at Cairo in July.* There are many lakes and ponds which are overflowed in the rainy season, and the river Sobat or Telky is very large and carries a great volume of water into the White Nile. Besides these there are many other tributaries from the west and east.†

I have never suggested that the inundation of the Nile is caused by snow, but only that snow is the chief sustaining source of that river, keeping it fresh throughout the year, preventing the lake into which it runs, if it runs into any, from stagnation. Captain Speke himself appears to agree with this view, when he states that the water of Lake Victoria is fresh and sweet, and that the natives prefer it to the water of the Tanganica. As to the inundation, I fully believe that neither the snow nor the tropical rains south of the Equator would be sufficient causes for producing it. Hence Mr. McQueen appears to be more correct than Captain Speke in one point, but the latter is right in another—the origin of the Nile south of the Equator.

Another statement of Captain Speke's I can confirm. He says :— " There must be some insurmountable difficulties between the east of Kifuga and Kikuyu, whither the Arabs go trading viâ Mombaz

---

* The Nile rises at Cairo about the beginning of July, increases during 100 days, till the middle of October, then subsides and reaches its lowest level near the end of April. It would fall earlier if the southern equatorial rains, from November to February, did not strengthen it a little. The prevailing winds from March to November are northerly, from December to February chiefly southerly.

† It is very probable that the White River receives also considerable part of its water from the lake Ufole or Zamburie, which lies near the Doko country, where a great mountain range seems to run from south to north, towards the countries Worata, Susa, and Caffa.

from Zanzibar; for if a passage were open by which they could get to Kikuyu, exactly one third of the distance which they now travel viâ Uniamuẹzi to Zanzibar would be saved." Now the reason of this is because the south and west of Kikuyu are infested by Wakuafi savages who have their head quarters in the vicinity of Kikuyu; besides which many tribes of Kikuyu and its vicinity are hostile to the Arabs, which hostility arises chiefly from the Wakamba, who consider themselves entitled to the monopoly of the trade of the interior coastwards, in the direction of Mombaz. Nor will they allow the Suahili and Arabs to trade with Ukambani, Kikuyu, Mberre, Uembu, Udaka, and other inland countries. By every means in their power they induce the inhabitants to keep off the Arabs, unless the latter have guides of the Wakamba nations. Once a caravan of Suahali penetrated into the territory of Wakambani and Kikuyu, but it was instantly repulsed and driven back. A few tribes of Kikuyu, it is true, would like the traders of the coast, but they are prevented by the jealous Wakamba, whose influence extends as far in a westerly and northerly direction, as it does eastward to Mombaz. A traveller, therefore, wishing to see the Kegnia and Lake Victoria or Buringu, must engage Wakamba, in addition to some Wanika, Suahili, and others from the tribes beyond Ukambani, unless he is backed by a strong body able to force its way through the latter place and the adjacent country. No doubt Mombaz or Malindi presented in ancient times the readiest route to the sources of the Nile, and to the Mountains of the Moon, which latter term Captain Speke has very ably explained, whilst Dr. Beke and myself had previously attempted to account for it. Captain Speke has actually seen a crescent-shaped mountain* to the northward of the Tanganyika, due west of the snow-capped Kilimanjaro and Kegnia, and west beyond Uniamesi, or the country of the Moon. The Waniamesi tribes have at all periods visited the eastern coasts of Africa; hence these hills, lying beyond their Moon-country, may have given rise to the term Mountains of the Moon. The Greek merchants, of course, translated it literally ὄρος τῆς Σελήνης.

In conclusion, I would add some late remarks of Dr. Petermann on the sources of the Nile:—" In spite of the glorious discoveries of

---

* See page xxviii, ante.

Captain Speke we have not yet reached the grand centre of all the geographical researches of equatorial Africa,—the decision regarding the site of the sources of the Nile; for it is not yet ascertained whether the Nile really has its rise from the lake discovered by Captain Speke. We readily believe that Captain Speke's view is founded on various and careful researches; but the ultimate solution of the question can only be expected by farther researches made on the spot. This shows that the solution of the old problem of the Nile's sources will yet require a good deal of labour; but in consequence of the travels and researches made by Captain Speke and the Protestant missionaries in the south, and by the Egyptians and the Roman Catholic missionaries, the region yet unsurveyed and in which the sources of the Nile must be situated, is so much circumscribed, that probably a single journey of a scientific traveller proceeding from Zanzibar to Gondokoro, or *vice versâ*, would suffice to solve definitely this famous geographical problem; and that such a journey will soon be accomplished is evidenced by the projects of Dr. Roscher, Friths, and especially by the Anglo-Indian expedition under Lieutenant J. D. Kenelly, at the recommendation of Lord Elphinstone, and which will proceed towards the scene of Major Burton and Captain Speke's discoveries, in order to circumnavigate and survey the whole of " Lake Victoria."

My countryman Dr. Roscher* will proceed by way of Kitui, a route first traversed by me in 1849, which will doubtless prove to be the nearest route from the coast to Victoria Nyanza, and to the final solution of the Nile problem, though it may be attended with some difficulties and perils from hostile tribes in the occupation of those regions. Should the Kitui route prove an abortive one, the route of Barava, $1\frac{1}{2}°$ N. of the Equator, must be selected. This route, besides the discovery of the sources of the Nile, will enrich our knowledge with much information respecting the Christian remnants existing in the countries south of Abessinia. By it we shall also derive much information respecting the Galla tribes, and in many ways new discoveries will reward the undertaking. Of this I feel so fully assured that, were I equipped and furnished with the requisite means, I should have no hesitation in entering upon such an enterprise at a few days' notice.

* See Introduction, page xxx.

The "Proceedings of the Royal Geographical Society" contain some curious and important information connected with the latter route, furnished by a French missionary, the Père B. P. Leon, dated Zanzibar, August, 1858. This missionary has been in Enarea. He states that there is a frequented route from Barava on the sea-coast to Kaffa, the journey occupying twenty-four days; the estimated distance being 360 geographical miles. Twelve days' journey south of Kaffa, he mentions a people nearly white, called Amara, who possess written books, and speak a language different both from the Ethiopic and Arabic. They build houses and villages, and cultivate the soil. These are conjectured to be the remains of the Christian nations which in early times spread far to the south of Abessinia, until they were overrun, massacred, or scattered, by the savage Galla. Four days' journey from the Amara there is a lake whence flows one of the tributaries of the White Nile. M. Leon supposes this to be the source of the Sobat, but it is more probable that it is the main stream of the Nile. The Amara, he says, dwell between 2° and 3° N. lat. and to them are subject some tribes of copper-coloured people, who dwell near the Equator. No Mussulman dare venture into that country.

THE PRESENT LITERATURE OF ABESSINIA.

THE literature of Abessinia has been slightly referred to at page 37. During my residence in Africa, I collected most of the following works, the greater part of which still exist only in manuscript.

1. THE BIBLE: the Old and New Testament, with the Apocrypha— both in Ethiopic and in Amharic. The Amharic is the text of the Bible Society. It is printed in 4to; there is an edition of the New Testament with the Psalms in 8vo. Dr. Augustus Dillmann is now publishing the Ethiopic text of the Old Testament in 4to.; and the Bible Society has printed the Ethiopic text of the New Testament also in 4to. Portions of the Scriptures have been printed at various times, both in Ethiopic and in Amharic, and the curious reader is referred to the Catalogue of Mr. David Nutt, of London, for such as are more easily obtainable. The Psalter in Ethiopic was published in 4to by Ludolf at Franckfort in 1701, (see No. 118) and in his history of Ethiopia he gives the history of the Bible of the Abessinians, pointing out its sources and contents, and exhibiting specimens of it with a Latin translation. The Amharic text, as issued by the Bible Society, was the translation of an Abessinian monk, Abu Ruhh, or Abu Rumi, a native of Godjam.

2. HAIMANOT ABAU (*the Belief of the Fathers*) or the Dogmas of the Abessinian Church, consisting of extracts from the Bible, from the Canons and Decrees of Synods and Councils, and from the writings of the Fathers of the Church,

particularly from Clemens of Alexandria, Theophilus of Antioch, John and Dionysius of Antioch (? John of Damascus, and Dionysius of Alexandria) Cyrill of Alexandria, John Chrysostom, and others. This book is said to have been compiled, or translated by Maba Zion, the son of Ras Amdu in the reign of Nebla Dengel.

3. RETUA HAIMANOT, the Orthodox Belief.

4. AMADA MISTER, Pillars of the Mysteries of Faith, in Amharic, treating of the Holy Trinity, the Manhood of Christ, of Baptism and the Holy Communion, and of the Resurrection.

5. KIRILLOS, a dogmatic treatise by St. Cyrill of Alexandria.

6. MASGABA HAIMANOT, the Treasury of Faith, a dogmatic treatise.

7. MAZHAFA TEMHERT, the Book of Doctrine, another dogmatic treatise.

8. AFA WORK, Golden-tongue or Chrysostomus, a life of St. Chrysostom, with his Exposition of the Epistle to the Hebrews. Anbakom, a native merchant of Arabia Felix in the time of king Naod, and of Tekla Haimanot is said to have rendered several treatises of St. Chrysostom into Ethiopic.

9. SINODOS, the Canons and Constitutions of the Holy Apostles. (This book has been printed in Ludolf's History of Ethiopia.)

10. FATHA NEGEST, the King's Court or Book of Laws, said to have

fallen from Heaven in the time of the Emperor Constantine, and to have been rendered into Ethiopic by Petros Abd Essaid, a native of Tigre, in the reign of Sara Jacob, about 1434—1468.

11. KEBRA NEGEST, Honour to Kings, an historical work written in praise of the kings of Ethiopia.

12. SERATA BIETA CHRISTIAN, Rules and Orders of the Church of Christ.

13. ABUSHAKER, the Abessinian Calendar, (printed in Ludolf's History of Ethiopia.)

14. KEDASIE, the Liturgy of the Church of Abessinia.

15. ARGANON (Hours of the Virgin). Prayers and Hymns of Praise to the Virgin Mary.

16. ARDEET, the last Words of Christ to the Apostles before his Ascension.

17. SIENA FETRAT, History of the World before the Flood, delivered to Moses on Mount Sinai.

18. SIENA AIHUD, Sacred and Profane History connected.

19. GENSET, the Burial of the Dead, said to have been written by St. Athanasius, and discovered by the Empress Helena at the finding of the Cross.

20. AKLEMENTOS, Discourses of St. Clement of Alexandria.

21. MAZHAFA FILASFA, Aphorisms of ancient Philosophers.

22. MAZHAFA ENOK, the Book of Enoch, (printed by Dr. Augustus Dillmann, in 1851.)

23. FAKERA JASUS, the Love of Jesus.

24. FEKARIE JASUS, Christ's Prophecies relating to the End of the World.

25. SINKESAR, Saints' Calendar, like the *Menæum* of the Greek Church, divided into 365 sections, to be read daily in the Churches.

26. KUFALIE, Hidden Secrets revealed to Moses on Mount Sinai, not contained in the Pentateuch.

27. ANTIAKOS, a Dialogue between St. Athanasius and Antiakos, a nobleman.

28. MAZHAFA TOMAR, a Letter written by the Saviour.

29. TOMAR KOPRIANOS, Letter of (?) St. Cyprian, or Koprian.

30. MEELAD, a dogmatic book.

31. MAZHAFER MISTER, Exposition of early Heresies.

32. MAZHAFA AKLIL, the Solemnization of Matrimony.

33. MAZHAFA TIMKAT, the Ministration of Baptism.

** See, No. 19, GENSET, Burial of the Dead.

34. MAZHAFA FAUES MANFAZAVI, the Book of Spiritual Medicine.

35. MAZHAFA GRAGN, an Amharic account of the life of Gragn, the fanatic king of Adal.

36. KALATA ABAU, the Council of Nice (with the opinions of the 318 prelates who attended it.)

37. SUASO, an Amharic Grammar and Dictionary (of little value).

38. DEGUA, a book of Hymns, which St. Jared is said to have compiled and set to music three hundred years ago. The saint is still supposed to be in the flesh, and to live somewhere the life of a recluse.

39. LEFAFA ZEDEK, Prayers and Exorcisms against evil spirits, a book much prized by the Abessinians, and often buried with their dead.

40. MAZHAFA DORHO; 41. ANKORITOS; 42. FARETSH; 43. LIK VANGEL; 44. GERA MOIE; 45. EPIPHANIOS; 46. AXIMAROS; 47. SAVEROS; 48. MAZHAFA BUNI; 49. DIDASKALIA; 50. TEKLA ZION.

51. TAMERA JASUS, the Miracles of Christ.

52. MEVASET, Dirges.

53. EKAMBANI, Prayer-book.

54. GERMAMA, Exorcisms against evil spirits.

55. DERSANA SANBAT, Life of St. Sanbat.
56. VUDASIE AMLAK, the Praise of God.
57. TURGUAMIE FIDEL (in Amharic.)
58. MELKA MIKAEL, Prayers to St. Michael.
59. MELKA GABRIEL, Prayers to St. Gabriel.
60. MELKA JESUS, Prayers to Christ, and the Virgin Mary.
61. ZELOTA MUSIE, the exorcisms of Moses against the Spirits of Evil.
62. ZOMA DEGUA, Fast-hymns.
63. KAL KIDAN, Words of the Covenant.
64. AUDA NEGEST, Book of Magic.
69. MAZHAFA JAI; 65. EGSIABHAR NEGES; 66. MAZHAFA SHEKENAT; 67. BARTOS; 68. DIONASIOS.
70. MAZHAFA BERHANAT, Book of Lights (Proofs.)
71. MAALA SALAT, Hours and Hymns.
72. MAZHAFA KEDER, Instruction for Renegates.
73. GEBRA HAIMANOT, Lessons for Passion-week.
74. VUDASIE MARIAM, Praise of the Virgin Mary.
75. NAGARA MARIAM, Words of the Virgin Mary.
76. NAIA MARIAM, Life of the Virgin Mary.
77. TAMERA MARIAM, the Miracles performed by the Virgin, whilst for three years and a half in Abessinia with the Infant Jesus.
78. DERSANA MARIAM, History of the Virgin Mary.
79. GEORGIS WOLDA AMID; 80. MANSHAK.
81. GADELA KEDUSAN, Lives of the Saints.
82. MISTIRA SAMAI, Mystery of Heaven.
83. SIENA ABAU, Lives of the Fathers.
84. ARAGAVI MANFASAVI, for the use of the Monks.
85. ZELOTA MONAKOSAT, Prayers of the Monks.

86. DERSANA MAHAJAVI, History of the Giver of Life.
87. FELIKISOS, for the use of the Monks,
88. DERSANA GABRIEL, History of the Angel Gabriel.
89. ZELOTA MUSADOD. Prayers against the Spirits of Evil.
90. TEBABA TABIBAN, Wisdom of the Wise, Hymns upon the Old and New Testament.
91. GADELA HAVARIAT, Lives of the Apostles.
92. GADELA MIKAEL, Life of St. Michael.
93. GADELA LALIBALA, Life of King Lalibala, who lived in the commencement of the thirteenth century after the fall of the Jewish dynasty Falasha, and is said to have conceived the notion of turning the bed of the Nile in order to destroy the Mohammedans in Egypt, who exercised great cruelty towards the Christians.
94. GADELA SENA MARKOS, Life of St Mark.
95. GADELA GIBRA MANFAS KEDUS, Life of Gibra Manfas Kedus, one of the nine saints of Abessinia. Nine Greek Apostles are said to have arrived in Abessinia in the reign of King Ahamada, in the fifth century, and to have spread Christianity further in the land, which had first been preached by Furmanatos, or Frumentius, during the reigns of Abreha and Azbeha, towards the middle of the fourth century. Frumentius, who is called Abba Salama in Abessinia, translated the New Testament into Æthiopic, the Old Testament already then existing in that language, as king Menelek, the son of Solomon by the Queen of Sheba, had brought, according to tradition, the Pentateuch and the

Psalms to Aksum, and the brothers Sakri and Pauli had translated the books of the Prophets after the birth of Christ. He was the first Bishop of Abessinia. These nine Greek Apostles were called : Panteleon, Likanos, Abba Asfie, Abba Schema, Abba Garima, Gebra Manfas Kedus, Abba Gubba, Aragavi, and Alef. In place of Gebra Manfas, St. Imata is sometimes included in the list of the nine Apostles of Abessinia.

96. GADELA TEKLA HAIMANOT, History of the great Abessinian Saint Tekla Haimanot, a native of Shoa, in the thirteenth century, who was the founder of the celebrated convent of Debra Libanos in Shoa. He decreed that all future primates (Abuna) should be Egyptian Copts and not Abessinians ; and that one-third of the entire revenues of Abessinia should go to the Church, for the support of the Abuna, the clergy, convents and churches. He also prevailed upon the Jewish dynasty Segue, under their King Naakueto Laab, to abdicate in favour of the Solomonian dynasty under king Jekuenu Amlak, by which the original family were again raised to the throne, and the usurpation of the Falash brought to an end.

97. GADELA ADAM, History of Adam.

98. GADELA SAMUEL, History of Samuel, who rode upon lions.

99. GADELA MEDHANALEM, Life of the Redeemer.

100. GADELOS KIROS, Life of St. Kiros.

101. GADELA ARAGAVI, or also, SAMICHÆL, the History of Aragavi, one of the nine Apostles of Abessinia, who at first took up their abode at Aksum for twelve years, and then spread themselves into the various provinces of the land.

Abba Aragavi reached Agame in Tigre, and founded a convent upon the lofty rock of Damo, to the summit of which, according to the legend, he was drawn up by a large serpent whose tail he had clutched. He is said to have converted the Prince of Darkness, and to have prevailed upon him to wear a monk's hood for forty years. Like Jared (in No. 37), he, too, is now living somewhere in the flesh the life of a recluse.

102. GADELA TOHANI, the Life of St. Tohani.

103. GADELA ANTONIOS, Life of Antonius, the Monk.

104. GADELA GEORGIS, Life of the celebrated Saint Georgis.

105. GADELA SANNEL ; 106. GADELA Ijob ; 107. GADELA ARSEMARO ; 108. GADELA AHIB ; 109. Gadela Nakod Volab—Lives of five Abessinian Saints.

110. GADELA GEBRA CHRISTOS, Life of Gebra Christos, the son of the Emperor Theodosius. (?)

111. Mazhafa Havi.

Of these writings I picked up about eighty in Shoa, either in manuscript or copied expressly for me, all of which I sent to Europe. No doubt, many works of similar character are scattered over other parts of Abessinia, with the titles of which I am not acquainted ; but in all there is such a preponderance of dross, and so little pure gold, that the labour and fatigue of perusal have but a sorry reward, unless one is possessed of the indomitable perseverance and learning of a Ludolph, who two hundred years ago earnestly desired to see the Protestant and the Abyssinian Churches united, and whose writings are even to this day the principal sources of information respecting Abessinia. I may as well enumerate the most useful of these :

112. LUDOLFI (SEU LEUT-HOLF JOBI) HISTORIA Ethiopica, sive brevis et succincta Descriptio Regni Habessinorum, quod vulgo male Presbyteri Joannis vocatur; sive de Natura et Indole Regionis et Incolarum; de Regimine; de Statu Ecclesiastico, Initio et Progressu Religionis Christianæ; de Rebus privatis; de Literatura, etc. *Francofurti ad Mœnum*, 1681, folio.

This volume was translated into English and into French.

113. LUDOLPHI (JOBI) COMMENTARIUS ad suam Historiam Æthiopicam in quo præter Res Æthiopicas multa S. Scripturæ loca declarantur, et Antiquitates Ecclesiasticæ illustrantur, etc. *Francofurti ad Mœnum*, 1691, folio.

114. LUDOLPHI (JOBI) APPENDIX ad Historiam Æthiopicam illiusque Commentarium ex nova Relatione de hodierne Statu Habessiniæ ex India nuper allata; *Francofurti ad Mœnum*, 1693, folio.

115. LUDOLPHI (JOBI) APPENDIX SECUNDA ad Historiam Æthiopicam continens Dissertationem de Locustis; *Francofurti ad Mœnum*, 1694, folio.

These four works form his complete history of Ethiopia, in the compilation of which Ludolf received great assistance from Abba Gregorius, the Amharic Patriarch, whose portrait is prefixed to the second, and who resided with him for a short time at the court of the ancestor of H. R. H. the Prince Consort, Duke Ernest of Saxe Gotha. His own portrait is given with the first, and with the third, the portrait of Gulanel Gabas Khan; besides which, there are plates of natural history, costume and antiquities scattered through all. In the first, amongst matters incidentally alluded to, is the correspondence of the Abessinian princes with the kings of Spain. The same volume also contains a very interesting catalogue of Ethiopic manuscripts, with specimens and translations, including much curious liturgical matter, prayers and ceremonies of the Church, in Ethiopic and Latin, &c. In the second he gives the Canons of the Apostles (see No. 9, ante); the Abessinian Calendar (No. 13); a curious Computus Ecclesiæ, and a most valuable dissertation upon the ancient language of Egypt and Northern Africa, with the names of animals, &c. in Ethiopic, Amharic, and Latin, and specimens of the Ethiopic, Amharic, and Galla dialects.

In 1683 he published:—116. EPISTOLA, Æthiopice, ad universum Habessinorum gentem; which was followed, in 1688, by the *Epistolæ Samaritanæ ad Jobum Ludolfum*, with a Latin version. And here may be mentioned his:—

117. FASTI ECCLESIÆ ALEXANDRINÆ; and his treatise *de Bello Turcico feliciter conficiendo*.

118. LUDOLFI (JOBI) GRAMMATICA Linguæ Æthiopicæ, *Francofurti ad Mœnum*, 1702, folio.

119. LUDOLFI (JOBI) LEXICON Æthiopico-Latinum, *Francofurti ad Mœnnm*, 1699, folio.

Nos. 116 and 117 were originally printed at London, in 1661. The Franckfort editions are much enlarged.

120. PSALTÉRIUM ÆTHIOPICUM; accedunt Hymni et Orationes aliquot, Canticum Canticorum, Æthiopice et Latine cura Jobi Ludolfi; *Francofurti ad Mœnum*, 1701, quarto.

121. LUDOLFI (JOBI) GRAMMATICA Linguæ Amharicæ, quæ vernacula est Habessinorum; *Francofurti ad Mœnum*, 1698, folie.

122. LUDOLFI (JOBI) LEXICON Amharico-Latinum cum Indice Latino copioso; *Francofurti ad Mœnum*, 1698, folio.

In the compilation of his Amharic Grammar and Dictionary, he was assisted by Abba Gregorius, the patriarch of Abessinia, a native of Makana-Selasse, in Shoa.

I do not enumerate the writings of Bruce, Salt, Rüppel, Gobat, Katte, Lefevre, Combes, Themasier, Rochet, Harris, Johnstone, Beke, Mansfield, and other modern travellers, whose works necessarily contain much illustrative both of the literature and languages of Northern Africa. The library of His Excellency Sir George Grey, K.C.B. is rich in all works appertaining to a knowledge of African linguistic development; and the second part of the first volume of his catalogue is devoted to the languages and dialects north of the Tropic of Capricorn (see No. 170).

123. ISENBERG'S (C. W.) GRAMMAR of the Amharic Language; *London*, 1842, royal 8vo.

124. ISENBERG'S (C. W.) DICTIONARY of the Amharic Language; in two parts, Amharic and English, and English and Amharic; *London*, 1841, quarto.

This work of my dear friend, the Missionary Isenberg, incorporates the manuscript Amharic vocabulary of Missionary Blumhardt, which was begun in 1837, at Adoa, and finished at Malta in 1839. It contains all the words which occur in the Bible.

125. YATEMEHERT MAJAMARYA, a Spelling and Reading-book in Amharic, by the Rev. C. W. ISENBERG; *London*, 1841, 8vo.

126. KATEGHISMOS, the Heidelberg Catechism in Amharic, translated by the Rev. C. W. ISENBERG; *London*, 1841, 8vo.

127. THE BOOK OF COMMON PRAYER, &c. of the Church of England and Ireland, in Amharic, translated by the Rev. C. W. ISENBERG, 8vo.

128. BAABNA BAWALD, Regni Dei in

Terris Historia, Amharice, in duabus partibus; inde Adami lapsu ad Hierosolymitarum Deletionem; et de Rebus Ecclesiasticis a S. Joannis Morte ad Tempora nostra. Auctore C. GUIL. ISENBERG; *London*, 1841, 8vo.

129. YA ΛALAMTARIK, Adumbratio Historiæ Mundi, Amharice. Auctore C. GUIL. ISENBERG; *London*, 1842, 8vo.

130. GEWOGRAFIYA YAMEDER TEMEHERT, a book of Geography in Amharic; by the Rev. C. W. ISENBERG; *London*, 1841, 8vo.

Besides these works enumerated above my dear friend Isenberg translated the Psalms, and the four Gospels into the language of Tigre, but this version has not yet been printed.

131. AN AMHARIC VOCABULARY, prepared for my own use, in manuscript.

I may here mention the existence of a Dictionary of the *Bari* language, which the Roman Catholic Missionaries at Khartum have prepared, and which, upon my visit to the Missionhouse in 1855, Mr. Kirchner, as mentioned at page 478, was kind enough to place in my hands. By what I saw of it, the *Bari* language does not appear to belong to the South-African family, but rather to incline to the Wakaufi, which is spoken in the Equatorial regions. Mr. Kirchner also showed me a Vocabulary of twelve dialects, which are more or less connected, and are spoken on the banks of the White Nile.

In the second volume of the *Proceedings of the London Philological Society* is an Essay on the Languages of *Abessinia*, by Beke.

Besides the *Old Testament*, now publishing, mentioned at p. 555, and the *Book of Enoch* (No. 22.), Dr. Dillmann has published an *Ethiopic Grammar*, in 1857; and the *LiberJubilæorum*, in 1859.

BOOKS ILLUSTRATIVE OF THE LANGUAGES OF EASTERN AFRICA.

I. KI-SUAHILI.

132. OUTLINE OF THE ELEMENTS OF THE KI-SUAHILI Language, with special reference to the *Kinika* Dialect, by the Rev. Dr. J. L. KRAPF ; *Tübingen*, 1850, 8vo.

133. SALLA SA SABUCI NA JIONI SASAL-LIWASO KATIKA Kiriaki ja Kienglese siku sothe sa muaka, Morning and Evening Prayers said in the Church of England, daily throughout the year, translated into *Ki-Suahili* by the Rev. Dr. J. L. KRAPF; *Tübingen*, 1854, 18mo.

134. THREE CHAPTERS OF GENESIS translated into the Sooahelee (*Ki-Suahili*) Language, by the Rev. Dr. J. L. KRAPF, with Introduction by W. W. Greenough, printed in the *Journal of the American Oriental Society* in 1847 (vol. i. pp. 259—274).

135. THE ENTIRE NEW TESTAMENT in *Ki-Suahili*, by the Rev. Dr. J. L. KRAPF ; still in manuscript.

136. COMPLETE DICTIONARY OF THE KI-SUAHILI TONGUE, by the Rev. Dr. J. L. KRAPF ; still in manuscript.

137. VOCABULARY OF THE SOAHILI (*Ki-Suahili*), by SAMUEL K. MASURY, printed in the *Memoirs of the American Academy, Cambridge, Mass.*, 1845.

138. DSHUO DSHA HERKAL, an Account of the Wars of Mohammed with Askaf, Governor of Syria to the Greek Emperor Heraclius, in rhyme ; a manuscript in *ancient Ki-Suahili*, written in Arabic characters.

139. DSHUO DSHA UTENSI, Poems and Mottoes in rhyme ; a manuscript in *ancient Ki-Suahili*, written in Arabic characters.

For an account of these curious linguistic treasures, in the dialect formerly spoken in the islands of Patta and Lamu, see the *Journal of the Oriental Society of Halle*, vol. viii. pp. 567—637. I presented these manuscripts to the library of that Society.

The Ki-Suahili language is spoken by some 300,000 or 400,000 Suahili, in the islands of Kiama, Tula, Patta, Lamu, Kau, Mombaz, Tanga, Pemba, Zanzibar, Kiloa, and all places on the mainland which are inhabited by the Mahommedans, from Barava to Cape Delgado.

II. KI-NIKA.

140. THE BEGINNING OF A SPELLING-BOOK of the *Kinika* Language, accompanied by a translation of the Heidelberg Catechism, by the Rev. J. L. KRAPF, D.Ph., and the Rev. J. REBMANN ; *Bombay*, 1848, 12mo.

141. EVANGELIO ZA AVIOANDIKA LUKAS, translated into *Kinika* by Dr. J. L. KRAPF ; *Bombay*, 1848, 12mo.

The Kinika language is spoken by from 50,000 to 60,000 Wanika, between the third and fourth degrees of southern latitude, about fifteen to twenty miles inland, at an altitude of 1200 to 2000 feet above the level of the sea. See No. 172 for the Wanika Dictionary of Missionary Rebmann.

III. KI-KAMBA.

142. EVANGELIO TA YUNAOLETE MALKOSI, the Gospel according to St.

Mark, translated into the *Kikamba* language by the Rev. Dr. J. L. KRAPF ; *Tübingen*, 1850, 8vo.

143. EVANGELIO TA YUNAOLETE MATTEOS, the Gospel according to St. Matthew, translated into the *Kikamba* language by the Rev. Dr. J. L. KRAPF ; still in manuscript. The Kikamba language is spoken by some 70,000 to 90,000 Wakamba, about 400 miles distant from the sea, in the rear of the Wanika.

IV. HINZUA.

144. A GRAMMAR AND VOCABULARY OF THE HINZUAN LANGUAGE, by the Rev. WILLIAM ELLIOTT, of the London Missionary Society, written during a residence in the Island of Johana, one of the Comoro Islands ; still·in manuscript.

V. SIDI.

145. IN MAJOR BURTON'S SINDH, and the Races that inhabit the Valley of the Indus, published at London in 1851, Appendix IV., is a *Vocabulary of the Sidi Language*, the language spoken by the slaves imported from Zanzibar, and other parts of the East-African coast, pp. 372—374, and *passim*, 253—257.

VI. GALLA.

146. TENTAMEN imbecillum Translationis Evangelii Joannis in *Linguam Gallarum*. Auctore J. L. KRAPF, Missionario, auxiliante Berkio, viro ex stirpe Gallarum, quam Gelan vocant, oriundo. Inceptum in urbe Ankober, quæ regni Shoanorum capitalis est, 1839 ; *Londini*, 1841, fcap. 8vo. The first five chapters of St. John's Gospel.

147. EVANGELIUM MATTHAEI translatum in *Linguam Gallarum*. Auctore J. L. KRAPF, Missionario

Ankobari, regni Shoanorum capitalis. 1841 ; *no imprint ;* fcap. 8vo.

148. GENESIS in Lingua Gallarum, J. L. KRAPF, Missionario, interprete ; not yet printed.

149. AN IMPERFECT OUTLINE of the Elements of the *Galla Language*, by the Rev. J. L. KRAPF. Preceded by a few Remarks concerning the nation of the Gallas, etc., by the Rev. C. W. ISENBERG ; *London*, 1840, 12mo.

150. VOCABULARY OF THE GALLA LANGUAGE, by the Rev. J. L. KRAPF ; together with an English-Galla Vocabulary, prepared from a MS. Gallo-German Vocabulary of Dr. Krapf, by the Rev. C. W. ISENBERG ; *London*, 1840, 12mo.

151. A GRAMMAR OF THE ʻGALLA LANGUAGE, by CHARLES TUTSCHEK, edited by Lawrence Tutschek, M.D., *Munich*, 1845, 8vo. The Grammar is followed by some native prayers and letters, in Galla and English (pp. 84—92). The Grammar was written in German, and the translation is by Mr. J. Smead, of Richmond, Virginia.

In the third volume of the *Proceedings of the London Philological Society* is an Essay on *Galla* Verbs, by Newman ; and in the *Transactions* of the same Society for 1859, an Essay by Hensleigh Wedgwood, Esq., " *On Coincidences between the Galla and different European Languages.*"

152. DICTIONARY OF THE GALLA LANGUAGE, composed by CHARLES TUTSCHEK, and published by Lawrence Tutschek ; (Gallo-English and German) 3 parts, *Munich*, 1844—5. 8vo

In the Catalgoue of Sir George Grey's Library (vol. i. p. 253), Mr. Bleek states that both the Grammar and Dictionary of Tutschek "are chiefly the fruit of an intercourse in Germany with three Gallas, one of whom was, together with an Umale, a Darfurian, and a Denka, intrusted by Duke Maximilian of Bavaria to the care of Dr. Charles Tutschek from 1838 to 1843, when the Doctor died, and Dr. Lawrence Tutschek, supplied his place, and edited these posthumous works of his brother. The Dictionary is dedicated to H. R. H. Maximilian, Crown Prince of Bavaria; and the Grammar to Sir Thomas Dyke Acland, Bart., who assisted materially in these publications." In the third volume of the *Proceedings of the Philological Society of London*, is an Essay by Dr. Tutschek on the *Tumali* language.

Respecting the people who speak the Galla language, consult pp. 72—84, *ante*.

VII. DANKALI.

153. A SMALL VOCABULARY of the *Dankali* Language, in three parts, Dankali and English, English and Dankali, and a selection of Dankali sentences, with English translations, by the Rev. C. W. ISENBERG; *London*, 1840, 12mo.

Compiled chiefly during a stay at Tadjurra. Dankali is spoken between Abessinia and the Red Sea, to the South of the Habab, and by the people of Arkiko, and tribes north of the Somal and the Ittu Gallas, from 11—58° Northern latitude at Tadjurra, to 15—40° at Arkiko; by numerous tribes of the Danakil or Affer,—the Shoho, Hazaorta, and Teltal in the North, and in the South by the Ad Alli, Burhanto, Dinsarra, Debeni, Weema Galeile, Tak'eel, Meshaich, Gidoso, and Mudiato.

VIII. SOMALI.

154. AN OUTLINE OF THE SOMAULI

LANGUAGE, with Vocabulary, by Lieutenant C. P. RIGBY, will be found in the ninth volume of the *Transactions of the Bombay Geographical Society*, (pp. 129—184), 1850, 8vo.

155. DE AZANIA Africæ littore Orientali, GEORGIUS BUNSEN ROMANUS scripsit; *Bonnæ*, 1852, with a map of Ancient Azania, 8vo.

The Somali is spoken in the whole Eastern Horn, from Cape Guardafui nearly to Cape Babelmandeb to the north, "where," says Mr. Bleek, "it is bounded by the dialects of the Danakil or Affer, and Ittoo Gallas, whilst to the south it ranges to the Suahali country, and westwards to a few miles of Harar.

IX. HARARI.

156. FIRST FOOTSTEPS IN EAST AFRICA; or an Exploration of Harar; by (Major) RICHARD BURTON; (with a Grammatical Outline, Dialogues and Sentences, Specimens of Poetry, Names of months and measures, and English-Hariri Vocabulary), *London*, 1856, 8vo.

The Hariri language is confined to the walls of the city of Harar, which is surrounded on all sides by the Gallas.

X. IL-OIGOB: 1. KAUFI, or KI-KAUFI.

157. VOCABULARY OF THE ENGUTUK ELOIKOB, or Language of the Wakaufi Nation in the Interior of Equatorial Africa, compiled by the Rev. Dr. J. L. KRAPF (in the Island of Mombaz, with the help of *Lemasegnot or Merduti*, a native of the Enganglima tribe).—It contains an English-Kaufi Vocabulary, a specimen of a translation of St. John, a free translation of Genesis iv., dialogues on Wakaufi stories, salutations, materials for grammar, etc., with Introduction of 28 pages.—*Tübingen*, 1854, 8vo.

Respecting the Wakaufi, see p. 358, *ante*. They call themselves *Il-oigob*, and are nicknamed by the Masai *Imbarrawuio*, or *Em-barawuio*.

2. MASAI.

158. VOCABULARY OF THE ENGUDUK ILOIGOB, as spoken by the Masai-tribes in East Africa, compiled by the Rev. J. ERHARDT (edited by the Rev. Dr. J. L. KRAPF), in two parts (Masai-English, and English-Kimasai, with a song of the Masai, with a literal translation)—*Ludwigsburg*, 1857, post 8vo.

Respecting the Masai, see p. 358, *ante*.

XI. MOZAMBIQUE.

159. THE LANGUAGES OF MOZAMBIQUE : Vocabularies of the Dialects of Lourenzo Marques, Inhambane, Sofala, Tette, Sena, Quellimane, Mozambique, Cape Delgado, Anjoane, the Maravi, Mudsau, &c. Drawn up from the Manuscripts of Dr. W. PETERS, and from other materials, by Dr. W. H. J. BLEEK. *London*, 1856, 8vo.

These dialects are spoken in the Portuguese possessions by a population of some 280,000 to 300,000 souls, inhabiting the country between 10 deg. and 26 deg. southern latitude, from Cape Delgado to Delagoa Bay, and stretching considerably inland. The chief towns are Mozambique, on an island at the entrance of Mesaril Bay, Inhambane, Sofala, Luabo, Quilimane and Ibo.

The materials for these Vocabularies were collected by Dr. Peters, during his stay in the Portuguese settlements of Eastern Africa in 1842—48, and were arranged by Dr. Bleek in 1853—54, and seen through the press by Mr. Norris, Dr. Bleek having left Europe before three sheets were printed. The book was printed at the expense of the Foreign Office. This work incorporates, with the exception of some doubtful words, the *Vocabulary of Captain White of the tribes inhabiting Delagoa Bay* at the close of the last century, which is contained in pp. 65 —70, &c. of his *Journal of a Voyage performed in the Lion Extra, Indiaman, from Madras to Columbo, and Da Lagoa Bay on the Eastern Coast of Africa*, in 1798 ; *London*, 1800, 4to., the words so omitted being given in Sir George Grey's Catalogue, vol. i., p. 163.

160. ALPHABETICAL INDEX of the English words in the Vocabulary of the *Languages of Mozambique*. Compiled by Dr. W. H. J. BLEEK, *Cape Town*, 1858, 4to. *In Manuscript.*

161. SPECIMENS OF THE CONJUGATIONS OF THE VERBS in the *Languages of Mozambique* (Inhambane, Sofala, Tette, Sena, Maravi, Makua, and Suaheli), collected by Dr. W. PETERS ; folio. *In Manuscript.*

162. GRAMMATISCHE TABELLEN der Nomina, Pronomina, und Adjektiva im Idiom von Sena. Aus Dr. W. PETERS Papieren zusammengetragen von W. H. J. BLEEK ; 1853, folio ; *in Manuscript*. Nos. 160, 161, and 162 are in the Collection of Sir George Grey, as are also the three following :—

163. O MUATA CAZEMBE e os povos *Maraves, Chevas, Muizas, Muembas, Lundas*, e outros da Africa Austral.—Diario da Expediçâo Portugueza commandata pelo MAJOR MONTEIRO, &c., redigido pelo MAJOR A. C. P. GAMITTO. *Lisboa*, 1854, 8vo.

Account of the Portuguese expedition of 1831—2 to the Cazembe. App. III. and IV. contain Vocabularies

of the dialects of Tette, Muiza, Ma-
shona, Ba-rotse, Maravi, and other
tribes of the interior. The subjects of
the Cazembe are Arunda, who, like
other African tribes, cultivate cassave
as their chief food; and the articles
they trade with are copper-bars, peltry,
ivory, salt, and slaves. The country is
fertile, and rain is regular and plentiful; but though they possess horned
cattle in abundance, cow's milk and
butter are luxuries still unknown to
them.

164. COLLECTIONS OF WORDS in the
    Languages of *Ba-rotse* and of *Tette*,
    by the Rev. Dr. LIVINGSTONE,
    1855—56. 4to. *In Manuscript.*
    Containing also words of the Zam-
    bezi generally, collected at Quil-
    limane, and *Malagasse* words, col-
    lected at St. Augustine's Bay,
    26th July, 1856.

165. VOCABULARY of the Language of
    the *Mashona*; by the Rev. R.
    MOFFAT; 4to. *In Manuscript.*

Perhaps, in addition to these, it may
not be out of place to mention Mr.
C. J. Andersson's "*Journey to Lake
Ngami, and an Itinerary of the prin-
cipal routes leading to it from the
Coast*," &c., published in 1854, at Cape
Town, which contains, at pp. 20—26,
a comparative Table of *Otjiherero,
Ba-yeye*, and *Chjilimanse*, the latter
spoken on some part of Zambezè, or
Kilimansi. The Lake itself is nearly
equidistant from the Eastern and the
Western Coasts.

XII. MISCELLANEOUS.

166. ANALYSE D'UN MEMOIRE DE M.
    EUGENE DE FROBERVILLE sur les
    Langues et les Races de l'Afrique
    Orientale au sud de l'Equateur
    (*Extraite du Mauricien.* 4 pp.)
    Port-Louis Ile Maurice, 1846, 4to.

167. VOCABULARY of Six East-African

Languages (*Ki-Suahili, Ki-nika,
Ki-kamba, Ki-pokomo, Ki-hiau,
Ki-Galla.*) Composed by the Rev.
Dr. J. L. KRAPF, Missionary of the
Church Missionary Society in
East Africa: *Tübingen*, 1850, 4to.

168. ON CERTAIN RECENT ADDITIONS
    to *African* Philology, by R. G.
    LATHAM, Esq., 2 parts; in the
    *Transactions of the London Philo-
    logical Society* for 1855, 8vo.

169. COINCIDENCES IN THE ROOTS of
    African and European Languages,
    by HENSLEIGH WEDGWOOD, Esq.;
    in the *Transactions of the London
    Philological Society* for 1858, 8vo.
    See also note to No. 151.

170. THE LIBRARY OF HIS EXCELLENCY
    SIR GEORGE GREY, K.C.B.—Phi-
    lology, Vol. I. Part 2. Africa,
    North of the Tropic of Capricorn,
    by Dr. W. H. J. BLEEK. *London,
    Trübner & Co.*, 1858, 8vo.

The following portions of this highly
interesting Catalogue of Books, illustrative of the languages of Africa,
Madagascar, Polynesia, Borneo, New
Zealand, Australia, &c., are now complete :—

VOL. I. PART 1. *South Africa*, within
    the limits of British influence;
    title-page and table, pp. 1—186.
    (*Dr. W. H. J. Bleek.*)

VOL. I., PART 2. *Africa*, North of the
    Tropic of Capricorn; title-page
    and table, pp. 191—261. (*Dr. W.
    H. J. Bleek.*)

VOL. I., PART 3. *Madagascar;* title and
    pp. 1—24. (*J. Cameron and Dr.
    W. H. J. Bleek.*)

VOL. II., PART 1. *Australia;* title-page
    and table, pp. 1—44. (*Dr. W. H.
    J. Bleek.*)

VOL. II., PART 2. *Australia and Poly-
    nesia*, Papuan Languages of the
    Loyalty Islands and New He-
    brides; pp. 1—12. (*Sir George
    Grey, K.C.B.*)

Vol. II., Part 3. *Feji Islands and Rotuma*, etc., title-page and pp. 13—32, and leaf not numbered. (*Sir G. Grey and Dr. W. H. J. Bleek.*)

Vol. II. Part 4. *New Zealand, the Chatham Islands, and Auckland Islands;* title page and table, and pp. 1—76, (*Sir George Grey and Dr. W. H. J. Bleek.*)

Vol. II. Part 4 (Continuation). *Polynesia and Borneo;* title-page, II.

and pp. 1—154 (*no name of compiler*).

The work is printed at the Cape of Good Hope, and is an elegant specimen of Colonial Typography.

171. De Linguæ Æthiopicæ cum cognatis Linguis comparatæ Indole universa. *Auctore* E. Schrader. 1860, 4to.

Prepared for Press.

172. A Complete Dictionary of the Wanika and Waniassa Language, by the Rev. J. Rebmann.

In Progress.

173. A Translation of the Herzbuechlein into Amharic, by the Rev. Dr. J. L. Krapf.

Just Published.

174. A Catalogue of a large Assemblage of Books, appertaining to Linguistic Literature, Ancient and Modern ; on sale by Trübner & Co. ; (*African Languages*, pp. 10—15.) *London*, 1860, 8vo.